D0323235

Empire and others

The Neale Colloquium in British History

Charity, self-interest and welfare in the English past
Martin Daunton (editor)

England's Long Reformation, 1500–1800
Nicholas Tyacke (editor)

Empire and others:
British encounters with indigenous peoples, 1600–1850
Martin Daunton and Rick Halpern (editors)

Empire and others: British encounters with indigenous peoples, 1600–1850

Edited by

Martin Daunton
University of Cambridge

and

Rick Halpern
University College London

First published in the UK in 1999 by UCL Press

Reprinted 2003 by Routledge
11 New Fetter Lane
London, EC4P 4EE

Routledge is an imprint of the
Taylor & Francis Group

ISBN: 1-85728-991-9 HB

British Library Cataloguing in Publication Data
A CIP catalogue record for this book is available from the British Library.

Printed and bound at T.J. International, Padstow, UK

Contents

CONTENTS

CONTENTS

Acknowledgements

Empire and others emerges from a joint meeting of the Neale Colloquium in British History and the Commonwealth Fund Colloquium in American History, designed to link the historiography of both sides of the Atlantic. The colloquium attracted a large number of historians to London for discussion of 38 papers. It was not possible to include all the papers in the limits of one volume, but the organizers are extremely grateful to everyone who gave a paper, acted as a commentator, and took part in the discussion. An important feature of each colloquium is the public keynote lecture that provides an overview of the topic. In 1997, we had two outstanding, wide-ranging lectures, by Chris Bayly and Philip Morgan; they helped to establish the agenda for the colloquium. We should in particular thank Linda Colley and Richard Dunn who prepared comments on the two keynote lectures, and Shula Marks who undertook the formidable task of summing up the entire event with her usual insight. We are very grateful to them.

The organization of the colloquium was made possible only by the generosity of the large number of people and organizations who provided administrative and financial support. In the Department of History at University College London, Nazneen Razwi and Simon Renton coped with a considerable burden of work in addition to their normal duties, and learned new skills of transmitting papers over the Internet. Financial support was provided by the British Academy, the Graduate School of University College London, the Institute of United States Studies of the University of London, the Mellon Fund of the University of Cambridge, the Robert Bruce Centre of the University of Keele, W. W. Norton, Jonathan Cape, and the *Journal of American Studies*. As a result of their support, and the enthusiastic discussion over the three days of the colloquium, the innovation proved a success that will be repeated at some future date.

Martin Daunton
Rick Halpern
Cambridge and London, March 1998

Notes on contributors

Andrew Bank is Lecturer in History at the University of the Western Cape. He is the author of *The decline of urban slavery at the Cape, 1806 to 1834* and has recently published articles on nineteenth-century Cape colonial racial discourse.

Christopher Bayly is Vere Harmsworth Professor of Imperial and Naval History at the University of Cambridge. His most recent book is *Empire and information. Intelligence gathering and social communication in India, 1780–1870.* He is associate editor of the *New Cambridge History of India.*

Hilary Beckles is Pro-vice Chancellor, office of the board of undergraduates studies at Mona Campus, University of the West Indies, Jamaica. He is the author of several books, including *Natural rebels: a social history of enslaved Black women in Barbados, White servitude and Black slavery in Barbados, 1650–1715,* and *A history of Barbados.* Currently he is working on a study of gender and slavery in the Caribbean.

Louise Breen teaches in the history department at Kansas State University. She is currently completing a book, *Transgressing the bounds: The Puritan mercantile and military elite in seventeenth-century Massachusetts,* which examines elite Puritan men who challenged dominant views of social or religious orthodoxy.

Kathleen Brown is an Assistant Professor of History at the University of Pennsylvania. She is the author of *Good wives, nasty wenches, and anxious patriarchs: gender, race and power in colonial Virginia.* Currently she is working on a history of cleanliness in British North America and the antebellum United States.

Martin Daunton was formerly the Astor Professor of British History at University College London, before moving to the chair of economic history at

Cambridge in 1997. He is the author of *Progress and poverty: an economic and social history of Britain, 1700–1850*, and is currently completing a book on the politics of British taxation from 1815 to the present.

Heather Goodall is an Associate Professor in Public Policy in the Faculty of Humanities and Social Sciences at the University of Technology, Sydney. She is the author of *Invasion to embassy: land in Aboriginal politics in New South Wales, 1770 to 1972*.

Catherine Hall is Professor of Modern British Social and Cultural History at University College London. Her *Family fortunes: men and women of the English middle class 1780–1850* was co-authored with Lenore Davidoff. Her recent work has focused on the intersections of race and gender in the history of empire. *Civilizing subjects: "race", nation and empire, 1830–1870* will be published in 1999.

Rick Halpern is Reader in the History of the United States. His most recent publication is *Down on the killing floor: Black and white workers in Chicago's packinghouses, 1904–1954*. He is currently working on a comparative study of race and labour in the sugar industries of the United States and South Africa.

Ruth Herndon is Assistant Professor of Early American History at the University of Toledo. Her most recent publication, written with Ella Wilcox Sekatu, is "The right to a name: Narragansett people and Rhode Island officials in the Revolutionary era", *Ethnohistory* **44** (3), Summer 1997. Currently she is revising for publication her doctoral dissertation on the social experience of New England townspeople during the Revolutionary war.

Madhavi Kale is Helen Taft Manning Assistant Professor of History at Bryn Mawr College. Her contribution to this volume is part of a larger project on history, archives and constructions of labour, entitled *Fragments of empire: capital, slavery, and India indentured labor in the Carribean* (Philadelphia, 1999). Her current project explores technologies of film, domesticity and women's education in India, 1910–65.

Anne McGillivray is Associate Professor of Law at the University of Manitoba. In addition to her continuing work with Russell Smandych on the colonization of aboriginal childhood, she has written on childhood, law and violence, violence against women, law and literature, and legal culture. She is guest editor of Mosaic's *Adversaria: Literature and the Law* and editor of *Governing Childhood*.

Philip Morgan is Editor of the *William and Mary Quarterly* and Professor of History at the College of William and Mary. His most recent publication is

Slave counterpoint: Black culture in the eighteenth-century Chesapeake and Lowcountry. He is working on a study of eighteenth-century Jamaica.

Greg O'Brien received the Ph.D. in History from the University of Kentucky and is currently Visiting Assistant Professor of History at the University of Southern Mississippi. He is presently revising for publication a manuscript entitled *Indians in a revolutionary age: the transformation of power and authority among the Choctaws, 1750–1781*.

Jean O'Brien is an Associate Professor in the Department of History at the University of Minnesota. She is the author of *Dispossession by degrees: Indian land and identity in Natick, Massachusetts, 1650–1790*.

Ann Marie Plane is Assistant Professor of History at the University of California, Santa Barbara. She is the author of several articles on New England Native American history, focusing on issues of gender and sexuality. Her forthcoming book is entitled *Family lives, colonial worlds: marriage and the making of race in Southeastern New England, 1620–1760*.

Andrew Porter is Rhodes Professor of Imperial History at King's College, University of London. His recent publications include *European imperialism 1860–1914*. He currently works on religion and empire, and is editing the forthcoming *Oxford History of the British Empire*, volume 3, *The nineteenth century*.

Nathaniel Sheidley is a doctoral candidate in American History at Princeton University. His dissertation, entitled "Preachers, prophets, and unruly men: religious upheaval and the meanings of manhood on the southern frontier, 1763–1815", is a study of Native American and Anglo-American religious revivals on the trans-Appalachian frontier of the early United States.

Russell Smandych is Associate Professor of Sociology at the University of Manitoba. He has published extensively in the fields of Canadian criminal justice and legal history. In addition to his current work in progress with Anne McGillivray on colonialism and aboriginal childhood, he is working on historical research on the application of colonial criminal law to aboriginal peoples, and contemporary research in the fields of youth justice, aboriginal justice, and community-based crime prevention.

Peter Way is Professor of American History at the University of Sussex. He authored *Common labour: workers and the digging of North American canals, 1780–1860*. Currently he is writing a class-based study of common soldiers and the British Army in the Americas during the Seven Years' War.

Chapter One

Introduction: British identities, indigenous peoples, and the empire

Martin Daunton and Rick Halpern[1]

Empire and others results from an innovation and establishes a precedent. In 1997, the two long-standing colloquia organized by the Department of History at University College London were merged: the Neale Colloquium in British History and the Commonwealth Fund Colloquium in American History. The ambition was to address themes linking the historiographies of both sides of the Atlantic in a way which would reframe chronologies, transfer insights, and redefine problematics.

British historiography has much to gain from this dialogue. Unlike American historians, who have long dealt with indigenous peoples as part of their own national history, historians of Britain have been able to avoid including encounters with colonized peoples within their domestic history. Metropolitan residents consumed the products, ideas and knowledge of the far reaches of empire, even if they did not directly encounter indigenous peoples. What needs to be stressed, to a greater extent, is the way in which imperialism became a significant constitutive element in British identities.[2] As C. A. Bayly argues in his recent historiographic survey, the next phase of scholarship should be to feed imperial history back into Britain. "The imperial history of the future will have to take seriously the question of how far, and in what ways, the imperial experience contributed to the making of national identity and regional identities in the British Isles itself."[3] The old meta-narrative of battles between Spanish, Portuguese, British, French, Dutch and German empires for ascendancy should remain part of the story, but it is only one part of a larger whole. As Linda Colley notes, the new emphasis is on "a complex saga of the collisions, compromises, and comings together of many different cultures". This saga should include the mutual definitions of fellow Europeans, as well as the similarities and divergences of European responses to indigenous peoples throughout the world. British perceptions of Native

1

Americans were not necessarily the same as French, and might well be contested within both countries; and the implications for British and French identities might well differ.[4] The problem facing historians is how to write this new history, and how to make it operational without descending into a chaos of imagined identities and cultural confusions. The challenge is to balance attention to discursive practices, while retaining a grounding in the material realities of political economy.

The rich and impressive American historiography offers much to historians of Britain and its empire; at the same time, the American literature would be strengthened by attention to the encounters with indigenes in other parts of the empire. A major aim of this volume is to reintegrate the history of colonial North America with British and imperial history. North America is over-represented in the book, owing in the first instance to the format of the two colloquia, drawing as they did upon the constituencies of British history and North American colonial history. There are two further intellectual justifications.

The first is that historians of North America need to be aware of the different chronology which emerges when their work is inserted into the larger context of the British empire. The American historiography is set within an internal chronology of the United States, in which the story of indigenous peoples in the North- and South-East comes to a tragic nadir in the Jacksonian period. A British imperial perspective offers alternative perspectives, with a collection of different chronologies. Not all the chronologies are pursued in this volume, and in particular the encounters in the African slave trade or in Asia. Clearly, encounters in India in 1750 or in China in 1850 were very different from North America in 1650 in terms of the relative power of the parties, and of metropolitan attitudes to forms of religion or political authority. Rather, the emphasis in the present volume is on the long chronology of encounters with indigenous societies which were seen as broadly comparable. The North American chronology continues with en-counters of soldiers, traders and settlers with the aborigines in Australia, the Maoris in New Zealand, and the Xhosa and the Zulu in southern Africa.

Indeed, the American experience fed into and informed these longer-term processes. As Andrew Porter shows in his contribution to this volume, the chronology was obvious to missionaries who reflected on the lessons of North America as they extended their attentions to other parts of the world. Similar continuities and connections existed between opposition to slavery in the Americas and protection of Aborigines in Australia. Evangelical reformers such as Thomas Fowell Buxton transferred their allegiance from emancipation of slaves to aboriginal land rights in the 1830s.[5] Legal continuities from the colonial to the post-imperial eras are evident in Chief Justice Marshall's decisions on native title in the United States; these developed from English legal traditions and were themselves cited in rulings of the courts in New South Wales and New Zealand.[6] Contemporaries were themselves creating typologies of similarities of encounters, testing how far the property rights, religious beliefs, and political forms of Aborigines in Australia or Maoris in New Zealand could be admitted within metropolitan definitions.

The second justification for the over-representation of American material is that historians of Britain and its empire have much to learn from the literature on colonial North America. The exciting and incisive conceptualization of the frontier in the American historiography informs the contributions to this book. In contrast to older notions of the frontier as a fixed geographic and temporal entity, the new scholarship views the frontier as a process of interaction between indigenes and Europeans taking place in "zones of contact" that are spatially and chronologically flexible, and within which social, economic and military dynamics intersect and interact.[7] Although imperial history has started to adopt a similar concern for "zones of contact" in Australia, Africa and Asia, this has taken place within the framework of distinct national histories, with the danger that connections and comparisons are often missed between different parts of the world and with the metropole.

A related point concerns the way in which American scholars have explored the shifting and historically contingent aspects of "white" identity. In recent years, a diverse group of historians and sociologists has begun to redefine the way in which race, racism and, indeed, anti-racism are understood.[8] Kathleen Brown, in her article "Using Native Americans to interrogate the category of race", revisits the classic work of Winthrop Jordan[9] to show how racial identity was subject to constant negotiation and renegotiation in early colonial North America. Rather than closed categories existing in simple relation to one another, "black" and "white" had multiple referents. Broadly speaking, this sort of approach to problems of identity and issues of self-perception can be applied to other parts of the empire and, indeed, to the metropolitan country itself.

British history itself has recently been transformed by a new emphasis on the "forging" of identities, a word that captures the ambivalence of the process as both creation and counterfeiting. Essentialist approaches to class, gender and nation have given way to a concern for social construction and imagination which has undermined the old meta-narratives of political, social and economic history. One of the strengths of recent British historiography has been its attention to the way in which discursive practices help constitute class and gender identities, religious communities, regional loyalties and economic interest groups.[10] Taking a cue from the American literature, British historians now need to consider how, where, and under what circumstances race should be inserted as a category of analysis. This is seen most clearly in Madhavi Kale's essay. Although the concrete situation studied is the British Caribbean, Kale's analysis reaches back across the Atlantic to the metropole as well as to India in an effort to understand the ways in which imperial agents constructed new identities for both emancipated slaves and indentured servants from the Indian subcontinent. Sensitivity to imperial location informs her analysis, and offers a lesson to historians of empire and metropole in their quest to understand the precise and contingent relations between class, gender and racial identities.[11]

During the eighteenth century, race was an important but not the primary category of identity within Britain. There was an emphasis on the need to moralize the manners of the "dissipated" elite and the "heathen" of the slums within Britain, as well as on the need to convert indigenous peoples in the empire. The creation of the Society for the Promotion of Christian Knowledge in 1698 reflected worries about the irreligion of the poor at home, and established charity schools as a form of metropolitan mission. Similarly, the formation of the Society for the Propagation of the Gospel in Foreign Parts in 1701 was part of the attempt to spread Christianity within the empire. The result was that "heathens" in the empire were defined within the same terms as "heathens" at home who wilfully rejected the benefits of revealed religion, so that the colonized abroad and the poor at home occupied similar moral space. The languages of race and class always operated in relation to each other, with constant slippage, and a major task for historians of metropolitan Britain is to pay much more attention to their interconnection. The way forward is suggested in this volume by two other pieces on the Caribbean that deploy complementary interpretative frameworks – Catherine Hall's essay on the constitution of a new Black subject after emancipation, and Hilary Beckles' examination of English–Kalinago relations in the seventeenth century. Other recent writing suggests that slave emancipation in the British Caribbean had important consequences for the racialization of "white" working-class identity in the metropole.[12]

A further development within British history, which complements the stress on identities, has been to re-think the nature of the state between the Civil War and the early nineteenth century. This work has pointed to the emergence within Britain of a powerful "fiscal-military state" from about 1680 with the capacity to apply domestic revenues to warfare. The expenditure was initially directed to the European theatre, but from the war of 1739–48 was increasingly turned to imperial pursuits. The creation of this new form of state affected the metropole in a variety of ways, by redrawing the boundary between local and central government, by developing new forms of fiscal extraction, and by creating new financial institutions and interests.[13] One dimension of the creation of such a state was the successful negotiation of the political tensions arising from the governance by one monarch of multiple kingdoms within the British Isles, and the way in which problems in one kingdom could destroy the delicate and unstable relation of the parts.[14] However, these concerns with the administrative and political complexities of the multiple kingdom did not disappear with union with Scotland in 1707, let alone with Ireland in 1801. The constitution of an imperial state re-invigorated these questions of identity and their relation to tensions within the political process. The "fiscal-military state" was not merely a domestic development. The search for revenue, and the mercantilist "navigation system" with which it was associated, were transferred across the seas and impacted upon the structures of both settler and indigenous societies in the Americas, Africa, and Asia. Moreover, the fiscal-military states within Britain and the empire were interconnected: a desire to reduce taxes at home might create tensions on the periphery, and resistance on the periphery might force up extraction at home at the cost of political conflict.[15]

This concern with multiple kingdoms within the British Isles and the construction of "British" communities in the New World can be linked with our stress on identities. How did a Scot in the Highlands or the Lowlands, or a Protestant or Catholic in Ireland, imagine their identity and construct their relationship with England? Furthermore, how did a Lowland Scot, educated at the University of Edinburgh, working as a physician on a slave plantation in Jamaica, see himself as "British"? A displaced Highland soldier fighting in Canada may have been serving in a British army, but probably in a Highland regiment with a high degree of Scottish identity; and the British army was often part of a multinational alliance of Europeans and indigenes. Meanwhile, the clans had to make their terms with the House of Orange after 1688; some offered their allegiance to the new regime, but others retained a commitment to the deposed Stuarts, at least in part as the result of a nationalist desire to reverse the union with England of 1707. When the uprising of 1745 came to a bloody end at Culloden in 1745, the Gaelic-speaking Highlands experienced a draconian policy of repression which had a clear ethnic dimension.[16]

A full answer to these issues of identity can be given only by moving beyond the British Isles to a consideration of empire. Irish Catholics or Highland Scots were subaltern peoples at home who also took part in imperial ventures abroad: they were both subordinate and dominant. The imperial project started beyond the Irish Sea before it crossed the Atlantic, and there were many parallels and continuities in responding to differences of language, culture, religion, legal systems, and social structures. This theme is echoed in Louise Breen's contribution to this volume. Her protagonist – Daniel

Gookin – was not alone in applying to Native Americans lessons from his encounter with Irish Catholics.[17] The multiple kingdoms reached across the oceans, where the identities of both British and indigenes were subject to constant re-negotiation. This process was more than a simple encounter between two stable, fixed identities, for both were fractured and various, changing over time and space in constant interplay and mutual redefinition. It should also be stressed that these identities were defined and took on meaning only in relation to each other. It was not merely that imperial power, springing from many sources, classified, defined and sought to dominate indigenous peoples, but that equally the identities of Britons themselves took shape in relation to the colonized "other".

Our two lead essays, by C. A. Bayly and Philip Morgan, explore the formation of identities, both British and indigenous, from imperial and New World perspectives. This process began within Britain and then unfolded, with both common tropes and significant variations, in different parts of the colonized world. At the most basic level, the acquisition of territory and the settlement of British people necessitated the adaptation, however hesitant and piecemeal, of metropolitan institutions and English legal forms to a variety of colonial settings. The creation of identities was played out in the definition of entitlement to welfare and to property rights, both within the metropole and on the periphery. Within the British Isles, a Scot moving to England or even English men and women shifting between parishes were "strangers" whose claim to support in old age or ill-health were limited or non-existent, and varied according to place and circumstance.[18] Similarly, property rights, mainly in land but also in persons and in hunting, were undergoing constant re-negotiation at least from the sixteenth century within the British Isles as well as in the colonies – a process affecting not only landlords and tenants, settlers and indigenes, but also the state's claim to tax revenues. These changing definitions of entitlement and of rights in property were contested both in the metropole and in the colonies, as the outgrowth of the same legal and ideological concerns, a process which forced both Britons and indigenous peoples to re-negotiate their position within the political nation and the economic system.[19]

This process of contestation is considered here in two essays that chart the implementation of the English poor law and the understanding of property rights in colonial North America. Ruth Herndon and Ann Marie Plane analyze the processes of inclusion and exclusion which defined entitlement to resources of relief and land, as well as membership within the community. These common processes unfolded simultaneously within Britain and many of its colonial possessions. Herndon's account of Native American women who lost their entitlement to poor relief in eighteenth-century Rhode Island was paralleled by the experience of many migrants within the British Isles who found themselves denied public support, as well as by colonists in Australia to whom the English system of tax-based public relief was not extended, or in Upper Canada where it was removed.[20] Similarly, Plane's narrative of the legal battles of Jacob Seeknout, who attempted to assert his rights to grazing land in colonial Massachusetts, could just as easily be drawn from the records of countless English parishes where commoners contested the appropriation of their customary rights.[21]

Outcomes varied. In some outposts of empire, the English legal system granted to indigenes some recognition of property rights, albeit within a different context which made land more marketable. Maoris in New Zealand, for example, secured a form of title to their land that was superior not only to that of Aborigines in Australia (considered by Heather Goodall in this collection) but also to that of Scottish Highlanders evicted from their clan lands. Although it was the result of changes within Scottish society rather than a simple imposition from outside, the conversion of clan lands into the private property of aristocrats shares common features with the redefinition of tribal lands in North America. The Scottish legal system gave less recognition to customary rights than the English courts, which made it easier for the clan chiefs to turn themselves into great landowners. In the Highlands, up to the early eighteenth century, clan members paid "tribute" of cattle to their chieftains who provided hospitality in return, and used the provisions to sustain feuding and warfare. The gradual conversion of this system from the later seventeenth century into part of a monetized and commercial economy imposed strains on social relationships; amongst the outcomes were migration to North America and service in the imperial army.[22] In the same way, as Nathaniel Sheidley and Greg O'Brien show in their essays on North America, the use of gifts within traditionally defined gender and generational structures gave way to commercial, market-oriented trade.[23] Similarly, there was a highly controversial debate that affected both Britain and the colonies over the criteria for the ownership of land. By what means was land considered to be "usefully" occupied, rather than being defined as *terra nullius* to be expropriated by newcomers? If the rights of indigenes were accepted, they might still be wrenched from their context and redefined within English perceptions of ownership.[24]

It is hoped that the articles in this collection will serve as a guide, pointing out to British historians approaches and conceptual developments animating the American literature that will help them advance their own research, and *vice versa*. A further benefit of bringing together papers covering different parts of the empire, with their own distinctive concerns, is that it can stimulate explicitly comparative work. Rather than treating each area in isolation, attention to the imperial perspective offers the corrective of a comparison by way of a negative check. Attention to the fate of the Khoi in the Cape Colony, for instance, or to the incorporation of the Maori into the sheep-raising economy of New Zealand, cautions scholars against too easy an assumption that there were no alternatives to the American outcome of extirpation by disease, military resistance, or relocation. The point is a modest but important one: in certain key regards, developments within the United States and the British empire diverged from a common starting point in respect of encounters between white settlers and indigenous societies. In this sense, imperial perspectives function as a variant of the cross-national comparative history envisioned by George Fredrickson. Such perspectives can undermine, in Fredrickson's words, "two contrary but equally damaging presuppositions – the illusion of total regularity and that of absolute unique-ness. Cross-national history, by acquainting one with what goes on elsewhere, may inspire a critical awareness of what is taken for granted in one's own country".[25]

Frederickson has also pointed out that cross-national comparative history "promotes a recognition that similar functions may be performed by differing means" in two or more cases.[26] His comment prompts identification of a profitable avenue for further enquiry: comparison of imperial systems. The work of Fernand Braudel and Immanuel Wallerstein suggests one approach, through the analysis of "world systems"; more recently, Robin Blackburn has focused on New World slavery and Anthony Pagden on imperial ideologies.[27] Much remains to be done, in taking comparisons further and applying them systematically on two levels. What is needed is explicit comparison of imperial systems as they operated within a fully global context, which ideally would entail comparisons not only of European empires but also of the Mughal, Russian, Japanese and Chinese empires. Secondly, it would be desirable to analyze the way in which various empires competed for influence or domi-nance in one area of the world, such as the French and British in the *pays en haut* of the Great Lakes, or in India.[28] Such an approach would have to include, at minimum, attention to the various ways in which imperial systems emerged over time, the different configurations of state power that both organized them and determined their limits, and the ways in which imperial administration and commerce impacted upon the process of class formation. Such a body of scholarship would, it is hoped, allow historians to isolate important variables and lead to greater theoretical and methodological rigour.

Several recent monographs exemplify this approach. Blackburn's recent analysis of slavery and the development of a "plantation complex" in the New World is suggestive of comparison between empires. Examining the experi-ence of the Iberian, Dutch, French and British empires, he highlights the

8

importance of state structures, relations within civil society, and the timing of commercial development within the world system. A similar, but more modest, comparison can be envisaged between the British and French empires, centring on the relationship between military and diplomatic imperatives on the one hand, and the commercialization of large areas of indigenous commodity production on the other. The contributions by Peter Way, Greg O'Brien and Nathaniel Sheidley contain material that can serve as a starting point for this sort of comparative project. By demonstrating how military imperatives in different situations, and within different imperial systems, connected with indigenous patterns of land holding, exchange and gender relations, these authors raise questions and point to themes that could guide a larger, fully worked-out comparison. Interactions between French and British military personnel and indigenous peoples took differing forms, but in both cases involved reciprocal influences. As Way shows, the decision by the British government to remove gifts to Native Americans and also to cut pay to soldiers destabilized both sides of the equation and related back to internal tussles within Britain over the costs of the imperial venture. French responses to Native Americans and to their own military were similarly connected with the distinctive structure of the *ancien régime*.

A further comparison in this vein could focus on the ability of the British and the French in India to extract tax revenue from land in the subcontinent. As Bayly argues in this volume, and at greater length elsewhere, the success of the former and the failure of the latter reflected in part the different structures of the imperial state – whereas Britain constructed an effective fiscal system both at home and, despite considerable difficulties, in India, the French faltered on the difficulties of completing this project of state formation. Where the British failed was in the Thirteen Colonies, for the attempt to pass more of the costs of imperial defence on to the white settlers led to resistance. Both in India and in the Thirteen Colonies, issues of identity were crucial. In North America, the settlers' claims to the rights of Englishmen led to a demand for representation and to hostility towards central government impositions which were similar to the sentiments expressed within England at the time of the excise crisis of 1733. In India, the *zamindars* were converted into a counterpart of the English gentry, in a way which eased the collection of land taxes by the East India Company.[29]

An altogether different, but equally promising approach would be to centre analysis upon the imposition of imperial authority and its constant policing and refurbishment through the agency of both colonists and indigenous peoples. Here, the trail blazed by the subaltern studies collective has provided some of the most exciting work in imperial history in the last twenty years. Drawing upon Gramscian theory and terminology, they maintain that relations between colonists and subalterns were based on "dominance" without achieving "hegemony".[30] The subaltern emerged from a discursive process, from the creation of colonial categories of knowledge which categorized and labelled the experience of the peoples of the colonies. Yet, despite the discursive genesis of the subaltern, it is also claimed that subalterns were able to act "on their own, that is, independently of the elite": their politics were "an autonomous domain, for it neither originated from elite politics nor did its existence depend on the latter".[31] Such an approach has been very fruitful, but it does have drawbacks. As Frederick Cooper comments, the subaltern historiographies on India and Africa confront but do not transcend the dichotomous vision characteristic of colonial ideologies. "The binaries of colonizer/colonized, western/non-western, and dominance/resistance begin as useful devices for opening up questions of power but end up constraining the search for precise ways in which power is deployed and the ways in which power is enjoyed, contested, deflected and appropriated." The challenge, Cooper asserts, is "to confront the power behind European expansion without assuming it was all-determining and to probe the clash of different forms of social organization without treating them as self-contained and autonomous".[32]

The point emerging from this volume, in common with subaltern studies, is that elites are almost axiomatically dominant and are rarely hegemonic. Nevertheless, the subaltern did not operate entirely apart from elite politics in an autonomous domain: there was always some room for a degree of manoeuvre within structures imposed by the imperial state. There were always limits to the extent of imperial power, as a result of constraints of cost, manpower, ideology and external threats from other European or indigenous states. British imperial power might be attained by force, either actual or threatened, but it was sustained by many other means. These might include trade or gifts, education and religious conversion, the incorporation of indigenous structures of authority within an imperial system, or the definition of tribes as "criminal". The essays by O'Brien, Sheidley and Way all show how indigenous people were able to exploit native diplomacy for their own ends, inserting themselves into European alliances and conflicts. The rule of the law might be about dominance, and it structured subaltern relations with the colonizers, yet it also created interstices within which subaltern people could exercise power. As Plane shows in her careful analysis of a court case on access to grazing land on Chappaquiddick, a Native American could operate through the courts and claim customary tenure. In the process, Native American categories and tenures were refracted through English legal principles, and the balance of power was grossly unequal. The significant point is that subaltern politics were not fully autonomous, but operated through the assumptions of the elite, which were themselves contested and changing over time. The discursive formation of the subaltern created a typology or classification of tenures to which the law gave more or less credence, and so gave the subaltern a greater or lesser degree of manouevre.

How is the concern for subalternity within the British empire to be linked with subalternity at home, in terms of class, gender, region, race and other categories? In Ranajit Guha's view, the metropolitan elite was dominant in the colonies but secured hegemony at home. The result, according to Gyan Prakash, was that "while the operations of power relations in colonial and metropolitan theatres have parallels, the conditions of subalternity were also irreducably different".[33] This raises the question of where parallels existed, and where differences; and it is essential to keep in view subalternity in both the metropole and the empire for they referred to each other.

A shortcoming of subaltern studies, and the recent emphasis on identities, has been a relative lack of interest in processes of capitalist development. Proponents of subaltern studies have been wary of economic history, on the grounds that it imposes a Western teleology on the history of the world, derived either from Marxism or from development economics, both of which imply a narrative of progressive capitalist advance. The criticism of much economic history is entirely justified, with its concern for patterns of trade and international flows of capital or revenues without an appreciation of the cultural implications for both parties in the transaction. But historians do need to analyze the process of capitalist development as a global phenomenon in order to understand how the system functioned and changed. Capitalism and the complexities and contingencies of its development should be brought back into the picture.[34]

In whatever way the attempt to insert imperial concerns into the making of national identities is written, one thing is clear: it must combine elements of the old narrative of the "clash of empires", in which indigenous peoples are given an important role, with a sensitivity to the discursive analysis of identities. This volume, we hope, suggests a possible avenue forward, an approach that is bound together by an emphasis on the changing formation and reformation of state-centred imperial systems and the extension of commercial networks across the globe. It is within this material framework that identities took shape, were tested against new realities, and re-negotiated. It is also within this framework that we can best see the ways in which identities and categories of existence were interrelated.

These processes continued to unfold as long as empires continued to exist and, indeed, they assumed new configurations once the era of decolonization opened. However, the present collection stops around 1850, and it is worth reflecting on the extent to which there was a major change at this point. The case made by Andrew Bank is that the 1840s and 1850s saw a "crisis of liberalism" within the empire, arising from a growing pessimism about the prospects of civilizing or converting indigenous peoples. He claims that there was a new racial conservatism by the 1850s, and that humanitarian and diplomatic views of relations on the frontier gave way to "iron-fisted militarism", resting on the assumption that the best way of improving the moral and material condition of indigenous peoples was through coercion and subjugation. The change was apparent in the policies of Sir George Grey in New Zealand and the Cape, where he adopted a programme of assimilation through dispossession. It is also argued that sexual relations between British men and indigenous women, which at least were tolerated in the eighteenth and early nineteenth centuries (as noted by McGillivray and Smandych in Canada), were no longer acceptable.[35]

The extent of any general crisis of liberalism in the empire needs careful delineation, and in particular the distinction must be drawn between colonies and dependencies. Representative government was granted to white settler societies, which gave political rights to Britons abroad in a similar way to the extension of the franchise to responsible property owners at home. There was a complex relationship between liberalism and racial discourse. In a sense, there was a triumph of liberalism both in the white settler colonies and in the metropole where new forms of state power and a new liberal political grammar emerged. A harsher punitive attitude was adopted towards indigenes, but also to the "residuum" at home.[36]

The fiscal-military state was reconstructed at home, with a shift to free trade and the introduction of the income tax. The reformed state of Peel and Gladstone gained in legitimacy through a stress on equity between classes and interests.[37] The relative tax burden fell as the costs of the national debt and warfare were reduced. There was a greater confidence in the use of the state within the empire and in the great cities of the metropole as an agent for progress and social reform. One way in which the benefits of free trade were secured for the British working class and a sense of "fairness" created was by the passing on of the costs of imperial defence from the centre to the periphery. Stability in London had its converse of strife and tension elsewhere in the empire.[38] What Bank terms the "crisis of liberalism" in the Cape had another side – a greater confidence in the benefits of state action which allowed the relations between missions and the state to be re-negotiated. The relationship was always rather ambivalent. On the one hand, state power was central to the creation of slavery and the dominance of a planter class in the Caribbean; it was possible to develop a radical critique of the state, at home and in the colonies, as exploitative and corrupt. On the other hand, missionaries and abolitionists could argue that access to the Colonial Office gave them some means of redress against the power of the planters in the Caribbean or white settlers in Australia who were expropriating the aborigines. They were highly critical of aspects of state power, but were also dependent on imperial protection. The relationship between the imperial state and missionary and abolitionist activity was therefore ambivalent: the state could be both the problem and the agent for its resolution. Some of these tensions emerge in Catherine Hall's discussion of the Baptist missionary William Knibb.[39] The abolition of slavery and the system of imperial protection could lead to a more positive attitude towards state action, which was now purified of interest: the irony was that it could therefore take a more intrusive line towards indigenous societies.

Such changes had implications at home as well as abroad, for race and class started to pull apart in the second quarter of the nineteenth century. The emancipation of slaves within the British empire contributed to the change, for evangelicals and humanitarians no longer viewed trade and commerce as the agents of degradation and exploitation, but rather as a means of civilizing and destroying indigenous slavery. Increasingly, the whiteness of the British working class was stressed and class conflict contained within a racialized language. Thomas Carlyle's essay of 1849 on the "negro question" reflected this shift, with its suggestion, still uneasy and cautious, that Blacks were somehow different. The tensions of the age of Chartism were resolved after 1848 in part by a stress on the virtues of English constitutionalism compared with continental despotism, which contributed to the legitimation of the British state and the triumph of liberalism at home.[40] But the "other" of English self-definition was not only European, for at the same time there was a greater emphasis on the racial superiority of "white" over "black". The implications of any crisis of liberalism in the colonies need to be thought through within the metropole.[41]

The innovation of bringing together the Neale and Commonwealth Fund Colloquia should be taken much further than has been possible here within the constraints of a single volume. It should be possible to continue beyond 1850, in order to appreciate the parallels and contrasts in attitudes to race within the United States and Britain. We need to analyze the ways in which capital and landed elites utilized indigenous labour on plantations, in mines and factories; we need to understand how indigenous peoples were constructed as consumers for exported goods; and we should consider the way in which politicians and the military, or educationalists and the churches, approached them. Themes identified here continued into the later nineteenth century, and indeed through to the present day. The coverage should also be extended to Africa, which was an obvious point of connection between English slave traders and American planters. However, the contributors to this joint meeting of the colloquia have provided enough to stimulate historians of both North America and Britain. Precedents exist to be followed rather than to foreclose discussion.

Notes

1 We wish to thank Julian Hoppit and Catherine Hall for their comments on an earlier draft.

2 For examples of the knowledge of empire, see J. Gascoigne, *Joseph Banks and the English enlightenment: useful knowledge and polite culture* (Cambridge, 1994) and P. J. Marshall & G. Williams, *The great map of mankind: British perceptions of the world in the age of enlightenment* (Cambridge, Mass., and London, 1982). See the plea for greater attention to imperial history by British historians from S. Marks, "History, the nation and empire: sniping from the periphery", *History Workshop Journal* **29**, 1990, pp. 111–19, and A. Burton, "Rules of thumb: British history and 'imperial culture' in nineteenth- and twentieth-century Britain", *Women's History Review* **3**, 1994, pp. 483–500.

3 C. A. Bayly, "The historiography of the 'second British empire' c. 1780–1995", in *Oxford History of the British Empire*, vol. 5, R. Winks (ed.), forthcoming.

4 L. Colley, "Clashes and collaborations", *London Review of Books* (18 July 1996), p. 8. For a discussion of some elements of different European responses to indigenous peoples, which does not consider the impact on European identities, see A. Pagden, *Lords of all the world: ideologies of empire in Spain, Britain and France, c. 1500–1800* (London, 1995).

5 H. Reynolds, *The law of the land* (Ringwood, Victoria, 1987), pp. 82–100.

6 *Ibid.*, pp. 46–8.

7 For example, R. White, *The middle ground: Indians, empires and republics in the Great Lakes region 1650–1815* (Cambridge, 1991) or C. G. Calloway, *Crown and calumet: British–Indian relations, 1783–1815* (Norman, Okla., 1971); also L. Thompson & H. Lamar, "The North American and South African frontiers", in *The Frontier in History: North America and South Africa Compared* (New Haven, Conn., 1981); W. Nugent, "Comparing wests and frontiers", in *The Oxford History of the American West*, C. A. Milner, C. O'Connor & M. A. Sandweiss (eds) (New York, 1994), pp. 803–33.

8 Renewed attention to white racial identity was inaugurated with the publication of D. Roediger's *The wages of whiteness: race and the making of the American working class* (London, 1991); see also the essays in his *Towards the abolition of whiteness: essays on race, politics, and working-class history* (London, 1994). Other key texts contributing to this revision include A. Saxton, *The rise and fall of the white republic: class, politics, and mass culture in nineteenth-century America* (London, 1990); E. Lott, *Love and theft: blackface minstrelsy and the American working class* (New York, 1993); N. Ignatiev, *How the Irish became white* (New York and London, 1994); and T. Almaguer, *Racial fault lines: the historical origins of white supremacy in California* (Berkeley, 1995); T. W. Allen, *Invention of the white race*, vol. 1: *Racial oppression and social control* (London, 1994).

9 W. Jordan, *White over Black: American attitudes towards the Negro, 1550–1812* (Chapel Hill, N. C., 1969).

10 For example, L. Colley, *Britons: forging the nation, 1730–1834* (London, 1990); D. Wahrman, *Imagining the middle class: the political representation of class in Britain, c. 1780–1840* (Cambridge, 1995) and P. Joyce, *Visions of the people: industrial England and the*

question of class, 1840–1914 (Cambridge, 1991); M. Kale, *Fragments of empire: capital, anti-slavery and Indian indentured labor migration* (Philadelphia, 1998); A. McClintock, *Imperial leather: race, gender, and sexuality in the imperial context* (London, 1995); J. Langton, "The industrial revolution and the regional geography of England", *Transactions of the Institute of British Geographers* n.s. **9**, 1984, pp. 145–67; J. Money, *Experience and identity: Birmingham and the West Midlands, 1760–1800* (Manchester, 1977).

11 For insightful discussion of "imperial location", see R. Gregg, "Apropos exceptionalism: imperial location and comparative histories of South Africa and the United States", in *American exceptionalism? US working-class formation in an international context*, R. Halpern & J. Morris (eds) (Basingstoke, 1997), pp. 220–306.

12 For example, S. Thorne, " 'The conversion of Englishmen and the conversion of the world inseparable': missionary imperialism and the language of class in early industrial Britain", in *Tensions of empire, colonial cultures in a bourgeois world*, F. Cooper & A. L. Stoler (eds) (Berkeley, 1997), pp. 238–62, and C. Hall, "Re-thinking imperial histories: the Reform Act of 1867", *New Left Review* **208** (November–December), 1994, pp. 3–29; see also R. Gregg & M. Kale, "The Empire and Mr Thompson: making of Indian princes and English working class", *Economic and Political Weekly* **32** (36), 6 September 1997, pp. 2273–88. For an interesting recent discussion of the shift from a stress on the common linguistic identity of Indians and Europeans to an emphasis on racial difference in the mid-nineteenth century, see T. R. Trautmann, *Aryans and British India* (Berkeley, 1997) and P. Robb (ed.), *The concept of race in South Asia* (Delhi, 1995).

13 J. Brewer, *The sinews of power: war, money and the English state, 1688–1783* (London, 1989); P. K. O'Brien & P. Hunt, "The rise of a fiscal state in England, 1485–1815", *Historical Research* **66**, 1993, pp. 129–76; P. Mathias & P. O'Brien, "Taxation in Britain and France, 1715–1810: a comparison of the social and economic incidence of taxes collected for the central government", *Journal of European Economic History* **5**, 1976, pp. 601–50; P. G. M. Dickson, *The financial revolution in England: a study in the development of public credit, 1688–1756* (London, 1967); J. Innes, "The domestic face of the military-fiscal state: government and society in eighteenth-century Britain", in *An imperial state at war*, L. Stone (ed.) (London, 1994), pp. 96–127.

14 C. Russell, *The fall of the British monarchies, 1637–1642* (Oxford, 1991) and J. Morrill & B. Bradshaw (eds), *The British problem c. 1534–1707: state formation in the Atlantic archipelago* (Basingstoke, 1996).

15 C. A. Bayly, "The British military-fiscal state and indigenous resistance: India, 1750–1820", in Stone, *Imperial state at war*, pp. 322–54; on the navigation system, see L. A. Harper, *The English navigation laws: a seventeenth-century experiment in social engineering* (New York, 1939) and J. B. Williams, *British commercial policy and trade expansion, 1750–1850* (Oxford, 1972); T. Keegan, *Colonial South Africa and the origins of the racial order* (Leicester and Charlottesville, Va., 1996).

16 A. L. Karras, *Sojourners in the sun: Scottish migrants in Jamaica and the Chesapeake, 1740–1800* (Ithaca, N.Y., 1992); A. I. MacInnes, *Clanship, commerce and the House of Stuart, 1603–1788* (East Linton, 1996); see the contribution to this volume by Peter Way.

17 See N. Canny, *Kingdom and colony: Ireland in the Atlantic world, 1560–1800* (Baltimore, 1988) and *The Elizabethan conquest of Ireland: a pattern established, 1565–76* (Hassocks, Sussex, 1978); see also D. B. Quinn, *The Elizabethans and the Irish* (Ithaca, N.Y., 1966).

18 For example, S. King, "Reconstructing lives: the poor, the poor law and welfare in Calverley, 1650–1820", *Social History* **22**, 1997, pp. 318–38; N. Landau, "The regulation

of immigration, economic structures and definitions of the poor in eighteenth-century England", *Historical Journal* **33**, 1990, pp. 541–71, and "The laws of settlement and the surveillance of immigration in eighteenth-century Kent", *Continuity and Change* **3**, 1988, pp. 391–420. These issues of entitlement were discussed in a previous Neale colloquium: *Charity, self-Interest and welfare in the English past*, M. J. Daunton (ed.) (London, 1996).

19   The classic accounts are R. H. Tawney, *The agrarian problem in the sixteenth century* (London, 1912) and E. P. Thompson, *Whigs and hunters: the origins of the Black act* (London, 1975) and *Customs in common* (London, 1991). The issue has revived more recently as a result of the debate over R. H. Brenner, "Agrarian class structure and economic development in pre-industrial Europe", *Past and Present* **70**, 1976, pp. 30–75, which points to the tussle between crown, lords and peasants over rent and taxes. See C. E. Searle, "The Cumbrian customary economy in the eighteenth century", *Past and Present* **110**, 1986, pp. 106–33; N. Gregson, "Tawney revisited: custom and the emergence of capitalist class relations in north-east Cumbria, 1600–1830", *Economic History Review* **42** (2nd series), 1989, pp. 18–42, and R. W. Hoyle, "Tenure and the land market in early modern England: or a late contribution to the Brenner debate", *Economic History Review* **43** (2nd series), 1990, pp. 1–20.

20   R. Smandych, "Colonial welfare laws and practices: coping without an English poor law in Upper Canada, 1792–1837", *Manitoba Law Journal* **23**, 1996, pp. 214–6, and R. Dare, "Paupers' rights: Governor Grey and the poor law in South Australia", *Australian Historical Studies* **25**, 1992, pp. 220–43.

21   For example, J. M. Neeson, *Commons: common right, enclosure and social change in England, 1700–1820* (Cambridge, 1993) and J. Humphries, "Enclosure, common rights and women: the proletarianization of families in the late eighteenth and early nineteenth centuries", *Journal of Economic History* **50**, 1990, pp. 17–42.

22   Thompson, *Customs in common*, pp. 165–6 on Maoris; on the Aborigines, see Reynolds, *Law of the land*; on Scotland, see T. M. Devine, "Social responses to agrarian 'improvement': the Highland and Lowland clearances in Scotland", in *Scottish society, 1500–1800*, R. A. Houston & I. D. Whyte (eds) (Cambridge, 1989), pp. 148–68, and I. Whyte, *Agriculture and society in seventeenth-century Scotland* (Edinburgh, 1979); R. A. Dodgshon, "West Highland chiefdoms, 1500–1745: a study in redistributive exchange", in *Economy and Society in Scotland and Ireland*, R. Mitchison and P. Roebuck (eds) (Edinburgh, 1988), pp. 27–37, and "'Pretence of blude' and 'place of thair duelling': the nature of Highland clans, 1600–1745", in Houston and Whyte, *Scottish society*, pp. 169–98; E. R. Creegan, "The tacksmen and their successors: a study of tenurial reorganisation in Mull, Morven and Tiree in the early eighteenth", *Scottish Studies* **13**, 1969, pp. 93–143; MacInnes, *Clanship, commerce and the House of Stuart*.

23   On this process, see also J. Axtell, "The first consumer revolution", in his *Beyond 1492: encounters in colonial North America* (New York and Oxford, 1992), pp. 125–51.

24   See Thompson, *Customs in common*, Chapter 3 on "Custom, law and common right"; W. Cronon, *Changes in the land: Indians, colonists and the ecology of New England* (New York, 1983), Chapter 4 on the definition of property rights; see also P. Langford, *Public life and the propertied Englishman, 1689–1798* (Oxford, 1991), for a discussion of property rights. Reynolds, *The Law of the land*, considers the debates within England and Australia over the property rights, if any, of Aborigines; on the Cape, see Keegan, *Colonial South Africa*; and on India, E. Stokes, *The English Utilitarians and India* (Oxford, 1959) and P. G. Robb, *Ancient rights and future comfort: Bihar, and Bengal Tenancy Act of 1885, and British rule in India*

(Richmond, Surrey, 1996). For an example of the redefinition of property rights in a different context which allowed alienation within England, see C. Fisher, *Custom, work and market capitalism: the Forest of Dean colliers, 1788–1888* (London, 1981).

25 G. Fredrickson, "From exceptionalism to variability: recent developments in cross-national comparative history", *Journal of American History* **82**, 1995, pp. 587–604; a similar methodological point is made by J. Breuilly in *Labour and liberalism in nineteenth-century Europe: essays in comparative history* (Manchester, 1992), introduction and conclusion.

26 Fredrickson, "From exceptionalism to variability", p. 604.

27 F. Braudel, *The perspective of the world* (1985) and *The wheels of commerce* (London, 1985); I. Wallerstein, *Historical capitalism* (London, 1983); Pagden, *Lords of all the world*; R. Blackburn, *The making of New World slavery: from the Baroque to the modern* (London, 1997).

28 For example, White, *Middle ground*.

29 Bayly, "British military-fiscal state"; see also Mathias and O'Brien, "Taxation in Britain and France".

30 G. Prakash, "Subaltern studies as postcolonial criticism", *American Historical Review* **99**, 1994, pp. 1475–90; G. Chakravorty Spivak, "Subaltern studies: deconstructing historiography", in *In other worlds: essays in cultural politics* (Princeton, N.J., 1988); and R. Guha (ed.), *Subaltern studies: writings on South Asian history and society, vols 1–5* (Delhi, 1982–7).

31 Ranajit Guha, "On some aspects of the historiography of colonial India", *Subaltern studies*, vol. 1, pp. 3–4, cited in Prakash, "Subaltern studies", p. 1478.

32 F. Cooper, "Conflict and coercion: rethinking colonial African history", *American Historical Review* **99**, 1994, p. 1517.

33 Prakash, "Subaltern studies", p. 1480.

34 See the debate between G. Prakash, "Writing post-orientalist histories of the Third World: perspectives from Indian historiography", *Comparative Studies in Society and History* **32**, 1990, pp. 383–408, and R. O'Hanlon & D. Washbrook, "After orientalism: culture, criticism and politics in the third world", *Comparative Studies in Society and History* **34**, 1992, pp. 141–67.

35 R. Hyam, *Empire and sexuality: The British experience* (Manchester, 1991), provides one, contentious, view of the shift in sexual attitudes. On the greater stress on "racial science", see Robb (ed.), *Concept of race*.

36 On attitudes to the poor and the "residuum" at home, see G. Stedman Jones, *Outcast London: a study in Victorian society* (Oxford, 1971).

37 For example, P. Harling, *The waning of "old corruption": the politics of electoral reform in Britain, 1779–1846* (Oxford, 1996) and E. Biagini, *Liberty, retrenchment and reform: popular liberalism in the age of Gladstone, 1860–80* (Cambridge, 1992).

38 R. Hyam, *Britain's imperial century, 1815–1914* (Basingstoke, 1993), notes a spate of uprisings in the late 1850s and 1860s. Bayly argues that the costs of the fiscal–military state were exported to the empire as well as reduced at home: see Bayly, "British military-fiscal state", p. 18.

39 Keegan, *Colonial South Africa*.

40 Biagini, *Liberty, retrenchment and reform*; M. Finn, *After Chartism: class and nation in English radical politics, 1848–74* (Cambridge, 1993).

41 For the connection between civilizing missions at home and the colonies, see A. L. Stoler, *Race and the education of desire: Foucault's history of sexuality and the colonial order of things* (Durham, N.C., 1995) and "Rethinking colonial categories: European communities and

the boundaries of rule", *Comparative Studies in Society and History* **31**, 1989, pp. 134–61; P. Hollis, "Anti-slavery and British working-class radicalism in the years of reform", in *Anti-Slavery, Religion and Reform*, C. Bolt & S. Drescher (eds) (Folkestone, 1980), pp. 294–315; Thorne, "The conversion of Englishmen and the conversion of the world inseparable".

Chapter Two

The British and indigenous peoples, 1760–1860: power, perception and identity

C. A. Bayly

A century or even two decades ago, the two terms used in the title of our conference, "the British" and "indigenous peoples", seemed solid enough. The term "British" was taken to refer to an old national entity; the term "indigenous peoples" to a set of fixed racial groups within the empire. These indigenous peoples were thought to have been condemned to global defeat by their genetic or, as later commentators argued, their economic failure. Now both terms seem unstable and contentious. Today's political arguments about the Union within the British Isles and about "native rights" in the Commonwealth and former empire have subjected both of them to close scrutiny. Meanwhile, historians have begun to expose the particular conjunctures of political and economic change which created both "the British" and "native peoples".

Historians now insist that, far from being a given, Britishness was a recent, fragile and contested ideology of power. The century between the accession of George III and Benjamin Disraeli's first ministry witnessed the creation of a still friable sense of British identity and British statehood, overriding regional patriotisms and local particularism. According to Raphael Samuel, Linda Colley and John Brewer,[1] the catalysts were several: domestic economic integration, international war, the revival of strenuous Protestant Christianity, the reinvention of the British crown, and of course, the experience of empire itself. Empire-building began in the British Isles and its outward expansion continued to help drive forward the forces of domestic British integration. Great new caches of patronage in civil offices, colonelcies, bishoprics and surveyor-generalships in India, the Cape, and Canada assuaged the hunger of embattled gentry from the English regions, the Irish Pale and the Scottish borders, confirming a sense of common Britishness.

In fact, during the century from 1760 to 1860, domestic economic expansion and the experience of empire were finally absorbing the "indigenous peoples" of the British Isles themselves. Scottish gentry and merchants became businessmen, soldiers and administrators across the empire.[2] Gaelic speakers from the North and West of Ireland entered the East India Company's army and medical services in large numbers.[3]

This pattern of assimilation was not a smooth one. It raised sharp conflicts about identity, language, and the control of local resources within Britain itself.[4] The very notion of "indigenous people" within the British Isles was fundamentally re-worked in the course of our period.[5] Scottishness within the empire was redesigned by Walter Scott and Robert Burns and annexed to the British crown through traditionalizing ritual at the very time when the last Gaelic-speaking communities were disappearing. Irishness was, on the other hand, redesigned as a predominantly Catholic force outside the empire as a result of the experience of the 1798 Rebellion and the Catholic revival.[6] Meanwhile, British subjects in the empire themselves played an important role in both strengthening British identity and, in some cases, insisting on the separateness of Ireland's "spiritual empire" of Christian teaching. Here is one illustration: an Irish doctor in the Bengal medical service advocated in the 1820s the spread of English among Indians. The process, he implied, was a natural progression, just as his own Celtic-speaking forebears had been anglicized in the preceding century.

Outside the British Isles, the years from 1760 to 1860 also saw the creation of a new concept of indigenous peoples. Eighteenth-century ideas about the unity of mankind and the diffusion through the world of the lost tribes of Israel were slowly being replaced by the vision of a ladder or hierarchy of development up or down which societies must pass.[7] The experience of governance and economic exploitation had encouraged British scholars and administrators to rank mankind hierarchically in this way. Moralizing movements of imperial reform and anti-slavery pointed in a similar direction.

Yet, as within the British Isles, so in the world outside, the term "indigenous peoples" was fractured and contested from the beginning. Were people of mixed race, or slaves or families long resident in the Caribbean or southern Africa, "indigenous" or not? Were the Khoikhoi or "Bastard Hottentots" of mixed race dwelling at the Cape "indigenous people" or not?[8] The same question was asked of the mixed-race Métis of Canada. Again, despite a parliamentary campaign from 1828 to 1834 the Eurasians of British India were denied the status of British subjects and debarred from voting and living in Britain.[9] Yet they held themselves increasingly separate from Indians. Particularly difficult to categorize were the so-called aboriginal or native peoples of southern and south-eastern Asia. These forest dwellers and nomads – now called *adivasis* in India and *orang asli* in south-east Asia – were populations anciently settled in their various regions.[10] But where was the line of demarcation with other Indians or Malays to be found and who had drawn it? This debate about origins has considerable resonance today, at a time when United Nations and other agencies are targeting economic resources at "indigenous peoples", often very narrowly defined.[11]

The argument of this chapter, then, is that the period 1760–1860 was a critical one in the epistemological and economic creation of "indigenous peoples" as a series of comparable categories across the globe. But it also argues that a consideration of the nature of British imperial expansion and of British intellectual history is central to an understanding of the invention of these "indigenous peoples".

Recently, studies of the encounter between the British and non-Europeans have tried to recover the decentred narrative, the local discourse and the particular experience of the oppressed and marginalized. Historians have understandably sought to distance themselves from the grand narratives of progress, state-building and capitalist development which held sway between the later eighteenth century and the so-called last "development decade" of the 1970s. But this project is in danger of foundering in its own particularism and of becoming a form of post-modern antiquarianism. For it is still necessary to ask what the "centre" was around which these decentred discourses revolved. What was the motive force of the juggernaut which rolled down on to Celtic Britain, Mediterranean Europe, Asia, Africa and North America between 1760 and 1860? The strong sense that the contemporary triumph of global capitalism and of Western-dominated global media was indirectly pre-figured by the events of the eighteenth and early nineteenth centuries only adds urgency to the need to locate the voices of the marginalized in a broader context.

Until large-scale territorial empire came into existence during the century from 1750 to 1850, British influence outside the West Indies and the Thirteen Colonies, where it was already brutally disruptive of indigenous peoples through the slave system, was limited to the economic and military ripples set up by the network of forts and markets scattered across the globe and periodically linked by the Royal Navy. Even on the frontiers of the denser English expansion in north America, settlers remained dependent on indigenous intermediaries. They were still forced to bargain with, to cajole and to accommodate indigenous powers.

Hereafter, the territorial expansion of the Seven Years' War and the later Anglo-French wars from 1756–1815 imposed a wholly new set of conditions on the majority of non-European populations worldwide. For all the talk of the high point of imperialism in the later nineteenth century, the basic system of British imperial dominance was put in place between 1760 and 1860. Not very much of economic value was added thereafter. Curiously, though, our present "theories of imperialism" have relatively little to say about this period, and until they do it will be difficult to analyze broadly the British impact on indigenous peoples.

Peter Cain and Anthony Hopkins recently reaffirmed that this critical period of expansion was relatively "neglected", drawing it into their picture of the military-fiscal empire of "gentlemanly capitalists", happy to live off, own and trade in an expanding national debt.[12] As indicated in my *Imperial Meridian* (London, 1989), I broadly accept that position for Asia. In other parts of the world, of course, the importance of British textile exports in the promotion of imperial interests should also be accorded considerable importance in the process of expansion, as recent revisions have suggested. But either way, a general characterization of the economic and cultural quality of expanding Britain is not the same as an account of the remarkable growth of territorial empire as such. Here historians need to be more precise about the causal mechanisms which linked metropolitan crises generated by the finance of warfare, or the imperatives of trade, with territorial acquisitions outside the metropolis.

Before considering the broader mechanics of empire, however, it is first necessary to point to a critical special case: the West Indies. In the Caribbean slave system there is no question that direct commercial interest continued to play a predominant role in the politics of empire throughout the period. About 1780 the West Indies system accounted for something like 15 per cent of Britain's total overseas trade and the economies of the western British and Irish ports and their hinterlands were dominated by the sugar and slave trades. If anything, the loss of the American colonies increased the dependence of Glasgow, Cork and Bristol on the West Indies. As the Elder Pitt said, the Caribbean estates were an essential part of the landed wealth of Great Britain. French rivalry in the region, particularly acute in the 1780s, was as dangerous to the national interest as French mastery in the English Channel. From this perspective, the enormous commitment of soldiers, sailors and treasure to fighting in the Caribbean, especially during the 1790s, giving rise to at least 60,000 casualties, was entirely rational, as Michael Duffy has recently argued.[13] Yet this should not lead us to resurrect a monolithic or simplistic argument about the imperialism of trade. For quite apart from its direct commercial importance, the strong British position in the West Indies also conferred a decisive military and fiscal advantage on Britain. Throughout the later eighteenth century, the value of the trade and investments in Caribbean sugar, tobacco and cotton production made it infinitely easier for the government to borrow money in order to fight its European and Asian wars. George III had said during the American conflict, "If we lose our sugar islands it will be impossible to raise money to continue the war." Pitt and Dundas echoed this sentiment in 1797. Later, without a secure British position in the West Indies, the slow British recovery in the Mediterranean and the Peninsula during the Napoleonic wars would have been impossible. Not least among the advantages the British gained from the continuation of the West Indian trades was the massive pool of ships and seamen which it provided for the navy in time of war. After all, this was the main reason why Horatio Nelson supported the slave trade against its enemies.

Geo-political and military concerns also overlaid strictly commercial interests in the Caribbean in another sense. After 1780, fear of slave rebellion and of French republicanism was a powerful incentive to aggression and expansion in the region which forged a common interest between the once mutually suspicious plantocracies of the islands and ministries in London. The capture of Martinique, San Domingue, Guadaloupe and Trinidad certainly put local British merchants into a strong position in the emerging trade with the Spanish colonies, but it was military and naval concerns which prompted their initial conquest.

Given the continuing economic importance of the West Indian trades through to at least 1815, however, what needs to be explained is the great increase of Britain's territorial empire *outside* this area, particularly since the value of British trade in itself throughout the Asian, African, Pacific and even Canadian worlds was neither as centrally important to the domestic economy nor significantly growing. This takes us back to the issue of the finance of warfare on the periphery of the British empire. Great as was the importance of the West Indies, it did stand as an exception in one significant sense. The islands could never adequately provide for their own security by raising local military or naval forces. The whites of the islands were too small in numbers and the use of slaves or freed slaves could only be envisaged to a limited extent without subverting their whole economic system.

By contrast, British territorial expansion throughout the empire beyond the West Indies between 1760 and 1830 was driven centrally by the need to finance and provision imperial armies from local resources. It was redoubled by the resistance of indigenous peoples to that very expansion. Military fiscalism on the periphery became a *perpetuum mobile* which far outran, and even endangered, the interests of the very trading concerns it was designed to protect.

Even during this period, the imperative of controlling trade and production remained very significant, of course, especially for the mercantile interests which worked on the fringes of the emerging colonial state. This became more evident after 1830 when free trade at last became an effective political

23

doctrine in domestic British politics and territorial empire came to be viewed with relative disfavour. In time, again, the industrial revolution set up powerful demands for new resources and for the seizure of captive markets during periods of domestic and European stagnation. The search for markets and for products such as opium, timber and raw cotton re-emerged as a powerful contributory factor to, and justification of, imperial expansion. By the 1840s statesmen hoped that colonies of settlement would provide raw materials for an expanding population at home and begin to accept British manufactured goods.

Over much of the globe, however, all this happened after territorial acquisition had occurred, and not before it. Indeed, it was as a consequence of the military and naval dispositions and requirements of this period of empire-building that the critical new links in international capitalism and methods of economic management were generated. It was military finance which initially set the juggernaut rolling. Why had it become such a pressing aspect of British and wider European external policy?

From the middle years of the eighteenth century the emerging European states were caught in the scissors of military fiscalism. Armies and navies increased in size and the costs of warfare escalated massively.[14] The very early part of the eighteenth century witnessed the ousting of the matchlock gun by the flintlock; the middle and later part of the century saw the development of the breech-loader, greater sophistication in rifling and new forms of heavy artillery. Military and naval costs spiralled upwards and the numbers of men needed to fight major land battles quintupled, particularly after the French revolution.

The costs of warfare outside Europe between competing groups of merchants and companies increased by the same degree.[15] New forms of statecraft, economic and military management and new weaponry were filtering into the non-European world. Some of these changes of scale by indigenous states preceded the new imperial age; indeed, the supposed "threat" from better organized indigenous states sometimes incited this expansion. The new styles of casting were adapted first by Persian and then by Indian princes. More sophisticated and costly French-style fortifications were built throughout India and the Middle East in the later eighteenth century, greatly prolonging and adding to the cost of sieges. In North America, the new rifles of American and British forces came into the hands of American Indians who used them with great effect against the European invader.

Problems of state financing, already acute, became critical as a result of these enhanced military and naval demands. Urban taxes and excise could not be raised too fast without jeopardizing the social peace of European cities, as Walpole and his French contemporaries found to their cost. Land tax could not be increased because of the resistance of territorial aristocracies. European powers had become world powers without the financial muscle to fill their expanded role. The answer in the eyes of domestic politicians was to off-lay the expenses of the new military organization and technology on to settlers, creoles and indigenous peoples wherever possible. After 1760, the British and the Spanish both tried to reorganize their American and Caribbean empires. Settler society was to be taxed for its own protection; indigenous peoples were to be subject to stricter controls, and if possible exploited as a labour pool; the profits of colonial trade and office were to be reappropriated in the form of quasi-monopolies by the hungry gentry of the metropolis.

As we know, the American settlers and the Spanish creoles revolted and destroyed these empires rather than submit to further metropolitan taxation.[16] By comparison, in the Asian world, the British off-laying of the costs of warfare and tighter administration on to peasants and princes brought about a great increase in the size of territorial empire. While a combination of fiscal and export interests may have provided the motor of British expansion in the metropolis, the form and sequence of territorial acquisition can only be understood as a series of conjunctures in the periphery. As Indian historians have shown in detail, the East India Company's demand for military subsidies in silver rupees pushed some rulers and peasantries into revolt. Others suffered a slow erosion of their resources and ceded swathes of their territory to the British to protect what remained.[17] The presence of large British military forces under treaty acted everywhere as a provocation and a cause for further intervention.

The advantages of trade were, of course, widely invoked to justify territorial acquisition whether it was in the Caribbean, the Canadian West or the Cape. Areas once conquered certainly provided markets for new manufactures as well as extra salaries for gentlemenly capitalists, as Martin Daunton has pointed out. But the pressures of what Douglas Peers[18] has called the imperial "garrison state" acted inexorably as a force for sub-imperialism. Peers is quite right when he discounts strictly commercial motives for the wars against Nepal (1814–16) and against Burma (1824–6). There was some interest in the teak of Tenasserim and the chimera of a new China trade in these cases, of course. But, in the words of Peers, "war arose because Anglo-Indian militarism demanded it".[19] Moreover, in the revived Ottoman empire, Konbaung Burma, Gurkhali Nepal and Ranjit Singh's Punjab, the British encountered several of the most prominent examples of the second generation of Asian military states, forced to expand their own land and revenues or perish.

The imperial garrison state also took root outside British Asia. At Versailles Lord Castlereagh bargained fiercely to hold on to the Cape Colony, St Helena and Mauritius not "for their commercial value" but "because they affect essentially the engagement and security of [British] dominion".[20] By 1808 the British garrison at the Cape had increased to 5,000 from the measly 1,500 maintained there by the Batavians during the peace of Amiens. The form of government and the economic measures of British government on the Cape before 1830, and in particular the tying of indigenous labour by pass laws, derived from the need to finance and service the garrison and transiting ships.

Even in the northern part of the old British North American empire, military and geo-political interests played an important secondary role to the direct commercial concerns represented by the Newfoundland fisheries, the timber industry and the Northwestern and Hudson's Bay Companies. As Elizabeth Mancke has recently pointed out,[21] the role of the domestic British state and of its military and naval forces in what became Canada had long been much more obtrusive than it was further south in the Thirteen Colonies. British ministries' fears of French, Russian and Spanish intrusion as much as the need to arbitrate between the quarrelsome companies and local entrepreneurs dictated this. After 1783, British territorial expansion into central and north-western Canada and treaty-making with native peoples continued to be driven forward by rivalries with the Americans and Russians and by the need to secure revenues to pay for an exaggerated military presence. These concerns continued to influence the nature of Canadian political culture until well into the nineteenth century. In Mancke's words, "the red coats of the army, rather than the red coats of the North West Mounted Police preceded British settlement" in nineteenth-century Canada.

The expanding imperial garrison state did not fade into insignificance with the dawn of the supposed era of free-trade imperialism and utilitarian government after 1830. Of course, more direct commercial motives played a role in the Arrow War against China of 1856–60 and the expansion of whalers across the Pacific. After 1815, the growing pressure of free white settlement in Canada, the Cape and Australasia certainly imposed different local pressures on indigenous land and polities, drawing in their wake more methodical and statistical methods of government. But these commercial interests still combined in explosive ways with the established military and garrison character of empire. New South Wales was run as an enlightened despotism of naval and authoritarian governors for its first decade. Later its character was powerfully influenced by the military *coloniae* of the New South Wales Corps. Governor Arthur's Tasmania had at its core a military-slave system, legitimated in English law as a penal colony.[22] Inside, convicts were subject to the brutality of martial law. Outside, the aboriginal people were corralled and exterminated like pheasants on an officers' hunt. The city of Auckland supported as many as eight thousand British troops in the 1860s and this military presence itself intensified the pressures which contributed to the wars with the Maori.

Can we generalize at all about the impact which this model had on indigenous societies over this long period and huge area? The earlier lightly armed trading-mart model which prevailed outside North America and the Caribbean up to the mid-eighteenth century had, of course, subtly changed local societies. Indigenous and mixed-race entrepreneurs – whalers, fur traders or merchants in calico – had benefited as intermediaries between the British and their own societies. The cash economy had made significant inroads in the hinterland of the port cities. Indigenous rulers had recruited themselves as allies and receivers of weapons and missionaries from the Europeans.[23]

The territorial military fiscalism of the following phase, however, vastly increased these pressures. With its civilian and commercial fellow-travellers, it wrought more profound changes in indigenous societies. The main determinants of this impact were disease, warfare and the differential effect that new military and commercial opportunities and disasters had on indigenous peooples. Of course, this was nothing new. On a smaller scale all this had already taken place in the West Indian islands, the colonies of mainland North America, and the societies of the West African coast which had been savaged and re-wrought by the slave trade over nearly two centuries. Now, however, this grim cycle was to be replayed on a much vaster scale, with slavery itself giving way over much of the world to new systems of revenue and crop extraction from African and Asian peasantries. It is true that the tried and tested ways of exploitation in the slave system continued to operate throughout this period. Figures put together by John Iliffe from the researches of Phillip Curtin, Barbara Solow and others suggest that the end of the eighteenth century may well have seen the European slave trade, and certainly the British slave trade, at its historic height. The very pressures for money making in a period of global war meant that slave extraction in Africa and slave exploitation in the Americas were redoubled in vigour. Initially, too, the abolition of the British and French slave trades in 1807 and 1793 effected little more than a cosmetic change. Slavery continued to distort African societies, with old slave ports and aristocracies going under while new ones came up. The move was from legal British and French ships to illegal ones, or to Spanish and Portuguese ones. Ironically also, new imperial holdings and new tied trades in palm-oil and cocoa along the African coast came into being as an indirect effect of the very attempt to suppress the slave system by the two powers.

Nevertheless, what was new about this era was the massive expansion of European interference with non-European societies and the forging of wholly new forms of dependency worldwide. The brutality of the slave system has naturally transfixed the gaze of historians. But when Charles Metcalfe went from his post as governor-general of India to take up his new one as governor of Jamaica, he remarked that the ex-slaves were vigorous and well fed, by comparison with the crushed and exploited peasantry of India.

Not surprisingly in this globalization of the Caribbean cycle, death was the main camp-follower. Supplied with new weapons, indigenous peoples fought each other with greater savagery as North American and Caribbean native peoples had done a century or more before. The Maori of the Bay of Islands area established a new military dominance over the North Island peoples of New Zealand.[24] During the East Indian wars of the early 1800s or the commando campaigns in the Cape under Lord Somerset, disruptions of trade and exchange created local man-made scarcities. Equally, the pressure of demands for cash revenues or labour services weakened populations everywhere and made them vulnerable to the famines that affected much of Europe, Asia and Africa during the 1780s, 1830s and 1840s. As Alfred Crosby pointedly demonstrated, disease spread in the trains of the great garrison armies and the Royal Navy.[25] Thomas Malthus considered that the death of population, of which he heard rumours all around him, was a general condition of mankind. What he was really hearing, however, were the cries of the distant victims of a quite specific set of historical conjunctures.

Yet military imperialism also brought in its wake change and adaptation, especially because many of the societies subjected to the new European deluge were both biologically and economically more resilient than the native peoples of coastal America and the Caribbean had been. Most of the new bazaars and marts which were established in the non-European world over this period were not initially the boons of free trade or places of free exchange. They were military posts and cantonments which were only later filled out by the commerce in tropical commodities, grain for the European table, furs or forest produce. Around the great military posts, however, contact with European soldiery and methods of warfare had encouraged the diffusion of new social and intellectual techniques. Hybrid medicines, printing presses, maps, better metallurgical techniques – all these spread round the rim of the military settlement.

Patterns of exchange, production and taxation were modified in similar ways across the empire. In the heat of war against European enemies, the British used large amounts of military labour, drawn not only from settled peasantries with a military tradition, but from nomadic and pastoral people on the colonial frontiers. The Khoikhoi farmers, North Indian Rajput and Bhumihar warriors, Nepali Gurkhas and, later, North Island Maori were enlisted as peasant mercenaries to reinforce the over-stretched British regiments. Supplementing landholding incomes with military service, such war-rior elites reinvented themselves as an indigenous gentry, and played an important political role for the British down to the end of the nineteenth century.[26] Since interests such as these were also critical intermediaries in the levying of rural taxation, the organization of labour or the supply of com-modities to the colonial state, they were vested with land rights and encour-aged to buy the products of British machine looms. Of necessity involved in transactions of trust with their white rulers, they also came to be seen as racially superior, as descendants of Aryans or sometimes Ethiopians or Jews, but certainly marked out by nature with superior virtue and physiques from their degraded populations.

The fate of the less settled and less agriculturally-based "tribal" people was very different. North American Indians and Khoisan or Xhosa warriors at the Cape were initially employed by British armies as allies and scouts. So too were members of East Indian and Malay "tribal" groups dwelling in the hills and forests.

In the longer run, however, many of these supposedly "predatory" mobile people came to be seen as a nuisance by the colonial regime. Their military importance to the empire declined after the end of the wars with the French, Spanish, Dutch and Americans. Mobile peoples were increasingly subjected to punitive raids. Their resources were seized by settlers, both indigenous and white, and their forest lands were walled off by interventionist colonial forestry departments, alarmed by the spectre of deforestation and climatic change. The appropriation and later abandonment of such peoples by the colonial power widened ethnic and social fractures within indigenous societies which had once functioned as interrelated polities. The new dispensation separated them from settled societies with whom they had traditionally traded, worshipped and fought. They were called savages, later to be reinvented as "indigenous peoples" in today's narrower sense.

We can, therefore, see two broad patterns in the global relations between the British and indigenous peoples over this critical century. These reflected changes in the nature of the imperial impact from early culture-contact and trade, through the era of military imperialism to the settler deluge and intrusive government after 1850.

First, we should consider those indigenous societies which could not reproduce themselves without resort to hunting or fishing and were socially structured by the life of the huntsman and warrior. This included not only societies such as the Australian Aborigine and the San of the Cape, which were fundamentally nomadic, but also semi-agricultural communities such as the Iroquois, the Maori or the East Indian Kolis, all of whom needed wild meat, fish, or forest produce to sustain themselves through the winter.[27]

29

In the case of such peoples, a period of early culture-contact and trade when the European needed indigenous protection gave way to the era of military imperialism, when substantial change in indigenous societies took place. As we have seen, the colonial power first selected out allies from among privileged sections of these peoples. Sometimes large rewards flowed to them for mercenary or guiding services for British armies. Internal warfare and depredation were encouraged, but many chieftains benefited from the possession of new weapons and trade goods. Sometimes this led to a short-lived cultural efflorescence, as among the North-West Coast Indians whose potlatch rites of gift-giving expanded after contact with the Europeans.[28] Ironically, it was these rites of friendship and beneficence which marked out the Indians as "degenerate" and spendthrift for the hard moralists of early Victorian Canada.

Communities with a more developed agriculture and a strong sense of territoriality survived best in this phase. Australian Aborigines and South African San, nomads with a feeling for the charisma of the land, but no strong territorial rootedness and no function in agricultural production, taxation or trade, were looted and driven away first.

This era of sharp differentiation was followed in such semi-agricultural and semi-hunting societies by a third phase of massive cultural and economic disruption. This accompanied the development of settler and settled government. It gathered pace from 1800 on the eastern side of North America, but a generation later elsewhere in the world. In this phase, encroaching white settlement drove away even more rapidly the animals – kangaroo, whales, beaver, bison or deer – which sustained the substance and culture of indigenous peoples. Their response could only be to fight and face extermination, to adapt to European husbandry and disintegrate culturally, or to withdraw, so leaving the land vacant for European settlement.

We can see analogous sequences in the other major type, the peasant, literacy-aware societies of Asia and North Africa which had domesticated animals for millennia before the European arrival. Here, the first stage of military imperialism once again offered some benefits to client rajadoms or military aristocracies, but also intensified conflict among them. In the second phase after about 1840, the harsher extraction of revenue or cash crops encouraged a dramatic levelling down of indigenous society, and a further "peasantization", or even proletarianization, of its populations.[29]

In these peasant societies, white farm and plantation settlement remained superficial by comparison with Australasia, the western Cape or North America. In them, Indians, Arabs, Chinese or Malays still controlled the vast bulk of capital and the means of agricultural production in their homelands. Nevertheless, the indirect pressures of the mature capitalist world economy, transmitted by the railways and steamboat, fell on the indigenous peasant peoples at much the same time as settler colonization impacted fully on the peasant-hunter populations mentioned earlier. This perhaps explains the apparent coincidence in the mid-nineteenth century of large-scale indigenous resistance in very diverse economic and cultural circumstances. This ranged from the Indian "Mutiny" to the Xhosa and New Zealand wars.

These two models of change are, of course, driven critically by economic assumptions. It is difficult to see how any worthwhile model of imperialism would not privilege economic elements in this period of colonial expansion. The British forward movement was powered by the need to secure revenue, produce and manpower for their military and naval forces and latterly for their settlers and merchants. Still, subtle discursive practices intervened to shape its impact, as we shall see, and not everything that occurred in this era can be seen simply in terms of European exploitation and indigenous resistance. Issues of politics and culture also intervened in these processes in critical ways. James Belich has shown that a more aggressive notion of British sovereignty contributed as much to the outbreak of the New Zealand wars as settler land hunger.[30] Governor Grey's period in South Africa supports the same point. Similarly, Lord Dalhousie's overweening intervention in Indian polities and disregard of Indian sovereignties helped spark the Indian rebellion. By now, the colonial state was driven by newly hardened ideological and positivistic legal norms as well as by economic imperatives. It is to ideology that the chapter next turns.

As we have seen, military power, demographic and ecological change shaped the relations between the British and indigenous peoples over the late eighteenth and early nineteenth centuries. But the way that these peoples were understood, represented and classified by European agents was an equally important part of their fate, indeed of the very creation of the concept of indigenous peoples. The ideologies and attitudes of soldiers, missionaries, administrators, politicians and scientists did not simply reflect the needs of colonial power. But they were invariably related dialogically to it. New maps of mankind and the natural world flowed outwards from Britain's universities and learned societies. These changes of mood often reflected broader changes in European sensibilities. Yet conflicts and constructions of society generated on the colonial frontiers played an active rather than a passive part in the creation of the new formulations. Indigenous voices penetrated these debates, though often distorted and sometimes to be discounted.

The styles of knowledge which the British constructed about indigenous peoples over the century between Plassey in 1757 and the Treaty of Waitangi in 1840 were strongly influenced by the nature of the imperial garrison state, even though they cannot be reduced to simple reflections of its needs.

Between 1760 and 1820 broad philosophical speculations about the outside world were given a sharper edge by innumerable articles in learned journals, official surveys and private memoirs. Naval and military officers provided the link between local observation and the circles of savants which congregated around Joseph Banks, H. H. Wilson and Alexander Dalrymple in London and Edinburgh, just as clergymen and local gentleman scholars were the watchers and informers in the British Isles. The military and naval survey provided the leading edge for the expansion of statistical knowledge about and taxonomies of indigenous people.[31] Medical topography, for instance, developed in the disease-ridden atmosphere of Pacific voyages and Indian cantonments.[32] Military surveys concerned to locate pinnacle fortresses and fields of fire preceded surveys of land revenue or crops. Military academies provided the models for civilian service training schools; Fort William College, the training school for Indian civil administrators, was specifically modelled on French military academies by Wellesley.[33] Knowledge of the peoples of British North America was accumulated initially in the files of the Department of Indian Affairs, a military-dominated body.[34]

There was also a broader sense in which the military and strategic nature of the empire over these years moulded its forms of knowledge. The encounter with native peoples could be as brutal as it was a generation later, racial disparagement as sharp. But, in an empire whose military strength depended still on huge numbers of native guides, indigenous soldiers, princely and chiefly levies, general disparagement of non-European customs, languages[35] and mores had to be restrained. Vigorous Protestant evangelization would not help much among Irish and Maltese Catholics, Hindus or Muslims. The intellectual style of the more learned officers and civil administrators of the imperial garrison state tended to be deistical and free-thinking. They looked for traces of the ancient common knowledge of man in the Hindu vedas or the Chinese annals.[36] They fancied they saw the dispersed tribes of Israel living along the Hudson or scattered through the pattern of islands of Polynesia. They tried to select out kings, coherent tribal structures and clans with which to make compacts. Where, as in the case of Australia, non-European peoples could play little role in imperial defence or in providing the labour, produce and revenue to support the garrison state, interest in them was more fitful, confined to clergymen and a few inquisitive administrators.

These concerns fitted well with those of the "men on the spot" who needed to trade and make transactions in land with the representatives of indigenous societies. From the very earliest days of English settlement in the New World the questions "Can the natives make a contract?", "What is the value of their oaths?" had been an issue when more than simple extermination and expropriation was at stake. In the seventeenth century William Penn had argued, contrary to the aggressive colonists of New England, that the king's patent was not sufficient to seize Indian land. To him these descendants of the Jews who "believed in God and immortality" had few wants. They were "not disquieted with bills of lading and exchange, nor perplexed with chancery suits and exchequer reckoning", but they were "exact observers of property", and their land must be purchased, not seized.[37]

The administrators, soldiers and antiquarians of the later eighteenth century still generally believed that mankind was sprung from one stock imbued with some knowledge of divinity. At the dawn of time, Indians and Chinese, in particular, had made great advances in the arts and sciences. It was still possible to make great discoveries in medicine, astronomy and divinity by taking note of their pharmacopoeia and star-charts.[38] Even peoples without benefit of a regular system of writing, such as the North American Indians or the Maori, possessed stable societies and a degree of ancestral knowledge. Since many believed them to be descendants of the lost tribes of Israel, while south Asians and Maoris were Aryans set adrift after the Flood, this was only to be expected.

British understandings of indigenous peoples and attempts to categorize them for the purposes of government were generated both out of such widely held sociological ideas and also by fractious issues arising from cultural and military clashes across the colonial frontier. These *causes célèbres* were employed more and more after 1815 to give a darker picture of indigenous peoples. The period from 1830 to 1860, in particular, saw a range of fierce debates about the barbarity of "heathen races" which took on a common pattern and served a similar role in the official mind. The British became concerned almost simultaneously with the following: Chinese foot-binding and prostitution, Indian widow-burning, infanticide, ritual murder and human sacrifice, cannibalism and tattooing in Australasia and the Pacific and polygamy and other sexual customs perceived as transgressive among Native Americans and Africans, where pictures of savagery had been painted much earlier.[39] Colonial wars on the frontiers of empire added sadistic savagery to these marks of Cain in the eyes of settlers and military officers. These debates may well have had the effect of making indigenous people "other". It is important to remember, though, that lesser depravities were being simultaneously ascribed to the English working class and the Scottish and Irish peasantries. The debate about the "condition of the native" cross cut, time and time again, with the debate about the condition of the British poor, long before eugenics and scientific race theory legitimated this elision in the later nineteenth century.

Everywhere missionary apologists seeking funds at home found allies in evangelical and modernizing members of the colonial administrations. Both groups found it politic to exaggerate and progagandize these practices. The latter sought not only pretexts for intervening in indigenous societies, but more often justifications for superseding the older, corrupt generation who had connived in heathenism and lax administration. Recent studies have, however, brought out two other points. First, this generally harsh re-evaluation of indigenous society was powerfully aided by the expansion of the medium of print.[40] Romantic and dreadful stories of alien depravity titillated both the godly and the lubricious market. Secondly, indigenous peoples themselves participated in these debates and began to re-examine and reinvent their tribal, regional or national traditions. Polynesian tattooing, a subject of wonder and disgust to Europeans, was cherished as a mark of true lineage even by those Maori chiefs who donned tailcoats, and whose pictures by European artists still peer down at us from the walls of Auckland's National Gallery. Though most modernizers came to reject it, widow-burning in India became the focus of one of the first national campaigns against British government in the 1830s and gave a powerful impetus to the indigenous press. Tribal totems retained their value to Native Americans and Fijians who had apparently succumbed to the preaching of Methodists or Baptists.

Of course, enlightened views of the unity of mankind, propagated by the military gentlemen, did not exclude violent diatribes against the corruption of polity and morals among indigenous people. But equally, the shift of attitudes when settlers, missionaries and Peelite administrators began to edge aside the gentlemen-soldiers was a complex one. In the new dispensation Europeans tended to rank indigenous peoples and to create hierarchies of them, rather than castigate them all as backward savages. While Macaulay's remark that a shelf-ful of European books was worth all the learning of the Orient has been constantly echoed by post-colonial theorists, the dominant attitude of missionaries and scholar-administrators, if not expatriate settlers, was more complex.

Their attitude reflected above all a practical implementation of the stage theory of the Scottish Enlightenment. It drew on the same intellectual roots as the earlier deistical understanding of the unity of human knowledge, but it was more sharply scientific and historical. It followed John Millar's statement that "There is in human society a natural progress from ignorance to knowledge and from rude to civilised manners, the several stages of which are usually accompanied with peculiar laws and customs."[41] In this vision of history, commerce expanded in conjunction with virtue. Thereafter, moral advance could only come through the combination of Christian revelation with a further growth of international trade to satisfy virtuous wants, though not idle luxury. This theory of the ascent of races directly reflected, of course, the domestic evangelical project of morally improving the lower classes of society. Very few observers joined James Mill in ranking most of the indigenous peoples of the British empire on the lowest rung of this ladder, but most wished to contain, reify and disarm Indian sovereignties and property rights so that the "rule of law" could diffuse civilization more widely.

This local understanding of the contractual basis of relations between people underpinned colonial ideologues and moderate settler opinion through to the early Victorian age. Many witnesses before the Parliamentary Committees of 1834–8 on the Aboriginal Peoples of the British Empire applied more or less sophisticated versions of these ideas. Truly savage peoples – and "savage" at this time did not mean bestial – had few if any wants. They had no fixed sense of property and had, consequently, no notion of the oath. Archdeacon Broughton of New South Wales remarked that the aboriginal populations around Sydney were not "dull of wit" but "They have no wants . . . and therefore have no inducement to remain under a state of restraint, nor are they ever willing to leave their children" to mission education.[42] By comparison another witness believed that the Caffrees (the Xhosa of the Eastern Cape) were nearer to the higher category of "barbarians" than to that of savages. "They have the elements of a civil community . . . respect for the ideas of meum and tuum." If someone was suspected of theft, the authority of the head of the village was needed before the inhabitants broke into the suspect's house.[43] But many witnesses argued that British colonial courts had not always observed these distinctions properly. If the native concerned was "a Hindoo or a Mahometan we adopt the form of oath he uses. But the New Zealander, the Australian, the Caffree and the [American] Indian, have no such usage".[44]

Liberal witnesses urged that the amounts of blood and treasure already spent in the Xhosa and Maori wars turned in part on the failure to understand that these peoples had a form of civil government. An officer of the Madras army, for instance, contrasted the burning and expropriation of Xhosa villages on the Cape with the supposedly humane treatment of frontier disputes between the Madras authorities and the domains of the Indian prince the Nizam of Hyderabad. Here military punitive parties could only be employed under the direction of the civil authority.[45]

Jane Samson has recently shown how these debates within the colonial system affected the indigenous inhabitants of Australia and the Canadian West Coast. Samson is the first modern commentator to note the large degree of ambivalence in British thinking about the capacity of native peoples to take oaths. She shows that in both regions administrators who had been influenced by humanitarian ideologies and abhorred the racial massacres which had taken place on the frontiers since the 1820s argued that native peoples' evidence should be taken in court cases even without oaths on the Bible. These people,

races. Paradoxically, the crushing of the indigenous political systems in the mid-century wars deepened the dependence of exiguous British forces and administrations on Sikh soldiers, Hindu merchants, Chinese compradors and Arabic writers. The intellectual conquests of the later Scottish Enlightenment and the classical political economists had, ironically, provided the tools with which indigenous scholars and public men could deploy self-strengthening movements. James Ballantyne's Brahmin pupils at the Benares College became Indian teachers and lawyers.[49] They joined British learned societies and lauded the virtue of the great Indian scientists and religious teachers of the past.[50] Chinese magnates educated by the Methodist missionaries in Hong Kong and Shanghai built the schools and orphanages which formed the seed-bed of overseas Chinese nationalism.[51] Jamal-al Din al Afghani and Mahomed Abduh, the Muslim reformers of the Near East, learned from their intellectual and physical bruising at the hands of British authorities and Christian apologists the value of global Islamic contacts and political aspiration.[52]

In all of these cases, the impact of the economic tools and mental systems of the West was profound. But in all of them, too, Western learning and expertise was combined with reworked patriotisms, home-bred sciences and sensibilities of the divine which derived from the native past. The birth of this new world order took place, almost unnoticed, at the high point of the Britannic deluge, as the imperialisms of the garrison state gave way to the dynamic forces of settler dominion and bureaucratic government.

Notes

1   L. Colley, *Britons. Forging the nation 1707–1837* (London, 1993); J. Brewer, *The sinews of power. War, money and the English state 1688–1783* (London, 1989); C. Emsley, *British society and the French wars, 1793–1815* (London, 1979); R. Samuel (ed.), *Patriotism. The making and unmaking of British national identity* (London, 1989).

2   L. M. Cullen & T. C. Smout, *Comparative aspects of Scots and Irish economic and social history, 1600–1900* (Edinburgh, 1977); J. Ritchie, *Lachlan Macquarie* (Melbourne, 1986).

3   The heavy representation of Scots and Irish (Catholic and Protestant) is revealed in D. G. Crawford, *A history of the Indian medical service, 1600–1913* [3 vols] (London, 1914).

4   E.g. Scot's denunciation of the 'clearances', anon., *The House of Binny* (Madras, 1969), p. 28.

5   C. O'Halloran, "Irish re-creations of the Gaelic past. The challenge of Macpherson's Ossian", *Past and Present* **124**, 1989, 69–95; C. Vallancey, *A vindication of the ancient history of Ireland* (Dublin, 1786); cf. the chapters by H. Trevor-Roper and P. Morgan in *The invention of tradition*, E. Hobsbawm & T. Ranger (eds) (Cambridge, 1983).

6   S. Clark & J. S. Donnelly, *Irish peasants. Violence and political unrest 1780–1914* (Dublin, 1983); B. Jenkins, *Era of emancipation. British government of Ireland, 1812–30* (Kingston, Ontario, 1988).

7   G. W. Stocking, *Victorian anthropology* (New York, 1987).

8   For contemporary opinions on the "Hottentots" (Khoikhoi), R. Percival, *An account of the Cape of Good Hope* (London, 1806), pp. 80–87.

9   C. J. Hawes, *Poor relations. The making of a Eurasian community in British India, 1773–1833* (Richmond, Surrey, 1996).

10 T. N. Harper, "The politics of the forest in colonial Malaya", *Modern Asian Studies* **31**(1), 1997, pp. 1–29; M. Rangarajan, *Fencing the forest. Conservation and ecological change in India's Central Provinces, 1860–1914* (Delhi, 1996); A. Skaria, *Hybrid histories. Forest, frontier and wilderness in western India* (Delhi, 1998).

11 See, e.g., Julian Burger, *Report from the frontier: the state of the world's indigenous peoples* (London, 1987).

12 P. Cain & A. G. Hopkins, *British imperialism. Innovation and expansion, 1688–1914* (Harlow, 1993); but cf. M. J. Daunton, "Home and colonial", *Twentieth Century British History* **5**(3), 1995, pp. 344–58 and earlier; F. Crouzet, "Towards an export economy. British exports during the industrial revolution", *Explorations in Economic History* **17**, 1980, pp. 48–93; R. Davis, *The Industrial Revolution and British overseas trade* (Leicester, 1979).

13 M. Duffy, *Soldiers, sugar and seapower. The British expeditions to the West Indies and the war against revolutionary France* (Oxford, 1987), p. 285, cf. p. 17 and Ch. 1 passim.

14 J. Black, *European warfare, 1660–1815* (London, 1994). The themes of the next section are explored in comparative perspective in my "The first age of global imperialism c. 1760–1830", *Journal of Imperial and Commonwealth History* **26**(2), May 1998, pp. 28–47.

15 D. B. Ralston, *Importing the European army. The introduction of European military techniques and institutions into the extra-European world, 1600–1914* (Chicago, 1990); G. Parker, *The military revolution. Military innovation and the rise of the West, 1500–1800* (Cambridge, 1988).

16 I. R. Christie and B. W. Labaree, *Empire or independence. A British American dialogue on the coming of the American Revolution* (Oxford, 1976), pp. 1–46.

17 See, e.g., R. Barnett, *North India between empires. Awadh the Mughals and the British, 1720–1801* (Berkeley, 1980); C. A. Bayly, *Indian society and the making of the British empire* (Cambridge, 1987), Chs 2 and 3; for a nuanced account which demonstrates the dialogue between trading and fiscal interests, P. J. Marshall, *Trade and conquest. Studies in the rise of British dominion in India* (Aldershot, 1993).

18 D. Peers, *Between Mars and Mammon. Colonial armies and the garrison state in India, 1819–1835* (London, 1995); J. Pemble, *The invasion of Nepal. John Company at war* (Oxford, 1971).

19 Peers, *Between Mars and Mammon*, p. 150.

20 Cited in S. Newton King, "The labour market of the Cape Colony, 1807–28", in *Economy and society in pre-industrial South Africa*, S. Marks & A. Atmore (eds) (Harlow, 1980), p. 172, cf. p. 173; L. C. Duly, *British land policy at the Cape* (London, 1964), p. 186; R. Elphick & H. Giliomee, *The shaping of South African society, 1652–1840*, rev. edn (Harlow, 1989); cf. J. S. Galbraith, *Reluctant empire. British policy on the South African frontier, 1834–54* (Berkeley, 1963).

21 E. Mancke, "Another British America. A Canadian model for the early modern British empire", *Journal of Imperial and Commonwealth History* **25**(1), 1997, pp. 1–36.

22 R. Hughes, *The fatal shore. A history of the transportation of convicts to Australia, 1787–1868* (London, 1987), pp. 414–34; L. Ryan, *The Aboriginal Tasmanians* (Brisbane, 1981).

23 T. Bayliss-Smith et al. (eds), *Islands, islanders and the world. The colonial and post-colonial experience of East Fiji* (Cambridge, 1988), pp. 48–50.

24 J. Belich, *Making peoples. A history of the New Zealanders* (London, 1995), pp. 158–69.

25 A. Crosby, *Ecological imperialism. The biological expansion of Europe, 900–1900* (Cambridge, 1986).

26 See, e.g., D. H. A. Kolff, *Naukar, Rajput, and sepoy. The ethnohistory of the military labour market in Hindustan, 1450–1850* (Cambridge, 1990); S. Alavi, *The sepoys and the company* (Delhi, 1995); Capt. D. C. Graham (Commanding the Bheel Corps), *Historical sketches of the Bheel tribes inhabiting the province of Khandesh* (Bombay, 1856), pp. 203–18; B. Craymont, *The Iroquois in the American Revolution* (Syracuse, N.Y., 1972), pp. 13, 54–8; Percival, *Account of the Cape*, pp. 80, passim, for the Hottentot Corps.

27 The model of this sequence has been drawn mainly from the North American material, though it seems to apply in Australasia, forest Asia and Africa also; see Craymont, *Iroquois*, pp. 10–11: L. F. Upton, *Micmacs and colonists. Indian–White relations in the Maritimes, 1713–1867* (Vancouver, 1979); J. M. Bumsted, *The peoples of Canada* [2 vols] (Toronto, 1992).

28 R. Fisher, *Contract and conflict. Indian–European relations in British Columbia, 1774–1890* (Vancouver, 1977); B. Gough, *Gunboat frontier. British maritime authority and the Northwest Coast Indians, 1846–90* (Vancouver, 1989); J. M. Bumsted, *The peoples of Canada*.

29 For India, see the bibliographical essay referring to C. A. Bayly, *Indian society and the making of the British empire*, Ch. 5; for Ceylon, K. M. de Silva, *History of Sri Lanka* (London, 1981), pp. 243–51, 308–14; for southern Africa, Elphick & Giliomee, *The shaping of South Africa*.

30 J. Belich, *The New Zealand wars and the Victorian interpretation of racial conflict* (Auckland, 1986), pp. 32ff.

31 M. Edney, "The patronage of science and the creation of imperial space", *Cartographica* **30**(1), 1993, pp. 61–7; M. Edney, "British military education, map-making and military 'map-mindedness' in the late enlightenment", *The Cartographic Journal* **31**(1), 1994, pp. 14–20; M. Edney, *Mapping an empire* (Chicago, 1997).

32 David Arnold (ed.), *Imperial medicine and indigenous societies* (Manchester, 1988); *Colonising the body. State medicine and epidemic disease in nineteenth century India* (Berkeley, 1993).

33 "College of Fort William", Wellesley Papers Add. 13,862, f. 29, British Library, London.

34 R. S. Allen, *His Majesty's Indian allies. British Indian policy in the defence of Canada, 1774–1815* (Toronto, 1992).

35 B. S. Cohn, "The command of language and the language of command" in *Subaltern Studies*, vol. 4, R. Guha (ed.) (Delhi, 1985), pp. 276–329; "Hottentot" and Malay were later standardized for similar reasons, though the military creation of language was powerfully aided by missionary activity.

36 P. J. Marshall & G. Williams, *The great map of mankind. British perceptions of the world in the Age of Enlightenment* (London, 1982). For one example, see F. Wilford, "On Egypt and other countries adjacent to the Coli River or Nile of Ethiopia from the ancient books of the Hindus", *Asiatick Researches* **iii**, 1799, pp. 295–9ff; for background, Frank E. Manuel, *The eighteenth century confronts the gods* (Cambridge Mass., 1959), and for the deeper deist tradition, R. Cudworth, *The true intellectual system of the universe* (London, 1678); David Hume, *Natural history of religion* (Edinburgh, 1757).

37 Anon., citing Penn, *Some account of the conduct of the Religious Society of Friends towards the Indian tribes in the settlement of the colonies of East and West Jersey and Pennsylvania* (London, 1844), p. 47; for a discussion of property and rights for a later period see Jane Samson, "British voices and indigenous rights: debating aboriginal legal status in nineteenth century

Australia and Canada", *Culture of the Commonwealth: Essays and Studies* **2**, Winter 1996–7, pp. 5–16.

38 C. A. Bayly, *Empire and information. Intelligence gathering and social communication in India, 1780–1870* (Cambridge, 1997), Chs 7–9.

39 e.g. A. London, *A selection of some of the most interesting narratives of outrages committed by the Indians in their wars with the white people* (London, 1808, and thereafter); M. van Woerkens, *Le voyageur étranglé. L'Inde des Thugs. Le colonialisme et l'imaginaire* (Paris, 1995); F. Padel, *Sacrificing human being. British rule and the Konds of Orissa* (Delhi, 1995); Anon., *A brief narrative of a New Zealand chief being the remarkable history of Barnet Burns* (Belfast, 1844), on tattooing and cannibalism.

40 Journals such as the *The Church Missionary Recorder*, *The Missionary Register*, *The Baptist Register*, etc., were important in that they reached a large audience, and also juxtaposed lurid observations on diverse societies.

41 John Millar, 1779, cited in J. Rendall, *The origins of the Scottish Enlightenment, 1707–76* (London, 1978), p. 145.

42 Evidence of Archdeacon Broughton, New South Wales, "Report from the Select Committee on Aborigines (British Settlements)", *Parliamentary Papers*, 1836 sess., vii, p. 20.

43 Evidence of Mr Saxe Bannister, *ibid.*, p. 184.

44 *Ibid.*

45 Evidence of Capt. C. Bradford, *ibid.*, pp. 177–8.

46 W. Robertson, *An historical disquisition concerning the knowledge which the ancients had of India* (Dublin, 1791), p. 302.

47 J. R. Ballantyne, *Christianity contrasted with Hindu philosophy* (London, 1859); J. R. Ballantyne, *Aphorisms of the Mimansa philosophy by Jaimini* (Allahabad, 1851); *Lectures of the Nyaya philosophy embracing the text of the Tarka Sangraha* (Benares, 1848).

48 Belich, *Making peoples*, pp. 164–78, 229–35; R. Ross, *Adam Kok's Griquas. A study in the development of stratification in South Africa* (Cambridge, 1976).

49 R. F. Young, *Resistant Hinduism. Sanskrit sources on anti-Christian apologetics in early nineteenth century India* (Vienna, 1981), pp. 49–101.

50 Bapu Deva Shastri, "Bhaskara's knowledge of the differential calculus", *Journal of the Asiatic Society of Bengal* **27**(3), 1858, pp. 313–16; Bapu Deva Shastri, "The sidereal and tropical systems", *ibid.*, pp. 205–15.

51 H. Lethbridge, *Hong Kong. Stability and change* (Hong Kong, 1978); cf. S. B. Bayly, "The evolution of colonial cultures: the Empire in Asia", in *Oxford History of the British Empire*, vol. 3, A. N. Porter (ed.) (Oxford, forthcoming).

52 A. Hourani, *Arabic thought in the liberal age, 1798–1939* (Cambridge, 1960); N. Keddie, *Iran and the Muslim world; resistance and revolution* (Basingstoke, 1995).

Chapter Three

Encounters between British and "indigenous" peoples, c. 1500–c. 1800

Philip D. Morgan

A noticeable trend in recent historical scholarship is the exploration of connections among what were formerly considered separate and discrete phenomena. Local events are often unintelligible in local terms only; national concerns assume full significance only when viewed through supra-national frames of reference. Scholars are increasingly interested in relationships between the nation-state and larger historical entities, in interdependent relationships among component parts of broader systems. Much modern historical work involves a broadening of horizons, an enlargement of scope. In a way, modern scholars are coming to terms with an early modern discovery, what J. H. Elliott calls the "sense of one interconnected world", a development much "assisted by the new conceptualization of space made possible by the Renaissance device of the globe."[1]

While this expansive reorientation of historical enquiry has its roots in the early modern era, it owes more to recent developments in modern life. As our world becomes more cosmopolitan, as our economy becomes more global, as international communications bring us closer together, our perspectives broaden and our ambitions soar. For this reason, courses on Atlantic, Pacific, and world history are now taking their place in university curricula. Imperial history, seemingly old-fashioned and outmoded, is resurgent. The empire has indeed struck back. Historians now tell us to focus on "'the area of interaction' between the component parts of imperial systems", and see imperialism as "a double-ended process, in which the colonies played as dynamic a role as the metropolis". Literary scholars tell us to reread the cultural archive "not univocally but *contrapuntally*", see the "shadow behind the country house", link that Antiguan slave plantation to Mansfield Park, place Jane Austen alongside Frantz Fanon, pay attention to creole Bertha Mason as well as to

English Jane Eyre. The injunction is to read in reverse, against the grain, between the lines, from below. The wretched of the earth are talking, and we are all trying to listen; we now aim for a bifocal vision, a bilateral history, a mirror-image ethnography. Consequently, intricate connections across national boundaries heave into sight. New configurations and patterns emerge from a mass of dispersed and scattered information. Intersections and parallels, contrasts and comparisons become evident. These "glowing moments of illumination," Bernard Bailyn notes, "suffusing at different times and in different ways the thought of many historians working on many problems, are where the real excitement lies".[2]

The excitement resides in tracing connections, identifying parallels, highlighting contrasts, describing patterns, and always attending to both sides of the encounter – in short reconstructing whole worlds and whole processes. Standing on mountain tops and surveying panoramic scenes is exhilarating, but it can also be dangerous. I am thinking less of the hazards of vast and ever proliferating scholarly literatures or even of the post-colonial angst that sees efforts to retrieve the experiences of indigenous peoples as doomed to failure. The problem goes deeper. It is all too easy to describe what the indigenous peoples shared – becoming objects of European history and no longer makers of their own history – in ways that seem to mimic colonization's robbery of the colonized's subjectivity. To describe native peoples – as many early modern visual and textual representations demonstrate – is to engage in a form of cultural appropriation, in what might be termed "ontological imperialism" in which otherness vanishes and becomes part of the same. With trepidation that I too fall into the trap of pouring the indigenous peoples into the same post-colonial pot, yet with excitement at seeing hitherto only vaguely glimpsed patterns, I offer five capsule ways of thinking about encounters between the British and indigenous peoples in the period *c.* 1500 to *c.* 1800. They are: identities, variations, metaphors, connections, and arenas.[3]

Identities

British history is now being practised; no longer is it English history writ large. But as scholars probe the interactions between England and its archipelagic cousins and imperial offspring, questions arise about exactly who the British were and when, if ever, they emerged as a distinct people. Who are these British? The very term, to paraphrase Raphael Samuel, is more redolent of Balmoral than Glasgow, Westminster than Hackney, "Rule Britannia" than "The roast beef of old England", swaggering John Bull than egalitarian Robin

Hood. "British" is abstract rather than concrete; its associations are diplomatic and military rather than literary and linguistic. "Britons" is no more helpful, asserts T. O. Lloyd, because it "still has too much of a suggestion of woad about it". Whatever the terminological inexactitude and unease, presumably the British included the Welsh, whose absorption goes back to the union of 1536–43. How about the Scots? Were they too absorbed? If not from 1603, then from 1707 onward with the union between Scotland and England (and Wales), technically yes, but Scotland was, as many historians have emphasized, an anomaly, neither kingdom nor province nor colony. Those who identified themselves as North Britons may have been at root assimilationist, but even they were somewhat ambiguous about their Britishness, sometimes prone to vehement Anglophobia, and often committed to traditional forms of Scottish patriotism. Furthermore, the Scots were deeply fractured. Well into the nineteenth century many Lowland Scots still referred to their Highland neighbours as savages, as essentially members of a different and inferior race.[4]

Other residents of that "Atlantic archipelago . . . from Shetland to Sark and from Dingle Bay to Dogger Bank" are even more crucial for probing the meaning of Britishness. If Scotland is an anomaly, Ireland is an enigma. In the early modern era, it resembled, in Thomas Bartlett's words, "not so much a model colony . . . but rather an unruly palimpsest, on which, though much rewritten and scored out, could be discerned in an untidy jumble – 'kingdom', 'colony', 'dependency', and, faintly, 'nation'". And what about other minorities: how British were people of African descent living in the so-called British Isles, or Jews never numerous but forever haunting the British imagination, or gypsies seen as of Egyptian origin in the sixteenth century and of East Indian descent in the seventeenth and eighteenth centuries, or the Dutch, French, and Italian communities in London against whom apprentices frequently rioted, or the Channel Islanders with their own parliament, or the Cornish, a few of whom continued to speak a separate language until the late eighteenth century? As with the Cornish, what importance should we attach to county and regional identities, still so powerful in early modern Britain?[5]

No matter how diffuse and always evolving was Britishness, it was unquestionably forged in a wide context. What most enabled Britain to emerge as an artificial nation and to be superimposed on to older alignments, Linda Colley has argued, was a series of massive wars between 1689 and 1815 that allowed its diverse inhabitants to focus on what they had in common, rather than on what divided them. Protestantism, and increasingly constitutional liberty, were two crucial ingredients of this new common identity, but insofar as the British defined themselves in the early modern era, they did it in conscious opposition to "the Other beyond their shores". In fact, the creation of a British identity emerged not just in opposition to the foreigner or outsider, but also in the emigration of these various island peoples who became inescapably British in the process. For exiles, Britishness became a reality abroad in ways it never did at home. John Dee, a Welshman, was allegedly the first person to use the term "British empire"; the idea of Britain was in large part a Welsh and Scottish invention; but early on, the Welsh and the Scots were as actively involved as the English – perhaps more so in proportion to their population – in settling, defending, administering, and profiting from empire. Irish involvement, both Catholic and Protestant, was considerable, even though Ireland, a dependent kingdom with its own parliament until 1801, was formally excluded from much imperial business. Just as prominent representatives of the so-called Celtic fringe preached the importance of a wider and more developed British consciousness at home, so provincials abroad identified themselves as Britons more consistently than anyone else in the empire.[6]

These brief reflections on the meaning of a British identity in a broad context underline that identities are, above all, invented and imagined in a complex and ever changing process of interaction. Identities depend on imagined communities, on constructed associations, on invented traditions, on manufactured myths. A sense of self is rooted in a collective consciousness of "us" versus "them". Neither "we" nor "they" are fixed, but rather are constantly negotiated and renegotiated, encompassing a multitude of shifting boundaries and subjective identities. Alongside a British identity, then, co-existed myriad alternative identities, sometimes complementary, sometimes contradictory, which were locally – but no less powerfully – articulated. People had many loyalties, many allegiances. For this reason, if no other, there never could be a single, unitary or monolithic British encounter with indigenous peoples.[7]

If the British were not monolithic, how much more must this be true of the so-called indigenous peoples. Let us ask our question again, then, now in reverse, exactly who are these indigenes? Are they simply the rest, once we discount the West? In a sense – if the insult is not too gratuitous – the short answer is yes, although if we want to spread around the insults, we might say that the Gaelic Irish, Highland Scots, and perhaps some Welsh-speakers had a foot in these two camps of West and Rest. But the non-Western indigenous peoples with whom the British come into contact are obviously an amazingly diverse array of peoples, because no empire was as far-flung as the British, a "vast empire on which the sun never sets", as Sir George Macartney put it in 1773. The staggering variety is evident, to take one example, in the range of pre-contact populations: from the 10–20 million in Bengal to the 86,000 in

New Zealand, from the 20–25 million in West Africa to the 750,000 in Australia, from the 6–7 million in North America and the Caribbean to the 90,000 in the Marquesas Islands.[8]

What can we say about the identities of these highly varied peoples? At the risk of gross oversimplification, two features might be highlighted. First, the sheer localism of life is impressive. In North America, east of the Mississippi, well over 150 Indian groups can be identified, speaking many more separate languages. On the Caribbean islands, scores of separate Indian societies and regional chiefdoms existed. At a minimum, about two hundred states – not including countless stateless societies – can be identified along the littoral of early seventeenth-century West and Central Africa. Perhaps a thousand separate languages could be heard from Senegambia to Angola. The peoples of the three great divisions of the Pacific – Polynesia, Melanesia, and Micronesia – had little in common either linguistically or culturally, and in any case the twenty-five thousand islands that they inhabited divided them even further. Hundreds of aboriginal societies, speaking at least 200 mutually distinct languages, inhabited Australia, some land-oriented, others sea–oriented, some living in rainforests, others deserts, some tablelands, others highlands. Tasmania, Australia's largest offshore island, was home to nine major linguistic and cultural groups, each comprising between five and fifteen bands. James Cook's six-month circumnavigation of New Zealand in 1769–70 vividly revealed the regional variability of Maori life: some were farmers, others fishermen, some did well, others poorly, some tattooed their buttocks, others their faces. Even this cursory survey, rudimentary and schematic as it undoubtedly is, fails to capture the reality of life in many parts of the globe into which the British penetrated. For among most of the indigenes, the most meaningful aspects of life took place in autonomous village communities composed of largely autonomous kin groups. What has been said about Australian natives has wider application: "The indigenous peoples never had a collective consciousness as 'Aborigines'; instead they defined themselves according to their specific clan relationships to land and kin, and were divided from one another."[9]

India and some parts of Africa would seem to be a major exception to generalizations about localism. In India's case, the Mughal empire is difficult to square with an emphasis on localism. In the second half of the seventeenth century, as Christopher Bayly puts it, "the Muslim power at Delhi still shook the world". But over the next century, the decline of Mughal power was spectacular, leading a number of scholars to question the degree to which it was ever a centralized state. On closer inspection, "empire" and "state" were always limited in India. As Bayly emphasizes, power was highly differentiated. In many ways, the Hindu kings of the localities, the rajas as guardians of the caste order, and the local notables controlled resources and authority in the villages. They were dependent in turn on the warrior farmers, the headmen and their subordinates. In short, layers upon layers of power existed in early modern India, and very often the hands on the levers of power were local ones. The same is true of the larger empires and states in early modern Africa – Mali, Great Fulo, and Mane in West Africa, Loango and Kongo in Central Africa – which in reality comprised a number of tributary states and semi-autonomous provinces. Centralized authority was limited. Nevertheless, this argument for localism should not be exaggerated. In India, British rule was superimposed on an already functioning system, taking advantage of the technical, commercial, bureaucratic, and military expertise of the natives. The British oversaw taxation and legal structures that were Hindu or Muslim in substance. In Africa, European traders entered into partnerships with indigenous elites, who set many of the rules for the trade in slaves.[10]

Still, the decentralization of the various worlds of indigenous peoples had obvious implications for contact with Europeans. In North America, headmen of particular lineages or clans forged economic connections with individual Euro-American traders, often at cross-purposes to the efforts of other leaders whose commercial alliances stretched in different directions. Among various Native American groups, generational conflicts often arose between older accommodationists and younger militants, between those who readily adapted to the introduction of new kinds of private property and those who did not, between Christians and non-Christians. In eighteenth-century India, many wealthy Indian merchants became the agents of private Europeans acting as their *banians* or *dubashes*, thereby posing a challenge to their own rulers' authority. Consequently, relations between Europeans and indigenous peoples assumed a vivid kaleidoscopic quality. Local divisions and interests created a variety of responses to the European presence; in many cases local divisions, as on the African coast, were fundamental, and the Europeans were almost an incidental presence. For all these reasons, far more intricate alignments arose than the often conventional intruding European ranged against retreating non-European.[11]

Second, if localism was the overriding feature of pre-contact indigenous life, then the encounter with Europeans was most significant for the enlargement of scale that it entailed and the reconstitution of identities that ensued. One obvious change is that the British and other Europeans generally imposed unifying misnomers on the peoples they met. Beothuks and Powhatans became Indians; Igbos and Nupes became Africans; Taipi and Teii became Marquesans; Nyungars and Arandas became Aborigines. The process in each case generally took centuries, with many twists and turns, but it occurred everywhere. Another obvious change is the uprooting of indigenous peoples, creating diasporas not just overseas but also in their homelands, which makes the very term "indigenous peoples" somewhat problematic. The Cape Colony, Mauritius, Trinidad, Sierra Leone were just some of the more dramatic examples of societies composed of multiple diasporas. Africans faced the most searing forced removal and created the most extended diaspora in the early modern world. Because many slaves came in tortuous ways from the interior to the coast, whatever identity they originally had was in flux. When they reached the Americas, they met other Africans from a much wider variety of societies than at home. New ethnic identities arose. Igbo-speakers, for example, who had never even heard the name Igbo in their homelands because there they identified with a smaller dialect or cultural group, became Igbo in the New World. This process was somewhat analogous to what would later occur in colonial Africa; as John Iliffe put it, because "Europeans believed that Africans belonged to tribes, Africans built tribes to belong to". But, more important than neo-African ethnicities, generalized African-influenced Black cultures – far more homogenous than anything in Africa – arose in the Americas. Uprooting and reconstitution was also the story of Native American life. By the eighteenth century, none of the major Native American societies that interacted with the British had existed a century earlier. Each was an amalgam of survivors, refugees, and war captives produced by demographic and military upheavals. According to Colin Calloway, the names of Native American communities "should often be regarded as 'addresses' rather than tribal designations". The Great Lakes area was what historian Richard White labels "a world made of fragments" where survivors from the Iroquois wars and the great early-contact-era epidemics had coalesced into new configurations. Something similar occurred in Australia. The death toll among Australian aboriginal groups around Sydney in the late eighteenth century caused a major social reorganization. Remnants of bands combined to form new groups known to Europeans by such names as the "Botany Bay tribe", the "Kissing Point tribe", and the "Broken Bay tribe". As Scots, Welsh, and Irish assumed a larger identity as British, so indigenous peoples moved in parallel, if far more traumatic, fashion, gradually becoming Africans, Indians, and Aborigines.[12]

Although the new identities of indigenous peoples arose in part from attempts to control and exploit, history was not made by the colonial masters alone. There was not always "a White man behind every brown", as Dorothy Shineberg puts it. The natives constructed their own heritages, sometimes subverting and sabotaging the classifications imposed upon them, sometimes ignoring them altogether. In the sixteenth century, Native Americans created various confederacies – Huron in southern Ontario, Powhatan in the Chesapeake, Iroquois in New York – to defend themselves against both

European and Native American enemies. These alliances strengthened internal cohesion and increased numbers in an age of demographic collapse. Two centuries later, Native Americans engaged in wider alliances. As Gregory Dowd notes, by the late eighteenth century "the idea of united Indian resistance to settler expansion had taken hold among the Eastern Woodlands peoples". Among slaves, hundreds of small runaway communities dotted the Americas where Africans from many different ethnicities built new more generalized cultures. In a few cases, they also built loosely co-ordinated organizations to confront colonial society. In Marshall Sahlins' words, "The local people articulate with the dominant cultural order even as they take their distance from it, jiving to the world beat while making their own music".[13]

Asking who the British and the various indigenous peoples are, probing their changing and multiple identities, takes us on to very difficult terrain. Yes, we recognize that identities are ever in flux, are plastic, fluid, fragile creations. Yes, that "Manichean showdowns" between an indigenous people and the imperialist force are much too simplified, that binary oppositions fail to capture the complicated intercultural zones where cultural differences were mediated. Yes, that alliances cross ethnic boundaries and correlate oppositions in the colonizing group to differences among the local people. Yes, that the encounter between British and indigenous peoples helped shape and create new, usually larger, identities. But the contested and unstable character of these formations should not be exaggerated. Not everything is indeterminate and permeable, not everything is contested, not everything is fragile. Multiple and hybrid these identities may have been, but their integrity, their totality, their continuities with a past, their ability to maintain boundaries should not be underestimated. The British, for all their diffuseness, were, after all, rather unified, linguistically and culturally. Native American groups did not commit cultural suicide; they made drastic adjustments to the British presence but all the while keeping intact the core of their ancient cultures. Even African-American slaves, denied the complex institutions of their ancestral societies – their kings and courts, guilds and cult-groups, their markets and armies – and heirs to the most "mangled pasts" imaginable, improvised and invented within a framework of a shared set of generative principles, which, while ever changing, like Proteus, were ever enduring.

Variations

Turning from the complicated question of how to make sense of the identities of the various peoples in our encounters, how do we get to grips with the dizzying variety of encounters? Some of the most obvious ways are essentially binary in character, which clearly run the risk of oversimplifying reality, but two at least are worthy of brief exploration.

One distinction that has preoccupied imperial historians and that has a direct bearing on relations between the British and indigenous peoples lies in the character of the imperial enterprise itself. The issue is usually posed in stark oppositional terms: was the empire more concerned with commerce than territory, trade than conquest? Establishing a trading partnership as opposed to military conquest, paying rent or tribute to local rulers rather than taking possession of their land are obviously drastically different ways of relating to indigenous peoples. These simple dichotomies, however, tend to dissolve on closer inspection. For one thing, the primary orientation of the British was simultaneously trade in some parts of the world (most notably Africa and Asia) and territory in others (most notably Ireland, North America and the Caribbean). A further moment's reflection and even this dichotomy is readily seen as simplistic. In Africa, for example, the British, weak though they were, always focused on more than trade. In their enclaves on the coast, British officials exercised a degree of political influence over African societies, less through direct military intervention than by supplying firearms and finance for the hiring of mercenaries both in intra-African conflicts and against other Europeans. Conversely, the British presence in the so-called territorial Caribbean was often far more commercial than territorial. And in many parts of the so-called territorial Americas, trade was an overriding priority, most particularly of course in the fur trading posts on Hudson's Bay, fishing settlements in Newfoundland, and log-cutting communities in Central America. Furthermore, everywhere trade was vital; not for nothing has the eighteenth-century empire been described as an "empire of goods". Realities, in short, were a lot muddier than simple dichotomies.[14]

Orientations also changed over time. In fact, in the prehistory of the British empire, plunder rather than either trade or territory was the primary orientation. When plunder was the goal, relations with indigenous peoples could often be remarkably pragmatic: witness Drake's alliances with the *cimarrons* in Panama. Furthermore, there were clearly shifts in emphasis in official policy over time. Over the course of the eighteenth century, the British presence in India, for example, undoubtedly changed in character, particularly after 1757, when territorial aggrandizement gradually supplanted commerce as the strategy of the East India Company. More generally, the official policy of Whitehall, especially before the middle of the eighteenth century, subordinated the territorial dimension of empire to a concern with naval power, but the logic of maritime empire readily led to territorial expansion and the exercise of territorial sovereignty. By the late eighteenth century, the militarization of the empire was formidable. In practice, the line between commerce and conquest was always permeable.[15]

From the perspective of indigenous peoples their relations with the colonizers always involved trade and warfare, even if the balance was constantly shifting. The key from the indigenes' vantage point was whether the terms of trade and military power, and most importantly their cultural autonomy, were under their control or not. Early trade was not always destructive of native life. Some foreign commodities enriched native life and were readily adapted to customary practices. European glassware and copper products, for example, were quickly integrated into Native American rituals since these could easily substitute for indigenous copper, shells and rare stones. The African demand for cloth with unusual colours and designs was motivated by prestige, fashion, and a desire for variety. The perfect symbol for the early Maori response to contact, James Belich avers, was the patu, or club, that Te Puhi, a chief, wielded in 1815: it had been created from bar iron. The demands of local peoples were almost everywhere selective rather than eclectic, even if they involved, from a European perspective, rather unusual notions of utility. As Sahlins puts it, "the first commercial impulse of the [indigenous] people is not to become just like us but more like themselves. They turn foreign goods to the service of domestic ideas, to the objectification of their own relations and notions of the good life". But the true break in their lives came with the moment of domination, never easy to pinpoint, perhaps when many natives saw the need to learn English, or when they became dependent on European goods, or when they began to alienate their land to pay for those goods, or when diplomatic relations abandoned native forms, when in short the natives assumed subaltern status. "This is the B.C. and A.D. of the [indigenous peoples'] world history," notes Sahlins, " 'Before Colonization' and 'After Domination'."[16]

A second way to categorize the varied encounters between British and indigenous peoples is to contrast casual, intermittent, fleeting contacts with sustained, routinized, long-term relationships. Uniformity characterizes many descriptions of first contacts, even though they may have taken place in very different parts of the globe. Read an early sixteenth-century description of a cultural encounter off the coast of Newfoundland and a late eighteenth-century account off the coast of New Zealand and many times the sense is of *déjà vu*. How often for example were the natives immediately divided into good and bad, whether in the Caribbean, the North American mainland, the African coast, or the Pacific? Some rituals of possession-taking – whether ground dug, trees carved, salutes fired, flags hoisted, crowns toasted, bottles buried, things renamed – vary little from place to place. The gesturing, the random violence, the usual attempt to kidnap a native or two – the drill seems much the same. One reason for this apparent sameness is that, in Judith Modell's words, ethnographies create encounters as much as *vice versa*. For example, when James Cook and Joseph Banks saw the aborigines of Botany Bay, they saw them, in part at least, through William Dampier's eyes, proving that Dampier's vivid description – a bestseller of its day – lived long in the European memory. Indigenous people had their own ethnographies. When the British encountered an indigenous people, they had invariably been preceded not only by many other indigenous peoples but often by other Europeans. When in 1733 Tomochichi, an elderly leader of the Yamacraw Indians, told the British that one of his predecessors had "entertained a great white Man with a red Beard" who had "expressed great Affection to the Indians", he was keeping alive – indeed, he was the sixth generation so to do – the memory of a red-bearded French captain who had visited the Georgia coast 171 years previously. And, more to the point, he no doubt told his story to make a point: he expected affection. As Dening notes, "the Other is rarely met in a present divorced from all the meetings that have gone before".[17]

First contacts often gave rise to European meditations on their supposed deification and on the Other's alleged cannibalism. These two stereotypes have prompted Gananath Obeyesekere to argue that cannibalism is as much "European fantasy" as native practice, and that the godlike European is "a myth of conquest". Obeyesekere is right to emphasize myth-making in European thought, but essentially his argument hinges on a view of natives as pragmatic, calculating, strategizing rationalists who were rather like Europeans, which in the final analysis seems a curiously ethnocentric interpretation. Marshall Sahlins' intricate argument that the Hawaiians viewed James Cook as the god Lono and Anne Salmond's realistic and matter-of-fact acceptance of Maori cannibalism rest on the more plausible view that the indigenous peoples had distinct cultures, different rationalities, and different cosmologies from the Europeans. What this debate vividly demonstrates is the value of a truly bilateral history as practiced by Sahlins and Salmond and the unhelpfulness of a unilateral interpretation – even if it is nominally from a subaltern perspective.[18]

The glitter of first contact inevitably catches the eye, but the long-term historical processes of intercultural negotiation of power and meaning are even more important to document. I confess to pausing at stressing negotiation, for it can seem too anodyne (encounter too has a neutral ring to it), not quite doing justice to the remorseless tide of dispossession and destruction that marked a large part of the relationship between British and indigenous peoples. Empire, it has been said, "meant no more than conjugating 'the verb to rob in all its moods and tenses'". But, as many now rightly stress, invasion, despoliation, and annihilation do not constitute the whole story. As peoples became familiar with one another, they found ways to live together. They established customary rules, they entered into reciprocal work arrangements, they created niches for themselves – Aborigines working for cattle herders, Native Americans peddling baskets and pottery, Fijians trading sandalwood, slaves growing food which they sold to their masters, and the like.[19]

The people who navigated across cultural boundaries were critical in facilitating familiarity between newcomers and natives. The terms used by historians and anthropologists to describe these intercultural travellers are legion and testify to their importance. We call them go-betweens, intermediaries, mediators, negotiators, brokers, middlemen, guides, beachcombers, liminal people – but their function as people who went back and forth, interpreted, translated, exchanged, and explained was clearly vital to the increasingly integrated worlds they inhabited. One such were what Ira Berlin calls Atlantic creoles, often Africans, sometimes Euro-Africans, most notable for their linguistic skills and their familiarity with the Atlantic's diverse commercial practices, cultural conventions, and diplomatic etiquette to negotiate across the cultural divide. Living on the African coast, along the edges of the North American continent, throughout the Caribbean islands, in European port towns, these intermediaries exhibited considerable "linguistic dexterity, cultural plasticity, and social agility". In James Cook's expedition to New Zealand in 1769, the Tahitian priest Tupaia played interpreter; from the Maori perspective, the *Endeavour* was Tupaia's ship. We could replicate examples of intermediaries from everywhere else the British and indigenous peoples came into sustained contact. Ideally, we need collective profiles of these crucial figures. We know some were women, as in western Canada and locales in Africa, but were most of them men? Were they suspended between worlds or were they firmly rooted on one side of the divide or the other? [20]

Metaphors

It is notable that these somewhat mechanical categorizations – commerce versus conquest, fleeting versus sustained contact, and one might multiply them to include formal versus informal rule – assume a binary character, seemingly appropriate for a "we" and "they" topic such as the British and indigenous peoples. Thinking in binary terms sets one to thinking about how the mind works, about apposite metaphors for conceiving of cultural contact. Some may say that metaphors are unimportant, somewhat trivial; explore the

fontier

real–life, on-the-ground, face-to-face encounters, they may urge. So we should, but metaphors are important: they shape the way we think.

One of the oldest, and still best, is the frontier. Not the frontier of a forward-advancing line, not a giant leap ahead bringing civilization and progress in its train. But, rather, a margin between peoples, a zone of interaction, a place where the rules of engagement were contested. Ever shifting frontiers existed wherever British and indigenous peoples met: the Pale in Ireland, the Highland–Lowland divide in Scotland, the longitudinal moving boundary separating Native Americans and colonists in North America. For Native Americans, as James Merrell has argued, the frontier was essentially between two worlds, one where Native American principles applied and one where British rules held sway. Both colonists and Native Americans talked of "their own country" and "the other world", "English ground" and "Indian ground", a people of the forest and a people of the field. The frontier in the case of European–Maori first encounters was the shore, for many times Maori and European encountered one another either around or on board ship.[21]

"Frontier" can mean many things and can be measured in many ways. Who laughed at whom, who was the stock comic character is one not insignificant guide to who was in control. In Indian country, the joke was often on the colonist; in colonial settlements, the shoe might be on the other foot. Ethnic jokes, slurs, and jingles repay close investigation across the intercultural divide. The Maori–European frontier was a rich zone of cross-cultural laughter. On one occasion, a Maori ventured close to Cook's ship and "civilly turned up his breach and made the usual sign of contempt amongst the Billingsgate ladies". Apparently, this was the first recorded instance of a ritual insult, exposure of the anus. Later that same day, a British sailor dropped his drawers and returned the taunting gesture, which only served to enrage another group of Maori canoemen. The joke gets better, for a few days later Cook and his men came across a beautiful rock arch, through which they are able to see the Pacific. They were in raptures at this natural wonder. One member of Cook's company sat down to draw it, and his sketch survives. What the Europeans did not realize is that the Maori name for this arch, this hole with a view of the ocean, was none other than "anus of the land". Watching the Europeans, the Maoris must have split their sides at "this grand cross-cultural joke". But, in certain frontier situations, laughing at others could be dangerous. When a group of Marquesans known as the Hapaa saw their arch-enemies the Teii provisioning Americans and their British prisoners, they climbed a nearby mountain and yelled down that "the Americans were the posteriors to the Teii privates". Calling whites arse-holes when they had Marquesan allies got five Hapaa killed.[22]

54

Another compelling metaphor, akin to frontier, is that of islands and beaches, the title of Greg Dening's evocation of that silent land, the Marquesas. "Island" can of course refer to a physical setting, the site of so many encounters between British and indigenous peoples in the early modern era, but it can equally apply to a continental enclave (the Cape Colony, the forts and factories in West Africa, Bengal, the Australian outposts, and almost all the seventeenth-century and many of the eighteenth-century North American settlements), and even to the invaders' ships, which some Native Americans and Maoris referred to as "floating islands". But the island Dening has in mind is less physical than cultural: it is a cultural world, a mental construction, which can be approached only across a beach, a cultural boundary, which divides "the world between here and there, us and them, good and bad, familiar and strange". In crossing a beach every voyager brings something old and makes something new. Beaches, therefore, "are beginnings and ends". Dening even sees the whole of European expansion in terms of islands and beaches. As he puts it, "Europeans discovered the world is an ocean and all its continents are islands. All its parts are joined by straits and passages. They encompassed the world".[23]

Dening's insights have, I think, even wider application. Islands are worthy of investigation both literally and metaphorically. In literal terms, islands were, in Oliver Sacks' words, "experiments of nature, places blessed or cursed by geographic singularity to harbor unique forms of life". Islands have seen far higher rates of animal, bird, and plant extinctions than mainlands. Humans might be added to the list. One thinks of the total, and in some cases near, extirpation of Tainos in the Greater Antilles, Lucayans in the Bahamas, and aborigines in Tasmania. Islands are also natural laboratories of extravagant experimentation. They are a catalogue of quirks and superlatives. Naturally, I am thinking mainly of animals and plants, but I don't see why humans should be too offended to be included in this galaxy. The Black Caribs and the gloriously mixed populations of places like Mauritius and Trinidad surely fit the bill. Metaphorically, the island is central to the history of colonies and colonization. One thinks of Oceana, Utopia, and New Atlantis, the whole "Edenic island discourse", of Prospero, Fletcher Christian, and Robinson Crusoe. The centrality of islands to colonization is gauged in one North American patriot's complaint that people in Britain thought of colonies only in terms "a parcel of *little insignificant conquered islands*". As a result, he maintained, colonists were thought to be no more than "a compound mongrel mixture of English, Indian, and Negro". As a "freeborn Briton" living on the mainland, he was much offended, but his indignation is just one of many clues that islands had powerful associations.[24]

A third metaphor, also closely related to frontier, is the concept of marchland or borderland. Marchland has the virtue of connecting the Welsh borderlands, the Scottish middle marches, the Irish Pale, the Caribbean, and the Australian outback, "one of the most unformed, raucous, and rambunctious Anglo-frontier societies that ever existed". All these typically disordered border countries were, in Bailyn's view, war zones. They were peripheries, ragged outer margins of central worlds, regressive, backward-looking places. Bailyn stresses their "primitiveness and violence, the bizarre, quite literally outlandish quality of life". He is impressed by their wildness, their extravagance. They gave rise to exotic experiments.[25]

If marchland tends to exaggerate destructiveness and cultural misunderstanding, the concept of middle ground – a fourth metaphor, popularized by Richard White – tends to exaggerate harmony and shared understanding. The middle ground is a place where cultures mingled and developed new forms through exchange. For White, the search is for accommodation and common meaning. As he puts it, "the middle ground is the place in between: in between cultures, peoples, and in between empires and the nonstate world of villages". White's most provocative argument, I think, is that, in his words, "no sharp distinctions between Indian and white worlds" existed on the middle ground. They were different peoples, he concedes, but "they shaded into each other".[26]

I confess to being sceptical on this point. The notion of boundaries, it seems to me, is vital even as we recognize the emergence of a more integrated world. Crossing common grounds after all bred not just familiarity but contempt. Even as people built bridges across cultural divides, the chasm that separated them came into sharper focus. In some cases, the gap widened; the chasm became a canyon.

Connections

Boundaries are important to an understanding of this early modern world, but so are connections. What happened in one area of this vast interdependent world affected others, so the linkages should be investigated. A single labour market emerged, highly regionalized and segmented to be sure, but one in which the distribution and redistribution of slaves, servants, convicts, and contract labourers can be understood only in relation to each other. Interesting comparisons might be explored: convicts' relations with indigenous peoples in North America and Australia might tell us a lot about these different frontier settings. Continuous exchanges between interrelated segments of an increasingly unified if extended global system involved material goods as well as people. Indian calicoes to Africa to purchase slaves; Caribbean molasses to New England to be turned into rum for trade with Native Americans; Tahitian breadfruit to the Caribbean to feed slaves; even such improbable linkages as the conches that the Moravians used in the North Carolina piedmont to call together their meetings, a borrowing from slaves in the Caribbean. Not only did products circulate, but diseases swarmed from one part of the globe to another. What happened to aboriginal populations in the Americas would occur later in Australia, Tasmania, New Zealand, and many Pacific islands. An empire of labour, goods and disease is just one of the ways of conceiving of this increasingly interconnected world.[27]

Connections should be thought of not just in metrocentric terms, in one-way directions from core to periphery, but rather in bilateral and multilateral directions among the peripheries themselves. Nor should we stop at the continent's edge, for we must also traverse that interconnected worldwide space of the seas. Since connections between peripheries and on the seas have been least well explored, I will concentrate on these two.

An important connection between peripheries is the way that relations with one set of indigenous peoples often served as laboratories for later colonial experiments. A number of historians have shown how attitudes developed in the conquest and colonization of Ireland influenced the process of colonization in America, but John Elliott has recently gone further and urged a more systematic and comprehensive analysis. Comparing the Spanish and British empires seems to suggest that the Spanish incorporation and British exclusion of Native Americans, while owing much to local conditions, can be seen in embryo in colonial precedents in Europe.[28] Less explored is the linkage between the Scottish Highlands and America, but it may have been no less real. In the sixteenth century, the image of the Scottish Highlands, one of those "dark margins of the western imagination" where primitivism, bestiality and satanism allegedly reigned, undoubtedly shaped, and to a lesser extent drew upon, the view of Native Americans. Highlanders were associated with those generic wild men of medieval and Renaissance lore, those creatures of the forest, often said to be from the north. "Wild" was a vital marker of Highlanders and Native Americans (and later of Black maroons). James VI even referred to Highlanders as "lascivious" and "barbarous cannibals",characteristics attributed to wild men. John White's representations of Algonkian life, usually described as remarkably scientific, should be viewed alongside his watercolours of Picts, portrayed as long-haired, naked, exotically tattooed, and armed, far more barbarous and ferocious than the Indians.

In the eighteenth century, a very different set of linkages can be discerned. The radical restructuring of agrarian society that the British government put into effect in the Highlands after the 1745 revolt was later influential in plans

for Canada, the Cape Colony, and India. Further, no sooner had the programme been put into operation than the Highlands became a place to search
for heroic ideals, archaic forms of social organization, and romantic scenery,
a myth with parallels to those constructed of Native Americans as they faced
their own radical restructuring.[29]

Just as the Scottish Highlands and Gaelic Ireland in some ways acted as
models for colonial experiments in the Americas, so the Americas in turn
served a similar purpose in the Pacific and elsewhere. The early explorers and
settlers readily referred to the indigenous inhabitants of the Pacific region as
"Indians" or, less frequently, "blacks". Comparisons were drawn from known
to unknown. Thus, one visitor to Botany Bay described the "Indians of this
country" as worse off than those he had witnessed on the Mosquito Shore of
Central America. Joseph Banks found the smell of bird or fish oil with which
Maoris anointed their hair reminiscent of Newfoundland and Labrador fishing
stations. Although "aborigine" and "aboriginal" were words in common
literary usage in this period – indeed, in the eighteenth century the words
were used to describe Native Americans, Indians in the subcontinent, and
ancient Britons – they were not used specifically to refer to the original
inhabitants of Australia until well into the ninteenth century. Rather, the
earliest observers and settlers used, more or less indiscriminately, "natives",
"blacks", "Indians" and "savages". Or to take another example, the most
powerful and most frequently cited legitimation of the British presence in
America was that aboriginal land was unoccupied. This argument of a *terra
nullius* (land of no-one) was later used as the primary justification for British
incursions into Australia and the Eastern Cape. Finally, the history of missionary encounters in North America almost certainly had an impact on later
encounters in Africa and the Pacific. What Andrew Porter says of missionary
studies is of more general importance: "Too many studies of missionary
enterprise focus on the transmission of missionary ideas from a single centre,
and fail to understand that most often missionary thought and plans were the
product of exchanges between several such centres."[30]

Seafaring not only linked the different parts of the world together, making
transoceanic relationships possible, but also stood as a world apart. The first
British empire was, in contemporary terms, an "empire of the deep". In many
places throughout the empire, maritime activities were more striking than
their slow expansion on land. Ports were the key nodal points of the empire;
a majority of people lived close to the sea. Ship news was a vital feature in
metropolitan and colonial newspapers. The number of sailings and amount of
tonnage expanded enormously in the seventeenth and eighteenth centuries;
people were brought closer together and the known world shrank. Yet, at the
same time that maritime communication connected people, the sailor was, in

the words of a contemporary, a "species of man abstracted from every other race of mortals". Looking, acting and speaking differently, the sailor seemed a special breed. "Seaman have always dwelt on the fringes of settled society", notes N. A. M. Rodger. "The Greeks hesitated whether to count them among the living or the dead." Narratives of sea-voyages were so popular in eighteenth-century Britain in large part because seafaring life itself was so profoundly strange.[31]

One way in which the maritime world was distinctive was its international character. Sailors came from many nations and many ethnicities. Maritime work blurred social boundaries and status definitions, scooping up in its net a remarkably polyglot group of people, who often worked aboard the same ships and shared similar duties and conditions. Sailors regularly crossed cultural boundaries, regional boundaries, and status boundaries. Of none was this more true than the buccaneers, a truly international collection of professional sea-marauders. But bands of rootless trans-nationals roamed all the oceans, sailing under any flag on any ship. A few Moskito "Indians" were generally found on most privateering vessels, eliciting much praise for working well, supporting crews through their fishing and harpooning, and fighting well, never seeming "to flinch nor hang back". Native Americans played a large role in New England whalers. Almost as soon as European vessels arrived in the Pacific, the islanders took advantage of the new opportunities to visit other islands. From the first, a few Pacific Islanders began to appear on the musters of almost every whaler and trader in the region.[32]

If the maritime world could readily incorporate Native Americans and Pacific Islanders, what about Blacks? Olaudah Equiano referred repeatedly to his being on good terms with British seamen. After being befriended by a slave, three white sailors "shook him by the hand". A visitor to Jamaica in the early nineteenth century noted that white sailors and Black slaves "are ever on the most amicable terms". He spoke of their "mutual confidence and familiarity". In "the presence of the sailor", he proclaimed, "the Negro feels as a man." The navy attracted Blacks because, in that service, a man's skill seemed to matter more than his colour. A naval court, for example, hanged two white men for sodomy on the evidence of a Black seaman. Colour was apparently unimportant in assessments of black William Brown, described in a newspaper story as "a smart well-formed figure, about 5′4″ in height and possesses a considerable strength", who served in the British Navy for over a decade and achieved the post of Captain of the Foretop. Exhibiting "all the traits of a British Tar", Brown and fellow messmates took grog together "with the greatest gaiety". Popular below decks, Brown also performed "highly to the satisfaction of the officers". Brown was only unmasked as an African woman when her husband claimed her prize money. One of the most famous incidents in the events leading up to the American Revolution involved a score or so men, mostly sailors, who assembled in Boston's Dock Square in 1769; one of the sailors, an Afro-Indian, Crispus Attucks, was the first to fall when the troops opened fire. Even in remote New Zealand, Black sailors could find haven; the Maori sometimes spared them in attacks on European parties. The maritime world seems to have fostered a measure of interracial tolerance.[33]

But interracial harmony should not be pushed too far. There was certainly "no questioning of the institution of slavery" on naval ships, and some British officers carried their own slaves to sea. On one naval ship at least, racial prejudice was definitely present. In 1780 a naval captain wrote to the First Lord of the Admiralty about his Black boatswain, a "good seaman but wants that great requisite . . . of making himself of consequence among the people – who have I find – taken a dislike to the man's colour". The boatswain wanted to exchange ships and the captain acknowledged how difficult it was to correct "a particular prejudice which has crept into a new ship's company". Even more tellingly, a white privateer, arguing before a judge that his captured Black prisoners were slaves, referred to their "vile and Cruel Colour". Rhetorically, he questioned, "Does not their Complextion and features tell all the world that they are of the blood of Negroes and have suckt Slavery and Cruelty from their Infancy?" The 330,000 or so British seamen who worked in the transatlantic slave exhibited little fellow feeling for Africans on board their ships. Similarly, few white New Englanders, who used Native Americans as oarsmen in either the offshore or the ocean-going whale fishery, developed much camaraderie for their companions. Rather, they seemed more intent on driving Native Americans into debt peonage. One reason why racial conditions on board ship may not have been as distinctive as some have suggested is that most sailors spent less than a decade at sea. As Daniel Vickers has noted, most sailors quit the sea before the age of thirty and returned to land. If seafaring was "merely an interlude in lives acted out primarily on shore", then all the more reason why exaggerated claims of interracial harmony are probably far-fetched.[34]

Perhaps a more plausible development than interracial internationalism may be that Blacks, and perhaps other minorities, used seafaring to develop their own international, sometimes subversive, perspectives. Paul Gilroy has written of a Black Atlantic culture, which he suggests is traceable to the eighteenth century. In the Caribbean, access to the sea had revolutionary potential. In 1758 a Dane living on St Croix complained of slaves who stole boats and sailed to Puerto Rico, and then sent back messages with other sailors to their slave companions. Julius Scott has described in great detail how black workers who crisscrossed empires by sea served as informants to local communities and spread ideas and information throughout the circum-Caribbean. Particularly during the Haitian Revolution, Scott sees the development of a "truly international" and potentially revolutionary "Afro-Atlantic perspective". So many influential African-Americans worked at sea. "Eighteenth-century black leaders frequently rolled out of the forecastle", Jeffrey Bolster observes, "a worldly origin eclipsed by the subsequent dominance of the pulpit as the wellspring of black organization." These spokesmen for Black people, by moving between and connecting local Black communities, helped define and knit together a larger Atlantic community of colour and foster the beginnings of what later came to be called Pan-Africanism. The careers of activist-seamen Equiano and, in the next century, Robert Wedderburn, point in that direction.[35]

Another aspect of the internationalism of sailors is their bodily decorations, specifically their tattooing. The tradition of maritime tattooing has a long history. It can be traced, apparently, to the Coptic Christians, who tattooed the Crusaders and Pilgrims to the Holy Land, marking their bodies as Christians. The techniques and designs of the Coptic Christian tattooists rubbed off, as it were, on the seafarers ferrying people across the Mediterranean. But later encounters with Native Americans (who seem to have tattooed, as well as used body paint and forms of scarification), perhaps Africans (who certainly scarified), and above all South Sea Islanders seem to have increased interest in this ancient art. *Tatau*, after all, is a Polynesian word and, as Greg Dening has noted, "a tattoo was a badge of any eighteenth-century sailor's ethnographic experience in the Pacific". In 1691 Jeoly, the "painted Prince", a tattooed South Sea Islander, was a show object in England long before the English saw their first Maori tattoo. Polynesian tattoos made a great impression on Europeans once the remarkable series of drawings from Cook's circumnavigation of New Zealand began to circulate. Europeans generally found full facial tattoos ugly, but Joseph Banks spoke for many when he said "it is impossible to avoid admiring the immence Elegance and Justness of the figures . . . finished with a masterly taste and execution". The designs of sailors' tattoos in the South Seas drew from Polynesian and Euro-American sources. Fletcher Christian had a star on his breast and an undescribed mark on his buttock, perhaps, as Dening speculates, "the broad black band that all Tahitian men wore". Another mutineer of the *Bounty* had a Tahitian feather gorget (*taumi*) on his chest. Those sailors who went native got extensively tattooed. One Frenchman who deserted in the Marquesas became "profusely tattooed in Marquesan style", though he left space on his stomach for a tattooed clay pipe. Even if most deep-sea sailors incorporated no specifically South Sea designs, "the relative popularity of tattooing among late-eighteenth-century mariners", as Simon Newman notes, "confirms that exposure to the ornate tattooing of the South Sea Islanders, in the wake of Cook's voyages of the 1770s simply increased interest and proficiency in a custom already well established among seamen".[36]

The maritime world was, in short, an ambiguous place. Some features justify Peter Linebaugh and Marcus Rediker's claim that sailors and slaves (and presumably other minorities) created "a vital world of cooperation and accomplishment within a multi-racial, multi-ethnic, international working class". Yet, this is also to claim too much for a privileged space at sea. Maritime culture and shipboard social structure never overcame the fissures of race. Few white sailors saw Blacks or Indians or South Sea Islanders as their equals, or wavered in their belief that men of colour were generally inferior. Seafaring blurred the binary terms in which British peoples generally encountered indigenous people on land, but hardly erased the divide altogether.[37]

Arenas

Relations between the British and indigenous peoples must be sought not just in the larger connections that drew them together but in the myriad meetings, the conversations, the encounters that occurred in a variety of different contact arenas. This is not a history of large-scale events, but rather of asides, silences, gestures, snatches of conversation, snippets of action. The traces of the colonized are inscribed in the margins of the colonizer's discourse. Language is one such sphere, particularly the misreadings, the transformations, and the recognition of meanings that occurred in linguistic contact; or the remarkable efflorescence of pidgins and creoles and the continuous invigoration of English that linguistic confrontation spawned; or the search for balance between linguistic imperialism on the one hand and the resilience of indigenous languages on the other. In the economic realm, the clash of different notions of property, the multiple economic arrangements, the fascination with material possessions that generally can be found on both sides of the encounter need to be explicated. The realm of material culture saw reciprocal borrowings between British and indigenous peoples, a process which informs too few archaeological and architectural studies, wedded as they generally are to static, positivistic views of ethnicity. The violence inherent in much cultural contact is a rich area for investigation: violence not just between but among peoples; violence of the gun, the introduction of which could be usefully compared from Africa to the Americas to the South Seas; violence in the contrast between populations readily disarmed and populations forever fighting back; and violence in the collaboration of Native American allies, sepoys, the

Carolina Corps, the West India Regiments, and the Cape Regiment. The issues are legion – and I have not even mentioned other vital contact arenas, such as religion and the law. All these are vital topics, well worthy of detailed investigation, but I will content myself with only one arena, perhaps the most basic, the sexual.

How should we characterize sexual encounters between British and indigenous peoples in the early modern era? According to one eminent historian, "In the British colonies miscegenation is known to have happened – but only occasionally, here and there, marginally." Another is even more categorical. The British, he asserts, "found the prospect of intermarriage with Native Americans abhorrent". John Elliott has probed the comparative context and sees pre-existing cultural attitudes as crucial. The long history of interpenetration of Castilian and Moorish worlds predisposed Spaniards to contemplate ethnic intermarriage in the New World, while the colonization of Ireland offered the English a legal precedent for the rejection of marriage with the native population, even if many Anglo-Irish marriages actually occurred. What seems impressive is that "almost from the start" the British were opposed to taking Native American mistresses. "The great divide was not ethnic but cultural", Elliott avers, a fear of cultural degeneracy, which seems in part at least a legacy of experiences in Ireland. Thus the British created pales in America, much as in Ireland, frontiers of exclusion, very different from the Spanish-American frontiers of inclusion.[38]

These historians confine their attention to sexual encounters between the British and Native Americans. Before broadening out our investigation, let us spend a minute on that subject. First, is it possible to argue that some English people believed that Native Americans could be incorporated through marriage alliances? One immediately thinks of course of the celebrated marriage of Rolfe and Pocahontas in 1614. But other marriages were proposed in early Virginia. Governor Sir Thomas Dale, for example, requested the hand of Powhatan's youngest daughter. Some of the women who accompanied Pocahontas to England went to be married, and at least one married an Englishman in Bermuda, an indication that, in Nicholas Canny's words, "attempts may have been underway from the moment of first contact in the Chesapeake to promote reform through intermarriage". That some English colonists "entertained the hope that Amerindian society could be gradually assimilated into theirs through marriage alliances" should be taken seriously, Canny thinks. Perhaps a brief privileged era did exist.[39]

One place where the British and Native Americans did cohabit on an extensive scale was Rupert's Land, the huge drainage basin of Hudson Bay. The Hudson's Bay Company attempted to prohibit marriage between its employees and Bay Indians, but the chief factors of the company took the lead in forming unions with Indians. For the most part, these were not casual, promiscuous encounters but rather developed into long-standing marital unions which gave rise to distinct family units. From the European perspective, the lack of white women – before the early nineteenth century there were virtually none present – meant that the loneliness of a trader's existence would have been unbearable unless, in the words of one contemporary, "softened . . . by the many tender ties, which find a way to the heart". The British found Cree women in particular physically attractive. Besides the obvious sexual advantages, Native American wives played vital domestic roles and also served as important intermediaries in the fur trade. From the Native American perspective, a marriage created a reciprocal social bond which consolidated economic relationships with a stranger. Eighteenth-century unions were more Indian than European in form; children mostly had Indian names and grew up as Indians. As the mixed-blood population grew, a shift occurred from the taking of Indian wives to mixed-race wives; and by the 1820s and 1830s, as white women and missionaries began to arrive, it became increasingly fashionable to have a European wife.[40]

The Hudson's Bay Company trading world was unusual, but trading posts throughout the British world bore more than a passing resemblance. To be successful, individual fur traders not just in western Canada but throughout the Americas usually cohabited with Native American women; how otherwise were they to gain access to a vital network of kinship and personal connections? Similarly, the mixed-race children of such unions often played important go-between roles, even if no Metis community arose like that of Red River. To jump from west to east, and to another trading company, the keeping of a mistress was of course a well established practice in British India; British travel literature had long portrayed Hindu women as sexually alluring; India, like other parts of the world, became "a playground for sexual fantasy". With the rapid increase in the numbers of ordinary British soldiers in India during the latter part of the eighteenth century both the size and character of the Eurasian population changed. The overwhelming majority of Eurasian children born to the British at that time were fathered by poor whites. Opposition to concubinage began to mount in the late eighteenth century; the arrival of missionaries perhaps played a role as in Rupert's Land, but more likely it owed more, first, to an increasing awareness that fortunes were to be made in India and that Eurasians should be excluded from this patrimony, and, second, to a growing belief that Eurasians posed a risk to British security, as the role of the coloureds in French Saint Domingue seemed to demonstrate. The frequency of concubinage and marriages involving British men and Indian and Eurasian women dropped dramatically at about the same time in Rupert's Land and India.[41]

The African coast too was in some ways analagous to Rupert's Land. Since there were almost no white women among the British in Africa, the men had to look toward the natives for partners. Some took slaves as concubines. Most, like the Owen brothers (impoverished Irish gentry reduced to slave brokerage in the Sherbro estuary), became integrated into their host society through intermarriage. They conformed to African norms and reinforced their business connections with ties of kinship. When the Irish trader Richard Brew died on the Gold Coast in 1776, his estate was divided between his African wife and their two mulatto daughters. As one European observer on the coast noted, "Once the black woman has given him [the European] some mulatto children, the white man loves them just as much as a man who cares for his lawfully wedded wife and his children in Europe." The major difference from Rupert's Land was that on the African coast, the mixed-race children came to assume positions of great authority. The mulatto children of British fathers in the Sherbro and Sierra Leone peninsula served as middlemen, collecting African produce and slaves at convenient points and in convenient quantities for loading on ocean-going ships. The Caulkers, Rogers, and Clevelands became important power brokers – "merchant princes" according to one historian – in their own right.[42]

Wherever whites and blacks encountered one another in the Americas – and this was after all by far the most numerically important eighteenth-century encounter that the British had with another people – sexual liaisons resulted. It is impossible to argue that miscegenation happened "only occasionally, here and there, marginally" if white–black relations are taken into account. There were, however, distinctive regional patterns of interracial sex. The most brutal and extensive sexual exploitation undoubtedly occurred in the plantation systems of the Caribbean. Part of the reason was the lack of white women, although the increasing presence of white women over time did little to inhibit West Indian planters' keeping of Black and mulatto mistresses; part too was the degree of absenteeism, the lack of rootedness; part too was the sense of being marooned in thoroughly Black societies. In the Caribbean, openly practised, widely accepted concubinage was part of the social fabric. White society on the mainland was never as sanguine about concubinage because whites were not as outnumbered by blacks, had more white women available, and put down firmer roots than in the islands. Eighteenth-century South Carolina was the closest approximation to West Indian patterns, exhibiting a fairly relaxed tolerance of interracial unions. In the eighteenth-century Chesapeake, on the other hand, a man's reputation, it was said, could be ruined by fathering a mulatto child, and public condemnation of miscegenation was frequent. Nevertheless, the fairly evenly matched white and black populations of the Chesapeake may have actually provided more opportunities for racial intermixture than the more imbalanced black–white ratios of South Carolina and the heavily imbalanced ratios of the Caribbean, a suggestion borne out by contemporary perceptions and rough measures of the proportion of mulattoes in the slave population.[43]

Although the British found beauty and sensuous appeal in a seemingly exotic East, Polynesia and in particular Tahiti set the standard for sexual allure. Girls standing on the prows of canoes, lifting their wraps and flaunting their nakedness, making unmistakable gestures to the seamen, a "sea of sexuality" in Dening's words or an "ocean of desire" in Smith's – such was the scene of perhaps the first European vessel, the HMS *Dolphin*, to arrive off Tahiti's shores on June 21, 1767 – and the image stuck. British voyagers to the region extolled the beauty of the women, their cleanliness, their "copper color", their youthfulness, their nudity. The uninhibited attitude to sex, the seeming lack of shame, the alleged indiscriminate giving of sexual favours of Polynesian women scandalized some, made most somewhat uneasy, and were taken advantage of by almost all. A stereotype arose and it has been labelled not the noble but the nubile savage – a sexually inviting and desirable woman. Again, the legend lived, for as British officials laid their plans for the settlement of Australia, one idea involved bringing Tahitian (and other Polynesian) women to become wives for the marines who wished to settle in the new land. The women would be free to choose husbands and on marriage to soldiers would receive grants of land. From the union of marines and island women would therefore arise sturdy yeoman farmers.[44]

Antipodean sexual encounters were somewhat more restrained than Tahitian. Early accounts of sexual behaviour between British men and Maori women indicate that high-born young women and married women were sexually inaccessible – although an exception might be made for an important guest as a gesture of hospitality and honour – but captive women might be made quite freely available and young women were generally at liberty to sleep with whomever they pleased. Confronted by wholly male invaders, some Maori apparently assumed that the newcomers must be homosexual and offered the requisite hospitality. Once sailors began regularly visiting New Zealand, the resulting heterosexual "sex industry" became "the leading earner of overseas exchange". The economic benefits and the ability of Maori women to gain some measure of control over the industry offset the disease and increasing exploitation that ensued.[45]

Australian Aborigines have been described as "the hard primitive to the soft primitivism of the Tahitian", that is, they were considered less beautiful, less seductive. Nevertheless, First Fleet officers often cajoled and entreated Aboriginal women to come within their grasp – ostensibly so they could decorate their naked bodies with gifts, as a form of erotic voyeurism. Aboriginal men, by contrast, were most concerned, when they encountered their finely and elaborately dressed British counterparts, to determine their sex. Gender specificity was crucial to Aboriginal diplomacy and when they met the British they pointed to their own penises and asked the British to reciprocate. When reassured, they "made a great shout"; when once presented with a young boy, they "burst into the most immoderate fits of laughter".[46]

This cursory survey of sexual encounters between British and indigenous peoples has suggested considerable variations over time and across space. There are continuities, to be sure: consider, for example, how often indigenous people are described as "naked", a cultural marker of real significance, rife with sexual and theological connotations; or how often indigenous men are said to treat their women badly as a way of legitimating a British "rescue" of those women; consider how important the relative demographic balance of white men and women was in shaping interracial encounters in many places in the world; or that trading posts tended to articulate certain patterns of sexual interaction and plantation slavery others. But equally there were important differences from one trading region to another, from one plantation region to another, and over time. But the claim that the British were especially reticent to engage in sexual relations with indigenous peoples cannot be sustained. Another extreme argument – that empire arose in part from bachelors taking out their sexual frustration in military aggression and imperial conquest – seems equally far-fetched. Similarly, the notion of empire as sexual paradise, as "an unrivalled field for the maximization of sexual opportunity and the pursuit of sexual variation", is a rather lurid and insensitive dismissal of those who were sexually exploited. Ronald Hyam is no doubt correct that empire could expand sexual opportunity for some, but try telling that to a sex-starved indentured servant in the early Chesapeake or early Caribbean, and servants were after all the vast majority of British emigrants in the seventeenth century and not an inconsiderable proportion in the eighteenth century. Further, Hyam's perspective is resolutely masculine. A new generation of scholars willing to explore gender in all its facets – the process is well underway, as witness for example Anne McClintock's *Imperial Leather*, which must stand as one of the better titles in this genre – are focusing on the role of women in empire, on masculinity, and on the gendered rhetoric and images of imperialism.[47]

This essay has offered five ways to think about encounters between the British and indigenous peoples in the early modern era. It has emphasized that identities must be deconstructed, variations over time and across space delineated, metaphors deciphered, links between core and margins dissected, and arenas of contact differentiated. In the space available, it has not been possible to offer a continuous master narrative, detailing how encounters changed from 1500 to 1800. Instead, the intent has been to present a variety of perspectives, a set of analytical tools, a range of approaches. Even these are hardly exhaustive – a strong argument, for example, could be made that British encounters with indigenous peoples can be understood only in a wide-ranging comparative context – but at least some of the more important modes of analysis, it is hoped, have been identified and illustrated.

To understand cultural encounters between the British and indigenous peoples, it will be necessary to use a full toolkit. Only by weaving together an array of interpretive strands, a series of perspectives, will the rich tapestry of cultural encounters take shape. We must, on the one hand, encompass whole panoramas, entire sets of interrelated systems, truly pan-global contexts, and on the other, attend to individual particularities, local settings, and specific situational sockets. The real challenge will be to connect the two; and to integrate the local and the general, we will need bifocal vision, a bilateral history, a mirror-image ethnography. Only then will we glimpse whole worlds, large or small, that have not been seen before. A synoptic view, bringing metropole and colony, colonizer and colonized, British and in-digenous peoples into one frame, into a single analytical field, will reveal not merely a catalogue of differences and similarities, not just a series of intriguing parallels, but whole configurations, general processes, an entire interactive system, one vast interconnected world.

Notes

Please note where notes list more than one reference the order they are cited in the note corresponds directly with the order they are given in the text.

1   J. H. Elliott, "Final reflections", in *America in European consciousness*, Karen O. Kupperman (ed.) (Chapel Hill, N.C., 1995), p. 404.

2   Bernard Bailyn, "The challenge of modern historiography", *American Historical Review* **78**, 1982, pp. 1–24; Daniel Walker Howe, *American history in an Atlantic context: an inaugural lecture delivered before the University of Oxford on 3 June 1993* (Oxford, 1993); David Fieldhouse, "Can Humpty-Dumpty be put together again? Imperial history in the 1980s", *Journal of Imperial and Commonwealth History* **12**, 1984, pp. 9–23 (quote on p. 10); P. J. Cain & A. G. Hopkins, *British imperialism: innovation and expansion 1688–1914* (Harlow, 1993); Edward Said, "Secular interpretation, the geographical element, and the methodology of imperialism", in *After colonialism: imperial histories and postcolonial displacements*, Gyan Prakash (ed.) (Princeton, N.J., 1995), pp. 21–39; Said, *Culture and imperialism* (New York, 1993); Maaja A. Stewart, *Domestic realities and imperial fictions: Jane Austen's novels in eighteenth-century contexts* (Athens, Ga., 1993), pp. 2, 26–31, 105–136; Antoinette Burton, "Recapturing *Jane Eyre*: reflections on historicizing the colonial encounter in Victorian Britain", *Radical History Review* **64**, 1996, pp. 59–72; Bailyn, "The idea of Atlantic history", *Itinerario* **20**(1), 1996, pp. 19–43.

3   Robert Young, *White mythologies: writing history and the West* (New York, 1990), p. 13; Dane Kennedy, "Imperial history and post-colonial theory", *Jour. Imp. and Comm. Hist.* **24**, 1996, pp. 345–63.

4   J. G. A. Pocock, "British history: a plea for a new subject", *New Zealand Historical Journal* **8**, 1974, pp. 3–21 and "The limits and divisions of British history: in search of the unknown subject", *AHR* **87**, 1982, pp. 311–36; Raphael Samuel (ed.), *Patriotism: the making and unmaking of a British national identity, vol. 1: History and politics, vol. 2: Minorities and outsiders, vol. 3: National fictions* (London, 1989); T. O. Lloyd, *The British empire 1558– 1983* (New York, 1984), p. xii; Gwyn A. Williams, *When was Wales? A history of the Welsh* (London, 1985), p. 119; R. Merfyn Jones, "Beyond identity? The reconstruction of the Welsh", *Journal of British Studies* **31**, 1992, pp. 330–57; Jenny Wormald, "The creation of Britain: multiple kingdoms or cores and colonies", *Transactions of the Royal Historical Society* **6th Ser.** (2), 1992, pp. 175–94; Colin Kidd, "North Britishness and the nature of eighteenth-century British patriotism", *Historical Journal* **39**, 1996, pp. 361–82; J. G. A. Pocock, *Virtue, commerce, and history: essays on political thought and history, chiefly in the eighteenth century* (Cambridge, 1985), pp. 127–30, 137; John Robertson (ed.), *A union for empire: political thought and the British Union of 1707* (Cambridge, 1995); R. R. Davies (ed.), *The British Isles 1100–1500: comparisons, contrasts and connections* (Edinburgh, 1987); Hugh Kearney, *The British Isles: a history of four nations* (Cambridge, 1989); Linda Colley, *Britons: forging the nation 1707–1837* (New Haven, Conn., 1992).

5   Pocock, "The limits and divisions of British history", *AHR* **87**, 1982, p. 318; Fynes Moryson, *An itinerary* (London, 1617), as quoted in David Quinn, *The Elizabethans and the Irish* (Ithaca, N.Y., 1966), p. 122; Thomas Bartlett, " 'This famous island set in a Virginian sea': Ireland in the British Empire", in *The Oxford History of the British Empire, vol. 2: The eighteenth century*, P. J. Marshall (ed.) (Oxford, 1998), pp. 253–75 (quote on p. 254); Nicholas Canny, *Kingdom and colony: Ireland in the Atlantic world, 1560–1800* (Baltimore, 1988) and "Irish, Scottish and Welsh Responses to centralisation, c. 1530–c. 1640: a comparative perspective", in *Uniting the kingdom?: The making of British history*, Alexander Grant & Keith J. Stringer (eds) (London, 1995), p. 147; Peter Fryer, *Staying power: the history of Black people in Britain* (London, 1984); Todd M. Endelman, *The Jews of Georgian England, 1714–1830: tradition and change in a liberal society* (Philadelphia, 1979); James Shapiro, *Shakespeare and the Jews* (New York, 1996); Judith Okely, *The traveller gypsies* (Cambridge, 1983); David Mayall, "The making of British gypsy identities, c. 1500– 1980", *Immigrants and Minorities* **11**, 1992, pp. 21–41; V. G. Kiernan, "Britons old and new", in *Immigrants and minorities in British society*, Colin Holmes (ed.) (London, 1978), pp. 23–59.

6   Linda Colley, "Britishness and otherness: an argument", *Jour. Brit. Stud.* **31**, 1992, pp. 316, 323, 324, and *Britons: forging the nation*, p. 6; Keith Robbins, "An imperial and multinational polity: The 'scene from the centre', 1832–1922", in *Uniting the kingdom?*, Grant & Stringer (eds), p. 253. See also Gerald Newman, *The rise of English nationalism: a cultural history, 1740–1830* (New York, 1987), pp. 75, 112–20, 133, 149–53, 160, 169–71.

7   R. R. Davies, "The peoples of Britain and Ireland, 1100–1400: I. Identities", *Trans. Royal Hist. Soc.* **6th Ser.** (4), 1994, pp. 1–20, and "The peoples of Britain and Ireland, 1100– 1400: II. Names, boundaries and regnal solidarities", *ibid.* **6th Ser.** (5), 1995, pp. 1–20; J. G. A. Pocock, "Contingency, identity, sovereignty", in *Uniting the kingdom?*, Grant & Stringer (eds), p. 300; Frederick Cooper & Ann L. Stoler, "Introduction. Tensions of empire: colonial control and visions of rule", *American Ethnologist* **16**, 1989, pp. 609–21. See also Nicholas Canny & Anthony Pagden (eds), *Colonial identity in the Atlantic world*

1500–1800 (Princeton, N.J., 1987); Benedict Anderson, *Imagined communities: reflections on the origin and spread of nationalism* (New York, 1991); R. F. Helgerson, *Forms of nationhood: the Elizabethan writing of England* (Chicago, 1992).

8   Sir George Macartney, *An account of Ireland in 1773 by a late chief secretary of that kingdom* (London, 1773), p. 55 as cited in Bartlett, " 'This famous island set in a Virginian sea' ", in *The Oxford History of the British Empire*, vol. 2, Marshall (ed.) (Oxford, 1998), pp. 262. Population figures are inevitably approximate: P. J. Marshall, "Empire and opportunity in Britain, 1763–1775", *Trans. Royal Hist. Soc.* **6th Ser.** (5), 1995, p. 112; P. J. Marshall (ed.), *The Cambridge Illustrated History of the British Empire* (Cambridge, 1996), pp. 16, 37, 38; James Belich, *Making peoples: a history of the New Zealanders from the Polynesian settlement to the end of the nineteenth century* (Honolulu, 1996), p. 178; Patrick Manning, *Slavery and African life: occidental, oriental, and African slave trades* (Cambridge, 1990), p. 72; William M. Denevan, *The native population of the Americas in 1492*, 2nd edn (Madison, Wisc., 1992), p. xxviii; Douglas H. Ubelaker, "North American Indian population size: changing perspectives", in *Disease and demography in the Americas*, John W. Verano & Douglas H. Ubelaker (eds) (Washington, 1992), p. 172; Greg Dening, *Islands and beaches: discourse on a silent land, Marquesas 1774–1880* (Honolulu, 1980), p. 239. For some rather overdrawn contrasts, see Anthony Pagden, *Lords of all the world: ideologies of empire in Spain, Britain and France c. 1500–c. 1800* (New Haven, Conn., 1995), p. 8.

9   William C. Sturtevant (ed.), *Handbook of North American Indians* (Washington, 1978–   ), especially vols 4, 5, 6, 9, 10, 14, 15, 17; Irving Rouse, *The Tainos: rise and decline of the people who greeted Columbus* (New Haven, Conn., 1992); William F. Keegan, *The people who discovered Columbus: the prehistory of the Bahamas* (Gainesville, Fla., 1992); William F. Keegan, "Creating the Guanahataeby (Ciboney): the modern genesis of an extinct culture", *Antiquity* **63**, 1989, pp. 373–9; John Thornton, *Africa and Africans in the making of the Atlantic world, 1400–1680* (Cambridge, 1992), pp. xii–xxxviii, 103–5, 186; Michael Mann & David Dalby, *A thesaurus of African languages: a classified and annotated inventory of the spoken languages of Africa* (London, 1987); Greg Dening, *Islands and beaches*, pp. 31–78; Derek J. Mulvaney & J. Peter White (eds), *Australians to 1788* (Broadway, New South Wales, 1987), pp. 120–365; D. J. Mulvaney, *Encounters in place: outsiders and Aboriginal Australians 1606–1985* (St. Lucia, Queensland, 1989), pp. xv, 2; Anne Salmond, *Two worlds: first meetings between Maoris and Europeans, 1642–1772* (Honolulu, 1991); Bellich, *Making peoples*, pp. 91–9; Bain Attwood, "Aborigines and academic historians: some recent encounters", *Australian Historical Studies* **24** (94), 1990, p. 127.

10 C. A. Bayly, *The New Cambridge History of India, vol. 2: 1. Indian society and the making of the British Empire* (Cambridge, 1988), pp. 7–32; Thornton, *Africa and Africans*, pp. 83, 91–4.

11 Daniel K. Richter, "Native peoples of North America and the eighteenth-century British empire", in *The Oxford History of the British Empire, vol. 2*, Marshall (ed.), (Oxford, 1998), pp. 347–71; Claudio Saunt, "A new order of things: Creeks and Seminoles in the Deep South interior, 1733–1816" (PhD dissertation, Duke University, 1996), especially Chs 3, 7, and 8; essays by Greg O'Brien and Nathaniel Sheidley in this volume; P. J. Marshall, "The British in Asia: Trade to Dominion, 1700–1765", in *The Oxford History of the British Empire, vol. 2*, Marshall (ed.), pp. 487–507, and "Masters and banians in eighteenth-century Calcutta", in *The age of partnership: Europeans in Asia before dominion*, Blair B. Kling & M. N. Pearson (eds) (Honolulu, 1979), pp. 191–213; S. Arasaratnam, "Trade and political dominion in South India, 1750–1790: changing British–Indian relationships", *Modern Asian Studies* **13**, 1979, pp. 23–6; P. E. H. Hair and Robin Law, "The English in

Western Africa to 1700", in *The Oxford History of the British Empire, vol. 1,* N. Canny (ed.), (Oxford, 1998), pp. 241–63.

12 Sean Hawkins & Philip Morgan, "Patterns of cultural transmission: diffusion, destruction, and development in the African diaspora", paper presented at York University, Canada, 1996; cf. Thornton, *Africa and Africans,* pp. 183–234; John Iliffe, *A modern history of Tanganyika* (Cambridge, 1979), p. 324; Colin G. Calloway, *The American revolution in Indian country: crisis and diversity in Native American communities* (Cambridge, 1995), p. xvi; Richard White, *The middle ground: Indians, empires, and republics in the Great Lakes region, 1650–1815* (Cambridge, 1991), p. 1; Mulvaney & White (eds), *Australians to 1788,* pp. 343–4.

13 Dorothy Shineberg, *They came for sandalwood: a study of the sandalwood trade in the south-west Pacific* (Melbourne, 1967), p. 214, as cited in Marshall Sahlins, "Goodbye to *tristes tropes*: ethnography in the context of modern world history", *Journal of Modern History* **65**, 1993, pp. 1–25 (quote on p. 5 and later quote on p. 19); I. C. Campbell, "Culture contact and Polynesian identity in the European age", *Journal of World History* **8**(1), 1997, pp. 29–55; Francis Jennings, *The ambiguous Iroquois empire: the covenant chain confederation of Indian tribes with English colonies from its beginnings to the Lancaster Treaty of 1744* (New York, 1984); Bruce Trigger, *The children of Aataentsic: a history of the Huron people to 1660* [2 vols] (Montreal, 1976); Gregory Evans Dowd, *A spirited resistance: the North American Indian struggle for unity, 1745–1815* (Baltimore, 1992), p. 49; Richard Price (ed.), *Maroon societies: rebel slave communities in the Americas,* 2nd edn (Baltimore, 1979).

14 Hair & Law, "The English in Western Africa to 1700", in *The Oxford History of the British Empire, vol. 2,* pp. 241–63; T. H. Breen, "An empire of goods: the anglicization of colonial America, 1690–1776", *Jour. Brit. Stud.* **25**, 1986, pp. 467–99.

15 I. A. Wright (ed.), *Documents concerning English voyages to the Spanish Main, 1569–1580,* Hakluyt Society, 2nd Ser., 71 (London, 1932); Kenneth R. Andrews, *The Spanish Caribbean: trade and plunder, 1530–1630* (New Haven, Conn., 1978), pp. 139–145; for the imperial garrison state, see the essay by C. A. Bayly in this volume; cf. Pagden's view that, by the second half of the eighteenth century, Britain viewed the empire as a predominantly commercial enterprise, *Lords of all the world,* p. 37. For the relation between trade and conquest, see Kathleen Wilson, "Empire of virtue: the imperial project and Hanoverian culture, c. 1720–1785", in *An imperial state at war: Britain from 1689 to 1815,* Lawrence Stone (ed.) (London, 1994), p. 132; Peter N. Miller, *Defining the common good: empire, religion and philosophy in eighteenth-century Britain* (Cambridge, 1994), pp. 172–80; and Margaret Steven, *Trade, tactics and territory: Britain in the Pacific 1783–1823* (Carlton, Victoria, 1983). More generally, see Cain & Hopkins, *British imperialism,* pp. 85–6, "The political economy of British expansion overseas, 1750–1914", *Economic History Review* **33**(4), 1980, pp. 463–90, and "Gentlemanly capitalism and British expansion overseas I. The old colonial system, 1688–1850", *ibid.,* **39**(4), 1986, pp. 501–25; John Brewer, *The sinews of power: war, money and the English state 1688–1783* (New York, 1989).

16 Christopher L. Miller & George R. Hammell, "A new perspective on Indian–white contact: cultural symbols and colonial trade", *Journal of American History* **73**, 1986, pp. 311–28; Ray Kea, *Settlements, trade and politics on the seventeenth century Gold Coast* (Baltimore, 1982), pp. 207–12; Bellich, *Making peoples,* 148–9; Sahlins, "Goodbye to *tristes tropes*", *Jour. Mod. Hist.* **65**, 1993, pp. 1–25 (quote on pp. 16–17).

17 Judith Modell, "From ethnographies to encounters: differences and others", *Journal of Interdisciplinary History* **27**(3), 1997, pp. 481–95; Glyndwr Williams & Alan Frost (eds),

Terra Australis to Australia (Melbourne, 1988), pp. 123–4, 133, 145; Glyndwyr Williams, "'Far More Happier than We Europeans': Relations to the Australian Aborigines on Cook's voyages", *Historical Studies* **19**, 1981, pp. 499–512 (Williams here notes that the earlier visit to Tierra del Fuego also influenced Cook's and Banks' impressions of Aborigines); Diane Bell, "An accidental Australian tourist: or a feminist anthropologist at sea and on land", in *Implicit understandings: observing, reporting, and reflecting on the encounters between Europeans and other peoples in the early modern era*, Stuart B. Schwartz (ed.) (New York, 1994), pp. 502–55; Peter H. Wood, "North America in the era of Captain Cook: three glimpses of Indian–European contact in the age of the American Revolution", in *ibid.*, p. 487; Greg Dening, "The theatricality of observing and being observed: eighteenth-century Europe 'discovers' the 'Pacific'" in *ibid.*, p. 464. For other recognitions of this distinction between fleeting and sustained contact, see Urs Bitterli's *Cultures in conflict: encounters between Europeans and non-European cultures, 1492–1800*, trans. Ritchie Robertson (Stanford, Calif., 1989), and P. E. H. Hair, "Outthrust and encounter: an interpretative essay", in *The European outthrust and encounter: the first phase c. 1400–c. 1700*, Cecil H. Clough & P. E. H. Hair (eds) (Liverpool, 1994), pp. 43–75. I am not suggesting, of course, that all first contacts were essentially the same over three centuries, but lessons from earlier encounters did influence later ones.

18 Gananath Obeyesekere, *The apotheosis of Captain Cook: European mythmaking in the Pacific* (Princeton, N.J., 1992); Marshall Sahlins, *How "natives" think about Captain Cook, for example* (Chicago, 1995) and *Islands of history* (Chicago, 1985); I. C. Campbell, "Polynesian perceptions of Europeans in the eighteenth and nineteenth centuries", *Pacific Studies* **5**(2), 1982, pp. 65–8. Salmond, *Two worlds*, pp. 129, 178–9, 228, 243–7, 249, 252, 351. The literature on cannibalism is large, but see Michael Palencia Roth, "Cannibalism and the new man of Latin America in the fifteenth- and sixteeenth-century European imagination", *Comparative Civilization Review* **12**, 1985, pp. 1–27, and "The Cannibal Law of 1503", in *Early images of the Americas: transfer and invention*, Jerry M. Williams & Robert E. Lewis (eds) (Tucson, Ariz., 1993), pp. 21–63; Peter Hulme, *Colonial encounters: Europe and the native Caribbean, 1492–1797* (London, 1986), pp. 13–43; Philip P. Boucher, *Cannibal encounters: Europeans and the island Caribs, 1492–1763* (Baltimore, 1992); Claude Rawson, "'Indians' and Irish: Montaigne, Swift, and the cannibal question", *Modern Language Quarterly* **53**, 1992, pp. 344–54; and Gananath Obeyesekere, "'British cannibals': contemplation of an event in the death and resurrection of James Cook, explorer", in *Identities*, Kwame Anthony Appiah & Henry Louis Gates, Jr. (eds) (Chicago, 1995), pp. 7–31.

19 St Francis Xavier, quoted in Geoffrey V. Scammell, *The first imperial age: European overseas expansion, 1400–1715* (London, 1989), p. 92; Ann McGrath, *'Born in the cattle': Aborigines in cattle country* (Sydney, 1987); James H. Merrell, *The Indians' new world: Catawbas and their neighbors from European contact through the era of removal* (Chapel Hill, N.C., 1989), pp. 210–11, 230, 267–70; Shineberg, *They came for sandalwood*; Ira Berlin & Philip D. Morgan (eds), *The slaves' economy: independent production by slaves in the Americas* (London, 1991).

20 Ira Berlin, "From creole to African: Atlantic creoles and the origins of African–American society in mainland North America", *William and Mary Quarterly*, **3rd Ser.** (53), 1996, pp. 251–88; for the best study of mediators between North American Indians and Europeans see James H. Merrell, *Into the woods: negotiators on the colonial Pennsylvania frontier*, in press; Margaret Connell Szasz (ed.), *Between Indian and white worlds: the cultural broker* (Norman, Okla., 1994); Colin G. Calloway, "Simon Girty: interpreter and intermediary", in *Being and becoming Indian: biographical studies of North American frontiers*, James A. Clifton (ed.)

(Prospect Heights, IL, 1993), pp. 38–58; J. Frederick Fausz, "Middlemen in peace and war: Virginia's earliest Indian interpreters, 1608–1632", *Virginia Magazine of History and Biography*, 95, 1987, pp. 41–64; Yasuhide Kawashima, "Forest diplomats: the role of interpreters in Indian–white relations on the early American frontier", *American Indian Quarterly* **13**, 1989, pp. 1–14; Alan Taylor, "Captain Hendrick Aupaumut: the dilemmas of an intercultural broker", *Ethnohistory* **43**, 1996, pp. 431–57; Bellich, *Making peoples*, p. 20. For more general works, see Jerry H. Bentley, *Old world encounters: cross-cultural contacts and exchanges in pre-modern times* (New York, 1993); Philip D. Curtin, *cross-cultural trade in world history* (Cambridge, 1984); Frances Karttunen, *Between worlds: interpreters, guides, and survivors* (New Brunswick, N.J., 1994).

21 Bernard Bailyn & Philip D Morgan (eds), *Strangers within the realm: cultural margins of the first British empire* (Chapel Hill, N.C., 1991), pp. 19–22; Gregory Nobles, *American frontiers: cultural encounters and continental conquest* (New York, 1997), pp. xii–xiii, 11–14, 19–96; James H. Merrell, "'The Customs of Our Countrey': Indians and colonists in early America", in *ibid.*, pp. 118–20; Salmond, *Two worlds*.

22 Merrell, "'The Customs of Our Countrey'" in *Strangers within the realm*, Bailyn & Morgan (eds), p. 120; Anne Salmond, *Two worlds*, pp. 187, 330; Dening, *Islands and beaches*, p. 27; see also Christie Davis, "Ethnic jokes and social change: the case of the Welsh", *Immigrants and Minorities* **4**, 1985, pp. 46–63, and "Ethnic jokes, moral values and social boundaries", *British Journal of Sociology* **33**(3), 1982, pp. 383–403; Keith Thomas, "The place of laughter in Tudor and Stuart England", *Times Literary Supplement* (21 Jan. 1977).

23 Greg Dening, *Islands and beaches*, pp. 3, 20, 23 (quote), 31, 32 (quote); Bitterli, *Cultures in conflict*, p. 25; Salmond, *Two worlds*, p. 123.

24 Oliver Sacks, *The island of the colorblind and Cycad Island* (New York, 1996); David Quammen, *The song of the dodo: island biogeography in an age of extinctions* (New York, 1996); Richard H. Grove, *Green imperialism: colonial expansion, tropical island Edens and the origins of environmentalism, 1600–1860* (New York, 1995); Diana Loxley, *Problematic shores: the literature of islands* (New York, 1990); Mary W. Helms, *Ulysses' sail: an ethnographic odyssey of power, knowledge, and geographical distance* (Princeton, N.J., 1988), p. 217; James Otis, *The rights of the British colonies asserted and proved* (1764) in *Pamphlets of the American Revolution, 1750–1776* [2 vols] Bernard Bailyn (ed.) (Cambridge, Mass., 1965), I, p. 435.

25 Bernard Bailyn, *The peopling of British North America: an introduction* (New York, 1986), pp. 112–31.

26 White, *Middle ground*, pp. ix–xi, passim.

27 Richard S. Dunn, "Servants and slaves: the recruitment and employment of labor", in *Colonial British America: essays in the new history of the early modern era*, Jack P. Greene & J. R. Pole (eds) (Baltimore, 1984), pp. 157–94; Paul E. Lovejoy & Nicholas Rogers (eds), *Unfree labour in the development of the Atlantic world* (London, 1994); Jon F. Sensbach, *A separate Canaan: the making of an Afro-Moravian world in North Carolina, 1763–1840* (Chapel Hill, N.C., 1998), p. 55. Studies of disease among Native Americans have influenced Australian history, best evident in N. G. Butlin, *Our original aggression: Aboriginal populations of Southeastern Australia 1788–1850* (Sydney, 1983), but the close attention that can be paid to the spread of disease in nineteenth-century Australia and New Zealand may well help us understand earlier experiences in America. See, for example, Judy Campbell, "Smallpox in Aboriginal Australia, 1829–31", *Historical Studies* **20**, 1983, pp. 536–56; N. G. Butlin, "Macassans and Aboriginal smallpox: the '1789' and '1829' epidemics", *ibid.* **21**, 1985, pp. 315–35; Judy Campbell, "Smallpox in Aboriginal Australia, the early 1830s", *ibid.* **21**(84),

1985, pp. 336–58; and Bellich, *Making peoples*, pp. 173–8. For a good case for connections, see Shula Marks, "History, the nation and empire: sniping from the periphery", *History Workshop Journal* **29**, 1990, pp. 111–19.

28   Howard Mumford Jones, *O strange new world. American culture: the formative years* (New York, 1964), pp. 167–79; Quinn, *The Elizabethans and the Irish*, pp. 106–22; Nicholas P. Canny, "The ideology of English colonization: from Ireland to America," *WMQ* **3rd Ser. (**30), 1973, pp. 575–98; James Muldoon, "The Indian as Irishman", *Essex Institute Historical Collections* **111**, 1975, pp. 267–89; Nicholas P. Canny, *The Elizabethan conquest of Ireland: a pattern established, 1565–76* (New York, 1976), pp. 117–36, 159–63; K. R. Andrews, Nicholas P. Canny, P. E. H. Hair (eds), *The westward enterprise: English activities in Ireland, the Atlantic and America, 1480–1650* (Detroit, 1978); John Gillingham, "Images of Ireland, 1170–1600: the origins of English imperialism", *History Today* **37** (February 1987), pp. 16–22; Canny, *Kingdom or colony*; Sir John Elliott, *Britain and Spain in America: colonists and colonized*, The Stenton Lecture (Reading, 1994).

29   Alden T. Vaughan, "Early English paradigms for new world natives", *Proceedings of the American Antiquarian Society* **102**, 1992, pp. 35–40, 50–56; T. D. Kendrick, *British antiquity* (London, 1950), pp. 121–5; Arthur H. Williamson, "Scots, Indians and empire: the Scottish politics of civilization 1519–1609", *Past and Present* **150**, 1996, pp. 46–83 (quotes on pp. 47 and 64); Paul Hulton & David Beers Quinn, *The American drawings of John White, 1577–1590, with Drawings of European and Oriental Subjects* [2 vols] (Chapel Hill, N.C., 1964), II, plates 64–8 (see also plates 139–43); C. A. Bayly, *Imperial meridian: the British empire and the world, 1780–1830* (Harlow, 1989), pp. 155–60; Peter Womack, *Improvement and romance: constructing the myth of the Highlands* (Basingstoke, 1989); John Lanne Buchanan, *Travel in the Western Hebrides: from 1782 to 1790* (London, 1793), pp. 4–5, as cited in Eric Richards, "Scotland and the uses of the Atlantic empire", in *Strangers within the Realm*, Bailyn & Morgan (eds), p. 80.

30   Williams & Frost (eds), *Terra Australis*, pp. 150, 166, 190; Salmond, *Two worlds*, pp. 142, 273; Robert King, "Terra Australis: Terra Nullius and Terra Aborigium", *Journal of the Royal Australian Historical Society* **72**, 1987, pp. 75–80; A. G. L. Shaw, "British policy towards the Australian Aborigines, 1830–1850", *Australian Historical Studies* **25**(99), 1992, pp. 265–85; Clifton Crais, "The vacant land: the mythology of British expansion in the Eastern Cape, South Africa", *Journal of Social History* **25**, 1991, pp. 255–74; Charles Grant to Henry Dundas, c. 1796, in *Britain at the Cape 1795 to 1803*, Maurice Boucher & Nigel Penn (eds) (Houghton, South Africa, 1992), p. 81. The OED notes too that *indigenous* or *indigene* was used to describe Highlanders, the Irish, and Native Americans in this period. Andrew Porter, "North American experience and British missionary encounters in Africa and the Pacific, c. 1800–1850" in this volume.

31   James Thompson, as cited by Richard Koebner, *Empire of the deep* (Cambridge, 1961), p. 81; P. J. Marshall, "Introduction", in *Oxford History of the British Empire*, Marshall (ed.), pp. 1–27; Bob Harris, "'American idols': empire, war and the middling ranks in mid-eighteenth-century Britain", *Past and Present* **150**, 1996, pp. 111–41; Kathleen Wilson, *The sense of the people: politics, culture, and imperialism in England, 1715–1785* (New York, 1995), pp. 38–9; Ian K. Steele, *The English Atlantic, 1675–1740: an exploration of communication and community* (New York, 1987); N. A. M. Rodger, *The wooden world: an anatomy of the Georgian navy* (Annapolis, Md., 1986), p. 15; Philip Edwards, *The story of the voyage: sea-narratives in eighteenth-century England* (New York, 1994).

32   Marcus Rediker, *Between the devil and the deep blue sea: merchant seamen, pirates, and the Anglo-American maritime world, 1700–1750* (New York, 1987), p. 76; William Dampier, *A*

new voyage round the world, ed. Albert Gray (London, 1927), pp. 11, 15–17, 32–5, 65–7; Dening, *Islands and beaches*, pp. 134–6, 150. The Moskito Indians had apparently black admixture: see Troy S. Floyd, *Anglo-Spanish struggle for Mosquitia* (Albuquerque, N.M., 1967), pp. 22–3, 64–7.

33   Paul Edwards (ed.), *The life of Olaudah Equiano; or Gustavus Vassa the African, 1789* [2 vols] (London, 1969 [orig. publ. London, 1789]), I, pp. 95, 98–100, 111, 123, 135–6, 138–9, 151, 171–3, 178–9, 184–5, 217, 252; William Butterworth, *Three years adventures of a minor in England, Africa, the West Indies, South-Carolina, and Georgia* (Leeds, 1822), p. 211; James Kelly, *Voyage to Jamaica, and seventeen years' residence in that island . . .* (Belfast, 1838), pp. 29–30; Rodger, *The wooden world*, p. 159; *Bristol Gazette*, Sept. 7, 1815, as cited in D. P. Lingaard, *Black Bristolians of the eighteenth & nineteenth Centuries* (typescript, n.d.), pp. 13–14; W. Jeffrey Bolster, *Black jacks: African-American Seaman in the age of sail* (Cambridge, Mass., 1997), p. 96; Bellich, *Making peoples*, 138. For black participation in pirate and privateering crews, see John Franklin Jameson, *Privateering and piracy in the colonial period: illustrative documents* (New York, 1923), pp. 222, 290–2 and James G. Lydon, *Pirates, privateers, and profits* (Upper Saddle River, N.J., 1970), p. 221.

34   Rodger, *The wooden world*, pp. 159–61; Capt. John Colpoys to Lord Sandwich, *Orpheus* off the Ooze, Aug. 14, 1780, SAN/F/24/47, Sandwich Papers, National Maritime Museum, reference kindly supplied by N. A. M. Rodger; Jameson, *Privateering and piracy*, pp. 407–14; David Barry Gaspar, "A dangerous spirit of liberty: slave rebellion in the West Indies during the 1730s", *Cimarrons* 1, 1981, p. 91n; Daniel Vickers, "The first whalemen of Nantucket", *WMQ* **3rd Ser.** (40), 1983, pp. 560–83; "Nantucket whalemen in the deep-sea fishery: the changing anatomy of an early American labor force", *JAH* **72**, 1985, pp. 277–96, and "Beyond Jack Tar", *WMQ* **3rd Ser.** (50), 1993, pp. 418–24 (quote on p. 423).

35   Paul Gilroy, *The Black Atlantic: modernity and double consciousness* (Cambridge, Mass., 1993); N. A. T. Hall, "Maritime maroons: *grand marronage* from the Danish West Indies", *WMQ* **3rd Ser.** (42) 1985, pp. 476–98; Julius S. Scott, "Afro-American sailors and the international communication network: the case of Newport Bowers", in *Jack Tar in history: essays in the history of maritime life and labour*, Colin Howell & Richard J. Twomey (eds) (Fredericton, N.B., 1991), p. 52 (quote); "Crisscrossing empires: ships, sailors, and resistance in the Lesser Antilles in the eighteenth century", in *The Lesser Antilles in the age of European expansion*, Robert L. Paquette & Stanley L. Engerman (eds) (Gainesville, Fla., 1996), pp. 128–43, and "The common wind: currents of Afro-American communication in the era of the Haitian Revolution" (PhD dissertation, Duke University, 1986); W. Jeffrey Bolster, *Black Jacks*, p. 2; Iain McCalman, *Radical underworld: prophets, revolutionaries and pornographers in London, 1795–1840* (Cambridge, 1988), pp. 50–72; Robert Wedderburn, *House of slavery and other writings*, Iain McCalman (ed.) (New York, 1991).

36   Dening, "The theatricality of observing and being observed", in *Implicit understandings*, Schwartz (ed.), pp. 470–72; Salmond, *Two worlds*, pp. 141–3, 214, 217, 225, 260, 272–3, 346; Greg Dening, *Mr Bligh's bad language: passion, power and theatre on the Bounty* (Cambridge, 1992), pp. 35–6; Dening, *Islands and beaches*, pp. 160, 278; Glyndwr Williams, "Buccaneers, castaways, and satirists: the South Seas in the English consciousness before 1750", *Eighteenth-Century Life* **18**(3), 1994, 118; Ira Dye, "The tattoos of early American seafarers, 1796–1818", *Proceedings of the American Philosophical Society* **133**, 1989, pp. 520–54; Simon P. Newman, "Wearing their hearts on their sleeves", in *American bodies: cultural histories of the physique*, Tim Armstrong (ed.) (New York, 1996), pp. 18–31, and "Reading the bodies of early American seafarers", *WMQ* **3rd Ser.** (55), 1998, pp. 59–

82. For general works on tattooing, see Robert Brain, *The decorated body* (London, 1979); Victoria Ebin, *The body decorated* (London, 1979); Frances E. Mascia-Lees & Patricia Sharpe (eds), *Tattoo, torture, mutilation, and adornment: the denaturalization of the body in culture and text* (Albany, N.Y., 1992); R. W. B. Scutt & Christopher Gotch, *Skin deep; the mystery of tattooing* (London, 1974), p. 65.

37 Peter Linebaugh & Marcus Rediker, "The many-headed hydra: sailors, slaves, and the Atlantic working class in the eighteenth century", *Journal of Historical Sociology* **3**(3), 1990, pp. 225–52 (quote on p. 225).

38 Bernard Bailyn, *The boundaries of history: The old world and the new*, The dedication of the Caspersen Building (Providence, R.I., 1992), p. 25 (pamphlet); Pagden, *Lords of all the world*, p. 150; Elliott, *Britain and Spain in America*, pp. 8–12. See also James Axtell, *The invasion within: the contest of cultures in colonial North America* (New York, 1985), p. 278.

39 Nicholas Canny, "England's New World and the Old 1480s-1630s", in *The Oxford History of the British Empire,* vol. 1, pp. 158–60; David D. Smits, " 'Abominable mixture': toward the repudiation of Anglo-Indian intermarriage in seventeenth-century Virginia", *Virginia Magazine of History and Biography* **45**, 1987, pp. 157–92, and " 'We are not to grow wild': seventeenth-century New England's repudiation of Anglo-Indian intermarriage," *American Indian Culture and Research Journal* **11**, 1987, pp. 1–32.

40 Sylvia Van Kirk, "Women of the fur trade," *The Beaver* **303**(3), 1972, pp. 4–21, and "The custom of the country": an examination of fur trade marriage practices", in *Essays on western history in honour of L. G. Thomas*, Lewis H. Thomas (ed.) (Edmonton, 1976), pp. 49–68, and *"Many tender ties": women in fur-trade society, 1670–1870* (Norman, Okla., 1980), p. 36; Jennifer S. H. Brown, *Strangers in blood: fur trade company families in Indian country* (Vancouver, 1980); Glyndwr Williams, "The Hudson's Bay Company and the fur trade, 1670–1870", *The Beaver* **314**(2), 1983, pp. 69–77. For a summary of frontier trading posts, see Ronald Hyam, *Empire and sexuality: the British experience* (Manchester, 1990), pp. 95–8. See also Jacqueline Peterson, "Prelude to Red River: a social portrait of the Great Lakes metis", *Ethnohistory* **25**, 1978, pp. 41–67; Jacqueline Peterson & Jennifer Brown (eds), *The new peoples: being and becoming metis in North America* (Lincoln, Neb., 1985); Dennis F. K. Madill, "Riel, Red River, and beyond: new developments in metis history", in *New directions in American Indian history*, Colin G. Calloway (ed.) (Norman, Okla., 1988).

41 Kathryn E. Holland Braund, *Deerskins and duffels: the Creek Indian trade with Anglo-America, 1685–1815* (Lincoln, Neb.); Merrell, *The Indians' New World*; Daniel Richter, *The ordeal of long-house: The peoples of the Iroquois League in the era of European colonization* (Chapel Hill, N.C., 1992); Hyam, *Empire and sexuality*, pp. 115–17; Kate Telscher, *India inscribed: European and British writing on India 1600–1800* (Delhi, 1995), pp. 50–51 (quote p. 51); Kenneth Ballhatchet, *Race, sex, and class under the Raj: imperial attitudes and policies and their critics, 1793–1905* (London, 1980), pp. 96–7, 144, 164–6; Margaret O. MacMillan, *Women of the Raj* (New York, 1988), p. 157; C. J. Hawes, *Poor relations: the making of a Eurasian community in British India, 1773–1833* (Richmond, Va., 1996), pp. 9–20, 56–62; Lionel Caplan, "Creole world, purist rhetoric: Anglo-Indian cultural debates in colonial and contemporary Madras", *Journal of Royal Anthropological Institute* (N.S.) **1**, 1995, pp. 743–62.

42 Nicholas Owen, *Journal of a slave-dealer . . .*, Eveline Martin (ed.) (Boston, n.d.), pp. 44, 70, 76, 102; Rodney, *History of Upper Guinea*, pp. 200–222; [L. F. Romer], *Le Golfe de Guinea 1700–1750: Recit de L. F. Romer marchand d'esclaves sur la cote ouest-africaine. Traduction,*

introduction et notes par M. Dige-Hess (Paris, 1989), as cited in Natalie Everts, "Cherchez la femme: gender-related issues in eighteenth-century Elmina," *Itinerario,* **20** (1), 1996, p. 45 (quote); Christopher Fyfe, *A history of Sierra Leone, 1400–1787* (London, 1962), p. 10 (quote); George E. Brooks, Jr., "The *Signares* of Saint-Louis and Goree: women entrepreneurs in eighteenth-century Senegal", in *Women in Africa: studies in social and economic change,* Nancy J. Hafkin & Edna G. Bray (eds) (Stanford, Cal., 1976), pp. 19–44; Margaret Priestly, *West African trade and coast society: a family study* (London, 1969); Adam Jones, "White roots: written and oral testimony on the 'first' Mr. Rogers," *History in Africa* **10**, 1983, pp. 151–62; David Henige, "John Kabes of Komenda: an early African entrepreneur and state builder", *Journal of African History* **18**, 1977, pp. 1–19. For Dutch relations, see J. T. Lever, "Mulatto influence on the Gold Coast in the early nineteenth century: Jan Nieser of Elmina", *African Historical Studies* **3**(2), 1970, pp. 253–62, and Larry W. Yarak, "West African coastal slavery in the nineteenth century: the case of the Afro-European slaveowners of Elmina", *Ethnohistory* **36**(1), 1989, pp. 44–60.

43 Winthrop D. Jordan, *White over Black: American attitudes toward the negro, 1550–1812* (Chapel Hill, N.C., 1968), pp. 136–78; Philip D. Morgan, *Slave counterpoint: Black culture in the eighteenth-century Chesapeake and Lowcountry* (Chapel Hill, N.C., 1998), pp. 398–412.

44 Dening, *Mr Bligh's bad language,* p. 193 (quote); Dening, "The theatricality of observing and being observed", in *Implicit understandings,* Schwartz (ed.), p. 478; Bernard Smith, *Imagining the Pacific in the wake of Cook's voyages* (New Haven, Conn., 1992), p. 210; Michael Sturma, "The nubile savage", *History Today* (April 1995), pp. 7–9; Williams & Frost (eds), *Terra Australis,* p. 164; Alan Bewell, "Constructed places, constructed peoples: charting the improvement of the female body in the Pacific", *Eighteenth-Century Life,* **18** (3), 1994, pp. 37–54; Bridget Orr, " 'Southern passions mix with northern art': miscegenation and the *Endeavour* voyage", *ibid.,* pp. 212–31.

45 Salmond, *Two worlds,* pp. 175–6, 251; Bellich, *Making peoples,* 146–7, 152–4 (quote p. 152).

46 Bell, "An accidental Australian tourist", in *Implicit understandings,* Schwartz (ed.), p. 551; Ann McGrath, "The white man's looking glass: aboriginal–colonial gender relations at Port Jackson", *Australian Historical Studies* **24**(95), 1990, pp. 189–206 (quote p. 192).

47 Lawrence Stone, *The family, sex and marriage in England 1500–1800* (New York, 1977), pp. 52–4, 379–80; Ronald Hyam, "Empire and sexual opportunity", *Jour. Imp. and Comm. Hist.* **14**(2), 1986, pp. 34–90; Mark T. Berger, "Imperialism and sexual exploitation: a response to Ronald Hyam's 'Empire and sexual opportunity' ", *ibid.* **17**(1), 1988, pp. 83–9; Ronald Hyam, " 'Imperialism and Sexual Exploitation': A Reply", *ibid.,* pp. 90–98; Hyam, *Empire and sexuality,* pp. 88–114, 211 (quote); Anne McClintock, *Imperial leather: race, gender and sexuality in the colonial context* (New York, 1995); Wilson, *The sense of the people,* pp. 44n., 185–205, 274. Most of this work has focused on the nineteenth and twentieth centuries: Ann Laura Stoler, "Rethinking colonial categories: European communities and the boundaries of rule", *Comparative Studies in Society and History* **30**(1), 1989, pp. 134–61, and "Sexual affronts and racial frontiers: European identities and the cultural politics of exclusion in colonial southeast Asia", *ibid.* **34**(3), 1992, pp. 514–51; Margaret Strobel, *European women and the second British Empire* (Bloomington, Ind., 1991); Nupur Chaudhuri & Margaret Strobel (eds), *Western women and imperialism: complicity and resistance* (Bloomington, Ind., 1991); Mrinalini Sinha, *Colonial masculinity: the 'manly Englishman' and the 'effeminate Bengali' in the late nineteenth century* (Manchester, 1995). For reviews, see

Jane Haggis, "Gendering colonialism or colonizing gender? Recent women's studies approaches to white women and the history of British colonialism", *Women's Studies International Forum* **23**(1/2), 1990, pp. 105–15, and Malia B. Formes, "Beyond complicity versus resistance: recent work on gender and European imperialism", *Journal of Social History* **28**, 1994–1995, pp. 629–41.

Chapter Four

Native Americans and early modern concepts of race

Kathleen Brown

In these islands I have so far found no human monstrosities, as many expected, but on the contrary the whole population is very well formed, nor are they negroes as in Guinea, but their hair is flowing and they are not born where there is intense force in the rays of the sun.
–Columbus's Letter to the Sovereigns on His First Voyage

This is also to bee consydered as a secreate woorke of nature, that throughout all Afryke under the Equinoctiall line and neare abowt the same on bothe sydes, the regions are extreme hotte and the people very blacke. Whereas contraryly such regions of the West Indies as are under the same line, are very temperate and the people neyther blacke nor with curlde and short woolle on theyr heades as have they of Afryke, but of the coloure of an olyve with longe and blacke heare on theyr heades; the cause of which varietie is declared in dyvers places in the Decades.
–Richard Eden, "Second Voyage to Guinea"

The Negro's complexion seemed more important than the Indian's not only because the Indian was less dark but because with the Indian attention was focused primarily on the question of origin. Indeed both in Europe and America white men belittled the importance of the Indian's tawny complexion or used it merely as a foil for proving certain points about the Negro's blackness . . . There was little dissent to the commonplace assertion that the Indians' tawny color resulted wholly or in part from their custom of daubing themselves with bear grease, oils, or the like from a well-stocked cabinet of natural cosmetics . . . White men seemed to want to sweep the problem of the Indian's color under the rug. The question of the color of man was pre-eminently the question of the color of the Negro.
–Winthrop Jordan, *White over black*

Christopher Columbus was the first European to compare the physical appearance and culture of West Africans, with whom he was familiar from his many voyages aboard Portuguese ships, with that of indigenous Caribbean dwellers, whom he first encountered in 1492. His reports of naive, generous, naked peoples, living in a sylvan paradise, laid the foundation for centuries of colonial discourse about Indians and shaped the mercantile and imperial agendas of many rising European nation-states. Columbus' accounts of a previously unknown (to Europeans) indigenous population were not easily reconciled with existing European frameworks for explaining variation in human appearance. Even in the brief quotations above, we can sense Columbus struggling to fit Indians into existing European categories of difference. He compares Indians to several other groups "known" from ancient texts and recent Atlantic travel accounts, including monstrous peoples, negroes from Guinea and, elsewhere in his logbook, Canary Islanders, and tries to reconcile the appearance of Indians with popular theories about skin colour and proximity to the Equator.

My purpose here is not to retell this well known event but to try to examine the issues it raises from a perspective informed by recent scholarship on race, ethnicity, difference, and the body. Briefly recounted, the insights of this scholarship include the following: that it is more useful to think of race as a historically rooted category of difference rather than as an essential characteristic of a natural body; that "race" is not synonymous with blackness and must be understood to include whiteness, which also has a history; that approaching race from the perspective of difference reveals similarities between the formation of ethnic and racial categories; that despite all efforts to study race as a socially constructed category of difference similar to ethnicity, the opposition between blackness and whiteness continues to emerge as a distinctive characteristic.[1]

As the title of my chapter suggests, I am interested in how the history of the European encounter with American Indians can be usefully employed to further complicate the understanding of race that emerges from this recent scholarship. I view this chapter as a preliminary attempt to re-think three aspects of this issue: the importance of blackness and whiteness to definitions of race; the possibility of conceptualizing racial difference differently; and the relationship between cultural differences (manners and fashions) and differences mapped on to the body.

This chapter considers the legacy of Columbus' comparison of Guinea and Caribbean natives both broadly and narrowly. First, taking the broad view, I will re-examine one of the most influential works about the history of race, Winthrop Jordan's *White over black*, in light of recent theoretical works on race and my own research on sixteenth- and early seventeenth-century European texts about West Africa. The critical question here is to what degree the opposition of black and white remains useful for understanding the early history of race. Then I will offer a brief comparison of the similarities and differences in European discourse about West Africans and Indians. Third, I will consider the impact of these different categories and discussions of difference in the formation of English ethnic and racial identities in the late sixteenth and seventeenth centuries. Were the people that we would today define as embodying racial identities necessarily the most important to the racial formations of the sixteenth and seventeenth centuries? Ultimately, I hope to reassess what we mean by "race" for this early period of cultural contact between African, Indian, and English peoples.

Thinking over White over black

Nearly thirty years after its publication, *White over black* remains unparalleled for the scope of its research and range of its interpretation of English racial attitudes. Leaving few stones unturned, Winthrop Jordan investigated a staggering number of English pamphlets, books, and travel accounts from the period of the early sixteenth-century forays to the West African coast to the early national period of the United States. Careful to avoid using the term "racism" anachronistically, Jordan offered a nuanced analysis of his sources that allowed for multivocality and contradiction as well as historical continuity. My critique of Jordan is in no way meant to impugn his research or diminish its significance. Rather, I want to suggest how we might amend or modify his conclusions about the early history of race based on the insights of recent scholarship and a re-examination of some of the evidence.

Like most other historians writing before the late 1980s, Jordan approached race as a physiological and genetic fact, immediately perceptible to the human senses, rather than an ongoing historical and cultural construction. "I assumed that when Englishmen met Negroes overseas there would be 'attitudes' generated", he wrote in his introduction, "and I first looked for evidence in the writings of English voyagers to West Africa and of their readers at home." Although in the careful exegesis of blackness that followed, Jordan emphasized the meanings English men brought to the encounter rather than the physical appearance of Africans, he never questioned that the racial differences of which English travellers wrote were real.[2]

For Jordan, the inescapable reality of racial difference and the source of

English racial attitudes could be traced to the difference between the skin colour of West African and English people. Even after English explorers had made contact with a variety of West Africans with different skin tones, Jordan argued, the "firmest fact about the negro was that he was 'black'". The explanation for the importance of blackness lay, in part, in the contrast it presented to English whiteness: "The impact of the Negro's color was the more powerful upon Englishmen, moreover, because England's principal contact with Africans came in West Africa and the Congo where men were not merely dark but almost literally black: one of the fairest-skinned nations suddenly came face to face with one of the darkest peoples on the earth."[3]

Ever the careful scholar, Jordan recognized that cultural factors also shaped English racial attitudes. Two of these, the concepts of Christianity and civility, appeared prominently in English travellers' negative assessments of West Africans. Like Muslims, Jews, and the partially converted Gaelic Irish, West Africans fell outside the bounds of the religious faith that defined European identity. Indeed, European encounters with West Africans greatly facilitated the emerging concept of Europeanness by serving as an important foil. Whereas West Africans were frequently described as "heathen", even Europeans of the lowest ranks might be labelled "Christian", a category whose meaning depended upon European contact with non-European peoples around the globe, especially as the rifts between European Catholics and Protestants became violent during the sixteenth century. European concepts of civility overlapped in certain respects with the concept of "Christian", but pointed more generally to standards of living, divisions of household labour between the sexes, manners, and mores. When Europeans described West Africans and other non-Europeans as being of "beastly living", they were simultaneously asserting their own civility. The alleged sexual virility of West African men, which Jordan noted was central to English assessments of African beastliness, thus suggested English men's own sexual restraint and discernment.

Despite the complexity of Jordan's interpretation of race, there are still grounds for scepticism about his claim that blackness was the overriding impression in the earliest English encounters with West Africans. I wondered how Jordan's assumptions about blackness as the essence of racial difference had affected his interpretation of these early sources. I also wondered whether the thematic organization of the first part of his study had led him to overemphasize the importance of blackness for the period before 1650.

I began reading the early (pre-1650) texts, some written by Englishmen, some only translated into English, that Jordan cited in the first hundred pages of *White over black*. As I waded through the material, my respect for Jordan's achievement grew. I was struck, however, by the feeling that I was searching for the proverbial needle in the haystack. Frequently, I examined pages and pages of material about trade negotiations, conflicts with the Portuguese, detailed discussions of flora and fauna, and pejorative descriptions of African manners, housing, diet, and costume, before I found commentary on blackness. In other texts, it was less difficult to identify the material Jordan had quoted, but it still seemed that blackness was only one of many topics English men turned to in delineating the ways Africans differed from themselves. In many texts, references to blackness seemed more neutral in tone than Jordan's conclusions had led me to expect.

The earliest chronicles of English voyages to West Africa that I examined, spanning the years 1530–62, reveal little focus on the issue of African blackness, with a few notable exceptions. The first is Richard Eden's version of Thomas Wyndham's "First Voyage to Guinea" in 1553, in which he described the king of Benin as "a blacke moore (althoughe not so blacke as the rest)"; and Eden's disquisition on human colour, quoted at the beginning of this chapter, in which he marvelled at the variation in human appearance, even among those peoples living close to the Equator. Blackness was not the major focus of either of these texts, however, nor was the discussion of blackness in either case infused with the emotionally charged, pejorative meanings that Jordan had uncovered in his exegesis of blackness. All of the other texts written before 1562 that I examined included lengthy discussions of the West African landscape and the manners of the people and detailed accounts of English efforts to engage in trade. There were other charged comments made about West Africans, which I will discuss below, but these did not concern blackness. The greatest source of anxiety in these texts concerned English attempts to compete with Portuguese and French traders and the forceful manner in which they were repulsed.[4]

The earliest account I found that offered strong support for Jordan's argument is also a document with a unique context. Robert Baker's 1562 rhyming couplet about a voyage to Guinea that resulted in a ferocious battle between the English and the Guinea natives is everything that readers of Jordan might expect from an early English text about indigenous West Africans. Baker described the residents of Guinea as "a number of blacke soules/ Whose likeliness seem'd men to be,/ but all as blacke as coles". Elsewhere in his poem, Baker described his Guinea opponents as "the blacke beast", "the brutish blacke gard", "fiends more fierce/ then those in hell that be", "brutish blacke people", and "blacke burnt men".[5] We can speculate about the reasons for these eruptions by Baker. First, the rhyme described an extremely bloody encounter in which the Guinea men often had the upper hand and many lives, English and African, were lost. Second, Baker was a man with a mission. His purpose in writing was to alert his friends in England to pay the ransom being demanded by his captors and deliver him from his French prison. Baker's second poem about a second voyage to Guinea supports this interpretation. Although not complimentary in its descriptions of Guinea natives, the second poem contained none of the inflammatory language about blackness that peppered the account from the previous year. Significantly, in the rhyme about the second voyage, in which Baker and his companions had successfully engaged in trade with Guinea residents, the West African climate – the scorching sun and suffocating heat – and a diminishing store of rations were the villains of the piece, killing many members of the English party and leaving the survivors sapped of strength with the threads of their rotting clothes barely covering their nakedness.[6]

After 1563, English travellers to the West African coast seem to have become somewhat more negative in their judgements of indigenous residents but blackness was rarely the central topic of their account. Often the pamphlet writer made no mention of African appearance. One of the exceptions seems worth discussing. George Best's "Experiences and reasons of the Sphere, to proove all partes of the worlde habitable", written in 1578, stands besides Robert Baker's rhyming account as an excellent example of Jordan's claims about blackness. Best devoted a sizeable portion of his disquisition on climate, torrid and frigid zones and the movement of the sun to the question of variation in human appearance. After using American Indians to cast doubt upon the theory that the black skin of Africans resulted from exposure to the burning heat of the sun, Best offered his own explanation: that black skin was the result of an infection, which was itself a consequence of the curse upon Ham's descendants for their father's sin of unlawful "carnall copulation" aboard the Ark. His best evidence for the infection theory concerned the seeming permanence of black skin even among the descendants of Africans born in England. Best somewhat nervously recounted, "I my selfe have seene an Ethiopian as blacke as a cole brought into England, who taking a faire English woman to wife, begat a sonne in all respects as blacke as the father was, although England were his native countrey, and an English woman his mother; whereby it seemeth that blacknes proceedeth rather of some natural infection of that man, which was so strong, that neither the nature of the Clime, neither the good complexion of the mother concurring, coulde any thing alter, and therefore, wee cannot impute it to the nature of the Clime".[7]

Best's extended discussion of blackness does not necessarily support the thesis that blackness was dominant in the English perception of Africans. Rather, Best sought to convince English investors and merchants that climatic theories about variations in human appearance which encouraged conservative policies of voyage, trade, and settlement were mistaken. He began his treatise with a discussion of previous English voyages "so much to proove that Torrida Zona may bee, and is inhabited, as to shew their readinesse in attempting long and dangerous Navigations". Troubling to Best but an important part of his case to his English readership was the fact that "Wee also among us in England have blacke Moores, Aethiopians, out of all partes of Torrida Zona, which after a small continuance, can well endure the colde of our Countrey, and why should not we as well abide the heate of their Countrey?" One of the most focused and sustained assessments of African blackness thus appears not to be the consequence of the shock Englishmen experienced when they saw Black Africans, but rather a somewhat convoluted attempt to encourage more English expeditions, trade, and investment in the torrid zone along the West African coast.[8] Like Baker's poem, Best's text reflected a concept of blackness that was as much inscribed upon African bodies as a consequence of other concerns as it was a natural characteristic of those bodies.

Few English writers followed Best's lead in the years before 1650. One of the notable exceptions was the physician Sir Thomas Browne, whom Jordan describes as "the first Englishman to discuss the Negro's color in great detail". Browne devoted a large portion of his book *Pseudodoxia Epidemia* (1646) to considering theories about variations in human skin colour. His discussion was, on the whole, remarkably free of judgements about savagery or physical deformity and included a long disquisition on the relative nature of beauty. More typical, perhaps, of the English travel literature between 1600 and 1650 were the pamphlets by Richard Jobson, *The golden trade* (1623) and Andrew Battell, *The strange adventure of Andrew Battell of Leigh in Essex* (1624). Both men engaged in extended descriptions of the manners and customs of the West Africans they encountered. Although Jobson engaged directly in a discussion of the skin colour of the Mandingoes and Fulbes, invoking the theory of Ham's curse, this was not a major preoccupation of his text. African religious practices, diet, economy, and the possibilities of trade for gold were far more important to Jobson. The villains of his text, England's Portuguese rivals, were more likely to be portrayed in stark moralistic terms than were West Africans, whom Jobson described as embodying a variety of skin colours, moral conditions, and degrees of civility. Although Andrew Battell was far less sanguine about African civility than Jobson and freely engaged in diatribes about the savagery of the Central African peoples who kept him captive, it was African mores, not the fact of black skin, that raised his hackles.[9]

Although these readings of early English texts suggest significant interpretive divergences from Jordan's *White over black*, some of these differences can be traced to different research strategies and methodologies. Taking only a portion of Jordan's vast research base and subjecting each text to a close reading, I evaluated the role of blackness as a theme within each text rather than trying to demonstrate continuities in a large number of texts. Second, I focused only on those texts published before 1650, whereas Jordan wove a thematic narrative that ranged from the sixteenth to the eighteenth centuries. Paragraphs in *White over black* that contain evidence from three centuries correctly demonstrate certain continuities in the English preoccupation with blackness over time, but are structurally predisposed to overemphasize the importance of blackness for the earlier period.

Despite my effort to raise questions about the salience of blackness as a dominant theme of early English texts about West Africa, I want to amend, not discard, Jordan's conclusions. As my research suggests, the theme of blackness may not have been as dominant a theme in the period before 1650 as his work suggested, but it was an important and oft-repeated theme. The question that remains is what exactly to do with blackness in light of these findings. Does blackness assume such significance in our readings of early English texts because of its significance for modern concepts of race? Can we start with the assumption that blackness is the essence of racial difference and still learn anything new about the history of race? Or does such an assumption simply entrench us deeper in racial polarities, offering us strange reassurance that antagonism, opposition, and hyper-awareness of difference have always been part of the history of race and are not merely an affliction of modernity?[10]

The point I wish to take from this discussion of *White over black* is that we need to keep an open mind when we think about the meaning of race in the early modern period. If we leave open the possibility that blackness is not the core meaning around which concepts of racial difference developed during the sixteenth and early seventeenth centuries, what will take its place? How else can we think about the meaning of race during this period? What role, if any, do peoples other than West Africans play in the emergence of racial concepts of difference? Armed with a healthy scepticism about the primacy of blackness to early English concepts of race but willing to acknowledge that commentary on skin colour was indeed an important part of the discourse of difference, let us now consider the different ways Africans and American Indians appeared in English texts about indigenous others. Are the discussions of these two groups different enough that we would wish to reserve the label "racial" for English perceptions of African difference? Where does blackness fit into English representations of indigenous American differences?

Sexual bodies, generative bodies

Before comparing sixteenth- and seventeenth-century English evaluations of African and Indian bodies, it is worth considering how these same authors evaluated indigenous cultures. These discussions of culture were often closely linked to those about physical appearance; indeed, it is sometimes difficult to tell where cultural difference ends and physical difference begins. For the purposes of this essay, however, separating these two discourses of difference makes it easier to discern how much of the burden of difference resided in bodies.

There were pronounced similarities in the ways English travellers wrote about all non-Anglo-Saxons – whether they be South Asians, Turks, Africans, Gaelic Irish, American Indians, or Inuit. Passages describing the manners, morals, and material culture of indigenous peoples often used similar language and hearkened to common criteria for otherness. Descriptions of West African and Native American cultures, in particular, reveal several common themes including indigenous peoples' wonder at European technology, their willingness to trade gold for trinkets, their proclivity to worship idols or devils or engage in cannibalism, their custom of assigning heavier manual labour to women than to men, and their susceptibility to being taken back to Europe as human souvenirs or enslaved for sale elsewhere in the Atlantic world.

Of these themes, that of indigenous amazement at European technology initially played better with Indians than with Africans, as the use of iron among the latter undermined the European technological edge. By the 1560s, many West Africans had already encountered European weaponry in the hands of the Portuguese and were no longer fazed by it. Native Americans who witnessed European demonstrations of muskets were shaken by the noise, the force of the projectile, and the smell of exploded powder. Eventually, these differences between Indian and African responses to European technology largely disappeared as Native Americans became more inured to European ways and gained access to guns.[11]

In similar fashion, initial differences between the malleability of Africans and Indians to the will of Englishmen in matters of trade faded as Native Americans became more experienced in dealing with Europeans. Early in the seventeenth century, when Englishmen landed in the Chesapeake and New England, Indians appear to have been as wary in trade as their African counterparts who were by then many decades more experienced in the European trade. Soon, Englishmen were describing Indians as a changeable people who could not be trusted to tell the truth, much as sixteenth-century English chroniclers had denigrated the honesty and trustworthiness of West Africans.[12]

English writers described both West Africans and Indians as idolaters, devil worshippers, and heathens but they had different interests in the "unenlightened" religious conditions of each group. The so-called barbarism of West Africans seems never to have troubled the consciences of English voyagers of the mid-sixteenth century and became an increasingly convenient rationale during the next century as the English became more involved in the slave trade. In contrast, English chroniclers of the North American voyages professed some desire to spread Christianity to Native Americans, although interest in this project subsequently waned.[13]

Discourses about African and Indian bodies followed closely from these evaluations of and responses to indigenous culture. One of the most constant refrains in early European accounts of people living in or near the so-called torrid zones was "the people goeth all naked". This phrase can be found in descriptions of "blackamoores", of American Indians, of Arabs, and of South Asians, and was usually followed by descriptions of cloths, gourds, or other materials used by men and women to cover their "privies" and of head coverings, animal skin wraps, and other accessories worn by distinguished persons.[14] Columbus' narrative was the foundational text for this discourse about Native Americans: "The inhabitants of this island, and all the rest that I discovered or heard of, go naked, as their mothers bore them, men and women alike. A few of the women, however, cover a single place with a leaf of a plant or piece of cotton which they weave for the purpose".[15]

The appearance of allegedly naked indigenous bodies signified for Europeans many often contradictory meanings. On the one hand, nudity suggested the state of mankind before the expulsion from the garden of Eden, and so communicated arrested development and innocence. Peter Martyr was perhaps most explicit in discussing this meaning of nudity for Europeans, explaining that the nude bodies of Indians were like unfinished furniture, capable of taking the imprint of those that finished them, in this case, the Christian Europeans who would enable them to shake off their barbarous ways. Nudity also communicated sexual promiscuity and an absence of civility to Europeans, which they sometimes described as "beastly" living.[16]

Lacking the protective layers of clothing worn by Europeans, the bodies of Africans and Indians were visible to English travellers and predictably became the subject of commentary. Certain topics related to the body appear in the accounts written about both groups of people: the overall form of the body, stature, stamina and suitability for specific tasks or labour, the colour and texture of hair, the colour of the skin, and adornment of the body with tattoos and jewellery. The content of these descriptions generally conformed to three major themes or patterns:

a) Europeans were more inclined to minimize the strangeness of Indian than African appearance;

b) the appearance of Indians was more likely to be attributed to cultural practices than the appearance of Africans;

c) both indigenous groups displayed physical characteristics for which Europeans could find no satisfying explanation.

From the moment of first contact, Europeans described Indians as a well formed people with limber, well conditioned, and well proportioned bodies. Columbus' comment, that "the whole population is very well made", was repeated by scores of other writers, including Englishmen who described indigenous Americans as "very handsome and goodly people, and in their behaviour as mannerly and civil as any of Europe" and skilful in hunting owing to their "swiftness of foot and nimbleness of body ..." Commentary about the stature of these well formed Indian bodies varied greatly, much as the actual height of indigenous peoples probably did. In contrast to these observations about Indians, English travellers found little to praise in the physiques of Africans. Although some observers did note variations in the height of different African people, as they did with Indians, they apparently found no population as pleasing to the eye as certain Native Americans.[17]

As Jordan has noted, Europeans who initially seemed unsure how to describe the skin and hair of Indians frequently exaggerated the Europeanness of their appearance for the benefit of readers back in England. Often, this exaggeration occurred in the midst of a comparison of Indians to Africans, as it did in Peter Martyr's assessment: "For the Ethiopians are all blacke, havinge theyre heare curld more lyke wulle then heare. But these people of the Iland of *Puta* (being as I have sayde under the clyme of Ethiope) are whyte, with longe heare, and of yelowe colour." Like Columbus, Martyr was puzzled by the light colouring of people whose proximity to the Equator should have resulted in dark skin. "They are whyte", he repeated, "even as owre men are, savynge suche as are much conversant in the sonne." The notion that Indians were born white like Europeans and became darker as a result of the sun's rays and cultural practices was repeated in several English texts.[18] The texture and colour of Indians' hair was similarly handled in early European texts. Martyr's tendency to Europeanize Indian appearance manifested itself in the belief that the great variety in Indian hair texture and colour had been masked by cosmetics which allowed them "by arte" to make their hair "long and blacke". Later chroniclers provided new evidence of variation in hair colour, claiming that although "their hair [was] black for the most part, and yet we saw children that had very fine auburn and chestnut coloured hair".[19]

Some European writers resolved the problem of how to fit Indians into the opposition of Black Ethiopian and white European by creating new categories and approaching the question of colour from the perspective of a continuum. Richard Eden, who is quoted at the beginning of this essay, noted that Indians were not "blacke nor with curlde and short woolle on theyr heades as have they of Afryke", but were "the coloure of an olyve with longe and blacke heare on theyr heades". Eden had earlier devoted considerable space to the discussion of the colour of Indians and to the larger mystery of variation in human appearance. After noting that whiteness and blackness were opposites on the continuum of human colour, Eden located "yelowe" skin somewhere in between, but left room for even greater variation: "even so it is to be considered howe they dyffer one from an other as it were by degrees, forasmuche as sum men are whyte after dyvers sortes of whytenesse: yelowe after dyvers maners of yelowe: and blacke after dyvers sortes of blackenesse". Eden described West Indians as "all togyther in general eyther purpole, or tawny lyke unto sodde quynses, or of the colour of chestnuttes or olyves: which colour is to them natural and not by theyr goynge naked as many have thought: albeit theyr nakednesse have sumwhat helped therunto".[20]

Writers about both groups of people devoted considerable space in their texts to descriptions of indigenous peoples' adornments of their bodies, the consequences of which were no less startling to English observers than differences which allegedly originated in nature. English people were astonished by the appearance of the Brazilian king brought back to England by William Hawkins during the early 1530s, "for in his cheekes were holes made according to their savage maner, and therein small bones were planted, standing an inch out from the said holes, which in his owne Countrey was reputed for a great braverie. He had also another hole in his nether lip, wherein was set a precious stone about the bignes of a pease: All his apparel, behaviour, and gesture, were very strange to the beholders." Travellers took equal interest in describing the tattoos, scarification, and dyes that decorated the skins of both Africans and Indians.[21]

In general, however, whereas English travellers tended to explain African appearance as the result of the hot climate ("scorched and vexed with the heat of the sunne") or infection, or to describe it as some type of deformity ("The people be tawnie, but not disfigured in their lippes and noses, as the Moores and Cafres of Ethiopia"), they were more likely to attribute the differences they saw between themselves and Indians to Indian culture.[22] Applying bear's grease to the skin, plucking facial and body hair to maintain a smooth, hairless appearance, piercing the body to wear jewellery, embroidering the skin with tattoos – all of these practices contributed to the strangeness of Indian appearance, in the European view, but left little about Indian appearance that needed further explanation. It is interesting to speculate about the differences

Europeans failed to remark upon and felt no need to explain. No traveller to the Guinea coast that I am aware of ever noted that compared to Indians, Africans and Europeans had similarly shaped eyes. No-one observed that both Native Americans and West Africans had relatively little body and facial hair compared to the more hirsute Europeans. Few bothered to comment on the size of feet, the form of ears, or the ratio of leg to torso length, perhaps because individual variations defied even the grossest of generalizations. Yet, when one considers the great variety in colour and stature that Europeans encountered and yet felt comfortable reducing to generalities, the silence about these other aspects of appearance becomes more curious.

Thus far we have discussed several discourses of Indian and African difference that were quite literally mapped on to indigenous bodies. Commentary on these aspects of indigenous peoples' physical appearance did not exhaust English observations on Indian and African bodies, however. In their discussions of Indian and African sexual mores, virility, and health, English travellers inscribed yet other differences on the bodies of indigenous peoples.

At first glance, English commentary on the sexual behaviour and demeanour of Indian and African women might appear to be identical in its tone. In describing the Garamantes people of Libya, observed by John Lok on his second voyage to Guinea, Richard Eden claimed that the women were "common", because "they contracte no matrimonie, neyther have respect to chastitie". This observation about Africans echoed those that appeared in an earlier translation of a Spanish text about the encounter with Native Americans: "These folke lyven lyke beste without any resonablenes and the wymen be also as comon. And the men hath conversacyon with the wymen who that they ben or who they fryst mete is she his syster his mother his daughter or any other kyyndred. And the wymen be very hoote and dysposed to lecherdnes. And they ete also one a nother." In yet another translation of the account of Vespucci's voyage to America, Eden countered the cleanly habits of Indians – "Theyr bodies are verye smothe and clene by reason of theyr often washinge" – with their "beastly filthy living". "They are in other thinges fylthy and without shame", he argued. "Thei use no lawful conjunction of mariage, but every one hath as many women as him listeth, and leaveth them agayn at his pleasure." Other evidence of "beastly living" included reports of an incestuous relationship between a brother and sister taken captive in New Spain, and anecdotes about cross-dressing and "unnatural" sexual activity among both African and Indian men.[23]

As fascinating as these similarities in the discussions of indigenous peoples' sexuality are, the differences are even more revealing. Indian women were much more likely to be described as beautiful and alluring by English writers than were their African counterparts. Travellers often communicated the aesthetic and erotic appeal of Indian women's bodies and demeanour, frequently casting Indian women as seductresses, playthings, or beautiful and virtuous allies of Europeans. In Eden's account of Vespucci's voyage, for example, he reported that Indian women "neyther have they theyr bellies wrimpeled, or loose, and hanginge pappes, by reason of bearinge manye children". John Hawkins claimed that Indian women maintained their pert, well-shaped breasts with great care: "they delight not when they are yong in bearing of children, because it meketh them have hanging breasts which they account to bee great deforming in them, and upon that occasion while they still bee young they destroy their seede, saving, that it is fittest for olde women".[24]

Spaniards, and even the reputedly less hot-blooded English, apparently found their dealings with Indian women to be erotically charged, at least on their end of the encounter. Eden's translation of Peter Martyr recounted the delight of Spanish men during an evening's entertainment performed by the Indian women:

> Fyrste there mette them a company of xxx women, beinge al the kynges wyves and concubines, bearinge in theyr handes branches of date trees, singinge and daunsinge: They were all naked, savynge that theyr pryvie partes were covered with breeches of gossampine cotton. But the virgins, havinge theyr heare hangynge downe abowte their shulders, tyed abowte the foreheade with a fyllet, were utterly naked. They affirme that theyr faces, brestes, pappes, handes, and other partes of theyre bodyes, were excedynge smoote, and well proportioned: but sumwhat inclyning to a lovely brown. They supposed that they had see those most beautiful Dryads, or the native nymphs or fares of the fountains whereof the antiquates speak so much.[25]

John Smith's account of Pocahontas' women entertaining him with a dance, performed in a semi-naked state, followed by "crowding, and pressing, and hanging upon him, most tediously crying, love you not mee?" offered English readers a similar tableau of Indian women with highly sexualized bodies. Although Smith and other English men claimed not to have taken sexual liberties with Indian women as their Spanish counterparts did, that did not keep them from looking and commenting. The author of "The First Virginia Voyage" was not above describing one Indian woman as "well favoured", and enjoying the hospitality of the wife of the king's brother. Sir Walter Raleigh's voyage to Guiana brought him face to face with a woman he deemed to be startlingly beautiful. "In all my life, I have seldom seen a better favoured woman", he declared. "She was of good stature, with black eyes, fat of body, of an excellent countenance, her hair almost as long as herself, tied up in pretty knots." Many people are familiar with the tales of beautiful and warm-hearted Indian women who allegedly became allies of down-and-out Europeans: La Malinche and Pocahontas are perhaps the best known, but there was also the aforementioned wife of Granganimeo on Roanoake island, the benevolent queen Anacaona who pleaded for the kind treatment of the Christians, and the sister who had apparently had enough of her incestuous relationship with her brother and decided to betray his knowledge of indigenous resistance plans to Vasco Nunez de Balboa.[26]

Englishmen's earliest descriptions of African women's bodies and their reactions to them make for a stark contrast with these anecdotes about Euro-Indian relations. West African women were rarely depicted as alluring. Their breasts and bodies were not described erotically but rather with distaste and disdain. William Towerson reported on his first voyage to Guinea that "the men and women goe so alike, that one cannot knowe a man from a woman but by their breastes, which in the most part be very foule and long, hanging downe lowe like the udder of a goate". Lest the reader miss his meaning, he reiterated the point in the middle of a description of oversized flora and fauna: "divers of the women have such exceeding long breastes, that some of them wil lay the same upon the grounde and lie downe by them, but all the women have not such breastes". There was also nothing erotic in Englishmen's descriptions of African women's attempts to entertain English visitors. Again, Towerson is the source: "divers of the women to shewe us pleasure daunced and sung after their manner, full ill to our eares . . . and with these wordes they leape and daunce and clappe their handes". When in Africa, Englishmen dealt not with warm-hearted native female beauties, but with male guides, interpreters, and merchants. Whereas West African women were described at best as a curiosity, at worst as creatures with deformed breasts, English reports of Indian women were saturated with sexuality.[27]

In the sixteenth and early seventeenth centuries, English travellers' different evaluations of Indian and African women's sex appeal was accompanied by similarly polarized views of the virility and sexual potence of their respective menfolk. Although the received wisdom about the sexual powers of Indian men varied greatly from account to account, one of the persistent themes was that their reproductive potential had been diminished owing to their access to too many women. Such accounts of Indian sexual excess and sexual impotence were only bolstered by early sixteenth-century theories about the New World origins of syphilis. In contrast, as Jordan has noted, African men were believed to have libidos and sexual organs of mythic proportions, a trait that English commentators considered additional evidence of African denigration.[28]

English writers kept a wary eye on the ability of Indians, Africans, and the

English themselves to reproduce offspring that bore the mark of its sire, especially in inter-ethnic/racial unions. George Best's comments on the effacement of Englishness that resulted from the union of an African man with an English woman remained influential throughout the first half of the seventeenth century, despite evidence from the colonies that unions of Africans with English men or women would produce offspring lighter than their darker parents. The most compelling evidence of African potence came not from British North America, however, but from Portuguese settlements in West Africa where, Richard Jobson claimed, although there were "Molatoes, betweene blacke and white", the vast majority of Portuguese offspring were as black "as the naturall inhabitants". English writers appear to have been convinced that their chances of producing offspring that looked English were much greater in unions with Indians. George Chapman gently mocked this concern in *Eastward Ho!* (1605) claiming that the Roanoake colonists had sired a generation of Indians with English faces. Even John Smith believed that Englishmen were capable of producing offspring who would eventually manifest an English appearance, in this case, a full beard. Curiously, the efforts of seventeenth-century English writers to find evidence of English parentage in the children of inter-ethnic/racial unions was not dissimilar from sixteenth-century efforts to find the European in the Indian, a similarity discussed in greater detail below.[29]

Perhaps the most basic challenge to ethnic and racial potence was the chance of premature death caused by disease, poor diet, cramped travel conditions, and exposure to new climates. George Best broached the subject most openly when he wondered why Africans could manage to survive a winter in England whereas English men seemed to be dropping like flies under the burning African sun. Other European writers struggled to come to terms with the vast toll the European presence took upon Indian populations. Indigenous constitutions appear to have differed in fundamental ways, with Indians as likely to die in their own land as they were to die in England (witness Pocahontas) and Africans able to withstand not only the hot climate that killed English men, but the chilly damp climate in which English men thrived.[30]

Once we look beyond skin colour and the texture of hair, the cultural differences between European and Indian appear to be nearly as clearly mapped on the indigenous body as the differences between European and African. One of the main discrepancies in the two discourses of difference during the late sixteenth and early seventeenth centuries is the sexualization of English representations of Indian women's bodies even though English men were somewhat reluctant, at least compared to their Spanish counterparts, to enter into sexual unions with flesh and blood women. It seems likely that these different views of indigenous women's bodies might have something to do with the proximity of English men to Indian women and with the initial European belief that Indians were culturally assimilable. In contrast, English travellers had little interest in transforming Africans, other than teaching them a few words of English, and had little faith that the core characteristics of Africanness could be eradicated through close proximity to the English. By the eighteenth century, this equation of difference was greatly altered by slavery. Enslaved Africans in British North America were viewed as culturally malleable compared to Indians but less easily physically transformed – owing in large measure to laws that naturalized racial separateness – by unions with the English. Indians remained culturally distant from the English, but less physically distant from whiteness.

Whiteness as a form of difference

Yet another consideration in this exploration of race and difference is the historical construction of whiteness. If we take seriously recent scholarship suggesting that whiteness rather than blackness is the category perpetually in crisis, then it is worth examining, briefly, what Indians had to offer in the way of definitional rigour. Despite Jordan's contention that Indians functioned mainly as foils for proving certain points about Africans, in whom the burdens of embodied racial difference resided, it seems that Indians also provoked English people to define themselves as white people.

One possible way to explore this "racial" relationship between Indians and the English is to study the place of whiteness in English texts about Anglo-Indian encounters. To what degree did the seeming ambiguity of the Indian's place in the continuum of human appearance provoke English explorers to define the meaning of whiteness and to embrace it as the category describing their own appearance? Comments like those of Peter Martyr, "They are whyte, even as owre men are, savynge suche as are much conversant in the sonne", suggest that Europeans may have been identifying themselves as white even as they were attempting to define the meaning of the term.[31] Martyr's comparison of Indians to Europeans invoked the presumed familiarity of "owre" men to communicate information about the appearance of an unknown population. That he chose to qualify the comparison, observing that Indians who spent a lot of time in the sun did not appear as white as their fellows, narrowed the meaning of whiteness and introduced the possibility of changing pigmentation. Martyr's subsequent comments about the native inhabitants of the island of Puta, who were "whyte, with longe heare, and of yelowe colour", raised the possibility that whiteness might be a matter distinct from hair colour and style. In the hands of Richard Eden, the issue became even more complex as "sum men are whyte after dyvers sortes of whytenesse". Although Eden initially defined whiteness in opposition to blackness, the location of Indian skin colour somewhere in the middle of his continuum forced him to acknowledge that even at the extremes, skin colour exhibited great variation, thus the phenomenon of "dyvers sortes of whytenesse".

Although evidence is scarce, there are some indications that indigenous peoples themselves contributed to the meaning of whiteness, defining the concept that Europeans would later embrace as an important component of European identity. In 1584, a group of English men of Roanoake island attempted to demonstrate that they were the first Europeans to reach the island, an accomplishment that would strengthen English claims to the land. One means of proving this, in the view of the author, was to show that the Secotan Indians had never before had contact with Europeans. The chronicler's observations of the Secotans' reaction to the English adventurers is fascinating, not only for what it possibly reveals about the attitudes of Secotan Indians towards Europeans, but for what it certainly revealed about European beliefs about the significance of whiteness. "Other than these", the Roanoake chronicler opined, "there was never any people appareled, or white of colour, either seen or heard of amongst these people, and these aforesaid were seen only of the inhabitants of Secotan. This appeared to be very true, for they wondered marvellously when we were amongst them at the whiteness of our skins, even coveting to touch our breasts, and view the same." One wonders, in this instance, what exactly Indians learned about the meaning of whiteness, and whether the Europeans whose skins they stroked had also learned something important about their appearance from the responses of indigenous peoples.[32] Certainly, if Indians thought they were "white" like Europeans, there would have been little reason for wonder at the sight of pale English skin.

Native Americans were not the only native peoples to contribute actively to the meaning of whiteness. Richard Jobson's 1623 account of his attempt to establish a trade outpost in The Gambia contained a unique reference by West Africans to European whiteness. After English explorers insisted on bathing in crocodile-infested waters, their Mandingo guides cautiously decided to join them, reasoning that "the white man, shine more in the water, then they did, and therefore if Bumbo [the crocodile] come, hee would surely take us [the English] first". Skin colour in Jobson's account thus appeared in Mandingo reactions to the English as well as in English impressions of Africans.[33]

As literary critic Kim Hall has observed, the construction of whiteness in early modern English texts frequently appeared in contexts in which whiteness was allegedly most threatened with erasure, as in the sexual unions of black men with English women. George Best's anxious musings about the offspring of such a union tellingly did not use "white" to describe the English woman who had taken an African lover, but "faire", a term that distinguished women as a sex from men, as in the phrase the "fair" sex. Best described the father as "an Ethiopian as blacke as a cole" and his child as " sonne in all respects as blacke as the father was". Despite having a "good complexion", Best contended, the mother passed on little of her fairness to her child, thus demonstrating the strength of the father's "blacknes". Hall's thesis, that whiteness and blackness were often represented as qualities embodied, respectively, by genteel English ladies and black men, usually of the servant class, alerts us to the gender and class implications in emerging meanings of race. That the authors of travel accounts should feature Indian women as sexually alluring and ignore or denigrate African women lends credence to Hall's claims about the uses of "faire" women to represent whiteness and African men to represent blackness.[34]

An important exception to Hall's argument and to the one advanced here points to the need for caution in the face of sweeping generalizations that ignore subtle changes in racial formations over time. In 1653, Richard Ligon's *A True and Exact History of the Island of Barbados*, contained several lengthy and frank accounts of the author's erotic interest in three women of African descent on the island of St Jago, part of the Cape Verde islands. Ligon's fascination with these women, none of whom was enslaved, and his admiration for their physical beauty stood in sharp contrast to his subsequent portraits of enslaved women working the cane fields in Barbados. Whereas the St Jago women flashed alluring smiles and revealed firm, bare flesh under colourful clothing, the enslaved field labourers had breasts that "hang down below their Navels, so that when they stoop at their common work of weeding, they hang almost to the ground, that at a distance you would think they had six legs". As Ligon's account suggests, by the middle of the seventeenth century, English accounts of African women had already become more complex, reflecting their entry into the transatlantic slave trade, and their interest in African women's productive and reproductive value. That the women he found appealing were free and not enslaved labourers might indicate that previous gender discourses of race had been put to the service of justifying the enslavement of African women and assigning them to the same kinds of arduous labour as African men. It also foreshadows the rise of the image of the "Sable Venus", which was to become popular during the eighteenth century.

Ligon's complex use of appealing and repulsive imagery further reminds us that with continued settlement of British North America, English discourses about Indian women might also be transformed.[35]

At this point, we might reconsider the quote by Winthrop Jordan with which this essay began. Jordan contends that the colour of Indians was never the issue for English people that the colour of Africans was. Yet why, if this was the case, was it necessary for English people to sweep the colour of Indians "under the rug"? And why was Jefferson so resolutely set on proving that every characteristic that distinguished Indians from Anglo-Americans was in fact a product of diet, environment, and culture rather than nature? Jordan may be correct that the question of variation in human colour was fundamentally a question of explaining the colour of the African. But it seems quite possible that, since the trail of ambiguous and confusing explanations for skin colour, of early assertions of whiteness, and of shrill denials of natural difference takes us to the Indian's door, there may be an interesting history of early modern racial formations yet to be written about the Englishman and the Indian.[36]

Notes

1   See Barbara Fields, "Ideology and race in American history", in *Region, race, and reconstruction: essays in honor of C. Vann Woodward*, J. Morgan Kousser and James McPherson (eds) (New York, 1982); Henry Louis Gates, Jr. (ed.), *"Race," writing and difference* (Chicago, 1986); Terrence Epperson, *"To fix a perpetual brand": the social construction of race in Virginia, 1675–1750* (PhD thesis, Temple University, 1990); Emily C. Bartels, "Imperialist beginnings: Richard Hakluyt and the construction of Africa", *Criticism* **34**, 1992, pp. 517–38; Evelyn Brooks Higginbotham, "African-American women's history and the metalanguage of race", *Signs* **17**, 1992, pp. 251–74; Stuart Hall, "What is this 'black' in Black popular culture?", in *Black Popular Culture*, Gina Dent (ed.) (Seattle, 1993); David Roediger, *The wages of whiteness: race and the making of the American working class* (New York, 1991); Michael Omi and Howard Winant, *Racial formation in the United States from the 1960s to the 1990s*, 2nd edn (New York, 1994); Kim F. Hall, *things of darkness: economies of race and gender in early modern England* (Ithaca, N.Y., 1995); Noel Ignatiev, *How the Irish became white* (New York, 1995); Kathleen M. Brown, *Good wives, nasty wenches, and anxious patriarchs: gender, race, and power in colonial Virginia* (Chapel Hill, N.C., 1996).

2   Jordan, *White over black: American attitudes toward the Negro, 1550–1812* (Chapel Hill, N.C., 1969), p. ix.

3   *Ibid.*, p. 6.

4   Richard Eden, "First voyage to Guinea", in *The first three English books on America*, Edward Arber (ed.) (Birmingham, 1885), p. 376; Eden, "Second voyage to Guinea" in *ibid.*, p. 386; William Hawkins in Richard Hakluyt, *The Principall Navigations, Voyages, Traffiques and Discoveries of the English Nation* [8 vols] (London, n.d.), VIII, pp. 13–14 [hereafter *PNVTD*]; Thomas Wyndham, "Voyage to Guinea", in Richard Hakluyt, *The Principall*

Navigations, Voiages and Discoveries of the English Nation [2 vols] (Cambridge, 1965), I, p. 83 [hereafter *PNVD*]; William Towerson, "First voyage to Guinea", in *ibid.*, pp. 98–112; Towerson, "Second voyage to Guinea", in *ibid.*, pp. 112–20; Towerson, "Third and last voyage to Guinea", in *ibid.*, pp. 120–30.

5   Hakluyt, *PNVD*, I, pp. 130–35.

6   *Ibid.*, pp. 135–42.

7   Hakluyt, *PNVTD*, V, p. 180.

8   *Ibid.*, p. 172.

9   Jordan, *White over Black*, p. 19; Sir Thomas Browne, *Pseudodoxia Epidemia* (London, 1646), in *The Works of Sir Thomas Browne*, Charles Sayle (ed.) (Edinburgh, 1927), II, pp. 367–95; Richard Jobson, *The golden trade; or, a discovery of the River Gambra, and the golden trade of the Aethiopians* (London, 1623); Andrew Battell, "The strange adventure of Andrew Battell of Leigh in Essex", in Samuel Purchas, *Hakluytus Posthumus: or Purchas His Pilgrimes* . . . (1625; reprint, New York, 1965), VI.

10 Jordan's framework continues to be an avenue for creative and compelling scholarship on the history of race. There is perhaps no better evidence of this than Hall's *Things of Darkness*. Hall contends that the trope of blackness, which is subsequently appropriated to mark other groups – American Indians, Irish, Spanish, South Asian Indians – as different, remains dependent on a concept of difference that originates with Africans.

11 See Eden's translation of Sebastian Munster's version of Vespucci's voyage in Arber (ed.), *First three books*, p. 33; Peter Martyr, "The first decade", in *ibid.*, p. 86; Thomas Hariot, "A brief and true report of the new found land of Virginia", in Richard Hakluyt, *Voyages to the Virginia Colonies*, ed. A. L. Rowse (London, 1986), pp. 126–7, 130; William Towerson, "A second voyage to Guinea", I, p. 115.

12 Martyr, "First decade", pp. 74, 94; William Towerson, "First Voyage to Guinea", in Hakluyt, *PNVD*, I, p. 101; Eden, "Second Voyage to Guinea," in Arber (ed.), *First three books*, p. 386; John Hawkins, "The unfortunate voyage", in *PNVD*, II, p. 553; George Fenner, "The voyage of M. George Fenner to Guinie", in *ibid.*, I, p. 145; John Smith, *Proceedings of the English Colonies*, in *Complete Works of Captain John Smith* [3 vols], Philip Barbour (ed.) (Chapel Hill, N.C., 1986), I, p. 246; William Bradford, *Of Plymouth Plantation, 1620–1647*, ed. Samuel Eliot Morison (New York, 1952), p. 26; Bartels, "Imperialist Beginnings", *Criticism* **34**, 1992, pp. 517–38.

13 Martyr, "First decade", 99; Hawkins, "The voyage made by the worshipful M. John Haukins Esq", in Hakluyt, *PNVD*, II, p. 527; William Strachey, *The Historie of Travell into Virginia Britania* (London, 1611); Jordan, *White over Black*, p. 89.

14 Arber (ed.), *First three books*, p. xxviii; Eden, "The fyrste viage of Americaus Vesputius", in *ibid.*, 37; Martyr, "First decade", p. 66; George Best, "Experiences and reasons of the sphere", in Hakluyt, *PNVTD*, V, p. 179.

15 Columbus, "Letter to various persons", in *Four voyages*, p. 117; the comment about Indian nakedness was repeated in Hariot's "Brief and true report", in Rowse (ed.), *Voyages*, p. 126, and in Richard Fisher's description of Newfoundland Indians in 1593, *ibid.*, p. 56; see also Martyr, "First decade", p. 95, about men using a gourd "cutte after the fashion of a coddepiece".

16 Martyr, "The second decade", in Arber (ed.), *First three books*, 106; Brown, *Good wives, nasty wenches*, pp. 53–64.

17 Columbus, "Letters to various persons", p. 121; "The first Virginia voyage, 1584", in Rowse (ed.), *Voyages*, p. 68; Bradford, *Plymouth Plantation*, p. 207; Eden, "Second voyage to Guinea", in Arber (ed.), *First three books*, p. 384. For an exception to this generalization,

see John Hawkins' comments on a particular group of Guinea natives who were "of stature goodly men, and well liking, by reason of their foode"; see Hakluyt, *PNVD*, II, p. 525 and Jobson, *The golden trade*, for his comments on the physiques of Fulbe women, p. 33. For a detailed discussion of English views of Indians as civil in their deportment, see Karen Ordahl Kupperman, "Presentment of civility: English reading of American self-presentation in the early years of colonization", *WMQ* **3rd Ser. 54**, 1997, pp. 193–228.

18 Martyr, "First decade", pp. 88, 89; John Smith, *Map of Virginia*, in *Complete Works*, Barbour (ed.), I, p. 160; Strachey, *Historie of Travell*, p. 70; George Alsop, *Character of Mary-land* (1666), p. 59, quoted in Jordan, *White over Black*, p. 241.

19 Martyr, "First decade", p. 91; Rowse (ed.), *Voyages*, p. 69.

20 Eden, "Other notable things as touching the Indies," in Arber (ed.), *First three books*, p. 338; Eden, "Second voyage to Guinea," in *ibid.*, p. 387. See also John Hawkins, in Hakluyt, *PNVD*, II, p. 530.

21 Hakluyt, *PNVTD*, VIII, p. 14; Eden, "Second voyage to Guinea", p. 386.

22 Thomas Stevens, "A letter written from Goa", in Hakluyt, *PNVD*, I, p. 162.

23 Arber (ed.), *First three books*, p. 37; Martyr in *ibid.*, pp. 121, 138; Eden, "First voyage to Guinea", in *ibid.*, p. 384; Battell, "Strange adventure", p. 376.

24 Eden in Arber (ed.), *First three books*, p. 37; Hakluyt, *PNVD*, II, p. 530.

25 Martyr, "First decade", p. 83.

26 Smith, *Proceedings*, in Barbour (ed.), *Complete works*, I, p. 236; Rowse (ed.), *Voyages*, pp. 69, 71; Charles Nicholl, *The creature in the map: Sir Walter Ralegh's quest for El Dorado* (London, 1995), p. 162; Martyr in Arber (ed.), *First three books*, pp. 85, 122.

27 Towerson, "First voyage to Guinea," in Hakluyt, *PNVD*, II, pp. 101, 102. For a detailed discussion of English representations of African women's breasts, see Jennifer L. Morgan, "'Some could suckle over their shoulder': male travelers, female bodies, and the gendering of racial ideology, 1500–1770", *WMQ* **3rd Ser. 54**, 1997, pp. 167–92.

28 Strachey, *Historie of Travell*, p. 116; Alfred Crosby, *The Columbian exchange: biological and cultural consequences of 1492* (Westport, Ct., 1972), p. 127; Jobson, *The golden trade*, pp. 52–3; Jordan, *White over Black*, pp. 32–40.

29 Jobson, *The golden trade*, p. 28; Smith, *A Generall Historie of Virginia . . .* , in Barbour (ed.), *Complete Works*, II, p. 173.

30 Eden, "First voyage to Guinea", in Arber (ed.), *First three books*, p. 377. See also Martyr, "First decade", p. 80; Hariot, "True report", p. 131; Bradford, *Plymouth Plantation*, p. 260; Patricia Seed, "Taking possession and reading texts: establishing the authority of overseas empires", *WMQ* **3rd Ser. 47**, 1992, pp. 184–209; Joyce E. Chaplin, "Natural philosophy and an early racial idiom in North America: comparing English and Indian bodies", *WMQ* **3rd Ser. 54**, 1997, pp. 229–52.

31 Martyr, "First decade", p. 89.

32 Rowse (ed.), *Voyages*, p. 74.

33 Jobson, *The golden trade*, p. 18.

34 Hall, *Things of darkness*; Best, "True discourse", in Hakluyt, *PNVTD*, V, p. 180.

35 Richard Ligon, *A true and exact history of the island of Barbados* (London, 1653), p. 51.

36 Jordan, *White over Black*, pp. 478–9.

Chapter Five

Praying with the enemy: Daniel Gookin, King Philip's War, and the dangers of intercultural mediatorship

Louise A. Breen

Late on the evening of 28 February 1676, the obscure Massachusetts private Richard Scott reached an emotional breaking point. Convinced that magistrate Daniel Gookin's solicitude for Christian Indians signified that the militia captain (and soon-to-be major) was little better than a traitor to his "country", Scott burst into Cambridge's Blue Anchor Tavern and launched into an impassioned diatribe against his foe. The chief witness to this incident, tavern proprietor Elizabeth Belcher, swore out a deposition several days later detailing the verbal contents of Scott's shocking tirade.[1] Not only had Scott "broak out into many hideous railing expressions against the worshipful Captain Daniel Gookin, calling him an Irish dog that was never faithful to his country, the sonne of a whoare, a bitch, a rogue, God confound him, and God rott his soul", but the disorderly soldier also gave voice to a violent fantasy involving Gookin: "if I could meet him alone I would pistoll him. I wish my knife and sizers were in his heart. He is the devil's interpreter."[2]

Scott's violent rage against Gookin, erupting at the height of King Philip's War, stemmed from his resentment of the captain's dogged insistence that the Christianized, or "praying", Indians be accepted as spies, guides, and soldiers, rather than eyed warily as potential turncoats richly deserving of internment, or even annihilation.[3] Although Scott was extraordinarily bold in his actions, his animosity toward Gookin, superintendent of the "praying" Indians, was widely shared. At one point, the doleful captain reportedly feared to "go along the streets" alone.[4]

Daniel Gookin's views on the "praying" Indians sparked intense, class-based controversy in a colony whose leaders had failed, in the decade prior to

101

Vincent Gookin's world, unlike Daniel's, elite factions were free to debate assimilationist policies with minimal reference to or input from ordinary men like Richard Scott. As Nicholas Canny has shown, Vincent Gookin, a political protégé of the Boyles, pressed for assimilation as a means of preserving the rights of those English colonizers who had established themselves in Ireland prior to 1641, and who feared displacement at the hands of the victorious soldiers who had put down the rebellion and were now seeking land.[14] Gookin, to counter their claims, stressed how "benevolent" policies would contribute to the Cromwellian empire as a whole, reducing the likelihood of future rebellions, and permitting Ireland, with its Catholics "swallowed up by the English and incorporated into them", to begin absorbing England's surplus population.[15] Still, advocacy of missionary projects offered tangible benefits to Gookin's local constituency, allowing them to retain an identity separate from, and superior to, that of brutal Cromwellian soldiers and degenerated "old" English settlers alike.

Daniel Gookin was every bit as hegemonic in his intentions for the local Algonquians as Vincent Gookin had been in his plans for the Gaelic Irish.[16] But in Puritan Massachusetts corporate identity never did, and never would, hinge on the "uplift" of indigenous peoples. Ever since the 1630s Bay Colonists had resented English "grandees" who questioned New England's primacy of place in the divine scheme of things, and who engaged in imperialistic projects – the colonization of Providence Island and Oliver Cromwell's Western Design, for example – that could draw off resources and colonists from Massachusetts.[17] Some of these same sorts of resentments toward internationalist projects attached themselves to the Puritan-led missionary enterprise of the 1640s and 1650s; and, after 1660, when the restored monarchy took over the New England Company, the potential threat that it posed to New England regional culture became that much more sinister. In the fateful year 1655, when Gookin had witnessed the "transplantation" debate, he had also agreed to carry out a mission for the Cromwellian Protectorate that he knew would be unpopular in Massachusetts: to promote the idea of re-settling Jamaica, whose recent conquest had been aided by Gookin's Massachusetts Artillery Company colleague Robert Sedgwick.[18] As a Boyle client, Gookin's New World career symbolized linkages among Puritan internationalism, Restoration imperialism, and missionary impulses, all of which were arrayed against Bay Colony provincialism.

The "middling" planters and freemen of Massachusetts viewed the privileging of local over imperial affairs, and the drawing of "tribal" social boundaries, as key components of their English "liberty". But the New England Company, under the influence of Robert Boyle, a member of the Council for Foreign Plantations, envisioned the missionary project in explicitly imperialistic terms. The economic expansion bound to occur, as non-productive indigenous peoples were transformed into disciplined, God-fearing workers and consumers, Boyle thought, would help to heal the residual animosities left over from the Civil War years; factions that had been at odds, and regional areas that had been at cross-purposes, could then unite under the banner of trade and civilized prosperity.[19] New Englanders continued to look to Boyle as one of the few figures of the Restoration government who occasionally lent a friendly ear to the concerns of dissenters; still, his larger commitments were at variance with theirs, expecially those of the common people. The Puritan internationalist agenda pursued during the Cromwellian era, and the altered imperial dream that Robert Boyle subsequently worked out as governor of the New England Company, were equally disturbing, for each gestured menacingly at how the transatlantic market and the frontier might one day coalesce and overrun the New England centre. Missionary work drew fire because it was perceived as the intrusive project of transatlantic elites, both Puritan and Anglican, who envisioned a heterogeneously constructed empire in defiance of the wishes of ordinary local residents.

The new roles Gookin limned out for converts as labourers and soldiers, meanwhile, threatened to collapse the distinction between Indians and ordinary English colonists, not only exposing the latter to danger in the case of Indian treachery, but also possibly denigrating the labour of Englishmen who already occupied the lower rungs of the colony's social ladder. At a time when the coveted status of landed "independency", connoting full "manhood", increasingly eluded the best efforts of many English colonists, Gookin, by protecting Indian claims to land, appeared to be extending hopes of economic "competency" to "savages" while depriving his own people of the same benefit.[20]

The assimilationist project may have seemed identity-affirming in Boyle's Ireland; but in Massachusetts, the concept of cultural conversion posed a direct threat to the distinct and particularistic (and now embattled) New World identity – homogeneous, roughly egalitarian, and provincially oriented – that had prevailed in Massachusetts since the 1630s. Intent on retaining their own identity as a separate people, ordinary folk, who had long shied away from those cross-cultural, transatlantic ties on which missionary work depended, resented Gookin's efforts to replace the ties of race and kin with those of religion alone. While the clear, visceral expression of these resentments depended on the charged atmosphere of war, the widespread feelings of insecurity on which the hatreds fed was rooted in the previous decade's debates over religious, and therefore communal, inclusion and exclusion.

Daniel Gookin's plans for transforming "others" into "brothers" coincided, inauspiciously, with the controversy over the "halfway" covenant. In 1662, a ministerial synod recommended that congregations remedy the problem of declining church membership by extending an attenuated, "halfway" status to those children of the "saints" unable to make the required conversion narrative. Because the "innovation" symbolically spoke to the broad issue of corporate identity and belonging, it became the subject of acrimonious debate.[21] Scholars have not yet examined how Anglo-Indian tensions may have shaped responses to the "halfway" covenant; but here I will argue that Gookin's high visibility as a champion of both "halfway" covenant and "praying" Indians inhibited acceptance of an innovation which, in the long run, tended to reinforce popularly based "tribalistic" urges.[22]

In the five years prior to King Philip's War, Bay Colonists witnessed the painful rupture of First Church Boston, when a faction of "dissenting brethren" withdrew from the church, and created a new congregation (Third Church, or Old South), in protest against the majority's rejection of the "halfway" covenant.[23] The break-up of this prestigious congregation, which contained a fair percentage of the colony's war leaders, caused deep and long-lasting political and social turmoil; but even more disturbing, from the perspective of ordinary colonists, was the fact that neither side was able (or willing) to articulate a vision of the "good life" acceptable to the commonalty. Daniel Gookin, together with leading proponents of the "halfway" covenant in Third Church, showed by word and deed that he did not equate the innovation with provincial "tribalism". First Church Boston, meanwhile, while retaining the old forms, represented a cosmopolitanism that comported even less well with the aims of the common folk.[24]

In 1671, the clergyman John Oxenbridge, returning from a missionary stint in Surinam, chose to accept the pulpit call of First Church Boston.[25] Oxenbridge, who recognized the "halfway" covenant's potential to underwrite a kind of "racial" exclusivity, would seem to have been attracted to First Church precisely because of its principled stand on this issue.[26] In his manuscript "Conversion of the Gentiles", completed in 1670, Oxenbridge warned pointedly that those Englishmen who despised or distrusted Indian converts ignored the Abrahamic covenant of grace, and wilfully reverted to the ideals of the Old Testament Jews, whose legalistic covenant of works necessarily confined the bonds of sacred fellowship to those within the nation, and the race.[27]

Although Daniel Gookin and John Oxenbridge concurred on the issue of "praying" Indians, the two men were political enemies. Oxenbridge's prominent flock, which included John Leverett and Edward Hutchinson, supported limited tolerationist goals which Gookin, an avid persecutor of anabaptists and

Quakers, adamantly opposed.[28] Still, while First Church Boston adhered to the rigorous standards of church membership associated with the founders, its vision of community was neither traditional nor appealing to the common people. In combining rigorous admissions practices with tolerationist beliefs, a dominant faction within the congregation had begun to conceptualize the churches of Massachusetts as non-coercive enclaves of purity within a diverse society – a formulation that figured the realm of spirit as individualistic, private, and unconnected to a specific people or geographic location. The cosmopolitan community envisioned by First Churchers was patently unpopular, resembling, to some extent, that advocated earlier by the "antinomians" of the 1630s.

Given the disturbing direction in which Oxenbridge's First Church contingent was moving, the promoters of the "halfway" covenant might have appeared like the more reliable guardians of communal identity.[29] These champions had, after all, suggested that a reinvented New England Way could still form the backbone of a provincial community defined by its homogeneous dedication to a single interpretation of Puritanism. Nathaniel Saltonstall, moreover, a "halfway" covenant partisan (and member of Third Church) who authored several King Philip's War tracts, warned that an open and variegated Christian community, such as that sought by First Church, would bring nothing but defeat and divine disapproval. In one of his more polemical efforts, Saltonstall implied that the ambush and rout of troops serving under Edward Hutchinson near Brookfield in the summer of 1675 represented God's rebuke of First Church; the doleful event occurred on the same day that First Church was holding a fast to propitiate divine aid, "which thing was taken especial notice of, by all those who desire to see the Hand of God in such sad Providences".[30] Hutchinson, as a frontier landowner who foolishly trusted the word of Nipmucks he employed to work his fields, was, Saltonstall reasoned, partially blamable for the tragedy.[31] The church, meanwhile, in its rejection of the "halfway" covenant, has forsaken the ideal of the homogenous locally oriented Christian community; it had effectively abandoned the "seed" while embracing in its stead a variety of dangerous strangers.

Gookin, like Saltonstall, was a political enemy of First Church, and an advocate of the "halfway" covenant. But Gookin could never agree with Saltonstall's substantive claims about the danger of intercultural contact; nor could he acquiesce in Saltonstall's efforts to manipulate popular opinion by presenting the "halfway" covenant as an engine of exclusion. Instead, Gookin understood the "halfway" covenant to be an innovation whose broad principles might inform the safe expansion, rather than the constriction, of the scope of community; and this was precisely why he became so unpopular. Gookin's patron Robert Boyle favoured, in England, a "comprehensive", latitudinarian Anglicanism that would harshly exclude abject heretics yet welcome all pure-hearted souls, regardless of their lack of theological sophistication.[32] Daniel Gookin, in his own colonial milieu, sought to strengthen Puritanism along these same lines, arguing that the faith should "comprehend" all would-be believers, including the Indians, who were sincere and well behaved, while, at the same time, weeding out and persecuting heretical followers of anabaptistry or Quakerism, in part because sectarian doctrines would confuse would-be converts.

Unlike fellow New Englanders, Daniel Gookin, with his roots in Ireland, failed to worry much about the consequences of uniting with possible hypocrites. Vincent Gookin, in writing about the benighted Catholics of Ireland, had minimized the dangers of hypocrisy, which New Englanders greatly feared, arguing instead that the external performance of Protestant practices, even if done only to gain worldly benefits, was sufficient to place converts on the right path: "The son may be sincere, though the father be a hypocrite, and what his earthly father intended only for the saving of his estate, his heavenly father may advance to the saving of his soul."[33] In Massachusetts, Daniel Gookin adapted this line of reasoning to his own converting ends; although Gookin admitted that some praying Indians, like some Englishmen, were no doubt hypocrites, he held that a "charitable" people must decline to delve into the "secret" things that "belong to God".[34] If religion and the churches had always symbolically defined community for Bay Colony Puritans, Gookin's formulation threatened pollution – a risk that many colonists remained resolutely unwilling to take, even when it might benefit their own relatives and friends.[35] Rank-and-file colonists may well have appreciated how the "halfway" covenant debate voiced and legitimated a "tribal" calculus. But Gookin showed how, with or without "halfway" measures, the bonds of community would continue to expand in alarming ways.

To be sure, Gookin never suggested that the "halfway" covenant be applied directly to Indian converts. In demanding that colonists accept proselytes as "true" Christians, however, Gookin did attempt to appropriate for them the same "charitable" feelings that ministers exhorted their flocks to extend toward "halfway" members. "Charity" in this context was meant to extend only to those "genealogical heirs to the covenant" who lived moral lives, understood religious tenets intellectually, and put forth a demonstrable effort to convert.[36] Gookin, however, inverted the hierarchy that privileged insiders over "others", insisting instead that new converts with no historical relationship to the covenant were, precisely because of their inexperience with Christian ways, equally, if not more, deserving of latitude.

John Oxenbridge, unlike Gookin, had correctly sensed the dangers in the new covenantal logic. As Massachusetts leaders gradually came to enjoy the "delights" of the "new learning", and to pursue ways of connecting themselves with religious networks in the metropolis, they also emphasized countervailing images and practices capable of endowing religion with a domestic, communal feel.[37] Ministers stumbled, perhaps unwittingly, upon this manner of rendering new forms of association non-threatening during the framing of the "halfway" covenant – a truly ambivalent "innovation", which could be read alternately as the very quintessence of provincialism or as an incomplete adaptation to nascent "latitudinarian" demands for "comprehensive" churches. At the same time, however, the emphasis on domesticity reinforced the notion that religion was a family affair non-inclusive of cultural "others", like the Indians, who increasingly came to symbolize all sorts of real and imagined enemies, from crafty courtiers to conspiratorial witches.[38] In this vein, the sophisticated William Hubbard described the vast majority of Indians as "hanging all together, like Serpent's Eggs", and sharing an "inbred Malice and Antipathy against the English Manner and Religion"; blood, in other words, was thicker than water – even baptismal water.[39] Ironically, as the early Enlightenment dawned in colonial Massachusetts, so too did an enhanced sense of "racial" difference, and a desire for exclusivity.

In the years following King Philip's War, Gookin regained popularity in Massachusetts by taking a firm stand against England's political encroachments upon the Bay Colony charter; but his missionary work, and his economic goals, had the opposite effect, connecting New England to a transatlantic web of commerce in which a unique Puritan culture would become difficult to maintain. Even Gookin's harsh stance against religious dissent, which could be interpreted as devoted commitment to the New England Way, may have been geared more toward helping the Indians gain a firm grasp on Puritan doctrine than policing boundaries.[40]

Missionary work, combined with other kinds of mediatorship, threatened the personal identity of would-be assimilators who, out of self-interest, occasionally tried to see the world through Indian eyes. Gookin, like the "cunning people", or popular healers of early New England, performed a kind of intercultural "magic" at the edge of a multivalent boundary.[41] His manipulations there were as likely to produce war and destruction as prosperity and trade. And, just as helpful "cunning persons" might easily be transformed into malevolent witches, so too might cultural mediators turn "traitor".

Gookin played a number of different roles on the frontier. He was an engrosser of land and developer of towns, particularly Worcester; he sat on General Court committees that regulated trade and licensed traders; he negotiated differences between colonists and Indians, both praying and "profane"; he distributed implements, and sometimes arms, from the New England

3 R. Slotkin, *Regeneration through violence: the mythology of the American frontier, 1600–1860* (Middletown, Conn., 1973; repr. New York, 1996), pp. 81–2. On the use of Indian adjuncts see R. R. Johnson, "The search for a usable Indian: an aspect of the defense of colonial New England", *Journal of American History* **64**(3), 1977, pp. 623–51.

4 For Scott's appearance before the Court of Assistants see J. Noble (ed.), *Records of the Court of Assistants of the colony of the Massachusetts Bay, 1630–1692* [3 vols] (Boston, 1901–   ), I, pp. 60–61.

5 For the argument that the rejection of "praying" Indians reflected leaders' temporary "loss of control", see J. H. Pulsipher, "Massacre at Hurtleberry Hill: Christian Indians and English authority in Metacom's War", *William and Mary Quarterly* **53**(3), 1996, pp. 459–86.

6 On the late seventeenth-century challenges to the "city upon a hill" see F. J. Bremer, *The Puritan experiment: New England society from Bradford to Edwards* (New York, 1976), pp. 125–68. For the classic account of the "halfway" covenant see R. G. Pope, *The halfway covenant: church membership in Puritan New England* (Princeton, N.J., 1969). On the tortuous intellectual adjustment that Puritan clergymen had to make at the end of the century see M. P. Winship, *Seers of God: Puritan providentialism in the restoration and early Enlightenment* (Baltimore, 1996).

7 On Puritan "tribalism" see E. S. Morgan, *The Puritan family: religion and domestic relations in seventeenth-century New England* (New York, 1966).

8 On the Gookins see J. W. Thornton, "The Gookin family", *New England Historical and Genealogical Register* **I**, 1847, pp. 345–52; Gookin *Daniel Gookin*; and H. Galinsky, "*I cannot join with the multitude*": *Daniel Gookin (1612–1687), critical historian of Indian–English relations* (Erlangen-Nuremberg, 1985).

9 For Boyle's ideology see N. Canny, *The upstart earl: a study of the social and mental world of Richard Boyle first Earl of Cork* (New York, 1982).

10 T. C. Barnard, "Lord Broghill, Vincent Gookin and the Cork elections of 1659", *English Historical Review* **88**(347), 1973, pp. 352–65, examines Gookin's efforts to get out from under the political domination of the Boyle family, but demonstrates that this did not imply any disagreement on the issue of "transplantation".

11 On Eliot's programme of assimilation see K. M. Morrison, "'That art of coyning Christians': John Eliot and the praying Indians of Massachusetts", *Ethnohistory* **21**(1), 1974, pp. 77–92. For subsequent use of Eliot's image to justify removal see J. D. Bellin, "Apostle of removal: John Eliot in the nineteenth century", *New England Quarterly* **69**(1), 1996, pp. 3–32.

12 On the history of the London-based missionary society that sponsored Eliot and Gookin, and its revival during the Restoration, see W. Kellaway, *The New England Company, 1649–1776: missionary society to the American Indians* (London, 1961). For an account of how Boyle's interests in economic "projecting", millennialism and science came together in missionary work see J. R. Jacob, "The New England Company, the Royal Society, and the Indians", *Social Studies of Science* **5**, 1975, pp. 450–55.

13 Daniel Gookin, *Historical collections of the Indians in New England*, ed. J. H. Fiske (1792; rep. Boston, 1970), p. 129. See also N. Canny, "The ideology of English colonization: from Ireland to America", *William and Mary Quarterly* **30**(4), 1973, pp. 574–98.

14 On the centrality of cultural conversion to planter identity see N. Canny, "Identity formation in Ireland", in *Colonial identity in the Atlantic world, 1500–1800*, N. Canny & A. Pagden (eds) (Princeton, N.J., 1987), pp. 159–212. For another view see K. S. Bottigheimer, "Kingdom and colony: Ireland in the westward enterprise, 1536–1660", in

The westward enterprise: English activities in Ireland, the Atlantic and America, 1480–1650, K. R. Andrews et al. (eds) (Liverpool, 1978), pp. 45–64.

15 V. Gookin, *The great case of transplantation in Ireland discussed* (London, 1655), pp. 30–31.

16 See, for example, J. P. Ronda, " 'We are well as we are': an Indian critique of seventeenth-century missions", *William and Mary Quarterly* **34**(1), 1977, pp. 62–82; N. Salisbury, " 'Red puritans': the 'praying Indians' of Massachusetts Bay and John Eliot", *William and Mary Quarterly* **31**(1), 1974, pp. 27–54; and W. S. Simmons, "Conversion from Indian to Puritan", *New England Quarterly* **52**(2), 1979, pp. 197–218.

17 See K. O. Kupperman, "Errand to the Indies: Puritan colonization from Providence Island through the Western Design", *William and Mary Quarterly* **45**(1), 1988, pp. 70–99.

18 H. D. Sedgwick, "Robert Sedgwick", *Transactions of the colonial society of Massachusetts*, vol. 3 (Boston, 1900), pp. 155–73.

19 See J. R. Jacob, "Restoration, reformation and the origins of the Royal Society", *History of Science* **13**(1), 1975, pp. 155–76.

20 On the centrality of "independency" and "dependency" as crucial "social categories" in British North America see J. P. Greene, *Pursuits of happiness: the social development of early modern British colonies and the formation of American culture* (Chapel Hill, N.C., 1988), pp. 186–9, 195–7. For the analogous concept of "competency" see D. Vickers, "Competency and competition: economic culture in early America", *William and Mary Quarterly* **47**(1), 1990, pp. 3–29.

21 Pope, *Halfway covenant*, stresses lay resistance. But see D. D. Hall, "The meetinghouse", in *Worlds of wonder, days of judgment* (Cambridge, Mass., 1990), p. 153.

22 For the importance of family in colonial America see H. M. Wall, *Fierce communion: family and community in early America* (Cambridge, Mass., 1990).

23 On this event see H. Hill, *History of the Old South Church, Boston, 1669–1884* [2 vols] (Boston, 1890), I, pp. 1–112; Pope, *Halfway covenant*, pp. 152–84; and P. Miller, *The New England mind: from colony to province* (Cambridge, Mass., 1953), pp. 93–118.

24 For evidence that the common people were trying to play one faction off against the other see [N. Saltonstall], *The present state of New England with respect to the Indian war* [1675], in *Narratives of the Indian wars, 1675–1699*, C. H. Lincoln (ed.) (1913; rep. New York, 1941), pp. 40–41.

25 On Oxenbridge see P. F. Campbell, *The church in Barbados in the seventeenth century* (Barbados, 1982), pp. 147–8.

26 K. O. Kupperman, "Presentment of civility: English reading of American self-presentation in the early years of colonization", *William and Mary Quarterly* **54**(1), 1997, pp. 193–228, argues that the concept of "race" did not begin to be constructed until the later part of the seventeenth century.

27 J. Oxenbridge, "Conversion of the Gentiles", 1670, Massachusetts Historical Society, Boston, Massachusetts.

28 On the divisions between First and Third Church partisans see R. C. Simmons, "The founding of the Third Church in Boston", *William and Mary Quarterly* **26**(2), 1969, pp. 241–52; E. B. Holifield, "On toleration in Massachusetts", *Church History* **38**(2), 1969, pp. 188–200; and S. Foster, *The long argument: English Puritanism and the shaping of New England culture, 1570–1700* (Chapel Hill, N.C., 1991), pp. 175–230.

29 For the argument that the "halfway" covenant helped to reinforce the new "orthodoxy", and the association of First Church with "antinomian" beliefs, see J. Knight,

Orthodoxies in Massachusetts: rereading American Puritanism (Cambridge, Mass., 1994), pp. 184–197.

30   [Saltonstall], *Present state*, p. 38.

31   *ibid.*, p. 35.

32   See J. R. Jacob, "Restoration, reformation and the origins of the Royal Society"; and Jacob, "The New England Company, the Royal Society, and the Indians", pp. 450–55.

33   V. Gookin, *Transplantation*, pp. 4, 5–6.

34   Daniel Gookin, "An historical account of the doings and sufferings of the Christian Indians in New England, in the years 1675, 1676, 1677", *Collections of the American Antiquarian Society* **2**, 1836, p. 515; see also Gookin, *Historical collections*, p. 62. On the distinction between the "godly" and the "merely civil" see R. Gildrie, *The profane, the civil and the godly: the reformation of manners in orthodox New England, 1679–1749* (University Park, Penn., 1994).

35   Hall, "Meetinghouse", pp. 144–5, has shown how "halfway" members of Puritan congregations were discomfited by their liminal condition, and would, in extreme cases, turn to witchcraft for a release from the religious demands that they felt unable to fulfill.

36   Pope, *Halfway covenant*.

37   H. S. Stout, *The New England soul: preaching and religious culture in colonial New England* (New York, 1986), pp. 127–47, has noted the prevalent use of the word "delight" in late seventeenth-century cosmopolitan circles.

38   A. Porterfield, *Female piety in Puritan New England* (New York, 1992), pp. 116–56, sets this emphasis on domesticity in the context of the women's growing numerical predominance in the churches.

39   W. Hubbard, *A narrative of the troubles with the Indians in New England (1677)* in *The history of the Indian Wars in New England*, S. Drake (ed.) [2 vols in one] (New York, 1969), I, pp. 119–23.

40   Vincent Gookin argued that theological in-fighting made Protestantism look less attractive to potential converts (Gookin, *Transplantation*, p. 3).

41   On the "cunning people" see J. Demos, *Entertaining Satan: witchcraft and the culture of early New England* (New York, 1970).

42   On Gookin's entrepreneurial land acquisition see J. F. Martin, *Profits in the wilderness: entrepreneurship and the founding of New England towns in the seventeenth century* (Chapel Hill, N.C., 1991), pp. 23–8. For Gookin's official position on committees that controlled trade, and sales of guns and ammunition, see N. Shurtleff (ed.), *Records of the governor and company of the Massachusetts Bay* [5 vols in six] (Boston, 1853), IV.2, pp. 329–30, 365, 399; for his role in developing Worcester and Sherborne see *ibid.*, V, pp. 23, 35, 37.

43   *Massachusetts Archives* 30: 258a.

44   Mary Pray to James Oliver, 20 Oct. 1675, *Massachusetts Historical Society Collections*, **5th ser.**(1), 1871, p. 105.

45   On the role of husbandry-related disputes in tensions preceding King Philip's War see V. Anderson, "King Philip's herds: Indians, colonists and the problem of livestock in early New England", *William and Mary Quarterly* **51**(4), 1994, pp. 601–24; and J. M. Marshall, "'A melancholy people': Anglo-Indian relations in early Warwick, Rhode Island, 1642–1675", *New England Quarterly* **68**(3), 1995, pp. 402–28.

46   Daniel Gookin to Governor Thomas Prince, 12 April 1671, *Massachusetts Historical Society Collections*, **1st ser.**(6), 1779, pp. 198–99; and 14 April 1671, Miscellaneous Bound, Massachusetts Historical Society, Boston, Massachusetts. This correspondence is also reprinted in Gookin, *Daniel Gookin*.

47 For treatment of how the 1671 crisis was averted see P. Ranlet, "Another look at the causes of King Philip's War", *New England Quarterly* **61**(1), 1988, pp. 89–100.

48 Gookin, Daniel *Gookin*.

49 For Ahauton's activities see "Instructions from the Church at Natick to William and Anthony", 1 August 1671, *Massachusetts Historical Society Collections*, **1st ser.**(6) 1799, pp. 201–3; I. Mather, "A brief history of the warr with the Indians in New England", in *So dreadfull a judgment: Puritan responses to King Philip's War, 1676–77*, J. Folsom & R. Slotkin (eds) (Middletown, Conn., 1978), p. 87; H. W. Bowden & J. P. Ronda (eds), *John Eliot's "Indian Dialogues": a study in cultural interaction* (Westport, Conn., 1980); and Gookin, "Doings and sufferings".

50 For full-length exposition of this case see A. M. Plane, " 'The Examination of Sarah Ahhaton': the politics of 'adultery' in an Indian town of seventeenth-century Massachusetts", in *The Algonkians of New England: past and present*, P. Benes (ed.) (Boston, 1993), pp. 14–25. For Sarah's sentence see Shurtleff, *Massachusetts Bay records*, IV.2, pp. 407–8.

51 Daniel Gookin, "The Examination of Sarah Ahhaton, Indian Squa Wife Unto William Ahhaton of Pakemit alias Punquapauge taken the 24th of October 1668 Before Daniel Gookin", Massachusetts Archives, 30: 152.

52 Gookin, "Examination".

53 For Philip's move to curtail religious efforts in Mount Hope, see H. W. Van Longkhuyzen, "A reappraisal of the Praying Indians: acculturation, conversion, and identity at Natick, Massachusetts, 1646–1730", *New England Quarterly* **63**(3), 1990, p. 420. On the struggle to establish independent Christian Indian identities see J. Lepore, "Dead men tell no tales: John Sassamon and the fatal consequences of literacy", *American Quarterly* **46**(4), 1994, 479–512; and E. M. Brenner, "To pray or to be prey, that is the question: strategies for cultural autonomy of Massachusetts praying town Indians", *Ethnohistory* **27**(2), 1980, pp. 135–52.

54 Gookin, "Examination".

55 On this legend see D. T. V. Huntoon, *History of the town of Canton, Norfolk County, Massachusetts* (Cambridge, Mass., 1893), pp. 23–4.

56 On the importance of reciprocity in Algonquian cultures see N. Salisbury, *Manitou and providence: Indians, Europeans, and the making of New England, 1500–1643* (New York, 1982), pp. 10–11. On Gookin's disdain for Algonquian culture see A. Cave, "New England Puritan misperceptions of Native American shamanism", *International Social Science Review* **67**(1), 1992, pp. 15–27.

57 Gookin, "Doings and sufferings", p. 447.

58 Gookin, "Doings and sufferings", p. 447; and Gookin, *Historical collections*, p. 82.

59 A. K. Nelson, "King Philip's War and the Hubbard-Mather rivalry", *William and Mary Quarterly* **27**(4), 1970, pp. 615–29. For a recent challenge to the argument that Hubbard was more "modern" or "rational" than other Bay Colony ministers, particularly Cotton Mather, see Winship, *Seers of God*, pp. 22–7.

60 Gookin, "Doings and sufferings", p. 495.

61 Shurtleff, *Massachusetts Bay records*, V, p. 71.

62 Hubbard, *Narrative*, I, pp. 113–14.

63 *Ibid.*, pp. 116–17.

64 *Ibid.*, pp. 175–8.

65 M. G. Hall, *The last American Puritan: the life of Increase Mather* (Middletown, Conn., 1988), pp. 310–13, emphasizes how the Indian work helped Mather to cultivate influential contacts in London.

66 See, for example, Mather, "An earnest exhortation to the inhabitants of New England", in *So dreadfull a judgment*, pp. 187–8.

67 Gookin, "Doings and sufferings", p. 454.

68 K. Z. Derounian, "Puritan orthodoxy and the 'survivor syndrome' in Mary Rowlandson's Indian captivity narrative", *Early American Literature* **22**(1), 1987, pp. 82–93, argues that the act of producing a narrative was a healing process for Rowlandson.

69 Mather, "Exhortation", pp. 189–90; and Mather, "Diary", *Massachusetts Historical Society Proceedings*, **2nd ser.**(13), 1899–1900, p. 358.

70 See R. Godbeer, *The devil's dominion: magic and religion in early New England* (New York, 1992), pp. 85–121.

71 F. Fausz, "Merging and emerging worlds: Anglo-Indian interest groups and the development of the seventeenth-century Chesapeake", in *Colonial Chesapeake society*, L. Carr et al. (eds) (Chapel Hill, N.C., 1988).

72 See, for example, G. E. Dowd, *A spirited resistance: the North American Indian struggle for unity, 1745–1815* (Baltimore, 1992).

73 See, for example, "The revolution in New-England justified [1691]", in *The Andros tracts*, W. H. Whitmore (ed.) [3 vols] (New York, 1868–74), I, 100–12.

74 P. Boyer & S. Nissenbaum (eds), *The Salem witchcraft papers: verbatim transcripts of the legal documents of the Salem witchcraft outbreak of 1692* [3 vols] (New York, 1977), I, pp. 51–5. For the connection between witchcraft and Indian war see J. McWilliams, "Indian John and the northern tawnies", *New England Quarterly* **69**(4), 1996, pp. 580–604; and J. E. Kences, "Some unexplored relationships of Essex County witchcraft to the Indian wars of 1675 and 1689", *Essex Institute Historical Collections* **120**, 1984, pp. 179–212.

75 According to R. St. George, "'Heated speech and literacy in seventeenth-century New England", in *Seventeenth-century New England*, D. D. Hall et al. (eds) (Boston, 1984), pp. 275–317, the epithet "dog", which was also hurled at Gookin, could be used to describe persons who "had no hope for redemption" or who "might be working with Satan" (p. 294).

Chapter Six

The cutting edge of culture: British soldiers encounter Native Americans in the French and Indian war

Peter Way

Nothing can be more contemptible than an Indian war in North America. – Adam Smith[1]

Soldiers from the 44th Regiment hunted down and killed Jerry near Schenectady, New York in August 1756. His head was "found next morning on a Post" in front of the regiment's encampment, the place reserved for the regiment's colours, and was thus meant to act as a badge of honour for the 44th. This murder was fraught with meaning, for "Jerry" was an Indian, an adopted member of the Tuscaroras, one of the Six Nations which were allied to the English in their war with the French. The perimeter of the 44th's encampment marked the boundary between the British and Indian peoples. Jerry's sightless eyes stared across this frontier, his truncated body at once marking a racial dividing point and a cultural meeting place. While this brutal act seems to lend credence to Adam Smith's assessment of Indian warfare, his meaning is reversed, with the British playing the contemptible part. It was perhaps this he was afraid of, that English manners would be scoured away in the encounter with the New World, that the art of war would be revealed as mere butchery. Such reflections were lost on the soldiers of the 44th, who acted out of revenge, and on army commanders more interested in a larger military effort that required Indian support, not to mention Native Americans with their own culturally rooted ways of war.

Jerry's murder caused a violent stir amongst the Iroquois, who were temporarily pacified by the presentation of scalps and gifts by William Johnson, Britain's Northern Indian Superintendent. But Lord Loudoun, commander-in-chief of His Majesty's Forces in the Americas, insisted that

Jerry's murderers be discovered. "Men, that can in cool-blood go out four miles & murder a Man, for an offence committed a Year before, and at the same time, to satisfy their own private Resentment, run the risk of throwing the Affairs of the whole Continent into the utmost Confusion, the loss of them can be no harm to the Service." He offered a £20 reward for information leading to the culprits' arrest.[2] Considerations of statecraft and military discipline thus superseded moral repugnance with violence. The covenant chain linking Britain with the Six Nations must remain firm, and military discipline must be preserved, otherwise the empire in America faced dissolution.

Loudoun's outrage was tempered, however, when he heard the whole of Jerry's story. It began with General Braddock's ill-fated 1755 campaign against the French on the forks of the Ohio River, when British regular soldiers and Native Americans first met as allies and enemies, and during which the 44th Regiment was decimated. Jerry had been one of the native scouts accompanying Braddock, but, when the tide turned against the British, he deserted and scalped several of his former allies. He then joined the Tuscaroras and came with them to Albany. But "considering who the Man was, and what Villainous Murders he had committed on the Companions of that Regiment, no later than last Summer", Loudoun felt he had been wrong to come to the English settlements, "especially after the Language he had held in this Town . . . before he left it; Owning all the People he had Murdered belonging to them, and bragging no Man dared touch him for it". Loudoun believed "a Publick Example" should have been made of Jerry. "But as the Authors of his Death now, had no right to be his Executioners, they shall suffer for their Crime likewise."[3] Yet Thomas Gage, lieutenant colonel to the 44th, reported that he could not get a satisfactory account of the murder. While it was generally accepted that Jerry's killers belonged to the 44th, officers within the regiment proved uncooperative, and his murderers escaped justice. Over a year later, Johnson wrote that "the Murder of Jerry Still Sticks in ye. Stomacks of the Tuscaroras" and this "has cooled their affections towards us", leading them over to the French.[4]

This episode is revealing of relations between the British army and Native Americans during the French and Indian War, usually examined on a diplomatic level, but which at base were experienced by flesh and blood beings motivated by basic human emotions such as revenge. In its essence cultural mixing is a personal matter, and Jerry, the ultimate man in between, is a symbol of the degree of that mixing: a Native American whose tribal background is not known, bearing only a diminutive European name, fighting for the British but not out of allegiance, becomes a traitor to a cause that is not his own, and is sacrificed in a way with both European and Native American meanings attached.

This article will examine the relationships that developed between the regular army and various Indian tribes during the war. This interaction took place on a number of planes. On an institutional level, the army sought to maintain formal relations with the natives as a component of empire-building. On the personal level, soldier encountered warrior as ally and enemy, and this led to both social intermingling and brutal bloodletting. At root economic, political and personal, this relationship was played out in a variety of symbolic ways. The military shifted from one stereotype of natives to another as need dictated, the "Indian" being made to play the savage, the cunning and treacherous ally, greedy *homo economicus*, the drunkard, and the highly skilled woodsman, all with an eye to squeeze the most benefit possible out of natives. Similarly, Native Americans were motivated by tribal, village, and kinship concerns to preserve and enhance their power within Native America as well as within Indian–European relations. To do so, they played on the paternalistic mindsets of Europeans to extract the trade goods and military support they desired, while enticing the British to partake of native forms of expression and social practice, from lessons in wilderness living to symbolic exchange such as the smoking of the peace pipe, to ritualistic torture and cannibalism. The two groups never wholly understood each other, as meaning went missing in the garbled exchanges. Still, in the process of commingling a synthesis occurred, producing New World cultural forms which led ultimately to the denigration of Native American society, but, to a much lesser extent, was also corrosive of hierarchical Europeanisms.

The war brought the British into closer contact with Native Americans, causing conflict over concerns of land ownership and equitable trade, and contributing to the construction of enduring racial stereotypes. But it also fostered communication between soldiers and Indians, as conveyed through microbes, drink, sex, kinship, hunting, and physical violence, elemental human language ripe with promise of commonality and co-operation that threatened the command structure of the army and the class system that was embedded in British imperialism.

In a time of warfare, bloodletting dominated the discourse; military tactics were exchanged, and cultural practices associated with warfare deplored or emulated. There is no doubting the feeling of difference that each felt for the other, but in outlining these differences more attention needs to be paid to bridging the divide between white and red, themselves symbols masking a shared humanity and a common history. This was a British and Indian war and the discrete historiographies of the military and Native Americans, with their emphasis on difference, need to be brought face to face.

The war has long been the stuff of romanticism, lending itself to the fabrication of national foundation myths. Wolfe and Montcalm personified the resourceful British and aristocratic French within Parkman's pulp history; Washington and Franklin embodied the nascent spirit of American independence, while Cooper's Natty Bumppo was the frontier everyman that out-Indianed the Indian. The story of the regular soldier has been less prone to mythologizing: stick figures marching in redcoated ranks through an unregimented wilderness. More perniciously, Cooper's Chingachgook and Magua – Mohican and Mingo respectively – codified the good Indian/bad Indian, the noble and the savage, stereotypes which matured in the eighteenth century, while the Indians' slaughter of the surrendered British garrison of Fort William Henry in 1757, centrepiece of *Last of the Mohicans*, revealed their supposed bloodthirsty nature. Such imagery has only recently begun to be expunged from the historical record.

Military history has been too long concerned with warfare in itself, with generals, strategies and battles marching in serried ranks, or has treated organized armed conflict as a mere adjunct to the political process, an acting out of statecraft, or has been too prone to treat the military as separate from society. Colonial American military history has had its eye too firmly cocked on the coming Revolution and its heart too besotted with the idea of an American national character. A "new military history" has developed since the 1960s that places greater emphasis on cultural content, but these traits persist.

In Britain much of the recent writing on the army in the eighteenth century has been institutional in nature, dealing with its place within the state, the development of bureaucracy, the nature of military justice, or with the professionalization of the officer class.[5] Sylvia Frey and Glenn Steppler have gone some way to revealing the social and economic experiences of the common soldier, conjuring up a harsh environment of deprivation and violence, one populated by real people of modest means set adrift by historical forces.[6] Yet both Frey and Steppler, in descending through the ranks, have lost something that used to elevate traditional military history: a sense of narrative. This does not mean that the historian should return to a canonical chronology of battles and heroes, but that the "new military history" is just as much in need of overarching themes as the old, of models for explaining historical change with the military acting as a causative agent rather than just a mere mirror to external social forces.

With regard to the French and Indian War, American historians' focus has been on the colonies' militias and provincial troops.[7] Amongst the best is Fred Anderson's study of Massachusetts, which argues that the provincials were not drawn from a displaced "marginal population" as were British regulars, but instead were young men who took advantage of relatively high wages and substantial bounties to set themselves up for the future. Moreover, provincial regiments were more fraternities than hierarchies, roughly egalitarian groupings of men with no embedded class divisions. In effect, the provincials were cultural fragments of developing American society, with its opportunities for self-advancement and essentially classless nature.[8] In effect, soldiers were the shock troops of American exceptionalism. Such a dubious treatment largely results from a similar assumption that the regular army was a monolithic representation of the failures of British society; i.e. hierarchical, rigid, cruel, and immoral.

A more pernicious Manichaean world view dominated representations of native people and led to their virtual extirpation from the historical record.[9] The "new Indian history" has undergone overlapping stages of development. First came moral awakening and a desire to chastise whites for their crimes against Indians. This type of history tended to emphasize the wholly destructive impact of white culture on native societies, creating in effect a cultural breakdown-assimilation model. Second came the wave of ethnohistory. While still acknowledging Europeans' imperialist thrust, ethnohistorians argued for Indian cultural integrity and the persistence of social forms to the present day. A potential weakness of this approach was its tendency to push Europeans to the sidelines, treating them more as curious onlookers than as active participants in native history.[10] The current trend in the writing of Indian history, particularly in the colonial period, argues for a dialectic of Native and European forces across what could be characterized as a permeable frontier. Richard White in *The middle ground* adopted an accommodation model. Europeans and Indians meet, consider each other as alien, and learn to live together over two centuries in "a common, mutually comprehensible world"; but accommodation eventually breaks down as whites gain the upper hand. Accommodation took place because whites for a long time could not force Indians to their will nor ignore them.[11] While accommodationist histories are acutely tuned to the rhythms of native village life, they are less so to the nuances of European societies, which tend to be taken at face value on an institutional or state basis. The soldiers of our story exist for them as nothing more than reflexes of imperial will.

The French and Indian War was implicitly fought over who would control North America's wealth, and British soldiers were the means to this end. Indians were intimately involved in the conflict, fighting to maintain, at the least, the *status quo ante*. Soldiers met warriors in places both political and personal, making this a war of collaboration as much as conflict.

Wars in North America had been traditionally fought with a minimum investment of regular troops and firm reliance on colonial militias and provincial soldiers. Outside Halifax, there was virtually no regular military presence, excepting the Independent Companies of New York and South Carolina, technically regular forces but notorious for their unpreparedness.[12] A series of defeats, however, prompted William Pitt to commit thousands of troops to the colonies. They came not only to a new theatre of operations but to an entirely new military environment. The army was expected to oversee relations with its native allies and to fight its enemies in novel ways in the strange wooded and relatively thinly settled North American interior.

The army's Indian diplomacy was infused with paternalist attitudes combining racialist and classist assumptions of natives as wilful dependants who must be brought to heel. Colonel John Forbes wrote from the Pennsylvania frontier: "Our Indians I have at length brought to reason by treating them as they always ought to be, with the greatest signs of scorning indifference and disdain, that I could decently employ." Others' fear and loathing ran deeper, mining psychological terrain. James Wolfe spoke of diverse native peoples as "the black tribe", and confessed that "As an Englishman, I cannot see these things without the utmost horror and concern". Wolfe's fright was not just at the otherness of native people, but at their ability to incite terror. Some British officers came to admire Indian effectiveness at the type of warfare waged in the New World. "The Indians are more cunning than the wisest of us", opined one. "Their patience is invincible [SIC]. They would lie for a Week to their skin in water before they would aim a blow they were not sure of."[13]

Indians felt the scorn of officers, yet equally looked down upon the British military, as revealed by the damning criticism levelled by Scarroyady, an Oneida sachem, against "the pride and ignorance" of General Braddock in the wake of his defeat.

> He is now dead; but he was a bad man when he was alive; he looked upon us as dogs, and would never hear anything what was said to him. We often endeavoured to advise him and to tell him of the danger he was in with his Soldiers; but he never appeared pleased with us, & that was the reason that a great many of our Warriors left him & would not be under his Command.[14]

Yet Indians were drawn more inextricably into the European contest for their lands. They sought to assuage these pressures in the same ways they always had with Europeans, by allying and trading with them. At the same time, they sought to insulate their interests by protesting at sharp trading or encroachments on their lands, by failing to live up to British expectations of their duties as allies, by remaining aloof and asserting neutrality when the English appeared weak, and by taking up the tomahawk against them if it was to their advantage. With interests at root opposed, it is no wonder that misunderstanding and conflict frequently emerged between the British military and Indian tribes, friendly or otherwise.

At the same time, however, a different discourse was taking place between soldiers and warriors. In the process of carrying out the wishes of their leaders and in acting out their own drives, these people came into very close contact. Communication took various forms, and, while mutual understanding may not have been any greater, it is clear that each group learnt from the other. I shall look more closely at a number of the more prominent features of exchange: military tactics; cultural practices like scalping, torture and cannibalism; and at the ways in which Indians adopted European forms and British troops "went native".

Troops shipped to the Americas during the French and Indian War came from diverse origins, but most were recent recruits, drawn from agricultural and handicraft occupations that were undergoing rapid change. We are thus talking about English weavers, Scottish crofters, Irish peasants, and German miners. The land they marched into would have seemed a veritable "wilderness", the Indians they encountered truly "savage", and the fighting that erupted horrible beyond their ken; it was a new world of warfare.[15]

The learning process began early, with the first mass infusion of soldiers under Braddock, who arrived in 1755 with the 44th and 48th Regiments, and with orders to resurrect the 50th and 51st with American recruits. Some of the officers and troops would have had some experience with irregular warfare, as the 44th and 48th had served with the Duke of Cumberland, the "Bloody Butcher" of the Scots, in the campaign of 1746 where guerrilla tactics had been used.[16] Yet, the vast majority of soldiers would have enlisted since then, and would have had experience, indeed where they had any, primarily of garrison duty.

The regulars were joined by 1,100 provincial troops from the southern colonies, but the expected Indian allies did not materialize. Only fifty warriors were sent by the governor of Pennsylvania, and the Virginians failed to bring the 400 natives promised. Braddock met with Delaware chiefs who agreed to join the army on its march, but failed to do so. In the end the expeditionary force was left with eight to ten warriors for the final push on Duquesne.[17] The Indian allies of the French were more forthcoming, as the British troops soon discovered. On 24 June, they found a recently abandoned Indian camp, where "They had stripped and painted some trees, upon which they and the French had written many threats and bravados with all kinds of scurrilous language". These were not idle taunts, as the next day three men were shot and scalped near camp at the Great Meadows, leading Braddock to offer a bounty: "If Any Soldr or follower of the Army bring into head Quarters An Indian Scalp shall Receive five pounds from the Genl for every Scalp." Yet on the 26th they found another abandoned camp similarly decorated with threats, and depicting the scalps that had been taken. Two weeks later, three to four people straggling in the rear of the grenadiers were killed and scalped by Indians.[18]

The British force, on the morning of 9 July, were attacked by a party of French and Indians (estimated at 300 by George Washington) after having crossed the Monongahela. Braddock ordered reinforcements to the vanguard. The front collapsed under the fierce assault, however, and fell back upon the reinforcements, "which caused such Confusion and struck so great a Panick into our Men, that Afterwards no Military Expedient coud [sic] be made use of that had any effect". The baggage train was then attacked. All the while cannons were firing, keeping off the Indians, but doing little damage in the wooded site. Many officers were killed and Braddock finally attempted an orderly retreat, "but the panick was so great that he could not succeed". Once the general and most officers were wounded and men had fired off all their ammunition, the soldiers "by one common consent left the field, running off with the greatest precipitation". They were pursued by about fifty Indians who killed several men. Jerry presumably chose this time to change sides and join in the chase. The troops fled all that night and the next day. On 13 July, Braddock died near the camp at the Great Meadows.[19]

In the frenzy of finger-pointing that erupted in the aftermath of Braddock's debacle two themes quickly emerged: the unfamiliarity of both regular officers and troops with the tactics practiced by the Indian allies of the French; and the cowardly conduct of the British private soldiers. William Shirley – Massachusetts politician, colonel of the 50th Regiment, and Braddock's successor – attributed the defeat to the French strategic advantage "and their Covert way of fighting in the Indian manner from behind Trees and Logs, which occasioned that Panick and confusion in the Troops that expos'd them not only to be shot down at pleasure by the Enemy, but to be destroyed by each other". George Washington, wishing to exculpate himself and his Virginia provincials, asserted that "the dastardly Behaviour of the English Soldiers, exposed all those who were inclined to do their duty to Almost certain Death, and at length in dispite [sic] of every Effort to the Contrary broke and run like sheep before the Hounds". Washington further imputed that two thirds of casualties at the Monongahela "received their shot from our Own Cowardly dogs of Soldiers". There has even been some suggestion that the private men were not just firing in a panic, but may have been shooting their officers to be able to escape the slaughter. This possibility was not raised by the Inquiry into the defeat, which blamed the troops' bad behaviour on a number of factors, but principally on the fact that fighting in the European manner was futile; on the want of natives and other irregulars to give warning; and "Lastly the Novelty of an invisible enemy & the Nature of the Country Which was intirely a Forest".[20]

Braddock's defeat has been re-fought numerous times since by historians. I return to the field of battle only to highlight the themes of this chapter: that much of the history of this war was generated by the coming together of Europeans and Indians; that most of the exchange was transacted in terms of flesh and blood; and that this was immensely important to the British "imagining" of the Indian and *vice versa*. Largely unseasoned troops marched into an unimagined "wilderness", there to have stragglers scalped or beheaded by a mostly unseen but certainly fierce and fearsome enemy, while the overweening pride of their commander alienated the native allies who were their only hope of survival. Conversely, enemy Indians, outnumbered by an invading European force, waged warfare of terror, taunting their opponents and dismembering those they caught for trophies, with an eye to amassing plunder and cementing a lucrative alliance with another distant European power. As one officer wrote, "the War in North America differs Widely from that in Europe".[21] The British soldiers were new to this type of warfare, but they were quick learners. Jerry's head stuck on a post outside the 44th's camp at Schenectady was a totem of sorts to their adaptation of New World ways.

It is important to place the conduct of native warfare in context, freighted as it is with racial and cultural assumptions. Indians were considered "bloodthirsty" due to their practices of scalping, torture, human sacrifice and cannibalism, all rituals which were rooted in native culture but were influenced by European contact. The notion that scalping was introduced by Europeans has been scotched by James Axtell and William Sturtevant, who demonstrate its existence in pre-Columbian native cultures. Scalps, heads, or captives taken from enemies in so-called "mourning wars" were meant to replace dead tribal members, to appease the spirits of the departed, and to ease the grief of those left behind.[22] Similarly, blood and sometimes body parts could be consumed on the battle field. Captives would be tortured on the return journey, killed if an encumbrance, and forced to run the gauntlet if they made it back to the village. Some of the survivors would be set aside for further torture, often involving the use of fire, which could go on for extended periods. Others would be adopted into families which had lost members recently. These adoptees would be expected to live according to Indian ways, or face punishment and death. Like scalping, these practices were meant to restore spiritual harmony, while adoption was intended to replenish the population.[23] At the same time, European bounties exacerbated scalping, and armed conflict necessitated further mourning wars to restock the tribe and restore spiritual harmony.

The experience of Thomas Brown gives a British soldier's perspective on these blood rituals. A member of Captain Spikeman's company of Rogers'

Rangers, Brown was wounded during a major engagement with the French and their Indian allies between Crown Point and Ticonderoga on 18 January 1757, and witnessed his captain "stripp'd and scalp'd" alive. Taken captive next day by Indians, his wounds were treated, and he was brought to their camp, where he saw Spikeman's head on a pole, thus experiencing the two extremes of native culture. The Indians removed Brown to their village. During the journey they "stripp'd off all my Cloaths, and gave me a Blanket. And the next Morning, they cut off my Hair and painted me, and, with Needles and Indian-ink, prick'd on the back of my Hand the Form of one of the Scaling-Ladders, which the French made to carry Fort William-Henry". Brown was here being transformed and given a mock totem. Another prisoner fared less well. When he refused to have his hair cut, the Indians "made a Fire, stripp'd and ty'd him to a Stake, and the Squaws cut Pieces of Pine, like Scures, and thrust them into his Flesh, and set them on fire, and then fell to powwawing and dancing round him". They ordered Brown to join in the dancing, and "Love of Life" made him comply; "for I could expect no better Treatment if I refus'd". Here, Brown is given entrance to native ritual as a means to further bind him to his captors. When Brown finally arrived at the Indian town about twenty miles from Montreal he was stripped naked and made to run the gauntlet, thereby metaphorically passing into the tribe. However, his "Indian master" was from the Mississippi country, so he was taken there with several other prisoners. Arriving in the Mississppi village on 23 August, Brown was placed with a squaw who was to be his mother, where he lived through the winter, employed in hunting, dressing leather, and "being cloath'd after the Indian Fashion". Later he was taken to Montreal by a French merchant, and worked on a farm as nothing more than a slave. Brown was finally exchanged in January 1760, after having been away almost four years.[24] This acount of capitivity, in many ways representative of such narratives in its emphasis on suffering and redemption, can be pried apart in an attempt to understand the social and economic instrumentality as well as cultural significance of native ritual, which Brown himself could not be expected to comprehend.

Soldiers in the French and Indian War experienced native ritual as physical threat, and none more so than scalping. After a battle with the Cherokee in 1761, a captive warrior was brought into the camp, and a Catawba ally of the British, whose relative was killed in the fight, knocked him down with a war club, "Tomahawk'd & scalp'd him, then Blew out his Brains, cut open his Breast, & Belly, & cut off his privy parts, & otherwise mangled him in a most Shocking manner".[25] However shocking it was for soldiers to see a helpless prisoner gutted by one's ally, knowing that the same treatment could be visited upon themselves was more worrying, for British troops were scalped regularly. From April 1755 to January 1756, the 50th Regiment lost about thirty men to scalping out of an initial total of 849 troops (roughly 3.5 per cent). Such skeletal numbers do not convey the flesh and blood horror. For example, two soldiers who went missing from Halifax one evening in 1757 were found the next day about three hundred yards from the fort in the woods, "one of them, his Head carried off, and one of his Hands mangled; the other had the Back part of his Head carried off". Infrequently, individuals survived scalping to bear testimony to the ordeal. In the winter of 1758, a group of men from Fort Edward were attacked by a party of mostly Indians; 13 men were killed, four wounded and three were taken captive. One scalped soldier escaped, "came into the Fort and saw some of the Officers and said by G-d Gentlemen I have lost my Night Cap". He suffered a contusion but was expected to survive.[26]

The British were not just the innocent victims of scalping, however, but encouraged it through the offering of bounties. Life was literally commodified by the army, but it took moral refuge in the assertion that since 1752 the French had been promoting scalping in return for the payment of "premiums".[27] We have already seen how Braddock offered a bounty of £5 to any soldier or camp follower who brought in a scalp. The following December, Shirley promised a "reward" for every scalp or prisoner taken by a party of Iroquois sent to attack French and native forces on the western frontier. The next year, General Loudoun promised Captain Jacob Cheeksaunkun, a Mohican from Stockbridge who commanded a company of his comrades, that "For each French and Indian Prisoner or Scalp, you shall be allowed Five pounds Sterling".[28]

British bounties could not but provide an incentive for Indians and soldiers to go out in search of human profit. For example, Robert Rogers' Ranger Company took 114 prisoners and scalps in less than a month in 1756, at £5 each, and two years later Major Rogers came into the camp at Lake George with fifty enemy scalps. Once learned, scalping became a norm of warfare for Europeans, who could appreciate the terror tactics that lay behind flaunting body parts. Recently arrived Scottish troops, perhaps having learned in the uprising against their English masters in the '45, took to terror tactics, though they were less adept at New World forms. After the fall of Louisbourg, "several Indians which the Highlanders took alive; they told them they did not understand scalping, but chopped off their Heads", which they of course would understand. It was then also reported that "We have killed a great many Indians, and the Rangers and Highlanders give no Quarters to anyone, and are scalping every where, so you cannot know a French from an Indian Scalp".[29]

At the same time, scalping did cause some moral concern among the high command. Despite offering a bounty in September 1756, Loudoun maintained in November that he would "give nothing for Scalps, which is a Barbarous Custom first introduced by the French, and of no use to the Cause". In June 1759, commander-in-chief General Jeffery Amherst ordered "that no scouting party or others in the Army under his command shall whatsoever opportunity they may have scalp any women or children belonging to the enemie. They are to bring them away if they can, if not they are to leave them unhurt". But, if the enemy should murder or scalp any British women or children, he promised to kill two of the enemy's for every one. General Wolfe, after rangers had scalped a local priest during the siege of Quebec, ordered all civilians to be spared, as "Cruelty is the most distinguishing characteristic of cowardice". Wolfe was willing to make exceptions, however, "Strictly" forbidding "the inhumane practice of Scalping, Except when the Enemy are Indians, or Kanadians dressed like Indians". Clearly being or going native exempted one from humane warfare.[30]

While British soldiers, like colonists before them, made a relatively painless adoption of scalping, they had greater difficulties dealing with Indians' ritual torture and cannibalism. Captives were routinely burnt, flayed, dismembered, and consumed in rites often involving community participation that could continue for days.[31] Rufus Putnam, a private in the Massachusetts provincials, recorded that on July 4, 1757 a soldier taken by the enemy was

> found barbecued at a most doleful rate, for they found him with his nails all pulled out, his lips cut off down to his chin and up to his nose, and his jaw lay bare; his scalp was taken off, his breast cut open, his heart pulled out and his bullet pouch put in the room of it; his left hand clenched around his gall, a Tomahawk left in his bowels and a dart stuck through him; the little finger of his left hand cut off and the little toe of his left foot cut off.[32]

Soldiers also witnessed the torture of enemies by Britain's native allies. Caleb Rea, another provincial, commented:

> I can't but take notice of ye Cruel Nature of our Indians, I look on'm not a whitt better than ye Canadians for when they took a Prisoner their custom was to confine him and making a Ring 'round him with their Company, then Scurging him with whips, or pricking with Sharp pointed Sticks, taring his Nails out by ye Roots, Sculping alive and such like torments, they wou'd shout & yell (as I may say) like so many Fiends, these Frolics they would sometimes Hold all Night long and perhaps be two or three Nights murdering one Prisoner.[33]

Soldiers had to watch these ceremonies without interfering, let the Indians turn against them.

Instances of cannibalism were perhaps the most difficult Indian cultural practice for soldiers to absorb. When rescuers arrived at Fort Bull near Oswego, which had been razed by the French and Indians, they were outraged to find bodies, "some partly Consum'd & others wholly, to the number of 18 more". And Richard Williams of the 51st Regiment, who was taken captive outside Oswego in March 1755 and removed to Oswegatchie (Ogdensburg), claimed to have seen "Lieut. Bulls Scalp brought in there, with his Leggs, and Buttocks which the Indians burnt".[34] Bull had commanded the ill-fated fort bearing his name.

When it came to partaking of human flesh, British soldiers were extremely loath. The only incident encountered occurred in January 1752. After a mutiny at Oswego amongst the New York Independent troops, several mutineers made for New France overland. They became disoriented, ran out of provisions, and began preying on each other; in the end four to five were consumed.[35] The difference was clear: Indians commonly ate flesh to absorb the enemy's spirit and to reinforce communal values; Europeans only consumed each other in dire straits as a means of individual self-preservation. It was a matter of a collective sacrament versus individual consumption.

There is a danger, in detailing Indian martial practices, of reinforcing the stereotype of the bloodthirsty savage. This is not the intention here, for Europeans had no stronger claim to being non-violent. They came from a culture in which torture and dismemberment had a long tradition and served both political and religious purposes as well as cultural. Although it could be argued that such practices were tailing off in the eighteenth century, state-sponsored executions were clearly in the ascendant, and heads and other body parts of thieves and traitors were regularly displayed on the walls of Britain's main cities.[36] When one talks of military discipline, the situation is exaggerated. Soldiers regularly saw men whipped 1,000 times or executed for desertion and any other number of offences. Francis Jennings aptly observed that soldiers were "disciplined by Torture", and suggests that it derived in part from the class divisions embedded in the army.[37]

Furthermore, European military tactics at this time tacitly sanctioned the destruction and pillaging of towns, and the rape and murder of non-combatants. During the siege of Louisbourg Wolfe confided: "tho' I am neither inhuman nor rapacious yet I own it would give me pleasure to see Canadian vermin sacked and pillaged and justly repaid their unheard-of cruelty." And a year later when it was rumoured that three grenadiers captured by Indians during the siege of Quebec were to be burnt, Wolfe threatened Gouverneur Vaudreuil: "If this be true, the Country shall be but one universal blaze." In effect, Wolfe sought to translate native expressions of "mourning war" to a European language of "total war".[38] Such scorch and burn tactics were not unusual, as when General Loudoun instructed Jacob Cheeksaunkun and his Stockbridge Indians to "take Prisoners and Scalps to intercept the Enemy's Convoys of Provisions, to destroy their Cattle, to Burn their Barns, and other Magazines and Storehouses of Grain and Forrage, and you are to take all Oppertunities to annoy and distress them".[39] The actions of the 1761 British expeditionary force against the Cherokees highlight European tactics. After an initial fight with the Cherokee, Lieutenant Christopher French was sent to take native villages with "orders to put every Soul to Death". He found them deserted, but the British took their revenge over the next month by burning fifteen settlements and all their plantations; over 1,400 acres of corn were destroyed and above 5,000 men, women and children were driven into the "Woods & Mountains to Starve". The army also was prepared to treat natives by European rules of military law. Thus Elias Pegan, an Indian prisoner judged a spy, was sentenced to death.[40] There is also the contentious, though now generally accepted, claim that the British intentionally infected the Delaware Indians with smallpox during Pontiac's Rebellion.[41]

Thus far, this study has concentrated on the cultural clashes between European and Indian formalities of war, but there was great scope for acculturation, both metaphorically and literally, for natives to don the redcoat and soldiers the buckskin. In the end, Indians were more successful at crossing and re-crossing the cultural divide, as they adapted European forms to traditional goals, whereas many troops who entered the forest were lost to Old World ways; this latter possibility chilled the regimented and class-conscious heart of the armies.

Commercial relations were the main ways in which natives acculturated to European ways. We have already seen how scalping became commodified, yet this largely entailed merely adding a price tag to established native warfare. Other tasks became formalized as "jobs" paid in wages at set rates; in this way Indians became workers, however temporarily. They were paid for providing accommodation and food, transporting supplies, carrying messages, patrolling, acting as guides, spying, guarding prisoners, etc. Rum sometimes substituted for cash, but wampum was only a secondary form of payment by this time.[42] Indians were also paid to hunt down deserters. A soldier who deserted from the expedition to Detroit in 1763 had a Mohawk and another man sent to bring him in "dead or alive; if he resisted to shoot him and bring in his head". Here, Indian practice was explicitly wedded to the army's concern for discipline, with the head to act as both a symbol of the Mohawk's tracking skills and a warning to other lightfooted soldiers.[43]

From paid army workers and hunters of deserters it was but an easy transition to fully fledged military status as a mercenary soldier. Indians thus perpetuated a long tradition of bought martial labour that gave the original definition to the word "soldier", its root meaning being one who is paid to fight. Joining the ranks usually was preceded by a more autonomous relationship in which military service was bartered for; thus, in return for promising to fight the French in 1758, some Cherokee were to receive "forty weight of Leather to each man, to make them amends for the Loss of the Summer hunt". A second destination for Indian recruits was the rangers, independent companies, and provincial forces, where they received wages and were expected to follow orders like their white comrades.[44]

Indians' increasing absorption within the British war machine was apparently matched by a growing desire for steady wages. It was complained in 1756 that, whereas formerly Indians would serve without money being paid, the expedition to Oswego the year before under the direction of William Shirley had "Spolt them by Giveing them Great wages So that they now all Expect to have the Same". In an attempt to wrest Indians of the Six Nations from the control of William Johnson, Loudoun felt Shirley had "taught them the use of Money, of which they are now insatiable". Johnson agreed: "The many precedents Mr. Shirley has Sett of giveing Indians pay, & Commissions, has, I find, run through the Six Nations, & River [Mohican] Indians. So that in short what goods &ca I give them (altho it amounts to a great deal) is thought nothing of." As well, a ranger officer had been recruiting among the Mohawks and offering $18 bounty with pay of 4s. a day. Johnson tried to talk the Mohawks out of taking up the offer, "but they being a verry mercenary People, it is not easy to do". They said they deserved at least as much as the rangers as they were better at that sort of service, and suggested forming their own companies with their own officers. Johnson thought the "Regimenting" of Indians was a good idea that would prove not much more expensive than the existing system of gift-giving and cash payments for specific tasks. He drew up a plan for a regiment of five hundred Indians complete with their own officers, for which the wage bill plus provisions would have amounted to £33,602 10s. currency per annum.[45] Lord Loudoun neither balked at the expense nor at the prospect of making Indians regular soldiers, but it was to be the Mohican of Stockbridge who were formally to join the army.

The Stockbridge were known as the "Civilized" Indians, as they had long had a Christian mission in their settlement and lived alongside colonists. The Mohican were first enlisted in Shirley's 1755 campaign against Niagara for $15 a month, a gun, a shirt and other supplies. They signed up again in 1756 when they began serving closely with Rogers' Rangers, but were largely inactive the next year. In February 1758, however, Jacob Cheeksaunkun and Jacob

Naunauphtaunk agreed to raise a company of rangers with fifty privates to be paid "British Pay". General Amherst was loath to use the "lazy rum-drinking scoundrels" in 1759, but was forced to, that year and the next, as the French were afraid of them. Three years later at the height of Pontiac's Rebellion, the Mohican offered their "Service to act offensively on pay", but Amherst refused. In 1764, with Amherst returned to England, a party of twenty went west with Johnson, but the uprising was all but over.[46]

Thus, while the desired regular regiment of five hundred Indian allies never materialized, the Stockbridge Indians provided regular reinforcements for the British war effort, taking the king's shillings in return. Although they never functioned like well-disciplined British soldiers – hiring on for the year, providing their own officers, ranging rather than ranking – they had clearly changed their pre-existing modes of warfare, absorbing European tactics and organization for the purpose of gain. They occupied a "frontier" of warfare which blended European form and acquisitiveness with native technique and ritual.

At the same time as the army encouraged Indians to fight more in accordance with European practice, it was not unmindful of the lessons to be learned from these allies. "Every Indian is a Hunter, expert in Arms, and very dextrous in Shooting consequently by being a good Marksman preferable to a Soldier in those immense Woods where European Discipline is of little Use."[47] Over the course of the war, initiatives were taken to make British soldiers into hunter warriors, equally adept in the forests and on the plains. Before sailing for North America Lord Loudoun instructed that the army wanted more "Irregulars", both rangers in the provincial troops and as many natives as possible. Upon his arrival he stated his intention to transform some regulars into rangers, as he found "there was a disposition in the Soldiers, to go out with Indians and Rangers".[48] The Duke of Cumberland concurred: "i [sic] hope that you will, in time, teach your Troops to go out upon Scouting Parties: for, 'till *regular* officers, with Men that they can trust, learn to beat the woods, & act as *irregulars*, You will never gain any certain Intelligence of the Enemy", as Indian and ranger information could not always be trusted.[49] Similarly the following year, Charles Hardy asked James Abercromby to consider "if leaving off square Elbows, and right heel to left, and in short the General Manuvire [sic] of regular Troops, was Changed, and the Troops, that is to say great part of them were broke into Irregulars, Used more to Scouting not render them more usefull for American Warfare".[50] As Hardy indicated, making British regulars more suitable for irregular warfare involved more than merely renaming them rangers; tactics, discipline and uniformity would all have to be altered. James Wolfe complained that "Our clothes, our arms, our accoutrements, nay even our shoes and stockings are all improper for this country. Lord How is so well convinced of it that he has taken away all the men's breeches".[51] Implementing the plan meant creating a soldier that not only fought unusually, but also looked very different from his redcoated comrades.

The transformation was first apparent with the rangers who donned a uniform in place of their own clothing. On their heads they wore a leather cap; over their shoulders rested a short cloak made of light canvas painted the same colour as tree bark, which covered their entire body; beneath this came a pattern cloak, and a coat similar to that of regulars, but shortened and with pockets on the inside of the breast and with lapels that went to the waist for warmth, all the colour of bark; next came a loose-fitting waistcoat. "The short trousers and Buskins are intended to let the Rangers have the free use of His Limbs when marching, that He may not be bound about the Knees, Leggs, or between the Thighs, that He may be drest sooner, and that He may be disencumbered from the weight and expence." The ranger carried a lighter, shorter, blackened firelock; a bayonet in the form of a knife; a scalping axe instead of a broadsword; and a tin-covered cartridge box to keep out the wet. All told, the ranger's arms, accoutrements, and clothing were 13 lb lighter than the regular's.[52]

The revolution of practice did not end with these adjunct troops, for Thomas Gage volunteered to raise a regiment of irregulars as part of the regular army. Loudoun was receptive, feeling that Gage's light infantry would greatly lessen expense and provide "a Corps of Rangers that would be disciplined, and have Officers at their head on whom I could depend". Gage's Light Infantry, the first light-armed unit in the British army, tended to attract a certain sort of soldier, more adventurous and independent, and perhaps with greater hunting skills. Amherst noted that the light infantry involved in the attack on Louisbourg were "chosen as marksmen from the different regiments". Irregulars also tended to come from a wide variety of ethnic and social backgrounds. "They are a mixt Nation, Even of all Sorts."[53]

The novelty of the rangers (or "Leather Caps") and irregular light infantry went further than their arms and clothes. For, in roaming the woods in small groups rather than ranks, and in trying to become part of the landscape rather than dominate it, they escaped to a degree the strict discipline and regimentation of regular soldiers. The camouflaging of their uniforms so as to blend in with the trees is a fitting symbol of the blurring of the two cultures. Yet it was never perfect or natural; in trying to pass as the other a new entity was created.

The irregulars were but the most extreme manifestation of the adaptation of Europeans' armed warfare to North American realities. Cultural blending was also evident amongst the regulars. "The Art of War is much changed and improved here. I suppose by the End of the Summer it will have undergone a total Revolution", noted an observer in 1758. "We are now literally an Army of round Heads. Our Hair is about an Inch long; The Flaps of our Hats, which are wore slouched, about two Inches and a half broad. Our Coats are docked rather shorter than the Highlanders. . . . The Highlanders have put on Breeches. . . . Swords and Sashes are degraded; and many have taken up the Hatchet and wear Tomahawks."[54] While this was said in admiration for this practical transformation, the degradation of European forms noted was a worry for officers. The limited freedom from commands offered by irregular duties and the increased interaction with Indians opened the door to a breakdown of discipline and, in the worst-case scenario, of soldiers "going native", either by fully embracing native martial practices or by deserting the army for life amongst the "savages". To the class-bound hierarchy of the military, this would lead not only to military defeat but to social chaos.

To the extent that European emulation of Indian warfare aided the war effort, it was tolerated and encouraged. Thus a captain in Gage's light infantry was allowed to go on a scout to Quebec in 1759 painted like an Indian with three native guides. In the landing at Martinique in 1762, a French militia officer was "Excessively Frightned [sic], mistaking the Rangers for Indians, they being Painted & drest as such & setting up the same hideous Yell". Similarly, during the battle for Havana the following year, a regular officer reported that his soldiers gave the "Indian Whoop" before assaulting a Spanish redoubt.[55] That soldiers exported cultural practice learned on the continent to the Caribbean signifies the hold it had on them.

Social interaction with Indians was more worrisome to commanders, as it could lead to drunkenness, dereliction of duty and physical conflict. In 1756, William Johnson asked Shirley to give strict orders to commanding officers to ensure their men "behave well towards the Indians, do not give them drink or drink with them & best to have nothing to say to them". Soldiers encamped at Rays Town, Pennsylvania, in 1758 were ordered not to go to the neighbouring Indian camp or to have any dealing with the natives, an order that proved ineffective as two sentries had to be placed at the camp to keep the men from visiting. That same year at Lake George, Amherst reported that Indians and rangers had become drunk together and "fell to handy Cuffs, but no great Mischief ensued". It was presumably such frolics that led Johnson in 1761 to order fort commanders to prevent soldiers from "having much intercourse with the Indians, or rambling abroad among them, as that often creates disputes & Quarrels between Soldier, & Indian for want of under-standing each other".[56]

Whether they understood each other or not, soldiers and warriors seemed to desire to socialize with one another. While officers undoubtedly were wary of the bad blood that could arise from drunken "handy cuffs", they also feared that the troops would take up the undisciplined ways of native allies and this would undermine their military effectiveness. Underpinning these concerns was a subconscious phobia that these two groups, both subject in different ways to the class control of a European elite, would combine and undercut the hierarchy that was the backbone of the British military and empire. This implied threat became explicit when enemy Indians became involved.

Indians routinely took soldiers captive. Those that survived would have undergone the same sort of cultural indoctrination that Thomas Brown had. If he is to be believed he went along with the process, biding his time to make an escape. But James Axtell has argued about Indian captivities in general that, after the traumatic incorporation into the tribe, many whites learned to love their new people and were reluctant to return to European society when given the chance, especially impressionable children who would be incorporated into native culture to maintain social and demographic stability.[57] Soldier captives offered Indians a different resource, as labour power, potential warriors, and bargaining chips for prisoner exchanges and ransom payments. Conversely, a native lifestyle offered some soldiers an escape from military discipline and possible access into society more open and egalitarian than British.

Richard Williams' story highlights the experience of soldiers forcibly inducted into Indian culture who found it difficult to return to their English ways. Williams was a 15-year-old drummer in the 51st Regiment taken prisoner near Oswego in March 1755. Brought to Oswegatchie, he met Roman Catholic deserters from the army at Oswego, and claimed to have witnessed the cannibalistic consumption of Lieutenant Bull. Williams was given to some Onondagas, with whom he resided for over a year. During his captivity Williams made a fur-trading trip to Schenectady with three Indians, during which he unsuccessfully tried to escape and was tied up. During the night he untied his hands and legs with his teeth and hid in a hollow log until late the next day. The Indians searched for him but eventually gave up the hunt, and Williams was free to return to the English.

Williams' deposition mirrors published captivity accounts of the period with its emphasis on an innocent taken by predatory Indians and exposed to various inhuman practices before making a valiant escape and return to civilization. Yet, ending as it does with his escape, it leaves out just how deeply he was marked by the experience. Taken up as a deserter on a vessel out of New Haven, Williams was described by a witness, James Swan, as "About five feet high, of a Ruddy Compexion [sic], Somewhat freckled, hawksbill Nose, a hole bored trou [sic] the Bridge of his Nose, both Ears Cut According to the Indian fashion, One of them torn Out (As he Says by an Indian)". Williams admitted to Swan that he had remained with the Indians for about two years, during which time he was taught to hunt and eventually allowed to go out on his own. He made his escape and claimed to have carried two scalps with him to Boston, where he bound himself as an apprentice to Swan, a pilot between New York and Sandy Hook. He ran away, however, leaving his clothes but taking with him a gun, hatchet, what he called his "Sculping knyfe", some powder, ball and flints, and two striped blankets. Williams had said "that he Could paint himself So As not to be known from an Indian".[58] Williams was taken up before he could complete his escape, so it is impossible to tell what his intentions were, but it is clear that he was caught between two worlds. His face reconfigured in native rituals, his skill in the woods broadened, he seemed more confident of being able to pass as an Indian than as a Caucasian, and certainly more drawn to the forest than to the garrison. He was a soldier only to the extent that the army refused to let him go.

Richard Williams escaped from his Indian captors, whereas other soldiers determined to remain with them, and more actually fled to them. In fact, so many deserting soldiers sought refuge with enemy natives that unsubstantiated claims of captivity rarely staved off punishment.[59] Whether convert or deserter, these pseudo-Indians posed a potentially greater threat to their former military masters in their rejection of the army, as a drain on manpower, and as potential enemies. Some sought to become Indian, like "Jemmy Campbell an Irish Lad who was taken at Oswego", but who took an Oneida "Squaw" as wife and lived with her kin, or the corporal in the South Carolina Independents who had deserted to live with the Cherokee when they besieged Fort Loudoun, only to return as an emissary of his new people. Some just stirred up trouble. William Williams reported that about twenty deserters, mostly Roman Catholic, had been adopted by the local natives around the Carrying Place, and were responsible for egging the Indians on to thieving cattle, and forcing the carpenters to give them rum. These "Devilish Deserters" must be taken care of, or they "will by & by become dictators", Williams warned. The pull of native ways is suggested by the fact that, as late as a year after the fall of New France, many soldiers were still living with Indians, some as unwilling captives, but others either through choice or fear of punishment, and Thomas Gage ordered that all white men should be discovered and seized.[60]

The most "Devilish" thing for a soldier to do was not only to desert and take up Indian ways, but also to serve his new people against the old in the war. Henry Hamilton of the 48th Regiment, who deserted to the enemy in

July 1759, was seen afterward with the French army in their white uniform and with Indians at St Francis. He later returned to the British to serve in the New York Independents, but was discovered and sentenced to death. John Boyd deserted from the 28th Regiment while standing sentry in 1759 and fought for the French. His claim that he was taken by the Indians and joined the French only to escape was dismissed, and, because of the "heinous" nature of his offence, he was ordered to be hung in chains "on the very Spot where he appear'd in Arms against those Colours which he had sworn to Defend".[61]

Jonathan Burns was one of the more notorious soldiers who went native. A Massachusetts provincial who was taken captive in 1756, Burns changed sides and fought for the enemy and was only taken up as a traitor when New France fell. His greatest sin, however, was his participation in the torture death of an English soldier who had been with Rogers' Rangers in their assault on St Francis and was later captured in the autumn of 1759 near Crown Point by Burns and his Indian comrades. The prisoner was taken to Isle aux Noix, where "the Indians came to a Resolution to sacrifice the said Prisoner: that he was led out by the Indians, to a small Distance from the french Encampment, and there tortured in a most barbarous Manner".[62] Burns assisted while many French watched. Soon after Burns came to Montreal where he received clothes and other rewards "for his Services". During his court martial Burns claimed that the Indians compelled him to take part in the sacrifice, but – true to form in published execution accounts – he was said to have confessed his crime before his own execution.[63]

English soldier dismembered English soldier in an Indian torture ritual meant to cleanse away the deaths inflicted on native people at St Francis by rangers emulating native tactics and punitive violence. This spectacle describes the cultural confusion wrought by warfare that brought very different people into close and bloody contact. Jonathan Burns was executed according to long-standing European traditions of punishment for the mortal sin of becoming an Indian; his fellow soldier and victim had been butchered according to native mourning rites to bring back the Indians he had killed. Jerry was killed as a traitor to an alien race, and his head stuck on a pike in a way that looked to both European and Indian practice; it was a form of punishment and a ritual to exorcize the ghosts of the Monongahela. And let us not forget the unnamed members of the 44th Regiment who hoisted his head; for in this act, where Tyburn met Indian palisade, a new, mute vocabulary of violence was being formed that spoke of the encounter of Briton and Indian. For all these individuals, as for many other soldiers and warriors, it was not the fall of New France that was the most significant result of the war, but the severing of traditional ties and the forging of new lives, often through killing and maiming, at the cutting edge of cultural change.

Notes

I would like to thank the Huntington Library, the British Academy, the Massachusetts Historical Society, and the University of Sussex for the funding and support they provided towards the researching of this chapter.

1   A. Smith, *The wealth of nations* (London, 1962), vol. 2, p. 183.

2   [Loudoun] to the Duke of Cumberland, 20 August 1756, Loudoun Papers, North American Series, Manuscript Department, Huntington Library, San Marino, California, LO 1525, Box 33 [hereafter all LO references apply to the Loudoun Papers]; see the definition of "Colours" in *The gentleman's compleat military dictionary . . .* , 18th edn (Boston, 1759), n.p.; Johnson to Loudoun, 6 August 1756, LO 1428, Box 32; Loudoun to Daniel Webb, 11 August 1756, LO 1466, Box 33.

3   [Loudoun] to Cumberland, 20 August 1756, LO 1525, Box 35; [Loudoun] to Johnson, 8 August 1756, LO 1442, Box 33; Johnson to Loudoun, 8 August 1756, LO 1444, Box 33.

4   Gage to Loudoun, 9 August 1756, LO 1449, Box 33; Loudoun to Gage, 8 August 1756, LO 1445, Box 33; Webb to Loudoun, 10 August 1756, LO 1459, Box 33; Johnson to Loudoun, 3 Sept. 1757, LO 4392, Box 97; S. Pargellis (ed.), *Military affairs in North America 1748–1765: selected documents from the Cumberland Papers in Windsor Castle* (New Haven, Conn., 1936; repr. Hamden, Conn., 1969), p. 252.

5   T. Hayter, "The British Army 1713–1793: recent research work", *Journal of the Society for Army Historical Research* **63**, Spring 1985, pp. 11–19; J. Brewer, *The sinews of power: war, money and the English state, 1688–1673* (Cambridge, 1989); A. J. Guy, *Oeconomy and discipline: officership and administration in the British Army, 1714–63* (Manchester, 1985); T. Hayter, *The army and the crowd in mid-Georgian England* (London, 1978); J. A. Houlding, *Fit for service: the training of the British Army, 1715–95* (Oxford, 1981).

6   S. R. Frey, *The British soldier in America: a social history of military life in the Revolutionary period* (Austin, Tex., 1981); G. A. Steppler. *The common soldier in the reign of George III, 1760–1793* (D.Phd. Thesis, Oxford University, 1984).

7   J. Shy, *Toward Lexington: the role of the British Army in the coming of the Revolution* (Princeton, N.J., 1965); E. W. Carp, "Early American military history: a review of recent work", *Virginia Magazine of History and Biography* **94**(3), 1986, pp. 259–84; D. Higgonbotham, "The early American way of war: reconnaissance and appraisal", *William and Mary Quarterly*, 3rd ser., **44**(2), 1987, pp. 230–73.

8   F. Anderson, *A people's army: Massachusetts soldiers and society in the Seven Years' War* (Chapel Hill, N.C., 1984). See also: J. Titus, *The Old Dominion at war: society, politics, and warfare in late colonial Virginia* (Columbia, S.C., 1991); J. Ferling, "Soldiers for Virginia: who served in the French and Indian War?", *Virginia Magazine of History and Biography* **94**(3), 1986, pp. 307–28.

9   As recently as 1989, James Merrell decried the absence of Indians from the writings of colonial historians. "Some thoughts on colonial historians and American Indians", *William and Mary Quarterly*, 3rd ser., **44**(1), 1989, pp. 94–119.

10 D. Brown, *Bury my heart at Wounded Knee: an Indian history of the American West* (New York, 1970); J. Axtell, *After Columbus: essays in the ethnohistory of Colonial North America* (New York, 1988).

11 R. White, *The middle ground: Indians, empires, and republics in the Great Lakes region, 1650–1815* (New York, 1991), p. x. See also J. H. Merrell, *The Indians' new world: Catawbas and their neighbours from European contact through the era of removal* (Chapel Hill, N.C., 1989);

D.H. Usner, Jr., *Indians, settlers, and slaves in a frontier exchange economy: the lower Mississippi Valley before 1783* (Chapel Hill, N.C., 1992), p. 6; D. K. Richter, *The ordeal of the longhouse: the peoples of the Iroquois League in the era of European colonization* (Chapel Hill, N.C., 1992), p. 2.

12 S. M. Pargellis, *Lord Loudoun in North America* (1933; repr. Hamden, Conn., 1968), pp. 17–22; Pargellis, "The four Independent Companies of New York", in *Essays in colonial history presented to Charles McLean Andrews by his students* (1933; repr. Freeport, N.Y., 1966), pp. 96–123.

13 Forbes to Abercromby, 24 Oct. 1758, Abercromby Papers, Manuscript Department, Huntington Library, no. 788, Box 15; Wolfe to George Sackville, 30 July 1758, and Wolfe to Amherst, 8 August 1758, in B. Willson, *The life and letters of James Wolfe* (London, 1909), pp. 388, 394; Henry Pringle to anon., 15 Dec. 1757, Henry Pringle Letterbook, MG 18, L 8, microfilm reel H-1954, National Archives of Canada, Ottawa [hereafter NAC], pp. 65–66.

14 Robert Morris, "Speach to Certain Indians . . . with a Reply, 22 August 1755", in G. E. Reed (ed.), *Pennsylvania Archives*, ser. 4, vol. 2 (Harrisburg, Penn., 1900), p. 485.

15 J. E. Ferling, *A wilderness of misery: war and warriors in early America* (Westport, Conn., 1980), Chapters 1–2, p. 197.

16 "Captain Orme's Journal", in *The history of an expedition against Fort Du Quesne, in 1755; under Major-General Edward Braddock, generalissimo of H. B. M. Forces in America*, W. Sargeant (ed.) (Philadelphia, 1855), p. 291; P. E. Russell, "Redcoats in the wilderness: British officers and irregular warfare in Europe and America, 1740 to 1760", *William and Mary Quarterly*, 3rd ser., **35**(1), 1978, pp. 630, 635–40.

17 Braddock to T. Robinson, 5 June 1755, LO 581, Box 13; Extracts from George Croghan's Journal, 14 March 1757, LO 3040, Box 67; "Captain Orme's Journal", pp. 309–11.

18 "Captain Orme's Journal," pp. 341; Daniel Disney Orderly Book, 26 June 1755, Manuscript Division, Library of Congress, Washington, DC [herafter LCMD]; "Captain Orme's Journal", p. 343; Disney Orderly Book, 27 June 1755; "Captain Orme's Journal", p. 350.

19 Orme to Governor Dinwiddie, 18 July 1755, LO 606, Box 13; "Captain Orme's Journal", pp. 355–7.

20 Shirley to Robinson, 11 August 1755, LO 622, Box 13; Morris to Shirley, 30 July 1755, in *Pennsylvania Archives*, ser. 4, vol. 2, p. 444; Washington to Dinwiddie, 18 July 1755, LO 605, Box 13; on the supposed shooting of officers, see F. Jennings, *Empire of fortune: crowns, colonies, and tribes in the Seven Years' War in America* (New York, 1988), p. 158; Robinson to Shirley, 26 August 1755, LO 640, Box 14; "Inquiry into the behaviour of the troops at the Monongahela, Statement of Col. Thomas Dunbar and Lt. Col. Thomas Gage", 21 Nov. 1755, LO 685, Box 151.

21 John St Clair [to Loudoun], 12 Jan. 1756, LO 753, Box 17.

22 J. Axtell and W. C. Sturtevant, "The unkindest cut, or who invented scalping?", *William and Mary Quarterly*, 3rd. ser., **37**, July 1980, pp. 451–72; T. S. Abler, "Scalping, torture, cannibalism and rape: an ethnocultural analysis of conflicting cultural values in war", *Anthropologica* **34**(1), 1992, pp. 7–9; Richter, *Ordeal of the longhouse*, pp. 32–7.

23 Abler, "Scalping, torture, cannibalism and rape", pp. 9–13; Richter, *Ordeal of the longhouse*, pp. 35–6, 65–70.

24 T. Brown, *A plain narrative of the uncommon sufferings, and remarkable deliverance of Thomas Brown. . . .* (Boston, 1760); quotations from pp. 7, 16–17, 19–20, 21.

25 Johnson to Shirley, 9 Sept. 1755, LO 644, Box 14; Christopher French Journals, vol. 1, 10 June 1761, LCMD.

26 Shirley, Petition to King George II [Jan. 1756], LO 2591, Box 59; Maj. Gen. Hopson to Loudoun, 21 Sept. 1757, LO 4513, Box 100; Abercromby to Loudoun, 14 Feb. 1758, LO 5594, Box 120; Eyre Massy to John Forbes, 14 Feb. 1758, LO 5596, Box 120.

27 [John Appy,] "Some Facts Stated, that prove the French to have been the Agressors in North America" [1756], LO 5177, Box 57; Anonymous, *The cruel massacre of the Protestants in North-America; showing how the French and Indians joined together to scalp the English . . .* (London, 1761); Axtell and Sturtevant argue that bounties commercialized what was formerly native ritual, thereby spreading the practice amongst both Indians and Europeans in the colonial era. "Who invented scalping?", pp. 468–70.

28 Major General Shirley's additional instructions to Major General Johnson, 20 Dec. 1755, LO 713, Box 15; [Loudoun] Instructions for Capt. Jacob Cheeksaunkun, 2 Sept. 1756, LO 1679, Box 38.

29 Muster Roll for Capt. Robert Rogers' Company, 28 Sept.–24 Oct. 1756, LO 2570, Box 54; John Noyes, "Journal of John Noyes of Newbury in the Expedition against Ticonderoga, 1758", Essex Institute, *Historical Collections* 45, 1909, p. 75; A Merchant at Halifax to Joseph Turner, 20 June, 1758, and Pilot of the English Admiral to his Friend at Halifax, 13 June 1758, in Samuel Hazard (ed.), *Pennsylvania Archives*, series 1, vol. 3 (Philadelphia, 1853), pp. 443–4.

30 *Orderly book and journal of Major John Hawks on the Ticonderoga–Crown Point campaign, under General Jeffery Amherst 1759–1760*, Hugh Hastings (ed.) (New York, 1911), p. 11; Col. Laurence Halloran, Diary, 23 August 1759, MG 18, N 52, mfm reel A-928, NAC; [Loudoun] to Abercromby, 11 Nov. 1756, LO 2196, Box 50; General Monckton's Orderly Book, 27 July 1759, Monckton Papers, Northcliffe Collection, MG 18 M, NAC, vol. 23, mfm. reel C-366.

31 Abler, "Scalping, torture, cannibalism and rape", pp. 9–12; Richter, *Ordeal of the longhouse*, pp. 35–6.

32 *Journal of Gen. Rufus Putnam kept in northern New York during four campaigns of the old French and Indian War, 1757–1760*, E. C. Dawes (ed.) (Albany, N.Y., 1886), p. 35.

33 *The journal of Dr. Caleb Rea*, ed. F. M. Ray (Salem, Mass., 1881), p. 31.

34 William Williams to all in Authority, 28 March 1756, LO 977, Box 21; deposition of Richard Williams, 5 Feb. 1757, LO 2780, Box 62.

35 CO/5/1064/140–42, Minutes of a General Court of Inquiry held at the City of Albany, 18 July 1752.

36 D. Hay, P. Linebaugh, J. G. Rule, E. P. Thompson, C. Winslow, *Albion's fatal tree: crime and society in eighteenth-century England* (New York, 1975); E. P. Thompson, *Whigs and hunters: the origins of the Black Act* (Harmondsworth, 1975).

37 A. N. Gilbert, "The regimental courts martial in the eighteenth century British Army", *Albion* 8(1), 1976, pp. 50–66, and "The changing face of British military justice, 1757–1783", *Military Affairs* 49, April 1985, pp. 80–84; Frey, *British soldier in America*, Chapter 4; Steppler, *Common soldier*, Chapter 4; Jennings, *Empire of fortune*, pp. 208–9.

38 Wolfe to Sackville, 30 July 1758, in Willson, *Life and letters of James Wolfe*, p. 389; Wolfe [to Robert Monckton], 25 July 1759, Monckton Papers, Northcliffe Collection, vol. 22.

39 Instructions for Cheeksaunkun, 2 Sept. 1756, LO 1679, Box 38.

40 Christopher French Journals, vol. 1, 10 June 1761, 12 June–2 July 1761; WO/34/40/95–8, Lt. Col. Grant's Journal of the Expedition against the Cherokee, 7 June–9 July 1761; WO34/39/93, Francis Grant, John Darby and Archibald Gordon to Amherst, 2 July 1759.

41 Francis Parkman and Howard Peckham both alleged that blankets from the smallpox hospital at Fort Pitt were given to Delawares in 1764 so as to cause an epidemic and undercut the Indian uprising. Bernhard Knollenberg disagrees, but acknowledges that Amherst certainly was not averse to such a tactic; Francis Jennings, however, accepts the account. Bernard Knollenberg, "General Amherst and germ warfare", *Mississippi Valley Historical Review* **41**, June 1954–March 1955, pp. 489–94; Jennings, *Empire of fortune*, pp. 447–8.

42 William Williams, Accounts from 22 Nov. 1755 to 10 June 1756, LO 686, Box 15; Richard Mather, Cash paid Indians for Publick Services, 21 March 1761, and The Crown to Thomas Hutchins, 21 March 1761, in Accounts, Receipts, etc., relating to Fort Pitt, Monckton Papers, vol. 40.

43 "Journal of John Montresor's expedition to Detroit in 1763", in J. C. Webster, *Life of John Montresor* (Ottawa, 1928), p. 12. There are numerous references to Indian trackers of deserters in the Courts Martial Records of the War Office Papers. See, for example: WO/71/71/147–57, 173–5.

44 William Byrd to Loudoun, 30 April 1758, Abercromby Papers, no. 217, Box 5; Warrants on William Johnson, 24 Nov. 1756, LO 2623, Box 52; [Eleazer Fitch] A Return of the New York Regiment to go on a Furlough, 10 Nov. 1756, LO 3464, Box 50.

45 Thomas Butler, 4 May 1756, LO 1106, Box 24; [Loudoun] to the Earl of Halifax, 26 Dec. 1756, LO 2416, Box 56; Johnson to Loudoun, 17 March 1757, LO 3073, Box 56; "Some Thoughts upon the British Interest in North America", nos. 1 and 2, 8 August, 4 Sept. 1755, in E. B. O'Callaghan (ed.), *Documents relative to the colonial history of the State of New York; procured in Holland, England and France*, vol. 7 (Albany, N.Y., 1856), pp. 29–31; [William Johnson,] "Expense of a Regiment of 500 Indians", 15 March 1757, LO 3063, Box 68.

46 P. Frazier, *The Mohicans of Stockbridge* (Lincoln, Neb., 1975), pp. 113–14, Chapters 10–11; Loudoun to Pitt, 14 Feb. 1758, LO 5598, Box 120; Jacob Cheeksaunkun and Jacob Naunauphtaunk to Loudoun, 14 Feb. 1758, LO 5592, Box 120; Engagement of the Stockbridge Indians [Feb.] 1758, LO 5799, Box 120; Warrants on Abraham Mortier, 19 July 1758, LO 934, Box 10; Amherst quoted in Frazier, *Mohicans of Stockbridge*, p. 129; WO/34/39/126, Robert Rogers to Amherst, 24 April 1760; WO/34/39/386, Johnson to Amherst, 22 July 1763; WO/4/39/391, Amherst to Johnson, 4 August 1763.

47 Notes relating to the Management of the Indians [Feb. 1756], LO 2476, Box 19.

48 Loudoun, Heads of Instruction for Col. Webb, 23 Feb. 1756, LO 848, Box 19; [Loudoun] to Cumberland, 20 August 1756, LO 1525, Box 35.

49 Cumberland to Loudoun, 22 Oct.–23 Dec. 1756 [15 Dec.], LO 2065, Box 47.

50 Hardy to Abercromby, 2 Dec. 1757, Abercromby Papers, AB 5, Box 1.

51 Wolfe to Sackville, 24 May 1758, in Willson, *Life and letters of James Wolfe*, p. 369.

52 Maj. George Scott, "Description of Arming and accoutring and cloathing Rangers", [13 Feb.] 1758, LO 6927, Box 120.

53 Abercromby to Loudoun, 18 Dec. 1757, LO 5038, Box 111; "Yearly Expences of a Company of Rangers" [18 Dec. 1757], LO 5039, Box 111; Loudoun to Pitt, 14 Feb. 1758, LO 5598, Box 120; Pargellis, *Lord Loudoun in North America*, p. 305; Jeffery Amherst, *A journal of the landing of His Majesty's Forces on the Island of Cape-Breton, and of the siege and surrender of Louisbourg . . .*, 3rd edn (Boston, [1758]), p. 6; Joseph Nichols, Journal, 3 Oct. 1758, HM 89, Huntington Library.

54 R[ichard] H[uck] to Loudoun, 29 May 1758, LO 5837, Box 124.

55 "Diaries kept by Lemuel Wood, of Boxford; with an introduction and notes", ed. S.

Perley, Essex Institute, *Historical Collections* **19**, July–Sept. 1882, p. 184; [Anonymous] Journal, 9 Jan. 1762, vol. 3, Mackenzie Collection; Christopher French Journals, 11 June 1763, vol. 2.

56 [Johnson] to Shirley, 25 May 1756, LO 1178, Box 26; Orderly Book of the 3rd Battalion of the Pennsylvania Regiment, 25 June, 11 July 1758, HM 613, Huntington Library; [Abercromby] to Johnson, 26 Sept. 1758, Abercromby Papers, no. 699, Box 13; WO/34/39/234, Minutes of the Several Proceedings, encl. Johnson to Amherst, 6 Dec. 1761, pp. 211–13.

57 J. Axtell, "The white Indians of colonial America", *William and Mary Quarterly*, 3rd ser., **32**, 1975, pp. 17–44.

58 Deposition of Richard Williams, 5 Feb. 1757, LO 2780, Box 62; Examination of James Swan concerning Richard Williams, 5 Jan. 1758, LO 5344, Box 115.

59 See: WO/71/68/8–9, 11–14; WO/71/70/281–3; WO/71/68/108–11, 143–44.

60 Henry Wendell to Johnson [17 Dec. 1757], LO 6861, Box 111; Christopher French Journals, 25 August 1761, vol. 1; William Williams [to Johnson], [March 1756], LO 994, Box 22; WO/34/5/90, 142, Gage to Amherst, 9 April, 26 May 1761.

61 WO/71/68/303–5; WO/71/68/9–11.

62 John Ogilvie, Chaplain to the 60th Regt., "The Substance of Jonathan Burns's Confession, a few Minutes before his Execution on the 7th of April last", n.d.

63 WO/71/68/147–55; WO/34/5/194, Gage to Amherst, 21 August 1761; WO/34/5/196.

Chapter Seven

Protecting trade through war: Choctaw elites and British occupation of the Floridas

Greg O'Brien

The conclusion of the Seven Years' War caused anxiety among Native Americans throughout eastern North America. As French troops withdrew from Canada, Louisiana, and the Ohio Valley, Indians wondered what a world with only one major European power would mean for them. In the South-East, Britain occupied former French territory along the Gulf Coast and up the eastern shore of the Mississippi River (West Florida) in addition to Spanish territory in Florida (then called East Florida). Only New Orleans remained in non-British hands, although it became Spanish, rather than French, in 1766. French abandonment of the continent forced Indians to confront Britain as the sole supplier of trade.

Choctaws found this adjustment particularly difficult. Prior to 1763, they relied upon trade with France to supply many of their necessities. Few Choctaw leaders had met any British traders or officials until a major conference at Mobile in 1765. At that meeting, all of the Choctaw speakers alerted their new neighbours to the importance of supplying Choctaws with goods. For example, Nassuba Mingo appealed to John Stuart, the British Southern Indian Superintendent, that

> I expect my people will receive presents in greater abundance, and if we do not, it must proceed from want of affection in their Father, & not from want of Ability, I do not speak for myself but for my Warriours, their Wives & their Children, whom I cannot Cloathe, or keep in order without presents.[1]

Britain failed, in the 1760s and 1770s, to equip Choctaw headmen with sufficient clothing, metal goods, paint, guns, and ammunition. This placed further strain on an already difficult relation and contributed to political instability.

By the 1760s, trade relations with Europeans affected Choctaw social stability directly. Since at least Mississippian times (*c.* 1100–*c.* 1600), southeastern Indian leaders maintained a level of non-coercive power and authority necessary to the preservation of social order by redistributing high-prestige items to their families and followers. France supported this ideal before 1763 by funnelling presents through established leaders. French trade with the Choctaws occurred once a year at Mobile, at which time Choctaw chiefs gave deerskins to French officials and French governors reciprocated with ample gifts of their own. Thus, trade took the form of an elaborate, ritualized gift-exchange that bolstered chiefly power through their control of goods which they redistributed according to the demands of kinship responsibilities and political needs.[2] The new British presence brought about a radically different trade relationship that centred on private enterprise and market values rather than diplomatic gift exchange. This threatened Choctaw chiefly authority.[3]

The problem for the chiefs was adjusting to a new set of rules. Independent British traders travelled directly to Choctaw villages and frequently bartered with non-chiefs for deerskins. Superintendent Stuart attempted to regulate the traders, but he faced stiff opposition as the southern colonies proved unwilling to relinquish their right to grant licences freely. Stuart found that although every Choctaw village (numbering between forty and fifty) had white people who traded and lived in it, only three traders in the nation held licences: "the rest were only authorized to trade by two or three Merchants in South Carolina and Georgia".[4] Abuses flourished as traders and their assistants assaulted Choctaw women, bartered with alcohol, and cheated Choctaws out of promised goods.[5]

At the same time, Choctaw chiefs no longer received annual presents as they had from the French. British officials understood perfectly well the difference between their system and that of France; West Florida Governor George Johnstone outlined the severe adjustments that would be necessary on the part of the Choctaws:

> The French have accustomed both the Upper Creeks and Chactaws to such large Presents, that it will be difficult to break that Custom, until they are convinced of Our Superiority and their Dependence, which can only be done by Time, and a well regulated Trade restraining the general Licences; Or, by an immediate War.[6]

Market-driven, British trade did little to maintain chiefly authority. The state, in the form of the British imperial system, managed the distribution of gifts to Indians when they visited British officials at Mobile or Pensacola, but left the more mundane trading activities to private individuals and companies. Thus, trade with the British supplied necessities to the Choctaws, but it failed to obey customs that enabled chiefs to maintain power by controlling the flow of goods.

Since the trade remained unregulated, this new structure threatened the redistributive roles of the chiefs and rendered them politically weakened. Choctaw leaders explained to the British that their young men were virtually uncontrollable unless they received presents that enabled them to fulfill their redistributive function. As early as 1764, they alerted the British that gifts of trade goods would quiet the "young men at home [who] will think the English look upon them as friends".[7] But the British did not agree that the worth of such assemblies matched the huge expense.[8] Only two major gift-giving conferences were held before the American Revolution; one in 1765, the other during the winter of 1771/1772.

Young men adapted by ignoring chiefly jurisdiction over the trade. Some of them circumvented British contact by trading with the Spanish and their French employees in New Orleans. Any man could acquire deerskins and exchange them directly with traders for the goods he desired. This loosening of control succeeded in putting more hunters in the woods in pursuit of deerskins. Whitetail deer supplied a vital source of food to Choctaws and their skins formed the basis of trade relations with Europeans. Also, Choctaw men hunted to gain prestige by showcasing their skills and proving their ability to contribute to a family's economic wellbeing. Successful hunting, as well as war exploits, further provided young men with the necessary accomplishments to acquire titles marking their transition from boys to men. Adult titles differentiated men from their mothers, who gave them their original boyhood name, and from women generally.[9] Direct participation in the trade gave non-elite males one way to handle a changed world, but there remained other options, such as preying upon British traders and outlying settlers.

Acts of violence and raids on European settlements escalated throughout the 1760s and the threat of armed conflict between the Choctaws and the British loomed ever larger. Both British and Choctaw leaders worked hard to avoid that scenario.[10] Choctaw headmen sought amicable trade relations in order to acquire the European manufactures on which Choctaws relied. War with the sole supplier of those goods promised disaster, but individuals and villages were entitled to behave as they saw fit to counteract the anguish engendered by the entrepreneurial system. Native groups throughout eastern North America felt these pressures owing to British ascendancy after the Seven Years' War. Several factors contributed to this, but "the withholding of gifts [by the British] must stand as one of the principal causes" of open tensions such as Pontiac's Revolt.[11]

British military and civil officials seized upon their own solution to the growing predicament. Their primary objective regarding south-eastern

Indians, after trade, aimed to prevent attacks on British settlers and traders. The numbers of potential Indian warriors in the South-East, from the Creeks in the East to the Choctaws in the West, easily surpassed the sum of British troops in the Floridas.[12] Creeks expressed much displeasure at British occupation of the Floridas, and had already killed British traders. British Indian policy initially sought to pacify them, with intimidation if necessary. At the same time, Britain could ill afford to enter into a war with a sizeable native enemy. Consequently, British officials encouraged the Choctaws to do their dirty work for them.

General Thomas Gage, the British military commander for North America, encouraged Superintendent Stuart to prompt a conflict between the Creeks and Choctaws:

> I therefore can't recommend it too strongly to you, so to foment the . . . bickering of the several tribes against each other and excite that jealousy so natural to all savages as shall be consistent with the peace security and welfare of His Majesty's subjects.[13]

From the British point of view, an inter-tribal war solved the problem of potentially dangerous Indian men. When the Creeks and Choctaws obliged British designs by getting into such a war, Governor Johnstone displayed his satisfaction:

> The present Rupture is very fortunate for us, more especially as it has been effected without giving them the least possibility of thinking we had any share in it. It was undoubtedly our Interest to foment the Disputes between those Nations . . . [and] I am of Opinion we should feed the war.[14]

British officials congratulated themselves for starting the war and did their part to see it continue. Accordingly, most scholarly explanations of this war have focused on the British role as instigators.[15]

Choctaw and Creek reasons for fighting the war, however, did not include British meddling. In fact, with a few recent exceptions, scholars have over-estimated the impact of European intruders, such as Gage and Johnstone.[16] From the point of view of Choctaw elites, ongoing assaults between their warriors and the Creeks presented a solution to a society in turmoil. Instead of permitting revenge killings to remain localized, headmen chose to escalate the conflict into a full-fledged war. Quickly, they realized the potential of war with the Creeks to bridge the growing generational breach with their young men. Young men sought honour and prestige by participating in successful war parties, and they also needed an outlet for their antagonism towards trade abuses. Inter-tribal war offered an opportunity for headmen and warriors to pursue a common objective, while attempting to avoid violence towards Europeans in order to protect the trade relationship. War parties also required the power and expertise of established war leaders and therefore automatically re-established a degree of chiefly authority. By promoting war, elites demonstrated that they were men of action, an essential characteristic for those who make claims to power.[17]

Choctaw reaction to the killing of a man named Suei Nantla by Creek Indians in the spring of 1766 supports this interpretation. Leaving no doubt of their identity, the Creek war party scalped the Choctaw and left "a Bloody War Stick and other hostile signals near [the body]".[18] The warclub produced its desired effect, for avenging Choctaw warriors soon killed six Creeks and captured a woman.[19] "Without doubt they'll have it Hot & Warm", John McGillivray, a British trader, predicted.[20] The warclub and a black bird's wing placed with Suei Nantla's body provided the needed spark – Choctaw leaders insisted the killing be punished in force:

> . . . the Chactaws have sent a Challenge to Emistecigo [Upper Creek leader from the village of Little Tallassee] & they say they have lost above twenty Men at different Times, which makes them send this Challenge, as they are sure the Creeks have killed them. The Chactaws say they will send 100 Men to lye between Pensacola & the Upper Creeks to kill all they can find, & 100 Men against the Wolf Kings Town [Upper Creek leader from the village of Muccolossus] to destroy it, & 100 More against Paucana Talakasa [Little Tallassee] & have reserved 500 in the Nation to guard the women & Children, & told them that they would fight them in the Plains & not behind Trees like Cowards.[21]

That the Choctaws issued this threat of well-planned massive retaliation, involving numbers of warriors beyond the capacity of any single village, establishes inter-village agreement among elites. Because warriors from all three Choctaw political divisions, the western, eastern, and Sixtowns, participated in the war from an early date, inter-divisional co-operation existed as well.

Consensus between the Choctaw divisions rarely existed in practice and makes the Choctaw decision to wage war on the Creeks exceptional. However, the turbulent situation faced by all elites united them in common cause. They told the British that inter-tribal war enabled them to control aggressive warriors, "who not having done any feats during the War, think to gain Reputation and Name of Warrior by not consenting to make peace".[22] Chiefs earned respect from their fellow villagers by acquiring needed European goods, organizing hunting expeditions, conducting sacred rituals, leading war parties, and supervising relations with outsiders. The expanding conflict with the Creeks empowered chiefs to perform all of those roles.

Creek chiefs agreed that "[the war] will be a means of giving our young Men full exercise by which means the Chiefs expect to be the better able to govern them".[23] As the Creek leader Wolf King put it, "I am not sorry for it [war with the Choctaws], I will keep them [young men] at Home and from doing Mischief to the White people who I look on as Brothers".[24] Another Creek leader, "Effatiskiniha", also known as "Mackay's Friend," told British agent David Taitt in 1772 that he led the first war party against the Choctaws and seized captives: "He says that he made war on purpose to keep his young people from falling out with the English, and as soon as his nation makes peace with the Choctaws he will spoil it again as he knows they must be at war with somebody." Such Creek sentiments describe the Choctaw position as well.[25]

Using war against the Creeks as the main method of protecting the trade relationship with Britain, Choctaw headmen never abandoned their lobbying efforts on behalf of gifts. Early in the war, all three Choctaw political divisions sent emissaries to Mobile. Mingo Houma Chito ("Great Red Leader") from the village of East Imongoulasha (eastern division) pleaded in 1766 that lack of supplies threatened social stability: "my extreme poverty alone obliged me to come and trouble you this Day, particularly Ammunition, as for want of it I may have my head cut off in my own Town, and not be able to help myself . . . [with] some ammunition to carry home; *I will send some work to my idle Warriors, who want it much.*"[26] Tomatle Mingo ("Leader who finishes or destroys") from Seneacha (Sixtowns division) promised that he could prevent contact between his young men and New Orleans traders if the British furnished supplies.[27] Shulustamastabé ("Red Shoes"), from the village of West Yazoo (western division) recalled the British promise to keep them well supplied:

> But I am sorry to find I am poor for ammunition, while I am surrounded with Enemies who are supplied it by the English toward the rising Sun [traders from Georgia and South Carolina], which gives them [Creeks] every Advantage they can wish for over us.[28]

Once having decided that war with the Creeks was both unavoidable and advantageous, Choctaw chiefs, warriors, and young men who wished "to gain Reputation and name of Warrior",[29] manipulated the war towards several purposes. In order to succeed, war parties required sufficient ammunition and guns from the British. British officials proved quite willing to dispense the necessary weapons to Choctaws who promised to use them against the Creeks, but many warriors desired the supplies in order to hunt and thus participate more fully in the trade.[30] Choctaw men rationalized that either use of the weapons would allow them to prove "that all the Chactaws are not old Women".[31] Success in either hunting or war awarded Choctaw men the "abi" (or "abé") suffix to their name, designating them as "killers" or "slayers", giving them higher status.[32] At times, the two methods of procuring rank overlapped one another and resulted in tragedy.

In the autumn of 1767, for instance, hundreds of Choctaw men from all three divisions flooded the British posts at Tombeckby, Pensacola, and Mobile asking for guns and ammunition. Choctaws started their annual deer hunts in the autumn, but the British insisted that they use the supplies to attack the Creeks. One chief, Red Captain, of the village of Shatalaya in the eastern division, heeded the call and paid the ultimate price.[33] Out of a reported eight hundred Choctaws who travelled to Tombeckby to get ammunition, only Red Captain and a force of 42 warriors stayed to strike the Creeks. Approximately 150 Creeks ambushed the party, killed 24 Choctaws and tortured Red Captain, skinning him alive.[34] Red Captain had a long record of working in the interest of the British, making his loss doubly profound. Most troubling from the British point of view, however, was the reluctance of other Choctaws to fight. Even the supposedly pro-British Shulustamastabé fled the battle soon after it began.[35] Although the deaths of 25 Choctaw warriors, including Red Captain's son and 12 others from his village, provoked cries for revenge, little retaliation took place. Prospective leaders were more interested in acquiring Red Captain's position as a British Great Medal Chief, which entitled them to extra gifts and greater access to trade goods.[36]

Young men certainly desired war titles and honours, but it seems that they often attempted the least dangerous method of attaining that higher status. In Red Captain's case, too few young men chose to attack the Creeks. In another instance, young men attacked a lone traveller too readily.

In February 1767, a war party led by the Small Medal Chief Chocoulacta, from the village of "Ebitabougoula ouchy" in the eastern division, accidentally killed a British settler while on the path from South Carolina to Natchez. Confused by the dark of night, Chocoulacta and "young men greedy of war names had flown to the man & scalped him before they knew him to be a white man".[37] The killing sparked an immediate reaction from divisional headmen. Several eastern division chiefs, including Olacta Houma, of "Iteokchakko", who was the "landlord" of Chocoulacta and his village, confirmed the killing and met to decide on punishment. Divisional chiefs, who were most responsible for overseeing relations with outsiders, perceived the murder as a serious threat to the maintenance of a mutually beneficial attachment to the British. Evidently, they had the authority to kill Chocoulacta in order to appease the British and prevent a rift from forming which jeopardized the trade relationship. Because he had admitted his mistake and reported it to Olacta Houma, the chiefs decided that Chocoulacta need not die.

Instead, Chocoulacta promised to bury the scalp and return the traveller's saddle and gun to the British commander at Fort Tombeckby. But the headmen remained extremely concerned about what the effects on the British might be, "in particular Olacta Houma his landlord, that he charged [Chocoulacta] to give no credits to the men that had been sent out to war with [him]".[38] Not only did the young men and warriors involved not receive recognition for a war exploit, but Olacta Houma confiscated Chocoulacta's British medal and even threatened to make him wear animal skins instead of his high-status manufactured clothing.[39] The eastern division headmen remained so concerned about this killing of an innocent British man that they sent a horse and deerskins to Superintendent Stuart as atonement, three years later! When it came to war and the honours to be gained by taking part, divisional headmen, even those like Olacta Houma who held no obvious recognition of status from the British, controlled the reins of power.[40]

The Choctaw division involved in the incidents concerning Red Captain and Chocoulacta (the eastern division) and the western division were the first to regard war with the Creeks as perhaps more harmful than beneficial. For five years war between the Choctaws and Creeks had continued, "in their manner, very few killed, but all in perpetual apprehension on both sides".[41] The Creeks were by far the more militant side, even going to the extreme of attacking the Chickasaws and the occasional British trader. Despite Chickasaw involvement on the side of the Choctaws and a Creek congress with the British in 1768 (during which they were resupplied with guns and ammunition), by 1770 both sides extended peace overtures. In particular, the western and eastern divisions of the Choctaws and the Upper Towns of the Creeks (the Creek political division located along the Coosa and Tallapoosas Rivers and closest to the Choctaws) sought peace. They exchanged tobacco, pipes, strings of white beads, and white swans' wings and the negotiations produced real progress. Yet, although most people of both sides desired peace, there were a few fellows excepted on both sides, who not having done any feats during the War, think to gain Reputation and Name of Warrior by not consenting to make peace".[42] In particular, men from the Choctaw Sixtowns division and the Creek Lower Towns (the political division of Creek villages located on the Chatahoochee River), who had largely avoided participation in the war to this point, hoped to gain prestige through success in battle. Both Choctaws and Creeks viewed an attack by any member of the other as a renewal of the war, and when the Creeks murdered four Choctaws and kidnapped the niece of Mingo Houma Chito, a Great Medal Chief, peace dissolved in an outburst of revenge.[43] Once again the autonomy of divisions and young men proved decisive in circumventing the chiefs' attempts at co-operation.[44]

Other circumstances worked against the peace as well. John Stuart insisted, and the Creek Upper Towns and Choctaw western and eastern divisions accepted, that he act as a mediator to end the war. The use of neutral third parties to end conflicts was a common feature of south-eastern Indian diplomacy.[45] Stuart attempted to bring about reconciliation until he received instructions from London that British imperial ambitions would be better served by keeping the two groups at odds. Because Britain had removed most of its troops from West Florida in the late 1760s to cut expenses, the government of West Florida feared that peace between Choctaws and Creeks would increase Indian visits and depredations. Additionally, Shawnee efforts to recruit Creeks into an anti-British confederacy increased British desires to see the Creeks occupied with an inter-tribal war. By December 1770, Stuart applauded himself for preventing the peace, notwithstanding the case that "Both Nations, with great reason, consider us as the Incendiaries who kindled the war".[46]

Choctaw leaders realized that peace was impossible as long as their destiny was so inextricably tied to British goals. Britain lacked the military capacity to defeat the Choctaws had they desired to do so, but they could disrupt relations between the Choctaws and Creeks and threaten to withhold the trade. Choctaw elites shifted their strategy after the peace failed; eastern division leaders abandoned the peace efforts, whereas chiefs of the western division preserved an open line of communication through the Chickasaws to the Creek Upper Towns. Leaders of both Choctaw divisions used the leverage of thousands of potentially uncontrollable warriors to chastise the British for supplying the Creeks while not doing the same for them. They demanded another gift-giving congress with which to reassert their redistributive authority and consequently keep young warriors in line.[47]

This time the pressure worked. Britain acquiesced finally in the winter of 1771/1772, holding a conference more than six years after the previous one. Several medal chiefs had died in the meantime, some like Red Captain at the head of war parties against the Creeks, and the rise of new contenders to chiefly status needed to be verified with medals. This, plus the necessary gift exchanges and ceremonies, reaffirmed the Choctaw–British relationship. Contingents from each village left Mobile in January 1772, well supplied with guns, ammunition, cloth, and other merchandise.[48]

Although they continued to pursue peace with the Creeks, western division leaders simultaneously sent war parties against them. The other two divisions also continued to war, largely unsuccessfully, with the Creeks. In one battle during 1772, for instance, Creeks killed 15 Choctaws while losing none of their own. Even Emistisiguo, who in the past had been very receptive to Choctaw peace overtures, led a party which scalped seven Choctaws. Two Choctaw Great Medal Chiefs, Tattoully Mastabé from Coosas and Cholko Oulacta from Ayanabe, and one Small Medal Chief, Yasi Mattaha from East Yazoo, lost their lives in the ongoing fighting. Despite the guns and other gifts received at the 1771/1772 congress, Choctaw fortunes in the war seemed only to worsen.[49]

Suddenly, in 1773, Choctaw prospects in the eight-year-old war reversed. Well supplied and probably incensed at the loss of more medal chiefs, they began to defeat large Creek war parties. For the first time in the war, Choctaw chiefs seemed to recognize that the conflict must be brought to a favourable conclusion, rather than merely allowing it to fester without a decisive end. Their aggressive pursuit of Creeks garnered still more material support from the British and in turn strengthened the position of leaders. Britain helped further, in 1774, by cutting off trade with the Creeks in response to the killing of Georgia settlers. British officials failed to employ that strategy earlier out of fear the Creeks would react violently. But attacks on settlers required imme-diate and drastic actions, and the war with the Choctaws weakened Creek retaliation. The beneficiaries, as expected, were the Choctaws. Knowing the Creeks were poorly armed, Choctaws assailed them with large numbers. Choctaw leaders, such as Taska Oumastabé from the western division and Captain Houma from the Sixtowns, journeyed to Mobile specifically offering their assistance to the British to punish the Creeks for killing Georgians. For the next two years they enjoyed stunning victories. They severely wounded Emistisiguo in an ambush, boldly attacked stragglers on the outskirts of Creek villages, and, most impressively, killed the staunchly anti-British Creek leader "The Mortar" and several of his men. Soon the Creeks suffered severe deprivation as they were unable to hunt safely. They appealed to the Chickasaws to help end the war once and for all.[50]

It so happened that a British imperial crisis aided the peace efforts. In 1775 instructions from General Gage and London urged Superintendent Stuart to promote peace between all of the southern Indian groups in order to en-able their possible deployment against American "rebels". Western division Choctaws and Upper Towns Creeks began negotiations, with the Chickasaws acting as intermediaries. Realizing that the two groups "are intent on making peace",[51] John Stuart initiated mediating efforts of his own.[52]

Stuart's efforts reached fruition in October 1776. Choctaw and Creek peace delegations, dominated by the Choctaw western and eastern divisions and the Creek Upper Towns, met in Pensacola and performed an elaborate diplomatic ritual to signify the end of fighting. Both groups, displaying white flags and white swan's wings, marched into an open area, stopping three hundred yards apart. The chiefs sang "peace songs" while waving eagle and swan's wings over their heads. In a clever acknowledgement of the part that warriors and would-be warriors played in starting and continuing the war, a "false battle" was performed by the Choctaw and Creek young men. Then the two groups met, joined hands, and presented two red warclubs to Stuart to signify laying down their arms.[53] Further negotiations lasted two days. Final reconciliation took place the following July when a Choctaw delegation, headed by western division leaders, travelled to Emistisiguo's village of Little Tallassee and invited Creek chiefs to visit and assure the nation, the "young people" in particular, that peace was a reality.[54] Headmen from both sides clearly dominated the peace proceedings, but British generosity made internal social cohesion possible as both groups enjoyed frequent and plentiful gifts. The influx of guns and other items helped ensure a degree of Indian loyalty to the British as the War for American Independence began and, more importantly, bolstered the position of native leaders within their respective societies.[55]

Choctaw chiefs weathered a nearly two-decade-long storm before they saw the return of gift-giving congresses on an annual basis. Spain, after defeating Britain in West Florida during the American Revolution, continued the annual congresses and regulated traders in Choctaw villages by giving the British Panton, Leslie & Company a monopoly on the Indian trade.[56] During the 1780s and 1790s, chiefs, especially those from the western division who came of age during the years of war with the Creeks, sought to establish additional trade relationships with Georgia and the United States, in part to satisfy disgruntled young men. Choctaws also continued to war with other native groups, especially those on the western side of the Mississippi River, as a way to channel animosities and provide opportunities for young men to acquire status.

Changed economic relations brought about by British occupation of the Floridas destabilized Choctaw political and social norms. Young men caused the anxiety which their chiefs, and many British traders and administrators, experienced. By attacking European property, they forced their chiefs to become more aggressive with the British and the Creeks. They ignored chiefly authority by interacting with British traders on their own initiative. Moreover, the power and authority that headmen exercised depended upon other Choctaws perceiving them as leaders. As abuses related to the trade relationship continued unabated, who were young men to turn to but themselves? Young men travelled to New Orleans to trade with the Spanish and French, and hunted ever greater numbers of deer to participate more effectively in the British trade. Choctaw elites demonstrated an inability to control their fellow villagers unless they acquired the presents of trade goods which made redistribution possible.

Nevertheless, headmen such as Olacta Houma, whose status did not rest upon British recognition, maintained their authority as the only legitimate decision makers and granters of war titles. The authority of such men rested in a sphere which originated solely within Choctaw culture. These men recognized the potential of an inter-tribal war to alleviate internal stress through a bonding of purpose with their young men. For some elites, such as Red Captain who did enjoy British recognition of his status, that bonding resulted in a fatal sacrifice to the goal of cross-generational cohesion.

We know that Native American inter-tribal warfare sometimes acted to remove competitors for trade resources or to replace population losses through adoption of war captives, as with the "Beaver Wars" between the Iroquois and Hurons.[57] Still others fought to conquer new lands, such as Lakota Sioux expansion on to the Plains.[58] In the Choctaw–Creek war, however, we are faced with reasons for fighting based upon generational conflict, the need to gain higher status, and the desire to transfer anxieties caused by changing economic relationships on to non-European targets, thus protecting access to value-laden goods. What is most striking is the sense that this solution to diverse predicaments by the Choctaws was not at all new. Archeological evidence shows us that there was inter-tribal warfare through-out the South-East before European arrival.[59] The reasons for those conflicts are perhaps forever obscure, but it is tempting to view Choctaw and Creek actions towards each other in the 1760s and 1770s as a manifestation of pre-contact notions of the proper way to handle a society-threatening crisis.

When Nassuba Mingo lost the power to "control" his "Warriours, their Wives & their Children",[60] he and other elites preserved their authority by the best means available; they deflected tensions away from one source of authority and used them to bolster another. By so doing, they exhibited the resourcefulness necessary for preservation in an altered and rapidly changing world.

Notes

1 Dunbar Rowland (ed.), *Mississippi provincial archives: English dominion, 1763–1766* (Nashville, Tenn., 1911), p. 242, hereafter cited as *MPAED*.

2 Small numbers of French traders ventured to Choctaw villages and affiliated themselves with village leaders, thus preserving chiefly control. See Patricia Galloway, " 'The chief who is your father': Choctaw and French views of the diplomatic relation", in *Powhatan's*

mantle: Indians in the colonial Southeast, Peter Wood, Gregory Waselkov, Thomas Hatley (eds) (Lincoln, Nebr., 1989), p. 271. For eighteenth-century references to Choctaw leaders' authority resting upon persuasion and redistributive abilities, see Jean Bernard Bossu, Travels through that part of North America formerly called Louisiana (English trans., London, 1771), pp. 294–5; Bernard Romans, A concise natural history of East and West Florida (1775; rpt. Gainesville, Fla., 1962), p. 76; and "Memoir on Indians by Kerlerec [French Governor in New Orleans]", 12 Dec. 1758", in Mississippi provincial archives: French dominion, Patricia K. Galloway, Dunbar Rowland, A. G. Sanders (eds) (Baton Rouge, La., 1984), vol. 5, p. 214, hereafter cited as MPAFD.

3   The disruptions of the Seven Years War prevented the French from holding annual congresses in the early 1760s, contributing further to Choctaw social disruption and exposing their utter dependence upon certain European goods. See Kerlerec to Berryer, 8 June 1761, Kerlerec to Choiseul, 10 Feb. 1762, MPAFD, vol. 5, pp. 271–2, 273; d'Abbadie to Farmar, 14 Oct. 1763, and "a Counsel Held with the Tchaktaw Nation, 14 Nov. 1763", Great Britain Public Record Office, War Office (Library of Congress photostat copy), v. 49; Kerlerec to Major Robert Farmar 4 Oct. 1763, and George Johnstone and John Stuart on 1765 Mobile Congress, 12 June 1765, both in MPAED, pp. 35, 187.

4   John Stuart to John Pownall, 24 Aug. 1765, Great Britain Public Record Office, Colonial Office, Class 5, America and the West Indies, v. 66, hereafter cited as CO5.

5   Choctaw complaints about these conditions are sprinkled throughout British, French, and Spanish records, but the most accessible are found in the transcripts of British–Choctaw conferences in 1765 and 1771. See "Congress with the Chickasaws and Choctaws at Mobile, 26 March 1765", MPAED, p. 216–55, also in CO5/66; and "1771–1772 Congress with the Chickasaws and Choctaws", in "Peter Chester: third governor of the province of British West Florida under British dominion, 1770–1781", Eron O. Rowland (ed.), Publications of the Mississippi Historical Society, Centenary Series, v. 5 (Jackson, Miss., 1925), pp. 134–59, also in CO5/73. For increased use of alcohol by traders after 1763, see also Peter C. Mancall, Deadly medicine: Indians and alcohol in early America (Ithaca, N.Y., 1995), Chapter 7.

6   Johnstone and Stuart on the 1765 Congress 12 June 1765, MPAED, p. 187.

7   "The talk of the head warrior of the Choctaws [unnamed]", in "A congress held at Pensacola with several Indian chiefs of the Creek nation and chiefs of other nations, 10 Sept. 1764", General Thomas Gage Papers, American Series, William L. Clements Library, University of Michigan, Ann Arbor, v. 24, hereafter cited as Gage Papers.

8   René Roi [interpreter to Indians] to John Stuart, 11 Aug. 1769, CO5/70.

9   Edmund J. Gardner Papers, Gilcrease Institute of American History and Art, Tulsa, Oklahoma, "Choctaw People File"; and Amelia R. Bell, "Separate people: speaking of Creek men and women", American Anthropologist 92, 1990, 336–7.

10 Daniel H. Usner, Jr. (Indians, settlers, and slaves in a frontier exchange economy: the lower Mississippi valley before 1783 (Chapel Hill, N.C., 1992), pp. 127–30) discusses the acts of banditry committed by Choctaws against outlying European settlements, but does not consider the Choctaw–Creek War and its potential to lessen the severity of these confrontations.

11 James A. Brown, "The impact of the European presence on Indian culture", in Contest for empire: 1500–1775, John B. Elliott (Indianapolis, Ind., 1975), p. 12.

12 Circa 1775, Choctaw and Creek total populations numbered approximately 14,000 each, with warrior populations estimated at slightly more than 4,000 each: see Peter H. Wood, "The changing population of the colonial South: an overview by race and region, 1685–

1790", in Wood et al., *Powhatan's mantle*, pp. 38, 72. British troops in West Florida, on the other hand, numbered just over 1,000 men in 1766: see "An estimate of the expense of provisions . . . [1766]", *Earl of Shelburne Papers*, William L. Clements Library, University of Michigan, Ann Arbor, v. 50, "Indian trade", hereafter cited as *Shelburne Papers*.

13 Gage to Stuart, 27 Jan. 1764, *Gage Papers* v. 13. Similarly, Gage remarked to the Northern Superintendent of Indian Affairs, William Johnson, that "it's my Opinion as long as they [Creeks and Choctaws] Quarell with one another we shall be well with them all And when they are all at Peace, It's the Signal for us to have a good look out," in *The Papers of Sir William Johnson*, Alexander C. Flick (ed.) (Albany, N.Y., 1921–65), vol. 4, p. 304, hereafter cited as *Johnson Papers*.

14 Johnstone to Shelburne, 19 May 1766, *CO5/67*. See also "Governor Johnstone's report to Mr. Conway, 23 June 1766", *MPAED*, pp. 511–12; Johnstone to John Stuart, 19 May 1766, *Gage Papers* v. 55; Governor Wright [of East Florida] to John Stuart, 10 July 1766, *CO5/67*; and Robin F. A. Fabel, *Bombast and broadsides: the lives of George Johnstone* (Tuscaloosa, Ala., 1987), pp. 54–7.

15 Clarence E. Carter, "The beginnings of British West Florida", *Mississippi Valley Historical Review* **4**(3),: Dec. 1917, pp. 337–8; Angie Debo, *The rise and fall of the Choctaw republic* (Norman, Okla., 1934), p. 31; John R. Alden, *John Stuart and the southern colonial frontier* (Ann Arbor, Mich., 1944), pp. 224–8; Robert S. Cotterill, *The southern Indians: the story of the civilized tribes before removal* (Norman, Okla., 1954), pp. 33–4; David H. Corkran, *The Creek Frontier, 1540–1783* (Norman, Okla., 1967), pp. 254–5; James H. O'Donnell, III, "The southern Indians in the War for American Independence, 1775–1783", in *Four Centuries of Southern Indians*, Charles Hudson (ed.)(Athens, Ga., 1975), pp. 49–50; Richard White, *The roots of dependency: subsistence, environment, and social change among the Choctaws, Pawnees, and Navajos* (Lincoln, Nebr., 1983), pp. 76–9; and Jesse O. McKee, *The Choctaw* (New York and Philadelphia, 1989), p. 30.

16 Current thinking on the causes of the war have taken seriously Choctaw and Creek motivations. Historian Kathryn Braund (in *Deerskins and duffels: Creek Indian trade with Anglo-America, 1685–1815* (Lincoln, Nebr., 1993), pp. 133–4) placed the onus of starting the war on the Creeks who acted to prevent Choctaw access to British trade. Clara Sue Kidwell follows this interpretation in *Choctaws and missionaries in Mississippi, 1818–1918* (Norman, Okla., 1995), p. 12. But she does not resolve why Choctaws willingly continued the war when British occupation of Mobile brought them unimpeded access to European trade. In the late seventeenth and early eighteenth centuries, Creeks often obstructed Choctaw access to British traders on the Atlantic coast, but the British occupation of the Gulf coast from Pensacola to the Mississippi River made their blockade ineffectual. Superintendent Stuart informed two Choctaw leaders as early as 1763 that traders could soon be expected from Mobile, thus circumventing the Creeks. (See Governors of Georgia, Virginia, Carolinas, and John Stuart on Southern Indian Relations 10 Nov. 1763, *CO5/65*.) Sociologist Duane Champagne *Social order and political change: constitutional governments among the Cherokee, the Choctaw, the Chickasaw, and the Creek* (Stanford, Calif., 1992), pp. 72–3 offered a scenario in which Choctaws and Creeks fought over hunting resources along the Choctaws' eastern boundary on the Tombigbee River. But at least one third of the Choctaws (the western division, which constituted one of three geographic and political divisions) held no claim to those lands, and they participated in the war as enthusiastically as any other group of Choctaws. Additionally, all Choctaws responded to a declining deer population by hunting in the west across the Mississippi River (see Lieut. John Ritchey to Brig. Colonel Taylor, 27

Dec. 1767, *British Museum: Additional Manuscripts* [Library of Congress photostat copy], No. 21671, Part 3, hereafter cited as *BMAM*; and Lawrence and Lucia B. Kinnaird, "Choctaws west of the Mississippi, 1766–1800", *Southwestern Historical Quarterly* **83**, April 1980, pp. 349–70).

17 Mary W. Helms, *Craft and the kingly ideal: art, trade, and power* (Austin, Tex., 1993), p. 136.

18 Elias Legardee to Governor Johnstone, 27 March 1766, *BMAM* No. 21671, Part 1.

19 William Tayler to General Thomas Gage, 1 June 1766, *Gage Papers* v. 52. Warclubs served as the main symbol of war and south-eastern Indians repeatedly left them at the scene of a killing in order to incite their enemies: see Charles Hudson, *The Southeastern Indians* (Knoxville, Tenn., 1976), pp. 245–7, and Wayne William VanHorne. *The warclub: weapon and symbol in Southeastern Indian societies* (PhD. thesis, University of Georgia, 1993).

20 John McGillivray to Charles Stuart [Deputy Superintendent to the Choctaws and Chickasaws], 10 May 1766, *Shelburne Papers* v. 60, "Indian trade", p. 81.

21 S. Forrester to Johnstone, 25 May 1766, *BMAM* No. 21671, Part 1. See also William Struthers to Johnstone, 20 May 1766, *MPAED* p. 522. British military officers mistakenly interpreted the "black wing" as a call for the Choctaws to join the Creeks in alliance against the English and expressed relief that war between them broke out instead: see Colonel Taylor to Gage, 18 Sept. 1766, *BMAM* No. 21671, Part 2.

22 Charles Stuart to John Stuart, 12 June 1770, *Gage Papers* v. 94.

23 Talk by "Molten" [the Mortar?] quoted in James Germany to Johnstone 28 June 1766, *BMAM* No. 21671, Part 1.

24 Wolf King to Johnstone, 28 June 1766, enclosed in *ibid.*

25 "David Taitt's journal to and through the Upper Creek Nation, 1772", in *Travels in the American colonies*, Newton D. Mereness (ed.) (New York, 1916), pp. 532–4, also in *Documents of the American Revolution, 1770–1783*, K. G. Davies (ed.) (Shannon, Ireland, 1972), vol. 5, pp. 265–6, hereafter cited as *DAR*.

26 "Mingo Houma Chito of Imongoulasha in the East. His talk to the deputy superintendent, 27 July 1766", *CO5/67*, emphasis added.

27 "Tomatle Mingo, Great Medal Chief of Seneacha, his talk to the deputy superintendent, 12 July 1766", *CO5/67*.

28 "Shouloustamastabe, alias Red Shoes, his talk to the deputy superintendent, 4 July 1766", *CO5/67*.

29 Charles Stuart to John Stuart, 12 June 1770, *Gage Papers* v. 94.

30 Lieutenant John Ritchey of Fort Tombeckby complained about this situation in a letter to Brigadier General Taylor dated 27 December 1766, *BMAM* No. 21671, Part 3.

31 "Shouloustamastabe, alias Red Shoes, his talk to the deputy superintendent, 4 July 1766", *CO5/67*.

32 Cyrus Byington, *A dictionary of the Choctaw Language*, ed. John Swanton & Henry S. Halbert (Washington, D.C., Bureau of American Ethnology Bulletin No. 46, 1909), p. 73; Henry C. Benson, *Life among the Choctaw Indians, and sketches of the Southwest* (Cincinnati, 1860; rpt. New York, 1970), p. 53; and John R. Swanton, *Source material for the social and ceremonial life of the Choctaw Indians* (Washington, D.C., Bureau of American Ethnology Bulletin No. 103, 1931), pp. 119–24.

33 Patricia Galloway (" 'So many little republics': British negotiations with the Choctaw Confederacy, 1765", *Ethnohistory* **41**(4), 1994, pp. 519, 528, and n. 37) lists Red Captain's village as "Chicktalaya" with no divisional designation. This is probably a version of "Shatalaya" as found in "Conferences with 73 Chactaw Head Warriors, 1 Nov. 1759",

Lyttelton Papers, when Red Captain attended negotiations with the British at the Creek village of Okfuskee. At that time, Red Captain was listed as the "Chief Leader of the Great Red Mingo of Betapoucoulou's Men". Betapoucoulou was an eastern division village. The eastern division affiliation is also evident from trader James Adair's description (*History of the American Indians* orig. pub. 1775, ed. Samuel Cole Williams (Johnson City, Tenn., 1930), pp. 292–3) of Red Captain's home as being in a "northern barrier town" that was within one day's ride from Fort Tombeckby on the eastern Choctaw boundary. This material further clarifies one of Galloway's arguments in the above article that most eastern division leaders (except Red Captain and another leader named Alibamon Mingo) wavered about whether to meet with the British in 1765. For maps of the Choctaw homeland, see especially "Part of the Purcell Map [by John Stuart] 1760s", reprinted as Plate 7 in John R. Swanton, *Early history of the Creek Indians and their neighbors* (Washington, D.C., Bureau of American Ethnology Bulletin No. 73, 1922); and Henry S. Halbert, "Bernard Roman's map of 1772", *Mississippi Historical Society Publications*, **6**, 1902, pp. 415–39.

34 Trader James Adair's well-known *History of the American Indians* (pp. 312–14) offers a compelling portrayal of Red Captain's last days which concurs with other documentary sources (listed below) including the statement that two white traders betrayed the Choctaw war party's whereabouts. Only ten Creeks died in the battle. See James Hewitt (trader to the Choctaws) to McGillivray & Struthers (Trading Co.), 16 Oct. 1767; Charles Stuart to John Stuart, 29 Oct. 1767; and John Stuart to Gage, 27 Nov. 1767, all in *Gage Papers* v. 72; Roderick MacIntosh (commissary in the Creek Nation) to John Stuart, 16 Nov. 1767, and John Stuart to Gage, 26 Dec. 1767, both in *Gage Papers* v. 73; John Stuart to Earl of Shelburne, 7 May 1768, *CO5/69*; John Stuart to Gage, 17 May 1768, *Gage Papers* v. 77; and John Stuart to Hillsborough, 28 Dec. 1768, *CO5/70*.

35 This probably happened because Shulustamastabé and Red Captain were war leaders from different divisions and therefore probably unwilling to serve under the other's command in a war party.

36 European governments recognized south-eastern Indian leaders on three levels: Great Medal, Small Medal, and "captains" or warriors with commissions.

37 "Deposition of John Farrell, packhorseman in the Choctaw Nation, 4 March 1767", *BMAM* No. 21671, Part 4.

38 *ibid.*

39 Trader Nathaniel Folsom reported that late eighteenth-century Choctaws wore European clothing when buried if they were an important person or chief, while others were buried in blankets or "sum other old worn out [animal] skin": "Discussion of Choctaw history by Nathaniel Folsom, [1798?]", *Peter Pitchlynn Papers*, Gilcrease Institute of American History and Art, Tulsa, Oklahoma, hereafter cited as "Folsom Discussion".

40 Chocoulacta regained his Small Medal Chief status at the 1771/1772 Mobile Congress at which he supplicated to Stuart while painted in white clay and accompanied by four Great Medal Chiefs and about a thousand other Choctaws. See Ritchey to Elias Legardére 4 March 1767, Legardére to Charles Stuart, 4 March 1767, both in *BMAM* No. 21671, Part 4; Taylor to Gage 22 March 1767, *Gage Papers* v. 63; Charles Stuart to John Stuart, 12 June 1770, *Gage Papers* v. 94; and John Stuart to Hillsborough, 7 Feb. 1772, *CO5/73*.

41 Taylor to Gage, 4 March 1767, *BMAM* No. 21671, Part 4.

42 Charles Stuart to John Stuart, 12 June 1770, *Gage Papers* v. 94.

43 Charles Stuart to John Stuart, 12 June 1770, *Gage Papers* v. 94. Mingo Houma Chito ("Great Red Leader") hailed from the village of East Imongoulasha in the eastern division.

44 See Upper House of Assembly [of West Florida] to Earl of Hillsborough, 24 Aug. 1768, in *The Minutes, Journals, and Acts of the General Assembly of British West Florida*, Robert R. Rea & Milo B. Howard, Jr. (eds) (Tuscaloosa, Ala., 1979), p. 146; John Stuart to Hillsborough, 8 June 1770, *CO5/71*; Emistisiguo to Charles Stuart (July–Aug.) 1770, *CO5/72*; Charles Stuart to John Stuart, 17 June 1770, 26 Aug. 1770, 27 Sept. 1770, and 26 Dec. 1770, *CO5/72*; Elias Durnford to Hillsborough, 8 July 1770, *DAR* vol. 1, p. 139; Charles Stuart to the Creeks 12 Dec. 1770, *CO5/72*; and Gage to Hillsborough 16 Jan. 1771, in *The Correspondence of General Thomas Gage* [2 vols], Clarence E. Carter (ed.) (New Haven, Conn., 1931), vol. 1, p. 289, hereafter cited as *Gage Correspondence*.

Richard White (*Roots of dependency*, 78) contended that, rather than fighting to gain war titles, the Sixtowns and Lower Creeks fought over hunting resources on the lower Tombigbee River. This is confirmed by Nathaniel Folsom who, at the end of the eighteenth century, cited an aged Choctaw man named "Osha humah" (aka "the Irish Man") who stated that the Creeks wanted too much Choctaw hunting territory ("Folsom Discussion"). However, both views are likely correct since it was access to hunting and the status it provided, as well as war and the rank it bestowed on successful warriors, that were at issue. Neither the Choctaws nor Creeks sought to occupy the disputed territory in any sense of the word; rather they both sought to preserve a boundary area that would continue to support game. Mississippian ancestors of the Creeks and Choctaws rarely fought to conquer territory: see Jon L. Gibson, "Aboriginal warfare in the Southeast: an alternative perspective", *American Antiquity* **39**(1), 1974, pp. 130–33.

45 See David H. Dye, "Feasting with the enemy: Mississippian warfare and prestige-goods circulation", in *Native American interactions: multiscalar analyses and interpretations in the eastern woodlands*, Michael S. Nassaney & Kenneth E. Sassaman (eds) (Knoxville, Tenn., 1995), pp. 300–1.

46 John Stuart to Hillsborough, 2 Dec. 1770, *CO5/72*. See also Gage to Hillsborough, 7 July 1770, *Gage Correspondence* vol. 1, p. 262; Charles Stuart to John Stuart, 12 June 1770, *CO5/71*; John Stuart to Hillsborough, 16 July 1770, *CO5/71*; Governor James Wright [Georgia] to Hillsborough, 8 Dec. 1770 and 20 July 1771, *DAR* vol. 1, p. 225, vol. 2, p. 151; Charles Stuart to John Stuart, 26 Aug. 1770, 27 Sept. 1770, and 26 Dec. 1770, *CO5/72*; Hillsborough to Gage, 28 Sept. 1770, *Gage Correspondence* vol. 2, p. 117; John Stuart to Head Warriors of Upper Creeks 25 Nov. 1770, *CO5/72*; John Stuart to Haldimand 23 Jan. 1771, *BMAM* No. 21672, Part 1; Hillsborough to John Stuart, 11 Feb. 1771, *DAR* vol. 1, p. 267; Governor Peter Chester [West Florida] to Hillsborough, 9 March 1771, *DAR* vol. 3, pp. 64–67; and Gage to Johnson 1 April 1771, *Johnson Papers* 8:58. For insistence that the war adversely affected trader's profits, see [Anonymous], "Survey of West Florida, 1768", in *Colonial captivities, marches, and journeys*, Isabel M. Calder (ed.) (New York, 1935), p. 230; and "Memorial of traders to Creek and Cherokee nations to Governor James Wright June 1771", *DAR* vol. 3, p. 126.

47 Peter Chester to John Stuart, 10 Sept. 1771, in Rowland, "Peter Chester", p. 102.

48 John Stuart to Hillsborough, 7 Feb. 1772, *CO5/73*; John Stuart to Gage, 16 Feb. 1772, *Gage Papers* v. 109; and "A list of towns in the Chactaw nation with the names of the Indians in each town receiving presents at the Congress, 1771–1772", *CO5/73*.

49 John Stuart to Gage, 15 May 1772 and 23 May 1772, *Gage Papers* v. 111; Charles Stuart to John Stuart, 17 March 1773, *Gage Papers* v. 118; and Gov. Sir James Wright [Georgia] to Earl of Dartmouth 17 June 1773, *DAR* vol. 6, p. 157.

50 See also note 46; Robert Mackay to John Stuart, 30 Nov. 1773, David Taitt to John Stuart, 3 Jan. 1774, 12 Jan. 1774, and 24 Jan. 1774, Wright to John Stuart, 27 Jan. 1774,

all in *CO5/75*; John Stuart to Haldimand, 3 Feb. 1774, *DAR* vol. 8, pp. 34–7; John Stuart to Earl of Dartmouth, 13 Feb. 1774, *DAR* vol. 8, p. 49; Charles Stuart to John Stuart, 12 May 1774, *Gage Papers* v. 119; same to same 19 May 1774 *CO5/75*; John Stuart to Gage, 3 July 1774, *Gage Papers* v. 120; John Stuart to Earl of Dartmouth 2 Aug. 1774, *CO5/75*; John Stuart to Gage, 19 Nov. 1774, *Gage Papers* v. 124; Charles Stuart to John Stuart, 12 Dec. 1774, *CO5/76*; John Stuart to Gage, 18 Jan. 1775, *Gage Papers* v. 125; "Letters from West Florida, 6 Jan. 1775", in *American archives: a documentary history* (Washington, D.C., 1837, fourth series), vol. 1, p. 1099; and *South Carolina Gazette* 24 May 1773.

51 John Stuart to Germain 6 June 1776.

52 Gage to John Stuart, 12 Sept. 1775, *CO5/76*; John Stuart to Gage, 3 Oct. 1775, National Archives Microfilm Publications, *Papers of the Continental Congress, 1774–1789* (M247, r65, i51, v1, p. 159); David Taitt to John Stuart, 20 Oct. 1775, Niaha Thlaco [Creek] to John Stuart, 20 Oct. 1775, John Stuart to Earl of Dartmouth, 6 Jan. 1776, John Stuart to Maj.-General Henry Clinton, 15 March 1776, same to same 23 Aug. 1776, and same to same, 16 Sept. 1776, all in *CO5/77*; and Germain to John Stuart, 5 Sept. 1776, *Lord George Germain Papers*, William L. Clements Library, University of Michigan, Ann Arbor, v. 5.

53 The "false battle" was likely performed as a ritualized hand-to-hand combat with warclubs, rather than with guns or bows and arrows. The warclub was absolutely vital to the prowess of a warrior in battle and provided a direct link to pre-contact Mississippian times during which skill in hand-to-hand fighting was far more important than proficiency in killing from a distance. See VanHorne, *The Warclub*, especially pp. 49, 105.

54 David Taitt to John Stuart, 3 Aug. 1777, *CO5/78*.

55 John Stuart to Germain 26 Oct. 1776; John Stuart to Brig.-General Augustin Provost, 24 July 1777, John Stuart to William Knox, 26 July 1777; Taitt to John Stuart, 3 Aug. 1777, and John Stuart to Germain, 22 Aug. 1777, all in *CO5/78*; and Charles Stuart to John Stuart, 7 March 1778, in Guy Carleton, *Lord Dorchester Papers, 1747–83* (microfilm copy).

56 See William S. Coker & Thomas D. Watson, *Indian traders of the southeastern borderlands: Panton, Leslie & Company and John Forbes & Company, 1783–1847* (Pensacola, Fla., 1986).

57 Daniel K. Richter, "War and culture: the Iroquois experience", *William and Mary Quarterly* **40**(4), Oct. 1983, pp. 528–59.

58 Richard White, "The winning of the West: the expansion of the western Sioux in the eighteenth and nineteenth centuries", *Journal of American History* **65**, Sept. 1978, pp. 319–43.

59 See, for example, David H. Dye, "Warfare in the sixteenth-century southeast: the de Soto expedition in the interior", in *Columbian consequences: volume 2: Archeological and historical perspectives on the Spanish borderlands east*, David Hurst Thomas (ed.) (Washington, D.C., 1992), pp. 211–22.

60 *MPAED* p. 242.

Chapter Eight

Hunting and the politics of masculinity in Cherokee treaty-making, 1763–75

Nathaniel Sheidley

In 1775, a delegation of Cherokee headmen turned over to Richard Henderson their claim to an enormous tract of land, virtually all of what is now central and western Kentucky.[1] It was the last in a series of dramatic cessions that marked a new direction in Cherokee diplomacy after 1770. Elder council members, called "beloved men", had once shown a remarkable reluctance to part with even small tracts of land. But in 1770 they granted thousands of acres of land in the New River Valley to Virginia. The next year they ceded land along the Savannah River to several traders and the Augusta merchants who backed them. This trend culminated in 1775 when beloved men granted 27,000 square miles of prime hunting land to Henderson and his partners.[2] In the course of five years, in exchange for trade goods that could not last, elder council members had renounced all claim to the last best hunting grounds known to Cherokee men.

The motives that underlay this pattern in Cherokee treaty-making have been difficult for subsequent observers to comprehend. Modern scholars have generally assumed that Indian diplomats agreed to part with a piece of land only when the preponderance of British military power left them with no alternative. But these particular cessions were made at a time of peace. British officials in fact hesitated before permitting the first of the three deals to take place, and they actively opposed the remaining two. A second explanation sometimes put forward is that Indians were defrauded of their land. By one theory, Henderson deceived Cherokee negotiators regarding the content of the document they signed.[3] This is precisely what Oconostota, Attakullakulla, and other council members implicated in the dealings later claimed. But given the number of interpreters present that day, it seems unlikely that all of these men could have been fooled. Nor can trickery explain the cession of 1771, which took place at the suggestion not of white land hunters but of Cherokee headmen.[4]

The notion that deception underlay the land cessions negotiated between 1770 and 1775 proceeds less from any concrete evidence than from a particular set of assumptions about the nature of Indian politics. From this perspective, Cherokees belonged to a monolithic "tribe", unified in its opposition to Anglo-American expansion. Reduced to a dichromatic portrait of Indian resistance to white domination, Native American history has no place for headmen who volunteered to give away land. Fraud becomes the only viable explanation for their behaviour.

By privileging tribal or even village units, however, this perspective effaces the often stark differences of power and interest that such units contained. Tribes, as Robert F. Berkhofer, Jr., suggested in a seminal article on Indian politics, were scarcely monolithic. Social relationships among Native Americans quite often extended beyond the tribe or hinged on smaller groupings within it.[5] Berkhofer's insight has helped to shape a "new Indian history" concerned less with the relations between Indians and whites than with those among Indians themselves, but it has discouraged historians from looking more closely at Native American diplomacy. That subject, so much a part of what Berkhofer called the history of "white–Indian relations", has been neglected in recent work. Informed by a different set of assumptions, however, the study of Indian treaty-making can shed new light on the principles, sometimes sacred, by which authority and interest have been organized within Native American societies.

To solve the mystery posed by Cherokee diplomacy between 1770 and 1775 requires that we set aside the fiction of a monolithic polity and admit that the leaders who negotiated these cessions may have acted for reasons not shared by their kinspeople in general. Like any collection of people, Cherokee villages embraced differences of wealth, colour, gender, age, and belief that rendered the political interests of their inhabitants heterogeneous. Divergent interests at times found expression in behaviour. As Colin Calloway has reminded us, older men negotiated the Henderson cession and younger men later rejected it.[6] But if Professor Calloway is right to focus our attention on generational conflict, his own approach leaves unsolved the conundrum of the older men's action. Indeed, it adds to this puzzle a related question: precisely what underlay the resistance of young Cherokee men to the land cessions made by their elders? This paper finds new answers to both questions in a politics of masculinity that preoccupied Cherokee villagers during the second half of the eighteenth century. It examines Cherokee thinking about the religious valence of hunting and about the problematic relationship between older and younger men, and connects these themes to a broader narrative of Indian–white relations that has too often obscured them.

Concerns about masculinity lie at the very heart of that narrative. The treaties of the 1770s inaugurated a new period of close and often violent interaction between Cherokees and their white and black neighbours. The course of this conflict destabilized the received meanings of manhood among both populations. Culturally freighted notions of young Cherokee men as hunters and also of white men as patriarchs became objects of great contention. Alternatives were slow to emerge from this meeting of cultures, but new meanings for masculinity and new roles for men would ultimately take shape in the evangelical and prophetic revivals of the early nineteenth century.[7]

A politics driven by these concerns was manifest in Cherokee villages even before 1770. Raids undertaken by young warriors had helped to ignite a devastating war with the neighbouring British colonies in 1760.[8] Although over by 1761, the War brought sickness and starvation in its wake. Perhaps fifteen out of every hundred Cherokees died.[9] Cherokee leaders drew a simple but compelling lesson from this experience: young men must no longer be permitted to raid their white neighbours.

How to achieve this goal was not immediately apparent. One approach was to separate the two populations. An unusual confluence of interests at first held out to elder council members some hope of success on this front. Following the Seven Years' War, British officials were anxious to avoid the expense of future conflicts with neighbouring Indians. In October 1763, the crown prohibited settlement beyond the Appalachian ridge and reserved the lands of the vast Mississippi watershed for Native American use, a policy that Cherokee councils ratified in a series of bilateral treaties negotiated with South Carolina in 1765, North Carolina in 1767, and Virginia in 1768.[10] Although these agreements required that modest portions of good hunting ground be surrendered, Cherokee negotiators saw this concession as the most conservative course available to them on the issue of land. Usteneka, a prominent Cherokee voice in the diplomacy of the 1760s, put it well: these treaties established "that there should be a line drawn to seperate [sic] our lands" from those belonging to Britain, and that "we might do as we pleased with ours".[11] If the border could forestall white encroachment west of the Appalachian mountains and preserve what remained of the still-extensive Cherokee hunting grounds, the bargain must have seemed a good one.

But not to young hunters, who went forth each winter and saw that the boundary line was ignored. Anglo-Americans continued to poach deer and other animals in prodigious quantities, while white farmers moved with alarming speed up backcountry riverbeds and on to Cherokee hunting grounds.[12] Even Thomas Gage, charged with enforcing British policy, had to admit that "the Frontier People of most of our Provinces are not to be limited by any Bounds".[13] Young Cherokee men could envision clearly a future in which they would no longer be able to hunt. If the memory of war guided the policies of established council leaders, a different set of imperatives came increasingly to dictate the actions of younger men. For these men, hunting was a fundamental component of masculinity, and one jealously to be guarded.

Cherokees believed that the power to take life was a dangerous but also a sacred power peculiar to men, a balance against the power of women to create life. The gendered alignment of these forces was as old as the world itself. According to one of the most sacred Cherokee myths, Selu (whose name means "corn") and her husband Kanati (the Great Hunter) came down to this world shortly after its creation. Here they became the first parents of human children (the two Thunder Boys). Each possessed the power to provide for their children's sustenance in a different way. Selu brought forth corn and beans as she brought forth life: from her womb. Kanati, by contrast, took life by killing the deer with which he returned each day.[14]

Because human survival depended on both forces, grave consequences attended any disruption in the balance between them. For instance, drought occurred when the sun, emblematic of a woman's power to create life, became too strong. To restore balance and end the drought, Cherokee shamans revivified male power. Using offerings of meat taken in a ceremonial hunt, they appealed first to the moon, the sun's brother but also her lover, asking that he cover her face and thus diminish her strength. If that failed, they invoked Kanati, the greatest icon of male power.[15]

Able to revitalize male or female power, human ceremony was enlisted also to preserve the balance between them. Proper balance required that the categories of men's and women's power be kept separate from one another and distinct. For one to bleed into and pollute the other inevitably weakened the latter and thereby disrupted the relationship between them. Cherokees thus practised a number of rituals designed to protect the boundary that divided male from female power. For instance, men consecrated for war or hunt were forbidden to interact with women. During menstruation and childbirth, women likewise kept away from men.[16]

Still, male and female power existed as distinct categories only so long as they were given meaning through ritual. In other words, the association between manhood and the taking of life could never be taken for granted; it had continually to be enacted. War-making was the most potent ritual by which Cherokee men gave meaning to their masculinity, but ideally war was not a frequent occurrence.[17] Thus hunting, the taking of *animal* life, came to have inordinate significance. The profound ceremonies by which men prepared for the act bore witness to its importance. Boys passing into man-hood commonly undertook a rigorous, four-year initiation under the super-vision of a shaman who specialized in rituals of the hunt. Only afterwards, when their potency as hunters and thus as men was secure, could the youths marry and have intercourse with their wives. Even men who neglected to undergo this initiation prepared themselves by similar ceremonies at the outset of each hunting expedition.[18] Through hunting, more than any other activity, young Cherokee men established and apprehended their place in the architecture of the world they inhabited.

Not surprisingly, young men complained bitterly about competition from white longhunters and encroachment by white farmers. "Our Young Fellows are very angry to see their Hunting Grounds taken from them," Oconostota told one British official in 1769.[19] But increasingly, young men did more than just complain. Some relieved white poachers of their pelts and delivered the men to British authorities.[20] Others exacted a more permanent price for such violations. In 1767 and again in 1768, hunting parties from Chilhowee returned home with the scalps of Virginians they had met and killed in the woods.[21]

This sort of action was precisely what elder council members sought most urgently to avoid. The cycles of murder and revenge that followed such unsanctioned raids threatened repeatedly to throw the frontier into open warfare. But how could unruly young men be restrained? This problem had a long pedigree in Cherokee thought. Indeed, Cherokees of the eighteenth century needed only to look into the night sky to be reminded of the tendency of young men to disobey their elders. Legend taught that the seven stars in what we now call the Pleiades cluster (or asterism) were brothers. As boys, they had stolen into their town's council-house and beaten the drum that was kept there for council meetings and public celebrations. A group of elders, presumably male council members, heard the drum and reproved the boys for their misdeed. But the brothers refused to stop. Instead, they grabbed the drum and "darted upwards with it, beating it in defiance as they ascended".[22]

This response made sense to Cherokees, for the councilmen had over-stepped the legitimate bounds of their authority by trying to discipline the boys. Matriliny and the law of clan revenge dictated that children might be disciplined by their mothers, grandmothers, and maternal uncles – in other words, by members of their own clan – but not by members of other clans.[23] Where daughters were concerned, this custom created few disciplinary prob-lems. Young women spent most of their time engaged in social tasks for which Cherokees organized themselves into clan units. Women were farmers, for example. Clans, or rather those lineages that represented a clan in a given

171

village, owned the cornfields and gardens and made all decisions regarding their use. Thus a young woman's mother or grandmother – an authority figure – could ask her to weed the garden or harvest green corn. There was little room for disobedience.[24] The making of war policy was another matter. Town councils and special war councils, not clans, decided whether to send warriors into the field or to keep them at home.[25] The directions that young men received thus came from non-kinsmen, from men who lacked authority over them. When council members asked warriors to refrain from making war, there was little guarantee that the younger men would obey. As Cherokee leaders repeatedly explained to British officials, the young men of their villages were "Rogues whom you know will not at all times listen to our Injunctions".[26] This is precisely what the myth of the seven stars was about: when young men beat the town council's drum, when they decided for themselves to go to war or become involved in village politics, elder men could not simply order them to stop.

But if young men could not be *made* to obey, perhaps they could be persuaded. This theme ran through the myth of Selu and Kanati. Kanati's relationship to the two sons, together with the structure of Cherokee kinship, made it impossible for him to act as their disciplinarian. All Cherokees belonged to one of seven clans, and segments of each of the seven clans existed in every village. Membership in these units – kinship – descended through the female line. A young man, in other words, belonged to his mother's clan. He in turn married outside that clan. His children thus belonged to his wife's clan, but never to his own. Strictly speaking, Kanati was unrelated to his own children, and he alienated the Thunder Boys whenever he scolded or reproached them. But by giving his sons gifts Kanati found that he could win their obedience after all. He brought bows and arrows for the boys to play with and birds for them to shoot at, and every day he disappeared into the woods and returned with a large deer for them to eat. Trouble surfaced only when Kanati failed to defend his position as the source of such gifts. When the Thunder Boys followed Kanati and discovered the cave in which he kept the deer and other animals, they immediately felt themselves relieved of the need to obey. "What need have we of our father now?" they asked. "We are as wise as he." But of course they were not. The Thunder Boys opened the cave and inadvertently permitted the animals inside it to escape into the woods. Ever since, it has been the burden of men to hunt when they are hungry for meat.[27]

To a reader raised in the values of a commercial society, it is tempting to regard Kanati's actions as bribery, but the moral of this story was in fact quite different. As recipients of their father's gifts, the Thunder Boys were bound to obey him, and their punishment upon violating this obligation was just. At the same time, however, the story contained a warning to fathers. When the Thunder Boys discovered their father's cave, his authority over them was in fact diminished. A father's authority hinged not on a single act of generosity but on his ability to continue giving.

Elder Cherokee men took this lesson to heart during the 1770s. Each time that the young men of their villages seemed restless and eager for war, council members tried to conciliate them with gifts. As one man explained, "it is the Duty of the Elder to clothe the younger".[28] The gifts that young men prized included not just clothing, however, but the materials that enabled them to hunt: muskets, powder, and shot. After the Seven Years' War, south-eastern Indians found that they could procure these items in sufficient quantities from only two sources: traders and British colonial officials. Traders were a potential threat. If permitted to do business directly with young hunters, they could undermine the authority of older men. Muskogean (or "Creek") leaders complained of traders who erected posts in the hunting grounds, far from the watchful eyes of village chiefs.[29] Such men, they thought, made young hunters "regardless of their Headmen", a concern that Cherokee beloved men frequently echoed.[30] By keeping traders close at hand and mediating between them and young hunters, elder Cherokees hoped to neutralize the threat to established authority that such men embodied. At the same time, headmen turned trading regulations themselves into a kind of gift extended to young hunters, trying at times to lever British officials into lowering the prices that hunters paid for firearms and other goods.[31]

Dealing with British officials was substantially less complicated. Council leaders usually turned to these men when young hunters became restless for war.[32] But to the British way of thinking, giving gifts to ensure peace smacked of bribery. Governors and Indian agents were instructed to refuse such requests where possible.[33] Thus when young men seemed poised on the brink of war, Cherokee councilmen found themselves with few choices but to sell land in exchange for the gifts they deemed crucial to preserving peace.

There are hints that elder council members used this strategy even before 1768. In May 1765, for instance, Anglo-Virginian vigilantes killed eight Cherokee men as they passed through Staunton in Augusta county. When news of the murders reached Cherokee towns, young warriors advocated swift retribution. Council leaders persuaded them to wait, hoping that Virginia might provide satisfaction by executing an equal number of its own citizens. But Attakullakulla returned from Williamsburg in October with sombre news: the murderers had been permitted to escape unpunished. To prevent young men from seeking revenge on their own terms would now be more difficult.[34] Just weeks later Cherokee leaders agreed to cede a contested tract of land to South Carolina, clearly assuming that they would receive a substantial gift of trade goods in return. Nowhere did Cherokee negotiators record what purpose they had in mind for these items, but the timing seems evidence enough. In all likelihood, the goods were to be redistributed in order to render young warriors obedient to the more pacific policies of their elders.[35]

After 1768, such efforts gained a new urgency. Meeting at Fort Stanwix that year, Iroquois leaders laid claim to the Cherokee hunting grounds that extended north of the Tennessee River and promptly ceded them to Britain. The crown rejected this provision, but not before news of it had brought great droves of land-hungry white farmers to the Holston River Valley, a fertile region particularly prized by Cherokee hunters.[36] Young men refused to sit passively by while such intrusions continued. Hunters from Chilhowee, customarily the most frequent Cherokee visitors to the Holston and its tributaries, were the first to call for action.[37] When Shawnee messengers arrived in the fall of 1769 and proposed a united Indian front to resist further encroachments on their land, Chilhowee residents tried to call a council to support the proposal. Cooler heads prevailed, but only temporarily. That winter, Chilhowee men could scarcely be restrained from killing a white hunter they found in the woods.[38] Nor did Chilhowee residents act alone. Throughout the so-called Overhill region of Cherokee settlement, young men were beginning to make war policy for themselves. Many attended the inter-tribal conference held at Scioto Plains in the spring of 1770, where plans for a war alliance were being laid.[39] Headmen had reason to worry.

The rising militancy of young hunters would shape Cherokee diplomacy over the next five years. In 1770, it prompted elder council members to grant land to Virginia. As early as January 1769, Virginia had requested that its border with the Cherokees be extended to the west. Cherokee headmen refused, stating plainly their wish "to keep the Virginians at as great a distance as possible".[40] In April 1770 they rebuffed a second request.[41] But six months later Cherokee negotiators reversed their position and agreed to cede a considerable portion of their northern hunting ground to Virginia.[42]

What had changed? In 1769, Oconostota's own son, Ahoweehee, had led a small delegation to the Iroquois council at Onondaga. His official mandate was to secure Onondaga's assistance in concluding a peace with the Algonquian villages farther west. Instead, Ahoweehee returned in September 1770 with more than two hundred Iroquois warriors. They carried Seneca war belts and proposed to join forces with the Cherokees against westering British settlers.[43] Oconostota, the principal Cherokee war chief, refused, but he must have known that he did not speak for his son's generation. And so in a desperate attempt to render young men obedient, elder leaders assumed Kanati's role as gift-giver. Meeting with British officials at Lochaber in the fall of 1770, they agreed to give up a substantial tract of land along Virginia's western border in exchange for an immediate supply of trade goods. When the young men of their villages angrily refused to ratify this agreement, council leaders asked British agents for still more goods. Only the giving of "a great Many presents" could persuade young hunters to accept such a cession of land, explained one member of the council at Chota. He and other leaders asked the British superintendent for two thousand pounds of powder, six thousand pounds of balls, plus firearms and other dry goods "of all kinds".[44]

The Lochaber cession, conceived as an effort to pacify young hunters, had served further to alienate them. As Oconostota reported, the hunters "Seemed Surprised that I would Agree to give away so much of their Land, that I would Consent to the White Peoples Settling so near to their Towns".[45] Cherokee headmen learned from their mistake, but as the crisis around them deepened, they refused to abandon altogether the strategy of gift-giving. Many Seneca warriors remained in the Overhill villages through the winter of 1770–1771. Shawnee and Delaware war parties arrived to join them. Again they urged Oconostota to make war on neighbouring whites, and once again he refused.[46] Young warriors from the Muskogean town of Coweta, neighbours with whom many Cherokees had intermarried, appeared ready to attack the Georgia frontier.[47] Fearing the worst, traders who lived among the Cherokees began to flee their homes in February 1771.[48]

Elder council members, no less apprehensive, seized the opportunity that presented itself. Traders were in too much of a hurry to pack their supplies back to Carolina. Offered land, these men might be persuaded to give the goods they had on hand to village headmen, who could then redistribute them among militant youths in an effort to avert war. This time, Oconostota, Usteneka, and the other headmen were careful to choose a location not coveted by young hunters. On February 22, they granted the traders sixty square miles of bottomland along the Savannah River, a region hunted primarily by Muskogees rather than Cherokees.[49] In return, the traders annulled all debts owed them by Cherokee hunters. Council members could represent this concession itself as a gift to younger men. More important, the traders also turned over to their Cherokee benefactors "all the goods they were possessed of in the nation". Mostly clothes and ammunition, these items were soon expended. But as one headman explained, "we could not do without them" at the time.[50] The strategy seemed to work. The Lochaber agreement had angered hunters, but this cession, according to Usteneka, was made "with the unanimous Consent of our young Men & Warriors".[51]

For the time being, at least, the crisis had been averted. But before long the links that young Cherokees had forged with militants throughout the trans-Appalachian woodlands again threatened to ignite a war. In September 1773, twenty Delaware and Shawnee warriors arrived in the principal Overhill town of Chota. Young Cherokees spoke darkly of joining them in a war against neighbouring whites. Oconostota was able to put an end to such talk in formal council.[52] But returning to the Ohio Valley in October, this party, accompanied now by two Cherokee men, attacked and killed a number of Virginians who were on their way to Kentucky.[53] William Crabtree, one of two survivors, avenged himself the following spring by killing a prominent Cherokee council member.[54] Young warriors advocated swift retribution. War belts arrived pledging Shawnee, Creek, and Seneca support.[55] While Cherokee Appalachia balanced uneasily between war and peace, council members rushed to locate a supply of gifts large enough to pacify their angry sons. Three years earlier, Attakullakulla had arranged to extend Virginia's boundary line hundreds of miles to the west. A commissioner named John Donelson had promised gifts worth five hundred pounds in exchange, but the goods had never materialized.[56] Now Attakullakulla hurried back to see Donelson and, as he put it, "hear the news".[57]

Donelson, however, remained unable or unwilling to deliver on his promise, and so as war came to their northern neighbours, elder leaders scrambled once again to locate a source of gifts. The conflict known to historians as Lord Dunmore's War involved mostly Shawnee and Delaware residents of the Ohio Valley, but some younger Cherokees also took part in the hostilities. Warriors from Chilhowee killed six white emigrants on the Ohio River. Seven more died at the hands of a group from Chota. Visitors to the towns of the Upper Tennessee watershed concluded that "their Chiefs are averse to War, but their Young Men are hardly restrainable".[58] Indeed, village leaders worried openly that they "were falling into contempt" among young warriors. Lacking the goods deemed necessary to restrain unruly youths, headmen made few efforts to assert their authority.[59]

Then Richard Henderson approached Upper Tennessee leaders. As early as the summer of 1774, observers thought Cherokee headmen seemed willing to sell land to a private interest.[60] Henderson proposed his purchase that same fall, offering four thousand pounds sterling in trade goods for all the land between the Cumberland and Ohio Rivers. By now desperate for a way to quiet their sons, Cherokee leaders found themselves in no position to refuse. Attakullakulla accompanied Henderson back to North Carolina to inspect the goods and returned at the head of a wagon train loaded with gifts – the last hope for peace, it must have seemed to elder council members.[61]

As before, the politics of masculinity created contradictory demands that left Cherokee negotiators little room to manoeuvre. Oconostota, Attakullakulla, and other elder councilmen understood that young hunters might not abide their selling the Kentucky country. The woods and canebrakes in that region "were their Hunting Grounds," they explained, and "their children who were then growing up might have reason to complain, if they sold that land".[62] And yet Henderson's purchase price seemed the only hope of pacifying these same sons.

Cherokee negotiators opened the proceedings with a proposal designed to resolve these contradictions. They proposed that Henderson purchase the land north and east of the Kentucky River – a tract that had been ceded to Virginia during the 1771 boundary survey, but for which Donelson still owed payment.[63] When Henderson declined, Cherokee negotiators announced that "they would look to Virginians for the price of [the] land".[64] But that avenue had already been tried. And so Oconostota, Attakullakulla, and the war chief of Chota reluctantly agreed to sign deeds for the land that Henderson wanted.[65]

With this act, it became impossible to contain any longer the contradictions imbedded in the Cherokee politics of masculinity. Young men rejected the Henderson purchase and with it the leadership of their fathers. Attakullakulla's own son, *Tsi'yu-gûnsi'ni* (Dragging Canoe), blamed the deal on "Old Men who . . . were too old to hunt".[66] In 1776, he led hundreds of young hunters into battle against the Anglo-Americans then settling Henderson's land. The war that Attakullakulla and his peers had made every sacrifice to avoid had come anyway. Cherokees would ultimately lose that war and the hunting grounds for which it was fought, thus leaving to a new generation the task of reconceptualizing male power in a world where large-scale hunting was a thing of the past.

Notes

An earlier version of this paper was presented in 1996 to the second annual conference of the Institute for Early American History and Culture at Boulder, Colorado. For their comments and suggestions, I would like to thank Stephen Aron, Ignacio Gallup-Diaz, Evan Haefeli, Jessica Meyerson, John Murrin, Nancy Shoemaker, and the participants in the 1997 Joint Neale and Commonwealth Fund Conference.

1   The depositions collected by Virginia authorities in 1776 and 1777 are the best record of what transpired. See W. P. Palmer (ed.), *Calendar of Virginia state papers and other manuscripts . . . preserved in the capitol at Richmond* [henceforth *CVSP*], [11 vols.] (Richmond, Va., 1875–93), I, pp. 271–315. For the illegality of Henderson's proceedings, see "A proclamation by Governor Martin against Richard Henderson and the Transylvania purchase", in *The Colonial Records of North Carolina, Published Under the Supervision of the Trustees of the Public Libraries, By Order of the General Assembly*, W. L. Saunders (ed.) [henceforth *CRNC*], [10 vols.] (Raleigh, N.C., 1886–90), IX, pp. 1222–5.

2   W. G. McLoughlin, *Cherokee renascence in the new republic* (Princeton, N.J., 1984), p. 19.

3 S. G. Parker. *The transformation of Cherokee Appalachia* (PhD thesis, University of California, Berkeley, 1991), pp. 164–7. More generally, see F. Jennings, *The invasion of America: Indians, colonialism, and the cant of conquest* (New York, 1976), pp. 144–5.

4 For the claims of Cherokee negotiators to have been deceived, see Isaac Shelby, deposition, 3 December 1777, *CVSP*, I, p. 297; and James Robinson, deposition, 16 April 1777, *ibid.*, I, p. 287. However, both sides made certain that there were other men present who could understand both languages: see Charles Robertson, deposition, 3 October 1777, *ibid.*, I, p. 291; Samuel Wilson, deposition, 15 April 1777, *ibid.*, I, p. 283; Thomas Houghton, deposition, 3 October 1777, *ibid.*, I, p. 290. Most of these interpreters were illiterate, and Henderson might simply have offered a verbal misreading of the document, which was then faithfully translated to the Cherokee signatories. But the available evidence militates against this interpretation. Henderson was surrounded at the moment of reading by literate men whose designs were in conflict with his own: see John Reid, deposition, 16 April 1777, *ibid.*, I, p. 284; and Charles Robertson, deposition, 3 October 1777, *ibid.*, I, p. 292. Furthermore, Henderson was aware that he would have difficulty persuading government to sanction his deal without having to answer to charges of fraud. See James Robinson, deposition, 16 April 1777, *ibid.*, I, p. 286. S. C. Williams, *Dawn of Tennessee valley and Tennessee history* (Johnson City, Tenn., 1937), pp. 408–9, assumes that this deposition was James Robertson's testimony, and that his name was misspelled; he is probably correct. On land hunters see S. Aron, *How the West was lost: the transformation of Kentucky from Daniel Boone to Henry Clay* (Baltimore, 1996), pp. 58–81.

5 Robert F. Berkhofer, Jr., "The political context of a new Indian history", *Pacific Historical Review* **40**(3), 1971, p. 363.

6 C. G. Calloway, *The American Revolution in Indian country: crisis and diversity in Native American communities* (Cambridge, 1995), pp. 182–212, esp. 190, F. Gearing, *Priests and warriors: social structures for Cherokee politics in the 18th century* (American Anthropological Association Memoirs 93, Menasha, Wisc., 1962), esp. p. 104.

7 My dissertation in progress at Princeton University, entitled *Preachers, prophets, and unruly men: religious upheaval and the meanings of manhood on the southern frontier, 1765–1815*, tells this story.

8 For Cherokee interpretation of the war as produced by young men's raiding, see "Journal of the Congress at Augusta with the Indians", in *Virginia treaties, 1723–1775*, W. S. Robinson (ed.), vol. 5 of *Early American Indian documents: treaties and laws, 1607–1789*, [18 vols.] (Frederick, Md., 1979–), p. 288; T. Hatley, *The dividing paths: Cherokees and South Carolinians through the era of revolution* (New York and Oxford, 1993), p. 114. Hatley, *The dividing paths*, pp. 119–40, argues that the cycle of raiding proved so explosive because it triggered far more fundamental hostilities between Cherokees and Carolinians. Also see D.H. Corkran, *The Cherokee frontier: conflict and survival, 1740–62* (Norman, Okla., 1962), esp. pp. 173–5.

9 Peter H. Wood has made the most systematic analysis of population in "The changing population of the colonial South: an overview by race and region, 1685–1790", in *Powhatan's mantle: Indians in the Colonial Southeast*, P. H. Wood, G. A. Waselkov, M. T. Hatley (eds) (Lincoln: Nebr., 1989), pp. 63–5. The Cherokee population declined by at least ten per cent and perhaps by as much as 33 per cent. The most reliable figures (9,000 before the war and 6,900 after it) translate approximately to a 15 per cent decline in population. Regardless of the precise figures, the subjective experience of the war was devastating for many of those who lived through it; see Hatley, *The dividing paths*, pp. 155–6.

10 On the proclamation of 1763, see L. De Vorsey, Jr., *The Indian boundary in the southern colonies, 1763–1775* (Chapel Hill N.C., 1961), pp. 34–40; For the South Carolina treaty, see "Minutes of a meeting with the Cherokee headmen", Fort Prince George, October 1765, encl. Ralph Phillips to Thomas Gage, 26 November 1765, *Gage Papers*, American Series, vol. 46; also "Cession of lands by the Cherokee Indians", Fort Prince George, October 1765, encl. John Stuart to Thomas Gage, 21 January 1766, *Gage Papers*, American Series, vol. 47. For the North Carolina treaty, see *CRNC*, VII, pp. 462–6, 502–5. For the Virginia treaty, which was supplanted by a new agreement in 1770, see John Stuart, "Journal of the Superintendant's Proceedings", Hard Labour, October 1768, *Gage Papers*, American Series, vol. 137, folder 8.

11 Proceedings "At a Meeting of a party of Cherokee Indians, chiefly Headmen and Rulers of their Nation, and most of the Cherokee Traders", near Fort Charlotte, 8 June 1771, Colonial Office Papers [henceforth CO], Public Record Office, 5/72/330.

12 Some white hunters took in excess of one thousand skins in a single year. Charles McLamore was found with 1,100 deerskins in the summer of 1769. Alexander Cameron to [John Stuart], Fort Prince George, 18 July 1768, encl. Stuart to Gage, 22 August 1768, *Gage Papers*, American Series, vol. 80. For more on McLamore, see Hatley, *The dividing paths*, pp. 135–8. On the longhunters in general see Aron, *How the West was lost*, pp. 21–7.

For one of the earliest attempts to settle west of the Holston Valley, see Joseph Martin to [William Symmes?], 9 May 1767, Tennessee Papers, Lyman C. Draper Manuscripts, Wisconsin Historical Society, Madison, Wisc. For a narrative of white settlement from the perspective of Cherokee hunters, see "The Deputy Superintendant Mr Henry Stuart's Account of his Proceedings with the Cherokee Indians about going against the whites", 25 August 1776, *CRNC*, X, pp. 765, 768–9.

13 Thomas Gage to John Stuart, New York, 26 January 1768, *Gage Papers*, American Series, vol. 73.

14 The most famous and most frequently used version is that collected by James Mooney: "Kana'ti and Selu: the origin of game and corn", in *Myths of the Cherokee*, J. Mooney, Nineteenth Annual Report of the Bureau of American Ethnology, 1897–1898, Part 1 (Washington, D.C., 1900), pp. 242–8. I have relied instead on an earlier version, collected in the 1830s by Daniel S. Butrick, a missionary among the Cherokees. The myth appears in two places in Payne's papers: typescript of Payne-Butrick manuscript, John Howard Payne Papers, Newberry Library, Chicago, I, pp. 26–31 [henceforth "Payne-Butrick typescript"; page numbers refer to the typescript and should not be confused with the manuscript's pagination]; and Payne-Butrick typescript, II, pp. 50–61.

Butrick identifies his informant as "Sickatower" or Sickatowa and describes him as "one of the most aged men in the nation". Sickatowa, claimed to have heard this myth when he was a boy (John Ross to Payne, 4 July 1837, Payne-Butrick typescript, IV, pp. 2–3). This would date the myth at least back to the 1760s and perhaps earlier. Butrick further stated that a Cherokee man named Big Cabin had told a similar story to another missionary. Big Cabin was 90 at the time, which would date his birth to some time about 1740. He said that he had first heard the story when he was 15 years old, thus dating it to approximately 1765. See *ibid.* typescript, II, p. 62. For more on Butrick's informants, see Butrick to Payne, 11 July 1837, *ibid.*, IV, pp. 5–6; Butrick to Payne, 29 December 1840, *ibid.*, IV, p. 9.

The earliest recorded version of the Selu–Kanati myth that I have been able to locate was taken down by Moravian missionaries to the Cherokees in 1810. See "*Diarium* von

Springplace vom 1. Jan. bis 31. August 1810", 20 May 1810, Cherokee Mission Papers: Diaries of Springplace, 1801–1814, Moravian Archives, Winston-Salem, N.C. [henceforth MAWS], M406, folder 3. Another version appears in "*Diarium* von *Springplace* vom Jahr 1815", 13 October 1815, Cherokee Mission Papers: Diaries of Springplace, 1815–1832, and Oochgeelogy, 1823–1831, MAWS, M408, folder 1.

The dating of this and other myths that structured how Cherokees thought about hunting and more broadly about masculinity is important. As Marshall Sahlins and others have pointed out, myths are fluid, constantly reinterpreted and refashioned when they seem out of step with a world which "is under no obligation to conform to the logic by which some people conceive of it". M. Sahlins, "Structure and history", in *Islands of history* (Chicago and London, 1985), p. 138. Also informative on this subject is A. Giddens, *Central problems in social theory: action, structure and contradiction in social analysis* (Berkeley and Los Angeles, 1979), esp. Chapter 2.

15 Payne-Butrick typescript, I, pp. 101–3. Moravian missionaries described exactly the same ceremony, performed in 1811: "*Diarium* von *Springplace* vom 1ten *Januar* bis 31. *December* 1811", 28 July 1811, Cherokee Mission Papers: Diaries of Springplace, 1801–1814, MAWS, M406, folder 3.

16 Payne-Butrick typescript, I, p. 38, III, pp. 42–5, 49, 64, 75–6, IV, p. 29; C. Hudson, *The Southeastern Indians* (Knoxville, Tern., 1976), pp. 319–22.

17 On the rituals of war-making and their relationship to male power, see Payne-Butrick typescript, III, pp. 58–75.

18 *Ibid.*, III, pp. 42–5, 49.

19 "Copy of a Talk from the Headmen & Warriors of the Cherokee Nation to John Stuart Esqr.", 29 July 1769, encl. Stuart to Gage, 25 September 1769, *Gage Papers*, American Series, vol. 87. For similar complaints see William Richardson, "An Account of my Proceedings since I accepted the Indian Mission in October 2d. 1758 to go & exercise my office as a Minister among the Cherokees or any other Indian Nation that wou'd allow me to preach to them", Wilberforce Eames Indian Collection, New York Public Library, 30 January 1759; John Stuart to [Thomas Gage], 30 March 1768, *Gage Papers*, American Series, vol. 75.

20 For example, see Gavin Cochrane, "Account of What Intelligence relating to the Indians I have lately received from Fort Prince George", 26 April 1765, encl. Cochrane to Gage, 26 April 1765, *Gage Papers*, American Series, vol. 35; also Cochrane to Gage, 23 January 1765, *Gage Papers*, American Series, vol. 30. In 1768, Cherokee hunters encountered a large number of Virginians hunting "within Forty Miles of their Towns" and confiscated their deerskins. See John Stuart to Gage, 30 March 1768, *Gage Papers*, American Series, vol. 75; CO 5/69/193, John Stuart to [Board of Trade?], 7 May 1768.

21 CO 5/67/246, "A Talk from Ouconnastatah or the great Warrior, Attacullaculla, and other Head Warriors and beloved Men of the Cherokees, to be sent to the Honble John Stuart Esqr, their Father in Charles Town", n.d. [1767?]; CO 5/1332/42, John Stuart to John Blair, 17 October 1768; John Stuart, "Journal of the Superintendant's Proceedings", 17 October 1768, *Gage Papers*, American Series, vol. 137, folder 8 (for another copy of this document, see CO 5/70/68–85).

22 Payne-Butrick typescript I, pp. 24–5 (quotation on p. 25). This version of the story was collected by Butrick in the 1830s. Mooney, *Myths of the Cherokee*, pp. 258–9, prints another version dating from the 1890s. Three informants told Mooney the same story, from which he concluded that "This myth is well known in the tribe" (Mooney, *Myths of the Cherokee*, p. 442).

23 Hudson, *Southeastern Indians*, pp. 185–96, provides a concise discussion of this kinship system, although he draws most of his evidence from Creek sources. Also see Gearing, *Priests and warriors*, pp. 15–23; John Gambold to Rev. Charles Gotthold Reichel, 4 August 1810, Cherokee Mission Papers: Misc. Cherokee letters, 1799–1831, MAWS, M411, folder 1; Gambold to Reichel, 22 May 1809, Cherokee Mission Papers: Springplace Letters, 1808–1809, MAWS, M411, folder 6B; Gambolds [Anna Rosel Gambold] to Rev. John Herbst, 10 November 1810, Cherokee Mission Papers: Springplace Letters, 1810–1818, MAWS, M412, folder 1, item 23. On clan revenge, see J. P. Reid, *A law of blood: the primitive law of the Cherokee nation* (New York, 1970).

24 On Cherokee women as farmers, see T. Hatley, "Cherokee women farmers hold their ground", in *Appalachian frontiers: settlement, society, and development in the pre-industrial era*, R. D. Mitchell (ed.) (Lexington, Ky., 1991), pp. 37–51; T. Purdue, "Women, men and American Indian policy: the Cherokee response to 'civilization' ", in *Negotiators of change: historical perspectives on Native American women*, N. Shoemaker (ed.) (New York and London, 1995), pp. 90–114. For the authority of clans over agricultural fields, see Gearing, *Priests and warriors*, p. 21.

25 Payne-Butrick typescript, III, pp. 58–9; Gearing, *Priests and warriors*, pp. 47–54.

26 Talk "from the Cherokee Chiefs & head men of the Nation to their Father in Charles Town", 22 September 1766, encl. Stuart to Gage, 19 December 1766, *Gage Papers*, American Series, vol. 60 (see CO 5/67/240–43 for another copy of this document). On the rhetoric of listening and hearing in another Native American context, see R. J. DeMallie, " 'These Have No Ears': narrative and the ethnohistorical method", *Ethnohistory* **40**(4), 1993, pp. 515–38.

27 Payne-Butrick typescript, II, pp. 56–61, quotation on p. 58.

28 Richardson, "An Account of my Proceedings since I accepted the Indian Mission", 30 January 1759.

29 See J. W. Martin, *Sacred revolt: the muskogees' struggle for a new world* (Boston, 1991), pp. 6–13, for a discussion of the problems associated with the term "Creek".

30 CO 5/75/17, "Abstract of Letters from David Taitt Esqr. Commissary in the Creek Nation to John Stuart Esqr.", 25 October 1773. For Cherokees, see CO 5/66/407, Alexander Cameron to [John Stuart], 1 June 1766; CO 5/1350/27, Attakullakulla, talk to [John Donelson], March 1772.

31 John Stuart, "Talk to the Headmen, & Warriors of the Cherokee Nation", 18 May 1767, in "Journal of the Superintendant's Proceedings", *Gage Papers*, American Series, vol. 137, folder 6; Oconostota, talk to John Stuart, 19 May 1767, in *ibid.*; Usteneka, talk to Stuart, 19 May 1767, in *ibid.*; and Saluy, talk to Stuart, 19 May 1767, in *ibid.*

32 In 1764, for instance, the headman of a neighbouring Creek village asked British agents for a substantial supply of goods. The pacification of young warriors, he explained, depended largely on gifts of ammunition and other goods "for the old people to distrbute to the young people by their Elders, & to acquaint them [of] the reason of these presents". See Emistisiguo, "Talk to Governor Boone and Superintendant John Stuart", 10 April 1764, encl. Stuart to Gage, 20 May 1765, *Gage Papers*, American Series, vol. 18. Also see R. White, *The roots of dependency: subsistence, environment, and social change among the Choctaws, Pawnees, and Navajos* (Lincoln, Nebr., 1983), pp. 68, 71.

33 See, for example, the opinion of General Thomas Gage, then commander of British forces in North America: "Tho' it may be necessary & right to give some Presents to the Savages to keep them in good Humour, & reconcile them to their new Neighbours [i.e. British settlers], it is not to be done profusely they are to be dealt out to them with Judgement

and Oeconomy": Gage to Major Ogilvie, 31 March 1764, *Gage Papers*, American Series, vol. 16. Also see White, *Roots of dependency*, p. 71; R. White, *The middle ground: Indians, empires and republics in the Great Lakes region, 1650–1815* (Cambridge, 1991), pp. 256–9.

34 CO 5/1331/6, Andrew Lewis to "the Chiefs of the Cherokees of the Over Hill Towns", 8 May 1765; CO 5/1331/8, Andrew Lewis to [Lt. Gov. Fauquier], 9 May 1765; CO 5/43/38, Andrew Lewis to [Lt. Gov. Fauquier], 3 June 1765; Alexander Cameron to Capt. Cochrane, 6 June 1765, encl. Cochrane to Gage, 5 August 1765, *Gage Papers*, American Series, vol. 40; Thomas Gage to Capt. Cochrane, 28 June 1765, *Gage Papers*, American Series, vol. 38; Francis Fauquier to Gage, 6 July 1765, *Gage Papers*, American Series, vol. 39; John Stuart to John Pownall, 24 August 1765, Shelburne Papers, William L. Clements Library, Ann Arbor, Michigan, vol. 60, pp. 39–67; CO 5/66/76, John Stuart to Halifax, 24 August 1765; Ralph Phillips to Gage, Charles Town, 9 October 1765, *Gage Papers*, American Series, vol. 44. John Stuart calculated that nine men had either been killed outright in Augusta or died later of wounds received there; see CO 5/68/100, Stuart's talk to "Kittagusta of Chote and to the Headmen & Warriors of the Cherokee Nation", 5 February 1767. Oconostota put the number at eight; see John Stuart, "Journal of the Superintendant's Proceedings", October 1768, *Gage Papers*, American Series, vol. 137, folder 8, p. 11 (for another copy of this document, see CO 5/70/68–85); CO 5/68/104, "A Talk from the Great Warriour, Oueconnastotah, to be sent to his Head Beloved Brother The Honble John Stuart Esq", 5 March 1767. Hatley, *Dividing paths*, p. 183, misdates the murders as taking place in 1766. On the Augusta incident, also see A. H. Tillson, *Gentry and common folk: political culture on a Virginia frontier* (Lexington, Ky., 1991), pp. 49, 182.

35 For cession of land, see "Minutes of a meeting with the Cherokee headmen", Fort Prince George, October 1765, encl. Ralph Phillips to Gage, 26 November 1765, *Gage Papers*, American Series, vol. 46. For the expectation that Cherokee headmen were to receive gifts, see John Stuart, "Journal of the Superintendant's Proceedings", October 1768, *Gage Papers*, American Series, vol. 137, folder 8, pp. 7, 9 (for another copy of this document, see CO 5/70/68–85).

36 On the connection between the Fort Stanwix treaty and white settlement in the Holston Valley, see De Vorsey, *Indian boundary*, pp. 71–4; Williams, *Dawn of Tennessee Valley and Tennessee history*, pp. 334–54. For Cherokee opinions of the Holston hunting ground, see CO 5/66/407, Alexander Cameron to [John Stuart], 1 June 1766.

37 As late as 1777 Cherokees continued to consider this region the primary hunting ground of men from Chilhowee and Settico. See speech of the Raven, 15 July 1777, in "The Treaty of Long Island of Holston, July, 1777", A. Henderson (ed.) *North Carolina Historical Review* 8(1), 1931, p. 83. Chilhowee had been hit particularly hard by the murders at Staunton, a factor that surely contributed to the unusual militancy of the village's young men.

38 For both incidents see John Stuart to Thomas Gage, 24 April 1770, *Gage Papers*, American Series, vol. 91.

39 John Stuart to Thomas Gage, 12 December 1770, *Gage Papers*, American Series, vol. 98. Militant Shawnees took the lead in inter-tribal diplomacy. Beginning in 1769, they and neighboring Delawares hosted a series of annual conferences at Scioto River, to which like-minded men from throughout the Eastern Woodlands were invited. Delegations of young Cherokee men attended, apparently without official sanction from town and regional councils, in 1769, 1770, 1771, 1772, and 1774. See G. E. Dowd, *A spirited*

resistance: the North American Indian struggle for unity, 1745–1815 (Baltimore, 1992), pp. 42–5; Gage to John Stuart, 19 September 1770, *Gage Papers*, American Series, vol. 96; Charles Edmonstone to Gage, 24 April 1771, *Gage Papers*, American Series, vol. 102; Gage to John Stuart, New York, 30 September 1772, *Gage Papers*, American Series, vol. 114; abstract, Alexander Cameron to [?], 18 June 1774, encl. Stuart to Gage, 3 July 1774, *Gage Papers*, American Series, vol. 120; John Stuart to Frederick Haldimand, 8 August 1774, *Gage Papers*, American Series, vol. 122.

40 CO 5/70/246, "Talk from Oucconnastotah & the other Head Men & Warriors of the Cherokee Nation, To John Stuart", 29 March 1769. For the request on behalf of Virginia, see CO 5/70/171, John Stuart, "Talk to the Head beloved Man of Chotéh", 19 January 1769.

41 Minutes, "Congress of the Principal Chiefs & Warriors of the Upper & Lower Cherokee Nation, Held at Congarees in the Province of South Carolina", 3 April 1770, *Gage Papers*, American Series, vol. 137, folder 11, esp. pp. 9–10, also in CO 5/70(1)/107–14.

42 Minutes, "General meeting of the principal Chiefs and Warriors of the Cherokee Nation with John Stuart Esqr. Superintendant for the Southern district of North America", 18 October 1770, *Gage Papers*, American Series, vol. 137, folder 10.

43 Alexander Cameron to John Stuart, Fort Prince George, 8 February 1771, in *Documents of the American Revolution, 1770–1783 (Colonial Office Series)*, G. Davies (ed.) [21 vols.] (Shannon, 1972–1981), III, pp. 37–8. For war belt, see Gage to John Stuart, New York, 24 April 1773, *Gage Papers*, American Series, vol. 118; and Sir William Johnson to Earl of Dartmouth, 4 November 1772, in Davies (ed.), *Documents of the American Revolution*, V, p. 212. Also see Gage to John Stuart, 19 September 1770, *Gage Papers*, American Series, vol. 96; Gage to Stuart, 16 October 1770, *ibid.*; Gage to Stuart, 20 November 1770, *Gage Papers*, American Series, vol. 98; Stuart to Gage, 12 December 1770, *ibid.*; Lord Botetourt, "Copy of the proceedings of a Council held at the Palace", 17 August 1770, encl. Stuart to Gage, 12 December 1770, *ibid.*

44 "General meeting of the principal Chiefs and Warriors of the Cherokee Nation with John Stuart Esqr. Superintendant for the Southern district of North America", Lochaber, 18 October 1770, *Gage Papers*, American Series, vol. 137, folder 10; abstract, Alexander Cameron to John Stuart, 19 March 1771, in Davies (ed.), *Documents of the American Revolution*, III, pp. 70–3. For preliminary discussion of a boundary extension, and Virginia's promise to pay for it, see CO 5/1332/103, Andrew Lewis & Thomas Walker, report to the Governor of Virginia, 2 February 1769.

45 Abstract, Alexander Cameron to John Stuart, 19 March 1771, in Davies (ed.), *Documents of the American Revolution*, III, pp. 70–3.

46 CO 5/72/177, abstract, Alexander Cameron to [John Stuart], 23 January 1771; Alexander Cameron to John Stuart, 8 February 1771, in Davies (ed.), *Documents of the American Revolution*, III, pp. 37–8; CO 5/72/221–2, talk of "Tistoe, Attakullakullah, The Wolf, Chinesto, The Terrapin, the Bear coming out of the tree, the Yellow Bird, and other Head Men of the lower Towns, To the Warriors and beloved Men over the Hills", 12 February 1771; CO 5/72/225, Alexander Cameron, talk to the Overhill Cherokees, 28 February 1771; "Proceedings of a Convention of the over Hill Cherokee Chiefs & Beloved Men &c.", 3 March 1771, *Gage Papers*, American Series, vol. 102 (see CO 5/72/227–8 for another copy of this document); abstract, Alexander Cameron to [John Stuart], 4 March 1771, *Gage Papers*, American Series, vol. 102 (same as CO 5/72/217–18).

47 CO 5/72/175, George Galphin to John Stuart, 19 February 1771.

48 CO 5/72/173, abstract, Richard King to John Caldwell, 1 February 1771; John Stuart to Gage, 8 February 1771, *Gage Papers*, American Series, vol. 99.

49 This cession became a bone of contention between provincial merchants and the colonial bureaucracy, which contested the right of British subjects to treat privately with any group of Indians. It also provoked a dispute between the Cherokees and their Muskogean neighbours, who claimed the land as their own. These issues were not resolved until 1773, when Cherokee and Muskogee headmen agreed to cede the land to the province of Georgia, which then gave a portion of the proceeds to the merchants and traders who were originally party to the deal. See J. R. Snapp, *John Stuart and the struggle for empire on the southern frontier* (Baton Rouge, La., and London, 1996), pp. 116–46.

50 CO 5/72/330, minutes, "Meeting of a party of Cherokee Indians, chiefly Headmen and Rulers of their Nation, and most of the Cherokee Traders", near Fort Charlotte, 8 June 1771.

51 CO 5/651/109, Judd's Friend, talk to [Alexander Cameron], 7 March 1771.

52 Abstract, Alexander Cameron to John Stuart, 11 October 1773, in Davies (ed.), *Documents of the American Revolution*, VI, pp. 231–2. Outside the council-house, Oconostota's control of the situation was less convincing. He later admitted to Stuart that young men with "no authority to call themselves deputies" had delivered war talks to Muskogulgee councils that fall. See Stuart to the Earl of Dartmouth, 21 December 1773, in *ibid.*, VI, p. 258.

53 This incident has been made famous as part of the lore surrounding Daniel Boone. Boone's son James was among the deceased. See J. M. Faragher, *Daniel Boone: the life and legend of an American pioneer* (New York, 1992). Isaac Thomas, deposition, 12 February 1774, and Thomas Sharp, deposition, 20 February 1774, encl. William Ogilvy to Frederick Haldimand, 8 June 1774, *Gage Papers*, American Series, vol. 119; CO 5/75/206–7.

54 Farragher, *Boone*, p. 95. For contemporary accounts, see CO 5/75/186–7, abstract, Alexander Cameron to John Stuart, 4 July 1774; Arthur Campbell to William Preston, June 1774, Draper Mss., 3QQ40; CO 5/75/202–3 Andrew Lewis, "talk to Oconostátó & the Chief of the [Cherokee] nation as well as Autosity", 9 June 1774; CO 5/75/204–5, William Preston, copy of a talk to the Cherokees, 11 June 1774; CO 5/75/206–7, Arthur Campbell to Alexander Campbell, 20 June 1774; Edward Wilkinson to [Alexander Cameron], 26 June 1774, encl. Ogilvy to Haldimand, 18 July 1774, *Gage Papers*, American Series, vol. 121.

55 For the anger of young Cherokee men, see CO 5/75/192, David Taitt to [John Stuart], 18 July 1774; John Stuart to Gage, 8 August 1774, *Gage Papers*, American Series, vol. 122; William Christian to William Preston, 9 July 1774, Draper Mss., 3QQ60. For war belts, see Edward Wilkinson to [Alexander Cameron], 26 June 1774, encl. Ogilvy to Haldimand, 18 July 1774, *Gage Papers*, American Series, vol. 121; John Stuart to Frederick Haldimand, 8 August 1774, *Gage Papers*, American Series, vol. 122.

56 Earl of Dunmore to Earl of Hillsborough, Williamsburg, [20] March 1772, in Davies (ed.), *Documents of the American Revolution*, V, pp. 51–3; CO 5/1350/27, Attakullakulla, talk to [John Donelson], March 1772; Charles Robertson, deposition, 3 October 1777, *CVSP*, I, p. 291; Williams, *Dawn of Tennessee valley and Tennessee history*, p. 349; De Vorsey, *Indian boundary*, pp. 81–5.

57 "Talk of the headmen of the Overhill Cherokee Nation to Alexander Cameron", n.d. [1774], encl. Ogilvy to Haldimand, 18 July 1774, *Gage Papers*, American Series, vol. 121. Cameron, the British official most familiar with Cherokee affairs, thought Attakullakulla

intended "to remind him [Donelson] of the Presents which the Colonel Promised to send out for the Chiefs when we parted"; CO 5/75/187, abstract, Alexander Cameron to John Stuart, 4 July 1774.

58 Alexander Cameron to [John Stuart], 25 August 1774, encl. Stuart to Gage, 14 September 1774, *Gage Papers*, American Series, vol. 123.

59 John Stuart to Earl of Dartmouth, Charleston, 15 December 1774, in Davies (ed.), *Documents of the American Revolution*, VIII, p. 244.

60 Arthur Campbell, deposition, 21 October 1778, *CVSP*, I, pp. 303–4; Patrick Henry, deposition, 4 June 1777, *ibid.*, I, p. 289; William Christian, deposition, 3 June 1777, *ibid.*, I, p. 288; Dunmore to John Stuart, 5 April 1774, encl. William Ogilvy to Frederick Haldimand, Charlestown, 8 June 1774, *Gage Papers*, American Series, vol. 119.

61 CO 5/76/93, Alexander Cameron to [John Stuart], 2 March 1775; A. L. Fries (ed.), *Records of the Moravians in North Carolina*, [11 vols.] (Raleigh, N.C., 1922–1969), II, pp. 835–6, 900. The timing and original offer are difficult to establish. When Henderson and Attakullakulla first passed through Salem en route to inspect the goods, they revealed that the Cherokees were contemplating a land sale and told Moravian leaders that the purchase price was "4,000 pounds in goods" (*ibid.*, II, p. 836). Oral tradition places the final purchase price at £10,000, but this figure cannot be verified. W. S. Lester, *The Transylvania Colony* (Spencer, Ind., 1935), pp. 35–6.

62 James Robinson, deposition, 16 April 1777, *CVSP*, I, p. 286.

63 Charles Robertson, deposition, 3 October 1777, *ibid.*, I, p. 291; Samuel Wilson, deposition, 15 April 1777, *ibid.*, I, p. 282; John Lowry, deposition, 16 April 1777, *ibid.*, I, p. 283; James Robinson, deposition, 16 April 1777, *ibid.*, I, p. 285.

64 John Lowry, deposition, 16 April 1777, *ibid.*, I, p. 283 (quotation); also see James Robinson, deposition, 16 April 1777, *ibid.*, I, p. 286.

65 J. P. Brown, *Old frontiers: the story of the Cherokee Indians from earliest times to the date of their removal to the West, 1838* (Kingsport, Tenn., 1938), pp. 553–6, reproduces the full text of the treaty, drawn from a copy of the deed filed "for recording" at Rogersville, Hawkins County, Tennessee, on 1 November 1794.

66 "The Deputy Superintendant Mr. Henry Stuart's Account of his Proceedings with the Cherokee Indians about going against the whites", Pensacola, 25 August 1776, *CRNC*, X, p. 764. This document has also been reproduced in Davies (ed.), *Documents of the American Revolution*, XII, pp. 191–208.

Chapter Nine

Racialization and feminization of poverty in early America: Indian women as "the poor of the town" in eighteenth-century Rhode Island

Ruth Wallis Herndon

In the late eighteenth century, New England town "fathers" and individual Native Americans dealt with each other repeatedly across the space of a council table. In these encounters, British-American officials used English poor laws to regulate a remnant of conquered and colonized people. The Native Americans concerned had not migrated north and west as had so many others intent on fleeing from the English presence. Nor did they dwell on the reserved lands marked off for native peoples here and there in New England. These indigenous people lived among the colonizers, laboured in their midst, and coexisted uneasily with officials who clearly considered them "the other". In the hands of local officials, the poor laws became a way of perpetuating poverty among these native people left behind the frontier. In the process, Native Americans became indistinguishable from African-Americans in official documents, as town fathers blurred the meanings of their encounters with two separate groups of people.

Native women suffered particularly from the actions of officials who applied the poor law, with the result that poverty became not only racialized but feminized. This essay argues that despite the gender-neutral and colour-neutral character of the laws, Indian women were among those least likely to benefit from the safety net deployed by town officials to rescue the poorest inhabitants in eighteenth-century Rhode Island. The social welfare system designed to provide "the necessities of life" for the neediest people seldom netted women of colour, whose lives as free people were circumscribed by economic vulnerability, community scrutiny, and official rejection. More often, town leaders targetted these women for removal rather than support.

This shifted the responsibility for poor relief to another town and simultaneously rid the town of women who were often seen as a threat to order.

In eighteenth-century New England, elected town leaders – councilmen, selectmen, and overseers of the poor – bore responsibility for identifying needy residents and alleviating their need. Town officials did not invent this system of local welfare; they inherited it, along with the rest of English law. Parliamentary legislation during the seventeenth and eighteenth centuries (referred to collectively as the Poor Law) codified and regularized the various means of poor relief that had sprung up in the sixteenth century after the dissolution of the manors, monasteries, and guilds that formerly had given aid to the needy. The Poor Law made local governments responsible for poor relief and implicitly assured all inhabitants that their basic material needs would be provided in times of crisis.

English Poor Law equipped governing officials with three principal instruments to manage the lives of desperately poor people. *Warning out* rid the community of people who "belonged" legally to another town – a home town – where they were entitled to poor relief. *Indenture* put poor children and adults into labour contracts with local residents, who agreed to provide the necessities of life in exchange for work. And *poor relief* put needy people into the care of "respectable" inhabitants, who would receive payment in money or goods from the town treasury for their support of the poor.[1] This essay draws on the records of warning out, indenture, and poor relief administration in fourteen Rhode Island towns between 1750 and 1800.[2] These records provide illuminating detail about the race and sex of people who came under the scrutiny of poor relief officials.

Analyzing the identity of the poor offers a new perspective on the New England town and on poor relief in early America. Most eighteenth-century town studies emphasize the homogeneous character of the townspeople and their prosperity relative to their English forebears. Poor and non-white townspeople, often hidden in town records, have been slighted by historians of the region. Further, classic studies of warning-out and indenture have not applied race and gender as categories of analysis.[3] And while studies of poor relief in early America have emphasized its utility as a means of social control, they have not analyzed the race and sex of the objects of that control.[4] This essay's focus on the racial and gendered aspects of warning-out, indenture, and poor relief illuminates the lives of people in the margins of these previous studies.

Indian women existed on the margins of New England town life then and on the margins of the remaining records now. They did not vote in town meetings or show up on tax lists or register the births of their children. Even their fleeting and shadowy presence in the poor relief, warning-out, and indenture records is complicated by the sensibilities of the record-keepers. In the latter half of the eighteenth century, town clerks routinely blurred the distinction between Indians and Blacks when they identified people of colour by racial designation in the town records. To make matter worse, there is clear evidence that town clerks *redesignated* Indians as Black, thereby virtually erasing "Indians" from the official records in most towns by 1800.[5] These records make it impossible to separate women of Native American descent from those of African descent; further, sexual liasons between Indians and Blacks resulted in children with a dual heritage. Therefore, to reconstruct the experience of women who were of Indian heritage, I have cast a wider net and have gathered in data pertaining to all women designated as non-white: "Black", "Negro", "mulatto", and "mustee", as well as "Indian".

The town leaders

Town leaders' treatment of Indian women reveals official sensibilities about race and gender. Local authorities upheld patriarchy, which gave them a particular view of women; and they upheld colonialism, which gave them a particular view of Indians. At the intersection of these two ideologies stood Indian women, who forced town leaders to shape a particular policy for dealing with them. That policy partook equally of officials' prejudices against non-white *women* (who threatened sexual disorder) and against vanquished *Indians* (who required management by whites).

New England town leaders acted within a communitarian understanding of patriarchy. Town councilmen and other officials functioned as the heads of a public family, and all inhabitants within their town came under their power and had claim to their care. From the moment of their annual election, the leaders of the towns assumed it was their right to manage the lives of others within the town, to claim their wealth to support the poor or to direct the details of their lives if they *were* the poor. It was with good reason that town leaders were called "fathers" of the town; they made it their business to act as surrogate fathers, husbands, and masters to all whose households did not function in accordance with European patriarchal tradition.

That patriarchal tradition was confounded by many households of the poorer sort: households headed by women. It was these households that town leaders targetted for removal through the warning-out process. Less than half (46 per cent) of the warned-out households conformed to the ideal European family structure of husband, wife, and children. In the majority of cases, separated spouses, single mothers, widows, and unmarried couples managed their own households and attempted to support their dependants with their own labour. Women sometimes grouped together and combined households – mothers with their adult daughters and young grandchildren, sisters raising their children together, wives of seafaring men sharing a house, and so forth. From the town fathers' point of view, these daughters, sisters, mothers, and wives were not in their proper place, disconnected as they were from the settled, patriarchal households on which white New England was officially built.

Indian women especially offended in this regard. Indian traditions of marriage and circumstances of colonial slavery often precluded the marriage ceremony that English people expected. When the South Kingstown councilmen grilled two native women who seemed to be in a needy and husbandless situation, they soon discovered that the women did indeed have mates. Mary Fowler testified that she had lived with James Fowler "for about thirty Years & had Ten Children by him" but she had not married him "in the Manner white People are married in these parts". Similarly, her daughter Mary Champlin told the councilmen that she had lived with John Champlin 11 years and had six children by him, "but never was Married to him according to the form Used by the White People in these Parts".[6] In another example, the East Greenwich councilmen granted a single settlement certificate to Winsor Fry ("an Indian Man") and Lucy Davis ("an Indian Woman"), indicating that officials acknowledged the two as belonging to the same household, even though they were not married according to white standards (hence two last names).[7]

Further, Indian women often lived in non-nuclear households, either out of preference for traditional native household forms or out of economic necessity. Indian men often supported their families through work as sailors[8] and soldiers,[9] two of the few occupations open to them, but occupations which kept men away from their homes for long periods of time. Naturally enough, women grouped together to support each other and to raise children together in the absence of the men. From the town leaders' point of view, those absent seafaring and soldiering men left their families vulnerable to poverty and trouble and necessitated the intervention of white officials. Dedicated attempts by Indian men to support their families thus resulted in their families coming under close scrutiny by town officials.

New England town leaders also acted within an understanding of colonialism that put whites in a superior position to Indian "savages". The seventeenth-century destruction and subjugation of Indians by English settlers in New England resulted in a sizeable population of Indians in positions of bound servitude or free poverty by the middle of the 1700s. This economic and social degradation signalled to white officials that the proper place for

Indians was under the rule of those who were both white and more prosperous. When deciding how to manage the lives of Indians, town leaders made arrangements they deemed "proper", "suitable" or "fitting" for "such persons". Some towns went so far as to acknowledge openly that all people of colour required white management. In 1757, the town meeting of Middletown voted that "all Indians & Molattos that are free born, residing in this Town, shall be under the Care and Government of the overseers of the poor, to be by them dealt with in all respects in the same manner as white people are who are under their care".[10]

Indian women, then, came under double scrutiny of town officials because they were female and because they were Indian. Both patriarchy and colonialism demanded that white officials monitor their lives and step in with appropriate measures when circumstances dictated. The story of Alice and Hannah Franklin at the hands of South Kingstown officials illustrates this double jeopardy for native women.

In May 1764, the South Kingstown councilmen learned that Hannah Franklin had given birth to an illegitimate child.[11] After hearing of this, the councilmen considered the evidence and decided that Franklin had "behaved in such a manner before ye authority" (perhaps refusing to tell the name of the father) that it would be useless to find and sue the father for maintenance; instead they ordered Franklin and her child bound out as indentured servants "for so long a Time as will Indemnify ye Town from any Expence, that was or has accrued on their account".[12] Six years later, Franklin bore a second illegitimate child. Again the council made no effort to find and penalize the father; instead, they ordered an overseer of the poor to "keep Hannah Franklin in his service until she pays him the charge of lying in, including of her maintenance and child".[13] Less than three years later, Hannah Franklin bore a third illegitimate child, a daughter named Alice. When Alice was 18 months old, the council ordered the mother put under indenture "not exceeding seven years" to pay the costs of her lying-in (an account of about £20) and they ordered the toddler bound out to townsman Caleb Gardner until she turned 18.[14]

In 1787, that toddler had grown into a 14-year-old who herself gave birth to an illegitimate son, Cato. Since Alice was still Gardner's bound servant, the town council authorized Gardner to "find a place and put out to board" this baby at the town's expense.[15] Young Alice was unable to care for the baby herself; she became "delirious" after Cato's birth and was "unable to support herself".[16] Faced with the long-term prospect of a non-productive servant (Alice was incapacitated for two years), Gardner tried to foist Alice on to the overseer of the poor, claiming she had turned 18 and was no longer bound to him by indenture. But the town council investigated, discovered that Alice was three years away from completing her indenture, and ordered Gardner to fulfill his contract. When Gardner refused, the council sued him for expenses and reluctantly took over the care of Alice until she could return to work.[17]

This story reveals the mentality of the white men who took responsibility for managing the lives of these women. Neither the master nor the town officials felt obliged to provide support for Hannah and Alice; both women were viewed primarily as labourers capable of earning their own keep. When it became clear that Alice could *not* labour, white authority fell into dispute about who should be burdened with her care. Town officials routinely covered the cost of lying-in and loss of work time for white women who gave birth to "bastard" children. Not so for women of colour. While white officials saw white women as suitable recipients of poor relief during the most vulnerable times of their lives, the same assumption did not apply to Indian women, whose identity as labourers eclipsed their identity as women.

Alice and Hannah Franklin's story also reveals the sexual nature of the threat to order posed by women of colour – at least, from the point of view of town officials. Official suspicions of prostitution among women of colour surface continually in the town records, as do official assumptions that the children of Black and Indian women were "bastards". Further, children of colour bound out as indentured servants are frequently designated in the record as "mustee" or "mulatto". These terms imply that officials had knowledge of the child's parentage, a knowledge that assumes sexual relations between Indian and white, Indian and Black, or Black and white persons. In the minds of town officials, Indian women signalled not only colonialism and patriarchy, but sexual disorder as well.

The poor of the town

A thin line separated the "the poorer sort" from "the poor of the town". The poorer sort were not bound servants or slaves, who constituted a separate category altogether. Many of the poorer sort maintained their own households and others paid for room and board in one place while they went out to day jobs elsewhere; in either case, they supported themselves by their own labour. Of all inhabitants, the poorer sort were most apt to need public support when misfortune visited in the form of illness or injury or death of a household member. The poorer sort became the town's poor when they needed the town's support to survive. When the town leaders spoke of "the poor of the town" or "the town's poor", they were referring to this smaller group of dependent people distinct from the larger group of the independent poorer sort.

Most of the poorer sort found ways of staying off public poor relief. When trouble loomed, some gathered up their household members and moved to another town in search of employment. Those who stayed might seek exemption from poll taxes, those taxes assessed on every head of household, however poor the household. Or they might turn for help to family members, who provided the first safety net in most instances, a natural situation underscored by Rhode Island law, which required grandparents and parents, if of ability, to take care of their grandchildren and children – and vice versa.[18] (If family members were slow to support their own, town officials prodded them along.) In addition, friends and neighbours might be counted upon to ease the financial difficulties of poor people in distress, or church congregations might help a long-time member. But when all outside resources failed, the poorer sort could "throw themselves upon the town" and ask for public support. In many cases, poor people took no action themselves; local officials stepped in after receiving information from neighbours about obvious distress in a household.

Whatever route they took to enter the ranks of the poor of the town, these neediest inhabitants soon found their lives managed and restructured by town officials, who questioned the poor, dissolved their households, and ordered new living arrangements. In taking these steps, leaders were driven by what they considered "suitable" for impoverished residents; and the meaning of "suitable" varied with the race, sex, and age of the poor person. For Indian women in particular, "suitable" meant a grim future.

Warning-out

The first action taken by poor relief officials was usually to verify that people in need were in fact the town's responsibility. English Poor Law stipulated how local officials should determine who were "legal inhabitants" in their towns and who were "transients". "Transient" conveyed very different meanings in the eighteenth century from those it does today. Then, it referred neither to travellers nor to homeless vagrants. Instead, it identified persons who had been living in a town but had not become legal inhabitants in that town. Inhabitants had rights and privileges associated with belonging; transients, however, remained in residence only by the permission of town leaders, and they were perpetually at risk of being sent away. Many of them would have ended their transient status, if only they could: the purchase of a "freehold" of real estate would have secured them a legal settlement in the town.[19] But these people were of the poorer sort; their search for work or for support forced them to leave their birthplaces, but their labour brought them little beyond the necessities of life. To purchase land and become legally settled inhabitants was beyond their means.

Every town contained numerous transients among its population, and many of these escaped the ignominy of being warned out. Town officials had to have plausible reasons for picking out certain transients for removal, and the usual explanation was complaint by neighbours of suffering and need in a particular transient household. But desperate poverty was not the only reason: officials issued numerous warning-out orders because "respectable" inhabitants had complained about transients' behaviour.[20] Negative interactions between transient people and legal inhabitants added the connotation of "undesirable" to the word "transient". For many propertied people of the late 1700s, "transient" signified noise, dirt, rudeness, illiteracy and disorder. To be a transient person was not only to be denied the legal privileges that inhabitants enjoyed; it was also to be regarded as a potentially troublesome person who represented the opposite of everything those respectable inhabitants valued. Thus "transient" status put people at risk of mean-spirited accusations, which could easily escalate into a warning-out.

To determine where a transient family "belonged", town officials often summoned the household head and conducted an "examination" during a council meeting. As they answered officials' questions, transients sketched out a small history of their lives: where they were born; where they had lived; what work they had done; the names of parents, masters, spouses; the number and ages of children. Transient examinations thus provide considerable detail about transient households, illuminate the circumstances of the poorer sort, and reveal tensions between the poor of the town and those who had official responsibility for them.[21]

The prevalence of women was perhaps the most notable characteristic of transient families.[22] Fully two thirds of the adult transients were female. Many of these women were wives who are hidden in the official record because only their *husbands* were questioned by officials following the usual patriarchal order.[23] But men headed only half the households (50.4 per cent). Women without husbands headed the other half (49.6 per cent): to conduct those interviews, officials were forced to deal directly with these widowed, separated, abandoned, and never-married women as persons responsible for their families.[24] Both as household heads and as wives, women dominated the ranks of adult transients.

Pregnancy made women particularly conspicuous to town officials and made them especially vulnerable to being warned out. The impending birth of a "bastard" child brought more female examinants before town officials and sent more female transients out of town via warning-out than any other cause. For example, when the East Greenwich officials were "Crediable Informed" that Almy Cooper ("an Indian woman") was "Prignant and Near the time of her Delivery", they ordered the town sergeant to go immediately and order Cooper to leave the town.[25] From an official perspective, such hurried removals on the eve of childbirth made good financial sense. Every council wanted to avoid both the immediate costs of caring for a recovering mother and her newborn and also the long-term costs of raising a fatherless child born within their jurisdiction. But even the most watchful officials were sometimes stymied. In 1800, Susan James (a "black woman") came into East Greenwich, "Taryed one Night and one Day and on the Second Night was Delivered of one other Child". The costs associated with James' month-long recovery and "Necessary Cloathing" for herself and her older child added substantially to the town's poor relief bill. This was the sort of expense councilmen hoped to avoid by removing women in the last stages of pregnancy.[26]

Suspicion of prostitution also tended to get immediate action from town officials. For example, Mercy Schooner (an "Indian" woman) was warned out of Jamestown several times in the 1760s. The councilmen considered Schooner and her two companions, Lydia Newberry and Mary Primus, to be of such "Infamous Charector" that the town sergeant was ordered to keep a watch out for them. If the three appeared in town again, the sergeant was to punish them by stripping them naked, tying them to the public whipping post and whipping them "fifteen Stripes on their Naked backs".[27] While continental army troops were stationed in East Greenwich during the Revolutionary war, the councilmen tried several times to rid the town of the numerous Black and Indian women who had come to work as prostitutes; they ordered that the town sergeant remove all the "Indians, Molatos & Negro Women" who did not "belong" to the army.[28] In Providence, the after-effects of a military presence included a bawdy house: in 1782, the councilmen warned out Sarah Gardner ("an Indian or Molatto Woman") who was one of the women living in that house where people had been "drinking, tippling, whoring, and misbehaving themselves to the damage and nuisance of the Town and great disturbance of the public peace".[29] Prostitution offended "respectable" people as much as bastardy offended the town treasury.

Just as women were over-represented in the transient population, so were people of colour. Between 1750 and 1800, about one fifth (21.9 per cent) of transient heads of household were identified as "Indian", "mustee", "mulatto", "Negro", "black" or "of colour". This percentage does not mesh with contemporary counts of Black and Indian people in the general population, which find people of colour as a declining presence in Rhode Island's population, from around 12 per cent of the population in 1755 to about 5 per cent in 1800.[30] The transient statistics show the opposite trend. The percentage of people of colour among transients rose significantly in the 1780s and 1790s, as increased emancipations resulted in former slaves leaving their places of bondage and resulted in official action to monitor the growing numbers of free Blacks and Indians. When "Boston Nance" (a "mulatto" woman) was warned out of Providence in 1800, people of colour constituted *half* of all those warned out of Rhode Island that year. This is an astonishing statistic in light of the census data that "Negroes" (including those Indians redesignated as Black) comprised only 5 per cent of the population that year.

Women of colour constituted over 13 per cent of all household heads warned out of town. These women were not vagrants; most were purposeful residents. Indian and Black female transients had been in place an average of seven years when they were warned out of town, two years more than the average for all transients. Some of them had spent lifetimes in a community. Sarah Greene (an "Indian" woman) had lived in Providence 24 years and Deborah Church (a "mustee" woman) 25 years.[31] At the time of warning-out, most non-white women had been in the town long enough to build a social and economic network and become an integral part of the community. But officials desired that they be elsewhere: the punishment for their poverty, their femaleness, and their colour.

Indenture of children

Warning-out rid the town of a considerable number of poor people, but not all. Every town was forced to acknowledge that certain needy persons were legitimately "the poor of the town". Officials' first response was generally to put those people to work in labour contracts and force them to contribute to their own support. Numerous adults were put into indentures to repay the town for this or that cost, but most frequently this labour system was used to maintain needy children.

Public indentures of children differed considerably from the more widely known contracts entered into by young adults trying to gain passage from Europe to the British American colonies during the 1700s. The indentures that brought Europeans to the colonies were voluntary contracts negotiated by adults; the local apprenticeships were negotiated by town officials to bind out children who were sometimes mere babies at the beginning of the contracts. These public indentures also differed from the private apprenticeships that parents frequently arranged so that their children might learn

specific skills from neighbours or relatives. Such private contracts were voluntary on the part of the parents, did not begin until the child had reached 12
or 13 years of age, and ran for no more than six or seven years. In the public
indentures, the town officials acted in the stead of the parents and made
arrangements based on the town's needs, rather than the needs of the child's
family; these contracts were in force until the child reached adulthood, a
matter of twenty years in some cases.

The 712 public indentures contained in the records of the study towns
specify the length and conditions of servitude and the obligations of both
parties to the arrangement.[32] The master's responsibilities included provision
of housing, food, work clothing, medical care, some education and training,
and a "freedom suit" of good clothing. The apprentice's obligations included
obedience to the master and the promise to avoid certain behaviours ranging
from telling trade secrets to committing fornication to playing with cards. The
clerk wrote out each contract, the contracting parties signed it, and the child
(average age: seven) was handed over to become part of a new household.

The sex and race of the child was almost always included in the indenture
records, and an analysis of those records shows that only one third of the
indentures applied to girls and that girls' contracts differed from boys' contracts in three particulars. First, very seldom did girls' contracts include
provision for training in a marketable skill. If anything specific was noted
about skills, it was usually that a girl should learn "to sew so well as to make
her own clothes" or "to knit, sew, and spin" or "to be brought up to
household business".[33] Second, girls' contracts seldom specified education
past reading. Writing was included only occasionally and cyphering
never.[34] Third, girls' contracts invariably ended before boys' contracts did. A
female apprentice usually received her freedom at age 18, a male apprentice at
age 21 or above.

Indian and Black boys were over-represented in these public indentures.
At least 23 per cent of the indentures were drawn up for children of colour,
but the great majority of these applied to male children. Access to indentures
did not necessarily indicate a rosy future, however. Indentures of children of
colour were often for longer terms than white children experienced: Indian
and Black girls were sometimes bound to age 21 (instead of 18) and boys to
23 or 24 (instead of 21). Further, if there was any education requirement at all
in indentures for Black and Indian children, it was that they be taught only to
read, not write and do math.[35] And contracts for Indian and Black children
rarely stipulated training in a marketable skill. Indentures for white boys often
contained some evocative phrase that indicated hopes for a good future: John
Teal was to be taught "some useful trade" that would "enable him to obtain
a livelihood in the world".[36] Nathaniel Luther was to be trained so that he

could "get a handsome living when free".[37] But only rarely did public indentures stipulate that non-white children were to be taught a specific skill. In a few cases, boys were to be taught "farming" or "husbandry"; in one case, a girl was to be taught "common household business". When Peter Norton, a "mustee" orphan, was indentured to learn the trade of a cooper and when Richard, "a Negro boy", was bound out to learn "the trade of a boat builder", these were notable exceptions.[38]

Although indentures primarily served masters' economic interests, the contracts could help children, who otherwise had no hope of independent living, through training in some skill and through connections established during years of labour beside a person of means. The dearth of girls of colour in the indentures illustrates how they were barred even from this dubious path to economic independence. In the rare cases where female children were given opportunities to learn marketable skills such as the work of a tailoress, it was white girls who received these advantages. When more elaborate freedom clothes were listed as "suitable" for a female servant, it was white girls who would receive the silk bonnet or extra pair of stays. What was "suitable" for girls of colour was to learn the work of a "house servant", as Sophia Havens' indenture stipulated when she was bound to David Vinton, "gentleman".[39] Or to be put under indenture as a punitive measure, as happened to "Indian Girl" Luranor, whom the New Shoreham councilmen deemed to be "an idle, luce, runagate hussey".[40]

Because they were given few opportunities as children, Indian and Black women were more likely to be economically vulnerable as adults. Women of colour certainly laboured as children, but not in contracts regulated by town authority. Instead, any recompense for their labour depended upon the good conscience of their white masters. As a result, when they reached the age of freedom, they faced severely limited economic futures.

Indentures affected Indian women's place in white society in another way. Indian women were viewed by officials as likely to produce the next generation of indentured servants. Numerous entries in the town records point to town leaders' perception that Indian women were prone to abandon their offspring to the care of whites, who would (of course) treat them as servant children. In a typical action, the South Kingstown councilmen bound "Indian Girl" Sarah as a servant to George Babcock, whose household had cared for the child since she was "left by an Indian Squaw" at Babcock's farm some nine months earlier.[41] In Jamestown, Daniel Weeden convinced the town council to bind two Indian children to him by indenture because he had cared for them for six months, since their mother − "an Indian Squaw called Betty Jack" − left them with him.[42] The town records do not address Indian women's motivations in putting their children in white households. Perhaps they were forcing the biological fathers to care for their children; perhaps they were rejecting children who were not fully Indian; perhaps they were too ill or too poor to care for their children themselves and sought out the second best alternative. But from the town leaders' point of view, Indian "squaws" were abandoning their offspring in an irresponsible manner. This provided more labouring bodies for prosperous white households and it reinforced the image of Indian women as disorderly.

Poor relief

If children or adults who belonged to the town could not labour for their own support, town leaders arranged that they receive "the necessities of life" at the town's expense. The local administration of welfare usually meant that those in dire need would be placed within another household for care and support. Town officials, acting in their capacity as guardians of the town treasury, tried to secure welfare arrangements that had the smallest effect on the public purse. Public poor relief thus was limited to the simplest forms of food, shelter, clothing, heat, and medical care, all meted out as was "suitable" or "appropriate" to the race and sex of the needy people. And because officials strived to keep to a minimum the number of persons on poor relief at any one time, most people received assistance only for a few months or perhaps for a few years; their condition was temporary and so was the remedy. People whom the town carried for decades, or a lifetime, were the exception.

Analyzing the sex and race of poor relief recipients is a frustrating task. No clerk ever noted down each individual relief recipient with any consistency. In general, clerks would record a few individual accounts, but then lump the next few accounts as expenditures for "the poor of the town" without further detail. A sampling of the poor relief expenditures in seven towns (the ones with the most detailed poor relief records) during three peak years of poor relief expenditures (1764, 1788, and 1791) shows that fully one third of the time, clerks noted only that money was granted for "support of the poor". But in those cases where adults were identified by name, women and men received money and goods in fairly equal proportions: women received 53 per cent of the disbursements in 1764, 61 per cent in 1788, and 46 per cent in 1791. This parity is surprising, considering how frequently women struggled to maintain households without the support of husbands and fathers. Women and men alike fell into ill health and feebleness in old age; but women alone bore the disruptions of childbirth and the attendant health problems. If poor relief accurately reflected the economic vulnerability of women, then disbursements on behalf of women – both in total cost and in number of expenditures – should far exceed those on behalf of men. But such was not the case.

As dismal as the poor relief situation was for those in need, it was even more so for people of colour, who are mentioned in poor relief records so rarely as not to form a useful statistical sample. When they are mentioned, they are usually women, and they are usually quite aged. The sexual disorder threatened by their presence in their younger years was gone; these women were incapacitated by age and infirmity. The poor relief supplied to them was most frequently the expenses of caring for them in a "final illness" and giving them a "decent burial". When Jamestown officials paid for "Indian squaw" Sarah Fitten's coffin and burial in 1755, for example, it was the only time the woman ever cost the town any money.[43] The same was true of "Indian or Negro Woman" Dorcas Fry, whose death in East Greenwich in 1780 prompted the councilmen to order that she be buried "in a Decent Manner".[44] No town supported an Indian or Black woman for more than a few months; only white men and women were virtually pensioned by the town, spending years on poor relief. Several white women who were mentally handicapped spent decades on support; no Indian or Black woman ever did.

Indian women and town officials

Indian women were in a precarious position in relation to town welfare. They were least likely to receive training in marketable skills as children; most likely to be warned out of town (and away from their workplace) in their labouring years; and least likely to receive poor relief when aged. They might receive "last rites" in the form of grave clothes and rum for those who watched over their corpse; but the record shows that they had few "living rights" as the poor of the town.

Despite such economic disadvantages and dismissive treatment at the hands of white officials, women of colour were not passive victims. The record is dotted with examples of Indian and Black women forging their own way in defiance of official dictates. Some women frustrated authorities by failing to appear in council meetings, by giving unintelligible answers to questions or changing their stories at each telling, by refusing to sign or mark the transcriptions of their testimonies, or by returning to town after being warned out. Sarah Gardner returned to Providence four times after being warned out. Even the threat of whipping didn't deter her or the four adult daughters who accompanied her. The council considered the five women to be "of bad

Character and Reputation" and clearly wanted them elsewhere, but the Gardners' determination to live in Providence was even stronger.[45] Sarah Mathewson, a "mulatto" woman, showed she had a sophisticated grasp of the system when, after returning illegally to Providence, she "concealed herself from the Officer until she got into her present Pregnant State when . . . it became improper to inflict the Punishment prescribed by Law".[46]

Ironically, it was just such assertive behaviour that cemented official perceptions of Indian women as "disorderly" and "unruly" and a threat to the peace and order of the "respectable" white community. The Indian women most visible to white officials were women who did not behave in ways approved by those "respectable" inhabitants. Indian women lived in households without a male head. They engaged in prostitution. They bore "bastard" children and abandoned them to the care of whites. In their illness and old age, they represented a cost to the town. They were not Indian princesses of romantic lore; they were troublesome "husseys" and "squaws". And their poverty aroused not official conscience and compassion, but official condemnation and exile.

Notes

I would like to thank Monique Bourque, Susan Klepp, Daniel Mandell, Karin Wulf, and the members of the Newberry Seminar in Early American History for their helpful comments on earlier drafts of this paper.

Abbreviations used in the notes: town meeting (TM); town meeting records (TMR); town council meeting (TCM); town council records (TCR). All TMR and TCR can be found in the town clerks' offices in the town halls of the respective Rhode Island towns. The Providence Town Papers (PTP) can be found at the Rhode Island Historical Society Library's manuscript collection, in Providence, Rhode Island.

1 Institutions such as poor houses and workhouses did not take root in Rhode Island until late in the eighteenth century, and then only in the most densely populated towns. For most of the eighteenth century, in most New England towns, officials made separate arrangements for each needy individual or family.

2 The study towns – Cumberland, East Greenwich, Exeter, Gloucester, Hopkinton, Jamestown, Middletown, New Shoreham, Providence, Richmond, South Kingstown, Tiverton, Warren, and Warwick – fairly represent the wealth, age, population, economic orientation and geographic location of the colony's 27 towns in the late eighteenth century. The methods used by town officials to deal with the poor varied little throughout the New England region, and the information drawn from Rhode Island towns applies as well to towns in Connecticut, Massachusetts, New Hampshire, and Vermont. Rhode Island towns enjoyed an unusual autonomy in relation to colony government, and town clerks took pains to document town business. The resulting richness of the town records allows Rhode Island to serve as a window into the entire New England region.

3   The first comprehensive study of warning-out was J. H. Benton, *Warning out in New England* (Boston, 1911), which primarily surveyed New England laws of legal settlement. Since then, only D. L. Jones has tackled the subject in "The strolling poor: transiency in eighteenth-century Massachusetts", *Journal of Social History* **8**, 1975, pp. 28–54, and *Village and seaport: migration and society in eighteenth-century Massachusetts* (Hanover, N. H., 1981).

    The classic studies of indenture in early America are R. B. Morris, *Government and labor in early America* (New York, 1946) and M. W. Jernegan, *Laboring and dependent classes in colonial America, 1607–1783* (1931). A more recent regional study is S. V. Salinger, *"To serve well and faithfully": labor and indentured servants in Pennsylvania, 1682–1800* (New York, 1987).

4   D. J. Rothman, *The discovery of the asylum: social order and disorder in the new republic* (Boston, 1971), deals primarily with the nineteenth century, but does provide an overview of poor relief before 1800. Studies of the poor and poor relief in particular regions include J. K. Alexander, *Render them submissive: responses to poverty in Philadelphia, 1760–1800* (Amherst, Mass., 1980); R. E. Cray, Jr., *Poverty and poor relief: New York City and its rural environs, 1700–1830* (Philadelphia, 1988); R. A. Mohl, *Poverty in New York, 1783–1825* (New York, 1971); and G. B. Nash, "Poverty and poor relief in pre-revolutionary Philadelphia", *William and Mary Quarterly* **33**, 1976, pp. 3–30.

5   For a full discussion of this problem, see R. W. Herndon & E. W. Seketau, "The right to a name: Narragansett people and Rhode Island officials in the revolutionary era", *Ethnohistory* **44**(3), 1997.

6   TCM 14 May 1796, South Kingstown TCR 6:230.

7   TCM 30 Jan. 1790, East Greenwich TCR 4:110.

8   Indian and Black men were common seamen in far greater numbers than their share of the general population. See R. W. Herndon, "The domestic cost of seafaring: town leaders and seamen's families in eighteenth-century Rhode Island", in *Iron men, wooden women: gender and seafaring in the Atlantic world, 1700–1920*, M. Creighton & L. Norling (eds) (Baltimore, 1996), pp. 55–69.

9   The record is peppered with evidence of native men enlisting as soldiers. For one example – Jack Sawnos – see TCM 26 Dec. 1759 to 13 May 1760, Exeter TCR 2:66–87.

10 TM 11 May 1757, Middletown TMR 1:63.

11 The record never identifies Hannah Franklin's race; but her daughter Alice and her grandson Cato are both identified as "mustee". TCM 11 Feb. 1790, South Kingstown TCR 6:167.

12 TCM 28 May 1764, South Kingstown TCR 5:150.

13 TCM 9 July 1770, South Kingstown TCR 5:230.

14 TCM 11 July 1774, South Kingstown TCR 6:24.

15 TCM 9 July 1787, South Kingstown TCR 6:135.

16 TCM 9 July and 31 Dec. 1787, South Kingstown TCR 6:135, 6:141.

17 TCM 31 Dec. 1787, 14 Jan. 1788, and 11 Feb. 1790, South Kingstown TCR 6:141–2, 6:167.

18 *Acts and laws of the English colony of Rhode-Island* (Newport, R.I., 1767), p. 201.

19 In eighteenth-century Rhode Island, a "freehold" meant real estate worth at least £40 sterling. Such a purchase gave most white men the privilege of voting and holding office in the town. Rhode Island's suffrage laws excluded Jewish and Catholic men, men of colour, white men without freeholds, and (of course) all women.

20 The limitations of the warning-out records make it impossible to determine the exact percentage of transients warned out because of objectionable *behaviour* instead of impov-

erished *condition*. Town clerks routinely wrote "likely to be chargeable" (meaning "likely to need poor relief") as the explanation for warning-out, even when other documents make it clear that someone had complained about the transient's behaviour. A sampling of the warning-out orders issued in Providence (where record keeping was especially detailed) shows that between 1780 and 1800 clerks specifically referred to objectionable behaviour in 18 per cent of the orders (84 of 470). The actual percentage of transients considered troublesome is probably higher.

21 Town records often provide only basic information about transients warned out and do not include the actual examinations, which are the richest sources of detail. The study town records contain over 1,900 warning-out records (which identify the race and sex of transient households' heads) and nearly 800 transient examinations (which give greater detail about the lives of transient people). For further information about warned-out and examined transients, see R. W. Herndon, "Warned out in New England: eighteenth-century tales of trouble", paper presented at the Philadelphia Center for Early American Studies, 22 September 1995.

22 For a detailed study of transient women, see my essay, "Women of 'no particular home': town leaders and female transients in Rhode Island, 1750–1800", in *Women and freedom in early America*, L. D. Eldridge (ed.) (New York, 1996), pp. 269–89.

23 92.8 per cent of the male heads of household were accompanied by their wives. The rest were widowed, never married, or cohabiting with women who were not their wives.

24 For white women: 39.8 per cent were never married; 34.1 per cent were abandoned, divorced, or separated; 20.4 per cent were widowed; and 0.5 per cent were cohabiting with their mates. For women of colour: 40.9 per cent were never married; 36.4 per cent were separated from their husbands; 12.1 per cent were widowed; and 9.1 per cent were cohabiting with their mates.

25 TCM 6 Jan. 1759, East Greenwich TCR 3:50.

26 TCM 1 and 24 Feb. and 29 Mar. 1800, East Greenwich TCR 4:331–5.

27 TCM 18 Oct. 1763 and 27 Jan. 1766, Jamestown TCR 1:154, 1:211.

28 TCM 4 Sept. 1779 and 26 Feb. 1780, East Greenwich TCR 3:198, 3:201.

29 "Warrant for sundry persons to appear before the Town Council", 23 July 1782, PTP 6:150. The warrant names "Elizabeth" Gardner but other documents indicate that the clerk meant Sarah. See the examination of Sarah Gardner, TCM 2 Sept. 1782, Providence TCR 5:215.

30 In 1755, people of colour constituted 11.6 per cent of the population in Rhode Island; in 1783, Indians constituted 0.9 per cent and Blacks 4.5 per cent. See E. B. Greene & V. D. Harrington, *American population before the federal census of 1790* (Gloucester, Massachusetts, 1966), pp. 67–70. Later counts show Blacks representing 6.3 per cent of Rhode Island's population in 1790 and 5.3 per cent in 1800 (us Bureau of the Census, *Negro population 1790–1915* (Washington, D.C., 1918), p. 51).

31 TCM 7 Aug. 1786 and 13 Aug. 1787, Providence TCR 5:393, 6:16.

32 For a detailed study of these indentures of children see R. W. Herndon, "'To live after the manner of an apprentice': public indenture as social control in eighteenth-century Rhode Island", paper presented to the Annual Conference of the American Studies Association, Boston, Massachusetts, 7 November 1993.

33 Indenture of Mary Floyd, TCM 12 May 1750, Exeter TCR, vol. 1; indenture of Betsy Brown, TCM 16 Feb. 1795, Hopkinton TCR, vol. 3; indenture of Mary Worden, TCM 31 Aug. 1751, Gloucester TCR, vol. 1.

34 Several contracts mentioned girls being taught to write, but the standard of accomplishment is severely limited. In an indenture contract for Martha Burdick, master Abel
Burdick is bound to teach her to "write so as to write her name intelligibly". Burdick was
under no obligation to bring her to any more sophisticated level of writing. (Indenture
contract of Martha Burdick, 5 Nov. 1787, Hopkinton town clerk's office.) The prevailing
convention dictated that female indentured servants not be taught arithmetic. In 1791,
Massachusetts gentleman Samuel Freeman published the first edition of *The town officer*,
which detailed both the published Massachusetts laws and the prevailing conventions that
governed the activities of each town official. Included in his discussion of the overseer
of the poor is a sample "Indenture to bind out a Poor Child", in which a male child is
presupposed. But at the end of the indenture form, Samuel Freeman added this: "Note.
– If the apprentice be a Girl . . . leave out the words 'and cipher as far [as] the rule of
three'." S. Freeman, *The town officer* (Portland, Me., 1791), p. 35.

35 In only one case was provision made for a non-white child to be educated as a white boy
would. In 1786, the Providence town council bound out Pero Gardner, "a Poor Negro
Child", stipulating that the master "teach him Reading Writing and Arithmetick". Pero
was also a special case in that "the Mother of the said Pero" had to agree to and sign the
indenture before it would be official. The presumed literacy of the mother and the special
consideration towards both mother and son suggest that Pero's mother was white. (TCM
17 Feb 1786, Providence TCR 5:363.)

36 Indenture of John Teal, 21 Dec. 1779, PTP 5:20.

37 Indenture of Nathaniel Luther, 7 May 1792, PTP 16:26.

38 TCM 16 Mar. 1780, Providence TCR vol. 5; TCM 21 Sept. 1772, Middletown TCR,
vol. 2.

39 Indenture of Sophia Havens, 7 Aug. 1797, PTP 28:48.

40 TCM 4 Apr. 1755, New Shoreham TCR 3:323.

41 TCM 9 Apr. 1770, South Kingstown TCR 5:228.

42 TCM 27 Aug. 1754, Jamestown TCR 1:75–6.

43 TCM 16 July 1751, Jamestown TCR 1:44.

44 TCM 14 July 1780, Jamestown TCR 3:204.

45 TCM 5 Mar 1770, 17 Feb. 1772, 20 Mar. and 4 Apr. 1780, and 1 Oct. 1787, Providence
TCR 4:299, 4:322, 5:168–69, 5:172 and 6:23; PTP 10:148.

46 Letter to Rehoboth Overseers of the Poor, TCM 18 May 1778, Providence TCR 5:113–
15. The punishment referred to was a public whipping.

Chapter Ten

"They are so frequently shifting their place of residence": land and the construction of social place of Indians in colonial Massachusetts

Jean O'Brien

The button-wood trees, in front of the south tavern, were set out in 1783 . . . Their being planted on the Indian burying ground gave offence to some of the few remaining individuals of the tribe; and one poor girl, with a mixture of grief and anger, endeavoured to uproot them; but they resisted her efforts, as they have many a violent storm, are still in a thriving condition, and measure 17 feet in circumference, at the height of two feet from the ground.[1]

This passage, from the section on "Remarkable Trees" in the first published history of Natick, Massachusetts (1830), describes a scene rich with symbolism. In planting buttonwood trees in front of a tavern and on the Indian burying ground, the relatively recently arrived English residents of the once all-Indian community engaged in a colonial act. In "grief and anger", an offended Indian girl defiantly resisted this deed of desecration and erasure, presumably hoping to defend the graves and memory of her people. By the 1780s, the Indian burying ground constituted one of the last places within the town that Indians could claim as their own.[2]

These were not the only trees Natick's first historian found remarkable. The others he wrote about served to mark the Indian-mission origins of the town. He noted two oaks that grew upon the place the English Calvinist missionary preached to the Indians in the seventeenth century. He also noted the elms Indians had planted in front of the houses of their two eighteenth-century English ministers as "trees of friendship".[3] In contrast to the buttonwood trees, these plantings symbolized co-operation between two peoples and reflected cultural changes Indians had made in order to survive the catastrophe of English colonialism.

Like the buttonwood trees and unlike the displaced Indians, English residents were firmly rooted in Natick by the end of the eighteenth century. The condition of the other trees Biglow surveyed paralleled the historical legacy of the Indian community in telling ways. The oaks that had grown at the inception of the Indian mission community had been decaying for forty years. The elms planted for one minister had died in the early nineteenth century. The other's vigorous elms stood ". . . in front of the house now occupied by Mr. Oliver Bacon", who was neither a minister nor a friend, but a Euro-American whose relatives had bought land from both Indian and English sellers in the last half of the eighteenth century. Land acquisition was a Bacon family tradition. Eight Bacons had bought land from Indians in Natick. At least six more got land from their relatives who had bought land from other English sellers in the speculative frenzy of late eighteenth-century Natick.[4]

The planting of buttonwood trees by English people who dispossessed Indians of their land mocked the dramatic transformation of Natick as an Indian place. Founded as a missionary experiment in 1650, Natick had endured as a largely autonomous Indian community well into the eighteenth century. But beginning in the 1740s when the commemorative oaks allegedly began to decay, so too did Indian ownership of Natick land start to erode.[5]

Biglow's narrative participated in a larger discourse of Indian extinction that pervading writings about Native Americans in the early nineteenth century. Local accounts like Biglow's did more than just chronicle the "glorious" accomplishments of English colonialism; they also included stories about Indians and Indian history which served to mark the "Americanness" of their places and sought to place the "Indianness" that partly informed that uniqueness firmly and safely in the past. Alluding to arguments over Andrew Jackson's removal policy, which used the trope of inevitable extinction, Biglow promised to reveal ". . . the circumstances which accompanied the gradual decrease and final extinction of the first tribe, that was brought into a state of civilization and christianity, by a protestant missionary". Still, in telling the story about the Indian girl and her companions, he contradicted his claim about extinction and undermined the simplistic narrative of decline.[6]

In fact, Natick's remarkable history as an Indian place reveals a complicated story of conquest and Indian resistance that serves as a counterpoint to stories of "extinction" that fuelled an emerging myth of the "vanishing Indian" in which Biglow's narrative participated. Writing more than two centuries after the English had begun to impose their colonial regime on the Native population of New England, which followed at least a century more of sporadic

contact and trade, his account naturalized the outcome of the colonial struggle
and advanced a story about Indians that failed to appreciate Indian resistance
and survival. Incontrovertible evidence for the failure of these narratives can
be found in legal struggles that began in the 1970s when still-present Indian
peoples pressed their claims for recognition and restitution and often succeeded.[7] In other words, Indian "disappearance" occurred in Euro-American
imaginations, or rather, in their failure to imagine how Indians struggled
and survived. Importantly implicated in this failure of imagination were
Euro-American assumptions about Indian cultures as static and race as
genetic purity.

In this chapter, I address the problem of the "vanishing Indian" by examining the ways in which the English used their own ideas about "proper" land
use and ownership to displace Indians, especially in the Indian town of Natick,
and to mark the place of Indians in the social order of colonial Massachusetts.
English notions about the social place of Indians were not monolithic and they
changed over time. The principal transformations can be read in the formulation of several shifting and sometimes overlapping categories the English
used to assign Indians their place in the colonial social order. From the
beginning, the English, invalidating Native mobile lifeways, viewed them as
"wandering Indians" who failed properly to fix themselves on the land. In the
seventeenth century, they developed the category "praying Indians" to describe Natives who (for their own reasons) responded to English religious and
cultural overtures. The secular version, "friend Indians", included Indians
who acted as military allies, cultural converts, and peoples contained within
the English colonial order. In the eighteenth century, after the English had
managed to impose their own legal and bureaucratic mechanisms for reckoning land "ownership" and almost completely dispossessed Indians of their
homelands, they reformulated the category "wandering Indians", whose persistent mobility testifies to their continued resistance to the English colonial
agenda of fixity and social place.

Different notions about land use and ownership, and how they figured in
properly constituting social relations, were central to the colonial encounter.
For the English, owning land as a commodity importantly structured their
notions about identity and place in society. Land ownership was thought to
be essential for social and political independence. Male heads of households
centred in nuclear families who owned this particular commodity were
conferred a place in a hierarchical social order thought to be divinely inspired.
The geographically bounded and "settled" New England town symbolized a
way of both ordering the landscape in an overwhelmingly agricultural society,
and replicating what the English viewed as the divinely-ordained social order
in a bounded place. Through colonization, the English imposed their notions

about property rights upon the landscape, bounded land differently from Indians, turned it and its products into commodities, altered its ecological uses, and eventually linked it to a new Atlantic economy driven by the market. Arrangements about land were underpinned by a legal system that enforced exclusive ownership, and contained bureaucratic procedures for property transfers and inheritance of property.[8]

English notions about property ownership and social order stressed "fixity" in both a geographical and social sense that starkly contrasts with Indian ideas and practices. Within the bounded homelands of the Wampanoag, Massachusett, Pawtucket, Nipmuck, Narragansett and other Native peoples of south-eastern New England, both "mobility" and "fixity" prevailed in structuring economic and social relations that, like the English, were considered to be spiritually mandated. Villages of a few hundred people included extended families from several lineages who were interconnected through kinship networks within and beyond the bounds of particular villages. Each group contained several such villages, and kinship connections provided individuals and families with options for relocating their village affiliation as well as a network of places for visiting. Central villages came together and fragmented into smaller units depending upon the season.[9]

Corporate ownership of a group territory was reckoned in the person of the hereditary sachem whose "ownership" of land was analogous to the "ownership" European monarchs asserted over their nations. Within this system of property, Indian usufruct principles delineated rights of ownership and use in a seasonally-mobile economy that included agriculture, hunting, fishing, and gathering of wild plant resources. Indian households "owned" the use of the land sachems assigned them for agriculture and they owned the crops of corn, beans, and squash grown by the women. Because Indians moved their fields every few years to avoid soil exhaustion, land ownership shifted over time. Ideas about property rights in hunting, fishing, and gathering related to ecological use: group members enjoyed the privilege of harvesting many resources wherever they found them, which in effect conferred their possession on them, although individuals or kin groups might enjoy exclusive ownership of traps, nets, and sometimes the location where they were placed.[10] Thus for Indians, economic and social relations that held "mobility" and "fixity" in tension formed a principal source of identity and a sense of place that included but also transcended natal village.

During the initial stages of English invasion, Indian mobility figured centrally in the development of an English ideology of conquest that justified dispossession on the basis of "proper" land use. Most English observers who looked at Indian mobility saw aimless "wandering", not seasonal migration pursued within elaborate notions of property that secured a livelihood. The expansive homelands required for Indians' diversified economies, homelands that included forests as well as fields, looked to the English like "unimproved" lands. Building upon these ideas so they could replicate their own social order on the land, seventeenth-century English colonists used two devices to dispossess New England Indians: they declared lands "vacuum domicilium" (empty of habitation), and (rejecting full Indian sovereignty over their lands) they "purchased" Indian land according to English legal principles. Even when they did "purchase" Indian lands, they assumed their land rights really emanated from crown grants secured through the "right of discovery", and the biblical directive to "subdue the earth and multiply". In this equation, "Wandering Indians" failed to "subdue the earth" because they did not use the land in European ways.[11]

English colonists could imagine a place for Indians within the colonial social order only as social, cultural, and religious converts fixed in bounded places where English notions of property and "propriety" would prevail. Missionary overtures the English extended to Indians beginning in the 1640s were predicated on the notion that Indians could have a place in the social order as converts to English Calvinism fixed and bounded in places they labelled as "praying towns", which stood as a metaphor for "Englishness". Indians who, for their own reasons, came to praying towns could occupy the social category "praying Indian". Here were the origins of Natick, one of more than a dozen such "praying towns" bounded in the mid-seventeenth century in Massachusetts. Indians who came to Natick and other praying towns understood the futility of military resistance against aggressive English colonists who proliferated rapidly and instead tried to use the institutions of the English colonial regime to defend their possession of at least some of their lands. As John Speen explained, one of his reasons for listening to missionaries was ". . . because I saw the English took much ground, and I thought if I prayed, the English would not take away my ground".[12]

Although the English tried to eliminate earlier Indian ways of belonging on the land by defining it as individually owned property transferable through the workings of the market economy, in Natick, Indians largely resisted these notions for seven decades after the mission community was bounded. But in 1719, the process of dividing the commonly held lands as commodities was begun (under somewhat mysterious circumstances), and the changed status of Indian land ownership in compliance with these English principles made possible the development of a market in Natick land. Natick Indians participated variously in this land market. Some entered the market to accomplish cultural transformations in keeping with English notions; others tried to avoid selling land at all, or if they did sell, to keep land within the Indian community. Even Indians who resisted often were forced to participate in the new market because English colonialism, complete with legal institutions that intruded on the day-to-day lives of Indian people, had created the conditions whereby they must participate. In particular, Indians who entered into debtor relationships with English creditors could not escape the resultant legal consequences, which often forced them to sell land. During the first two decades after land had been individualized (1720 to 1740), Indians bought and sold nearly 700 acres among themselves, and transferred just over 600 acres to English purchasers. After 1740, sales out of the Indian community rapidly outstripped transactions that kept land in Indian hands. In 1762, land transactions between Indians eclipsed Indian sales to English purchasers for the final time. By 1790, Indian land holdings had been virtually liquidated.[13]

The emergence of the Natick land market that set the stage for gradual Indian dispossession from Natick intensified persistent patterns of Indian mobility and created the conditions whereby the category "wandering Indian" would take on new meaning. Indian mobility included dimensions rooted in earlier ways as well as aspects that had been reformulated in the colonial context. Extra-local marriage persisted, and now sometimes included African-American partners. Outmarriage rose from a low of 27 per cent to a high of 82 per cent after the 1760s as Indian dispossession proceeded. Service in colonial militias, wage labour at sea, and migratory selling of Indian-crafted baskets and brooms redefined mobile economic activities that resonated with older Indian ways. Other forms of wage labour and Indian indentured servitude constituted innovations that also often entailed mobility.[14]

Within Natick, Indians had enjoyed relative autonomy in shaping their own political and social institutions until after the 1740s, when the land market drew substantial numbers of English residents who made claims for inclusion. Struggles over the social arrangements that followed starkly reveal English attitudes about the place of Indians within the social order. In the case of local governance, once they outnumbered the Indians, English residents persuaded commonwealth officials to disenfranchise Indians and bar them from holding local office. They also altered town boundaries and manipulated Indians into supporting several efforts to move the location of the church more conveniently for themselves.[15] This battle they lost: commonwealth authorities, citing the persisting Indian population of the community and the fact that the church was mostly supported by donations to the missionary cause, declared that ". . . the House for publick Worship should always be placed convenient for them".[16] English spokesmen from Natick replied that: ". . . we think it might have been as well pleaded that the Town house in Boston ought to Stand where it would accommodate the Indians, because this Province was formerly an Indian place, and there is many Indians living in it now."[17] Imbedded in this retort was an important commentary about English displacement of Indians in Massachusetts. For the English, even though "many Indians" persisted in the "formerly" Indian places of Natick and Massachusetts more broadly, an argument that Indian interests ought to prevail in ordering social institutions was so ludicrous that it could only be answered with sarcasm.

More than a numbers game, the battles of the 1740s represented a two-fold struggle over place: whose place Natick would be, and what place Natick Indians would occupy in the community. Around the same time, English town and commonwealth officials engaged in a further reconfiguring between "place" as a physical location, and the "place" of Natick Indians in the colonial social order more generally. Originally categorized as "praying Indians", once the missionary fervour had calmed in the late seventeenth century they were thought of in more secular terms as "friend Indians", who had earned protection from the English because they acted as cultural and military allies, but also needed to be bounded, settled, and controlled. In these arrangements, Natick had become one Indian place that symbolized the position of Indians within the now-dominant New English society, and emphasized the importance of Indian fixity there. By the mid-eighteenth century, a further redefinition of the place of Natick Indians in Massachusetts had occurred, which can be seen most graphically in the creation of a separate system of poor relief for Indians which involved the problem of defining "proper inhabitance" in New England towns and which revisited the thorny tension between English "fixity" and Indian "mobility" in structuring social order.

The issue of "proper inhabitance" received its fullest hearing during a protracted debate over responsibility for the debts of the impoverished Indian widow Sarah Wamsquan, who was born in Natick in 1702, and also married, bore children, owned land, and died there. But Sarah Wamsquan's life history was not so simply contained by her deep roots in Natick. Sarah was born during one of her parents' occasional visits to Natick from their residence in Billerica, and when she was seven, she had been made an indentured servant in Woodstock, Connecticut, then Cambridge, Massachusetts, then Boston, before marrying an Indian man from Cape Cod in Natick.[18] Sarah's life embraced both "fixity" in Natick, and an Indian pattern of "mobility" that had reconciled earlier Indian prerogatives (such as visiting and extra-local marriage) and the newer circumstances of English colonialism (such as getting a living through the institution of indentured servitude).

In Massachusetts, colonists drew upon English poor laws by locating responsibility for the impoverished in their town of origin, which served to underscore English ideals of fixity and order. In the debate over Sarah Wamsquan, Natick's minister attested that ". . . it cannot be made to appear that she is properly an Inhabitant of Natick or indeed of any other Town since she was freed from bond Service in Cambridge at the usual Age of Life". A petition that bore her mark asserted that she had ". . . no Pretentions to a legal Residence" anywhere, never living in one place for the 12 months required under poor relief laws.[19] This petition made an argument that attended to the niceties of English regulations about poor relief, entirely invalidated Indian patterns of mobility, and emphatically denied that Sarah Wamsquan had any real place in Natick. Given her circumstances and the colonial relations of power, even though she made her mark on the petition, it is impossible to know what she really thought about her "proper inhabitance".

The problem of providing charity for Natick Indians was met by the commonwealth by erecting a parallel system of poor relief based upon a complicated accounting system that categorically denied that Indians could claim "proper inhabitance" in any particular English-dominated place. If Indians owned land, the land was sold to cover the debts. If any proceeds remained, English guardians held the assets and paid future debts as they arose. If Indians could be shown to be connected with Indian groups who owned corporate assets, costs were recovered from those funds (also managed by English guardians). And finally, the province itself became the source for poor relief in the last resort, but only after all other sources of Indian capital had been exhausted.[20] This practice served to relocate the burden of poor relief from towns to the commonwealth. Towns thus avoided the costs of poor relief for Indians, and erected a barrier to discourage needy Indians from congregating in particular places. A spokesman from Natick summed up English concerns nicely when he commented on the Sarah Wamsquan situations: if forced to pay, ". . . [it] will prove an inlet to as many other Indians to come, as shall here of it – And towns that shall have an Indian in them will be likely to send him when he shall want relief".[21]

The commonwealth, using sleight of hand to create this separate Indian poor relief system, declared that Indians were not really residents of any town, despite instances where very clear connections were established. They even regarded as rootless Indians who had been born and married in a single town and had owned land there. The 1759 comment of Natick Indian Joshua Ephraim recited the assumption succinctly and ironically: ". . . the Indians, *Native* of this Province, are not accounted the proper burthen of any one Town."[22] Ephraim's commentary may or may not have been deliberately sarcastic in underscoring the fundamental tension in the claim that aboriginal people had no legal claim to particular places in the province. But what is clear is that as Indian dispossession from Natick proceeded, the English, almost none of whom had been there before 1740, apparently saw no contradiction in simply behaving as if Natick had never been an Indian place at all. Their official actions thus confirmed in practice their emerging stereotype of Indians as aimless wanderers without geographic origins, which configured assumptions English colonists brought with them in the first place, and justified their displacement of the Native population. Eighteenth-century "wandering Indians" differed from their seventeenth-century counterparts in that the colonial encounter divorced their "wandering" from actual Indian possession of their lands rather than reflecting English invalidation of Indian mobile economies. By the end of the eighteenth century, the English had done more than give up on the larger colonial project of culturally transforming Indians so as to assign them places in the colonial social order: they defined them as entirely extraneous to that social order.

In effect, the English, who as colonists were rootless people by definition, displaced their own dislocation on to Indians. This occurred first, by gradually dispossessing Indians, and then by the creation of various political institutions and administrative mechanisms for poor relief that equated this dispossession with a lack of geographic origin or place. In contrast to the missionary venture, which was premised on fixing Indians in a bounded location, the establishment of a separate social welfare system for Indians entailed a complete discount of the Indians' place. The manoeuvre disclosed deep ironies of a project that began by imposing a construction of place as property and fixity upon Indians, and then dispossessing Indians of their property and defining them as rootless in order to establish themselves in their place. The transformation is quite explicit in the successively worked out (and sometimes overlapping) categories of "praying Indian", "friend Indian", and "wandering Indian" which the English deployed to assign Indians to their place in the colonial social order.

Looking back in 1790, Natick minister Stephen Badger reflected on his nearly forty years in Natick. Though it mystified him as well as his contemporaries, Badger astutely narrated many of the dynamics of eighteenth-century Indian mobility, identity, and place:

> It is difficult to ascertain the complete number of those that are not here, or that belong to this place, as they are so frequently shifting their place of residence, and are intermarried with blacks, and some with whites; and the various shades in between those, and those descended from them, make it almost impossible to come to any determination about them I suppose there are near twenty clear blooded, that are now in this place, and that belong to it.[23]

As Badger unwittingly suggests, the story of Natick Indians is not a simple tale of extinction, but a complicated narrative of dispossession, displacement, and dispersal. Although his enumeration of twenty "clear blooded" Indians left in Natick sums up a story of extinction, his remarks upon the difficulty of counting Indians who "belong to this place" tells a different story that acknowledges a larger Indian sense of place that continued to transcend Natick's physical bounds. Badger's confusion in coming "to any determination about them" both embraced and rejected ideas about racial purity as a criterion of "Indianness" as well as Indian ways of placing themselves on their land which importantly included "wandering" that had been transformed by the colonial encounter. In "so frequently shifting their place of residence", Indians continued regional kinship networks that sustained them and they incorporated African-Americans as well, which blurred the picture for those who looked for Indians through the lens of "racial purity". The imposed colonial regime altered the connection between Indian mobility and Indian ways for getting a living: landless Indians increasingly occupied marginal niches permitted them as soldiers, whalers, wage labourers, indentured servants, and itinerant sellers of baskets and brooms.[24]

Only by striving to understand Indian ways of belonging on the land can we really see the complex ways Indians continued to negotiate their identity in relationship to the land. Within the changing circumstances of the New England Indian landscape, Indians perpetuated their lineages, and even under the constraints of English colonialism placed upon Indian families, kinship and a larger regional community composed of Indian places sustained the Indian truth that you are who your relatives are. The extinction story, readily sustained if the proof for persistence is only to be found in growing Indian populations in fixed locales, disregards the persistence of Indian difference in colonial New England.

The rhetoric of Indian "declension" and inevitable "extinction" has misunderstood changing Indian identity in New England and elsewhere, and reinforced ideas about Indian societies as rigidly bounded and fixed in the past. By the end of the eighteenth century, Indian ownership of the vastly restricted land base of Natick had entirely evaporated, and English people like Oliver Bacon had managed to root themselves firmly in that formerly Indian place. The arrival of a growing and disdainful English population reduced the Indian incentive to stay there to the vanishing point, and eventually they left Natick out of the geographically broad itineraries that continued to inscribe their social order on the land. In the case of Natick and New England more broadly, what had vanished was not Indian people but, instead, Indian power to define the terms for possessing the land. With Indian power thus in eclipse, the heirs of English colonialism could construct New England Indians as "vagrant", marginal, and about to disappear. But the heirs of that defiant

Hassanamisco Trustees Accounts, 1718–1857, American Antiquarian Society, Worcester, Mass., 15 (1731), 17 (1733) and throughout. On commonwealth expenditures, see, for example, AR 18:339, Appen. 13, Chap. 14, 6 June 1768; AR 18:383, Appen. 13, Chap. 17, 1 July 1769, MA 31:255, 1738; MA 33:164, 1761, MA 33:597, 1774; JH 42:227–8, 28 Jan. 1766; JH 44:95, 5 Jan. 1768; AR (1788–9): 932–3, Chap. 172, 23 Mar. 1786; AR (1794–5): 296–7, Chap. 116, 28 Feb. 1795; and MA 33:533, 1771.

21 MA 33:513–14, 1770.
22 Emphasis added. MA 33:104, 1759.
23 S. Badger, "Historical and characteristic traits of the American Indians in general, and those of Natick in particular; in a letter from the Rev. Stephen Badger, of Natick, to the corresponding secretary", *Collections of the Massachusetts Historical Society*, 1st ser., **5**(1) 1790, pp. 39–40, and 43.
24 O'Brien, *Dispossession by degrees,* Chapters 5 and 6.

Chapter Eleven

Legitimacies, Indian identities and the law: the politics of sex and the creation of history in colonial New England

Ann Marie Plane

In 1718, an Indian named Jacob Seeknout appealed against the verdict of the county magistrates at Edgartown, Massachusetts, who had ordered him to return 420 sheep, with damages, to their supposed owner, an Indian man named Sassechuammin. Seeknout knew that this case was not really about stealing sheep. He was the acknowledged *sachem* or political leader of the Indian community at Chappaquiddick, a small island at the easternmost end of the larger island of Martha's Vineyard, off the southern coast of Massachusetts.[1] Serving in this position since the death of his father, Joshua, in 1716,[2] Jacob Seeknout had the power to approve the requests of any English colonists who wished to put livestock to graze on Indian lands. But now he found that Sassechuammin, his cousin, had disputed his right to the sachemship, challenging the sachem's authority by allowing several Englishmen to run their animals on the island. When Seeknout impounded these sheep, Sassechuammin and his English allies attacked, winning reparations in the county court.[3]

Assisted by his English lawyer, Benjamin Hawes, the sachem Seeknout appealed to the Superior Court on the mainland. The two insisted that Sassechuammin's attack formed the latest round of a long-standing feud between the Martha's Vineyard Englishmen and the Wampanoags of Chappaquiddick. Sheep raising had been a staple of the island's economy, almost from the arrival of the first colonists from Massachusetts in 1642. English husbandmen had long sought greater control of the winter grazing lands on Chappaquiddick. In a successful appeal, Seeknout and Hawes asserted that, having failed in more direct challenges to Seeknout's "sachem's rights",

217

these Englishmen were now trying a more indirect route – finding a co-operative Indian ally, Sassechuammin, to put forward as a rival.

If this case truly concerned only sheep, we might leave it to a well-deserved obscurity. But the argument crafted by Benjamin Hawes in defence of Jacob Seeknout reveals the intricate connections between the law and the many cultural, political and economic appropriations that mark colonial societies. Until recently most historians have assumed that New England's Indians were vanquished by disease, warfare, and English economic domination within a generation or two after the English colonists arrived in 1620. However, a growing body of literature on New England Indians has documented native cultural survival well after King Philip's (Metacom's) war of 1675–1676.[4] Scholars have also uncovered increasing tensions between Indian sachems and their followers in the years that followed the war. Internal divisions and tensions amongst competing leaders were not uncommon because of the extreme stresses they faced. As open lands became scarce, sachems who sold lands to meet English demand found themselves under pressure from their own people, who worried about the loss of subsistence grounds.[5] The Seeknout case resulted from these tensions, and the history of arguably insignificant events on a remote island in a distant time takes on a much larger importance – revealing both the complexities and the strange alliances of such colonial struggles.

Benjamin Hawes fought for Jacob Seeknout's *political* legitimacy by deploying concepts of *sexual* legitimacy – he intertwined the two, proving Seeknout's sovereignty by detailing the marriage, paternity, and succession of his ancestors. Hawes' argument wove European concepts of legitimate paternity together with his understanding of Indian "custom". Thus, Hawes helped to forge one of the earliest instances of customary law in the British colonial experience. While well known to scholars of Africa and the Indian subcontinent, such customary law has never been explored in the seventeenth- and eighteenth-century American context. Even the best analyses of early American law have failed to mention the fate of indigenous legal systems or their transformation into "custom".[6] Students of English customary law in later periods have largely dismissed North America as a precedent.[7] Yet in Seeknout's appeal, Hawes articulated a distinct realm of Indian marital customs. Nor is this the only such eighteenth-century example of this phenomenon amongst New England Indians.[8] Thus, the Seeknout case exposes some of the ways in which Indian legal cultures may have been altered and then erased by English colonization.

Finally, the case also reveals the role of legal processes in creating historical narratives of Indian identity and Indian invisibility. Professional lawyers were relatively new in New England's courts.[9] To earn his keep and to advance his client's cause, Hawes spun a story about Seeknout's ancestors, paying particular attention to Seeknout's great-grandfather, the seventeenth-century sachem Pokepanessoo. Hawes' historical narrative differed dramatically in tone and substance from that authored by his close contemporary – the early eighteenth-century Martha's Vineyard missionary and historian Experience Mayhew. Where Mayhew used Pokepanessoo as the archetype of the defiant pagan, Hawes painted a self-serving portrait of a chaste and law-abiding sachem who begat only one legitimate heir, Seeknout, the grandfather of Hawes' client Jacob Seeknout. Hawes's legal arguments thus asserted a particular vision of seventeenth-century Chappaquiddick history, an idealized picture of Indian national identity that was contested even by his own close contemporaries. In this way, the case reveals some of the processes at the local level through which the complementary racial identities of "civilised" and "savage" were forged. It places the lawyer Hawes alongside earlier missionaries, as one who helped to forge Indian identity through the "cultural work" of colonization.[10] In appealing to history to construct his legal arguments, Hawes managed to bring an order and a "civility" to Indian practices of marriage in the seventeenth century that Calvinist missionaries had failed to achieve.

The chief beneficiary in this case was Benjamin Hawes himself – not Jacob Seeknout, and certainly not the ordinary Chappaquiddicks. Thus, having constructed nascent boundaries of race, having developed the sketchy outlines of a separate and unequal system of customary law,[11] and having "reduced" a past native society to English-style "civility" with a success never achieved in its own day,[12] Benjamin Hawes next performed the most obvious colonial act – appropriating native lands in compensation for legal services engaged to preserve them.

In order to understand the full implications of Hawes' arguments, we must read them in a series of contexts – economic, religious, criminal, and historical – each contingent upon all the others. This exploration of the Hawes' argument reveals that the intellectual colonization of native peoples – including the construction of racial, gender, and national identities – can never be divorced from material considerations such as the appropriation of Indian lands that occurred when Seeknout "won" his case. Indians may have had more to lose than to gain in their encounters with English courts.[13] Close analysis of Hawes' argument reveals the complex nature of the colonial struggle – a struggle that is never an uncomplicated dialectic between colonizer and colonized, English sheepowners and native cultivators, or Christian and heathen opponents. Chappaquiddick, so isolated and unimportant, suddenly seems located at the heart of early modern colonial discourses, and the words of one man, the lawyer Benjamin Hawes, enable us to unravel them.

"They Raise another dark Cloud": sovereignty, sheep, and the politics of legitimacy

Sassechuammin claimed the sachemship by virtue of primogeniture – he argued that his father, Pecosh, was the eldest son of the universally acknowledged seventeenth-century sachem of Chappaquiddick Island, Pokepanessoo. His English partisans argued that this made him the obvious heir.[14]

Through the attorney, Hawes, Jacob Seeknout responded by defending the legitimacy of his political leadership. He claimed that his father, Joshua Seeknout, and grandfather, Seeknout, had ruled without challenge. He brought in witnesses to attest to their peaceable tenure, and claimed that neither Sassechuammin "nor his father before him", nor even, indeed, the English sheepowners had ever "thot of" challenging "the Right Sachem, Joshua Seekenout" [father of Jacob] until they realized that there was a chance that Sassechuammin might thereby gain control of the Chappaquiddick grazing lands. In Hawes' flowery metaphor, just as Seeknout seemed the victor in the court battle, "and that the Cloud was Like to settle and the storm blow over and the sachem to hold something of his owne", the Englishmen raised "another dark Cloud and put . . . near one thousand sheep upon said Island, pretending that there is one Sassachumet who they have Just now found to be sachem of sd Chappequiddick".[15] (See Figure 11.1.)

Indeed, the dispute over sheep had raged for years. The English first purchased rights to graze animals on a peninsula controlled by the Chappaquiddick in 1653, paying the sachem an annual tribute or rent in corn, goats, and whale flesh.[16] Because the water formed a natural barrier, cattle and other animals could be left to range freely with only limited fencing. Every fall the

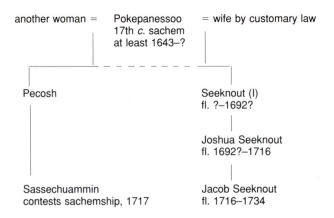

Figure 11.1 Genealogy of the Chappaquiddick sachems

English took their animals to pasture and each spring swam them back across the short channel. Englishmen obtained the use of these lands by virtue of their proprietor's rights in Edgartown's common lands.[17]

Struggles over these rights had a long history. As early as 1695 Matthew Mayhew, scion of the founding English family on the main island, described a violent dispute over grazing on Chappaquiddick. According to Mayhew, during the Glorious Revolution of 1689, the English had tried to steal some sheep belonging to the Indians. These Englishmen thought that as "there was not a King in Israel" (the government and courts were disrupted by the political crisis), they might do "what they saw good in their own eyes". While the English claimed that they were simply recovering animals stolen by the natives, the Indians knew better. The sachem, Seeknout I, and his men repulsed them with force. He then sent a written notice to Mayhew to make sure that the governor understood the Indians' version of events. In this document, Seeknout reminded Mayhew of the peace that had been estab-lished in the time of his father (Pokepanessoo) and Mayhew's grandfather (Gov. Thomas Mayhew, Sr.), and reminded the English leader that the Indians were entitled to "equal Justice, being the King's Subjects". In a bold assertion of Chappaquiddick sovereignty and legitimacy, he hoped that the "Violence and Riot committed on our People by the English" might be judged of "the same nature and quality as ours against them". He ended with a request that Mayhew and the other justices might consider the matter with "speedy care".[18]

But the English sheepowners continued their assaults on the Seeknouts' domain. During the sachemship of Joshua Seeknout, who came to power in 1692 and governed for the next quarter-century, the disputes over sheep flared up again. In 1708 the town proprietors appointed a committee "to treaty with the present Indian sachem . . . that therein may be done [what] as to right doth appertain".[19] Apparently the conflict only deepened, perhaps spurred in part by the involvement of Benjamin Hawes, who was sworn in as an attorney in the county in 1711,[20] and who thereafter appears to have represented Joshua and Jacob Seeknout, serving as their legal guardian in their dealings with the English. In October of 1712 the cause was heard before members of the Massachusetts' Governor's Council.[21]

This did little to quiet the controversy, which, if anything, proceeded even more vigorously. A series of actions between Joshua Seeknout and various English proprietors between 1712 and 1714 provoked additional interven-tions by the governor's council and the General Court (provincial assembly) in October of 1713 and May of 1714, and resulted in a final arbitration in December of 1715.[22] With Joshua Seeknout's death in 1716, a new round of suits and countersuits began. These can be described as essentially parts of two larger actions – one an attack on Jacob Seeknout's political legitimacy by Sassechuammin and the English, producing both the brief that we will examine and a series of cases that ran from 1716 to 1718; the other a suit for back rent payments brought by Hawes and Jacob Seeknout against the town of Edgartown, beginning in 1717 and continuing until 1720. In both cases, Hawes and his clients prevailed when the cause ultimately reached the Superior Court on the mainland, perhaps in part because the appeals court justices had much less to lose in upholding Seeknout's rights than did the justices on Martha's Vineyard, who may have felt an obligation to the English sheepowners. Thus, Benjamin Hawes' brief about the political and sexual legitimacy of Jacob Seeknout can only be understood as a small but critical part of the much larger controversy over grazing rights that raged almost continuously from 1712 to 1720.

Despite Hawes' and Seeknout's eventual victory, the suit represented a real loss for the Indians of Chappaquiddick. By 1718, Jacob Seeknout deeded over one eighth of the grazing rights to Hawes,[23] presumably because the attorney had earned the equivalent in legal fees and services.[24] Sassechuammin was briefly jailed, as he scrambled to make restitution to Jacob Seeknout for the costs of several hearings and appeals.[25] Hawes died in 1722;[26] in 1724 Jacob Seeknout finally sold his rights to annual tribute from the English for £5.[27] Just two years later his people complained that Seeknout had "in great measure forsaken us his poor people", having recklessly sold away "above halfe the Island", endangering the "planting previlege which is our life". His people attributed this to Seeknout's "Excessive Drinking" and to the undue influence of an unscrupulous English guardian, perhaps a reference to Hawes or to his successor. The long struggle of the Chappaquiddicks against English-men's livestock now took an all too familiar turn, as sheep owned by both the sachem and his English guardian damaged natives' crops and devastated local resources.[28] In the end, it would be colonists like Benjamin Hawes who benefited most from disputes over Indian concepts of "legitimacy" in English courtrooms. Seeknout may have won, but at the price of alienating both his native following and his English allies.

"With whom he lived beded and boarded": toward a customary law of Indian marriage

This lengthy dispute, then, provides the material context in which Benjamin Hawes crafted his arguments about Indian identity, customary marriage, and both political and sexual legitimacy. In Seeknout's appeal, Hawes summed up Sassechuammin's claims. Sassechuammin had argued that his father, Pecosh, "was begotten by sd [Pokepanessoo] on another woman (not his wife)". The appellants' first tactic, then, was to deny this point of fact, vigorously rejecting the notion that Pokepanessoo had fathered any child before Seeknout I (Jacob Seeknout's grandfather). Bristling in self-righteous indignation, Hawes accused Sassechuammin of slandering Pokepanessoo by claiming that the former sachem "did get a bastard . . . A Reproach indeed cast on not only the liveing but the dead and on [a] nation who are known to be as Chast as most . . . as our Captives from among them Testifie."

But because Hawes could not count on the court rejecting Pecosh's descent from Pokepanessoo, he next argued that this elder child must have been illegitimate. Launching a defence of Indian customary marriage, Hawes cast Seeknout as the only legitimate heir, because he was born of "the woman that was pekepesso['s] wife with whom he lived beded and boarded as such; allmost the only things by which that Relation [of marriage] was known amoung that people in that day".

Finally, Hawes separated legitimacy for purposes of inheritance from the question of succession to the sachemship. Using the words of customary law, he argued that in former times the Indian sachemship had never simply descended to the eldest, but had always gone to the heir best suited for office in the eyes of the people. In summation, the lawyer broadened the base of his argument, claiming that Jacob Seeknout was the "Rightfull heire to the Sachem-ship" according to both the natives' "tradition and the Course of the Comon Law".[29]

The arguments of the appellants are striking because they link Jacob Seeknout's political legitimacy to issues of his ancestors' sexual legitimacy. In order to establish Jacob Seeknout's right to be sachem, Hawes had to make an argument that extended back two generations. He maintained that one could find a legitimate marriage in that past (a wife with whom Pokepanessoo "lived beded and boarded as such"), for without this, English judges might have awarded the post to Sassechuammin as the eldest son. He also dismissed the well-documented native practice of polygynous marriage, asserting that in the Chappaquiddicks' experience, "a pluralitie of wifes at the same time has carss [scarce] been know[n] among them".[30] Hawes knew that the justices might find either that Sassechuammin's father, Pecosh, was indeed a legitimately born elder son or that both Pecosh and Seeknout were illegitimate. In either case, Hawes had to define a peculiarly Indian "custom" in which the principles of primogeniture (as understood by the English) could be overridden. It was for this reason that his summary argument noted that "in those days" (Pokepanessoo's day), the sachemship was not "inseparably Connected" to the eldest son, but did "depend arbitrarily on the Capasitie of the person[,] the dessposition of the sachem[,] and the conceurrence [sic.] of the people".[31]

As an English lawyer arguing in an English court of appeals, Hawes made sure that Indian "custom" never strayed too far from English common law (also based on an established body of customs),[32] at the same time as he wove together disparate rationales with promiscuous abandon. Hawes gave his argument weight by appealing to common law principles, scriptural precedent, and Indian "customary" practices. For example, most English men and women probably would have agreed that without any formal ceremony, the wife with whom a man "beded and boarded as such" might for all practical purposes be considered his legal wife. Elsewhere Hawes departed from common law precedent, as, for example, when he argued that sachems could be younger sons. To bolster this (to the English) unorthodox claim, Hawes turned to scripture, citing: "Solomon who was king of Israel was not Davids eldest son".[33] The appeal to the Bible referenced both its earlier importance to New England's legal history (Mosaic law lay at the heart of the first Christianized Indian communities) and European beliefs in linguistic and cultural connections between American Indians and the ancient Israelites.[34] To further bolster Jacob Seeknout's claim, Hawes introduced himself and Benjamin Norton as deathbed witnesses that Joshua Seeknout had asked Norton, Hawes and Matthew Pease "to take notice and remember that when he died he made Jacob sachem".[35]

In addition to establishing the sexual legitimacy of Seeknout's ancestry in Indian "custom", Hawes also had to make the case that Jacob Seeknout, his father, and his grandfather had always been the legitimate rulers of Chappaquiddick. Thus he stressed that the Seeknouts had been "accepted and acknowledged" as sachems "by both Indian and English", having always had "quiet possession" of the sachemship.[36] In a separate but related case, Hawes introduced testimony from both Englishmen and Indians that they paid tribute to the Seeknout sachems for the use of lands to graze animals and grow crops. James Pease recalled that Mr Mayhew told him that at each year's slaughtering time, "I should be sure to pay the Sachim a piece of bieff".[37] Sarah Natick, an Indian woman, noted that she had often seen "a great deal of meat" at the sachem's house, "that I understood the English payd to him for their cattle going to Chappaquiddick in the fall of the year . . . & I knew severall Indians pay him Corn and beans for useing his land".[38] Natick acknowledged as well the universal acceptance of both Seeknout and his son, Joshua Seeknout, as sachem. In her words the sachem "Has married[,] Ruled[,] and Judged and ordered the indians".[39] It was through such testimony of Seeknout's demonstrable authority that Hawes established the sachem's legitimacy in wielding political and economic power. His argument reveals the variety of legal traditions embraced within colonial law, as well as the ways in which the British colonial legal system defined custom so that it never diverged too far from English values and expectations.

"Begotten by sd Pekenoso on another woman (not his wife)": paternity and legitimacy in Chappaquiddick kinship

In order to be persuasive, Hawes had to present a coherent history of the Chappaquiddick sachems, a history of both sexual and political legitimacy that English authorities found plausible. But when we examine Hawes' particular interpretation of the Indian past closely, our reading of the historical record contradicts Hawes' version of the seventeenth century in a few important respects. Hawes couched Seeknout's defence in a familiar English discourse that linked legitimacy, paternity and property, recasting earlier polygamous practices as fornication or adultery. The circumstances of Pecosh's birth in the mid-seventeenth century now gave rise to a complicated set of claims in the first decades of the eighteenth. But would Indians in the mid-seventeenth century have recognized their experiences in Hawes' account?

Take Sassechuammin's claims as an example. Benjamin Hawes complained that the upstart's accusations suggested that Pokepanessoo had begotten a "bastard" on another woman, not his wife. But given what we know about the kinship system of the indigenous people of southern New England, it is difficult to see how a "bastard", in the sense that Hawes meant, might exist. Natives seem to have emphasized social rather than "biological" bonds of paternity within a system of clan or kin group relations. Some evidence points toward the existence of matriclans.[40] While the intricacies of native kin relations are unlikely ever to be revealed to us, they were clearly different from those of the English. Roger Williams' famous 1643 account of another southern New England group, the Narragansett, suggested that the clans may have provided for all children, regardless of their paternity. Ever critical of English society, Williams noted of the natives: "There are no beggars amongst them, nor fatherlesse children unprovided for."[41] He provides no term for bastard in his glossary, although he does offer the word "Towiúwock" which he translates as "Fatherlesse children".[42] Undoubtedly corporate land tenure, regular redistribution of community resources, and the existence of a clan structure begat attitudes towards "bastards" much different from those of the English.[43]

Benjamin Hawes also rejected the notion that the Chappaquiddick sachems had ever practiced polygamy ("a pluralitie of wifes at the same time has carss [scarce] been know[n] among them"). Yet seventeenth-century missionaries active in southern New England all noted polygynous marriages, especially by sachems. In fact, missionaries set out to change these practices as part of the conversion process. Clerics asked that native men give up hunting for farming and that native women abandon farming for spinning and other domestic chores; they encouraged natives to settle down on fixed plots of land in "praying towns", each centred around a native church or teacher; they worked hard to eradicate sexual encounters outside marriage; and they attacked polygamous marriage, asking elite male converts to "put away" all but one wife.[44]

But as the missionaries tried to eliminate the "gender frontier",[45] rendering native forms of marriage, gender, and property-holding more like those of the English, they ran into unforeseen complications, potentially creating rather than reducing the number of "bastard" children. In a fund-raising tract of 1648, the Reverend Thomas Shepard noted "a case now among them [Christianised natives]", that was so difficult that the ministers were reluctant to give an answer until they had received "the concurrence of others with us". The question posed a paradox – that in converting to Christianity and dutifully "putting away" all but one wife, the missionaries might actually be creating new "bastards":

> . . . suppose a man before hee knew God, hath had two wives, the first barren and childlesse, the second fruitfull and bearing him many sweet children, the question now propounded was, Which of these two wives he is to put away [divorce]? if hee puts away, the first who hath no children, then hee puts away her whom God and Religion undoubtedly binds him unto, there being no other defect but want of children: if hee puts away the other, then he must cast off all his children, with her also as illegitimate, whom hee so exceedingly loves.[46]

Neither Shepard nor later missionary authors record any response.

In fact, English ministers may have been forced to compromise. Important converts sometimes refused to abandon their wives, as revealed by a man named Wattapahtahinnit. In May of 1668 he challenged the Plymouth, Massachusetts missionary, John Cotton, Jr., asking: "How shall I know I have Gods seeing [of his sin?] I that am a Non-praying man never had but 1 wife, & some that are xians [Christians] have kept 3 wives?" High-status converts like sachems brought many of their followers into the fold. Since they were also the most likely to practice polygyny, missionaries like Cotton faced compromise or the loss of a large number of souls.[47] Their failure to bring even the most devout native converts to English "civility" created complications for those who later tried to determine legitimate descent. Indeed, in one case heard by the Martha's Vineyard courts in 1717, a property dispute between two landholders – one Indian, one English – arose because of duplicate land sales by different descendants of a polygynously married seventeenth-century sachem.[48]

While we do not know his marital history, Seeknout's great-grandfather, Pokepanessoo, initially resisted early missionizing efforts and their "civilising" effects. In fact, the Martha's Vineyard missionary Experience Mayhew featured Pokepanessoo prominently in his account of the island's Christian Indians. Pokepanessoo starred in the very first story, as the stoutest opponent of the first Christian convert, Hiacoomes. According to Mayhew, the "surly Sagamore" (Pokepanessoo) challenged Hiacoomes "for his Communion with the English in things both *civil* and *religious*", and railed at him "for being obedient to them".[49] In Mayhew's cautionary conclusion, Pokepanessoo was literally "smitten with Thunder" by "the just Hand of God" while repairing his wigwam (house) during a rainstorm. Burnt terribly before any of his companions "could *pluck the Brand out of the Fire*",[50] the old sachem "afterwards renounced his Heathenism, and became a Worshipper of the only true God".[51]

Such a traditionalist – a "surly Sachem" – could easily have fathered children by several women, despite all of Hawes' protestations to the contrary. In the context of historic polygyny, both Sassachuammin and Seeknout could craft plausible claims to the sachemship. Certainly English rules of legitimacy could not be applied simply to such a complicated situation.[52] Pecosh could have been born of an extramarital relationship, of an earlier or concurrent wife, or of a wife of the wrong family background to produce an heir.[53] Perhaps native husbands and wives did define themselves as those who "lived beded and boarded as such; allmost the only things by which that Relation [of marriage] was known amoung that people in that day". But more probably Hawes ignored the subtleties of seventeenth-century Indian marriages. Whatever the circumstance of Pecosh's birth, polygamy posed real problems for English legal definitions of legitimacy. Hawes' rejection of polygamy out of hand reveals more about what he wished were true than about the historical complexities of seventeenth-century native marriages.

"A Reproach indeed cast on not only the liveing but the dead": the criminal context of legitimacy

Hawes' argument also conflicted with local and contemporary understandings of Indians. We have already seen that Hawes contradicted Mayhew's unflattering portrait of the unregenerate Pokepannessoo. But Hawes swam against the current of local prosecutions as well. Early eighteenth-century English courts mostly left Indian "fornication" to the haphazard management of missionaries, local justices of the peace, and the fragmented Indian magistracy. Indeed, the case of *Seeknout v. Sassechuammin* was a rare instance in which the English superior court heard arguments of any sort about native bastardy. Of the literally hundreds of southern New England colonial and county court trials on bastardy and fornication, only a handful involved Indian defendants. Legal prosecutions of fornication and bastardy show that most English officials did not monitor Indian fornication. For example, in Plymouth Colony, a mainland region close to Martha's Vineyard, the period from 1633 to 1730 saw 184 fornication proceedings; at most, nine of these involved Indians.[54] In fact, because of this, historians of the family have described fornication and bastardy almost entirely within the frames of English society.[55] In most cases, including *Seeknout v. Sassechuammin*, the court investigated sexual legitimacy among the Indians only when other issues – land tenure and political office – were directly at stake.[56] Thus we might conclude that discourses about bastardy had no connection at all to contemporary criminal prosecution of Indian fornicators.

But this essay is about the importance of attending to the meanings of legal actions at the local level, and the Seeknout matter may have held different meanings on Martha's Vineyard from those it held in the Superior Court. The magistrates of Martha's Vineyard were unusual for southern New England's judiciary in that they *did* prosecute ordinary Indian men and women for fornication and bastardy. Thus, at the same moment that Benjamin Hawes was crafting his arguments about the chastity of seventeenth-century Indians, his peers on the Quarter Sessions bench were meting out punishments to Indian fornicators. How did these different courtroom discourses about fornication resonate against each other? How might we read Hawes' indignation at the "Reproach" cast by Sassechuammin on both "the liveing and the dead" in the context of real early eighteenth-century prosecutions of Indian fornicators? To answer these questions, first we need to examine the history through which premarital sexual activity was criminalized for New England Indians, and then turn our attention to the specific patterns of prosecution employed on Martha's Vineyard.

As with marital reform, Protestant missionaries were the first to inscribe English ideas of fornication into a new legal code aimed at Indians – to hold native converts responsible for their actions in much the same way that English Puritans watched over members of their own communities.[57] On the mainland, praying Indians began to formulate laws, to appoint Indian "magistrates", and to hold courts modelled after English practice.[58] The law code adopted by the "Praying town" at Noonanetum (Concord) in 1646 both reformed native manners – requiring Indians to give up gaming, lying, powwawing (curative rituals), and polygyny.[59] Item 18 specified: "If any commit the sinne of fornication, being single persons, the man shall pay 20s and the woman 10s."[60] Indian courts meted out punishments in the Christian communities of the 1640s to 1660s and in the resettled Indian communities (or "plantations") after King Philip's (Metacom's) war of 1675–1676. Since these Indian courts rarely if ever kept written records, scholars may never assess either how effectively they enforced these new laws or to what degree Indians internalized English notions of the crime of fornication.[61]

There is some evidence that Christianized Indians on Martha's Vineyard attempted similar reforms. They certainly appointed rulers in much the same way as the mainland.[62] But by the early eighteenth century, the Vineyard's English courts had done away with separate plantation jurisdictions and, in at least some cases, actually prosecuted individual Indians for fornication and bastardy.[63] From 1702 to 1728, about one third of all fornication cases involved Indian women and men; this was still disproportionate to their representation in the island's total population (Indians constituted roughly half), but strikingly more than in mainland jurisdictions.[64] Mostly these are terse entries, similar in tone to those involving English colonists. One of the earliest suggests the social distance between natives and Englishmen, because the court clerk neglected to enter the names of those involved.[65] But most court actions showed a more intimate knowledge of the participants and their crimes – as in the 1711 prosecution of Abel Ossoowit [Howwosswee] and Elizabeth Pomit, "being accused for being in bed together, and upon Examination they confesed the charge".[66]

Such legal actions had long helped to constitute particular social identities. In the hands of Puritan authorities, the old ecclesiastical court traditions of England took on a new reformed Protestant twist, shaping the identities of Puritan communities and individual sinners within them. At first such prosecutions affected both men and women equally. But by the early eighteenth century women began to take on the burden of moral shame, while courts increasingly held men accountable only for child support.[67] Fornication prosecutions and support proceedings became tied to accepted "natural" differences between men and women – helping to construct gendered identities of groups out of prosecutions of individuals. We would then want to ask how such prosecutions might also construct boundaries of "nation" around Indians like the Chappaquiddicks?

Indeed, fornication and bastardy cases could ritually affirm a variety of boundaries, marking groups as English, Christian, Puritan, civilized, or converted.[68] By the late seventeenth century, fornication prosecutions began with the discovery of sin and the maintenance of a "constant accusation" against a particular man by an unmarried pregnant woman. The ritual of swearing a bastard concluded with a courtroom encounter between the mother and the "reputed father", who, if found guilty, would be responsible for support.[69] In addition to criminal prosecution, fornicators who belonged to church congregations were also often required to confess sin and suffer "admonition" before being restored to good standing in the congregation.[70] Those who participated in these legal or religious rituals affirmed their membership in various communities (as English subjects, as Christians, or as church members) even as they passed through the classic phases of a *rite de passage* – of separation, *limen* (a state of flux) and reincorporation. In the end, they were restored to these communities.[71] Indeed, these real prosecutions of individuals contemporary with Jacob Seeknout doubtless shaped the reception of Benjamin Hawes' arguments about the character of Indians in general. If such real prosecutions made it difficult for such arguments to succeed before the island's justices, the comparative distance in time and space between the Indians of Martha's Vineyard and the appeals court justices may have aided Hawes' success.

"On [a] nation who are known to be as Chast as most . . . as our Captives from among them Testifie": legitimacy and Indian "nation"

Hawes thus worked hard to prove the entire "nation" of the Chappaquiddicks were "as Chast as most". Such a refutation recognized the very real dangers posed by negative perceptions. Even amongst the English, neighbourhood, religious, political, or cultural rivalries were oftentimes expressed in the language of fornication and bastardy. For example, two late seventeenth-century pamphlets attacked the unusual charter of the Massachusetts Bay Colony, employing the language of bastardy first to disparage the moral character of the authorities and people of the colony, then to heap scorn on their faith, and ultimately to use these moral failings to present political authority itself as "illegitimate".[72]

As Seeknout and Hawes fully realized, similar attacks on personal chastity might easily undermine Indians' political sovereignty. To avoid this, sachems adopted English understandings of bastardy, at least superficially. In a few instances, Indian leaders changed their behaviour in order to conform to English law. Thus, in 1734, the sachem of Rhode Island's Narragansett tribe, Charles Ninegret, married his last wife, Kate, solely to prevent the child she carried from being born a bastard. According to English witnesses, "George Babcock of South Kings Town Told him [the sachem] that if he did not Marry Her before the sd Child Was Born sd Child Would be A Bastard and Would not have his Estate After him". In haste, Charles arranged for their marriage, inviting both English and Indian witnesses and arranging for a magistrate to perform the service. As in Seeknout's contest with Sassechuammin, a long legal battle ensued, in which the legitimacy of Charles and Kate's marriage was challenged in light of Indian customs about the sachemship. Ironically, in the end, this son never did inherit, for though he was now a legitimate heir by English standards of inheritance, the Narragansetts themselves rejected his mother's ancestry as inadequate. In this way, Charles Jr. was still born a "bastard" despite his parents' civil marriage performed according to the English law.[73]

But Seeknout's protest not only defended his personal legitimacy. He also defended the sovereignty of a whole nation against the increasing identification of Indians with fornication and other sexual crimes. Seeknout's contemporary, Experience Mayhew, thought Indian serving women were especially prone to such failings, giving as an example the case of Elizabeth Uhquat who, prior to conversion, had born "two Children, before ever she had a Husband to be the Father of them".[74] Rapes and infanticides – the latter a crime long linked to illegitimacy – now enmeshed a disproportionate number of African and Indian defendants in the English legal system.[75]

Against this backdrop, Jacob Seeknout's lawyer stressed an alternative reading of Indian sexual practice, one that came from the new genre of English "captivity" narratives, the popular accounts of English men and women taken in wartime raids.[76] In order to convince English jurors of Pokepanessoo's chastity and of orderly, if odd-looking, rules of Indian succession, Hawes shifted the focus away from real fornicators and the increasing identification of Indians with even more serious crimes, appealing instead to the ethnographic knowledge judges might have gained from reading the popular narratives. Neal Salisbury suggests that perhaps the most famous account, that of Mary Rowlandson, a captive during King Philip's (Metacom's) war, was written to counter "coy phantasies" regarding her experiences in captivity, including rumours of a forced marriage to a native man. He notes that Rowlandson stressed that no Indian had ever offered "the least imaginable miscarriage".[77] In turning to such accounts, Hawes participated in the telescoping processes of colonialism, collapsing several divergent native identities into a single "Indian nation". In one breath he linked the narratives of captives taken in wartime – often by northern New England natives of a much different cultural tradition from those of Martha's Vineyard

– with the "chastity" of Chappaquiddick's sachems. With this bit of revisionist history, Hawes erased the individual miscreants that the justices knew, and replaced them with nobler "savages", of whom they had read. He erased both Pokepanessoo's documented rejection of Christianity and the more wide-spread complications accompanying the transition from polygynous marriage to English-style patrilineal descent. While Seeknout's situation was indeed quite typical, Hawes' arguments about history were not. Ironically, in substituting captivity narratives for local experience, he contributed to the erasure of New England's Indians, an erasure that would eventually culminate in their almost total invisibility to generations of colonial historians.

Hawes' appeal on behalf of his client linked Seeknout's political legitimacy to the sexual legitimacy of his ancestors. The appeal also replaced highly individualized social identities (the "real" individuals) with the distant but powerful divides of "nation". With a few strokes of his pen, Hawes created a new history for Pokepanessoo and his heirs, participating in a larger pro-gramme of intellectual colonization. Through his argument, law "reduced" the seventeenth century to "civility" in a way that the evangelists of that century had never been able to accomplish.

Indeed, the case was never about the real practices of real natives, but rather about the construction of ideal Indians, both individuals and a "nation". At the same time, this successful brief reveals the diverse array of sources – English, Indian, biblical – that informed early American law. Surely we need to recognize this legal culture as grounded in the inequities and formative identities of colonialism. In addition, Hawes stood to make real-world per-sonal gains (winning grazing rights in lieu of payment) from his intellectual colonization of the past. Seeknout too won a reprieve from English assaults – at least until he sold his grazing rights a few years later. But behind these legal victories, the Chappaquiddick people lost much. Seeknout's contest with Sassechuammin only further eroded the land base on which Chappaquiddick sovereignty ultimately rested. For scholars, the real significance of *Seeknout v. Sassechuammin* lies in the ways in which we see colonialism – both material and intellectual – play out at the local level in all its complexity. In the legal argument constructed by Benjamin Hawes to defend Jacob Seeknout against the predation of his English neighbours, we see constructions of nation and race, sexuality and gender, law and custom in combination, as the lawyer convinced the appeals court to uphold both the legitimacy of Seeknout's ancestors and the political authority of Seeknout himself. That the Chappaquiddicks ultimately lost extensive landholdings to their sachem's lawyer must simply have underscored for them the dangers inherent in resorting to the colonial courts.

Notes

The author gratefully acknowledges the thoughtful reactions of Kathleen Brown, Trevor Burnard, Richard Godbeer, Alan Karras, Ann McGrath, David Lowenthal, Joanne Pope Melish, James H. Merrell, Edith Murphy, Mary Beth Norton, Patricia Rubertone, Gail S. Terry, and Laurel Thatcher Ulrich, as well as the comments of participants at the joint Neale/Commonwealth Fund conference.

1   The Seeknouts' sachemship also included claims to territory on other nearby islands: E. A. Little, "Daniel Spotso: a sachem at Nantucket island, Massachusetts, circa 1691–1741", in *Northeastern Indian lives, 1632–1816*, R. S. Grumet (ed.) (Amherst, Mass., 1996), pp. 194–5.

2   I. Goddard & K. J. Bragdon (ed. and trans.), *Native writings in Massachusetts*, vol. 2 (Philadelphia, 1988), p. 766, index entry: *Seiknout, Joshua.*

3   This contest ran at least from 1713 to 1720. See Superior Court of Judicature hereafter SCJ) Record Books for 1700–1714 and 1715–1721, Massachusetts State Archives, Columbia Point, Boston, Massachusetts.

4   Some important recent works on Indians in New England after the war include: C. G. Calloway (ed.), *After King Philip's war: presence and persistence in Indian New England* (Hanover, N. H., 1997); D. R. Mandell, *Behind the frontier: Indians in eighteenth-century eastern Massachusetts* (Lincoln, Nebr., 1996); J. M. O'Brien, *Dispossession by degrees: Indian land holding and identity in Natick, Massachusetts, 1650–1790* (New York, 1997); W. S. Simmons, *Spirit of the New England tribes: Indian history and folkore, 1620–1984* (Hanover, 1986).

5   W. S. Simmons, "Red Yankees: Narragansett conversion in the Great Awakening, *American Ethnologist* **10**(2), 1983, pp. 257–9; J. W. Sweet *Bodies politic: colonialism, race and the emergence of the American north – Rhode Island, 1730–1830* (PhD thesis, Princeton University, 1995), Ch. 1; A. M. Plane, *Colonizing the family: marriage, household and racial boundaries in southeastern New England to 1730* (PhD thesis, Brandeis University, 1995), p. 170, n. 74.

6   See especially S. E. Merry, "Legal pluralism", *The Law and Society Review*, **22**(5) 1988, pp. 869–70, on the well-established literature on legal pluralism in nineteenth- and twentieth-century colonial societies. For the best review of early American law, but one that makes no mention of indigenous legal systems, see S. N. Katz, "The problem of a colonial legal history", in *Colonial British America: essays in the new history of the early modern era* J. P. Greene & J. R. Pole (eds) (Baltimore, 1984), pp. 457–89.

7   For example Bernard Cohn "Law and the colonial state in India", in *History and power in the study of law: new directions in legal anthropology*, J. Starr & J. F. Collier (eds), (Ithaca, N.Y., 1989), pp. 140–48.

8   See D. W. Conroy, "The defense of Indian land rights: William Bollan and the Mohegan case in 1743", *Proceedings of the American Antiquarian Society* **103** (pt. 2), 1993, pp. 395–424; and A. M. Plane, "Lawful marriage and customary marriage: intercultural negotiations in colonial New England", paper presented at "The many legalities of early America", Institute for Early American History and Culture and the American Bar Foundation conference, Williamsburg, Virginia, 22 November 1996.

9   J. M. Murrin, "The legal transformation: the bench and bar of eighteenth-century Massachusetts", in *Colonial America: essays in politics and social development*, 3rd edn, S. N. Katz & J. M. Murrin (eds) (New York, 1983), pp. 550–53.

10   I. Silverblatt, "Becoming Indian in the central Andes of seventeenth-century Peru", in

After colonialism: imperial histories and postcolonial displacements, G. Prakash (ed.) (Princeton, N. J., 1995), p. 279; see also J. Collier, B. Maurer, L. Suárez Navaz, "Sanctioned identities: legal constructions of modern personhood", *Identities: Global Studies in Culture and Power* **2**, 1995, pp. 1–27.

11 J. Starr & J. F. Collier, "Introduction: dialogues in legal anthropology", in *History and power in the study of law*, p. 9.

12 J. Axtell, "The invasion within: the contest of cultures in colonial North America", in *The European and the Indian: essays in the ethnohistory of colonial North America* (New York, 1981), pp. 45–6.

13 J. Comaroff & J. Comaroff, *Ethnography and the historical imagination* (Boulder Colo., 1992), p. 33.

14 Appellant's reasons of appeal from the decision of the Court of Common Pleas for the County of Dukes County, held at Edgartown, Massachusetts, to the SCJ, *Seeknout v. Sassechuammin*, April 29, 1718, Suffolk Files MSS case 12965, vol. 119, p. 101; Massachusetts State Archives, Columbia Point, Boston, Massachusetts. Hereafter cited as Appellant's reasons of appeal, Suffolk Files 12965.

15 *Ibid.*, p. 101;

16 For similar practices on nearby Nantucket Island, see Little, "Daniel Spotso", 200–202, 204–7.

17 C. E. Banks, "Annals of Edgartown", in *Town annals*, vol. 2 of *The history of Martha's Vineyard, Dukes County, Massachusetts* (1911 repr. Edgartown Mass., 1966), p. 203.

18 M. Mayhew, *The conquests and triumphs of grace: being a brief narrative of the success which the gospel hath had among the INDIANS of Martha's Vineyard* (London, 1695), pp. 43–4; Goddard & Bragdon, *Native writings* 2: 766, index entry: *Seiknout*.

19 Banks, "Annals of Edgartown", p. 204.

20 Copy of certificate, Benjamin Hawes sworn as attorney, Court of Common Pleas, County of Dukes County, 30 June 1711, in file papers, *Benjamin Pescosh v. John Swain, Jr.,* 26 April 1720, action of Appeal, SCJ: Suffolk Files 14045, vol. 128, p. 92. In a reversal of loyalties, Hawes represented Sassechuammin's ward in this case of wrongful indenture.

21 Banks, "Annals of Edgartown", p. 204. Seeknout and Hawes pressed their case in the county court as well: Court of General Sessions, October 1712, Dukes County Court Records, vol. 1, misc. bound (Dukes County Court House, Edgartown, Mass.), p. 209 [hereafter cited as DCCR. vol. 1, misc. bound].

22 See Banks, "Annals of Edgartown", pp. 205–6; see also *Seeknout v. Town of Edgartown*, DCCR, vol. 1, p. 251 (reverse).

23 Banks, "Annals of Edgartown", pp. 205–6.

24 Hawes was also responsible for keeping track of which animals went on to the island and by whose rights.

25 Order to Dukes County Sherriff, Suffolk Files 12965, vol. 119, p. 99 (reverse).

26 C. E. Banks, *Family genealogies*, vol. 3 of *The history ol Martha's Vineyard*, p. 194.

27 Banks, "Annals of Edgartown", p. 201.

28 Petition of Chappaquiddick Indians to the Honorable William Dummer, Esq., 29 Nov. 1726; MSS, Massachusetts Archives Series (Massachusetts State Archives, Columbia Point, Boston, Massachusetts), vol. 31: 129, Microfilm.

29 Appellant's reasons of appeal, Suffolk Files 12965, p. 101.

30 *Ibid.*, p. 101.

31 *Ibid.*, p. 101.

32 See P. Fitzpatrick, *The mythology of modern law* (New York, 1992), pp. 60–1.

33 Appellant's reasons of appeal, Suffolk Files 12965, p. 101.

34 cf. Axtell, "Invasion within", 56–7, 65.

35 Deposition of Benjamin Norton and Benjamin Hawes, 3 Oct. 1717; Suffolk Files 12965, p. 103.

36 Appellant's reasons of appeal, Suffolk Files 12965, p. 101.

37 Deposition of James Pease, no date, *Seeknout v. Town of Edgartown*, appeal, SCJ, Suffolk Files 14047, p. 100.

38 Deposition of Sarah Natick, copy March 21, 1712/13, *ibid.*, p. 107; Natick also noted that both she and "her husband when he kept sheep" had "payd" the sachem for that privilege. Natick noted that the English had put so many cattle on the island and left them so late in the spring "that we can neither plant much nor sow in season".

39 *Ibid.*, p. 107.

40 W. S. Simmons & G. F. Aubin, "Narragansett kinship", *Man in the Northeast* **9**, 1975, pp. 29–30; K. J. Bragdon, *Native people of southern New England, 1500–1650* (Norman, Okla., 1996), pp. 156–68.

41 R. Williams, *A key into the language of America* [1643], ed. J. J. Teunissen & E. J. Hinz (Detroit, 1973), p. 29.

42 However one early eighteenth-century source listed "Nanwetue" as "A Bastard": J. Cotton, "Vocabulary of the Massachusetts Indians" [1707], *Collections of the Massachusetts Historical Society*, 3rd ser., **2**, 1830, p. 162.

43 N. Salisbury, *Manitou and Providence: Indians, Europeans, and the making of New England, 1500—1643* (New York, 1982).

44 Axtell, "Invasion within", pp. 45–9, 55–6. See also N. Salisbury, "Red puritans: the 'praying Indians' of Massachusetts Bay and John Eliot", *William and Mary Quarterly*, 3rd ser., **31**, 1974, pp. 27–54; H. W. Van Lonkhuyzen, "A reappraisal of the praying Indians: acculturation, conversion, and identity at Natick, Massachusetts, 1646–1730", *New England Quarterly* **63**(3), 1990, pp. 414–15.

45 K. M. Brown, *Good wives, nasty wenches, and anxious patriarchs: gender, race, and power in colonial Virginia* (Chapel Hill, N. C., 1996), Ch. 2, *passim*.

46 T. Shepard, *The clear sun-shine of the gospel breaking forth upon the Indians in New England* (London, 1648), pp. 33–4.

47 Cotton recorded no response: J. Cotton, Jr., MSS Diary [1665–1678], Entry for May 1 [1668] (Massachusetts Historical Society, Boston, Massachusetts).

48 Deposition of Obediah Paul (copy), March 1717, *Manhit v. Rogers*, Appeal of decision of Dukes County Court of Common Pleas, SCJ Suffolk Files 12248.

49 E. Mayhew, *Indian converts, or, some accounts of the lives and dying speeches of a considerable number of the Christianized Indians of Martha's Vineyard* (London, 1727), p. 3.

50 *Ibid.*, p. 4.

51 *Ibid.*, p. 4.

52 J. L. Comaroff & S. Roberts, *Rules and processes: the cultural logic of dispute in an African context* (Chicago, 1981), pp. 39–41.

53 Plane, "Lawful marriage", p. 24.

54 Plymouth colony courts heard over fifty cases in the period from 1630 to 1686 (Shurtleff, below) and the Plymouth County Court of General Sessions heard over 120 cases in the period from 1686 to 1730 (Konig, below); Nine cases is a generous estimate, reflecting cases where white men attempted the chastity of Indian women, and cases of adultery. In the same period, Indians appeared for all types of actions at least 145 times in the years

235

from 1633 to 1686, and 89 times from 1686 to 1730. Drawn from N. B. Shurtleff (ed.), *Records of the Colony of New Plymouth* [12 vols.] (Boston, 1854–1861; repr. New York, 1968) and D. T. Konig (ed.), *Plymouth Court Records, 1686–1859* (Wilmington, Del., 1978), vols 1 and 2. Hereafter *RCNP* and *PCR*, respectively.

55 R. V. Wells argues that "the records that exist for colonial America on illegitimate fertility tend to focus on births to white women who were not living with a white man in some sort of ongoing, stable relationship". See his "Illegitimacy and bridal pregnancy in colonial America" in *Bastardy and its comparative history: studies in the history of illegitimacy and marital nonconformism in Britain, France, Germany, Sweden, North America, Jamaica and Japan*, P. Laslett, K. Oosterveen, R. M. Smith (eds) (Cambridge, Mass., 1980), p. 351.

56 Of course the defendent's socioeconomic status played an increasingly important role in fornication proceedings against English colonists: C. H. Dayton, *Women before the bar: gender, law, and society in Connecticut, 1639–1789* (Chapel Hill, N. C., 1995), pp. 213–15.

57 A. M. Plane, " 'The Examination of Sarah Ahhaton': the politics of 'adultery' in an Indian town of seventeenth-century Massachusetts", in *Algonkians of New England, past and present*, P. C. Benes (ed.) (Boston, 1994), pp. 14–25.

58 Y. Kawashima, *Puritan justice and the Indian: white man's law in Massachusetts, 1630–1763* (Middletown, Conn., 1986), pp. 28–32; K. Bragdon, "Crime and punishment among the Indians of Massachusetts, 1675–1750", *Ethnohistory* **28**(1), 1981, pp. 23–32.

59 Item 8 recorded: "They desire that no Indian hereafter shall have any more but one wife"; "Conclusions and orders made . . . amongst the Indians at Concord . . . 1646", in Shepard, *Clear sun-shine*, p. 4.

60 "Conclusions and orders made . . . amongst the Indians at Concord . . . 1646", in Shepard, *Clear sun-shine*, p. 4.

61 A few records survive and are translated: see Goddard & Bragdon, *Native writings* (vol. 1). Others were transcribed into English records on Nantucket: cf. A. Forbes, *Other Indian events of New England* (Boston, 1941), pp. 17–18. In one 1707 Massachusett glossary, *adultery, fornication* and *whoredom* were all glossed by variants of the same word, *nanwunwudsquas*. Cotton, "Vocabulary", p. 165.

62 J. P. Ronda, " 'Generations of Faith': the Christian Indians of Martha's Vineyard", *William and Mary Quarterly*, 3rd ser., **38**(3), 1981, pp. 369–94.

63 See Kawashima's discussion of Indians' individual, plantation, and tribal legal identities in colonial New England law: Kawashima, *Puritan justice*, p. 21 and Chapter 1, *passim*.

64 Compiled from DCCR vol. 1, misc. bound; for population see [Rev. J. Freeman], "Description of Dukes County, August 13th, 1807", *Collections of the Massachusetts Historical Society*, 2nd ser., **3**, [1815] 1968, p. 92.

65 October 1703, DCCR vol. 1, misc. bound, p. 135 (reverse).

66 October 1711, DCCR vol. 1, misc. bound, p. 203. Each was ordered whipped.

67 Dayton, *Women before the bar*, pp. 194–9.

68 On colonial identities and boundaries being created through sexual behaviour and selective prosecution, see A. L. Stoler, "Carnal knowledge and imperial power: gender, race, and morality in colonial Asia", in *Gender at the crossroads of knowledge: feminist anthropology in the postmodern era*, Micaela Di Leonardo (ed.) (Berkeley, 1991); and I. Silverblatt, *Honor, sex and civilizing missions in the making of seventeenth-century Peru* (Latin American Studies Center Series, No. 7, the University of Maryland, 1994), p. 10.

69 See Dayton, *Women before the bar*, pp. 184–5, 201–6.

70 See Discipline of Abigail Billington, *Plymouth Church Records, 1620–1859*, Publications

of the Colonial Society of Massachusetts, No. 22, *Collections* **1** (pt. 3), 1920, pp. 196–7.

71 A. Van Gennep, *The rites of passage*, S. T. Kimball (ed.), trans. M. B. Vizedom & G. L. Caffee (Chicago, 1960).

72 See G. P. Winship, *Boston in 1682 and 1699: a trip to New England by Edward Ward and a letter from New-England by J. W.* (1682; repr. Providence, R. I. 1905). A Congregationalist elder was defined here as "a Mungrel begot by a Jack Presbyter upon the body of an Independent Sister": J. W., facsimile p. 2.

73 Deposition of William Bassett and Experience his wife, Charlestown, R. I., in File Papers, *C. Ninegret v. S. Clarke*, Newport Superior Court, September 1743, Supreme Court Judicial Records Center, Pawtucket, Rhode Island. Kate's family was not of the "high" or "royal" blood; their marriage had not been performed with the consent of the tribe. See P. R. Campbell & G. W. LaFantasie, "Scattered to the winds of heaven – Narragansett Indians 1676–1880", *Rhode Island History* **37**(3), 1978, pp. 72–3.

74 Mayhew, *Indian converts*, p. 194.

75 cf. Dayton, *Women before the bar*, p. 265; P. C. Hoffer & N. E. H. Hull, *Murdering mothers: infanticide in England and New England* (New York, 1981); B. S. Lindemann, "'To Ravish and Carnally Know': rape in eighteenth-century Massachusetts", *Signs* **10**, 1984, pp. 63–82.

76 See J. Namias, *White captives: gender and ethnicity on the American frontier* (Chapel Hill, N.C., 1993). For the best narrative contemporary with the Seeknout case, see Mary Rowlandson, *The sovereignty and goodness of God, together with the faithfulness of His promises displayed, being a narrative of the captivity and restoration of Mrs. Mary Rowlandson and related documents*, Neal Salisbury (ed.) (Boston, 1997), pp. 38–43.

77 N. Salisbury, "Introduction", in Rowlandson, *The sovereignty*, p. 43. See also L. T. Ulrich, *Good wives: image and reality in the lives of women in northern New England, 1650–1750* (New York, 1980), p. 97.

Chapter Twelve

Images of aboriginal childhood: contested governance in the Canadian West to 1850

Russell Smandych and Anne McGillivray

Introduction

Until Philippe Ariès introduced a way of thinking about childhood as a sociopolitical or imaginal concept rather than a universal biological condition,[1] childhood was largely excluded as a subject of history. Childhood and its connection to society was not a central interest of writers of indigenous cultures. As Erik Erikson observed in his study of childhood among the Sioux and Yurok, "Even anthropologists living for years among aboriginal tribes failed to see that these tribes trained their children in some systematic way."[2] Studies of changing perceptions of childhood and the status and treatment of children in Western European and Eurocolonial North American societies constitute the bulk of the new childhood discourse.[3] While ethnohistorical and sociolegal studies have focused attention on many of the ways in which the arrival of Europeans affected the lives of North American First Nations peoples,[4] aboriginal childhood and its attempted transformation by processes of colonization have only recently begun to receive academic attention by way of the study of capitivity narratives, missionaries and travellers' accounts, and the records of Christian-based residential and mission schools.[5]

The study of the colonization of aboriginal childhood cannot be undertaken in isolation from the study of the impact of colonialism on other central aspects of aboriginal social organization and culture, including native spirituality, economic and gender relations, ideas about law and justice, and the treatment and valuation of childhood. Centrally, a broader consideration of developments in Europe must also inform the study of aboriginal childhood in the "New World". Childhood was subject to special interventions from the time of the earliest contact with missionaries, but later interventions were closely related to contemporaneous efforts of European "child-savers" to introduce new methods of childhood management for the "normalization" of European children, especially the urban poor.[6] The present study examines how aboriginal children in North America were viewed and treated by European colonizers in the period from first contact to the mid-nineteenth century. We also look at how aboriginal peoples may have viewed their own child-rearing practices, and at how they responded to missionaries' efforts to control the education of their children. The study explores European images of aboriginal childhood reflected in the accounts of travellers, fur traders, and missionaries who visited and lived in the northern United States and western Canada before 1850. Specific attention is given to the encounters between aboriginal peoples and missionaries in and around the Red River settlement, the first outpost of a mission and settler population in western Canada.

Central to our approach is the recognition that the assessment of European images of aboriginal childhood requires awareness of the threat of a hidden Eurocentrism which seeks to find the underlying "truths" about history revealed in the European historical record.[7] Recent post-colonial critics and First Nations historians have demonstrated the harm inflicted on indigenous peoples through Eurocentric historical writing, and investigators must make a conscious effort to adopt a more critical and intercultural approach to interpreting the records left by the colonizer.[8] Edward Said argues: "Without significant exception the universalizing discourses of modern Europe and the United States assume the silence, willing or otherwise, of the non-European world. There is incorporation; there is inclusion; there is direct rule; there is coercion. But there is only infrequently an acknowledgement that the colonized people should be heard from, their ideas known."[9] We are similarly reminded in the work of ethnohistorians that it is imperative that we not only document these images, but also try to understand the historical contexts in which they were articulated.[10] To do this, we need to form an understanding both of the various cultural and ideological world views and socio-structural forces that influenced the lives of Europeans who came to North America,[11] and of how these cultural sensibilities and practices were modified and reshaped by the encounters they had with indigenous peoples.[12] Prescriptively, Klaus Neumann notes in his recent essay on "Renegotiating first contact", that:

It is dangerous to focus on European colonial discourses and, in particular, on European representations of non-European peoples: by avoiding or accidentally ignoring Native Americans or Pacific Islanders other than as objects of European gazes, we would ascribe an autonomy to

European discourses and thus uphold one of the basic assumptions of the texts we set out to deconstruct. A critique of European colonial discourse must not be self-referential, but ought to take into account how European perceptions have been shaped both by what Europeans were conditioned to see and by what there was to be seen.[13]

Early missionary and travel accounts

Vivid images of aboriginal childhood were left by missionaries and travellers. One particularly rich source of these images is the 73 volumes of *Jesuit relations and allied documents*[14] generated by the Jesuit missionaries of New France. Numerous references are made to children within the context of other aspects of aboriginal social organization and culture, including the role of women and mothers, gender relations, and family structure. Children are central in discussions of missionary efforts at Christianization.

Foremost among these writers, in accuracy of observation and insistence that cultures be described in their own terms as well as compared with others, is the Jesuit Father Lafitau, missionary among the Iroquois in New France from 1712 to 1717. His *Customs of the American Indians compared with the customs of primitive times*[15] followed a scholarly trend of comparing old and new world paganism. Comparing new and old world cultures was an established convention: Lafitau's work was the most thorough and methodological and his observations are balanced and careful. The work received good reviews and a wide popular readership but it failed to impress the great minds of the day. Although Lafitau "invented" comparative ethnology and influenced later writers, his work is rarely cited, and the 1974 Champlain Society edition is the first complete English rendering of the work. Lafitau's treatment of aboriginal life advanced a concept of primitivism which would lead directly to later eighteenth-century concepts of the "noble savage". His work is characterized by close observation and cultural comparisons which denied certain European assumptions about New World peoples.

> I have seen, with extreme distress, in most of the travel narratives, that those who have written of the customs of primitive people have depicted them to us as people without any sentiment of religion, knowledge of a divinity or object to which they rendered any cult, as people without law, social control or any form of government; in a word, as people who have scarcely anything except the appearance of men. This is a mistake made even by missionaries and honest men who . . . have

written too hastily of things with which they were not sufficiently familiar . . .[16]

To prove the existence of spirituality, government, laws and systematic social practices among First Nations in North America, Lafitau drew extensive comparisons with the practices of "the ancients". Sources included his predecessors Le Jeune and the martyr Brebeuf, and other writers on the "customs of the ancients" and the practices of other aboriginal peoples including the Carib, the Florida and "the Indians of Middle America".

Lafitau's depictions of childhood span conception (Iroquois couples live together for a year before sexual congress), childbirth (often unassisted, with only minor disruption of daily life), naming, games and education, and initiation into adulthood.[17] His description of the cradleboard is a good example of the close attention he gave to New World practices and his admiration of the care given to infants.[18] But Lafitau's depiction of infant headbinding among the Flatheads in the region of Louisiana suggests that, not all aboriginal infancies were quite so free of pain. He also mentioned that headshaping was so common that the Canada "forest people" were called "round heads", *Tetes de Boule*, by other aboriginal peoples.

Early childcare is integrated with maternal work, with the help of the cradleboard, prolonged breastfeeding and continuous and prolonged mother–infant contact. Lafitau saw children take milk as late as age four. He makes a rare comparison with European practices, turning the gaze of the observed upon the observer. Women "are careful not to give their children to others to be nursed. They would think that they were cheating themselves out of the affection due a mother and they are much surprised to see that there are nations in the world where such a practice is accepted and sanctioned". Should the mother of a young infant die, "nurses are found in their family and what seems still more astonishing, old grandmothers who have long passed the age to bear children and yet still have milk, take the mother's place". Again making a European connection, Lafitau observes that "The Indian women love their children extremely passionately and, although they do not give them signs of their affection by such warm caresses as the Europeans, their tenderness is no less real, solid and lasting."[19]

Lafitau recognized the destructive impact of European contact on the education of children. In particular, he commented on how the traditional education of aboriginal children in learning the skills needed to survive under often harsh conditions had been eroded since the arrival of Europeans. In comparing the child-rearing practices of the ancient Greeks and aboriginals, he wrote that:

diaries, travelbooks, and other forms of literature in which newcomers left images of aboriginal childhood.[25]

In 1699, Father Lewis Hennepin published a two-volume account of his travels across "the Vast Country in America" from New France to New Mexico.[26] Among the 76 chapters of his first volume are "the Temper and Manners of the Illinois, and the little Disposition they have to embrace Christianity"; "The Advantages which the Savages of the North have over those of the South"; and a discussion of the difference in the manners of "Savages" of the south "from the Savages of Canada, and of the difficulties, or rather impossibilities attending their Conversion". Hennepin, like Lafitau, noted that the "Savages" of the south "differ from those of *Canada* both in their Manners, Customs, Temper, Inclinations, and even in the Shape of their Heads".[27] Obstacles Hennepin saw to converting the Illinois were the practices of polygamy and sodomy with young boys. Although he was not able to "boast . . . of many Conversions", the Illinois were sometimes (most often just before death) ready "to baptize their Children, and would not refuse it themselves".[28] In the second volume, reserved for a more complete "discourse" on the subject of conversion,[29] Hennepin wrote of other "barbarous and uncivil Manners of the Savages" including their nakedness, "Incivility" to "their Elders", and the behaviour of their children. Unlike Lafitau, Hennepin saw only negative results of the lack of corporal punishment. "The Children shew but small Respect to their Parents: Sometimes they will beat them [parents] without being chastised for it; for they think Correction would intimidate them, and make them bad Souldiers."[30] Children ruled the household.

> As soon as they enter a Cabin (or tent), they fall a smoking. If they find a Pot covered, they make no difficulty to take off the Lid to see what's in it. They eat in the Platter where their Dogs have eaten, without wiping it. When they eat fat Meat, they rub their Hands upon their Face and Hair to clean them: They are perpetually belching . . . I was surprised one day to see an old Woman bite the Hair of a Child, and eat the Lice . . . [and] When the Children have pissed their Coverlets, [their mothers] cast away their piss with their hands.[31]

Despite his disapproval of child-rearing practices, Hennepin grudgingly praised "honest and civil" attributes of Indians, as in their ethic of sharing with strangers.[32]

Hennepin's account was widely read by other newcomers to North America, although some questioned its accuracy.[33] One image portrayed consistently by Hennepin and his contemporaries was the great and unjudgemental love of aboriginal parents for their children. From the story of

Pocahontas, described once again in the 15th edition of Samual Drake's *The aboriginal races of North America* (1860), newcomers learned that John Smith's life was saved because "Powhatan was unable to resist the extraordinary solicitations and sympathetic entreaties of his kind-hearted little daughter".[34] This love of children is reflected in another account in Drake of "[a]n Indian of the Kennebeck tribe" who received a grant of land from the state for his "remarkable . . . good conduct". After he had settled near a number of white families, his son died.

> Though not ill-treated, yet the common prejudice against Indians prevented any sympathy with him. This was shown at the death of his only child, when none of the people came near him. Shortly afterwards he went to some of the inhabitants and said to them, "When white man's child die, Indian man he sorry – he help bury him – when my child die, no one speak to me – I make his grave alone. I can no live here." He gave up his farm, dug up the body of his child, and carried it with him 200 miles throughout the forests, to join the Canada Indians.[35]

The overwhelming grief of aboriginal parents at the death of a child is reported in numerous accounts of missionaries, captives and travellers in many different parts of North America.[36] These accounts are consistent with observations of the attachment of aboriginal parents to their children[37] and the sentiments expressed by European men who fathered children with aboriginal women.

"As fine Children as one wou'd Desire to Behold": children of the fur trade in the Canadian West

A unique feature of the early post-contact period in the Canadian West is the extent to which Europeans became acculturated to aboriginal ways of life. The first to arrive were fur traders in the employ of the Hudson's Bay Company, or, later, its competitor, the North-West Company.[38] The harsh climate made existence extremely difficult and for many years the "servants" of the Hudson's Bay Company depended on aboriginal peoples to provide the knowledge and material resources they needed to survive.[39] The most notable feature of the fur trade communities of western Canada over the course of 150 years of regular trade contact is the "country marriages" of fur traders and aboriginal women.[40] Some idea of the lives of these "mixed-blood" (English or Scottish) and Metis (French) children of the fur trade can be gained from examining the record left by traders.[41]

245

The most famous of the North-West Company employees, the explorer David Thompson, had a mixed-blood wife, Charlotte, and several children who accompanied him on most of his trade and map-making journeys in western Canada and the north-west United States.[42] Although Thompson was known as a somewhat prudish Christian who went to the trouble of sending at least one of his daughters back to Lower Canada for a Christian education,[43] he admired the way in which aboriginal people raised their children. In his *Narratives*, published after his retirement and return to Lower Canada with his family in 1812, Thompson painted a familiar picture of the children of the "Nahathaway" (or Cree):

> The children are brought up with great care and tenderness. They are seldom corrected, the constant company and admonition of the old people is their only education, whom they soon learn to imitate in gravity as far as youth will permit; they very early and readily betake themselves to fishing and hunting, from both men and women impressing on their minds, that the man truly miserable is he, who is dependent on another for his subsistance.[44]

Many accounts of explorers and travellers of "the manners and customs" of Indians in the north-west part of North America before the 1840s[45] record similar images. Such accounts evidence the extent to which Europeans shared a common picture of aboriginal childhood, an often idealized image of the Other. How fur traders themselves felt about raising their country-born children provides a more intimate paternal view of childhood.

James Isham, an employee of the Hudson's Bay Company, made a special effort to record his experiences. Isham was born in London in 1716 and died at York Factory, the Company's major trading post on Hudson Bay, in 1761 at the age of 45. Isham joined the Company in 1732 and was sent to York Factory to work as a "writer", or clerk-bookeeper, under Chief Factor Thomas White. White reported to the London Committee that Isham was "a very Sober, honest, & Diligent, young man" who worked hard and showed great promise as a Company officer.[46] In 1741, Isham was promoted to Chief Factor at Fort Prince of Wales on the Churchill River and worked actively in that capacity until the following trading season, when he became ill and was confined to the fort for three months during the winter of 1742–1743. During this period, Isham spent much of his time writing his account of daily life on the shores of Hudson Bay, giving detailed descriptions of the social organization and culture of the Cree and Chipewyan peoples.

Images of aboriginal childhood recorded in his *Observations and Notes* resonate with those of Lafitau and others. Isham read Hennepin's (1699) book and quoted his observation that Indian parents do not correct their children because they think it will "make them bad Souldiers" to support his own observation that "[t]hese Natives are Very Loving and fond of their Children".[47] Discreetly, without naming names, Isham remarked that mixed-blood children living around Company posts were "pretty Numerious". Describing their physical appearance, he wrote that "they are of a Sworthy complextion, and [I] have seen Europians not so fair, Especialy those Indians that has had copulation with the English, has Brought forth into the world as fine Children as one wou'd Desire to hold".[48]

In 1750, Isham returned from a two-year sojourn in England to take over as Chief Factor of York Factory. In the formal letter of instruction he received from the London Committee, Isham was reminded that he was "not to harbour or Entertain any Indian Women or Women in our Factory or permit others under you so to do, and that you be an Example to your people of Sobriety, diligence & whatever else is commendible and praise worthy".[49] Isham did not comply. Although he left a young wife and daughter in England in 1750, he entered into a country marriage which produced a son, Charles Price Isham. Two years after Isham's death in 1761, the London Committee ordered Ferdinand Jacobs, the new governor of York Factory, to carry out the terms of his will by sending his son to England to be educated. In 1766, Charles Isham returned to Rupertsland as a Company apprentice and remained in the service of the Company until 1814. Like his father before him, Charles Isham was "loved and respected by the Indians".[50]

While Isham thought it was proper for his son to be sent back to England for his education, his successor Jacobs believed that his children and those of other "Englishmen" (as all Company servants were known in Rupertsland) should be raised in a way that prepared them for an Indian life.[51] Writing in the 1770s, Samuel Hearne compared Ferdinand Jacobs' approach to child-rearing with that of other Company employees, in particular Moses Norton. Norton tried to raise his country-born daughter Mary as she would have been raised in England. Hearne, perhaps revealing his fondness for Mary,[52] noted that he admired her distinctiveness from other Indian women but her father was "very blamable from bringing her up in the tender manner which he did", for she lacked resistance to fatigue and hardship and the skills to provide for herself.[53] Hearne preferred Jacobs' method of raising country-born children as culturally aboriginal rather than English. Like Lafitau, Hearne recognized that aboriginal children were raised to be able to cope with hardship and austerity. Too often, European fur traders brought up their children "in so indulgent a manner, that when they retire, and leave their offspring behind, they find themselves so helpless, as to be unable to provide for the few wants to which they are subject".[54] According to Hearne:

The late Mr. Ferdinand Jacobs . . . was the only person whom I ever knew that acted in a different manner; though no man could possibly be fonder of his children . . . as there were some that he could not bring to England, he had them brought up entirely among the natives; so that when he left the country, they scarcely ever felt the loss, though they regretted the absence of a fond and indulgent parent.[55]

The Hudson's Bay Company initially tried to enforce a policy of prohibiting marriage with aboriginal women. Until the 1770s, the journals and correspondence of Company employees were almost silent on the practice. With the loosening of the policy in the late eighteenth century, Company employees began to write more openly about their country wives and children.[56] The later-established North-West Company encouraged country marriages, and employee accounts are more candid.[57] Significantly, prior to the 1820s, we see clear signs that European and aboriginal methods of child-rearing coexisted in many fur trade families of the Canadian West. Given this development, it is conceivable that, had it not been for the arrival of missionaries in the 1820s, a different type of society – one more free of racism and based on mutual cultural enrichment and respect – might have emerged from the children of the fur trade in western Canada.

Missionaries, Indians, and the Company: contested governance, 1820–1850

The arrival of the first Protestant missionaries at Red River marked the onset of a new phase in the colonization of aboriginal childhood, the result of Protestant evangelism in England aimed at Christianizing "heathens" throughout the Empire.[58] A unique feature in western Canada was that missionaries did not arrive until 150 years after first contact. The Hudson's Bay Company and other fur traders followed a practice of non-interference with aboriginal cultural and religious practices, generating contesting images of childhood among the Company employees, missionaries and aboriginal peoples who came together at Red River after 1820.

In 1820, Reverend John West was sent to Rupertsland as the first chaplain of the Hudson's Bay Company and the first representative of the Church Missionary Society in the region. When West arrived at Red River, he was faced with the scepticism and outright resistance not only of the Saulteaux and Cree but also of Company servants who feared the impact of missionary activity on the fur trade. The outcome was a period of at least thirty years in which missionaries, Company employees, and aboriginal peoples themselves articulated different views of aboriginal childhood and the need for educating aboriginal children.[59]

West had begun to recruit children for the school he planned to establish at Red River for aboriginal children soon after arriving at York Factory from England in August 1820.[60] In his journal, he wrote that the "corrupt influence and barter of spirituous liquors" at the Factory made it "peculiarly incumbent" upon him "to seek to ameliorate [the natives'] sad condition, as degraded, emaciated, and wandering in ignorance". Given that "little hope could be cherished of arresting the adult Indian in his wanderings and unsettled habits of life", he concluded that the "most extensive field, presented itself for cultivation in the instruction of the native children".[61] With the aid of an interpreter, West convinced one Withaweecapo to give him two of his boys for the mission school he planned at Red River. The decision to focus on children was not one that West made alone. The Church Missionary Society hierarchy believed that evangelism and civilization could best be achieved by focusing on the education of children[62] and the establishment of a native ministry to carry on the teaching of the gospel. Missionaries were instructed to keep an eye on promising students who could be "educated to be Native teachers or Assistants in the Mission".[63] The way to spread the word of God to "heathens" was to educate their children.

Despite initial optimism, West wrote in his private journal of his frustration and uncertainty about his mission during his three years at Red River.[64] Most of this was carefully expunged from his *Substance of a Journal*, published to raise funds for the Church Missionary Society at Red River.[65] There were also embellishments. In his private journal entry for 25 May 1821, West wrote of an Indian boy "about 7 years old" who was brought to Red River by his father from Qu'Appelle as a result of West's visit the previous January. The father, West wrote, said that "as I had asked for his son, and stood between the Great Spirit and them, he would send him to me".[66] In his published journal, West added, "Thus was I encouraged in the idea, that native Indian children might be collected from the wandering tribes of the north, and educated in the knowledge of the true God, and Jesus Christ whom he hath sent."[67]

West exaggerated his success in recruiting children. Contrary to the claims he made in his published journal, his private journal showed resistance by aboriginal people to his plans. At his first meeting with Chief Peguis in the fall of 1820, West tried to convince him of the benefits of education.[68] Two years later in October of 1822, West said he "was glad of the opportunity of assuring him", through the aid of an interpreter, "that many, very many in my country wished the Indians to be taught white man's knowledge of the Great Spirit, and as proof of their love to them, my countrymen had told me to provide for the clothing, maintenance, and education of many of their children".[69] West claimed that Peguis responded by telling him that, although he was not easily persuaded that he acted "from benevolent motives; he said *it was good!* and promised to tell all his tribe what I said about the children, and that I should have two of his boys to instruct in the Spring, but added, that 'the Indians like to have time to consider about these matters'".[70] After taking some time to smoke the calumet together, the Chief shrewdly asked again about his motives and goals. West recorded that Peguis

> asked me what I would do with the children after they are taught what I wished them to know. I told him that they might return to their parents if they wished it, but my hope was that they would see the advantage of making gardens, and cultivating the soil, so as not to be exposed to hunger and starvation, as the Indians generally were, who had to wander and hunt for their provisions. The little girls, I observed, would be taught to knit, and make articles of clothing to wear, like those which white people wore; and all would be led to read the Book that the Great Spirit has given them, which the Indians had not yet known, and would teach them how to live well and die happy.[71]

West left this meeting with the understanding that Peguis would bring two of his own children to his school, but when they next met, at Red River in early January 1823, Peguis was not convinced. Instead, Peguis was accompanied at this meeting by his widowed sister, who asked West to take her eldest boy into his school. According to West, Peguis and his sister were very fond of the boy, and "took an affectionate leave of him, remarking that they were sure I should keep him well".[72] A week later the mother returned for her son, saying that she had only left him because they had no provisions and it was already a long time since they had seen the boy. West seems to have viewed this as fraud.

> He was permitted to go from the school-house to their tent, which they had pitched near me in the woods, almost daily without restraint, till at length he refused to return. I repeated my request for him without effect; and having my suspicion excited, that they would take him away for the sake of the clothing and blankets which I had given him, I determined upon having them again, as an example to deter others from practising the like imposition. The parties were angry at my determination . . . [however] I insisted . . . on the return of the articles I had given to the boy, and obtained them; at the same time promising that if he would go back to the school-house, he should have his clothes again; but added that "it would never be allowed for Indians to bring

their children to the school, which was established to teach them what was for their happiness, merely for the purpose of getting them clothed and provided with blankets, and then to entice them to leave it".[73]

Chief Peguis never sent his own children to West or to his successors. He did begin having them baptized in 1837[74] and was himself baptized in 1840 after agreeing to give up three of his four wives.[75] Despite this slow shift toward Christianity (or perhaps Peguis' desire in old age to hedge his bets), what is significant is the way in which, in the 1820s, aboriginal people were resistant to the efforts of Protestant missionaries. The Saulteaux people around Red River, and others who sent children to West's school, held a notably different view of the needs of their children. Of the initial group of ten students recruited,[76] at least five were surrendered for economic reasons, as orphans or the children of poverty-stricken parents.[77] In fact, few children were recruited.

In the summer of 1823, John West left Red River with the intention of returning to England to bring his wife and child back to Red River. But he was dismissed from his position as Company chaplain by the London Committee for his open criticism of Governor George Simpson and other Company officers who refused to commit funds to his cause.[78] Relations between Church Missionary Society agents at Red River and officers of the Hudson's Bay Company improved when West was replaced by the Reverend David Jones for two years. Jones was succeeded by the Reverend William Cockran, who remained active as a missionary at Red River and other Manitoba settlements for forty years, from 1825 until his death in 1865.[79] Cockran left a large correspondence detailing his career, much of which is contained in the archives of the Church Missionary Society.[80] Cockran disagreed with the low priority West gave to teaching farming and husbandry. In 1832, he took over West's Indian school at Red River, and established a school of industry for "country-born" children. The school "trained boys in weaving, carpentry and husbandry, and instructed girls in spinning and other domestic duties".[81] Shortly after, Cockran established a mission school and church for Chief Peguis' band on the northern edge of the Red River settlement. According to Cockran's biographer, "The Saulteaux were far less responsive to the missionary's efforts than the Country-born settlers. But with patience and compassion Cockran instructed, pleaded, cajoled, and, on one occasion at least, threatened physical coercion to win the support of a hesitant few."[82] Cockran's punitive pedagogical style and his frequent recommendation that "children must be systematically broken, normally by corporal punishment",[83] would have been a profound shock

251

to aboriginal and perhaps country-born children. This pedagogy, premised on European images of appropriate child-rearing, was experienced by subsequent generations of aboriginal children whose parents were convinced or forced to send them to government-funded mission and residential schools.[84] Even with later backing from the Canadian government, missionaries were never able to completely extinguish traditional aboriginal beliefs about childhood.

Conclusions

This study provides an understanding of the spread of European images of aboriginal child-rearing practices across North America, and how these images influenced missionary efforts to transform aboriginal children. We have seen that images of aboriginal childhood may lurk in the interstices of records left by travellers and traders or come to the forefront in, for example, agonies of paternal choice in the education of country-born children. Transforming aboriginal childhood was at the forefront of missionary work, as shown in the efforts of John West and William Cockran at Red River. Mission education paved the way for subsequent residential schools. But, as we have also seen, these efforts were contested, and, in the course of this resistance, counterpoised images of childhood come into view. For Hennepin, the tolerance shown to aboriginal children made them obnoxious rulers of the household without respect for their parents.[85] Lafitau learned, to the contrary, that children respected their elders and did quite well despite the lack of corporal punishment. For fur traders like Samuel Hearne, raising country-born children in an indulgent manner ill-prepared them for later hardships. For some parents who sent children to mission schools, what mattered most was that their children would be properly fed and that they would not be kept from them any longer than was needed.

At a more general theoretical level, the study of the colonization of aboriginal childhood reveals the complicated ways in which the British encounter with North American First Nations is bound up with the colonization of childhood. Transforming childhood would, it was hoped, transform the people. Where transforming adults failed because of the fixity of adult ways and opinion, childhood, infinitely mutable, would transform the future adult. After 1850, when childhood became a statist or governance concern in Europe and its colonies,[86] the imaging of aboriginal childhood froze into a simple dichotomy. Children were smart but wild, both the origin and solution of "the Indian problem".

Notes

1   P. Ariès, *Centuries of childhood* (London, 1962).

2   E. Erikson, *Childhood and society*, 2nd edition (New York, 1963).

3   See A. McGillivray (ed.), *Governing childhood* (London, 1996); R. Smandych, G. Dodds, A. Esau (eds), *Dimensions of childhood: essays on the history of children and youth in Canada* (Winnipeg, 1991).

4   See for example J. Axtell, *Beyond 1492: encounters in colonial North America* (New York, 1992); O. Dickason, *Canada's First Nations: a history of founding peoples from earliest times* (Toronto, 1992); R. Smandych & G. Lee, "Women, colonization, and resistance: elements of an Amerindian autohistorical approach to the study of law and colonialism", *Native Studies Review* **10**(1), 1995, pp. 21–49.

5   See A. McGillivray, "Therapies of freedom: the colonization of aboriginal childhood", in *Governing childhood*, A. McGillivray (ed.) (London, 1996); A. McGillivray & R. Smandych, "Capturing childhood: the aboriginal child in the European imagination", paper presented at the joint meetings of the (US) Law and Society Association and the ISA Research Committee on the Sociology of Law, Glasgow, 1996; A. McGillivray & R. Smandych, "Governing aboriginal childhood: Canadian Indian policy and the aboriginal child in western Canada, 1870–1930", paper presented at conference on "Law and society in the middle kingdom: Canada's North-West Territories and prairie provinces", Calgary, 1997; J. R. Miller, *Shingwauk's vision: A history of Native residential schools* (Toronto, 1996).

6   McGillivray, "Therapies of freedom".

7   For a more detailed argument in support of this type of post-colonial deconstructionist approach, see J. Brown & E. Vibert, "Introduction", in *Reading beyond words: contexts for Native history*, J. Brown & E. Vibert (eds) (Peterborough, Ont., 1996).

8   For example, C. Breckenridge & P. van der Veer (eds), *Orientalism and the postcolonial predicament: perspectives on South Asia* (Delhi, 1994); J. Emberley, *Thresholds of difference: feminist critique, Native women's writings, postcolonial theory* (Toronto, 1993); N. Thomas, *Colonialism's culture: anthropology, travel and government* (Princeton, N.Y., 1994); B. Cohn, *Colonialism and its forms of knowledge: the British in India* (Princeton, N.J., 1996); E. Said, *Culture and imperialism* (New York, 1993); E. Said, "Secular interpretation, the geographical element, and the methodology of imperialism", in *After colonialism: imperial histories and postcolonial displacements*, G. Prakash (ed.) (Princeton, N.J., 1995); D. Scott, "Colonial governmentality", *Social Texts* **5**, 1995, pp. 191–220.

9   Said, "Methodology of imperialism", p. 28.

10 Brown & Vibert, *Reading beyond words*.

11 J. Appleby, *Economic thought and ideology in seventeenth-century England* (Princeton, N.J., 1978); C. Bayly, *Imperial meridian: the British empire and the world, 1780–1830* (London, 1989); M. Pratt, *Imperial eyes: travel writing and transculturation* (London, 1992); G. Scammell, *The first imperial age: European overseas expansion c. 1400–1715* (London, 1989); O. Dickason, "Europeans and a New World: cosmography in the 1500s", in Brown & Vibert, *Reading beyond words*.

12 Smandych & Lee, "Women, colonization, and resistance"; G. Sioui, *For an Amerindian autohistory: an essay on the foundations of a social ethic* (Kingston, Ont., 1992); O. Dickason, *Canada's First Nations*; C. Miller & P. Churchryk (eds), *Women of the First Nations: power, wisdom, and strength* (Winnipeg, 1996);

13 K. Neumann, "'In Order to Win Their Friendship': renegotiating first contact", *The Contemporary Pacific* **6**, 1994, pp. 111–45.

14 R. G. Thwaites (ed.), *The Jesuit relations and allied documents* [73 vols] (New York, 1959).

15 Latfitau, *Moeurs des sauvages ameriquains, comparés aux moeurs des premiers temps* [2 vols] (Paris, 1724) ed. and trans. William N. Fenton & Elizabeth L. Moore (Toronto, 1974).

16 Lafitau, vol. 1, pp. 28–9.

17 The discussion is developed further in McGillivray & Smandych, "Capturing childhood".

18 J. F. Lafitau, vol. 1, p 357. According to Lafitau, "The children are very warmly and gently cradled in these boards; for, besides the furs which are very soft, a quantity of down [from reed spikes or powder of slippery elm bark] is put in them to serve as a lining . . . by means of a little skin or piece of linen put between their thighs and hanging out in front, they can provide for their natural needs without soiling or spoiling the inside except for the down which can easily be replaced."

19 *Ibid.*, p. 356.

20 *Ibid.*, p. 360.

21 *Ibid.*, p. 361. An editor's footnote verifies the practice of throwing water into a baby's face as surviving into the nineteenth century; Seneca informants on this practice thought it cruel (p. 360).

22 *Jesuit relations and allied documents*, vol. 6, pp. 153–5. Even earlier than Le Jeune, Samuel de Champlain wrote about the Indians of New France: "The children have great freedom among these tribes. The fathers and mothers indulge them too much, and never punish them. Accordingly they are so bad and of so vicious a nature, that they often strike their mothers and others. The most vicious, when they have acquired the strength and power, strike their fathers. They do this whenever the father or mother does anything that does not please them. This is a sort of curse that God inflicts upon them." In *Voyages of Samuel de Champlain. Translated from the French by Charles Pomeroy Otis, Ph.D., with historical illustrations and a memoir by the Rev. Edmund F Slafter, A.M. Vol. III, 1611–1618* (Boston, 1882), pp. 170–71.

23 This may be a mistaken observation he made based on his comparisons with "the ancients", but Lafitau said he found support for this claim in the remarks of older Iroquois.

24 The idea that European colonizers, including the British, experienced this process of reshaping their identities is discussed in several of the essays contained in N. Canny & A. Pagden (eds), *Colonial identity in the Atlantic world, 1500–1800* (Princeton, N.J., 1987); especially M. Zuckerman's essay on "Identity in British America: unease in Eden". The process of forging new colonial identities, separate from England, and influenced by their associations with Indians, is also alluded to in J. Merrell, "'The Customes of Our Countrey': Indians and colonists in early America", in *Strangers within the realm: cultural margins of the first British empire*, B. Bailyn & P. Morgan (eds) (Chapel Hill, N.C., 1991), Smandych & Lee, "Women, colonization, and resistance", note the way ethnohistorians have used the concept of "syncretism" to come to a similar understanding of the way in which Europeans changed their own values and behaviour because of what they learned from aboriginal peoples.

25 Many accounts of this type can be found in the Canadian Institute for Historical Microreproductions, *Early Canadiana Microfiche Series/Native Studies Collection* (Ottawa, 1993), which lists over 1,400 primary historical documents (written prior to 1900) that have been microfilmed and made available to researchers at Canadian university libraries. Many of the primary historical documents cited in this chapter come from this collection.

26   L. Hennepin, *A new discovery of a vast country in America, extending above four thousand miles, between New France & New Mexico; with a description of the Great Lakes, cataracts, rivers, plants, and animals. Also, the manners, customs, and languages of the several Native Indians, and the advantage of commerce with those different nations* [vol. 1]; *with a continuation giving an account of the attempts of the Sieur de la Salle upon the mines of St Barbe, &c. The taking of Quebec by the English; with the advantages of a shorter cut to China and Japan* [vol. 2] (London, 1699).

27   *Ibid.*, vol. 1, p. 135.

28   *Ibid.*, pp. 102–3.

29   *Ibid.*, p. 136.

30   *Ibid.*, vol. 2, pp. 120–21.

31   *Ibid.*, p. 121.

32   *Ibid.* "When any one enters into their Cabins, when they are eating, they commonly present him with a plate-full of Meat, and they are extremely pleased when all is eaten that they give. They had rather fast two days without Victuals, than let you go without heartily presenting you with part of all they have. If by chance the Portions be distributed when one comes in, the Wife who makes the Distribution orders the matter so, that she gives (a) share to the New-comer."

33   In a book written 150 years later, G. Copway criticized Hennepin for his "fertile imagination", including his claim that "he paddled a canoe with the aid of two men, from Illinois to the Gulf of Mexico, and back, more than two thousand five hundred miles, in forty-nine days". Gopway alleged that it was only after he was questioned about the exaggerated claims he made in the French edition of his book published a decade earlier, that Hennepin travelled to England and had his book translated in the hope it would increase his chances of entering "into the pay of England's Protestant King, William III., who was anxious to be the rival of France in colonizing the banks of the Mississippi." G. Copway, *The traditional history and characteristic sketches of the Ojibway nation* (Boston, 1851), pp. 212–13.

34   Samuel G. Drake, *The aboriginal races of North America; comprising biographical sketches of eminent individuals and an historical account of the different tribes from the first discovery of the continent to the present period, with a dissertation on their origin, antiquities, manners and customs* 15th edn. Revised with valuable additions by J. W. O'Neill (Philadelphia, 1860), Book IV, p. 350.

35   *Ibid.*, p. 37.

36   See, for example, S. T. Rand, *A short statement of facts relating to the history, manners, customs, language, and literature of the Micmac tribe of Indians, in Nova-Scotia and P. E. Island: being the substance of two lectures delivered in Halifax, in November, 1849, at public meetings held for the purpose of instituting a mission to that tribe* (Halifax, 1850), p. 17; P. S. Ogden, *Traits of American-Indian life and character by a fur trader* (London, 1853), pp. 50–56; E. R. Young, *Indian life in the great North-West* (London, circa 1900), pp. 31–8; G. Catlin, *Illustrations of the manners, customs, and condition of the North American Indians with letters and notes written during eight years of travel and adventure among the wildest and most remarkable tribes now existing,* [2 vols]. 10th edn (London, 1866), vol. 2, p. 133.

37   See, for example, J. Buchanan, *Sketches of the history, manners & customs of the North American Indians, with a plan for their melioration* (New York, 1824), pp. 63–9; J. McIntosh, *The origin of the North American Indians: with a faithful description of their manners and customs, both civil and military, their religions, languages, dress, and ornaments: including various specimens of Indian eloquence, as well as historical and biographical sketches of almost all the distinguished nations and*

celebrated warriors, statesmen and orators among the Indians of North America (New York, 1853), pp. 186–7, 191; E. S. Brooks, *The story of the American Indian: his origin, development, decline and destiny* (Boston, 1887), pp. 143–4.

38   In 1670, a Royal Charter granted by Charles II gave the Hudson's Bay Company exclusive right to trade furs in the territory of Rupertsland, which included all of the lands whose rivers drained into Hudson Bay. In 1821, the Hudson's Bay Company, following its merger with the North-West Company, was granted a licence to extend its trade monopoly to encompass the territory known as "Indian country", which included all of the land beyond Rupertsland whose rivers drained into the Pacific and Arctic oceans. Although giving up its claim to parts of the north-western United States in 1846, the Company continued, at least nominally, to maintain its trade monopoly and legal authority over the rest of the Canadian West until 1870.

39   D. Francis & T. Morantz, *Partners in furs: a history of the fur trade in Eastern James Bay, 1600–1870* (Kingston, Ont., 1983); A. Ray & D. Freeman, *Give us good measure: an economic analysis of relations between the Indians and the Hudson's Bay Company before 1763* (Toronto, 1978); D. Russell, *Eighteenth-century western Cree and their neighbours* (Hull, Quebec, 1991); P. Thistle, *Indian–European trade relations in the lower Saskatchewan River region to 1840* (Winnipeg, 1986).

40   J. Brown, *Strangers in blood: fur trade company families in the Indian country* (Vancouver, 1980); J. Brown, "Children of the early fur trades", in *Children and family in Canadian history*, J. Parr (ed.) (Toronto, 1982); M. Clarke, *Reconstituting the fur trade community of the Assiniboine Basin, 1793–1810* (MA thesis, University of Manitoba, 1996); J. Foster, *The country-born in the Red River Settlement, 1820–50* (PhD thesis, University of Alberta, 1972); L. Gullason, "'No less than 7 different nations': ethnicity and culture contact at Fort George–Buckingham House", in *The fur trade revisited: selected papers of the sixth North American fur trade conference*, J. Brown et al. (eds) (East Lansing, 1994); S. Van Kirk, "'The Custom of the Country': an examination of fur trade marriage practices", in *Essays on western history*, L. Thomas (ed.) (Edmonton, 1976); S. Van Kirk, *"Many Tender Ties": women in fur trade society in western Canada 1670–1870* (Winnipeg, 1980).

41   A significant portion of this record has been preserved in the Hudson's Bay Company Archives (HBCA), which now exist as part of the Provincial Archives of Manitoba (PAM) in Winnipeg. It exists in many different forms, including Hudson's Bay Company post journals written by post governors and clerks, the official and private correspondence of Company employees, and the consistently maintained wills and powers of attorney of HBC employees. Many employees of the North-West Company, which included famous explorers like David Thompson, Simon Fraser, and Alexander Mackenzie, also left fragments of a written record of their lives which tell us something about their country marriages and children.

42   Van Kirk, *"Many Tender Ties"*, p. 138.

43   *Ibid.*, p. 99.

44   *David Thompson's narrative of his explorations in western America, 1784–1812*, ed. J. B. Tyrrell (Toronto, 1916), pp. 93–4. Thompson's *Narrative* is also rich with other observations about the role of women and children in the fur trade before 1812.

45   *The Kelsey Papers* (the papers of Henry Kelsey, circa 1690–1701) (Regina, Sash., 1994); *The journals and letters of Sir Alexander Mackenzie*, ed. W. Kaye Lamb (Toronto, 1970); *The letters and journals of Simon Fraser, 1806–1808*, ed. W. Kaye Lamb (Toronto, 1960); "First journal of Simon Fraser, 1806", and "Letters from the Rocky Mountains from August 1, 1806, to February 10, 1807, by Simon Fraser", in *Report of the Public Archives for the year*

1929 (Ottawa, 1930), pp. 109–59; J. Long, *Voyages and travels of an Indian interpreter and trader . . .* (London, 1791); D. W. Harman, *A journal of voyages and travels in the interior of North America . . . (with) a concise description of the face of the country, its inhabitants, their manners, customs, laws, etc.* (New York, 1822); and *Sixteen years in the Indian country, the journal of Daniel Williams Harmon,* ed. W. Kaye Lamb (Toronto, 1957).

46 Thomas White to London Committee, 27 August 1736; cited in *James Isham's observations and notes, 1743–1749,* ed. E. E. Rich (Toronto, 1949) p. 318. Appendix C, biography of James Isham.

47 *James Isham's observations and notes,* pp. 92–3.

48 *Ibid.,* pp. 78–9.

49 *Ibid.,* p. 322, London Committee to James Isham, 16 May 1751.

50 *Ibid.,* p. 325. When hearing of the news of the death of James Isham in April 1761, his friend Humphrey Marten wrote in his post journal at Fort James: "I cannot help Condoleing the lose of a Man who was the Idol of the Indians, and whose name will be dear to them as long as one is alive that knew him." Charles Isham's service to the Company is recorded in many documents written during his 48 years with the Company. Notable are the post journals for Cumberland House, which was established by Samuel Hearne in 1774 as the first inland Company trading post. See *Cumberland House Journals and Inland Journals, 1775–82,* ed. E. E. Rich (London, 1952).

51 Brown, *Strangers in blood,* p. 72.

52 Hearne knew Mary well. Brown, *Strangers in blood,* p. 71.

53 *Samuel Hearne's journey from Prince of Wales' Fort in Hudson's Bay to the Northern Ocean 1769–1772,* ed. J. B. Tyrrell (Toronto, 1911), p. 160; cited in Brown, *Strangers in blood,* p. 72.

54 *Ibid.*

55 *Ibid.*

56 Brown, *Strangers in blood,* pp. 70–74.

57 Sylvia Van Kirk in *"Many Tender Ties"* and Jennifer Brown in *Strangers in blood* draw attention to the place of children in the fur trade communities of the Canadian West through meticulous and well-documented studies of the country marriages of hundreds of fur trade company employees.

58 The Church Missionary Society (CMS) was established in 1799 by a group of evangelical Anglicans. Unlike other gospel-spreading societies tied to the Church of England such as the Society for the Propagation of the Gospel in Foreign Parts and the Society for the Propagation of Christian Knowledge, the aim of the CMS was to educate and civilize "heathens". It is also significant to note that the conversion of North American Indians was not the first priority of the CMS, as most of its missionary efforts were initially carried out in Asia and Africa. See E. Stock, *The history of the church missionary society: its environment, its men and its work* [3 vols] (London: Church Missionary Society, 1899).

59 While a good amount has been written about both Protestant and Catholic missionary activity in the North-West of North America, for the purposes of our present study we have decided to restrict attention mainly to Anglican-based missionary efforts at Red River. However, in doing this, we are in no way implying that we can generalize from Red River to missionary experiences elsewhere in western Canada, or in other countries.

60 There is a sizeable secondary literature on John West and later Protestant missionaries at Red River and elsewhere in western Canada. Representative studies include: V. Fast, *The Protestant missionary and fur trade society: initial contact in the Hudson's Bay Territory, 1820–*

1850 (PhD thesis, University of Manitoba, 1984); N. Goossen, *The relationship of the Church Missionary Society and the Hudson's Bay Company in Rupert's Land, 1821 to 1860, with a case study of Stanley Mission under the direction of Rev. Robert Hunt* (MA thesis, University of Manitoba, 1974); J. Foster, *The Anglican clergy in the Red River Settlement, 1820–1826* (MA thesis, University of Alberta, 1966); C. Podruchny, *Indians and missionaries in encounter: the Peguis band and the Church Missionary Society at the Red River, 1820–1838* (Graduate studies paper, University of Toronto, 1992); R. Coutts, "Anglican missionaries as agents of acculturation: the Church Missionary Society at St Andrew's, Red River, 1830–1870", in *The Anglican Church and the world of western Canada, 1820–1970*, B. Ferguson (ed.) (Regina, Sask., 1991); V. Fast, "A research note on the journals of John West", *Journal of the Canadian Church Historical Society* **21**, 1979, pp. 30–38; J. Foster, "Program for the Red River mission: the Anglican clergy, 1820–1826", *Histoire Sociale/Social History* **4**, 1969, pp. 49–75; W. Stevenson, "The Red River Indian mission school and John West's 'little charges', 1820–1833", *Native Studies Review* **4**, 1988, pp. 129–65; G. van der Goes Ladd, "Father Cockran and his children: poisonous pedagogy on the banks of the Red", in *The Anglican Church and the world of western Canada*.

61   J. West, "The British North West American Indians with free thoughts on the Red River Settlement, 1820–23", typescript copy of original held at St John's College Library, University of Manitoba.

62   Church Missionary Society Archives (CMS) A75, p. 9, Joseph Pratt to George Harbidge, London, 10 March 1824; cited in N. Goossen, *Relationship,* p. 28.

63   Church Missionary Society Archives (CMS) A75, p. 29, Edward Bickersteth to David Jones, London, March 1825; cited in N. Goossen, *Relationship,* p. 29.

64   *Ibid.*

65   J. West, *The substance of a journal during a residence at the Red River Colony and frequent excursions among the North-West American Indians, in the Years 1820, 1821, 1822, 1823* (London, 1824). For a more detailed discussion of these, along with other changes, made by West in the process of rewriting his private notes to form a published journal, see V. Fast, "A research note on the journal of John West".

66   West, "Free thoughts on the Red River Settlement", p. 11.

67   West, *Substance of a journal,* p. 20; Stevenson, "John West's 'little charges', 1820–1838", p. 136.

68   *Ibid.*

69   Podruchny, *The Peguis Band and the Church Missionary Society*, p. 22. West met with Peguis and his band at the mouth of the Red River on 5 October 1822, while returning from his second fall visit to York Factory.

70   West, *Substance of a journal,* pp. 102–4.

71   *Ibid.*, pp. 103–4.

72   *Ibid.*, p. 118.

73   *Ibid.*, pp. 118–20.

74   Stevenson, "John West's 'little charges', 1820–1833", p. 139.

75   Hugh Dempsey, "Peguis", *Dictionary of Canadian Biography*, vol. 9, p. 626.

76   Stevenson, "John West's 'little charges', 1820–1833", table 1, p. 137, notes that during his three years in the colony, West managed to recruit eight boys and two girls, from Swampy Cree, Plains Cree, Assiniboine, and more northern Chipewyan bands.

77   Miller, *Shingwauk's vision*, pp. 67–8. Drawing on information from West's published journal and Stevenson, *ibid.*, Miller argues that "At least three others were sent to school for differing reasons. A Plains Cree was sent to learn about the white people's religion, an

Assiniboine-Cree to learn to read and write, and a Chipewyan to be 'taught more than the Indians knew,' all suggesting a desire to learn the ways of the strange newcomers."

78 Stevenson, "John West's 'little charges', 1820–1833", p. 151. According to most accounts, within a short time of arriving at Red River, West managed to alienate George Simpson and most other Company officers by the evangelical approach of his missionary work. See, for example, Coutts, "Anglican missionaries as agents of acculturation", p. 53.

79 J. Foster, "William Cockran", *Dictionary of Canadian Biography*, vol. 9, pp. 134–7.

80 Although clearly much too voluminous to deal with in the present study, a close examination of Cockran's correspondence would be required in a more detailed study of European images of aboriginal childhood in the context of the Red River Settlement.

81 J. Foster, "William Cockran", p. 135.

82 *Ibid.*, p. 135.

83 See, for example, George van der Goes Ladd, "Father Cockran and his children: poisonous pedagogy on the banks of the Red".

84 Considerable support for this argument can be found in Miller, *Shingwauk's vision*, alongside numerous other histories of and commissions of inquiry which have looked at the operation of Canadian Indian residential schools.

85 Another negative image of the aboriginal child found in the accounts of newcomers was the "Indian-hating" image of the aboriginal child as a heathen savage, who, among other "savage behaviours", was taught from an early age how to participate in the torture of captives. This genre of "Indian-hating" literature, found often in captivity narratives, is covered in more detail in McGillivray & Smandych, "Capturing childhood: the aboriginal child in the European imagination".

86 For a more detailed account of this post-1850 history, see McGillivray, "Therapies of Freedom".

Chapter Thirteen

Authority under challenge: Pikampul land and Queen Victoria's law during the British invasion of Australia

Heather Goodall

Seen across time, invasions come to look like simple, two-sided struggles. When underway, colonial invasions were more likely to appear confused, riven with antagonisms within the contending camps and frayed with doubts. This paper explores a crisis of conscience experienced by Richard Bligh, a British official administering a frontier district on the Macintyre River in Australia during the late 1840s.[1] His distress was recorded in a large body of reports, justifications, confessions, accusations and counter-accusations. This outpouring in turn allows a brief glimpse of the experiences of the Pikampul people whose land was under attack. Reading the archives, one raises questions about what circumstances might draw or force someone like Bligh to step outside the comfortable alignments of their known community, and about why they might once more retreat behind its defensive stockade. More broadly, what are the forces and currents of thought which make it possible to see beyond the conventional oppositions of conflict? In this example, the question of contested authority was pervasive, but it had many levels. There was the question of whose authority over land was to be affirmed: the invading British crown's or the traditional landowners'. And the question of the authority of the law: was it a fixed, established code to be applied punitively or protectively to all, or was it a shifting, malleable process to apply only to those within certain boundaries?[2] More intimately, how was the authority of personal relationships to be negotiated in this tense situation, where manhood and paternal responsibilities were entangled in complicity with violence and dispossession?

The Macintyre River is the country of the Pikampul people, who call themselves Murris.[3] It forms the border of what are now the eastern states of

New South Wales and Queensland but it was on the frontier during the 1840s. Situated on the great belt of Aboriginal-created fire-farmed grasslands which arcs around the south-eastern half of the continent, the Macintyre faced a rapid invasion as sheep and cattle herders took up pastoral runs and claimed the fertile grazing land as their own. Major resistance by indigenous land-owners further south against the incoming herders had resulted in the British declaring martial law during the 1820s, and then in military as well as civilian punitive expeditions during the 1830s and 1840s, with many Aboriginal lives as well as some white lives lost. The events on the Macintyre were unique but their complexities, brutalities and ambiguities have resonances with many other episodes in this long invasion saga.[4]

In the Macintyre story, there were a number of individuals and groups in contestation. Richard Bligh was a commissioner for Crown Lands; his primary role was to oversee the orderly use of the land claimed by the British crown in a newly invaded district, but because of his frontier situation, he was also responsible for implementing civil and criminal law. He is the sole crown official in this local study, but his experience was mirrored in the frustrated careers of a number of the other Crown Lands commissioners of the period.[5] Both his mother's and father's families were named Bligh, but they imparted different traditions. Richard's maternal grandfather was William Bligh, whose style of imposing order had famously generated mutiny twice, when he was captain of the *Bounty* and again when he was Governor of New South Wales. Richard's father was a London barrister, giving him a legacy of awareness of black letter law.[6] Having arrived in the colony in 1838, a year of dramatic conflict between settlers and Aborigines, Bligh stayed in the longer-settled areas until his first position of authority, as the Commissioner at Warialda, which included the Macintyre on its northern boundary. He shared the suspicion many officials felt for the herders, the entrepreneurs who had so rapidly overrun the inland grazing country, demanding entitlement to free-hold over areas so vast that they staggered English imaginations. The herders were called "squatters", not only because there was not yet any administrative framework for their extravagant claims, but mainly because pastoralism was seen as a strictly temporary precursor to the real business of colonization, the fostering of dense agricultural land settlement.[7]

The landowning Pikampul had already been battered by invasion and their numbers had been reduced to some hundreds when Bligh arrived. Their law bound them very directly to their land, involving a complex set of relation-ships between people and land, which linked politics, society and culture to well-defined areas of country. Law was enacted in ceremonies and recorded in the oral traditions which explained social rules in terms of landforms. So for the Pikampul, trying to evaluate the practices and law of the intruders, it must have seemed sensible that Bligh was both a land administrator and a criminal investigator.[8]

The squatters and their employees were the final group on the Macintyre frontier. In this remote and densely wooded area, there were few white women, and children were only beginning to be brought into the area. There were no established civil or religious structures: Richard Bligh was expected to initiate all of that. Transportation had ended in 1840, but the white population in the area were viewed from Sydney not only as squatters but as undisciplined and unsavoury characters, ex-convicts and outlaws. These people saw themselves as pioneers, deserving support for their work of dispossession, resentful of control and reluctant to concede to any "law" that did not fit their interests in the new and disorderly conditions of the Macintyre.[9]

The invasion did not leave these groups separate. Rather, it brought them all into increasing interactions, and it is important to recognize that these were pervasively shaped by gender. Sex itself was the most common form of contact across racial lines. Gender and age as well as race determined the likelihood of becoming a victim of violence. Gender relations and the roles played out by each sex were central. For Murri women, it was not only sex but their gendered "women's" work as servants and nursemaids which made them vulnerable to violence, while the men on all sides struggled to fulfill (and to represent themselves as fulfilling) a responsible masculine and paternal role. Finally, gendered experiences shaped the perceptions and memory of the participants.

English colonizers and missionaries, as Catherine Hall has demonstrated, perceived their role and their relations with Africans in Jamaica through the lens of their own understanding of gendered relations, and particularly through their conception of the proper role for a responsible, Christian, English man and father.[10] She has argued that the metaphor of "the Family of Man" was central in shaping nineteenth-century British reformers' perceptions and self-representations, because it combined protective and paternal responsibilities with finely graduated hierarchies between men and women, between employers and servants and between cultures and races.[11] Ideas about gendered family relationships are important in understanding much of the interaction between Aboriginal people and the British on the Macintyre. But not only were the circulating familial metaphors those from the English (emerging) middle-class family and particularly that of the father; there were also ideas of proper social relations arising from Pikampul Murris, whose very different extended kin relations and familial responsibilities for land were shaping forces behind their actions.

The Pikampul of the Macintyre were in a complex struggle with the incoming British when Richard Bligh and his new wife arrived in their country early in 1847. Sheep herders there were a minority, but they needed labour, and if the Pikampul chose to take up work with these squatters they were readily accepted. Many Murri men and women worked as shepherds, using their knowledge of the land to keep sheep on best feed and water, find lost stock and protect them from dingos. Aborigines were employed also as general servants, carrying messages and goods between white squatting out-posts and shepherds' camps, adapting a role by which they had always communicated between encampments of their own people. There had al-ready been a white child born on the Macintyre, and Aboriginal women were beginning to work as nurses and carers to the children of the runholders.[12]

The more numerous squatters running cattle had less need of constant labour. Many of them argued that Aborigines frightened the cattle, and the managers and stockmen of most cattle herds were instructed to shoot any Aborigines they saw within the ill-defined boundaries of the squatting run. This strategy was known locally as "keeping them at a distance" and was carried further to justify hunting parties which threatened or attacked camps of Murris on sheep runs.[13]

This meant that the region was an uneven patchwork. Some Murris were able to access their traditional lands, harvesting its produce at the same time as they managed the flocks of the sheep holders. Many others, who might own immediately adjacent land, were ruthlessly driven off it by cattle herders and left without the economic resources to which they were entitled by traditional right. These locally dispossessed Murris did not disappear or move far away. They continued to assert their close identification with their own land, each group being known among the whites of the area by their collective affiliation to place. There was a Boobera mob, for example, much of whose land around Boobera Lagoon was taken up with cattle-fattening runs, and so they camped on the few sheep runs close to their own country. From more secluded camps along the river, dispossessed landowners might raid the cattle runs, not only to support their families but killing far more than they could eat in a clear strategy of economic harassment against their dispossessors. The leaders were known by name among whites, and communication between pastoral camp Murris and those in the river camps was no doubt strong.

In October 1847, the Pikampul began a regular and central ritual in their society, the *Bora*, the initiation of young boys into adult manhood. This ceremony united affirmation of authority over land with responsibility for the care of that land and for the kin linked to it, and with the responsibility to renew social relations between people and land by "making new men". The *Bora* was a responsibility of both mothers and fathers, with each performing particular roles defined simultaneously by their relationship to land and to the initiates. But after the women had delivered up their sons for the symbolic

263

death of ritual seclusion, it was the men who were charged with the ultimate responsibility of passing on the knowledge and the awe of the law of their society, in a process marked by both the intense pain of physical trials and the intense euphoria of new knowledge and new, powerful roles.[14] The ceremony must have been difficult to organize, given the hostilities in the area, but over four hundred Murris from the Pikampul and their surrounding neighbours gathered on a property between the Gwydir and the Macintyre, where they camped for eight weeks to conduct the proper ritual. The land of the hosts had always been called on to support such gatherings, and over this period, many raids on surrounding cattle runs had taken place to feed the participants involved in the intense and absorbing ceremonies.

Bligh had little awareness of the significance of these rituals in demonstrating and reaffirming Pikampul authority over land and society. For him, the gathering was not only an irritation but threatening, coming just before his wife gave birth to their first child. He was uneasy, his confidence in his new paternal role as protector of a young family undermined by what he interpreted as a show of strength and defiance on the part of the Pikampul. The oppressive and menacing atmosphere Bligh described in relation to the *Bora* ceremony was echoed in his account of the country as "interspersed with dense Brigalow scrubs, affording an impenetrable retreat to the Natives". He called for urgent reinforcements and for the formation of a "Native Police", composed of Aboriginal trackers from other areas, to control the Aboriginal bands.[15]

Bligh's first report on the state of the Aborigines was written after a year at his post.[16] He wrote dismissively of the potential for Aboriginal labour in the pastoral industry, describing them as having only ". . . a readiness for occasional desultory labour in the service of the whites". On the recently invaded Macintyre, he warned that "the Natives are in that state of semi-civilisation in which they have always [been] found most dangerous . . ." Most cattle properties had been subject to raids, but far more alarming was that "the lives of unoffending individuals have been taken in a most wanton manner by these Savages". Bligh described the circumstantial evidence linking Aborigines to the deaths of two adults, found dead after being robbed. He expressed deepest concern at the death of an 11-year-old boy, son of Mr James Mark, who "was most cruelly murdered and mutilated by the Aborigines". There had been no witnesses to the death, which had been reported by the boy's father, but Bligh accepted this unquestioningly, acknowledging no excuse for the abhorrent brutality of the Aboriginal murder of the young boy. The role Bligh wrote for himself was as a man of law protecting children from irrational savagery, and indeed this paternal role must have seemed very close to him, as he and his new wife embarked on caring for their first child.

By mid-year, Bligh had heard a rumour of an outrage of a different kind, against Aboriginal women. Early in June, there had been an attack on the Aboriginal shepherds at the Lanarch property, Carbucky, which took in part of Boobera Lagoon. The outcome was the critical wounding of a woman. Bligh had barely begun to inquire when he heard a report of the deaths of two Aboriginal women on 11 June at Umbercollie, a cattle property managed by Jonathan Young.[17]

The stories were very similar. Aboriginal people had lived peacefully in camps on each property, and had given valuable service over a number of years, not only as shepherds, cattle stockworkers and domestic servants but in the intimate roles of nannies and wet-nurses. These were people who had decided to camp on the new squatting runs and work closely with the invaders, in order to stay on their land. At Umbercollie they had had the good fortune of having a cattle run which nevertheless tolerated Aboriginal owners continuing to live there. On both runs, the victims had been sleeping only metres from the manager's huts when they were set upon in the early hours of the morning by a group of mounted men who had fired guns, chased down the slower members of the group, calling them by name till they turned, then shooting or bludgeoning them to death.

Bligh was assisted particularly by Margaret Young whose young child had been nursed by one of the women killed. This close contact led the manager's wife into a defiant challenge to the prevailing silence about attacks on the Pikampul, making her a more vocal defender of her servants than any of the white men who had taken Murri lovers. The detailed and intimate knowledge involved in these killings began to emerge. This was not an impersonal frontier where the killers never knew the names of their victims. Instead, here the most familiar were the easiest to find and the least likely to resist, so they were the most likely to die. The killers could name their victims and the witnesses, both Aboriginal and white, could name the killers. Yet none of the white witnesses would swear to the identity of those killers.

For the first time, Bligh began to turn his attention to the Aborigines for evidence. He was rapidly given eight names of people who were clearly identified by those Pikampul witnesses as the killers at Umbercollie, and most were implicated in the Carbucky attack as well. At Umbercollie the attackers included an Aboriginal man named "Billy" from the coast, but in each case, the ringleader was identified as James Mark, the squatter who had reported his son's death to Bligh in the previous year. A very different picture of that death too began to emerge from Aboriginal information. It became clear that James Mark had a reputation as a violent man, who was known to have killed two Aboriginal men in the months prior to his son's death. While both were mourned, one death had particularly angered the Pikampul, and Bligh

265

described this as a "most treacherous murder". This man had been carrying fresh meat from one white settler's camp to that of Mark. Not only was the British code of gratitude for a gift broken, but as the Pikampul explained, their law gave absolute protection to any messenger carrying news or goods between encampments of their own people or across the territory of others. Mark's treachery was a transgression against two laws. It was this, the Pikampul argued, which had led to the death of the boy. The accusations of mutilation never were substantiated. Bligh was convinced by the Pikampul accounts and at the end of August began to arrest those accused of the Umbercollie murders. Daniel Maclean confessed in a detailed statement.

Within days of Bligh's return to Warialda, on 2 September 1848, the murderers had struck again, this time at a sheep run owned by Augustus Morris, who graphically described the events. Here again the victims were two women and the baby one of them was holding, while a young boy was murdered nearby. The mother, Izabella, and her infant had been the family of a Pikampul man named by whites as "Pantaloon", who had worked as a trusted and skilled worker for Morris for over two years. The tensions of the invasion were suggested in this pantomime clown's nickname: "Pantaloon" had both trivialising and sexualizing implications, and must have revealed a derision of the masculinity of a conquered people. Pantaloon had been sent off two days previously to carry out an instruction from his employer, and Mary, who had nursed the Morris children, had gone to sleep with Izabella to keep her company in her nightly guard duty at the sheep pens. Morris was angered that the intruders must have known that the women were guarding the sheep, as their bedding was laid out in the gate of the pen. Curiously, however, the white witness was unable to assist with a sworn statement on the identity of the killers. Aboriginal witnesses were more observant and co-operative, identifying Mark and his associates. Bligh had no doubt the killings had occurred in retribution for his arrest of Maclean and his continuing investigation of the Umbercollie and Carbucky attacks.

Doggedly, Bligh continued to pursue the accused, arresting five of the eight suspects by early October. Mark himself had escaped, resisting arrest violently and then persuading the gullible constables that he would surrender himself to Bligh within a week. He had failed to do so and Bligh issued a warrant for murder. The pressure was mounting as Bligh continued to take statements, however, and Jonathan Young found that his neighbours were complaining about his co-operation with Bligh's investigation. Although Young denied that any threats had been made against him, Bligh was suspicious that this had occurred. On 4 November all his horses, both private and government issue, were stolen and destroyed. Bligh was in no doubt this was done as a warning to him to cease his enquiries.

By now, the charged men were rallying support to defend themselves. Bligh's depositions were being unsympathetically scrutinized in the office of the Attorney General, where the view was recorded that without further evidence Bligh was unlikely to obtain a conviction.[18] James Mark had eluded arrest but was still in the district. Buoyed by Bligh's failure to secure new evidence, Mark began a counterattack, complaining to the Colonial Secretary and the Governor that Bligh had unfairly accused him and had allowed the district to sink deeper into chaos. Now it was Bligh who found himself under attack, with little support from his superiors and only wavering backing from the whites who had originally offered statements to expose the killings. In January 1849, to defend himself, Bligh wrote a series of reports which detailed the events of the past year, but also revealed his own troubled attempts to analyze them.[19]

Richard Bligh began by admitting that he had been duped by local whites. The Pikampul were denied the opportunity to give sworn evidence in courts, but Bligh believed:

> . . . could these miserable savages give evidence in a court of justice or even set forth their case with a little of the eloquence employed against them the balance of injury and crime would be fearfully against the white population.

Bligh had reshaped his paternal role of protector and defender of women and children so that it now explicitly included Aboriginal people. He had stepped far outside the comfortable assumptions of his earlier report that Europeans were bringing civilization to the continent. His report gave accounts of the attacks, suggesting the horror which the murders had evoked in him.

> The method pursued has been that of stealing upon the natives in large parties in the night when sleeping in their camp at the stations of the few individuals who afford them protection and discharging upon them a volley of firearms. The victims selected have been almost without exception women and infants and generally valuable servants to the residents of the station which they frequented. And this circumstance proves in itself that the object is not the punishment of offenders but the exasperation of the natives and the gratification of the wanton brutality of the assailants by the degree of moral pain inflicted on the survivors.

Yet he was just as horrified by the evidence of "combination" and systematic planning which had gone into the murders themselves and the process of covering them up. His accusation of "combination" suggested the magistrate's anger at criminal conspiracy, but also class-based fears of Chartism and trade unionism. Bligh's main explanation for the horror he was witnessing was to

267

blame the ex-convict and working-class population of the area. Although transportation had ended in 1840, Bligh described the Macintyre as so remote a district that it had been:

> ... occupied by stockmen and hutkeepers generally chosen from the oldest hands, that is to say from the most depraved class, and these men have been hitherto beyond anything more than a nominal control ... here runaways and disorderly persons of every kind found acceptance and refuge.

These people not only had criminal intent, but used the tensions between Aborigines and squatters to serve their own labour interests:

> These men became united together by the bond of their common villainy having an interest in exciting and maintaining the violence of the natives and exaggerating the dangers to which they were exposed which formed a plea for demanding excessive wages for themselves as a compensation for the risk of life which they were supposed to incur ...

Bligh repeated the accusations against working people, "old hands" and ex-convicts frequently, suggesting it must have been important to him to find a class-based explanation. Yet Mark was a squatter, not an employee, and at one point Bligh uneasily admitted that he was being obstructed in bringing criminals to justice not only by the criminals themselves, but by the "respectable" members of society who refused to testify against those they knew to be guilty:

> It may give some idea of the state of combination and system of terrorism existing in the locality when I state that though the murderers in all these cases are known to everyone by the common fame of the country, though the Government have offered large rewards for information and I have used every effort in my power to bring the offenders to justice and have caused the arrest of six persons accused by an accomplice, yet not the smallest additional evidence has been given nor is there any probability that corroborative testimony will be obtained and persons of respectability who I am confident secretly abhor this atrocious system have actually joined in a subscription set on foot for the defence of the parties accused.

Bligh again called for the urgent reinforcement of the police force, but now it was to control not the Aborigines but the whites. In the longer term, he saw the only hope as the establishment of the class order in which he had had confidence in England and Sydney:

The great root of the evil however is the non-residence of the proprietors and the almost total absence of material from which a resident
magistracy could be formed, through whom alone it would be possible
to exercise that immediate control and prompt investigation which
would lead to the prevention or punishment of outrage on either side.

His developing communication with the Pikampul was suggested in the deep
sympathy of his writing, just as much as in its pervasive paternalism. The
Pikampul were worthy of his protection because he saw them as the defeated
and largely innocent victims of squatters who had defied British law. Yet
beyond revealing Bligh's ambivalent relationship with the Pikampul, his
report was further evidence that Aboriginal landowners were not leaving their
embattled lands for far distant areas, but were staying on, moving around their
land to find safe places:

> . . . there can be no doubt that the natives or more properly speaking a
> small number of the worst disposed amongst them have during the past
> year committed considerable aggressions on the cattle of the settlers in
> this quarter, but when I consider that they are forbidden on pain of
> death to show themselves upon most of the cattle runs because their
> presence disturbs these animals and that they are followed and attacked
> when they take refuge on the sheep stations it can hardly excite surprise
> that they should avail themselves of any safe opportunities for revenge.
> I do not know that their wretched state can be more clearly described
> than in the words of one of themselves, when told to go away from a
> sheep station at which so large a number of these creatures had congre-
> gated as to make it impossible for the well disposed owner to supply
> them all with food:

> > "Which way blackfellow yan [i.e. go]? Supposing this way you
> > shootem. Supposing that way you shootem. All about shootem."

Bligh was defeated by the local refusal to accept his vision of an orderly society
where the law was applicable to all. This vision of a law which was available
to all across the empire, regardless of race, had become one of the central
tenets of the anti-slavery movements which had held political and ideological
ascendancy in England since the 1820s but whose power was declining by
mid-century. Bligh's experience of rejection in the colony of New South
Wales in 1849 was to be echoed in the defeat of this principle in England itself
over the defence of Edward Eyre's savage repression of Jamaicans at Morant
Bay in 1865.[20]

The squatters on the Macintyre were, along with other colonists across the

British empire, precursors of a rising, racially exclusive version of British law. They were voicing thinly veiled criticisms of Bligh for not being harsh enough to control the "hostile natives".[21] While Bligh did eventually force James Mark out of the area, the universal refusal by "respectable" squatters to give corroborating evidence left the Commissioner for Gwydir vulnerable to official lack of interest and low-level corruption. The Maitland magistrate hearing the case insisted that further proceedings could not be taken without more evidence, and drunken, perhaps bribed police at Maitland jail allowed the confessing Maclean to escape.

Some Pikampul Murris took their own lessons from this failure of Queen Victoria's law to offer them either protection or retribution. Pantaloon, still mourning the slaughter of his family, moved off the sheep run and into the camps of the cattle raiders. The strong familiarity he had developed with the British was put to good use when he took up the role of spokesperson and negotiator in later contacts with whites.

The Colonial Secretary had finally arranged for the Native Police to be sent to the border, but when they arrived early in 1849, they were acting on the assumptions of Bligh's first report. The troop was made up of Aboriginal men from distant Victoria, and was led by Frederick Walker, a British officer who had served in the Native Police units in the southern areas. The troop was deployed without contact with Bligh. Walker's first announcement was that he was going to seek out "the hostile Natives" responsible for "a most atrocious murder", that of James Mark's son.[22]

Walker encountered local Aboriginal sabotage, complaining about "treacherous guides" who failed to lead him to the "notorious murderers", but he received enthusiastic support from the graziers who were angry with Bligh. Because of Pantaloon's prominent negotiating position, Walker assumed he was "one of the ringleaders" and scoffed when Pantaloon came to offer peace. Walker told the Pikampul delegation, "I make no terms with murderers," which must have struck Pantaloon with some irony. Over the next weeks, Walker's men pursued groups of Murris through the brigalow scrub. On July 9, the police troop came across the "Boobera mob" cutting up a beef carcass on Carbucky station. This run was the homeland of those Pikampul people, but Walker had been introduced to it by local squatters like Morris as "a place where five men are buried who were killed by blacks". With such inflammatory justifications in mind, and with no reference to the recent murders of Murris in the vicinity, Walker attacked those he called "hostile blacks", killing at least one man and severely wounding others who left clotting blood on the earth as they crawled away on their hands and knees. He wrote excitedly to the Colonial Secretary: "I much regretted not having one hour more daylight as I would have annihilated that lot."[23] Yet even Walker could see that the conflict was exacerbated by settler actions, as he wrote to the Colonial Secretary, in June 1849:

> I have to call your attention to the iniquitous practice carried on at some stations, which is to drive off all the blacks from there, this system they call keeping them at a distance. As every black has his own hunting ground from which he is thus expelled, and he is not allowed to trespass for any length of time on that of others, he is compelled for his own subsistence to kill cattle. It is my wish that the marauding parties which now infest the brigalow should be broken up, which can only be done by allowing each native to return to his own ground.[24]

Defeated and isolated from the whites in the area, Bligh continued his contact with Murris. He had used his growing communication with them, on the instructions of the Governor, to inquire about their response to a proposal to reserve small areas of "crown" land for Aboriginal use. He had learnt enough to give detailed recommendations for four significant places with good water, which would satisfy the different language and land affiliations of the Murris in the district.[25] One of these sites was Boobera Lagoon, that place of so much conflict but still a rich living area and the focal point of many powerful narratives in Pikampul tradition.

In a decision which was a partial recognition of native title to property, the New South Wales Governor announced the creation of around forty "Aboriginal reserves", including Bligh's four suggested sites, in September 1850. Commissioners were to inform Aborigines that the Queen had given them these reserves forever, so long as they limited their residence to the boundaries of those small areas. Bligh followed his instructions but observed repeatedly that the Pikampul regarded themselves as being "in possession" of their wider country, so that the bounded patches of reserved land meant little to them when they continued to feel they had rightful authority over all their lands. Decades later, as intensifying agriculture encroached further on to Aboriginal lands during the 1880s, people in all the areas where such reserves had been notified began calling on the government to fulfil Victoria's promise to save some of their land so they and their children could live securely. It is clear that Murris had been listening intently to the explanations and offers made by Bligh and his fellow commissioners, but they had been drawing very different meanings from those the Queen's officials had intended. It was this interpreted communication, refracted through the cultural prisms on all sides, which was the basis for later action and belief.[26]

Depressed and pessimistic not only about Aboriginal people but about his dissatisfactions with the remote and disturbing society to which he was posted, Bligh frequently sought leave or transfer to escape. He is remembered in the writings of other residents at the time as a solitary man, "just but severe", an indication of his distance from white society in his district.[27] His sense of inevitable decline was dramatically altered late in 1851, however, when the discovery of gold in the south of the colony led to a rapid and almost total loss of white labour in the remote pastoral areas.

The Crown Land Commissioner's reports for Gwydir for 1852, 1853 and 1854 demonstrate a remarkable change of tone, revealing the new dependence of the district and of himself on Aboriginal co-operation:

> . . . the services rendered by the Natives to the Settlers during the difficulties consequent upon the present dearth of labour have been of the utmost importance amounting in some cases nearly to the absolute preservation of the flocks from destruction . . . I have found the services of the Natives during the past year of the most essential importance, having been for months without other domestic servants and having been obliged when absent on duty to commit the Crown Lands Office to the charge of a Solitary Native who remained at his post with exemplary fidelity, sometimes for weeks at a time . . .[28]

This report from the Gwydir region was not unique. From all over the pastoral districts, commissioners for Crown Lands began to report dramatic changes in relations with Aboriginal landowners. Hostilities declined almost overnight as graziers of both sheep and cattle welcomed Aboriginal people back on to their own country, encouraging (and sometimes forcing) them to apply their detailed knowledge of the land to the work of a pastoral run.[29] Bligh now retracted his earlier assumptions that Aborigines were incapable of productive involvement in the settler economy. What had changed, he pointed out, were settler attitudes and preparedness to offer better conditions and pay for Aborigines and this had led to new co-operation from Aboriginal workers.[30]

As his personal contact with Murris was increasing, and as he became less pessimistic about their role in the labour market, Bligh began to intervene in the lives of the Aboriginal servants and employees around him. Reflecting his private position as the father of a growing family, as well as his role as an employer and official, he tried to convince Aboriginal parents that their children should be trained in apprenticeships, as working-class children would have been at that time. Bligh organized local apprenticeships for two children of Aboriginal people close to him: one young boy was indentured to a sawyer, while a young girl was apprenticed as a domestic servant. Yet as Bligh became more interventionist, he encountered more strongly a competing paternal authority. For Bligh, the result was rising frustration, which began to emerge as irritable complaints:

> I fear that only on the very young members of the Tribes can any permanently useful impression be made and only upon them when wholly withdrawn from the mischievous influence of the old men and Native Doctors.[31]

Early in 1856 Bligh succeeded in escaping the tensions of the North-West with a transfer to the coast, to the township of Grafton in the spectacularly beautiful Clarence River pastoral district. Here the more structured society for which he had been yearning was well established. Bligh began to apply himself energetically to supporting the Anglican church and re-entering a familiarly class-ordered world.[32]

As Commissioner for Crown Lands, he still needed to report on the state of relations with Aborigines, and his report for 1856 was in a very different tone from any of his Gwydir reports since 1848.[33] The situation in the Clarence was unlike that in the West, but perhaps Bligh had also reshaped his approaches, seeking to avoid the isolated position into which his defence of Aboriginal people had led him in Gwydir. The Bandjalang peoples of the coast were not a victimized and defeated minority of only 300, which was the way Bligh had come to represent the Pikampul. Instead, the Bandjalang and their allies were a very large surviving population, amounting to at least 2,000 people in the vicinity of Grafton, a figure so large that it shocked the London Colonial Office clerks who annotated the report in concerned disbelief. The area was well endowed with traditional food sources and the wilder high backcountry ravines offered safe close refuges. Not only were their numbers relatively large, but the Bandjalang peoples were well organized and continued to challenge British pastoral occupation of their country. While they were heavily involved by 1856 in employment with settlers in timbering, agriculture and stockwork, the Bandjalang were also continuing to raid cattle runs, spear cattle, rob shepherds' huts and take corn and pumpkins from farms in punitive attacks on the economy of the British settlers.

Bligh's predecessor had described the conditions in the district as "tranquil" only the year before, but Bligh was shocked at such strength and assertiveness, writing "the amount of outrage on the part of the Aborigines has far exceeded that which I have been accustomed to notice in Districts more remote than that of the Clarence River". Bligh was angered and affronted by the Bandjalang, accusing them of "evincing a predatory disposition and a consciousness of the extreme difficulty which attends the legal punishment of such offences by the Aborigines". By far the gravest concern for Bligh, however, was that there had been two sexual attacks on "respectable" white

273

women by the Bandjalang during 1856. In Bligh's writing about these incidents, there was undoubtedly genuine concern, but it was also an opportunity to demonstrate a realignment. He affirmed himself in the role of law bringer who protects women and children, but it was again white women and children whom Bligh sought to protect. Bligh knew that in Gwydir his outrage at the murder of James Mark's son had been the carefully orchestrated product of deception by Mark and other whites, but he made no inquiries at Grafton to find out whether the Bandjalang might have been acting in response to provocation or in retribution for actions already carried out against them. Bligh clearly never sought nor made the personal contact with these coastal people into which he had been almost forced while on the Macintyre. In 1859, the British Colonial Office washed its hands of any attempt to fight New South Wales colonists and improve Aboriginal peoples' conditions or rights, leaving "this important question to the local Government in whose hands it now entirely rests".[34] In his orderly and quiet years of retirement, in Grafton and then Sydney until his death in 1869, Bligh may have sought an escape from the unresolved moral difficulties he had opened up for himself at Warialda.

In this encounter both British and Aboriginal law was challenged. There were no unambiguous positions. The British were not united in any common goal: Bligh found his most difficult struggle over the nature of the Queen's authority coming from his own fellow British settlers. Yet his sympathy for and risk-taking on behalf of Aborigines was fraught with misunderstanding, paternalism and irritation. The Pikampul too took differing decisions among themselves about how to deal with the invasion, about whether to work with squatters or to attack them. Beyond this, they faced the threat of Aboriginal people from other areas transgressing their laws either in the service of individual squatters like "Billy", the accomplice in the Umbercollie killings, or of the state, like the troopers of the Native Police.

Bligh tried to implement an established law, imported from Britain, already formed in the historical moment of the earlier anti-slavery ascendancy, which was to be exercised equitably across racial boundaries as one element of a just colonialism which recognized native property rights as well as entitlements to justice. In a small precursor to the defeat of this view of British law in England itself, when John Stuart Mill and the Jamaica Committee failed to have Governor Eyre censured after the Morant Bay uprising in 1865, Bligh's attempts were rejected by many of the squatters, who had a different view of order, guilt and criminality.[35] In their colonial situation, they wanted only those aspects of British law which endorsed their property claims and protected their goals. They forced a recognition of the fluidity at the heart of common law, that law is not fixed and transportable, but remade constantly, shaped by the disorder of new and competing interests and powers. In this case, the squatters forced a reshaping of the law to endorse the embedding of racial limits to equal justice.

A central current of this complex encounter was gender. The violence of the invasion in the Macintyre was strongly gendered, with most of the killing by whites aimed at women and children. The way in which Bligh composed his role and identity in his official writing was through a view of masculinity, of the proper role for a responsible man in public life. On a small scale, there are parallels here between the colonial experience of Richard Bligh and, ironically, no longer that of John Stuart Mill but that of Edward Eyre. Bligh's conception of the paternal role of protector of women and children justified for him his transgression of colonial boundaries as long as the colonized people could be seen as defeated and weak. Frustrated by cultural resistance among the Pikampul, then faced with the military and cultural assertion of the powerful Bandjalang, Bligh retreated, defensively recomposing his paternal role so that he continued to present himself as a defender of women, but withdrew behind colonial race-defined boundaries once again, as Eyre had done in Jamaica well before the Morant Bay uprising.[36] In Bligh's contradictory experiences there are glimpses of the processes Catherine Hall and Ann Laura Stoler have explored, in which rather than the values of the metropolitan power being imposed on the colony, the colonial experience shapes and transforms the metropolitan ideas, not only as they appear in the colony but in the colonizing metropolis itself.[37]

There is another account of challenged understandings of masculinity in these events, but we can see only glimpses of it. Pantaloon, like many other Pikampul men, was facing the struggle to sustain a responsible manhood, even as the settlers mocked that idea in the name they called him. The determination of the Pikampul to reaffirm their authority over land and responsible manhood was clear in the Bora, yet Pantaloon like his other countrymen faced violent obstruction of his access to the country for which he was a custodian despite his decision to work with the invaders. Then his family was slaughtered. Pantaloon's response may be read in his shift to an active role in the cattle-raiding resistance groups, in which he tried to use what he had learnt about white men, as well as what he could learn from and about "native troopers", to negotiate peace. Although we have no way of observing this process, it must have raised searing questions for Pantaloon about his responsibilities and roles as a Pikampul man.

Yet although opening up the complexity of the experience of invasion, these incidents in the years from 1847 to 1856 on the Macintyre also give us an example of the intensity of the pressures to conform, to concede to the dominant narratives among colonizers. Bligh expended intense efforts, and faced attack and ostracism because of his defence of Aboriginal people and his attempt to expose James Mark. Yet the mythology which Mark propagated, that his family was blameless and that his son had been brutally murdered for no other reason than irrational savagery, was of far more use to the "pioneers" than Bligh's alternative narrative of a frustrated pursuit of justice. Only Margaret Young, the manager's wife on Umbercollie, supported Bligh's view when she wrote in her journal that Mark was "a great hater", a killer who had provoked his son's death, then used it to organize further massacres which led to the calling in of the Native Police.[38] In the public domain, however, the prevailing narrative reiterated the mythology of the innocent, murdered and mutilated white boy, killed by treacherous "hostile blacks". In newspaper articles demanding harsh penalties against Aborigines through the 1850s, in hearings before parliament justifying the Native Police atrocities in the 1860s and in reminiscences of heroic pioneering in the early twentieth century, the story appears again and again.[39]

There were many levels on which this engagement was concerned with authority: that of individuals trying to assert or claim power; that of "men" seeking to assert their public roles; of lawholders and law bringers; that of landowners, usurpers and administrators. One of the very few aspects of this fluid engagement which has proved to be unchanging is the tenacity of the association between the Pikampul and their land. It is now 1998, but the Pikampul are still seeking to secure and protect their land, focally Boobera Lagoon, which continues to hold powerful stories which are well known among surrounding Murri communities. The stillness of the Lagoon is being violated and its banks and wildlife severely damaged by irrigation and by heavy use of power boats. Shire government and white people's recreation clubs are locked in dispute with local Murris, and both state and federal governments have sent judicial adjudicators. The authority of all continues to be under intense challenge.

Notes

1 Much research into the events of 1848 has been carried out by local researchers, notably Dick Buchhorn, when a priest to the Catholic parish at Boggabilla, and Mark Copland, a teacher who has worked at Boggabilla and whose honours thesis investigates the killings at Umbercollie (*A System of Assassination*, University of Queensland, 1990). Work on Richard Bligh's biography has also been begun by Mervyn Williamson, a local historian at Inverell. This analysis would not have been possible without their dedicated work. Earlier drafts of this paper have been read by Dr

Paula Hamilton at UTS and by Dick Buchhorn, and I am grateful for their insights and suggestions.

2   A valuable account of the nature and fluidity of colonial law in Australia, although focused in urban Sydney and at an earlier period than Bligh's residence, is Paula Jane Byrne, *Criminal law and colonial subject: New South Wales, 1810–1830* (Cambridge, 1993).

3   Aboriginal words are pronounced with the stress on the first syllable, with short vowels, and there is no distinction in meaning between the voiced and unvoiced consonant pairs of b/p, d/t and g/k. "Pikampul" could also be spelt "Bigambul", but in general Aboriginal language groups have chosen to use the unvoiced letters [p, t and k] in their spelling systems. "Murri" was a term used in local languages of north-west NSW (New South Wales) and Queensland to mean human being, but after the invasion, the word usually became used to specify an indigenous person, "one of us". The word is pronounced with a short 'u' as in 'cut', and sounds like the English surname 'Murray'.

4   H. Goodall, *Invasion to embassy: land in Aboriginal politics in NSW, 1770 to 1972* (Sydney, 1996).

5   Notably Commissioner W. C. Mayne; see R. Millis, *Waterloo Creek: the Australia Day massacre of 1838, George Gipps and the British conquest of NSW* (Ringwood, Australia, 1992).

6   Biographical details on Richard Bligh from Bligh Family Bibles and genealogical material, Mitchell Library, Sydney and M. Williamson, "Richard Bligh", *Warialda Standard*, 3 June 1970.

7   This issue is discussed in Goodall, *Invasion to embassy*. An example of the concerns of officials is Commissioner for Crown Lands (hereafter CCL) Fry, Clarence River: "Like the Native, the European [pastoralist] occupies without possessing the soil. He has never appropriated it by agriculture, his pursuits are pastoral, of all others the least likely to generate industrial habits." 20/11/48. NSW Archives Office (hereafter AO) 48/13475.

8   Goodall, *Invasion to embassy*.

9   Reports of Richard Bligh, Commissioner for Crown Land, Warialda to Chief Commissioner for Crown Lands, 1848 to 1855; Margaret Young's Journal, MSS, Oxley Library, Brisbane.

10 C. Hall, "The case of Governor Eyre", in *White, Male and Middle Class* (New York, 1992); and "Imperial man: Edward Eyre in Australasia and the West Indies, 1833–50", in *The expansion of England: race, ethnicity and cultural history*, B. Schwarz (ed) (London and NY, 1996).

11 C. Hall: Discussion, "William Knibb and the constitution of the new Black subject", Commonwealth Fund and Neale Conference, 1997.

12 This information emerged from all Bligh's reports later quoted.

13 F. Walker to Col Sec, 13/6/49, 49/5553, Colonial Secretary's In-Letters (hereafter CSIL) NSW AO 4/2920.

14 For relations between land, law and ceremony in nineteenth-century NSW, see Goodall, *Invasion to embassy*.

15 CCL R. Bligh to Chief CCL, 7 May 1848, *Historical Records of Australia*, vol. XXVI, pp. 396–8.

16 *Ibid.*

17 The following account is based on a series of reports and letters Bligh wrote when defending himself early in 1849, including R. Bligh to Chief CCL, 8 Jan. 1849, letter 49/1; R. Bligh to Colonial Secretary, rebuttal of James Mark's complaints, 10 Jan. 1849, letter

49/2; R. Bligh to Bench Magistrate, Maitland, 23 Jan. 1849 and 6 Feb. 1849, all in Gwydir CCL Letters Sent, 1849–1852, NSW AO 2/7634; Warialda papers, Maitland Court Depositions, NSW AO 9/6354.

18 Undated annotation on prisoner Martin Cummins' deposition 10 Nov. 48, Maitland Court Depositions, NSW AO 9/6354.

19 The following quotations are from four letters with very similar content all written by Bligh in Jan. and Feb., 1849. These are: Bligh to Chief CCL, 8 Jan. 1849, letter 49/1; Bligh to Colonial Secretary 10 Jan. 1849, letter 49/2; Bligh to Bench Magistrate, Maitland, 23 Jan. 1849 and 6 Feb. 1849, all in Gwydir CCL Letters Sent, 1849–1852, NSW AO 2/7643.

20 Hall, "The case of Governor Eyre" and "Imperial man".

21 Statement of Augustus Morris in support of the aggressions of the Native Police under Frederick Walker, Morris to Col Sec, 18 Oct. 1849, 49/10488B, CSIL NSW AO 4/2920.

22 Walker's correspondence suggests strongly that he saw himself avenging the murder and alleged mutilation of the young boy. Margaret Young, Jonathon Young's wife, wrote in her journal that Walker's Native Police actions, including the killing of 12 Murris on Umbercollie, were seen as being in direct retribution for Mark's son's death: MSS, Oxley Library, Brisbane.

23 F. Walker to Col Sec, 12 July, 1849, 49/7305, CSIL NSW AO 4/2920.

24 F. Walker to Col Sec, 13 June 1849, 49/5553, CSIL NSW AO 4/2920.

25 R. Bligh, CCL Gwydir, 27 Oct. 1848, 48/12590, CSIL NSW AO 2/7634.

26 Surveyor General, to Col Sec, 27 Nov. 1848, CSIL Special Bundle, NSW AO; Bligh to Chief CCL, 28 Jan. 1851, Gwydir Letters Sent, 1849–1852, NSW AO 2/7634 4/1141.2; discussion of the "Queen Victoria" narratives in Aboriginal oral tradition in Goodall, *Invasion to embassy*.

27 *Warialda Standard*, 3/6/1970.

28 CCL Bligh to Chief CCL, 24 Jan. 1853, Gwydir Letters Sent, 1852–1856, NSW AO 2/1951.

29 Goodall, *Invasion to embassy*.

30 CCL Bligh to Chief CCL, 28 Jan. 1851, Gwydir Letters Sent, 1849–1852, NSW AO 2/7634; Bligh to Chief CCL, 21 Jan. 1854, 54/10, Bligh to Chief CCL, 30 Dec. 1854, 54/148, Gwydir Letters Sent, 1852–1856, NSW AO 2/1951; CCL Bligh, Gwydir, to Chief CCL, 12 Jan. 1856, NSW Governor's Despatches, Public Records Office, vol. 494 (pt. 1), reel 662.

31 "Native Doctors" are known in local Aboriginal English as "clever men", meaning a man (or occasionally woman) who is learned in traditional healing and philosophy. CCL Bligh, Gwydir, to Chief CCL, 30 Dec. 1854, 54/148, Gwydir Letters Sent, 1852–1856, NSW AO 2/1951.

32 Papers of Rev. A. E. Selwyn, A736, A737, Mitchell Library, Sydney.

33 Bligh to Chief CCL, 19 Jan. 1857, 57/3, NSW Governor's Despatches, Public Records Office, vol. 498, reel 666.

34 Lord Carnarvon to NSW Governor Fitzroy, 19 Feb. 1859, response to Governor's Despatches for 1857, Public Records Office, vol. 503, reel 671.

35 Hall, "The case of Governor Eyre".

36 Hall, "Imperial man".

37 *Ibid.*, A. L. Stoler, *Race and the education of desire* (Durham, N.C., 1995).

38 Margaret Young's Journal, MSS, Oxley Library, Brisbane.

39 *Sydney Morning Herald*, 30 Oct. 1852, letters to editor from Macleay squatter; Queensland Parliamentary Select Committee into the Native Police, 8 May 1861, evidence of a Goondiwindi squatter; John Watts, personal reminiscences, MSS, Oxley Library, Brisbane; William Telfer's recollections in *The Wallabadah Manuscript*, R. Millis (ed.) (Sydney, 1980).

Chapter Fourteen

The genocide policy in English–Karifuna relations in the seventeenth century

Hilary Beckles

Nation-building is a deeply contested political project in Dominica (Waitukubuli before Columbus). It has, nonetheless, claimed considerable ideological credit for facilitating the reversal of the genocidal effects of British colonialism upon the native Karifuna (Caribs) population. The immediate pre-Columbian community on the island stood at an estimated 8,000 persons, fell to fewer than 600 in 1730, and stayed about that level into the early twentieth century. The European population increased from 351 in 1730 to just over 2,000 by the end of the century, while the African population rose from an estimated 500 to 5,872 between 1730 and 1763. By the end of the Second World War when the Black-led nationalist movement challenged white elitism domestically, and prepared the masses to reject British colonial rule, the Karifuna population had increased to just under 900. In 1960 it had reached 1,136 out of a total population of 59,916.[1]

Dominica finally became an independent nation-state in 1978. Three years later the first national census registered the Karifuna population at 1,944 – 1,076 males and 868 females. Anthony Layng, an American sociologist, suggested subsequently that the turning point in Karifuna population growth performance coincided with the ending of colonialism. In 1983 he estimated that during the politically turbulent pre-independence decade there was a 39.4 per cent increase in their numbers in contrast to a 17.3 per cent increase for the island as a whole. The post-independence decade witnessed additional growth with higher birth rates and lower infant mortality as significant casual contributors. Projected estimates for the start of the next millennium suggest a population of just over 3,000.[2]

The history of British colonial rule in Dominica, which commenced as late as 1763 on account of over two hundred years of Karifuna resistance, came under considerable intellectual and political scrutiny during the mid-nineteenth century. Debates on the (im)moral economy of slavery and outrage at continuing Black dispossession and exploitation in post-slavery reconstruction invoked the allegedly more disturbing process of Karifuna genocide. Restructuring the plantation economy to accommodate a Black peasantry and proletariat was the principal discourse. But some colonial administrators experienced noticeable anxiety in contemplating the possible annihilation of surviving Karifuna.[3]

Frederick A. Ober, the reputable American ornithologist, visited the colony in 1877 and highlighted in metropolitan political circles the continuing process of Karifuna cultural and demographic genocide. His subsequent writings focused global attention on Karifuna decline as a moral crisis of British and European colonialism, and called for a positive policy response from both colonial and imperial government. Ober reported that only a few Karifuna still spoke the ancestral language, and that their cultural identity and ethnic distinctiveness were rapidly fading under the challenges thrown up by colonialism (racist hostility and imperial neglect) and African cultural dominance.[4]

Colonial administrators, however, were divided on the question of the cultural integrity of Karifuna ethnic identity. Most noted that Karifuna were fully assimilated through miscegenation into the African genetic pool, and that any claim to cultural distinctiveness was at best a strategic political response to adversity in the white-dominated society. Governor Bell, nonetheless, represented the minority opinion, and spoke persuasively in support of Karifuna claims to a distinct historically constructed ethnicity. He recognized the strong evidence in support of the "Africanness" of Karifuna physical and cultural identity, but considered the social making of their identity sufficiently discrete to warrant their special consideration as an autochthonous community.

In 1902 Governor Bell recommended that the Karifuna be empowered – or compensated – by the imperial government with dedicated resources in the form of a "native reserve". The Colonial Office agreed to settle the matter of privileging indigenous ethnic identity and interests in this way. The reserve came into constitutional effect on 30 June of the following year. Three thousand seven hundred acres of mostly splendid rainforest that embraced Karifuna villages on the periphery of the plantation lands were made available exclusively to them. In addition, their political leadership, in the form of a chief, was to receive a nominal stipend (£6 per year) to facilitate the administration of the reserve.[5]

The political history of the reserve now yields abundant evidence that attests to endemic crisis in the historical relations between Karifuna leadership and British colonialism, and Karifuna identity within post-coloniality. Successive chiefs challenged hegemonic imperial authority over the management of the reserve, and protested at attempts at non-Karifuna (largely Black) encroachment. Three generations of ethnic political conflict and social cohabitation on the periphery of the reserve between Blacks and Karifuna preceded the independent government of Dominica. In the first sitting of the national parliament on 29 November 1978, Black political representatives of the nation passed the Carib (Karifuna) Reserve Act which settled in the Karifunas' favour most outstanding border disputes as well as officially recognizing the authority of the chief. The objective of the Act was to consolidate the provisions of 1902 and secure Karifuna territoriality. Prime Minister Patrick John, however, was certainly dancing to an Afrocentric drum when he handed over the land title to Chief Faustulus Frederick on Independence Day, 3 November 1978.[6]

The euphoria over the epic return of the land title, stated Crispin Gregiore et al., "led the politically conscious Caribs [Karifuna] to drop the term 'reserve', which had all the trappings of colonial arrogance, and adopt instead 'territory', hence Carib Territory". This action constituted a clear signal that the Karifuna were willing to break with colonialism in all its guises and assert ancestral notions of political and cultural autonomy. Under the Reserve Act, the minister with responsibility for local government was given power in the territory over the chief as well as the council established to ventilate matters pertaining to "native affairs". In effect, the minister had replaced the colonial governor as final arbitrator with respect to judicial matters.[7]

Chief Hilary Frederick succeeded Chief Faustulus in 1980. While receiving his education as a young man in the United States, he had established working contact with autonomous organizations of indigenous peoples, and on returning home sought to stimulate and advance debate on representations of Karifuna ethnicity and identity. The discursive technique he used was to articulate the political notion that his people were occupying a colonial status within the nation-state. Prime Minister John conceded that "complete autonomy" was denied them under the Reserve Act because it was not the intention of his government to relinquish fully responsibility for public facilities such as schools, roads, hospitals and postal services. He denied, however, that the Karifuna were a colonized people within the Dominican nation and described them as free citizens with a new nationalist responsibility.[8]

Chief Hilary was not satisfied with the prime ministerial edict, and campaigned publicly on the theme that the independent nation of Dominica had consolidated the colonial subjection of indigenous people whose historic achievement as the "first" nation-builders on the island was ignored in order to sanction their long-standing status as marginalized inhabitants. He argued that the indigenous community in Dominica was part of a wider Karifuna nation which preceded both English colonialism and the oppressive Afrocentric nation-state. He urged, furthermore, that the "national" government should recognize their special status as a "State within the State", or at least a "nation within the State".[9]

Prime Minister John, while respectful of the historic aspect of the discourse, saw no way forward in resolving what for him was a "contradiction of Caribbean modernity", and opposed the concept of a "State within the State". Eugenia Charles, who succeeded John as prime minister, was less tolerant of the debate. In 1983 Chief Hilary was forced by the Charles government to resign following an orchestrated political dispute over an alleged unauthorized deployment of "Reserve" funds. Charges were less than convincing, but Prime Minister Charles pursued policy reforms designed to promote debate on the Karifunas' integration into national citizenship and full subordination to the constitution. Chief Hilary's successor, Chief Auguiste, however, intensified the discourse by reminding the government that their vision of a "State within the State" had preceded the project of national independence.[10]

The Dominica debate on contested nationhood found fuel in the 1992 Atlantic celebration of the quincentennial of Columbus' first voyage to the Caribbean. His second voyage in 1493 took him to Dominica, and the Karifuna used 1993 in order to stage a number of public events that promoted knowledge of the genocidal war waged by Europeans against their ancestors, and to celebrate their survival of the holocaust that engulfed other regional ethnic groups in the Greater Antilles such as the Lucayans and the Arawaks. They proposed that discussion of the history of their resistance and survival be made mandatory in public schools, and intimated that this record constitutes the basis of their moral right to political independence within the new, but still colonial, nation-state.

The text of Karifuna resistance, however, has not been systematically set out. This chapter examines their regional oppositional postures and strategies in the immediate post-Columbian dispensation, and takes the narrative through to their retreat and consolidation in Dominica's mountains at the end of the eighteenth century. Over the period they launched a protracted war of resistance to colonization, slavery and genocide.[11] They held out against the English and French until the mid-1790s, protecting some territory, maintaining their social freedom, and determining the economic and political history of the region in very important ways.[12] To some degree the analysis dichotomizes the autochthonous encounters with Europeans – the Taino (Arawak) experience in the Greater Antilles and the Karifuna in the Lesser Antilles. This effect is not intended to be the basis of a theoretical position. Rather, it recognizes in part that the distinctions between the two groups were blurred in the records produced by early colonial ethnographers.

According to recent archaeological evidence, the Karifuna were the last migrant group to settle in the Caribbean prior to the arrival of the Europeans in 1492. The Columbus mission found three native groups, of different derivation and cultural attainments, but all of whom entered the Caribbean from the region of South America known as the Guianas. These were the Ciboneys, the Taino (Arawaks) and the Karifuna. The Ciboney had arrived about 300 BC, followed by the Taino, their ethnic relatives, about 500 years later, who by AD 650 had migrated northwards through the islands establishing large communities in the Greater Antilles. Starting their migration into the islands from about AD 1000, Karifunas were still arriving at the time of the Columbus landfall. They were also in the process of establishing control over territory and communities occupied by Tainos in the Lesser Antilles, and parts of the Greater Antilles. When the Spanish arrived in the northern Caribbean, therefore, they found the Tainos to some extent already on the retreat, but later encountered Karifunas who they described as more prepared for defensive aggression.[13]

Karifunas, like their Taino cousins and predecessors, however, had been inhabiting the islands long enough to perceive them as part of their natural, ancestral survival environment. As a result, noted G. K. Lewis, they prepared themselves to defend their homeland in a spirit of defiant "patriotism", having wished that the "Europeans had never set foot in their country".[14] From the outset, however, European colonial forces were technologically more prepared for a violent struggle for space since, in real terms, the Columbus mission represented, in addition to the maritime courage and determination of Europe, the mobilization of large-scale finance capital, and science and technology for imperialist military ends. This process was also buttressed by the frenzied search for identity and global ethnic ranking by Europeans through the conquest and cultural negation of others.

European colonization did not focus initially upon the complete destruction of indigenous society. Preference was given to the reorientation and integration of local resource use, particularly land and labour, into the imperial economic order. In the Greater Antilles Europeans succeeded in imposing settler institutions upon Taino communities in order to extract productive value. In the Lesser Antilles, however, the persistent violent resistance of the Karifuna to the first settlement phase resulted in an European policy shift that called for their complete destruction.

In the Greater Antilles, Tainos offered a spirited but largely unsuccessful military resistance to the Spanish even though on occasions they were supported by the Karifuna. In the case of the early struggles for Puerto Rico Karifunas from neighbouring St Croix came to Taino assistance. In 1494, Columbus led an armed party of 400 men into the interior of Hispaniola in search of food, gold, and slaves, for resistance to which Taino caciques (chiefs) mobilized their armies. Guacanagari, a leading cacique, who had tried previously to negotiate an accommodating settlement with military commander Alonso de Ojeba, marched unsuccessfully in 1494 with a few thousand men upon the Spanish. In 1503, another forty caciques were captured at Hispaniola and burnt alive by Governor Ovando's troops; Anacaona, the principal cacique, was hanged publicly in Santo Domingo.

In Puerto Rico, the Spanish settlement party, led by Ponce de Leon, was attacked frequently by Taino warriors; many Spanish settlers were killed but Tainos and Karifunas were defeated and crushed in the counter-assault. In 1511, resistance in Cuba, led by Cacique Hatuey, was put down; he was captured and burnt alive. Another rising in 1529 was also crushed. In these struggles, Taino fatalities were high. Thousands were killed in battle and publicly executed for the purpose of breaking the spirit of collective resistance; some rebels fled to the mountains and forests where they established maroon settlements that intermittently continued the war against the Spanish.

Commenting on the accelerating depletion rate on Hispaniola, caused by disease, violence and famine, Richardson noted that Spanish slave-raiding parties tapped the aboriginal populations of adjacent islands, notably Jamaica and Puerto Rico. In addition, he added, Spanish slavers also brought an estimated 40,000 Arawaks from the Lucayas (Bahamas) to work the mines of Hispaniola in the first decade of the sixteenth century. In 1511 they had ranged as far south as Trinidad where enslavement practices eventually led to similar famine and human population decline.[15] By the middle of the sixteenth century, however, Taino and Karifuna resistance had been effectively crushed in the Greater Antilles; their community structures were smashed, and members reduced to various forms of enslavement in Spanish agricultural and mining enterprises.

In the Lesser Antilles, however, the Karifuna were more successful in defying first the Spanish, and then later the English and French, thereby preserving their political freedom and maintaining control of their territory. According to Carl Sauer, "As the labor supply on Espanola declined, attention turned to the southern islands" which, from St Croix and neighbouring Puerto Rico to the Guianas, were inhabited by the Karifunas. Spanish royal edicts dated 7 November 1508 and 3 July 1512 authorized settlers to capture and enslave Karifunas on "the island of Los Barbudos [Barbados], Dominica, Matinino [Martinique], Santa Lucia, San Vincente, La Asuncion [Grenada], and Tavaco [Tobago]", because of their "resistance to Christians".[16] By the end of the century, however, the Spanish had decided, having accepted as fact the absence of gold in the Lesser Antilles, and the inevitability of considerable fatalities at the hands of Karifuna warriors, that it was wiser to adopt a "hands off policy" while concentrating their efforts in the Greater Antilles. As a result, the Greater and Lesser Antilles became politically separated at this time by what Troy Floyd described as a "poison arrow curtain".[17]

The English and French initiating their colonizing missions during the early seventeenth century, therefore, had a clear choice. They could confront either the Spanish north of the "poison arrow curtain" or Karifuna forces south of it. Either way, they expected to encounter considerable organized armed resistance. They chose the latter, partly because of the perception that Karifunas were the weaker, but also because of the belief that Karifunas were the "common enemy" of all Europeans and that solidarity could be achieved for collective military operations against them.

Having secured some respite from the pressures of Spanish colonization by the end of the sixteenth century, then, Karifunas were immediately confronted by the more economically aggressive and militarily determined English and French colonists. Once again, they began to reorganize their communities in preparation for counter-strategies. This time it would be a clear case of resistance on the retreat. By the 1630s, their rapidly diminishing numbers were concentrated around a smaller group of specially chosen islands – mostly in the Windwards but also in the Leewards. Barbados, identified in a Spanish document of 1511 as an island densely populated with Karifunas, no longer had a native.

Europeans took advantage of this reorganization and resettlement of Karifuna communities, and established infant colonies in peripheral parts of the Leeward Islands where their presence was less formidable, and in Barbados where it was absent. The English and French, then, were aware that most of their settlements would have to come to terms with Karifuna resistance. This expectation, however, did not deter them, and they continued to seek out island niches where an effective foothold could be gained until such time as Karifuna forces could be subdued or destroyed by their respective imperial forces.

The English and French sought the pacification of the Karifuna for two distinct, but related reasons, and over time adopted different strategies and methods but maintained the ideological position that they should be enslaved, driven out, or exterminated. First, lands occupied by the Karifuna were required for large-scale commodity production within the expansive, capitalist, North Atlantic agrarian complex. The effective integration of the Caribbean into this mercantile and productive system required the appropriation of land through the agency of the plantation enterprise. Finance capital, then, sought to revolutionize the market value of Karifuna lands by making them available to European commercial interests. By resisting land confiscation Karifunas were therefore confronting the full ideological and economic force of Atlantic capitalism.

Second, European economic activities in the Caribbean were based upon the enslavement of indigenes and imported Africans. The principal role and relation assigned to these and other non-Europeans within the colonial formation was that of servitude. Europeans in the Lesser Antilles, however, were not successful in reducing an economic number of Karifuna to chattel slavery, or other forms of servitude. Unlike the Taino, their labour could not be effectively commodified, simply because their communities proved impossible to subdue. It was not that the Karifuna were more militant than the Taino. Rather, it was because the nomadic nature of their small communities, and their emphasis upon territorial acquisition, in part a response to the geographical features of the Lesser Antilles, enabled them to make more effective use of the environment in a "strike and sail" resistance strategy. Karifuna, then, while not prepared to surrender either land or labour to Europeans, were better placed to implement effective counter-aggression.

Primarily because of their irrepressible war of resistance, which intimidated all Europeans in the region, the Karifuna were targeted first for an ideological campaign in which they were established within the European mind, not as "noble savages", as was the case with the less effective Tainos, but as "vicious cannibals" worthy of extermination within the context of genocidal military expeditions.[18] Voluminous details were prepared by Spanish and later English and French colonial chroniclers on the political and ideological mentality of the Karifuna, most of whom called for "holy wars" against "*les sauvages*" as a principal way to achieve their subjugation.

This literature, dating back to Columbus in 1494, in a contradictory fashion, denied Karifuna humanity while at the same time outlining their general anti-colonial and anti-slavery consciousness and attitudes. In the writings of Jean-Baptiste du Tertre, Sieur de la Borde, and Père Labat, for example, all late seventeenth-century French reporters of Karifuna ontology, they are presented as a people who would "prefer to die of hunger than live as a slave".[19] Labat, who commented most on their psychological profile, found them to be "careless and lazy creatures", not at all suited mentally to arduous, sustained labour. In addition, he considered them a "proud and indomitable" and "exceedingly vindictive" people whom "one has to be very careful not to offend", hence the popular French Caribbean proverb, "fight a Carib and you must kill him or be killed".[20]

The French discovered, like the Spanish before them, noted Labat, that it was always best, if possible, "to have nothing to do with the Karifuna".[21] But this was not possible. Relations had to be established, and here Europeans discovered, Labat noted, that the Karifuna knew "how to look after their own interests very well".[22] "There are no people in the world", he stated, "so jealous of their liberty, or who resent more the smallest check to their freedom."[23] Altogether, the Karifuna world view was anathema to Europeans; thus the general view, echoed by Labat, that "no European nation has been able to live in the same island with them without being compelled to destroy them, and drive them out".[24]

The English and French started out simultaneously in 1624 with the establishment of agricultural settlements in St Kitts. From there, the English moved on to Barbados in 1627, and between 1632 and 1635 to Antigua, Montserrat and Nevis, while the French concentrated their efforts during the 1630s at Martinique and Guadeloupe. The first three years at St Kitts were difficult for both English and French settlers. They were harassed and attacked by Karifuna soldiers, and in 1635 the French at Guadeloupe were engulfed in a protracted battle. French success in their war with Karifunas at Guadeloupe encouraged them during the remainder of the decade to expand their colonial missions, but they failed to gain effective control of the Karifuna-inhabited islands of Grenada, Marie Galante, and La Desirada. Meanwhile, a small English expedition from St Kitts to St Lucia in the Windwards, the heart of Karifuna territory, was easily repelled in 1639. The following year Karifunas launched a full-scale attack upon English settlements at Antigua, killing fifty settlers, capturing the governor's wife and children, and destroying crops and houses.[25]

While English settlements in the Leewards struggled to make progress against Karifuna resistance, Barbados, alone of the Windwards, forged ahead uninterrupted. Unlike their Leewards counterparts, early Barbadian planters rapidly expanded their production base, made a living from the exports of tobacco, indigo and cotton, and feared only their indentured servants and few African slaves. By 1650, following the successful cultivation of sugar cane with African slaves, the island was considered by mercantile economic theorists as the richest agricultural colony in the hemisphere.

St Kitts colonists, both English and French, determined to keep up with their Barbadian competitors, were first to adopt a common military front with respect to Karifuna resistance. During the 1630s they entered into agreements, in spite of their rival claims to exclusive ownership of the island, to combine forces against Karifuna communities. On the first occasion, they "pooled their talents", and in a "sneak night attack" killed over eighty Karifunas and drove many off the island. After celebrating the success of their military alliance, the French and English continued their rivalry over the island until 1713 when the matter was settled in favour of the English by the Treaty of Utrecht.[26]

The success of Karifunas in holding on to a significant portion of the

Windwards, and their weakening of planting settlements in the Leewards, fuelled the determination of the English and French to destroy them. By the mid-seventeenth century, European merchants, planters and colonial officials were in agreement that Karifunas "were a barbarous and cruel set of savages beyond reason or persuasion and must therefore be eliminated".[27] By this time it was also clear that the slave-based plantation system demanded an "absolute monopoly" of the Caribbean, and tolerated no "alternative system".[28] What Richard Dunn referred to as "Carib independence and self-reliance" consti-tuted a major contradiction to the internal logic of capitalist accumulation within the plantation economy.[29] As a result, therefore, the economic leaders and political representatives of this increasingly powerful production and trade complex were determined to bring the contradiction to a speedy resolution by any means necessary or possible.

By the mid-seventeenth century, the need for a full-scale war against the Karifunas, though clearly established and articulated in Spanish colonial think-ing during the sixteenth century, now assumed greater urgency with the English and French. By this time the English were first successfully to establish productive structures based on sugar cultivation and Black slavery, and not surprisingly took the lead in attempting the removal of principal obstacles to the smooth and profitable expansion of the system. Also, the English, with the largest number of enslaved Africans in the region, were concerned that efficient control on their plantations would be adversely affected by the persistence of Karifuna resistance.

It did not take long for the Africans to become aware of Karifuna struggle against Europeans, and to realize that they could possibly secure their freedom by fleeing to their territory. Labat, who studied inter-island slave marronage in the Lesser Antilles during this period, stated that slaves knew that St Vincent was easily reached from Barbados, and many escaped there "from their masters in canoes and rafts". During the formative stage of this develop-ment, between 1645 and 1660, the Karifuna generally took "the runaway slaves back to their masters, or sold them to the French and Spanish", but as the Karifuna came under more intensive attack during the mid-century, Labat noted, their policy towards African maroons changed. They refused to return the Africans, he stated, and began regarding them "as an addition to their nation".[30]

By 1670, Labat estimated that over five hundred Barbadian runaways were living in St Vincent. This community was reinforced in 1675 when a slave ship carrying hundreds of Africans to Jamaica via Barbados ran aground off the coast of Bequia. Survivors came ashore at St Vincent and were integrated in the maroon communities. By 1700, Labat stated, Africans outnumbered Karifunas at St Vincent. In 1675, William Stapleton, governor of the

Leewards, noting the significant presence of Africans among the Karifunas, suggested that of the 1,500 native "bowmen" in the Leewards six hundred of them "are negroes, some runaway from Barbados and elsewhere".[31]

Throughout the second half of the seventeenth century Europeans tried unsuccessfully to exploit the sometimes strained relations between Karifunas and Africans by encouraging the former to return runaways to their owners. Miscegenation between the predominantly male African maroon community and Karifuna females was a principal cause of social tension between the two ethnic groups.[32] Both the French and English alleged that Karifuna leaders occasionally sought their assistance in ridding their communities of Africans.

The significance of such allegations, however, should be assessed against the background of two important developments in African–Karifuna relations. First, by the mid-seventeenth century, the group of mixed bloods, now known as the Garifuna, was increasing rapidly in numbers, and by 1700 had outnumbered both parent groups in St Vincent.[33] Second, joint African–Karifuna military expeditions against the French and English were common, and represented a principal characteristic feature of anti-European activity – on both land and sea.[34] The full-scale attack on the French at Martinique during the mid-1650s, for example, involved both African and Karifuna forces.[35] The warriors who attacked French settlements at Grenada during the same period and kept them in a weak and defensive condition were also described as having an African component. Similarly, noted Labat, the English expeditions from Barbados sent to capture St Vincent during the 1670s were repelled by both Africans and Karifunas.[36]

The presence of effective anti-colonial Karifuna communities on the outskirts of the slave plantations, therefore, constituted a major problem for slave owners in so far as they fostered and encouraged African anti-slavery. The merging of Karifuna anti-colonial and African anti-slavery struggles, therefore, represented the twin forces that threatened the very survival of the colonizing mission in the Windwards. As such, Europeans with the greatest economic stake in the enterprise of the Indies wasted no time in adopting a range of measures to suppress the Karifuna. Both the English and French pursued an initial policy characterized by the projection of anti-Karifuna social images in Europe, while seeking at the same time to promote diplomatic efforts to settle territorial claims.

In 1664 a Barbados document entitled "The state of the case concerning our title to St Lucia", described the island as being "infected" with Karifunas who were "abetted by the French" in their war against English settlers. In this document, Barbadians sought to reject French claims to the island by stating that they had purchased it from du Parquet, the governor of Martinique, who had bought it from the Karifunas in 1650 for 41,500 livres.[37] Likewise, in

1668, Thomas Modyford, governor of Jamaica, former Barbados governor and sugar magnate, described St Vincent, another Karifuna stronghold in the Windwards, as a place which "the Indians much infect".[38] These statements represent part of the ideological preparation of the English mind for what would be a genocidal offensive against the Karifuna that London merchant houses were eager to finance.

But a full-scale war, the English and French knew, would be costly, in terms of both human life and capital, and they hoped it could be averted. The significance of an ultimate military solution was clearly perceived by Karifuna leaders and colonial officials alike. By participating in tactful diplomatic intrigue designed to exploit differences and conflicts between Europeans, the Karifuna sought to advance their own interests. In 1655, for example, Captain Gregory Butler informed Oliver Cromwell, the Protector, that the settlement at Antigua was unable to get off to a good start on account of frequent molestations by the Karifunas, who at that time seemed to be in league with the French.[39]

Again, in 1667, Major John Scott, an imperial commander-in-chief, reported that he led an expedition against Dutch settlements in Tobago with the "assistance of a party of Caribs".[40] During the second Dutch War, 1665–7, in which France and Holland allied against the English in the Caribbean, the Karifuna played an important role in shifting the balance of power between Europeans while at the same time seeking to expand the scope and effectiveness of their own war of resistance.[41] In June 1667, Henry Willoughby stationed in the Leewards informed his father, William Lord Willoughby, governor of Barbados, that when he arrived at St Kitts he received "intelligence" of further atrocities committed by the Karifunas against the English which were "instigated" by the French. European rivalry, Michael Craton concluded, was effectively used by the Karifuna nation, as evident in the delayed loss of St Lucia and Grenada, and in the longer retention of full control over St Vincent and Dominica.[42]

The English and French also targeted the Karifuna for diplomatic offensives. The first systematically pursued diplomatic effort by the English to establish a footing within Karifuna territory in the Windwards was the Willoughby initiative of 1667. William Lord Willoughby, governor of Barbados, had long recognized the great financial gain that would accrue to himself, Barbados, and England, if the Windwards, the last island frontier, could be converted into slave-based sugar plantations. For over a decade, the sugar kings of Barbados had been signalling their demand for lands on which to expand their operations, and the Windwards were the perfect place, given prevailing economic concepts about the conditionalities of slave-based sugar cultivation. Small-scale military expeditions had been repelled by the Karifuna since the 1630s, and so Willoughby, not yet organized for a large-scale military assault, opted to send emissaries to open negotiations with Karifuna leaders.

The Karifunas, in response, showed some degree of flexibility, as is often the case with peoples involved in protracted struggles. Willoughby wanted a peace treaty that would promote English interests by removing obstacles to slave plantation expansionism, but the Karifuna were suspicious and vigilant. In 1666, they were tricked by the English to sign away by treaty their "rights" to inhabit Tortola, and were driven off the island.[43] The Windward Islands were their last refuge, and their siege mentality was now more developed than ever.

On 23 March 1667, Karifuna leaders of St Vincent, Dominica and St Lucia met with Willoughby's delegation in order to negotiate the peace.[44] At the signing of the treaty were Anniwatta, the Grand Babba (or chief of all Karifunas), Chiefs Wappya, Nay, Le Suroe, Rebura and Aloons. The conditions of the treaty were everything the Barbadian slavers wanted at that particular stage of developments:

1. The Caribs of St Vincent shall ever acknowledge themselves subjects of the King of England, and be friends to all in amity with the English, and enemies to their enemies.
2. The Caribs shall have liberty to come to and depart from, at pleasure, any English islands and receive their protection therein, and the English shall enjoy the same in St Vincent and St Lucia.
3. His Majesty's subjects taken by the French and Indians and remaining among the Indians, shall be immediately delivered up, as also any Indian captives among the English when demanded.
4. Negroes formerly run away from Barbados shall be delivered to His Excellency; and such as shall hereafter be fugitives from any English island shall be secured and delivered by as soon as required.[45]

The Willoughby initiative was designed to pave the way for English colonization of the Windwards, using Barbados as the springboard for settlement. In essence, it was an elaboration of a similar agreement that was made between the defeated Karifuna and victorious French forces at Martinique after the war of 1654–6. On that occasion, noted Jean-Baptiste du Tertre, who described in detail the nature of the conflict and its resolution, the French were able to obtain settlement rights from the Karifuna, as well as guarantees that they would assist in the control of rebel slaves by not encouraging, and, more importantly, returning all runaways.[46] Within two months of the Karifuna–Willoughby Treaty, a party of 54 English colonists from Barbados arrived at St Vincent in order to pioneer a settlement. The Karifuna, Garifuna, and Africans objected to their presence, drove them off the island, and broke the treaty with Barbados.

The collapse of the Barbados diplomatic mission angered Governor Willoughby, who swiftly moved to the next stage of his plan – a full-scale military offensive. His opportunity came in March the following year when English military commander Sir John Harman left behind in Barbados a regiment of foot and five frigates. Willoughby informed the Colonial Office that since he knew not how to "keep the soldiers quiet and without pay" the only course open to him was to "try his fortune among the Caribs at St Vincent".[47] Once again, the Karifuna proved too much for Willoughby, and the expedition returned to Barbados having suffered heavy losses.

English awareness of Karifuna solidarity and efficient communications throughout the islands of the Lesser Antilles meant that they had reasons to expect reprisals for the Willoughby offensives anywhere and at any time. Governor Modyford of Jamaica, a most knowledgeable man about Eastern Caribbean affairs, had opposed Willoughby's war plan. He told the Duke of Albemarle that while Willoughby was "making war with the Caribs of St Vincent" he feared the consequences for settlers at Antigua, and other places. Such an untimely war, he said, "may again put those plantations in hazard, or at best into near broils". "It had been far better", he continued, "to have made peace with them", for if they assisted the French against the English the result would be "the total ruin of all the English islands" and a "waste of the revenue of Barbados".[48]

Modyford was perceptive in his assessment of Karifuna responses. A report sent to the Colonial Office in London from officials in Nevis dated April 1669, entitled "An Intelligence of an Indian Design upon the People of Antigua", stated that "The Caribbee Indians have lately broken the peace made with Lord Willoughby, and have killed two and left dead two more of His Majesty's subjects in Antigua." Reference was made to 28 Karifuna warriors who arrived from Montserrat in two canoes and who participated in the raid upon Antigua in response to Willoughby's war in St Vincent.[49]

In addition, Governor Stapleton of the Leewards, in a separate document, outlined his fear for the lives of Leeward Islanders, including those who had gone to work in a silver mine in Dominica under an agreement with the Karifuna.[50] The Barbadians also offered their criticisms of Willoughby's war effort. In 1676, Governor Atkins described it as a "fruitless design", whose overall result was that there remain "no likelihood of any plantations upon Dominica, St. Vincent, St. Lucia and Tobago".[51] Meanwhile, the Antiguans were forced to keep "fourteen files of men", "doubled three days before and after a full moon" as a protective measure against Karifuna warriors.

Governor Stapleton, reflecting on the collapse of the Willoughby initiative, and considering the prospects for English settlements in the Leewards and Windwards, quickly moved to the frontstage what had been Willoughby's hidden agenda. Only the destruction of "all the Caribbee Indians" he concluded, could be the "best piece of service for the settlement of these parts".[52] In December 1675 a petition of "Several Merchants of London", addressed to the Lords of Trade and Plantations in support of Governor Stapleton's extermination thesis, called for the granting of a commission to Philip Warner, Stapleton's deputy, to raise soldiers to go into Dominica to "destroy the barbarous savages".[53]

Stapleton, however, had pre-empted the Colonial Office in their response to the London merchants and had already sent Warner "with six small companies of foot", totalling 300 men, into Dominica to "revenge" on the "heathens for their bloody perfidious villanies".[54] One William Hamlyn, who participated in the Warner expedition, described the assault upon the Karifuna as a massacre. At least thirty Karifuna, he said, were taken and killed on the first round, not including "three that were drawn by a flag of truce" and shot. After these executions, Hamlyn reported, another "sixty or seventy men, women and children" were invited to Warner's camp to settle matters over entertainment. These were given rum to drink, and when Warner "gave the signal", the English "fell upon them and destroyed them".[55] Included in those killed by the English was Indian Warner, Philip Warner's own half-brother, whose mother was a Karifuna, and who had risen to become a powerful Karifuna leader. Warner was imprisoned in the Tower, tried for the murder of his brother, but found not guilty. The decision pleased the London merchants who described him as "a man of great loyalty" whose service to the crown in the destruction of the Karifunas "who have often attempted to ruin the plantations" should be commended.[56]

In spite of losses sustained in Dominica, Karifunas there continued to use the island as a military base for expeditions against the English. In July 1681, 300 Karifunas from St Vincent and Dominica in six periagos, led by one who named himself Captain Peter, and who was described as a "good speaker of English having lived for some time in Barbados", attacked the unguarded English settlements in Barbuda.[57] The English were caught by surprise. Eight of them were killed, and their houses destroyed. The action was described as swift and without warning.

Frustrated again by his inability to protect the lives and property of Leeward Islanders, Stapleton reiterated his call for a war of extermination against the Karifunas. He wrote to the Colonial Office: "I beg your pardon if I am tedious, but I beg you to represent the King the necessity for destroying these Carib Indians." "We are now as much on our guard as if we had a christian enemy, neither can any such surprise us but these cannibals who

294

never come '*marte aperto*' . . ." If their destruction cannot be "total", insisted Stapleton, at least we must "drive them to the main".[58] He was aware, however, of the inability of Leeward Islanders to finance a major war effort, and had also become respectful of Karifunas' ability to obtain "intelligence" with respect to their plans. Given these two circumstances, Stapleton instructed London to order the Barbados Government to prepare the grand design against the Karifunas. Barbados, he added, was closer to the Karifuna-"infested" islands of St Vincent and Dominica; also, on account of the colony's wealth, it would be the "best piece of service" they could offer England whilst there was "amity with the French".[59]

Colonial officials in London accepted Stapleton's plan in its entirety. They instructed him to make plans to "utterly suppress" the Karifunas or "drive them to the main".[60] They also directed Governor Dutton of Barbados to make all possible contributions to the war effort. Dutton, however, would have no part of it, but, not wishing to contradict the king's orders, he informed the Colonial Office that though he was in agreement, Barbadians would support no such design against the Karifunas for three reasons. First, they considered the affairs of the Leeward Islands none of their business. Second, they did not consider the advancement of the Leewards as a good thing: indeed, they considered it in their interest for the Leewards to decline rather than progress. Third, planters considered peace with the Karifunas in the Windwards a better objective as this would assist them in securing cutwood and other building materials from those islands.[61]

The Leeward Islanders, therefore, had to look to their own resources to finance their military operations. In June 1682, a bill was proposed to the Leewards Assembly requesting funds to outfit an expedition against the Karifunas in Dominica. The Council agreed, but the Assembly of Nevis dissented on the grounds that since they had not been attacked by the Karifunas in over "twenty years" they did not intend to endanger their peace.[62] Months went by and Stapleton failed to get his planters to agree on a financial plan for the expedition. By 1700, the grand design had not yet materialized.

When on 11 April 1713 England and France settled their "American" difference with the Treaty of Utrecht, Karifuna were still holding on tenaciously to considerable territory. St Vincent and Dominica, though inhabited by some Europeans, were still under their control, and they were fighting a rearguard war to retain some space at St Lucia, Tobago and Grenada. Since the French feared that successful English settlement of Dominica would lead to the cutting of communications between Martinique and Guadeloupe in times of war, they continued to assist the Karifunas with information and occasionally with weapons in their anti-English resistance. The best the

English could do was to continue the attempt to settle private treaties with the French, as they had done during the Peace of Ryswick in 1697, which enabled them to go unmolested to Dominica for the sole purpose of purchasing lumber from the Karifuna.

Karifunas, then, succeeded in preserving some of their territorial sovereignty and by so doing were able to maintain their freedom from European enslavement. While other native Caribbean peoples suffered large-scale slavery at the hands of Europeans, the Karifuna were never found in large numbers working the mines, latifundia, or plantations in the Lesser Antilles. Though Spanish slave raids during the sixteenth century did take many into the Greater Antilles to supplement Taino labour gangs, European-controlled productive structures in the Lesser Antilles were not built and maintained on the basis of a Karifuna labour supply.

The involvement of Karifunas into the colonial economy, then, tended to be small-scale, and confined to areas such as fishing, tracking and hunting, agricultural consulting and a range of petty domestic services. When, for example, a group of Barbadian sugar planters, concerned about the shortage of white indentured servants and the rising cost of African slaves, encouraged Captain Peter Wroth in 1673 to establish a slave trade in Karifunas from the Guianas, colonial officials instructed Governor Atkins to make arrangements for the return of all those "captured and enslaved". The reason, they stated, was that "considering the greater importance of a fair correspondence between the Carib Indians and the English" in establishing settlements on the Amazon coast, it was necessary that "provocation be avoided" and all proper measures be taken to gain their "goodwill and affection".[63] Governor Atkins, in informing his superiors of his compliance, indicated his agreement that it was necessary to "keep amity" with the Karifuna, since they have "always been very pernicious, especially to the smaller Leeward Islands".[64]

Between 1492 and 1730 the Karifuna population in the Lesser Antilles may have fallen by as much as 90 per cent, noted Michael Craton, but they had done much to "preserve and extend their independence".[65] By this time, adult Karifuna at St Vincent and Dominica, according to Labat, "did not exceed 2000" and warriors were "too weak in numbers to do any serious harm" to European colonies.[66] Nonetheless, colonists in the "outlying districts" still had reasons to believe that any night Karifuna warriors could take them by surprise and "cut their throats and burn their houses".[67]

In 1972 Lord Hillsborough, Secretary for State in London, issued instructions for the launching of a military offensive against Karifuna at St Vincent, and a major naval force arrived at the island. The English governor of the island reported that the Karifuna struck against the English settlements as soon as they saw the fleet approaching, killing 72 men and wounding 80;

another 110 lost their lives to diseases within a month of the outbreak of war. Unable to hold out against increasing military pressure, however, Chief Chatoyer and 27 other leaders found it necessary to settle a peace treaty with the English in May 1773. The Karifuna were promised amnesty and sovereignty over a stretch of land in the north of the island (35 per cent of the island) in return for their allegiance to King George III.[68]

Peace could not be maintained. The expansion of the sugar plantation sector, and persistent racist postures by the English, made for a volatile political environment. The French revolution, and British reactions to it in the Caribbean, offered a further opportunity for Karifuna strategic adjustment. The treaty of 1773, which never settled well with the Karifuna, was rejected and war was declared against the English. The English, however, were better prepared this time to handle the possibility of an alliance between the Karifuna and the French. The enormous build-up of English military power in the region easily swept away Karifuna resistance before the French were finally defeated in the Caribbean. In the second half of the eighteenth century, then, developments in local and international affairs had created a context within which imperial modernity resolved to push aside all indigenous claims to life, liberty and land. The Seven Years' War offered the last opportunity for Karifuna to maximize opportunities for resistance by forging alliances with the French against the English. Signing the peace treaty with imperial interest in 1773 permitted white settlement, and was subsequently used as the basis of English proprietary claims upon their lands. Once the Anglo-French War in the Caribbean was over, the matter of the victor's appropriation of all lands in possession of the Karifuna assumed top priority.

The British wasted no time after the war in encouraging Sir William Young, Chief Commissioner for the sale of lands in the Carib territories of St Vincent, to accelerate the pace of white settlement. The Commissioner's position was that either a full-scale war against the Karifuna or a strictly enforced peace treaty was a precondition for settler expansion. He informed the Colonial Office:

We have the greatest reason to think that suffering the Charaibs to remain in their present state, will be very dangerous, and may at some period prove fatal to the inhabitants of the country, as their situation, surrounded with wood, makes any access to them for the purpose of executing justice impracticable; and they will from thence be capable of committing all outrages unpunished; or harbouring the slaves of the inhabitants of this island, as well as of all the neighbouring islands; of sheltering amongst those, vagabonds and deserters from the French, and in case of a rupture with France, it is probable they will join in distressing the inhabitants, and in an attempt to conquer the colony.[69]

The final defeat of the Karifuna in St Vincent and St Lucia during the 1790s drew whatever poison was left from the arrows of the Dominica community. Joseph Chatoyer, paramount chief in St Vincent, was put to death during a bloody clash with English soldiers in March 1795. Hundreds fled to sanctuary in Dominica. Those who could not do so amounted to some five thousand. These were rounded up by English troops and herded together on the tiny island of Balliceaux in the Grenadines pending imperial instructions for a final destination. One third of them starved to death on the island during the four months of incarceration before being transported to Rattan, an island off the coast of Honduras on which, it was said, not even iguanas easily survived.[70]

The transportation of Karifuna communities from St Vincent and St Lucia left the Dominica community as the Caribbean island core of the fragmented, militarily defeated nation. In 1804, lands in St Lucia and St Vincent conceded to the Karifuna by treaty with the British government were forfeited by the crown. In Dominica, the surviving community eked out a tenuous living in the rainforest and took whatever advantage they could find in selling their craftware in towns and their labour on neighbouring plantations. By refusing to capitulate under the collective military pressure of Europeans, however, Karifunas had kept the Windward Islands in a marginal relation to the slave plantation complex for two hundred years, and in so doing made a principal contribution to the Caribbean's anti-colonial and anti-slavery tradition.

Despite the liberating ideological effects of contemporary politics that call for a "nation within a State", the contradictions of Karifuna identity within Dominica's post-colonial modernity continue to militate against community development in their territory. Today, historic representations of Karifuna identity do not excite the imagination of the younger generation to the same degree as they did their parents; teenage Karifuna's preference for Afro-Caribbean socio-cultural life is openly displayed. Those who are obviously divided in their identity by miscegenation are socially pressured to choose between two worlds – life on the reserve or in mainstream urban and rural contexts. Many, however, have created a stable life as "in-betweeners", straddling both worlds as commuters with fluidity despite the endemic politics of ethnic prejudice. Karifuna men commonly keep two sets of family: one on the reserve with a Karifuna or Black woman, and one off the reserve with a Black woman. Custom allows Karifuna men to locate their Black spouses on the reserve but forbids women to do the same.[71] Both processes of miscegenation, nonetheless, continue to problematize traditional notions of ethnic identity and reproduction and suggest that the genocidal effects of colonialism remain evident.

Notes

1   See J. Borome, "Spain and Dominica, 1493–1647" and "Dominica during French occupation: 1778–1784", in *Aspects of Dominican history*, J. Borome (ed.) (Roseau, 1967); C. Gregoire et al. (eds), "Karifuna: the Caribs of Dominica", in *Ethnic minorities in Caribbean society*, Rhoda Reddock (ed.) (Trinidad, 1996), pp. 133–4. Commission Report, "Conditions in the [Dominica] Carib reserve and the disturbances of the 19th September, 1930".

2   *Report on the Census of Dominica, 1981* (Roseau, 1982). A. Layng, "The Caribs of Dominica: prospects for structural assimilation of a territorial minority", *Ethnic Groups* **2–3**, 1985, pp. 209–21; "Religion among the Caribs", *Caribbean Review*, **8**(2), 1979, pp. 36–41; *The Carib reserve: identity and security in the West Indies* (Washington D.C., 1983), pp. 42–64.

3   E. Banks, "A Carib village in Dominica", *Social and Economic Studies* **1**, 1956, pp. 74–86; J. Carew, "Columbus and the origins of racism in the Americas", *Race and Class* **39**(4), 1988; P. Fermor, "The Caribs of Dominica", *Geographical Magazine* **32**(6), 1950, pp. 256–64; N. Owen, *Land and politics in a Carib Indian community: a study of ethnicity* (PhD thesis, University of Massachusetts, 1975).

4   Frederick A. Ober, *Camps in the Caribees: the adventures of a naturalist in the Lesser Antilles* (Boston, 1886), pp. 46–52; *Aborigines of the West Indies: proceedings in American Antigrarian society*, vol. 9, pp. 1893–4.

5   See Sir Henry Hesketh Bell, *Report on the Caribs of Dominica* (London, 1902); also "The Caribs of Dominica", *Journal of the Barbados Museum and Historical Society* **1**, Nov. 1937, pp. 36–82; *Glimpses of a governor's Life* (1944). Gregoire et al., "Karifuna", pp. 121–2.

6   Gregoire et al., "Karifuna", pp. 157–8.

7   *Ibid.*, pp. 155–7.

8   *Ibid.*, pp. 154–5.

9   *Ibid.*, pp. 155–7.

10 *Ibid.*, pp. 155–6.

11 B. Richardson, *The Caribbean in the wider world, 1492–1992* (Cambridge, 1992), pp. 22–8. M. Craton, *Testing the chains: resistance to slavery in the British West Indies* (Ithaca, N.Y., 1982), pp. 21–3; H. Beckles, "The 200 years war: slave resistance in the British West Indies: an overview of the historiography", *Jamaican Historical Review* **13**, 1982, pp. 1–10.

12 See J. Paul Thomas, "The Caribs of St. Vincent: a study in imperial maladministration, 1763–73", *Journal of Caribbean History* **18**(2), 1984, pp. 60–74; Craton, *Testing the chains*, pp. 141–53, 183–94; Richard B. Sheridan, "The condition of slaves in the settlement and economic development of the British Windward Islands, 1763–1775", *Journal of Caribbean History* **24**(2), 1991, pp. 128–9; B. Marshall, "Slave resistance and white reaction in the British Windward Islands, 1763–1833", *Caribbean Quarterly*, **28**(3), 1982, pp. 39–40.

13 D. Watts, *The West Indies: patterns of development, culture and environmental change since 1492* (Cambridge, 1987) pp. 41, 51–2. W. Borah, "The historical demography of aboriginal and colonial America: an attempt at perspective", in *The native population of the Americas in 1492* W. Denevan (ed.) (Madison, Wisc., 1976), pp. 13–34. J. M. Cruxent and I. Rouse, "Early man in the West Indies", *Scientific American* **221**, 1969, pp. 42–52. B. Meggers & C. Evans,

"Lowland South America and the Antilles", in *Ancient Native Americans*, J. D. Jennings (ed.) (San Francisco, 1978) pp. 543–92.

14 G. Lewis, *Main currents in Caribbean thought: the historical evolution of Caribbean society in its ideological aspects, 1492–1900* (Kingston, 1983), p. 41.

15 Richardson, *Wider world*, pp. 22–8. On Karifuna assistance to Tainos in Puerto Rico, see C. Sauer, *The early Spanish Main* (Berkeley, 1966), pp. 158, 192; Richardson, *Wider world*, p. 25. See E. Williams, *Documents of West Indian history, 1492–1655* (Port-of-Spain, 1963), pp. 62–70, 89–94. R. Greenwood, *A sketchmap history of the Caribbean* (London, 1991), pp. 18, 23. See also Sauer, *Early Spanish Main*, p. 32.

16 Sauer, *Early Spanish Main*, pp. 35, 180, 193; see also Lewis, *Main currents*, p. 64. See also P. Boucher, *Cannibal encounters: Europeans and the island Caribs, 1492–1763* (Baltimore, 1992); P. Hulme, *Wild majesty: encounters with the Caribs from Columbus to present day* (Oxford, 1992).

17 T. S. Floyd, *The Columbian dynasty in the Caribbean, 1492–1526* (Albuquerque, N.M., 1973), p. 97. For an account of the Spanish "hands off" policy with respect to the Lesser Antilles, see K. R. Andrews, *Trade, plunder and settlement: maritime enterprises and the genesis of the British empire, 1480–1630* (Cambridge, 1986), p. 282.

18 See Sauer, *Early Spanish Main*, p. 35; Lewis, *Main currents*, p. 64.

19 See Lewis, *Main currents*, p. 64; R. Dunn, *Sugar and slaves: the rise of the planter class in the English West Indies, 1624–1713* (New York, 1973), p. 24; Sieur de la Borde, *Relacion des Caraibes* (Paris, 1694); Jean Baptiste Du Tertre, *Histoire generale des Antilles habitées par les Francais* (Paris, 1667–71); J. Eaden (ed.), *The memoirs of Père Labat, 1693–1705* (London, 1970).

20 *Memoirs of Pere Labat*, p. 75.

21 *Ibid.*, p. 83.

22 *Ibid.*, p. 98.

23 *Ibid.*, p. 104.

24 *Ibid.*, p. 109.

25 Watts, *West Indies*, pp. 171–2. R. Sheridan, *Sugar and slavery: an economic history of the British West Indies* (Bridgetown, 1974), pp. 80, 85, 87, 456.

26 See Dunn, *Sugar and slaves*, p. 8

27 Lewis, *Main currents*, p. 104.

28 *Ibid.*, p. 105.

29 Dunn, *Sugar and slaves*, p. 246

30 *Memoirs of Père Labat*, p. 137.

31 Governor Stapleton of the Leewards to the Lords of Trade and Plantations, 22 Nov. 1676, *Calendar of State Papers, Colonial Series* (*CSPC*), 1676, p. 499.

32 See C. Gullick, "Black Caribs origins and early society", in *Transactions of the Seventh International Congress on Pre-Columbian Cultures of the Lesser Antilles* (Quebec, 1978), pp. 283–7.

33 See W. Young, *An account of the Black Charaibs in the island of St. Vincent's* (London, 1795), pp. 5–8; also V. Gonzalez, *Sojourners of the Caribbean: ethnogenesis and ethnohistory of the Garifunia* (Chicago, 1988).

34 See V. Murga (ed.), *Historia Document de Puerto Rico*, vol. 1 (Rio Pedras, n.d.), p. 227.

35 For an account of the battles at Martinique, see Du Tertre, *Histoire General*, p. 467–8.

36 See H. Beckles, *Black rebellion in Barbados: the struggle against slavery, 1627–1838* (Bridgetown, 1988), p. 36.

37 "The state of the case concerning our title to St. Lucia", 1664, *CSPC*, 1661–8, no. 887.

See also Rev. C. Jesse, "Barbadians buy St. Lucia from Caribs", *Journal of the Barbados Museum and Historical Society (JBMHS)* **32** (February), 1968, pp. 180–2.

38 Governor Sir Thomas ModyFord to the Duke of Albemarle, 16 March, 1668, *CSPC*, 1661–68, no. 1714.

39 V. L. Oliver, *The history of the island of Antigua* (London, 1894–99), vol. 1, pp. xix, xxv; also Sheridan, *Sugar and Slavery*, p. 87.

40 Petition of Major John Scott to the King, 1667, *CSPC*, 1661–68, no. 1525.

41 Governor William Lord Willoughby to the King, 11 Feb. 1668, *CSPC*, 1661–68, p. 547; Watts, *West Indies*, pp. 242–3. Henry Willoughby to William Willoughby, 15 June 1667, *CSPC*, 1661–68, no. 1498.

42 Craton, *Testing the chains*, pp. 22–3.

43 Governor William Lord Willoughby to the King, 9 July 1668, *CSPC*, 1661–68, no. 1788.

44 "Copy of a treaty between William Lord Willoughby and several of the Chief Captains of Caribs", 23 March 1668, *CSPC*, 1661–68, no. 1717.

45 *Ibid.*

46 Du Tertre, *Histoire Generale*, pp. 467–8.

47 Lord Willoughby to the King, 13 March 1668, *Colonial Papers*, vol. 22, no. 5, *CSPC*, 1661–68, no. 1710.

48 Governor Sir Thomas Modyford to the Duke of Albemarle, 16 March 1668, *CSPC*, no. 1714.

49 Governor Stapleton to the Lords of Trade and Plantations, 17 May 1672; *Colonial Papers*, vol. 28, no. 61.

50 *Ibid.* The English claimed that the Dominica silver mine was "lawfully purchased" from the Karifunas who recognized the contract. Leolin Lloyd to Secretary Arlington, *Colonial Papers*, vol. 29, no. 46; also *Colonial Papers*, vol. 28, no. 12.

51 Governor Atkins to Lords of Trade and Plantations, 4 July 1676, *Colonial Papers*, vol. 37, no. 22.

52 Governor Stapleton to Council of Trade and Plantations, Dec. 1675, *Colonial Papers*, vol. 35, no. 63.

53 "A Petition of Several Merchants of London Adventurers to the Caribbee Islands to the Lords of Trade and Plantations", 1676, *Colonial Papers*, vol. 36, no. 5.

54 Governor Stapleton to the Council for Plantations, 8 Feb. 1675, *CSPC*, 1675–76, no. 428.

55 Sir Jonathan Atkins to Secretary for Colonies, 17 Feb. 1675, *CSPC*, 1675–76, no. 439.

56 "Petition of Several Merchants of London Adventurers to the Caribbee Islands to Lords of Trade and Plantations", 10 Jan. 1676, *CSPC*, 1675–76, no. 774.

57 Governor Stapleton to Lords of Trade and Plantations, 16 Aug. 1681, *Colonial Papers*, vol. 46, no. 45; see also *CSPC*, 1681–85, nos. 410, 411.

58 Sir William Stapleton to Lords of Trade and Plantations, 16 Aug. 1681, *CSPC*, 1681–85, no. 204. See also *Journal of Lords of Trade and Plantations*, 18 Oct. 1681, no. 259.

59 *Ibid.*

60 The King to Sir William Stapleton, Feb. 1682, *CSPC*, 1681–85, no. 411.

61 Sir Richard Dutton to Lords of Trade and Plantations, 3 Jan. 1682, *CSPC* 1681–85, p. 181, no. 357; also *Colonial Papers*, vol. 48, no. 1.

62 *Journal of the Assembly of Nevis*, 14 June 1682, *CSPC*, 1681–85, no. 557.

63 The King to Sir Jonathan Atkins, 30 Dec. 1674, *CSPC*, 1675–76, no. 401.

64 Sir Jonathan Atkins to Secretary of Plantations, *CSPC*, Feb. 17, no. 439. See Jerome Handler, "Amerindians and their contribution to Barbados life in the seventeenth

century", *JBMHS* **35**, 1971, pp. 112–17; "The Amerindian slave population of Barbados in the seventeenth and early eighteenth centuries", *JBMHS* **33**(3) (May), 1970, pp. 111–35. For an account of this attempt to establish a Barbados–Guianas slave trade in Karifunas, E. G. Breslaw, "'Price's – His Deposition': kidnapping Amerindians in Guyana, 1674", *JBMHS* **39**, 1991, pp. 47–50.

65 Craton, *Testing the chains,* p. 23.
66 *Memoirs of Pere Labat,* p. 115.
67 *Ibid,* pp. 110–11.
68 Craton, *Testing the chains,* pp. 151–2; 190–91.
69 *Ibid.,* p. 149.
70 *Ibid.,* pp. 206–7.
71 N. Owen, "Land, politics and ethnicity in a Carib Indian community", *Ethnology* **14**, 1975; "Conflict and ethnic boundaries: a study of Carib–black relations", *Social and Economic Studies* **29**(2–3), 1990. Douglas Taylor, "Kinship and social structure of the Island Carib" *Southwestern Journal of Anthropology* **11**(2), 1946, pp. 180–212; "A note on marriage and kinship among Island Caribs", *MAN* **53**(175), 1953, pp. 117–19.

Chapter Fifteen

William Knibb and the constitution of the new Black subject

Catherine Hall

This essay argues that part of the colonial project, the making of the British empire, was the making of new subjects, colonizer and colonized.[1] Colonies could not operate without military and naval support, economic systems, administrative machinery and all the other apparatus of rule. But any stability depended also on the construction of a culture and the constitution of new identities, new men and women who in a variety of ways would live with and through colonialism, as well as engaging in conflict with it. The success of the colonizers depended on the creation of new subjects, colonized men and women who internalized particular relations of power. Like Fanon's African in *Black skin, white mask*, the colonized were only to know themselves through the eye of the colonizer. For Fanon, decolonization involved not only a military, political and economic struggle but also a struggle to free the mind and the psyche from the trammels of colonialism, to liberate the self from the feelings of inferiority and inadequacy which were part and parcel of being a Black man in a white man's world. But it was not only the colonized who had to be re-made, as Fanon suggested, it was also the colonizers. The task of ruling the unruly, of civilizing subjects, required particular disciplines too, particular frames of mind and fields of vision as well as technologies of power. In the categorization of other peoples and marking of difference between the British and their others, new selves were constructed, new identities demarcated for those who were ruling as well as those who were ruled.[2]

The idea that colonizers and colonized could be "made", new identities constituted at particular historical moments in particular places, depends on a particular understanding of identity. As post-structuralist, post-colonial and feminist theory has suggested, identities can be understood as strategic and positional rather than essential. They are constantly transformed and re-worked, shifting and unstable rather than fixed, never unified, constituted within representation and derived from narratives of the self, narratives which are also performative. Those identities are constructed through difference, for it is only in relation to the other that positive meanings can be constructed for the self. Points of identification and attachment only work because of the capacity to exclude and leave out, to mark difference through relations of power.[3] Colonizer and colonized were themselves unstable categories with multiple forms. There were many different colonizers and many different colonized.

This essay focuses on the moment of transition from slavery to freedom in the British Caribbean, on the island of Jamaica, and on the constitution of two particular sets of identities: that of a new-style colonizer, the emancipatory missionary, and two new colonial subjects, the freed man and the freed woman. Its premise is that for the "great experiment" of emancipation to work, it was vital that new colonial subjects were formed, the subjects of a new cultural order and a new gender order. Those new orders were quite as central to the working of the new colonialism associated with emancipation as were the new economic system devoted to the extraction of labour, and the new political system which protected oligarchic power. It briefly examines the case of the Baptist missionaries in Jamaica, especially William Knibb, and their belief in the possibility of creating Africans anew, as new Christian subjects, babes in Christ washed clean, capable of transformation into labouring men and domesticated women. Both Madhavi Kale's and Andrew Bank's essays in this volume deal with closely related phenomena. Kale's essay explores the emergence of the category of "indentured labourer" as a response to the need for new forms of labour in post-slave economies and the reaction of anti-slavery forces to this. Andrew Bank is also concerned with questions of humanitarianism, this time on the Cape. My focus is on what might be described as the most utopian moment, on the moment of transition to freedom, on a particular group of missionary abolitionists in Jamaica and the work they did to represent their case in Britain. It suggests that the missionaries occupied a very different place in the "colonial order of things"[4] from that which the planters had occupied. Yet they too were colonizers, committed to the project of empire, wanting to protect British interests whilst recognizing the brotherhood and sisterhood of black people, convinced that a reformed and revitalized Christian Britain could offer leadership to the globe. Whilst never at one with the Colonial Office on the one hand, or the planters on the other, the missionaries longed for a new moral world which they envisaged as led by themselves, the fathers and patriarchs of the new Jerusalem. Their worst enemies were those planters who had become anti-Christ, who had enslaved others and rejected the teachings of Christ, who had stained the good name of Britain with the national sin of slavery and who were prepared to stop the preaching and teaching of dissenting missionaries in any way they could. Their best friends were those freed slaves who flocked to the Baptist chapels in the 1830s and seemed ready to become responsible, industrious and domesticated people.

The moment of emancipation, fully completed on 1 August 1838 with the termination of apprenticeship, marked a particularly utopian moment for the missionaries. The ending of slavery meant the building of a new society. Slavery was a whole social order and that order had to be made anew: enslaved labour transformed into free labour; the plantation turned into a unit of the free market; the slave code replaced by a legal system guaranteeing the rights of British subjects; the political system which had secured slavery turned into a political system which could gradually adapt itself to the demands of those same British subjects for political rights; the culture of the plantocracy re-worked for new times; concubinage and prostitution replaced by marriage and domesticity; a new familial order secured. While "Old Corruption" could only gradually be critiqued and disassembled in Britain, emancipation marked a truly new beginning. Jamaica could be a new moral world.

Emancipation was linked in the missionary mind with conversion. Emancipation gave men and women their political, social and economic freedom. But only conversion gave them a new life in Christ, the possibility to be born anew, to be new Black subjects, washed clean of old ways, new Black men and women. This was the abolitionist dream – a society in which Black men would become like white men, not the decadent planters with their dissolute habits but white men like the abolitionists, responsible, industrious, independent, Christian. Black women would become like white women; not the indolent ladies of plantation society, locked into their debasing acceptance of concubinage, but the white women of the middle-class English abolitionist imagination, occupying their small but satisfying separate sphere, married and living in regular households. The gender order of the abolitionists was central to their vision of the new Jamaica; Black men would survey their families with pride, Black women would no longer be sexually subject to their masters. A new marital economy would emerge, modelled on that of the English middle classes. The mission family, both literally – the missionary, his wife and his children – and symbolically – the linked families of all those attached to missions – provided the keystone for the new utopias. Congregations constituted families and were all part of the family of man whether black or white. Each family would be dominated by a patriarch, connected through a chain of male power to God the Father.

The period between 1838 and 1845 marked a transitional moment between the old and the new in Jamaica. As with revolutions, the major upheavals of the slave rebellion of 1831 and the legislation of 1834 and 1838 ending slavery and apprenticeship resulted in the unsettling of many economic, social, political and cultural relations and institutions. In this period of flux and instability new possibilities emerged, new dreams were envisaged, whilst aspects of the old order were re-vivified and re-worked.[5] It was in this moment that William Knibb, pre-eminent amongst the Baptist missionaries, was able to imagine a new nation, Jamaica, peopled with new Black subjects, subjects of the British empire, Black Britons with full legal rights, the men soon to be citizens with political power, for the terms of the franchise meant that small peasant proprietors should be able to have the vote.

In the Knibb Baptist Chapel in Falmouth, Jamaica, an impressive marble monument hangs on the wall behind the communion table. As the *Baptist Herald* reported in February 1841:

> The emancipated Sons of Africa, in connexion with the church under the pastoral care of the Rev. W. Knibb, have recently erected in this place of worship a splendid marble monument, designed to perpetuate the remembrance of the glorious period when they came into the possession of that liberty which was their right, and of which they have proved themselves to be so pre-eminently worthy. It is surmounted with the figure of Justice, holding in her left hand the balances of equity, whilst her right hand rests upon the sword which is placed at her side. Beneath this figure the likenesses of Granville Sharp, Sturge, and Wilberforce are arrayed in bas-relief, and that of the Rev. W. Knibb appears at the base. The inscription reads:

DEO GLORIA

ERECTED
BY EMANCIPATED SONS OF AFRICA
TO COMMEMORATE
THE BIRTH-DAY OF THEIR FREEDOM
AUGUST THE FIRST 1838
HOPE
HAILS THE ABOLITION OF SLAVERY
THROUGHOUT THE BRITISH COLONIES
AS THE DAY-SPRING OF
UNIVERSAL LIBERTY
TO ALL NATIONS OF MEN, WHOM
GOD "HATH MADE OF ONE BLOOD"

"ETHIOPIA SHALL SOON STRETCH OUT HER HANDS UNTO GOD" LXVIII PSALM 31 VERSE

Immediately under this inscription two Africans are represented in the act of burying the broken chain, and useless whip – another is rejoicing in the undisturbed possession of the book of God, whilst associated with these, a fond mother is joyously caressing the infant which for the first time she can dare to regard as *her own*.[6]

This monument, made in Birmingham, tells something of the complex and historic relation between Jamaica and Britain, a history which needs new narratives for post-colonial times. Granville Sharp, William Wilberforce and Joseph Sturge are well known figures in the British abolitionist hall of fame. Knibb's name is well known in Jamaica, "King Knibb" as he came to be called, his chapel still an imposing building in Falmouth, his descendants celebrated for their contributions to Jamaican education. His story provides one way into re-thinking the relations of Britain and Jamaica.

The monument celebrates 1 August 1838, the moment of full emancipation when "apprenticeship" was abolished. Apprenticeship was the system introduced alongside compensation for the planters by the imperial government, to soften the blow of emancipation for those who had lost their "property". Those once enslaved were now fully free. That moment marked the end of a prolonged struggle both in Britain and the Caribbean to secure the abolition of slavery: a struggle which always had both its British and its Caribbean forms. In Britain, efforts to abolish the slave trade and question the whole system of slavery were launched by Granville Sharp amongst others in the 1770s, sustained under the leadership of William Wilberforce in the late eighteenth and early nineteenth centuries, and culminated in the abolition of the slave trade by the imperial parliament in 1807. Popular pressure was central to the winning of that legislation. The recognition by the 1820s that the demise of the British slave trade had not been effective in transforming the system of slavery resulted in a revival of anti-slavery activity in Britain. In the Caribbean the resistance of the slaves peaked in Demerara in 1823 and in Jamaica in 1831. Both rebellions were widely reported in Britain, partly because of the central involvement of missionaries in the events and of the way in which they were held responsible by planters and colonists for the eruptions which took place.

In 1832 the Baptist missionaries in Jamaica decided to send one of their brethren, William Knibb, to Britain. Knibb was pastor of the mission in Falmouth, once a thriving slaving port and now a town at the heart of a network of sugar estates. He was to answer the charges which had been made against them and raise support following the destruction of their churches which had taken place as a part of the backlash. Once arrived in Britain Knibb defied the authority of the Baptist Missionary Society, which like all missionary societies cautioned their agents against any form of political involvement, and came out publicly against slavery. His subsequent public speaking tour mobilized large numbers for the campaign against slavery, a campaign which was finally successful in 1833 when slavery was abolished from 1 August 1834. A subsequent campaign against apprenticeship, in which Joseph Sturge, the Birmingham Quaker and corn merchant, played a vital part, resulted in the abolition of that system from 1 August 1838, as the monument records.[7] Sharp, Wilberforce, Sturge and Knibb were key figures in the anti-slavery movement in Britain. Neither Sharp nor Wilberforce ever went to Jamaica but Sturge visited the West Indies in 1837 and William Knibb lived there from 1825 to his death in 1845.

Born in Kettering, the Northamptonshire boot and shoe town, in 1803, Knibb's father was a tradesman and his mother the member of an independent church. He attended a dame school and then the town's grammar school as well as Sunday school at a local chapel. In 1816 he was apprenticed, along with his brother Thomas, to J. G. Fuller, the brother of Andrew Fuller, then the Baptist minister in Kettering and the secretary of the Baptist Missionary Society (BMS). The BMS had a particular relation to Kettering since it was there that the Society was formed in 1792, and it was some time before it moved its administration to London. J. G. Fuller lived in Bristol and the Knibb brothers became attached to the Baptist chapel there, a refuge for anti-slavery sentiments in a strongly pro-slavery town. In 1820 Thomas was baptized and two years later William followed in his footsteps for, as he put it,

> Having enjoyed the unspeakable advantages of a religious education, and of being trained under the care of a pious and affectionate mother, I was early taught my state as a sinner, and the necessity of flying to Jesus Christ as the only hope of escape from that punishment which my sins had deserved . . .[8]

In 1822 Thomas decided to become a missionary, thinking "that it would be far more delightful, more honourable, to go to heaven from a heathen country than a Christian one". Affected by the revival of the anti-slavery movement of the 1820s he chose to go as a schoolmaster to Kingston rather than to the more familiar Baptist pastures in India.[9] Thomas' choice inspired William and he too began to dream of a future in which he could minister to "the swarthy sons of Africa" and become an instrument for Christ with "the poor degraded negroes", "unfolding to them the wonders of redeeming love".[10] In 1823 Thomas died and William was accepted to replace him. After learning the Lancastrian system he sailed for Jamaica with his new wife Mary, a fellow member of the Baptist Church. A long delay off the south coast meant that he was able to preach a couple of times on the Isle of Wight, and encounter that "heathenism" at home which always stood as a counterpoint to heathens abroad. Niton, one of the villages in which he attempted to preach, was "deplorably dark and benighted", Knibb recorded in his journal. "Mud was thrown at the door but I escaped unhurt. Felt thankful that I had the opportunity of unfolding to them the word of life." His first encounter with a slaveholder was with a fellow passenger whose very attempts to justify the system showed "it to be complete with every enormity", from cruelty to immorality.[11]

Having landed in Port Morant the Knibbs took a boat to Kingston and had their first taste of Jamaica. "I have now reached the land of sin, disease, and death", wrote Knibb to a friend,

> where Satan reigns with awful power, and carries multitudes captive at his will. True religion is scoffed at, and those who profess it are ridiculed and insulted . . . The poor, oppressed, benighted, and despised sons of Africa, form a pleasing contrast to the debauched white population. Though many of them seem to have lost nearly every rational idea, such is the beautiful simplicity of the gospel, that though fools, they understand it, and joyfully accept the truth as it is Jesus . . . They are bursting through the thick gloom which has long surrounded them, and it will be a long time ere they may be denominated by any other name than babes in Christ.[12]

Knibb's anti-slavery sentiments, bred in the nonconformist culture of provincial England, and replete with the images of "poor negroes" and benighted souls awaiting enlightenment from white missionaries, were fully confirmed by his experience of Jamaica. He was shocked by the moral degradation of slavery and the mindless existence, as he saw it, to which slaves were condemned, reduced to stupidity, locked in a thick gloom, emerging only as "babes in Christ". No doubt his assumptions as to the "barren wastes" of their minds would have had a good deal to do with his difficulties in understanding their forms of speech and making sense of their customs and rituals. But he was convinced that his own people, white people, carried the responsibility for this appalling system and felt ashamed "that I belong to a race that can indulge in such atrocities". "The white population", he concluded, "is worse, far worse, than the victims of their injustice."[13]

Knibb soon started to preach, though the BMS was hesitant in giving him the requisite papers since he did not have the usual academic qualifications. In his early years on the island he struggled, as did all the missionaries, with the hostility of the planters who did not want Christianity, especially of the dissenting variety, taught on their properties. Family life and mission life were the only supports available. Other missionaries were the only white people who were likely to be friendly. The everyday associates were Black people, for the most part slaves, and this raised difficulties even for the most committed abolitionist. Working on behalf of Black people was one thing, intimacy was another. In 1825 Mary Knibb had twins and her husband was troubled at having a Black wet-nurse, a sign of the difficulties associated in his mind at this time of very intimate relations between the races. "Dear Mary is pretty well," he wrote to his mother in the following year after the birth of another daughter, "and we are truly happy in each other, which is a great mercy in this place, where all temporal pleasure is concentrated in home. Here are no fields to walk in, and few, if any, friends to visit."[14] The image vividly evokes some of the physical differences between England and Jamaica – Jamaica with its great houses and plantations, its acres of sugar cane, its tropical vegetation, its coffee and cocoa groves and its beaches had indeed few green pastures to walk in.

By 1826, when the Jamaica Baptist Association was formed to link the churches across the island, Knibb was well established amongst the missionaries and he served as its secretary. In 1829 he and his family left Kingston to set up a new mission on the west coast, in Savanna-la-Mar. The Consolidated Slave Law had been passed by the Jamaican House of Assembly in 1826. Tensions had increased between missionaries and planters, and the pattern of appeal to "the government at home" and British public opinion became increasingly important. James Stephen at the Colonial Office had become convinced that complaints of cruelty and injustice to the slaves should be investigated and that slaves were being denied religious freedom, a right which the ameliorative legislation of 1823, designed to improve the condition of slaves, had supposedly secured.[15] Despite the opposition of many planters, however, by 1833 there were 16 Wesleyan, 14 Baptist, eight Moravian and five Presbyterian missions on the island, 44 missionaries in all, most of whom were assisted by their wives.[16]

In 1830 the Knibb family moved to Falmouth, a well established station in the heartlands of plantation society. Here Knibb worked hard on the estates on which he was allowed to preach. He was soon involved in a case that raised political temperatures considerably. Sam Swiney, a slave and a deacon in Knibb's previous congregation in Savanna-la-Mar, had been sentenced to whipping and hard labour for preaching and teaching. Knibb was outraged since to his mind there was no evidence of Swiney either preaching or teaching, and he contacted the BMS as well as telling the local press what he had done. In Knibb's view, and that of the Colonial Office which investigated the case, Swiney had only prayed. The punishment was excessive, a warning to Black people not to become involved with Christianity.[17]

Not far from Falmouth, in St Ann's Bay, lived the Rev. George Bridges, the rector of that parish. Bridges was a leading advocate of slavery, an Englishman, a member of both Oxford and Cambridge who had gone to Jamaica as a young man. Having been educated to critique slavery, he discovered on arrival in Jamaica that he had been misinformed. He "found their masters a most injured and slandered race of men" and set to work to defend them. His particular enemies became the dissenting missionaries, men whom he accused of being of "the lowest and most dangerous description", only too capable of stirring the specious superstitions of ignorant people. It was "the poison of sectarianism" which had disrupted the unity and purity of the church.[18] In 1829 the Secretary of the Anti-Slavery Society sent an anonymous letter to the Colonial Office about Bridges' treatment of a woman slave, Kitty Hilton, owned by him. She had appealed for help and accused him of severely kicking and flogging her, leaving her naked. Bridges became a leader and spokesman for slavery on the island.[19] In July 1831 he formed the Colonial Union, an organization to protect the planting interest and the established church against the depradations of slaves and missionaries.

Bridges' anger against the missionaries had its roots in a virulent defence of the established church against all others. "The want of employment in the fields or manufactures of England", he raged, "sent crowds of ignorant and itinerant preachers to these shores, where they found, or expected to find, a rich harvest, or a glorious martyrdom." "This cloud of itinerant preachers hastened to exchange a parish pittance in England for a lucrative profession in the West Indies," he expostulated. The effect of this was that the pulpit,

> that safe and sacred organ of sedition, resounded with the ambiguous tenets, or at least the words, of freedom and equality; and the public discontent might be inflamed by the promise of a glorious deliverance from a bondage which the slave would rather apply to his temporal, than to his spiritual condition.[20]

This was indeed the heart of the complaint against the missionaries, the slippage that occurred between temporal and spiritual freedom. For Bridges the task of the colonizer was to rule those who were clearly inferior. Faced with the challenge from dissenting missionaries who saw their task as to evangelize all "heathens", whatever their colour, and were prepared to risk the inevitable dangers which would go with this, he reasserted the significance of racial difference and mobilized pro-slavery support. Missionaries as harbingers of a new form of colonial order, new colonizers, provoked a vituperative reaction and the articulation of identities which could stand as counterpoint to this, the defenders of the status quo.

In 1828 Bridges had published his *Annals of Jamaica*, an attempt to reclaim the high ground from the forces of anti-slavery in Britain and to strengthen planter resolve in Jamaica. He sought to justify racial inequalities. His case was that abolition was impractical but he did not defend slavery on principle. Rather he assumed, as did most protagonists of the system, that eventually it would melt away if there were no outside interference.[21] Africans needed the civilizing hand of Europeans for much longer before they would be anywhere near ready for freedom. Bridges' polemic had become more shrill as the tensions had increased between planters on the one hand and slaves and missionaries on the other. He could not tolerate the claim which slaves were making: the right to worship a Christian God, for that God was a dissenting God. Planters did not want slaves to learn to read any more than conservatives in England in the 1780s and 1790s had wanted working-class adults or children to learn those skills. They did not want them treated as equals, partaking of communion, addressed as "brother" and "sister". They heartily disliked the idea of leaders interpreting the Bible to their classes. They did not believe in universal rights. They knew all too well that some forms of religious belief had long been a source of radical thinking on the individual. For Bridges, African slaves were not the same as white people, they were different and inferior. Yet they were claiming the right to religious freedom.

It was well known in Jamaica that there were continuous efforts being made in Britain to abolish slavery. The slave rebellion which broke out in December 1831, led by Black or native Baptists who had been in contact with the missionaries, focused on the question of freedom. Native Baptists had derived their inspiration from the African-American Baptists who had come to Jamaica in the aftermath of the War of Independence. They had established congregations across the island and their practices, associated with Africa, were abhorred by orthodox Baptists.[22] The rebellion united the Europeans across the island and the governor took no steps to restrain white violence. The missionaries were blamed for the outbreak and were threatened with lynching and worse. They were forced to recognize that their work could not survive unless slavery was abolished and that whatever the rules of their societies they would have to take a public stand against the system. It was at this point that the Baptists met and decided to send William Knibb to make their case in the "mother country".

From 1823 a propaganda war had been waged between planters and abolitionists in Britain. At stake was the question as to what was the truth about the system of slavery. Both sides were interested in mobilizing public opinion, that increasingly powerful phenomenon. Missionaries began to publish material giving their accounts of slavery. A significant body of eye-witness material thus began to challenge the planter orthodoxy that they were the ones who knew. Missionaries, many of whom had gone to the West Indies in the 1820s with anti-slavery sympathies, were fuelling the abolitionist flames with vivid accounts of the refusal of planters to countenance Christian worship amongst their slaves. Christianity and slavery began to seem more clearly at odds.

Crucial to this war of representation was the disputed figure of the African – what kind of a man was he, what kind of a woman was she? While the supporters of anti-slavery claimed that African men and women were brothers and sisters, the plantocracy claimed that they were fundamentally different from, and inferior to, their white superiors. While the icon of the planters was the imagined figure of 'Quashie' – evasive, lazy, childlike and lacking judgement – the missionaries and their allies constructed new figures, the Black Christian man and woman.[23] Both discourses constructed stereotypes of the African, figures which reduced complex individuals and collectives with cultures and histories to a few simple characteristics. The new Black Christian man and woman were childlike, and in that sense linked to planter discourse, but also able to accept guidance, ready to learn, ready to labour and to live in families. These men and women were human beings, with feelings and thoughts, and with the capacity for redemption. The attempt to construct these new Christian subjects was at the heart of the missionary enterprise in Jamaica, just as it was at the heart of evangelical activity at this time in Britain. Black subjects were potentially both the same and different, equal and unequal. They were human beings with souls, men and brothers, women and sisters, but for the abolitionists they were also marked by their racial characteristics, by their uncultivated minds, by their need for guidance, by their capacity to labour in the burning sun.

The war over representation took place on many sites: in the press, in pamphlets, in fiction, in poetry, in public meetings. One key site in 1831 was the House of Lords, which had instituted a select committee on slavery – a select committee which gained urgency when the Jamaica rebellion took place at Christmas. In the Commons a select committee was also established in the wake of this, taking as one of its framing propositions the view that there would be more danger if emancipation were withheld than if it were granted.[24] Both committees focused on Jamaica. The House of Lords took evidence on the condition and treatment of the slaves, their habits and dispositions, the means of improving and civilizing them. Their findings, they concluded, "were of the most contradictory Description".[25] The House of

Commons committee was formed to discuss the ending of slavery in the safest possible way and wanted to investigate particularly whether slaves, once emancipated, would be industrious and maintain themselves. Their inquiry was unfinished but they concluded that there was an urgent need for serious legislation.[26]

Both plantocracy and abolitionists had marshalled their forces and made full use of the public platforms which the select committees offered them. While overseers and attorneys, planters and managers, naval and military men told one story, dissenting missionaries told another. The missionaries, encouraged by the Anti-Slavery Society, were determined to use this platform to counter the claims of the planters and discredit that old story of slave prosperity. There was now a sufficient body of white knowledge, from those who knew the island and had witnessed slavery at first hand, to tell a different story. Jamaica had been a "sealed country" and the plantations a "sealed book", for white people rarely visited them.[27] Those missionaries who gave evidence systematically refuted the notion that slaves were better off than British labourers, or that their intellect was inferior. Furthermore, it was vital for them to be able to claim that slaves were being Christianized, thus civilized, and that once freed they would work. The Black Christian subject had feelings and thoughts, was open to redemption, did accept the guidance of Christian missionaries, did want to buy clothes and items for their houses, would labour.

William Knibb gave evidence to both select committees. In January 1831 he had been harassed by the authorities and arrested in Jamaica. "Value your privileges, ye Britons" was his message to his anti-slavery supporters in the mother country. "Feel and pray for those poor Christian slaves who are entirely under the control of such beings. No Algerine pirate or savage Moor, would have treated me worse than I was treated by Englishmen."[28] The order of civilization had been turned upside down, Englishmen were savages and the slaves and missionaries were the victims. Knibb had been threatened and pressured to leave the island, chapels were burnt and a number of men "came dressed in women's clothing to tar and feather me", the cross-dressing a sign of the complete breakdown of social order.[29] Britishness, and whiteness, in the discourse of the missionaries and their allies, should mean order, civilization, Christianity, domesticity and separate spheres, rationality and industry. When it carried another set of meanings it was deeply disturbing. White people then became "savages", uncultivated and uncivilized.

The Colonial Church Union of Bridges and his friends was the quintessential example of such a den of infidels: their task, to burn the houses of God and lynch his servants. It was composed, as Knibb put it, "of nearly all the fornicators in the island". The organization was designed to stop the march of mind and religion, to protect the white rebels from deserved punishment, and to dry up the streams of religious instruction; infidels, clergymen, slave owners, newspaper editors, high and low, have joined hand and heart . . .[30]

The missionaries decided, though not without disputes amongst themselves and with the parent society, that they must break their vows of silence on political matters and represent the case against slavery to the British public. "My duty in the West Indies", said Knibb, "was to instruct the Slaves in Religious Matters; when in England, I am speaking to Free People."[31] Knibb's agenda became, as he put it at a great meeting at Exeter Hall, to "stand forward as the advocate of the innocent and persecuted", to speak for the African in England.[32] In the process he empowered himself by representing others; positioning Black men as potentially independent, albeit guided and defended by their missionary fathers, Black women as dependants. No Englishman, in the proper meaning of that term, could stand aside and see a woman flogged. Indeed, Englishness and slavery could not go together. Knibb insisted that the question was not one of politics but of morality. "All I ask", as he put it at Exeter Hall to thunderous applause,

> is that my African brother may stand in the family of man; that my African sister shall, while she clasps her tender infant to her breast, be allowed to call it her own; that they both shall be allowed to bow their knees in prayer to that God who has made of one blood all nations – the same God who views all nations as one flesh.[33]

It was the family of man which provided the key image, a family structured like the desirable English family with patriarchal father and domesticated mother.

In his evidence to the select committees Knibb had his larger audience ever in mind. But he was also concerned to persuade the lawmakers that they could delay no longer. He wanted to see the end of slavery and he wanted the British parliament to give emancipation as a kindness, not a right. This way the freed slaves would be bound to Britain for ever. If something was not done the slaves would take their own freedom by violence, he warned. Knibb demonstrated to his audience their embeddedness in the colonial system. Slavery was not something out there, it was linked to Britain in the most intimate ways. Many of the slaves, he pointed out, were the sons and daughters of Englishmen and Scotsmen, "they get English feelings and long for English knowledge"; they in turn influenced other slaves, opening their minds to English things he suggested.[34] Christian values, moreover, were spreading fast, a crucial indicator of African humanity and capacity for freedom.

Knibb was also anxious to separate the BMS from the Native Baptists, whom he saw as certainly party to the rebellion. The new Black subjects he desired to create were to be clearly marked off from such dangerous infidels. "We have no connexion with them," he insisted, "they hate us with the most perfect Hatred." "I am sorry to speak of any Body of Men," he continued to their lordships, "especially because they may be considered inferior on account of their Colour; but it is a lamentable Fact, that both their Doctrine and Example are very bad." They derided the Bible, they called themselves "spirit Christians", the mind of God was revealed to them by dreams. They had their own churches, their own papers, thousands of members, and deluded Black preachers who lived unholy lives and allowed sins of varied kinds in their flocks.[35]

He had one further concern which shaped his evidence, his desire to speak for and represent others who could not represent themselves. No Black person was invited to address the select committees, despite their being the subject matter. Knibb went so far as to read from his examinations of Black witnesses after the rebellion, thus introducing the only African testimony, mediated through his editorial voice.[36] At the same time Mary Prince's *History* was reaching the British public, the first narrative of an enslaved Black woman from the Caribbean. Mary Prince's story, as Moira Ferguson has shown,[37] was editorialized by Thomas Pringle, the Secretary of the Anti-Slavery Society, and Sarah Strickland, who wrote down her account of Mary Prince's words. The narrative immediately became a site of the war over the representation of Black women. Pro-slavery critics attempted to subvert her legitimacy while her female anti-slavery supporters were anxious to prove the validity of her claims. Both Pringle and Knibb were intimately involved in the constitution of new Black subjects – the labouring man and the domesticated woman.

Emancipation was granted by the imperial parliament in 1833 and became effective from 1 August 1834. Great celebrations were held across the island, marking the death of slavery. Freed slaves joined the Baptist chapels in large numbers in the years after 1834, demonstrating by their attendance, membership, and contributions their judgement of the part played by the Baptist missionaries in emancipation. Orthodox Baptist membership went up by 200 per cent between 1834 and 1839, and there was a similar increase in the number of inquirers.[38] The dream of freedom was soon, however, destroyed by the realities of apprenticeship. Apprenticeship turned out to be slavery with another name. Joseph Sturge, long-time abolitionist and celebrated in the Falmouth monument, had been concerned to monitor the system from the beginning and this he did mainly through his contacts with the Baptist missionaries on the island.[39] The missionaries activated their anti-slavery friends to alert the British public and by 1838 enough pressure had been mounted to force through full emancipation.

On 1 August 1838 celebrations were held in Falmouth, orchestrated by Knibb and his trusted Black deacons, to greet the end of apprenticeship, the dawning of freedom. A great procession with portraits of the emancipators, Clarkson, Wilberforce and Buxton amongst others, gathered around the coffin of slavery an hour before midnight. On one side of the coffin was painted in large letters *Cornwall Courier* and on the other *Jamaica Standard*, two of the hated pro-slavery papers. On the plate of the coffin was inscribed "Colonial Slavery, died July 31st, 1838, aged 276 years", and on the lower part, "the name of Sir John Hawkins, who first brought Africans into the colonies as *slaves*". Just before midnight, the assembled multitude sang,

> The death-blow is struck – see the monster is dying,
> He cannot survive till the dawn streaks the sky;
> *In one single hour*, he will prostrate be lying,
> Come, shout o'er the grave where so soon he will lie.

As the clock struck the final note of midnight Knibb cried out, "THE MONSTER IS DEAD! THE NEGRO IS FREE! THREE CHEERS FOR THE QUEEN!" There was a great burst of cheering and then the congregation sang,

> Restored the negro's long-lost rights,
> How softened is his lot!
> Now sacred, heart-born, dear delights
> Shall bless his humble cot.

The coffin was then buried, along with a symbolic chain, handcuffs and iron-collar. A flag reading *FREEDOM* together with the British Union Jack was then raised and a tree of liberty planted, evocative of the reframed imperial project and of the connections between Jamaica and the liberty-lovers of England. Services were then held in all the chapels in Falmouth, followed by a public meeting in the Baptist chapel at which all the speakers, except Knibb who was in the chair, were of African descent.[40]

These events were celebrated in the British missionary and evangelical press, demonstrating to that public the upright and responsible character of freed Black men. After the chairman's opening Andrew Dickson spoke first. He thanked the people of England. "I do truly thank God for the light of the everlasting gospel," he said. "I present my thanks to the people of England for the gospel." William Kerr spoke next:

> I stand up to give hearty thanks to the people of England for send us the gospel. The gospel bring we to see this day, the gospel bring we free. No

317

one can tell what we see one time, and what we was suffer; but the gospel bring us joy. We bless God, we bless the Queen, we bless the Governor, we bless the people of England for the joy we have. Let we remember that we been on sugar estate from sunrise a–morning till eight o'clock at night; the rain falling, the sun shining, we was in it all. Many of we own colour behind we, and many before: we get whip, our wives get beat like a dog, before we face, and if we speak we get the same; they put we in shackle; but thank our heavenly Father we not slave again. (Cheers)

He was followed by Edward Barrett, who was to accompany Knibb to England in 1840 for the Anti-Slavery Convention, who recalled the terrible ways in which slavery had divided families, forced men to maltreat their wives.

The next day a huge procession of school-children paraded round Falmouth. This was another ritual moment in the constitution of the new Black subject. It was led by a carriage, "in which were six children, sons and daughters of ministers, drawn by two horses, gaily caparisoned". The chapel was decorated with branches, flowers, pictures of Clarkson, Wilberforce and Buxton. Afterwards there was a banquet and more trees of liberty were planted.[41] The two days marked the beginnings of a new Jamaica, the possibilities of a new Christian patriotism, as Knibb called it in one of his sermons, one still shaped by the colonial relation but with benevolent and emancipatory colonizers heralding a new dawn.[42] As an editorial in the *Herald* put it, addressing the Baptist Convention in New York, "with all our souls, we say, come over and see the BLACK standing erect in the family of man".[43]

Emancipation made it possible for Black men, and it is almost always men, was to enter the public arena as speaking subjects. The existence of the *Baptist Herald and Friend of Africa* from 1839 meant that in the Baptist family there was a platform from which they could speak, which allowed their words to circulate beyond the local to the national arena, and even to Britain, to other Caribbean islands and to the United States. They were no longer being represented but were representing themselves. That representation was still mediated by the powerful hand of the missionary, chairing the meetings at which they spoke, editing the journals in which they were reported, claiming to shape the perspectives from which their new thinking emerged, protecting them, defending them, applauding them, and, if it was felt necessary, correcting and reproving them.

At a public meeting in Falmouth in July 1839, by which time it was abundantly clear that all was not going to be plain sailing in the transition from apprenticeship to freedom, Knibb reported to his Black audience that he had been in touch with Sturge and had "felt it my duty to endeavour to cover you with the mantle of British protection". Help was going to be needed to resist the planters' attempts to tie wages and rent. "I pledge myself", he vowed,

> by all that is solemn and sacred never to rest satisfied until I see my black brethren in the enjoyment of the same civil and religious liberties which I myself enjoy; till I see them take a proper stand in society as men!

What he sought for them was decent wages and some independence from the estates. Deliberately addressing them as negroes he defended the use of the word, "because it means black, and you have no reason to be ashamed of it". "I hail the labouring population of Jamaica with joy", he continued,

> and I trust that the propriety of their conduct will at all times inspire me with confidence in their behalf. Be kind to your wives; lighten their labours. I was glad, some time ago, to hear one of my people say that he wished his wife to refrain from hard labour, and turn her attention to domestic affairs, so that when he came home he might sit down and take his meals like a gentleman.[44]

Black men could be independent, not slavishly dependent, could have their own land and cottages, could marry and live with their families. As Deacon Andrew Dickson said, "let them act as freemen had a right to do". Let them claim their rights as voters which as peasant proprietors with a certain amount of land they could formally do. In the words of James Allen Senior, let them "assert their just rights . . . and defend their characters".[45] But those rights were still framed by missionaries, still dependent on their teaching.

In 1840 an auxiliary branch of the BMS was established at Salter's Hill, in the mountains above Montego Bay, the station run by Walter Dendy which was to be the site of an outbreak of mayalism, a practice associated with Africa and with the Native Baptists, in 1842. Mr John Grey, an elder of the Black community, spoke at the inaugural meeting, welcoming the change which now made it possible for Black men to think of providing salvation to other heathens. "This was a sinful country", he said,

> but through the goodness of God, Missionaries were sent to tell us about our souls; the Gospel has made a great change for us – it has changed our hearts. We are thankful that we have heard Baptist missionaries preach. What a pleasure, what a happiness, what a comfort it is to have the Gospel. If we did not know the Gospel we should still be as the beasts, and we do not know what we might have been doing this Christmas. It was good to get freedom.[46]

Meanwhile, William Knibb asked, to the fury of the planters, "Had the black man not the same right to every privilege of a British subject that white men had?"[47] In Lucea a celebration was held for the anniversary of emancipation in August 1838 at which the greatest cheer was for "Britons never will be slaves".[48] Black men and women could think of themselves and be thought of as Black Britons (a term almost forgotten until one hundred and fifty years later), part of the same greater nation, part of the empire.

In a symbolic moment in 1841 the foundation stone was laid for the new chapel at Mount Carey, high in the hills above Montego Bay, one of the free villages initiated by Burchell and named after the founder of the BMS. The stone was laid, reported the *Herald*, by Miss Burchell, daughter of the Baptist missionary Thomas Burchell, and a "fine, grey-headed old Christian negro" who thus symbolized the unity of white and black, the vision of a new Jamaica.[49]

Central to this vision was a particular notion of the family of man. Manhood meant independence, the capacity for a man to stand on his own feet, to look after those who were properly dependent on him, his wife and children. Negro women needed to learn new forms of dependence, not on their owners but on their lawful husbands. Slavery had produced an unnatural phenomenon: male slaves who were entirely dependent on their masters, who could not, therefore, truly *be* men. Emancipation marked the moment at which they could cast off that dependence and learn to be men, in the image of the Englishman.[50] Being independent "in pecuniary matters" was a central part of that new masculinity: becoming a householder with all the responsibilities attached to it, enjoying the freedom associated with the old maxim that "an Englishman's home is his castle", paying for medical care and for education, celebrating the "voluntary principle" which was at the heart of dissenting politics, the refusal of state intervention in church, in schools, in welfare. Jamaica offered an exceptional opportunity to carry this voluntary principle fully into effect. With a weak established church and a strong dissenting presence, with a state which had depended on the plantation to provide basic forms of care, the breakdown of the old system provided a moment to build a new society.

Knibb's dream was shaped by his encounter with Jamaica, his recognition that Africans as they had been represented in Britain were not the people he came to know, the island not the place he had imagined but a home he came to love. His daughter Annie was to marry a "coloured" man, the contemporary term for mixed-race, a clear indicator that the most intimate relationships could be with those of other "races". His understanding that Black men could and should exercise the vote depended on a conviction that they were equal to white men, that God's family was universal. In this sense Knibb learned from his colonial encounter and that encounter was dialogic. He was himself a new white subject, and critical to the construction of a new identity, the colonizer who rejected slavery but believed in empire. Jamaica became for him a more likely utopia than Britain. Slaves and freed men proved far more receptive to the Christian message than Englishmen. The Christian message he preached became marked by the new world he had seen. Knibb's dream was transported back to England by Joseph Sturge and fed his vision of a more co-operative and egalitarian society.[51] As C. L. R. James argued in *The Black Jacobins*, metropolitan politics were shaped by the colonies; the colonial encounter never worked only one way despite the unequal relations of power.[52]

Knibb's vision was of a harmonious racially mixed society which would operate like a family and be led by missionaries. "Children are we all of one great Father", claimed those missionaries.[53] The metaphor of the universal family of man was a critical one, for it contained both equality and difference. Black people were both the same and different from white people, women were both the same and different from men. Families were places of love, affection and belonging, but they were also sites of authority, regulation and discipline where children were trained for the grown-up world. Colonial encounters, whether between soldiers and rebels, colonial officials and supplicants, planters and cane workers, or pastors and their congregations, were always articulated through relations of power, across the axes of "race", class, ethnicity, gender and sexuality. The familial metaphor eloqently captures the uneven and ambivalent nature of the particular encounter between radical abolitionist missionaries and their Afro-Jamaican flocks. All belonging to the same organism, yet with their particular places, all having the capacity to grow and change, yet with the authority of the father firmly in place.

In 1845 Knibb died. His death symbolized the death of a particular "great experiment", that of creating a new moral world in Jamaica, peopled by Baptists and led by missionaries. His power and charisma had held together a vision which did not survive his death. The new Black subjects he had envisaged were less industrious and domesticated than he would have liked. The new-style colonizers could not displace the old, whose power was maintained, albeit in different ways. The decline of sugar production brought economic distress: the power of the missionaries declined, their congregations split, their leadership was rejected and Native Baptists flourished. The identities constituted in this transitional moment could not hold. In Britain the new Black subject, briefly encountered in abolitionist discourse, in their meetings and their literature, was transposed into more familiar stereotypes, re-worked for the 1850s: the oppressed and misguided victim of the plantocracy, the dupe of misguided Black leaders, or "the nigger" of Carlyle's fevered imagination. The moment of a new Jamaican nation, marking a new kind of contract between colonizer and colonized, was over. For the British the island could only be a colony, ruled from "home".

Notes

1   This essay is part of a longer project to be published as *Civilising subjects: the place of "race" and empire in the English imagination 1830–1867* (Cambridge, forthcoming). I am grateful to the Economic and Social Research Council which funded this research between 1990 and 1992 and to the Nuffield Foundation for the fellowship which they awarded me in 1995–6. Thanks to Gail Lewis for her comments on this essay.

2   Frantz Fanon, *Black skin, white masks* (London, 1986). On the relation between culture and imperialism see Edward W. Said, *Orientalism* (Harmondsworth, 1985); *Culture and imperialism* (London, 1993). For a critique of the new histories of imperialism and their focus on cultural identities see P. J. Marshall, *Imperial Britain* (London, 1994).

3   Stuart Hall, "Who needs 'identity'?", in *Questions of cultural identity*, Stuart Hall & Paul du Gay (eds) (London, 1996).

4   The phrase is Ann Laura Stoler's, *Race and the education of desire: Foucault's* History of Sexuality *and the colonial order of things* (Durham, N.C., 1995).

5   On this period see particularly Thomas C. Holt, *The problem of freedom: race, labor and politics in Jamaica and Britain 1832–1838* (Baltimore, 1992); William A. Green, *British slave emancipation. The sugar colonies and the great experiment 1830–1865* (Oxford, 1976).

6   *The Baptist Herald and Friend of Africa*, 17 February 1841.

7   For an introduction to some of the key debates see David Brion Davis, *The problem of slavery in the age of revolution* (Ithaca, N.Y., 1975); Robin Blackburn, *The overthrow of colonial slavery* (London, 1988). On slaves and missionaries in Demerara and Jamaica see Emilia Viotti Da Costa, *Crowns of glory, tears of blood. The Demerara slave rebellion of 1823* (Oxford, 1994); Mary Turner, *Slaves and missionaries. The disintegration of Jamaican slave society, 1787–1834* (Urbana, Ill., 1982).

8   John Howard Hinton, *Memoir of William Knibb, missionary in Jamaica* (London, 1847), pp. 6–7. There is a considerable amount of writing on Knibb. See particularly Turner, *Slaves and missionaries*; Philip Wright, *Knibb "the notorious". Slaves' missionary 1803–1845* (London, 1973); Catherine Hall, *White, male and middle class: explorations in feminism and history* (Cambridge, 1992) Chap. 9; "White visions, black lives: the free villages of Jamaica", *History Workshop* 36, Autumn, 1993 pp. 100–32.

9   Hinton, *Memoir*, p. 9.

10 *Ibid.*, pp. 19, 21, 29.

11 "William Knibb's journal of his first voyage to Jamaica", BMS Archive, Angus Library, Regent's Park College Oxford, WI/3.

12 Hinton, *Memoir*, pp. 45–6.

13 *Ibid.*, pp. 48–9.

14 *Ibid.*, p. 75.

15 Turner, *Slaves and missionaries*, Chap. 6.

16 *Ibid.*, p. 21.

17 CO 137/179, July–Dec. 1831, Belmont to Goderich, 23 August 1831, and Goderich to Belmont. See Philip Wright's chapter on 'Deacon Swiney' in *Knibb*, pp. 41–55.

18 CO 137/180, Offices and Individuals, 1831, Bridges to Goderich 5 May 1831; George Wilson Bridges, *The annals of Jamaica*, first published 1828 [2 vols] (London, 1968), vol. 2, p. 268.

19 Wright, *Knibb*, pp. 51–2.

20 Bridges, *Annals*, vol. 2, pp. 294, 301.

21 J. R. Ward, *British West Indian slavery, 1750–1834* (Oxford, 1988), p. 2.

22 See Turner, *Slaves and missionaries*, and Robert J. Stewart, *Religion and society in post-emancipation Jamaica* (Knoxville, Tenn., 1992).

23 Edward Long's use of the name 'Quashie' brought it into common use. See Edward Long the history of Samaica [3 vols] (London, 1774). Horace O. Russell, "The emergence of the Christian Black. The making of a Stereotype", *Jamaica Journal* **16**(1) February 1983.

24 Select committee on the extinction of slavery throughout the British dominions, House of Commons, 1831–2, vol. 20, August 1832, p. 2.

25 Select committee on the state of the West India colonies, House of Lords, 127, vols 11 and 12; 1831–2, vol. 11, p. iii.

26 Select committee, House of Commons, p. 4.

27 Select committee, House of Lords, vol. 11, p. 629.

28 Hinton, *Knibb*, p. 145.

29 Select committee, House of Commons, p. 254.

30 *Ibid.*, p. 268.

31 Select committee, House of Lords, vol. 12, p. 776.

32 Hinton, *Knibb*, p. 154.

33 *Ibid.*, p. 155.

34 William Knibb, *Speech on the immediate abolition of British colonial slavery* (Newcastle, 1833), p. 13.

35 Select committee, House of Lords, vol. 12, pp. 774, 757, 767, 776; Select committee, House of Commons, pp. 271, 273, 278.

36 Select committee, House of Commons, pp. 271, 273.

37 *The history of Mary Prince a West Indian slave, narrated by herself* (first published 1831), ed. Moira Ferguson (London, 1987).

38 Stewart, *Religion and society*, p. xvii.

39 Henry Richard, *Memoirs of Joseph Sturge* (London, 1864); Alex Tyrrell, *Joseph Sturge and the moral radical party in early Victorian Britain* (London, 1987).

40 Rev. F. A. Cox, *History of the Baptist Missionary Society* [2 vols] (London, 1842), vol. 2, pp. 248–52.

41 Cox, *History*, vol. 2, pp. 252–4; *Falmouth Post*, 15 August 1838.

42 *Baptist Herald*, 26 October 1839.

43 *Ibid.*, 28 September 1839.

44 *Parliamentary Papers 1839*, XXXVI, Feb–Aug 1839, 523, part 1, Jamaica, Enclosure 50 in no. 29, p. 147.

45 *Baptist Herald*, 13 May 1840.

46 *Ibid.*, 8 January 1840.

47 *Ibid.*, 4 March 1840.

48 *Ibid.*, 29 August 1840.

49 *Ibid.*, 6 January 1841.

50 On the construction of English middle-class manliness and femininity in this period, see Leonore Davidoff and Catherine Hall, *Family fortunes: men and women of the English middle class 1780–1850* (London, 1987), especially Part 1.

51 Tyrrell, *Joseph Sturge,* especially "White and black slaves".

52 C. L. R. James, *The Black Jacobins. Toussaint L'Ouverture and the San Domingo revolution* (New York, 1963).

53 The quote is from James Mursell Phillippo's *Jamaica: its past and present state* (London, 1843), p. 150.

Chapter Sixteen

"When the saints came marching in": the Anti-Slavery Society and Indian indentured migration to the British Caribbean

Madhavi Kale

I am sure that the House will feel the necessity of observing some analogy and proportion in its method of dealing with different questions, and with the several classes of her Majesty's subjects. Compare the child of nine yrs old – and some say, under – entering your factories to work eight hours a day – and some say, more – for a livelihood, with the child of nine years old [sic] in British Guiana, supported without labour by the proprietors of the soil. What shall we say of the Irish peasant with his six-pence a day; of the handloom-weeaver [sic] with his four shillings a-week? – what shall those of us who have such poor constituents say to them, when next we go among them, and see their wasted frames stooping to their toil for twelve or fourteen hours in the day to procure a bare subsistence, when we tell them we have no aid to afford them, but that we have been busy in rescuing from his seven-and-a-half daily hours the negro of British Guiana, who can employ his extra time at the rate of three shillings and sixpence, or four shillings a-day? (William E. Gladstone, 1838)[1]

In June 1840, the British and Foreign Anti-Slavery Society (BFASS) convened the first World Convention on Anti-Slavery at Exeter Hall, London. At the same time, parliament was considering the Bill proposed by the Whig government and endorsed by Colonial Secretary John Russell for lifting a ban it had imposed on indentured migration from India to Mauritius in 1838.[2] When Stephen Lushington reported on the last day of the Convention that Russell's Bill had been defeated the previous evening, it was proclaimed a victory in the cause that had brought together the scores of delegates from the British empire, France, and the United States. For this success, Lushington told the Convention, "we must all congratulate each other, all be thankful to Providence, that for the present, at least, a stop has been put to what I conceive to be little less than the renewal of the traffic in man."[3]

Ostensibly because they feared abolition would provoke debilitating labour shortages, a few metropolitan owners of sugar plantations in British Guiana had sought indentured workers from British India as early as 1836 – that is, less than two years after abolition. Unabashedly suspicious of West Indian plant- ers' motives in seeking Indian indentured labourers, the BFASS mobilized colonial knowledge on India to oppose the migration to Mauritius and British Guiana in this period.[4] They argued that the very conditions that made Indian indentured workers attractive to some colonial plantation owners – poverty, ignorance of where and how far they would be going and of the conditions of life and labour they would encounter there, vagueness of provisions for redress of grievances and return to India – made them peculiarly vulnerable to the wiles of unscrupulous recruiters and employers, and incapable of respon- sibly entering into long-term labour contracts with employers overseas. They also argued that introducing Indian labourers would contribute to corrupting the eminently corruptible morals of those freed people with whom they would come into contact – especially if male migrants outnumbered women as dramatically as they had in the now-suspended migration to Mauritius. Finally, they argued, introducing Indian workers (duped, kidnapped, cheated as they were and would inevitably be) would disrupt establishment of free labour in the sugar colonies, hamper the progress of civilization there and compromise the Great Experiment itself, on which the British nation had staked its reputation and £20 million.[5] Daniel O'Connell, Irish MP and crusader for Irish and Catholic rights in the empire, captured the BFASS position on Indian indentured migration when he declared at the Conven- tion, "I am fully persuaded that you might as well proclaim the slave-trade again as proclaim the admission of the Hill Coolies into our West India colonies; and I am equally convinced that the planters in the Mauritius are the worst guardians that could be appointed to protect these labourers. I would rather be a part to the total annihilation of that unfortunate race, than to their being subjected to a new species of slavery" (p. 383).

While such anti-indenture efforts and sentiments were successful in the short run, the migration to Mauritius was resumed in 1843, expanded to include Trinidad, British Guiana and Jamaica in 1845, and other colonies in the Caribbean, Africa and the Pacific in the next forty years before it was finally abolished during the First World War. By 1843, when the BFASS convened the second World Anti-Slavery Convention, the British abolitionist opposition to Indian indentured migration had splintered, as disagreement over proposals to eliminate tariff protections for British colonial sugar – often expressed in terms of the relative and competing claims to abolitionist sympathies of British working-class consumers and colonial working-class producers – polarized anti-slavery opinion and strained the anti-slavery leadership's credibility.[6] By 1843, ostensibly because Caribbean and Mauritian plantation owners' resistance to free labour threatened the success of British emancipation and the prospects for eliminating slavery elsewhere in the world (most notably Cuba, Brazil and the United States South), some British abolitionists had concluded that "East Indian" labour, duly regulated by colonial and imperial governments, might rescue the Great Experiment and the anti-slavery cause.

The minutes of the 1840 Convention suggest how empire enabled the BFASS to manage this compromise and the contradictions generated by their gendered and race-inflected assumptions about labour, as well as their abolitionist objectives and strategies. The minutes of the Convention suggest that the divisions among British anti-slavery activists over the course the BFASS ought to take in the wake of emancipation in the British Caribbean, Mauritius and the Cape Colony were informed by competing visions of the custodial obligations and moral and material opportunities afforded by empire. This essay presents four moments in the proceedings of the 1840 World Anti-Slavery Convertion that highlight the crucial significance of empire and capitalism to British anti-slavery thought in the post-emancipation period and the ongoing significance of anti-slavery critiques of both to the emergence of an imperial division of labour anchored in notions of racial/national hierarchy and patriarchal domesticity.[7]

"With his wife in her proper place and the Bible on the table"

A primary objective of the first World Anti-Slavery Convention was to develop strategies and resources for the ongoing campaign to eliminate slavery throughout the world, most particularly in Spanish and French colonies in the Americas, in the United States and Brazil. In the course of the first day's proceedings, committees were appointed to review the condition and state of knowledge on various issues considered of significance to the problem of slavery and its eradication. On the seventh day of the Convention, the first moment on which I focus in this essay, the committee on free labour presented its evaluation of the progress of free labour in the British Caribbean, Mauritius and Cape Colony, planters' efforts to limit its success (through evictions from houses and provision grounds, legislative actions that sought to limit freed people's mobility within and between colonies, and so on), and the best means for protecting and further amplifying the advances made. The report argued that, unfettered by restrictions imposed by a reactionary plantocracy, the production of sugar under free labour would bring about an end to slave-production of sugar in Cuba and Brazil where it was then flourishing. The report sought to turn accounts of diminished British Caribbean sugar output since emancipation to the advantage of the anti-slavery cause. It argued that scarcity and higher prices would accelerate sugar production under free labour in those parts of the world where conditions were suitable and the soil not yet exhausted by years of excessive cultivation, thus increasing supply and lowering prices, and in the longer term undermining sugar industries based on slavery and the slave trade. The committee identified Trinidad, British Guiana, and British India as the crucial sites for such take-off and redemption.[8]

Sounding remarkably like leading planters and advocates for immigration in Trinidad and British Guiana, this committee of abolitionists had noted that in these two Caribbean colonies, "there is a vast extent of unoccupied land of almost boundless fertility, sufficient to grow sugar for the whole world. In these colonies, the cultivation is at present immensely profitable, and labour is in such great demand, that there is reason to believe the planters would grant us any concession or securities we can ask, if we will only aid them in obtaining it".[9] The committee added that, while "we deprecate the introduction of ignorant and helpless beings" from India and Africa to these British Caribbean colonies, they felt that "if a sufficient guarantee can be obtained for securing entire freedom, and equal rights to free black immigrants from our other West India colonies, and the United States of America, immense advantage would ensue", and that while getting these would be difficult, it would not be impossible.[10] They went on to say that such free immigration, once started, would continue to the benefit of all concerned: immigrants, planters, and benevolent citizens of the empire. "Thanks to the efforts of our missionaries", they continued, free immigrants from other West Indian colonies as well as from the United States "would reach the shores of British Guiana, intelligent, and civilized, and christianized". There, improved cultivation technology and techniques would soon make immigrant labour "productive beyond example". Sugar would be raised in

> unlimited quantity, and at a price which, after a fair profit to the planter, would still be low enough to undersell in all the markets of Europe, the blood-stained produce of Cuba and the Brazils [sic]. If there be any truth

in the principles we have endeavoured to explain, the transport of human beings to these charnel houses of death would then cease, as it would no longer repay the risks of the passage. The slave-trade would thus be at an end, and as the competition of free labour held on its course, these nations would ultimately relinquish slavery itself.[11]

Trinidad and British Guiana, along with India, were central to the drama outlined above: they were at the crux of BFASS agendas for ending slavery worldwide.

After the report of the committee on free labour had been read, the Reverend William Knibb, a British Baptist missionary who had lived and worked since the mid-1820s among Jamaican slaves, apprentices and free Blacks, addressed the gathered abolitionists. Bitterly rejecting the defamatory accounts of freed people's post-emancipation behaviour circulated in the colonial and metropolitan press by planters and their sympathizers, Knibb took this opportunity "to clear the character of my brethren, the negroes, who cannot speak for themselves, from the aspersions which are continually cast upon them".[12] Knibb noted with concern that the free labour committee's report and the debate it had so far generated had focused on the record and prospects for post-abolition sugar production, and on how best to persuade stubborn planters who did not recognize their own best interest, of the abolitionist tenet that free labour was bound to out-perform slave labour. Under the circumstances, he said, it was left to him to show that, along with plantation-owners, "those most interested in emancipation, the suffering negroes", had also benefited from emancipation, despite the malicious efforts of the very men to whose reason and self-interest the free labour committee's report had appealed.

For Knibb, the success of emancipation would have to be measured by freed people's socialization to the roles and places he and his associates envisioned for and assigned them. Knibb told the Convention that in Jamaica, contrary to planters' claims, "emancipation has produced an increase of morality, social order, and domestic happiness". He reported that the "brethren" with whom he was involved had "since freedom came, celebrated nearly six thousand marriages. Many have said, 'Now our wives and children will be our own, and the lash will no more torture them'".[13] He argued, "if we can prove that his morality, his virtue, his industry, his every comfort has been improved, we prove all that we need in reference to this great object". Knibb's description of the good society is captured in the images of the single-family home (founded in those six thousand marriages performed since emancipation) and the free village, several of which had been developed under Baptist patronage and guidance, and sometimes named after prominent English abolitionists like Buxton, Sturge and Wilberforce, or after Queen Victoria. Knibb recalled for his audience one such village he had visited before he left Jamaica, where a handful of houses had been built, and where "I saw the man there with his wife in her proper place, and the Bible on the table. 'Step in', said they, 'Mr. Knibb, and sit down and see how happy we are'".[14] Knibb insisted that both the moral and the material bases of freedom in the British West Indies lay in the patriarchal peasant household – the very unit that, according to leading sugar planters, would ruin colonies like Trinidad and British Guiana and threaten colonial society if it were allowed to develop.[15]

Knibb sought to steer the Convention toward his perspective, invoking the philanthropy of the "Saints" who had worked so long and hard to end the horrors of the slave trade, and the perversions of slavery, and reminding them that "It is not with us a matter of pounds, shillings, and pence, but of stern principle, and to this we must come, and by this issue we must abide."[16] He argued that "we have in the emancipation of the peasantry in the West Indies, the foundation of that independence which alone can secure permanent prosperity". He invited the gathered abolitionists to Jamaica, where he and his associates and brethren would take them to "the freeman's cot, to the freeman's house, to the freeman's castle, where the Petty Debt Act cannot reach him for unjust and iniquitous rent [and] where the Ejectment Act cannot take hold of him, because he does not choose to work for less than labour is worth".[17]

In thus asserting freed men's right to participate in establishing the market price of their labour, Knibb enunciated a radical free labour position that challenged some abolitionists' approach to the wages, conditions and demands of labourers in their own shops and factories – as William Gladstone had pointed out in his speech against early termination of the apprenticeship in 1838 (see note 1). However radical this particular proposition may have been, Knibb (like the rest of the delegates to the Convention) remained committed to gender- and race-inflected social hierarchy. That he assigned freed men in Jamaica a role subordinate to his, and freed women a role subordinate to them, is abundantly clear in his language and assignment of roles, not only to freed people, but also to himself and his audience. He passionately proclaimed that "there does not exist, under the canopy of heaven, a more industrious, more orderly, more peaceful peasantry than those *things* whom you have made *men*".[18] Knibb concluded his narrative of the ordeal of free labour in Jamaica by once again invoking his authority to speak for the colony's newly emancipated people: "In the name of 300,000 negroes in Jamaica, I return you all the thanks which grateful hearts, which happy wives and children can give, surrounded by all the domestic comforts which their husbands and fathers feel proud to impart."[19]

"Keeping up a supply of sugar"

The second moment I present here immediately followed Knibb's speech. Responding to Knibb, Stephen Lushington agreed that the Convention should persuade the imperial government to ensure that the laws passed in British Caribbean colonies were just and impartially administered. He worried, however, that it was beyond the power of the BFASS and the Convention to effect the changes in social attitudes and values that would make it possible to successfully implement Knibb's programme for post-emancipation development in the British Caribbean. He argued that abolitionists' only influence lay in revealing the impediments introduced by the old plantocracy to the operation of free labour, and in successfully demonstrating its superiority over slave labour. Knowing, he observed, "that the world at large are not impressed with the same convictions that abolitionists entertain", he was most anxious "to find continuous labour throughout our colonies in the production of sugar". Endorsing Knibb's portrait of the positive social effects of emancipation in Jamaica, Lushington warned him to remember the horrors of the slave trade, and begged Knibb to "bend his efforts upon all just and fair principles, to the encouragement of the home growth of sugar". He added that "considering the enormous demand for sugar in this country compared with the supply, and knowing the feeling which pervades the minds of so many elsewhere", he feared that failure to maintain the level of supply would give further impetus to the Brazilian and Cuban sugar industries, and to the slave trades and slavery on which they were based.[20]

The response of subsequent speakers to Lushington's plea on behalf of British consumers and victims of the transatlantic slave trade overwhelmingly favoured the free labour committee's development agenda for the British Caribbean colonies (staple-crop production for a world market) over the kind of peasant subsistence production that Knibb envisioned, even as they further sanctified those notions of domesticity – with the wife in her proper place and the Bible on the table – he had enunciated.[21] The settlement negotiated between the internationally-minded wing of the BFASS and the Convention, and those more particularly focused on the British Caribbean colonies and the condition and prospects of their emancipated populations, is best represented by Daniel O'Connell ("the Great Emancipator"). He told the delegates and audience in Exeter Hall that other governments needed to be assured that abolishing slavery was "safe", and that the only proof that would be sufficiently convincing was the continued, preferably expanded, production of sugar in the post-emancipation British Caribbean colonies:

> Free labour in abundance affords the only chance of the experiment working well; but you cannot have free-labour in abundance, because the planters in Jamaica calculate upon the labour of both sexes in the field, while the negroes with great propriety keep their wives at home in their proper province, to attend to the domestic concerns of the family. . . . There is, therefore, naturally a decrease in the quantity of labour there; and how can it be supplied? Only by healthful emigration from North America, where the free negro is treated with unbecoming indignity, and by none treated worse than by my own unhappy countrymen, who having suffered persecution, ought to have learned mercy. The only prospect we have of keeping up a supply of sugar, equal to the consumption of this island, is by encouraging emigration.[22]

Inadvertently echoing John Gladstone – William's father who was the first to introduce Indian labourers to his plantations in British Guiana in 1837 and with a bow to Knibb, O'Connell placed the ordeal of free labour in the British Caribbean squarely in its multiple, overlapping and mutually constitutive gender, race, national and imperial contexts.

Immigration, even indentured immigration, was not in itself what these British abolitionists objected to. They agreed with planters that immigration could solve problems of underproduction in some British Caribbean sugar colonies – but only if prospective migrants could be trusted to enter the contracts voluntarily and fully understanding the rights and responsibilities these engendered. Representations of Indian indentured migration called into question Indian recruits' ability to take on these responsibilities – indeed, as I have shown elsewhere, some abolitionists argued that the very fact that thousands of Indian men had migrated to Mauritius without their wives and children proved how intrinsically unreliable and irresponsible they were.[23] A particular gender division of labour was being naturalized not only for the conjugal family, but also for the imperial family of nations and races, where those with labour power to sell were not equally free to do so – as supporters of Indian indentured migration were quick to point out.[24]

"They have retained in chains, those whom they found in chains"

The third moment, moving back in time, comes from the second day of the Convention, when Professor Adam of Cambridge, Massachusetts, had given a paper on the condition of slavery in British India. In Adam's account, Hindu and Muslim custom, and the British East India Company (EIC), emerged as the prime architects of Indian slavery. He argued that while slavery was allowed under both Hindu and Muslim law, the circumstances under which it was considered legal under the latter were limited to conquered infidels and their descendants, and that the bulk of the approximately one million slaves in India did not meet this criterion, and were therefore, according to Muslim law itself, illegally enslaved. Adam argued that, in effect, slavery had been made legal in British India "by a doubtful interpretation of [Muslim] law, the spirit of which is supposed to embrace slavery, and the letter of which is acknowledged to be wholly silent on the subject. It is by means of this confessedly doubtful, and it is believed wholly erroneous, interpretation, that the entire system of East India slavery has been perpetuated under the British government . . . [and] illegal custom has been invested by the British government of India, with the desecrated forms and sanctions of law and justice".[25] Adam recommended that the only remedy was immediate abolition of slavery in India, noting caustically that it would be "safe for the government" of British India to do this, "for all experience shows that danger to the government has arisen only from innovations introduced for the increase of revenue, while no danger can be shown to have ever arisen from innovations, such as this would be, plainly tending to, and designed for, the welfare of the people". Adam added that Mauritius and Demerara planters' innovations with Indian indentured labour were "merely another form" of the slave trade.[26]

Familiarly, India emerges in Adam's report as a place to be rescued, cultivated, civilized, itself emancipated from the thralldom of Muslim and Hindu pasts. More interesting than these familiar representations is the context in which Adam enunciates them and their effects in this forum. Adam's report, presented on the second day of this first international Anti-Slavery Convention, laid the groundwork for an anti-slavery vision of imperial obligation and resources that temporarily managed dissension among abolitionists. Abolishing slavery in India and expanding production there of sugar, cotton, and indigo cultivation through free labour was seen to solve several problems at once. The blot on British national philanthropy would be removed, while production of sugar and cotton through free labour could be tested without the burdens of planter nostalgia for slavery. Cash-crop production in British India under conditions of free labour and British imperial administration, and the vigilant eyes of British citizenry, would not only lift the veil of ignorance, poverty and despotic custom under which India languished but also redeem British enterprise in India and accelerate the end of Cuban, Brazilian and American slavery by proving once and for all the superior cost-efficiency and productivity of free labour. As Joseph Sams put it, if the British, "as a nation, were to use only free labour produce, it would be one of the severest blows which could possibly be given to slavers. Our fellow-subjects, the natives of British India are exceedingly oppressed; and I think measures might be adopted by the Convention, which, while they went even to destroy slavery, would tend very materially to their benefit".[27]

Amplifying Adam's criticism of the Indian and imperial governments, Joseph Pease of Darlington told the Convention that slavery was flourishing in India not because British legislators and ministers were unaware of it, but because "the government of this country has profited by the continuance of the system". He added that all could yet be set to right if more land were brought under cultivation, and if the government were to ease the revenue demands it made on Indian cultivators:

> Sufficient evidence upon the subject was taken in the committee of the House of Commons; it was proved that the land-tax was most oppressive, leading to want and starvation, and compelling millions to become slaves for a long series of years. I have stated these things before the Directors of the East India Company, and now hope that the statements made will go forth to the country, and that abundance of petitions will be sent in to Parliament, praying that one-third of the land, which is now in possession of wild beasts, may be brought into cultivation, that the wants of the human population may meet an adequate supply.[28]

Three further speakers then moved that the committee appointed to make recommendations for action to the convention be authorized to "turn minutely to the state of British India", and its government. The chairman of the day's proceedings summarily rejected this proposal, arguing that the Convention would "gain nothing by mixing up the subjects".[29] However, the next several days of debate and discussion would prove him wrong. Indian slavery, mis-government of India by the East India Company, the ordeal of free labour in the British West Indies, the threat of competition from Cuban and Brazilian slave-produced sugars and increasingly insistent demands from metropolitan British consumers for cheaper sugar, the dilemma posed by the British textile industry's reliance on American slave-produced cotton, the Convention's commitment to ending slavery and the slave trade throughout the world, and the imperatives of capitalism were inextricably entangled in delegates' understanding of the challenges they faced, and the strategies they proposed for attacking them.

When the committee on Indian slavery presented its report a few days later, it accepted and reiterated Adam's argument that the EIC had resurrected and legalized a moribund and practically illegal condition in its administration of Indian laws. The committee condemned both the EIC and the imperial government for this, noting especially that in the very year when slavery had been abolished in Mauritius, the British West Indies and the Cape Colony, a clause that had been in an early draft of the 1833 charter renewal bill, requiring abolition of slavery in British India by 12 August 1837, was eliminated from the final version that was passed by parliament, and replaced by one calling for amelioration and gradual abolition, "as soon as such extinction shall be practicable and safe", and by the stipulation that a committee would be appointed to determine how the end of slavery in British India could best be pursued. The committee on Indian slavery echoed Adam and Pease in concluding that, under these circumstances, it was "for the British nation to direct their immediate attention to this important subject, and to seek the immediate and entire abolition of personal slavery throughout the whole of British India".[30]

As discussion of Indian slavery proceeded, the British nation was simultaneously distanced from the British imperial state and the special interests that sought to influence it (monopoly and privilege, favourite free-trade foes) and assimilated to BFASS and its agendas and assumptions. BFASS emerged in its members' discussions as the active embodiment of civic virtue, the voice and conscience, the nerve-centre of civil society. The state was corrupt or at least eminently corruptible (and this comes through in all BFASS publications and pronouncements of its leadership), but the virtuous citizenry, animated by spirits of Christian justice and humanity, were not.[31] The state's corruptibility by privilege was brought home to delegates by the Rev. James Peggs of Bourne, who had been a missionary in Orissa, and had just published *The present state of East India slavery, chiefly derived from the Parliamentary Papers on the subject*. He made the Duke of Wellington the instigator, and the House of Lords the site where the slavery abolition clause was removed from the 1833 EIC Charter renewal bill. Peggs charged Wellington with having abused the authority to interpret and represent India that was accorded him by Britons on the strength of his years in the subcontinent when he assured his fellow-peers that the anti-slavery clause was unnecessary, saying, "I have served in that country, and lived among the people, and I never knew an instance of cruelty being practiced towards the slaves, if slaves they ought to be called".[32]

Clearly, in 1833 there had been some ambiguity and disagreement about what constituted slavery – and what constituted empire.[33] Parliament had recognized as slavery the perpetually heritable condition of legal bondage under which large proportions of transported and creole Africans in the Caribbean lived, and voted to end the legal condition throughout the British empire. Freedom was defined as slavery's opposite: as the absence of the legal conditions that characterized servile status.[34] Yet, in the same year, parliament agreed not to require abolition of what appeared to be a similar condition in India, on the authority of an architect of British empire in India and a peer of the realm, who defined slavery by cruelty, which he associated with the systems of the British Caribbean, and not with bondage in India. Wellington recognized, and persuaded parliament to recognize, degrees of unfreedom – at least in India, which though governed by Britons was not yet part of Britain's empire – when abolitionists were insisting there were only the absolute, mutually constitutive conditions and opposite poles of slavery and freedom. In calling attention to the problem of slavery in British India, the British abolitionists who organized the 1840 World Anti-Slavery Convention joined in the chorus challenging the ambiguous position of British India and the privileged position of the East India Company in the British empire. This anti-slavery annexation of India to the British empire helped to contain the inconsistencies and contradictions that threatened to overwhelm anti-slavery as a free-labour ideology palatable to the employers and patriarchal heads of household who formed the bulk of the BFASS membership, and make it an emancipatory political one that threatened the bases of their authority.[35] However, such a strategy had its own contradictions and hazards, and negotiating these further involved BFASS members and other delegates in enunciating and ascribing national as well as racial, class, and gender categories and identities.

Responding to an American delegate's comment, Reverend R. R. R. Moore complained that it was unfair to say the British were not abolitionists "because we cannot get rid of East India slavery". After all, he said, "In order to effect it, we must go to the East India Company, and they must consult Mohammedans and Hindoos." In effect, Moore blamed Indian culture and customs for slavery, downplaying the role that the East India Company had been assigned in its perpetuation by Adam, Pease and others. He added, by way of explanation, that "A slave in the East Indies belongs to a servile caste, and is, therefore, much oppressed. He cannot approach within 50 or 60 yards of a man of a higher caste".[36] Abolishing slavery, some argued, would have little practical effect, and while the convention and the BFASS should continue to raise the issue of Indian slavery with the public, in parliament and with Her Majesty's Government, they should also attend to the implications of freedom for people with no means of subsistence/support beyond the patronage of their masters. Pease argued that abolition had to be sustainable and that the only way to do that was to bring under cultivation the third of the subcontinent still given over to "wild beasts". He added that if this were done, "You would then, by free labour, be able to produce such a supply of cotton and rice, as would put down slavery and the slave-trade throughout the world".[37] Again, the East Indies would redeem the West.[38] Another delegate added that climatic and political conditions combined with moral imperatives made India an ideal laboratory for decisively proving the abolitionist article of faith that free labour was more productive and efficient than slave labour, and thus a site of redemption for both the freed people of the British Caribbean and their abolitionist supporters, and an endless source of sugar for English consumers and working classes. Held hostage by the short-sighted machinations of the old plantocracy, free labour would be redeemed through another act of abolition. India would redeem the British Caribbean – but not through migration of indentured labourers from one to the other, as had been proposed by Gladstone and his associates in Demerara.

"The whole tide of benevolence . . . stopped by a straw"

Still moving back in time, the final moment comes from the first day of the Convention. On that day, Wendell Phillips, an American abolitionist from Massachusetts, had introduced a motion questioning the BFASS's decision not to recognize the credentials of the American women delegated by their anti-slavery societies to represent them at the Convention. Phillips argued that the BFASS's invitation had been issued to "friends of anti-slavery" everywhere, and that in the United States, this had been assumed to include women abolitionists, as well as men. Professor Adam, who would present his paper on slavery in British India the following day, seconded his motion, noting that since his own credentials proceeded from the very societies that had appointed the excluded women, he could not proceed as a delegate if theirs were not recognized.[39] The gendered assumptions on which Adams, Knibb, Lushington, O'Connell and all other speakers built their cases had not only been challenged on the first day of the Convention, but were recognized as having been so challenged by the men who spoke for and against Phillips' motion. These speeches illuminate the ways freedom was being cast at the Convention as a patriarchal virtue and privilege, rooted in bourgeois notions of domesticity and its gendered hierarchies and division of labour.[40]

On that opening day, Reverend J. Burnet warned the assembled abolitionists that "the Convention itself is imperiled in this discussion", and he pleaded with them to "take a calm and deliberate view of the question – one of the most important that can be discussed in connexion with the mere forms of this Convention".[41] The motion, along with the calls for recognizing the American women abolitionists' claim to equal representation at this anti-slavery convention, was amended and evaded in the long run, but not before abolitionist men had enunciated the gender and national frameworks with which their variously hierarchical, free-labour ideologies were articulated.

English abolitionists who opposed Phillips' motion implicitly claimed national seniority over – even paternity to – their American counterparts when they insisted that the latter respect local custom and usage. Burnet argued that "our American friends would add another laurel to those they have already reaped in the Anti-Slavery field, amid their deep self-denial and great suffering, were they to say at this moment, 'Let us not make shipwreck of our vessel, let us, not even for a moment, put her in a perilous sea. As we are in England let us act as England does; and when English abolitionists come to America, we shall expect the same ready conformity'". He insisted, presumably calmly and firmly, that while Phillips and other American abolitionists were entitled to interpret the invitation sent by the BFASS according to their own national custom and usage, the British abolitionists were entitled to proceed with the Convention that they had organized as they had intended, without the introduction of American innovations. He told the delegates that it had never occurred to the BFASS invitation committee that "they were inviting ladies from any part of the globe, to take an essential part in the proceedings of the Convention. It never was contemplated in the formation of the Society; it never was practised in the doings of the Society; it never was intended in the resolutions of the Society".

Burnet further insisted that the BFASS intended no disrespect to the American women whose credentials it refused to recognize, averring that "We place them on a level with our own ladies". He observed, "Our wives and our daughters are in the same position with them. And surely, if they are placed in the same position as the ladies of England, it cannot be said that we have cast indignity upon them".[42] He added, for the benefit of those who might invoke against his arguments the English precedent and present condition of rule by a queen, that "It is not necessary, because we have a QUEEN, henceforth to clothe all the ladies with office in the general management of our social affairs".[43] The Reverend Elon Galusha of New York echoed Burnet's sentiments on this matter, submitting "to the consideration of our American female friends who are so deeply interested in the subject, the example of your noble QUEEN", who had, "by sanctioning her consort", Prince Albert, to chair an Anti-Slavery meeting, "showed her sense of propriety by putting her Head foremost in an assembly of gentlemen". Speaking for himself, Galusha added, "I have no objection to woman's being the neck to turn the head aright, but do not wish to see her assume the place of the head".[44]

Supporters of Phillips' amendment were quick to point out that custom was, as George Thompson put it, "flimsy" grounds for abolitionist arguments against including women in their proceedings. An American delegate, Bradburn asked the Convention "if it be right to set up the customs and habits, not to say prejudices, of Englishmen, as a standard, for the government, on this occasion, of Americans" and other nationals. He concluded, "I deprecate the principle of this objection. In America it would exclude from our Conventions all persons of colour; for there, customs, habits, tastes, prejudices, would be outraged by *their* admission".[45] This point was reiterated some time later by Ashurst, the radical lawyer and Owenite sympathizer, who asked, "What would be the result of such an argument employed in Virginia? Would they not say that slavery is the custom here, and therefore you have no right to place yourselves in opposition to the prejudices and customs of society in attempting to put it down? . . . You are convened to influence society upon a subject connected with the kindliest feelings of our nature; and being the first assembly met to shake hands with other nations, and employ your combined efforts to annihilate slavery throughout the world, are you to commence by saying, 'we will take away the rights of one-half of creation?'"[46]

Reverend A. Harvey of Glasgow rejected this line of reasoning, saying that, as for Phillips, it was with him "a question of conscience". He continued, "I have certain views in relation to the teaching of the word of God, and of the particular sphere in which woman is to act. I must say, whether I am right in my interpretation of the word of God or not, that my own decided convictions are, if I were to give a vote in favour of females sitting and deliberating in such an assembly as this, that I should be acting in opposition to the plain teaching of the word of God".[47] So it came to this: one man's conscience against another's, and in the interest of unity and advancing the higher cause for which they had convened, the apple of discord was to be voted out of sight and mind, even if it could not be banished from their proceedings. Phillips' motion was dropped, after some further emotional debate and flag-waving. This is not surprising perhaps, but read against this opening day debate, both Knibb's patriarchal visions of freedom and post-emancipation conditions in Jamaica, and their assimilation to other speakers' ends are harder simply to take for granted than they otherwise might be. The "woman question" was embedded in anti-slavery strategies and compromises in this post-emancipation period, and by extension in those involving colonial sugar production and labour, empire and race, as well. The race, class, sex hierarchies embodied in the BFASS's membership and reinforced in the Convention's delegates became synonymous with citizenship, while the people absent or banished from them (whether by oversight or design) were affirmed in their ancillary roles, subjects not citizens.[48]

Conclusion

The expansion of British empire and capitalism constrained and enabled British abolitionists' conflicting strategies for ending slavery, as well as their contradictory enunciations of freedom in the period immediately following emancipation in the British Caribbean, Mauritius and the Cape Colony. The ways the British empire in India was being acquired and consolidated were vexing to British abolitionists who learned from Professor Adam's paper not only that slavery still thrived there, but also that the British East India Company's servants had been complicit in legalizing and perpetuating it. However, the possibilities for abolition of slavery worldwide that India might offer were so enthusiastically advertised by boosters like Adam, Pease, Sams and other interested parties that even American delegates seemed to be persuaded. Obliquely reminding British associates that the British textile industry made cotton King, Wendell Phillips announced, "if we are successful in our present East Indian scheme, we shall terminate American slavery". He added, "It is my conviction that the success of their enterprise in regard to East Indian cotton, has bound up with it the death warrant of slavery, and that [that] is to be signed in Liverpool."[49] The visions of freedom offered by Jamaica-based Reverend Knibb were lost to those abolitionists who looked to the newer British colonies and to free labour and free trade to achieve their common goal of universal abolition.

Some abolitionists agreed with plantation owners trying to recruit Indian workers for British Guiana that Trinidad and British Guiana had the land to produce sugar in abundance, but lacked adequate supplies of labour. They argued, however, that this labour could be recruited from among the op-pressed, Christianized free Black populations of the United States and those Caribbean islands that had more labourers than land on which to employ them. Others proposed that India had both land and labour enough to grow sufficient sugar and cotton not only to meet the demand for both in Britain, but also indeed to prove that free labour was more economical than slavery, and so provoke its speedy demise in Brazil, Cuba and the American South. It would not be too much of a stretch for such British abolitionists to agree, however reluctantly, that perhaps Indian labourers could be transferred to the Caribbean, where so much had already been invested in sugar production, and where the success of the Great Experiment was at stake. As Stephen Lushington observed when he announced the defeat of the Bill to allow again Indian indentured migration to Mauritius:

> Whether the time may come hereafter when it may be of advantage to that large population to emigrate from our territories in Hindostan to other parts of the globe, I will not say; but this I will say, that I trust the hour will not arrive when permission will be granted by the Gov-ernment of this country, for one individual to quit that shore, until there is perfect safety against fraud and kidnapping, until there is security, that

upon their passage they shall be supplied with the necessaries and the conveniences of life, and until upon their landing, they may have justice . . .[50]

When Indian indentured migration resumed in 1843, the concerns enunciated by anti-slavery activists were addressed in the regulations and requirements stipulated in the enabling legislation, and elaborated over the next seventy-odd years of migration not only to Mauritius, British Guiana, Trinidad, and Jamaica, but also to British colonies in Africa and the Pacific and other British, French, and Dutch colonies in the Caribbean. Colonial governments were charged with the responsibilities of ensuring that those poor, rural Indians recruited for overseas plantations understood the terms and conditions of their contracts before they left India, and with impartially enforcing those terms and monitoring those conditions after they had arrived in the sugar colonies. Thus were the queen's Indian subjects freed to enjoy the opportunities of empire: to potentially improve their condition by participating in an imperial labour market, their civilizational "deficiencies" compensated for and immortalized in legislation and archives of empire.

Notes

1 Willian E. Gladstone, "Speech delivered in the House of Commons on the motion . . . for the abolition of the Negro apprenticeship", Friday, 30 March 1838 (London, 1838).

2 See Madhavi Kale, *Fragments of empire: capital, slavery and Indian indentured migration in the British Carbbean* (Philadelphia, 1998), Chapter 1.

3 "Minutes of the World Anti-Slavery Convention, Exeter Hall, London, June 1840" (London, 1840), Stephen Lushington, day 10, 1840.

4 The BFASS had been opposed to Indian indentured migration from the moment it had been reported on by its secretary, John Scoble. The tenor of his criticisms is captured in the title of one of Scoble's pamphlets, *A brief exposure of the deplorable conditions of the hill coolies, in British Guiana and Mauritius, and of the nefarious means by which they were induced to resort to those colonies* (London, 1840).

5 *Anti-Slavery Reporter* **I**(3) (12 February 1840), p. 17; **I**(4) (22 February 1840), p. 25; **I**(5) (11 March 1840), p. 44; "Immigration to Mauritius", "Memorial to the Right Honorable Lord Stanley", and "Petition to the House of Commons", from the British and Foreign Anti-Slavery Society, *Reporter* **III**(5) (9 March 1842): pp. 33, 34–5, 40. Kale, *Fragments of empire*, Chapter 5. "Minutes", p. 383.

6 Debates on "Introduction of slave-grown produce from Cuba and Brazil", and "Emigration from Africa to the British West Indies", Proceedings of the General Anti-Slavery Convention Called by the British and Foreign Anti-Slavery Society and held in London, 13–20 June 1843 (London, 1843), pp. 127–73, 238–64; *Anti-Slavery Reporter* **V**(7) (4 April 1844).

7 This discussion of British abolitionism is indebted to the secondary literature on the topic, especially Eric Williams, *Capitalism and slavery* (London, 1964); Howard Temperley,

British antislavery, 1833–1870 (Chapel Hill, N. C., 1972); Christine Bolt & Seymour Drescher (eds), *Anti-slavery, religion, and reform: essays in memory of Roger Anstey* (Folkestone, 1980); Claire Midgeley, *Women against slavery: the British campaigns, 1780–1870* (New York, 1992); David Turley, *The culture of English antislavery, 1780–1860* (London, 1991); Robin Blackburn, *The overthrow of colonial slavery, 1776–1848* (London, 1988); Thomas C. Holt, *The problem of freedom: race, labor and politics in Jamaica and Britain, 1832–1938* (Baltimore, 1992); Frederick Cooper, *From slaves to squatters: plantation labor and agriculture in Zanzibar and coastal Kenya, 1890–1925* (New Haven, Conn., 1980); John L. Comaroff, "Images of empire, contests of conscience: models of colonial domination in South Africa", in *Tensions of empire: colonial cultures in a bourgeois world*, Frederick Cooper & Ann Laura Stoler (eds) (Ann Arbor, Mich., 1997), pp. 163–97; Susan Thorne, " 'The Conversion of Englishmen and the Conversion of the World Inseparable': missionary imperialism and the language of class in early industrial Britain", in Cooper & Stoler (eds), *Tensions of empire*, pp. 238–62. Students of British abolitionism appear to agree that the movement lost momentum and influence after emancipation and, indeed, some abolitionists publicly worried about this at BFASS's 1843 Anti-Slavery Convention. It seems to me, however, approaching the issue from my research and focus on Indian indentured migration, that their influence was less noticeable after 1838 because at this juncture, the critiques of and accommodations to British capitalism and imperialism they had made earlier in the century became mainstream, the stuff of conventional liberalism.

8   "Minutes", pp. 342–61.

9   For analysis of planters and their associates' positions on labour migration, see Kale, *Fragments of empire*, Chapters 1 and 2, especially the propositions of John Gladstone and William H. Burnley.

10   "Minutes", pp. 360–1.

11   *Ibid.*, p. 361.

12   *Ibid.*, p. 364.

13   *Ibid.*, pp. 365–6.

14   *Ibid.*, p. 368.

15   See, for example, Dowson's and Grant's separate minutes dissenting from the report of the majority of the committee appointed by the Governor of Bengal to investigate allegations of abuse in recruitment of indentured migrants to Mauritius in IOR V/26/820/1–2, "Coolie export enquiry; Dickens committee report, evidence and dissenting minutes" (Calcutta, 1839).

16   "Minutes", p. 364.

17   *Ibid.*, p. 370.

18   *Ibid.*, p. 364: emphasis in original.

19   *Ibid.*, p. 374.

20   *Ibid.*, pp. 379–80.

21   For analysis of colonialism as development, see David Ludden, "India's development regime", in *Colonialism and culture*, Nicholas B. Dirks (ed.) (Ann Arbor, Mich., 1992), pp. 247–88.

22   "Minutes", p. 382.

23   Kale, *Fragments of empire*, Chapter 7.

24   Kale, "Casting labor in the imperial mold: empire and Indian indentured migration to British Guiana and Trinidad, 1836–1910", paper presented at the ISER-NCIC conference *Challenge and change: the Indian diaspora in its historical and contemporary contexts*, University of the West Indies, St. Augustine, Trinidad and Tobago, 13 August 1995. See

also John Kelly, *A politics of virtue: Hinduism, sexuality, and countercultural discourse in Fiji* (Chicago, 1992); and Brij Lal, "Kunti's cry: indentured women on Fiji plantations", *Indian Economic and Social History Review* **22**(1) (January–March 1985), pp. 55–72, and "Veil of dishonour: sexual jealousy and suicide on Fiji plantations", *Journal of Pacific History* **20**(3–4) (July/October 1984); Rhoda Reddock, "Freedom denied: Indian women and indentureship in Trinidad and Tobago 1845–1917", *Economic and Political Weekly* **20**(43) (26 October 1985), pp. 79–87; Patricia Mohammed, "Writing gender into history: the negotiation of gender relations among Indian men and women in post-indenture Trinidad Society, 1917–1947", in *Engendering history: Caribbean women in historical perspective*, V. Shepherd, B. Brereton, B. Bailey (eds) (New York, 1995), pp. 20–47.

25 "Minutes", pp. 80–81.
26 *Ibid.*, p. 86.
27 *Ibid.*, p. 90.
28 *Ibid.*, p. 87.
29 *Ibid.*, p. 90.
30 *Ibid.*, p. 450.
31 See, for example, Lord Brougham's speech in 1838 in the House of Lords condemning Colonial Secretary Glenelg's Order in Council allowing migration from India to the British Caribbean under terms and conditions expressly forbidden by British law for ships leaving Britain; "Speech on Eastern slave trade", 6 March 1838, p. 31.
32 "Minutes", p. 451.
33 Gyan Prakash, *Bonded histories: genealogies of labor servitude in colonial India* (New York, 1990), pp. 8–12, 218–25.
34 David Davis, *The problem of slavery in western culture* (Ithaca N. Y., 1966); Eric Foner, *Nothing but freedom: emancipation and its legacy* (Baton Rouge La., 1983); Blackburn, *The overthrow of colonial slavery*; Holt, *The problem of freedom*, Chapters 1–3; and Prakash, *Bonded histories*.
35 Ambivalence over the Indian empire persisted, however. In the 1843 Convention, John Scoble noted that while the Convention could congratulate themselves on having effected the abolition of slavery in British India, this should not be mistaken for approval of the way India had become British.
36 "Minutes", pp. 453–4.
37 *Ibid.*, p. 453.
38 The reverse flow of benefits was imagined by some observers in later years. In the aftermath of the 1857–9 rebellion in northern India (including regions of most intensive recruitment for indentured labour migration), some Indian and imperial government officials suggested that many rebels might be banished to the British Caribbean colonies to labour on sugar plantations for the remainder of their lives. In 1913, Archdeacon Josa suggested in an article in *Timheri* that since Indian women's prospects improved so dramatically in emigration, the government should encourage it for their sakes. *Timheri* **III**(1) (Sept. 1913), p. 28; see also Kale, *Fragments of empire*, Chapter 7.
39 "Minutes", p. 24.
40 This discussion is informed by: Mary Poovey, *Uneven developments: the ideological work of gender in mid-Victorian England* (Chicago, 1988); Leonore Davidoff & Catherine Hall, *Family fortunes: men and women of the English middle class, 1780–1850* (London, 1987); Judith Walkowitz, *Prostitution and Victorian society: women, class and the state* (New York, 1980); Catherine Hall, "Competing masculinities: Thomas Carlyle, John Stuart Mill and the case of Governor Eyre", pp. 255–95, and "'From Greenland's Icy Mountains . . . to Afric's Golden Sand': ethnicity, race and nation in mid-19th-century England", in *White,*

male and middle class. Explorations in feminism and history (London, 1992); Clare Midgley, *Women against slavery: the British campaigns* (New York, 1992); Moria Ferguson, *Subject to others: British women writers and colonial slavery* (New York, 1992); Lata Mani, "Contentious traditions: the debate on *sati* in colonial India", and Partha Chatterjee, "Nationalist resolution of the woman question", in *Recasting women: essays in Indian colonial history*, Kumkum Sangari and Sudesh Vaid (eds) (New Brunswick, N. J., 1990), pp. 88–126, 233–53; Antoinette Burton, *Burdens of history: British feminists, Indian women and imperial culture, 1865–1915* (Chapel Hill, N. C., 1994); Ann Laura Stoler, "Making empire respectable: the politics of race and sexual morality in twentieth-century colonial cultures", *American Ethnologist* **16**(4), 1989, pp. 634–60; Rhoda Reddock, "Freedom denied"; Patricia Mohammed, "Writing gender into history"; Mrinalini Sinha, *Colonial masculinity: the "manly Englishman" and the "effeminate Bengali" in the late nineteenth century* (Manchester, 1995).

41 "Minutes", p. 26.
42 *Ibid.*
43 *Ibid.*, p. 27.
44 *Ibid.*, p. 28.
45 *Ibid.*, p. 29.
46 *Ibid.*, p. 37.
47 *Ibid.*, p. 38.
48 Hall, *White, male and middle-class.*
49 "Minutes", p 414.
50 *Ibid.*, p. 540.

Chapter Seventeen

North American experience and British missionary encounters in Africa and the Pacific, c. 1800–50

Andrew Porter

The history of Anglo-American relations in many different forms – colonial and constitutional, military, economic, diplomatic, religious and humanitarian – has long been a staple ingredient of historical scholarship in the English-speaking world. The richness of the field is such that it has proved amenable to almost infinite reconsideration and extension. In such circumstances, therefore, it may be foolish to think that there exist significant issues still to be addressed at any length. However, this essentially impressionistic study is designed to consider one area which has apparently been little explored. It focuses on the question of the ways in which North American experience of religious encounter with indigenous peoples, both at home and overseas, influenced British missionary outlooks and enterprise from the 1790s, when the modern missionary movement finally got under way, to the 1840s, when it entered its second great wave of expansion. Equally, although not my purpose in this article, it would be possible to turn the question about, and to enquire into the influence of British experience on North American missions.

Studies of the evangelical revival, of the Great Awakening, and the origins of voluntary lay missionary societies on both sides of the Atlantic, from the Baptist Missionary Society (formed in 1792) to the American Board of Commissioners for Foreign Missions (established in 1810), have not only expanded enormously of late but have made much of the Anglo-American connection.[1] Over the past half-century, they have, not surprisingly, shed much light on the sources of inspiration, the theology, and the personal connections not only of evangelical leaders, like George Whitefield, John Wesley and Thomas Coke, but also the rank and file of what was fundamentally a transatlantic movement.

Recent study of the development of American protestant missionary thought has highlighted the replication in North American debate of those conflicting approaches to the relationship of "Christianity and Civilization" which equally divided British missions.[2] The world of Anglo-American evangelicalism has itself been shown to be part of a still greater Protestant network of influence and personal contacts embracing continental Europe.[3] Work now in progress is revealing much more of the significance of the Moravian Brethren, in bringing together the disparate communities of evangelicals on both sides of the Atlantic, and contributing not only to the global missionary enterprise but to the establishment of the new missionary societies of the 1790s.[4] Historians of religion are now familiar, for instance, with the impetus given by the writings of the Massachusetts pastor, Jonathan Edwards (1703–58), to religious revival and the reassessment of Protestant missions to the non-Christian world. This was not confined to the traditional media of preaching and published sermons or theological commentary. Edwards' publication of the diaries of his prospective son-in-law, David Brainerd, portraying his earnest but less than fruitful struggles to convert the Delaware Indians, became a classic of missionary literature influencing many in both Britain and North America.[5] Even studies of Anglo-American religious divergence serve to illustrate the extent of the interlocking, common religious culture which existed until the 1840s and in many respects well beyond.[6]

However, despite the growth in understanding of the transatlantic evangelical world, still hardly any work seems to exist throwing light on those Anglo-American connections which may either have influenced the development of attitudes to indigenous peoples as the object of missionary endeavours, or have contributed to the interplay of events and experience between one mission field and another. This apparent absence is the more striking because the importance of transatlantic exchanges has been commented on in related areas of study. The work of D. B. Davis, for instance, on western thought about slavery and anti-slavery in the eighteenth and early nineteenth centuries, or, most recently, Turley on English abolitionism, is shot through with such material and discussion.[7] Support for humanitarian causes and missionary enterprise were from the late eighteenth century onwards very closely connected.

Historians of Africa have also shown an awareness of the role of Black Americans and their society in the interchange. Philip Curtin, for instance, in his important study *The image of Africa*, commented that "In the trans-Atlantic exchange of ideas, Britain gave the anti-slavery crusade to America in the 1830s and received back the American racism of the 1850s."[8] Scholars interested in both indigenous American peoples and southern Africa have produced illuminating comparative studies, both of the "frontier" of settlement and encounter there and in America, and of the parallel development of segregated societies in both countries at the end of the nineteenth century.[9] They have also drawn their own explicit parallels and comparisons between the experience of American Indians and those of the Cape Colony's Khoisan and Xhosa in the face of white expansion.[10] However, they have very rarely seemed aware that early nineteenth-century contemporaries made similar observations and were also inclined to draw their own conclusions.

My first question is therefore what influence, if any, the history of missionary encounter, in the British colonial societies of North America, had on later similar encounters elsewhere, in Africa and the Pacific. What transference was there of missionary thought across the geographical and chronological "imperial meridian"?[11] Perhaps the eventual answer will be "very little". Perhaps the complexity of evangelical networks and intellectual influences is too great to be unravelled.[12] Interdenominational competition, of the sort which in the 1760s made the Society for the Propagation of the Gospel and the Society for the Promotion of Christian Knowledge work to prevent Indians in the North American colonies coming under the influence of local nonconformists, may have prevented fruitful co-operation. However, before the inquiry is dismissed as not worth pursuing, it is important to recognize in it one particular form of a more general question about the formation and transmission of missionary ideas and experience. Too many studies of missionary enterprise focus on the transmission of missionary ideas outwards from a single centre, and fail to understand that most often missionary thought and plans were the product of exchanges between several such centres. The influence, for example, of American revivalism on British evangelicalism had critical consequences for British missionary operations in many parts of the world in the years after 1870.[13] At the same time, writers rarely seem to remember that mission organizers at home and many missionaries in individual fields overseas were acutely conscious of operating in a global setting. They considered their world as a single arena for the working out not only of the Divine Command[14] but also of divine promises, with the result that developments in one region could be of great significance for the course to be adopted in another. In the later nineteenth century, events in India, China, and parts of Africa impinged on each other to influence missionary strategy in important ways. There seems no obvious reason why such cross-currents should not have been equally a feature of the early century. Indeed, the likelihood is that they were at least as powerful then as they were later on, when frequently denominational divisions had hardened and international competition was often more stridently expressed.

Early in the nineteenth century, there was already a sense among mission enthusiasts that Britain and America were developing in complementary ways. Thomas Haweis, for example, who played a key part in the formation of the London Missionary Society (hereafter LMS), hoped for great co-operation to follow from this. "America is still a land of real Protestants", he wrote, "so that the American colonies appear, not only rising into a vast consolidated empire, but reviving in efforts to promote the kingdom of the Lord . . . and are, I hope, destined with us to spread the everlasting gospel to the ends of the earth, whither their commerce next to our own extends . . ."[15] In the same spirit, between 1809 and 1817, the British and Foreign Bible Society contributed financially to the growth of local American societies, and encouraged the work of the American Bible Society, established in 1817.[16] As secretary of the Church Missionary Society and editor of the *Missionary Register*, Josiah Pratt assisted in the establishment of an American missionary society.[17]

Among the earliest writers of the 1790s, past American experience was seen as offering a few simple object lessons. One of the foundation documents, as it were, of the modern missionary movement, William Carey's famous pamphlet of 1792, emphasized the North American precedents as evidence of the possibility and likely success of Protestant missions.[18] By contrast, Melville Horne discerned across the Atlantic clear evidence of how not to proceed. In the record of Roman Catholic activity in Spanish America, in "the Missions among the Cannadian [sic] Indians, whilst that country made a part of the French dominions", and in Britain's former colonies, the proper missionary task had been ignored in favour of linking religion to the interests of the state in political and economic conquest, leaving the survivors "to be exterminated, as tribes of their brethren have been, by the English bayonet and the American rifleman". For Horne, the model to be followed was that of the Moravians.[19] It is also not especially difficult at a later date to find contemporary analogies being drawn by British observers from American experience, for example, with reference to southern Africa. "The history of the Cape is already written in that of America", William Hogge wrote confidently in 1851; "the gradual increase of the white race must eventually though slowly ensure the disappearance of the Black". Similar views were expressed that same year in *The Times*.[20] The problem for historians now is rather to identify the growth of such ideas, information and influence, and the channels along which they flowed.

One such series of channels was provided by the organizers of the London Missionary Society, formed in 1795, and their missionaries in the field, particularly in areas, such as the Pacific or southern Africa, where they came into close contact with those of the American Board of Commissioners for Foreign Missions (hereafter ABCFM). George Burder, LMS secretary from 1803 to 1827, established a correspondence with his opposite number at the

ABCFM, Jeremiah Evarts, which continued to grow under their successors. A significant part was played in this development by William Ellis, LMS foreign secretary from 1831 to 1841.

Ellis was originally sent in 1816 to join the LMS's Tahitian mission, and first made his acquaintance with the Americans when he accompanied an LMS deputation in 1822 to visit the recently-established ABCFM Sandwich Islands mission in Hawaii. Ellis was so well liked, and his linguistic skills so valuable, that he was invited to stay by the American missionaries and the local rulers, and the two mission boards agreed to his transfer to Hawaii. Ellis returned to Britain from the Sandwich Islands in 1824 on account of his wife being seriously ill, and found it necessary to travel eastwards, first taking ship via Cape Horn to New Bedford, Massachusetts. He spent four months in Boston and New York, preaching, lecturing and forming important friendships, especially with Rufus Anderson, about to become the American Board's foreign secretary. Ellis' wife meanwhile recovered sufficiently in the homes of American Board committee members to face the rest of their homeward voyage.[21]

Once back in Britain, Ellis gained a reputation not only as an expert on Polynesia, but as the chronicler of the local "progress" in Christianity and civilization brought about by the missionary societies.[22] In the preface to his *Polynesian researches*, he explained how his volumes showed the transformation of "the barbarous, cruel, indolent, and idolatrous inhabitants of Tahiti, and the neighbouring islands, into a comparatively civilized, humane, industrious and Christian people. They also comprise a record of the measures pursued by the native governments, in changing the social economy of the people, and regulating their commercial intercourse with foreigners, in the promulgation of a new civil code . . . the establishment of courts of justice, and the introduction of trial by jury".[23] However, Ellis was also acutely aware that this Anglo-American achievement was seriously threatened by the incursion of other Europeans, many of whom were far less willing than most missionaries to admit the existence of indigenous "interests".

In these circumstances, as he explained to Rufus Anderson when exchanging with him portrait drawings of the mission secretaries, Ellis regarded their correspondence as vital to their effective work in the field and to increasing or maintaining support at home. "The better we understand each other," he wrote, "the more effectually shall we be enabled to cooperate."[24] The two secretaries shared a common positive perception of Pacific islanders' capacities and a common diagnosis of the threats to their realization. Their correspondence offered one means of co-ordinating a successful defence.

This was not just a routine performance. Information exchanged was often inspiration shared. In Ellis' words, "The accounts we continue to receive from your side of the Atlantic are very encouraging and give increased energy to our exertions here. Your *Herald* I look for with great anxiety and receive with much satisfaction."[25] Exchanges of letters easily spilled over into mutual assistance with publication. Anderson and Ellis discussed the exchange of their own and others' manuscripts; the inclusion of material of particular interest to different audiences for separate British or American editions; how to outwit pirate publishers; obtaining books on particular subjects from the other's country; and the steps each was taking to refute the calumnies of missionaries' critics.[26] This was a continuous refrain, spanning the years from Ellis' vigorous *Vindication of the South Sea missions* in 1831 to his equally forthright defence of the Americans' Hawaii mission in 1866.[27]

Information and inspiration also went hand in hand with extended perspectives. The 1820s and 1830s witnessed a growing appreciation among the missions of the need for pressure behind the scenes to secure official protection in the face of the most serious threats. Shortly after his return to England, Ellis was telling his Boston friends of the efforts being made to persuade the British government to appoint a consul to the islands.[28] But it was not long before his outlook widened. His own early experience had included spending the latter months of 1816 involved with Samuel Marsden's work at Paramatta. No one in his position could ignore the cumulative evidence – from South Africa, the West Indies, New South Wales, and New Zealand, as well as other Pacific islands – of the combined threat to both indigenous societies and missionary activity posed by uncontrolled white expansion. It is scarcely surprising to find Ellis in 1830 voicing a general concern that aboriginal tribes should "be preserved and protected in the occupation of the lands of their fathers".[29]

These were, of course, issues with enormous resonance for anyone aware of North America's past, as Ellis himself realized. Together with the other mission secretaries, Dandeson Coates of the CMS and John Beecham of the Wesleyans, Ellis became steadily more involved with the political movements orchestrated by Thomas Fowell Buxton, which culminated in the appointment of the parliamentary select committee on aborigines in 1837. In preparing himself and his colleagues to give evidence to the committee, Ellis again called on Anderson, asking him for advice on the history of North American Indian relations with the white settlers: "I am desirous of obtaining all the information I can on the subject." Anderson's generous response not only gave Ellis much pleasure but was to the great benefit of the London Missionary Society's library.[30] As a further result of Ellis' concern, the missionaries' case to the select committee, perhaps even its final recommendations, were also significantly strengthened. North America's own record, both north and south of the 49th parallel, was interpreted as providing more than sufficient proof that indigenous peoples and invading white communities could not be brought to adapt to one another unless the missions and Christianity were guaranteed a central place in the process of adjustment. North America's failure to date should not be repeated. Ellis also took the opportunity in his own evidence to use material drawn directly from American sources and experience in the Pacific, including his own recent correspondence with Hiram Bingham, leader of the Hawaii mission.[31]

Ellis also had no doubt as to the value of discussing general missionary problems or dilemmas with Anderson. Some of the most serious had to do with their common, if sometimes touchingly naive, aversion to "political" involvement. Both men regarded Roman Catholic missionaries as a dire threat to their societies' efforts, and were deeply resentful of their contribution to the eventual French seizure of Tahiti in 1842. However, for both secretaries the wish to exclude Catholics conflicted with their equally fervent wish to avoid supporting any infringement by the state of the principles of political and religious liberty. They agonized too over the implications, for their principled avoidance of politics, of local rulers' wishes to take the missionaries' advice on matters of state.[32] At other times, Ellis pressed for ABCFM help in the LMS's attempts to curb the trade in spirits; he discussed the division of territorial spheres, the practical problems of recruiting unmarried females, and the desirability of medical missionaries.[33] Knowing of Ellis' close relationship with Anderson, LMS missionaries felt free to confide in Anderson and to use him as a safe post box for despatches they feared might otherwise be interfered with en route.[34]

Of a slightly older generation than Ellis, and from a very different background although likewise embraced by the LMS, was Dr John Philip. Philip has been the subject of several recent studies, and his career as director and superintendent of the London Missionary Society's work in South Africa from 1819 to 1851 is well known. However, he too corresponded widely with the organizers of other missionary societies and their employees in the field, and his contacts, for example, with the ABCFM, have been far less carefully scrutinized.[35] What, for example, lies behind W. M. Macmillan's passing observation that Philip was "consultant in chief to . . . American Mission Boards", and that "it was on his suggestion that the Americans . . . settled in Natal" in 1835?[36]

John Philip had come to American attention as a result of both his struggle in the 1820s to secure recognition of the legal equality and civil rights of the Khoisan, and the persecution he experienced in the Cape Colony for the publication of his book *Researches in South Africa* (1828). As superintendent of the London Missionary Society's stations, he was approached in 1832 by a

351

group of students at the Princeton Theological Seminary intent on becoming missionaries. In asking him for information about opportunities for missionary work in Africa, their motive was twofold: a wish to take advantage of the revivals then sweeping the eastern United States, and to atone for the guilt of American involvement with slavery and the slave trade.[37] Philip's lengthy reply eventually reached the American Board in Boston; published by them in the November 1833 issue of *The Missionary Herald*, it helped to shape their eventual decision in July 1834 to send two missionary parties, one inland to Mzilikazi's Ndebele, the other to the Zulu in Natal.[38] Philip received the new arrivals at Cape Town, introduced them to the country, and made many of the arrangements for their onward journeys. He continued to act as their adviser and an important link with their home society.

Philip's own reputation, and perhaps the interdenominational as well as Congregationalist sympathies characteristic of both the ABCFM and the LMS, help to explain these early moves. However, the readiness of Philip's response, and his interest thereafter in maintaining a regular correspondence with the Bostonians, reflected more than an obliging nature. Something of the Anglo-American outlook can be traced in his surviving letters to Rufus Anderson, the ABCFM's principal secretary.[39]

At root, Philip undoubtedly felt that he and the Americans were partners in the same enterprise. Embattled as he so often was, and sensing that his *Researches* had gained him less support at home than he felt he deserved, the interest and enthusiasm of the Americans provided welcome encouragement. Sensing their seriousness, appreciating both their willingness to plan carefully and their awareness of a need for patience, he was, he wrote, "particularly pleased with the views entertained in America, as to the means by which missions to savages and barbarians should be conducted. . . ".[40] Subsequent events during the 1830s only confirmed his conviction that "We are engaged in a common cause. . . ".[41]

In part this conviction rested on a sense of shared principles and a common background. A widespread belief in the universality of human nature, in the essential sameness of people everywhere and their equal accessibility to divine grace, is commonly recognized as the foundation for evangelicals' anticipation of worldwide conversion. For Philip, it was this uniformity which also made possible co-operation between missionaries of different nationalities. Differences between Americans and Englishmen, such as the former's partiality to revivalist meetings, might often occasion comment, but were essentially superficial. After all, Philip wrote, "Human nature is the same in its grand leading principles in all the countries of the world."[42]

Together with common principles, a shared history also united British and American endeavours. Philip felt able to draw on a common stock of analogies with the past. He not only referred to a shared experience of work in the Pacific as providing lessons in missionary strategy; when obliged to warn that the "same spirit which contributed to the years of Eliot and Brainerd's labours threatens" to isolate the missions and their work, he was clearly confident that his references would be understood and his fears taken seriously.[43] Events which he encountered on the frontiers of contact and settlement beyond the Cape Colony only too frequently had their parallels, as he knew Anderson and his colleagues would appreciate. On an earlier occasion, Philip had seen fit to celebrate "the savage American", who, "forgetting the sound of the war-whoop", had "joined the sweet singers of Israel". Together with his own subsequent study, however, twenty years at the Cape had sobered his judgement. "From what you have seen in America, you can judge of the results in Africa and other countries colonised from Europe."[44] The ABCFM was not only well versed in the gloomy history of white contact with North American Indians, but was extensively engaged in its own programme of Indian evangelization. Along with other societies in the 1830s, it was beginning to extend its operations beyond the Mississippi. Indeed, when the retreat of its mission to Mzilikazi in 1837 brought about the concentration of the Americans in Natal and removed the immediate need for reinforcements, the Board was clear as to the consequences. Anderson wrote to Natal telling his agents that "Since the amalgamation of your two missions, the designation of the two missionaries, appointed to S. Africa, has been changed to the Rocky Mountain Indians."[45]

With such foundations, Philip saw no difficulties and much to be gained in cultivating close relations with the ABCFM and its workers. Throughout the 1830s and 1840s his missionary efforts were intimately bound up with his prolonged battle to check the unregulated expansion of white settlement. At an early stage he emphasized the problems to Anderson. "Since the Hottentot question was settled and since my return to the Colony, there is another evil of great magnitude which I have had to contend against. In the second sentence of my *Researches* you will perceive in what manner the colonial boundary has been extending for the last thirty years. This system is as much opposed to sound policy as it is to the interest of justice and humanity; but the colonists will think of nothing but an extension of territory and more land, so long as they can hope that they will be indulged in their wishes. . . . The indulgence of those feelings by the extension of the colonial frontier is attended with . . . the destruction of the natives who have been killed in defending their territories, or have perished by the evils which have followed their expulsion."[46]

Philip's aim was to stabilize the frontiers of white settlement, perhaps by means of imperial government intervention, and beyond them to establish mission communities, under either imperial protection or that of local rulers. This missionary presence he believed would secure time for the conversion and civilization of African peoples, who would in the process establish peaceful relations with the Cape Colony. Philip felt that the American ventures had a place in this grand design, one reinforced by the Americans' own explicit concern to avoid areas already populated by whites.[47] He had welcomed the Paris Evangelical Missionary Society in 1829, the Rhenish and Berlin Societies shortly afterwards. In 1833 he was responsible for the Paris Mission's approach to Moshweshwe and the Sotho people. Now the ABCFM's involvement would contribute further to his plan. Not only was there safety in missionary numbers when facing up to both whites and Africans, but the concentration of missionary effort in particular centres rather than the diffusion of isolated individuals had other advantages. Conversion was more likely to result, and working together would help Philip, as he put it, "to introduce between the Colony and the natives and Zulus beyond our colonial limits a system of international law. . . ".[48] After his visit to London to give evidence to the aborigines committee, Philip wrote "We have got a breathing time and that should be sedulously improved [?] by setting among them [the Zulus] the seeds of divine truth which will in a short time raise them to a condition that will command the tempest of white power and set bounds to their encroachments." It was a time for optimism. "If you can but evangelize the Zoolahs you will be able to raise native agencies among that people that will be felt across a great portion of Africa."[49]

Pleased with what he felt was the high quality of the American missionaries,[50] Philip hoped to benefit from the connection in other ways. Sensitive to the cool reception of his own Society to his *Researches*, and its lack of interest in promoting it, he was hopeful that an abridged edition might be published through the Board's good offices in the United States. "You understand things of that kind better in America than they are understood in England", wrote the expatriate Scot.[51] More important still to Philip was Anderson's frequent provision of American missionary literature, and the latest "approved books and journals". "You cannot do us a greater service than to send us your publications and in that way to [press?] upon us that portion of the American mind and American policy which they contain." Too many British societies failed to see the importance of this kind of communication, with the result that missionaries "have returned to a state of childhood in which nothing interests, beyond the barren localities of their immediate neighbourhood". Few people he felt appreciated "how much of our active benevolence we owe to our sympathy with the great affairs of the great world, and these great things cannot affect us if they are not made known to us".[52]

Of course, this was a two-way process. Philip reciprocated with information, accounts and papers which "will, I doubt not, surprise and interest Americans", and even sent exhibits for the American Board's museum.[53] He arranged the earliest possible despatch to Boston of materials relating to the aborigines committee, seeing their importance at a time when "great questions such as this . . . are agitating England and America".[54] The Americans' knowledge of their own country, as well as their local practical experience, confirmed for them the wisdom of much in Philip's diagnosis of South African conditions. In particular, the Boer migration out of the Cape Colony on their Great Trek northwards had serious repercussions. Not only was the American mission to Mzilikazi destroyed in 1837, but even the regrouping of the missionaries with their colleagues in Natal seemed for a time to be threatened by white expansion.

Indeed, the leader of the American party, Daniel Lindley, saw little promise in their situation. "The emigration of the Boers was a thing, we believe, unthought of, when we first came into the country; and a thing by which we would have been in no way affected, had Moselikatsi [sic] not attempted their entire destruction. . . . The Emigrant Boers at present think they will settle not far from Natal, in order that they may trade at that port; and . . . It is now quite evident that no very long period will elapse before a considerable white population will be settled at and around that port; and when this shall take place, we may expect that the natives : . . will be compelled to give way to the wishes and interests of white men. We cannot think of the American Indians and of the natives in this country, without fearing that years of missionary labor among [them] may yet be sacrificed to what is called the enterprise of civilized man."[55] Without British intervention to protect the Zulus, their state and the mission would be destroyed.

Lindley and his colleagues increasingly came to believe that nothing could control the movement of Boers and other settlers in southern Africa. Analogy buttressed experience. After all, wrote Lindley, "what can prevent the emigration of Americans to the west? . . . The boundaries of the Cape Colony . . . are not impassable, and it is not in the power of government to make them so . . . The natives of this region are sinking for the last time". This was a still more pessimistic prognosis than Philip's, assuming as it did a repetition of the consequences of American conflicts, rather than reflecting on the numerical preponderance and resilience of local South African peoples. Nevertheless, it pointed in the same direction, towards the immediate need for many more missionaries if conversion were to be achieved. "There is no other hope for them."[56]

As war engulfed Natal in 1837–8, the American mission was for a time compelled to retreat once more, on this occasion to the Cape. Against this background, as an essential guarantee of missionary security and hence of the preconditions for conversion, members of the ABCFM came to accept, as Philip had previously done, that imperial intervention was inescapable. The mission eventually adapted itself both to the British annexation of Natal in 1842–3, and to working in an imperial rather than an independent African setting.[57] The advantage of so doing was finally accepted by Rufus Anderson himself. In 1836 he was already concerned that South African peoples might experience the same fate as that of North America's Indians in confrontation with settlers expanding westward. After the troubles of 1837–8, he even told Ellis, "The prospect now is, that we shall be driven out of South Africa; and what is far more important, that the whole aboriginal population will vanish before the emigrant white man!" However, writing to the members of the Zulu mission in 1852, he had attained a new calm. "Perhaps each one of you will do more for the world to come, by having an Anglo-Saxon empire growing up around you, than if you had the natives all to yourselves. I really suppose that it will be so. . . . It is a great thing to plant the gospel and its institutions in a great, fertile, and healthy country in advance of colonization, and so to shape the infancy of empires."[58]

Dr Philip was only one of the best known missionaries whose activities either developed under the influence of American evangelicalism or at least brought them into close connection with friends across the Atlantic. Missionaries' travel often involved visits there, and a wealth of good feeling was generated by American hospitality and other kinds of assistance. This was far from unusual in a period when British missionaries heading for India or China often found it easier to go via America, so minimizing difficulties with the East India Company.[59] Robert Morrison, for instance, travelled westwards to China in 1807, and lived in Canton with American merchants. Fund-raising for a new college at Serampore (Bengal) took the Baptist William Ward not only to Holland and north Germany but to the United States for six months in 1820–21.

Rather less direct but nonetheless notable was David Livingstone's contact with America. Ultimately, as he put it in his *Missionary travels and researches*, he looked to the "Anglo-American race" to promote liberty and progress. However, well before his great travels from 1853 onwards, the ABCFM's continuing efforts in Natal impressed him as they had others in the 1830s. Like Philip, he sensed the common endeavour in which they were engaged, and was also keen to use American outlets to report on South African develop-ments and mobilize public opinion against colonial abuses.[60] His brother sent him works of American theology, and, noting American generosity to Robert Moffat, Livingstone considered presenting to Amherst College the manuscript of Moffat's Setswana translation of the Bible.[61]

Although attention has been drawn here to these varied and persistent channels of communication within the missionary world, it is not intended to suggest that Anglo-American cross-currents were missionaries' exclusive preserve. Similar analogies and imagery were employed by colonial administrators, such as Lord Glenelg and Earl Grey, as well as military and naval figures. Nor were they even monopolized by the nonconformist or dissenting sections of British evangelicalism. From the mid-1830s, the idea of the "missionary bishop", one sent by the church to organize and direct its missionary work and build up its presence in new areas, was taken up in High Church circles, finding its first important British manifestations in the establishment of the Colonial Bishoprics Fund (1841) and the consecration of G. A. Selwyn as Bishop of New Zealand in October 1841. The sending out of missionary bishops appealed to those who were concerned to preserve episcopal authority and leadership, those who were hostile to the growth of lay and state control over the Church of England, and those anxious for its future in the face of aggressive expansion by rivals at home and abroad. A further 14 colonial and missionary bishops were consecrated by 1850, and the role found its fullest expression in 1861 when Bishop Charles Mackenzie led the first party of the Universities' Mission to Central Africa up the Zambezi.[62]

However much the concept of the missionary bishop suited English needs, it nevertheless seems to have originated in the preoccupation of the Protestant Episcopal Church in the United States with America's own westward expansion, and to have received its definition in George Washington Doane's sermon at the consecration in September 1835 of Jackson Kemper as Bishop of Missouri and Indiana.[63] Doane's English connections and correspondence were extensive, dating back at least to the mid-1820s, and on his visit to Britain in 1841 he was widely welcomed, meeting Selwyn amongst many others "and talked much with him of his plans for Missions". Although it is clear that British churchmen were excited by the American ideas, their transmission and the links between the two churches seem to have remained unexplored by modern scholars.[64]

Daniel Wilson, for example, as Bishop of Calcutta corresponded with Elijah Bridgeman and was both friend and admirer of the famous ABCFM worker in Burma, Adoniram Judson. The American Board's own close connections with the CMS had pre-dated the growth of those with the LMS.[65] Evidently there were many who, starting from very different points on the spectrum of Anglican churchmanship, could find interest and inspiration in American missionary activities.

No overview or rounded assessment of early nineteenth-century Anglo-American missionary relations can be attempted here. Nevertheless it is clear that North American experience, past as well as present, was widely seen as worth serious consideration. It could offer insights into the problems of dealing with "savage" or "barbarous" peoples, as well as those of managing white expansion. Both its successes and its failures were felt to be relevant in planning British missionary enterprise, and, although there is so far no evidence of significant transfers of funds from one country to the other, in general the international missionary alliance was seen as worth cultivating. Mutual support bred confidence; discussion of shared problems was thought to improve chances of finding effective solutions. While it may often remain difficult for historians to know whether among so many influences these connections made much practical difference, there can be no doubt that contemporaries felt them to be important, and regarded themselves in consequence as more effective and better informed. In terms of the images held of North American Indians, it seems likely that the missionary experience of the early nineteenth century revived the view of them as victims rather than heartless savages.[66] As earlier sufferers from the same processes of white settlement now being experienced by Pacific islanders and Bantu peoples, their example added to the growth of British humanitarian and missionary pressure for decisive action by the imperial government.

These are, of course, only tentative suggestions. The subject invites recall of the caution with which two eminent imperial historians concluded their study showing how, in the preceding period, "views about the world's peoples and an increasingly active British role in their lives went together".

> The processes of ordering the world both in the minds and by the actions of Englishmen were not necessarily connected. Scholars could work on areas where British influence was negligible, and men of action could be largely oblivious of the peoples among whom they conducted their operations. But in most cases the two activities clearly did have connections with each other . . . Yet if there are connections between assumed knowledge of the world and the growth of British power and influence, they are not simple ones . . . The relationship of idea and action is in our view a confused mixture of cause and effect.[67]

The reservations pinpointed in this quotation are obviously central to the concerns examined above. To enquire what knowledge of other societies the British acquired will also involve one in asking how that knowledge was obtained. The manner in which knowledge was transmitted and added to inevitably has implications for the way in which it was applied. That the

patterns of Anglo-American contact and experience of evangelization contributed to the ordering of the world and the global activities of the early
nineteenth-century missionary community on both sides of the Atlantic can
scarcely be doubted. It also deserves fuller investigation.

Notes

This is the revised version of a paper originally written for the conference
on "The British Encounter with Indigenous Peoples, *c.* 1600–1850", held at
University College, London, in February 1997. I am grateful for comments on that
occasion and also for those made by members of the imperial history seminar at the
Institute of Historical Research, London, and the modern British history seminar,
St John's College, Oxford. The citation in this essay of material from the papers of
the American Board of Commissioners for Foreign Missions is by permission of the
Houghton Library, Harvard University.

1 Most recently, see M. A. Noll, D. W. Bebbington, G. A. Rawlyk (eds), *Evangelicalism:
   comparative studies of popular Protestantism in North America, the British Isles, and beyond,
   1700–1990* (New York and Oxford, 1994).
2 W. R. Hutchison, *Errand to the world. American Protestant thought and foreign missions*
   (Chicago and London, 1987).
3 W. R. Ward, *The Protestant evangelical awakening* (Cambridge, 1992).
4 For example, J. Mason, *Moravian connections with Evangelical Calvinists during the missionary
   awakening in England, 1770 to 1790* (Position Paper 3, North Atlantic Missiology Project,
   University of Cambridge, 1996).
5 D. W. Bebbington, *Evangelicalism in modern Britain: a history from the 1730s to the 1980s*
   (London, 1989); R. E. Davies, *Jonathan Edwards and his influence on the development of the
   missionary movement from Britain* (Position Paper 6, North Atlantic Missiology Project,
   University of Cambridge, 1996); Edwards, *The life of David Brainerd* (1749), constantly
   reprinted thereafter, most recently as vol. 7 of Norman Pettit (ed.) *The works of Jonathan
   Edwards* (New Haven, Conn., 1985).
6 L. Billington, "British and American Methodisms grow apart", in *The end of
   Anglo-America: historical essays in the study of cultural divergence*, R. A. Burchell
   (ed.) (Manchester, 1991), pp. 113–36. For further illumination of the common
   religious world, R. Carwardine, *Trans-Atlantic revivalism: popular evangelicalism in
   Britain and America, 1790–1865* (Westport, Conn., 1978); J. F. C. Harrison, *The
   second coming: popular millennarianism 1780–1850* (London, 1979); R. H. Martin,
   Evangelicals united: ecumenical stirrings in pre-Victorian Britain, 1795–1830 (Metuchen,
   N. J., 1983).
7 D. B. Davis, *The problem of slavery in western culture* (Ithaca, N.Y., 1968); *The problem
   of slavery in the age of revolution, 1770–1823* (Ithaca, N.Y., 1975); *Slavery and human
   progress* (New York and Oxford, 1984); Howard Temperley, *British anti-slavery
   1833–1870* (London, 1972); D. Turley, *The culture of English anti-slavery, 1780–1860*
   (London, 1991).

8   P. D. Curtin, *The image of Africa: British ideas and action, 1780–1850* (London, 1965), p. 372.

9   H. Lamar & L. M. Thompson (eds), *The frontier in history: North America and South Africa compared* (New Haven, Conn., 1981); John W. Cell, *The highest stage of white supremacy: the origins of segregation in South Africa and the American South* (Cambridge, 1982).

10   W. M. Macmillan, *Bantu, Boer, and Briton: the making of the South African native problem*, rev. edn (Oxford, 1963), pp. 73, 276, 347–8; *The Cape colour question* (London, 1927), pp. 16, 83.

11   C. A. Bayly, *Imperial meridian: the British empire and the world, 1780–1830* (London, 1990).

12   Consider, for example, Andrew Walls' observation, in "The evangelical revival, the missionary movement, and Africa", in Noll, Bebbington & Rawlyk (eds), *Evangelicalism*, pp. 310–11: "The chain that led to William Carey's pioneering missionary initiative of 1792 was forged by a gift from a Scottish Presbyterian to an English Baptist of a book by a New England Congregationalist. Another New Englander, David Brainerd, became the principal model of early British missionary spirituality; his own work had been supported by the Society in Scotland for Promoting Christian Knowledge. An unending stream of correspondence, criss-crossing the Atlantic, reveals just how important as a missionary factor were the African-Americans and Afro-West Indians. The Church Missionary Society was hauled back from the point of absurdity through the pastor of a German congregation in London who put them in contact with a seminary in Berlin. Magazines on two continents gathered and disseminated 'missionary intelligence' without regard to denomination or country of origin."

13   Cf. A. N. Porter, "Cambridge, Keswick and late nineteenth-century attitudes to Africa", *Journal of Imperial and Commonwealth History* 5(1), 1976, pp. 5–34.

14   "Go ye into all the world, and preach the gospel to every creature", St Mark, 16: 15.

15   Thomas Haweis, *A view of the present state of evangelical religion throughout the world; with a view to promote missionary exertions* (London, 1812), pp. 53–4.

16   W. Canton, *A History of the British and Foreign Bible Society* [5 vols] (London, 1904), I, pp. 242–9, and II, pp. 49–57.

17   Entry in *The Dictionary of National Biography Vol. XLVI*, Sidney Lee (ed.) (London, 1896), p. 294.

18   W. Carey, *An enquiry into the obligations of Christians to use means for the conversion of the heathens* (1792; facsimile edition, London, 1891), pp. 36, 69–71.

19   M. Horne, *Letters on missions adressed to the Protestant ministers of the British churches* (Bristol, 1794), pp. 26–7, 34–7.

20   John S. Galbraith, *Reluctant empire: British policy on the South African frontier, 1834–1854* (Berkeley and Los Angeles, 1963), pp. 257–8, 248–9.

21   J. E. Ellis, *Life of William Ellis missionary to the South Seas and to Madagascar* (London, 1873), Ch. 6; W. Ellis, *Memoir of Mary M. Ellis* (London, 1835), pp. 151–3; also Ellis' correspondence with Anderson, contained in the ABCFM Papers which are held at the Houghton Library, Harvard University. For a fuller treatment of Ellis' early career, Andrew Porter, "British missions, the Pacific, and the American connection: the career of William Ellis", in *Pacific empires: essays in honour of Glyn Williams*, Alan Frost & Jane Samson (eds) (Melbourne, 1998).

22   Based on his *Narrative of a tour through Hawaii* (London, 1826); and *Polynesian researches, during a residence of nearly six years in the South Sea islands* [2 vols] (London, 1829).

23   *Polynesian researches*, p. ix.

24   ABCFM Papers, Houghton Library, Harvard University (hereafter ABC) ABC/14/1, Ellis

to Anderson, 19 July 1832. Unless otherwise stated, all Ellis letters cited are from this archive. The series ABC 14, "Miscellaneous foreign letters", consists of seven volumes covering principally the years 1831–99 and 1910–19; it contains the extensive correspondence addressed to the board and its officers in Boston by members of foreign missionary societies and other individuals overseas.

25 ABC/14/1, Ellis to Anderson, 27 March 1830.

26 ABC/14/1, Ellis to Anderson, 20 April 1830; 14 November 1830; 31 March 1831; 28 February 1833; ABC/14/2, Ellis to Anderson, 24 November 1838.

27 *Vindication of the South Sea missions from the misrepresentations of Otto Von Kotzebue* (London, 1831); *The American mission in the Sandwich Islands: a vindication and an appeal in relation to the proceedings of the reformed Catholic mission at Honolulu* (London, 1866).

28 ABC/14/1, Ellis to Jeremiah Evarts, 29 November 1828.

29 ABC/14/1, Ellis to Anderson, 20 April 1830. For a recent consideration of the contemporary South African debate, Elizabeth Elbourne, "Freedom at issue: vagrancy legislation and the meaning of freedom in Britain and the Cape Colony, 1799 to 1842", *Slavery and Abolition* **15**(2) 1994, pp. 114–50; and Timothy Keegan, *Colonial South Africa and the origins of the racial order* (Leicester and Charlottesville, Va., 1996).

30 Ellis to Anderson, ABC/14/1, 12 April 1837, and ABC/14/2, 7 February 1838.

31 *Report from the select committee on aborigines (British settlements), PP (1837) VII.* 425, QQ.4294-5, 4304–6, 4320, 4328 et seq., 4365, 4375, 4389, 4396–4402, 4416.

32 Ellis to Anderson, ABC/14/1, 22 June 1831, and ABC/14/2, 25 April 1843.

33 Ellis to Anderson, ABC/14/1, 2 June 1833, 16 December 1833, 18 April 1835, and ABC/14/2, 7 February 1838.

34 See, for example, George Pritchard's letters to Anderson, 1835–43, in ABC/14/1–2.

35 For example, Andrew Ross, *John Philip (1775–1851): missions, race and politics in South Africa* (Aberdeen, 1986) refers only in passing to his role in the establishment of the American Board Mission in Natal, pp. 95, 244.

36 Macmillan, *Bantu, Boer and Briton*, pp. 13, 95 n.2. Also *Cape Colour Question*, pp. 105–6.

37 J. B. Purney to Philip, 16 March 1832, in *Letters of the American Missionaries 1835–1838*, D. J. Kotze (ed.) (Cape Town, 1950), pp. 21–7; Kotze also gives Philip's reply, pp. 28–45. For the best known of the American missionaries to the Cape, see E. W. Smith, *The life and times of Daniel Lindley (1801–80)* (London, 1949).

38 ABC/2.01/2 f.363–66, Rufus Anderson to Rev. Dr John Philip, 10 August 1833; ABC/2.01/3 f.89–93, *ibid.*, 16 July 1834.

39 Unless otherwise stated, all Philip's letters cited here are to be found in the ABCFM Papers, Houghton Library, Harvard University.

40 ABC/14/1, Philip to Anderson, 13 December 1833.

41 ABC/14/1, *ibid.*, n.d., from London; received in Boston 26 June 1837.

42 ABC/14/1, *ibid.*, 18 March 1835.

43 *Ibid.*, ABC/14/2, December 1839, and ABC/14/3, 7 January 1845. In 1837, Ellis had made similar references in his evidence to the aborigines committee, Q.4416.

44 J. Philip, *Necessity of divine influence. A sermon preached before the Missionary Society . . . May 12, 1813* (London, 1813); ABC/14/1, Philip to Anderson, n.d., from London; received in Boston 26 June 1837.

45 Anderson to the Brethren of the South African Mission, 24 January 1838, in Kotze (ed.), *Letters*, p. 221. For the beginnings of the American advance, see J. D. Unruh, *The plains across: emigrants, wagon trains and the American West* (Urbana, Ill., 1979).

46 ABC/14/1, Philip to Anderson, 13 December 1833.

47 See N. Etherington, "An American errand into the South African wilderness", *Church History* **39**, 1970, pp. 62–71.

48 ABC/14/1, Philip to Anderson, 18 March 1835, and 11 March 1836. For local white hostility to the connections of Philip and the American missionaries, Kotze (ed.), *Letters*, pp. 116–17.

49 ABC/14/1, Philip to Anderson, received 26 June 1837.

50 ABC/14/1, *ibid.*, 27 May and 29 October 1835; Robert Moffat agreed, Kotze (ed.), *Letters*, p. 85. Also Robert Moffat to J. S. Moffat, 14 January 1836 (copy), ABC New Series 5, Special Collections, Livingstone and Moffat Correspondence 1807–58.

51 ABC/14/1, Philip to Anderson, 26 January 1834 (continued 14 March 1834).

52 *Ibid.*, ABC/14/1, 29 October 1835, and ABC/14/3, 7 July 1848. Anderson had started to send material to Philip with his very first letter in 1833: see n.38 above.

53 *Ibid.*, ABC/14/1, 18 March 1835; ABC/14/2, December 1839, 26 October 1842; ABC/14/3, 30 July 1846, 7 July 1848.

54 *Ibid.*, received 26 June 1837.

55 American missionaries (Daniel Lindley) to Anderson, 2 May 1837, in Kotze (ed.), *Letters*, pp. 173–4.

56 Lindley to Anderson, 1 December 1837, Kotze (ed.), *Letters*, p. 213.

57 This was only achieved with difficulty, and on several occasions Philip anticipated their withdrawal from South Africa: Philip to Anderson, ABC/14/2, 18 May 1838; ABC/14/3, 26 January 1844, 7 January 1845.

58 ABC/2.1/1 f.130–33, Anderson to Philip, 5 July 1836; ABC/2.1/2 f.116–17, Anderson to Ellis, 9 June 1838 (private); letter of 1852 quoted by Etherington, "American errand", p. 69.

59 Alan Frederick Perry, *The ABCFM and the LMS in the nineteenth century: a study of ideas* (PhD thesis, Washington University, 1974), p. 51 et seq.

60 David Livingstone to Charles Livingstone (brother), 1 February, 16 May, 19 August 1849, 10 September 1852, ABC New Series 5, Livingstone Correspondence. Charles was at this time living in Boston.

61 *Ibid.*, 6 February 1853 (copy; original sent to the Blantyre Memorial). For Charles Livingstone, see G. W. Clendennen, *Charles Livingstone: a biographical study, with emphasis on his accomplishments on the Zambezi Expedition, 1858–63* (PhD thesis, Edinburgh University, 1978).

62 H. Cnattingius, *Bishops and societies. A study of Anglican colonial and missionary expansion 1698–1850* (London, 1952), pp. 200–203; D. Newsome, *The parting of friends: a study of the Wilberforces and Henry Manning* (London, 1966), pp. 215–18, and T. E. Yates, *Venn and Victorian bishops abroad. Studia Missionalia Upsaliensia XXXIII* (Uppsala and London, 1978), pp. 99–100.

63 G. W. Doane, "Sermon VIII: The missionary bishop", in *The life and writings of George Washington Doane, D.D., LL.D., Bishop of New Jersey*, W. C. Doane (ed.) [4 vols] (New York, 1860), II, pp. 399–425.

64 One starting point would be W. C. Doane (ed.), *Life and writings*, I, Ch. 5. "English correspondence – visit to England". For the meeting with Selwyn, p. 282.

65 J. Bateman, *The life of the Rt. Rev. Daniel Wilson, D.D.* [2 vols] (London, 1860), I, pp. 280, 320–1, 394–8, II, pp. 149, 153; ABC/2.01/3 f.93, Rufus Anderson to Dr John Philip, 16 July 1834.

66   For a discussion of the earlier images, P. J. Marshall & G. Williams, *The great map of mankind. British perceptions of the world in the age of the Enlightenment* (London, 1982), Ch. 7.

67   *Ibid.*, p. 303.

Chapter Eighteen

Losing faith in the civilizing mission: the premature decline of humanitarian liberalism at the Cape, 1840–60

Andrew Bank

Studies of racial attitudes in Victorian Britain and her colonies have portrayed the mid- to late nineteenth century as an era of humanitarian retreat and transition towards the strident racism of the age of high imperialism. A wide body of scholarship documents a decisive change in British metropolitan and colonial settler images of non-Europeans in this era, whether Africans, Indians, West Indians or Maoris. In 1965 Philip Curtin identified this broad shift in racial discourse as a movement from "the age of humanitarianism" to "the age of imperialism".[1] More recent literature has written of it as the "transition from the altruism of antislavery to the cynicism of empire".[2]

It was in Christine Bolt's work on Victorian attitudes towards race, written in the early 1970s, that this interpretation was most fully elaborated. Bolt took the middle of the nineteenth century as her point of departure and argued that Victorian attitudes towards indigenous peoples grew increasingly pessimistic and hostile over the following two decades. It was in these decades that the ideological foundations for the new imperialism were laid: "ironically, during a period of apparent recoil from overseas commitment, the aggressive assertion of white superiority, which is such a pronounced feature of the 1850s and 1860s, prepared the way for the next great phase of British expansion towards the end of the century".[3]

These were decades of ascendant scientific racism and the more widespread acceptance in Anglo-American intellectual circles of polygenetic arguments for human racial difference. The ethnological studies of languages and the physical anthropologist's analyses of brains entrenched ideas of racial hierarchy. In the 1860s budding anthropologists began to apply Darwinian ideas about the survival of the fittest to the different "races" of humanity.[4]

Events in the colonies seemed to provide ample justification for this new theoretical racism. The Indian Mutiny of 1857 is seen as a major turning point in metropolitan and colonial attitudes towards other races. The mutiny heralded more than an end to Company rule: it was perceived as a point of transition between an era of romanticism and an era of realism and caution. Indian armed resistance was interpreted by Victorians as evidence of oriental treachery and ingratitude, and after the mutiny Indians became branded as "niggers" and spoken of with a "coarse contempt and vulgar hatred". The traditional image of the tractable, mild Hindu was undermined by an emergent stereotype of the cruel, scheming oriental. A contemporary comment in 1859 is seen by Bolt to express "the absolute quintessence of the post-Mutiny re-evaluation of the Indian character": "It used to be said of the Hindoos that they were such a mild, amiable and gentle race . . . But what is the disclosure? That greater liars do not exist in the world than the Hindoos; that you cannot always trust them out of sight; that they are deceptive; and we have seen by recent events such outbursts of fanaticism, cruelty and bloodshed."[5]

Military conflict in the West Indies generated deep-seated antagonism towards Blacks who were soon viewed with even greater contempt than their treacherous Indian counterparts. The Morant Bay Rebellion of 1865 was taken as an explicit demonstration of the failure of British civilizing policy and evidence of the ex-slaves' incapacity for responsible citizenship. It was this moment of rebellion and alleged betrayal in Jamaica, more than events in Africa or fears associated with reconstruction and the ending of slavery in the United States, that pushed Victorian thinking about "the negro" to pessimistic conclusions.[6]

Later studies have endorsed this chronology. According to Lorimer's 1978 work, the mid- to late nineteenth century was one of "transition from ethnocentrism to racism" and saw changing attitudes towards Black people within Britain as well. The close interaction of colour and class prejudice meant that the idea of a "Black gentleman" became a contradiction in terms in English society after mid-century. Lorimer drew similar connections between humanitarian decline, rising racism and later imperial expansion: "During the 1850s and 1860s, a reaction set in against the sentimental caricature of the abolitionists, and a more derogatory stereotype of the Negro became more prevalent. This change occurred before the exploits of explorers and the search for colonies revived interest in the African continent."[7]

The case for humanitarian disillusion and rising racism at home has been applied to European attitudes in the colonies in the 1850s and 1860s. In his influential revisionist study of the New Zealand wars, James Bellich proposes that frontier wars with the Maori precipitated a major shift in settler racial ideology in these decades. In contrast to the mythologized view of the wars

365

as a breeding-ground for mutual respect, Bellich maintains that military conflict bred contempt. Emerging hostility towards the Maori went beyond the conservative settler core who had always doubted "bungling and theoretical philanthropy". Hitherto "friends of the natives" reversed their judgements in the face of highly successful military resistance by indigenes: "Many who had fearlessly argued the justice of the Maori case in the Taranaki War of 1860 . . . felt that the Waikato War of 1863 was the 'sharp lesson' which, sadly, the Maoris both needed and deserved. By 1864 the Church Missionary Society in New Zealand was supporting, in principle, the confiscation of Maori land."[8] There was an emergent conviction among "missionaries and philanthropists" in New Zealand by the mid-1860s that coercion was the only means to effect the civilizing mission.

The trajectory of imperial expansion and shifting racial attitudes in the southern Africa context unsettles this conventional periodization. The British–Xhosa wars predated imperial conquests in New Zealand or India and bred a pessimism and hostility towards Africans decades before the shift in attitudes towards Indians, Jamaicans and Maoris. The transition towards a more strident racism among the nascent British settler community on the eastern frontier after the 1835 Xhosa War has been well documented.[9] But, as this chapter attempts to demonstrate, wars with the Xhosa bred a rising racism amongst those who had once been self-styled champions of the African cause. By the middle of the nineteenth century the political influence of Cape humanitarians and, even more strikingly, their very faith in their civilizing mission had eroded. This premature demise of humanitarian attitudes and rising racism at the Cape needs to be integrated into the standard account of racial attitudes in the Victorian era and suggests that the Xhosa wars on the Cape Colony's eastern frontier may well have been a more formative experience for British imperialism than has generally been acknowledged.

The early disillusion of the Cape humanitarians also qualifies the conventional periodization of the rise and fall of Cape liberalism in South African historiography. Liberal and revisionist historians of the 1980s concurred that the Cape liberal tradition was ascendant in the mid-nineteenth century and only went into decline in the closing decades of the century.[10] In Trapido's influential article on the "Friends of the Natives", the great tradition of Cape liberalism, associated with merchants, missionaries and colonial officials and their vested interests in bolstering an African peasantry, remained ascendant until the end of the nineteenth century. It was only in the 1880s and 1890s, as the South African peasantry declined under the impact of heightened demands for labour by Western Cape farmers and Witwatersrand miners, that the Cape liberal tradition was sent into crisis.[11] The story presented here indicates that Cape liberalism was thrown into crisis by wars with the Xhosa almost half a century earlier and that the disillusion of merchants, missionaries and colonial officials with Africans was largely a *fait accompli* by the middle of the nineteenth century.

The disillusion of the Cape humanitarians

In the 1820s and 1830s humanitarian attitudes and policies had their heyday in the Cape Colony. The missionaries and merchants that galvanized the liberal reform movement at the Cape enjoyed an unprecedented era of political ascendance with metropolitan influence, both in the British parliament through evangelical reformers like William Wilberforce and Thomas Fowell Buxton, and in the Colonial Office through sympathetic imperial policy-makers like James Stephen. The emancipation of the Khoikhoi through Ordinance 50 of 1828, its safeguarding by an Order in Council in 1829, the freeing of the slaves in 1834 and the introduction of Glenelg's Treaty System on the Cape Colony's eastern frontier in the late 1830s represented major victories for the humanitarian liberals in these decades.[12]

There was every reason for the first generation of Cape liberals to feel buoyantly optimistic about their civilizing mission at a theoretical as well as a practical level. In the 1820s the Cape's leading liberal campaigner, the controversial London Missionary Society Superintendent Dr John Philip, insisted that it is only "the discipline of education and the circumstances under which we are placed, which create the difference between the rude barbarian and the polished citizen – the listless savage and the man of commercial enterprise – the man of the woods and the literary recluse".[13] This environmental theory of difference was circulated by the newly established liberal newspaper, the *South African Commercial Advertiser*, which was edited by Philip's energetic son-in-law and political ally, John Fairbairn. In the late 1820s and early 1830s Fairbairn publicly derided those who attempted to "search for new principles of action in the minds of men who differ from us only in the colour of their skin".[14]

If the early 1840s was a "utopian moment" in Jamaica, as Hall suggests in her article in this volume, it was in an earlier decade that the realization of new possibilities seemed infinite for humanitarians at the Cape. But at the Cape, as in Jamaica, hierarchies were already inscribed within the liberal language of equality. The humanitarian strand of early liberal thinking, which galvanized around abolitionist issues, was always in tension with a more latent authoritarian strand, and notions of cultural hierarchy, derived from Scottish Enlightenment models of progressive stages of societal development, were embedded within Cape liberal ideology from the outset.[15] There was always the latent potential for disillusion when faced by actual contacts and conflicts with Africans, and with their failure to conform to humanitarian ideals.

By the early 1840s, there were already signs that the optimism of the Cape humanitarians was waning. The self-assured language of reform, the passion, zeal and combative spirit, the philosophical theorizing over "savage and civilised varieties of man" at the height of the abolitionist campaigns were noticeably muted, if not wholly absent, from editorials and columns of the liberal press. After the emancipation of the Khoikhoi and slaves (1828–38), local liberals showed remarkably little interest in the meaning of freedom for the coloured underclass, evidently viewing it in narrowly legal terms as a *fait accompli.*

It is striking that the liberal press expressed far greater enthusiasm for compensation payments to ex-slave-owners than for the freedom of ex-slaves. Editorials dismissed the ending of apprenticeship for the colony's 38,000 slaves on 1 December 1838 as an economic non-event.[16] There were no echoes in subsequent years of the great boom and massive rise in productivity in the transition from unfree to free labour that had been anticipated in the earlier utopian moment. The passing of the Masters and Servants Ordinance of 1841, legislation which re-enforced rigid control over the coloured underclass,[17] evoked none of the censure about restrictions on Khoikhoi mobility that Fairbairn had expressed in the debate over Ordinance 50.

The liberal press also steered clear of contention in reporting on the frontier conflict between Xhosa and colonists in the late 1830s and early 1840s. This was probably partly an attempt to restore shaken public faith in the newspaper. Fairbairn's ambivalence and expressions of sympathy towards the Xhosa viewpoint in his coverage of events leading up to the 1835 Frontier War[18] had provoked a petition by hundreds of outraged British frontier settlers demanding the suppression of his newspapers. Under these pressures George Greig, the Cape Town merchant and Fairbairn's erstwhile ally, had withdrawn from his established position as publisher of the *Commercial Advertiser* in 1835.

Subsequent liberal writings on frontier issues were more circumspect and less critical of the British colonists in the Eastern Cape. By 1840 the tone had already changed. Fairbairn now wrote with implied remorse that "It is because we have always viewed the defence of the frontier, *ever since the last war,* in this serious light, that we have so often pleaded for the presence of a strong force in that quarter" [emphasis added]. Despite some critique of the "political liars" of the Eastern Cape and a dogged defence of the Treaty System, Fairbairn was beginning to articulate greater concern for the security of colonists and there was little, if any, recognition of colonial culpability in breaches of trust across the colony's borders: "By a great force properly distributed we hope to see the real thieves checked and rooted out . . . For we firmly believe that the evils complained of, and the dangers to which we [colonists] are exposed, arise entirely from loose and abandoned Caffers and not from their chiefs or the people at large."[19]

By the late 1840s the humanitarian liberal position on frontier relations had been completely overturned. It was in their transformed attitude to the Xhosa and frontier policy after the Seventh Frontier War of 1846–47 that the humanitarian liberals' loss of faith in an earlier model of interaction was most dramatically demonstrated. The continued advocacy of diplomatic solutions to the frontier problem, albeit in more cautious terms, in the late 1830s gave way to a stridently imperialistic language of conquest, appropriation and punishment from the late 1840s. If the 1835 Frontier War prompted leading humanitarian ideologues to qualify their assessments of frontier relations, the War of the Axe sparked an outright reversal of earlier ideas and a rejection of the idea that frontier relations could be mediated through negotiation and treaties.

In direct response to the alleged "betrayal" of the Xhosa,[20] Fairbairn and his supporters came to insist that it was necessary to "add Cafferland to the dependencies of the Cape". This was followed up with demands for severe retribution: "both chiefs and people have to learn that the effects of an unjust war are not to end with the termination of actual resistance in the field. They have forced the British government most reluctantly to declare, that not victory but conquest is to be the end of this outbreak".[21] Later editorials called for punishment in even more vindictive terms: "before the sword is sheathed – the Caffers, chiefs and people, must be made to feel that the Colony is too strong for them . . . [T]hey must be made to feel at their throat the impartial sword of Justice".[22] The insistence of liberals like Fairbairn that the Xhosa should be "subdued and humbled" by punishing all the guilty was ironically even more thorough-going than the post-war retribution scheme proposed by their expansionist rivals of the 1830s, the British settler imperialists on the eastern frontier.[23]

This articulation of the transformed liberal attitude towards frontier policy was accompanied by an equally dramatic philosophical *volte face*. In a remarkable reassessment of his views on the relation of Xhosa to colonial "varieties of man", Fairbairn expressed his new conviction that: "In race, colour, language, customs [the Xhosa] differ as much [from the colonists] as any two varieties of the same species ever did or can do. To this difference is added a gloomy jealousy on the part of the natives, who have seen for generations the steady and irresistible progress of the white man towards the interior, not only as a master, but as sole proprietor of the country."[24]

While Fairbairn, like almost every other colonist, remained committed to a belief in a single human "species", his post-war emphasis on the nature and extent of difference between Xhosa and colonist diverges markedly from his earlier views of the intrinsic similarity between Africans and Europeans. Whereas in the early 1830s he was proclaiming that "Knowledge and Mental improvement are not hereditary",[25] by the late 1840s he had come to insist on the importance of innate features, the distinctions of "race" and "colour", as well as the cultural boundaries of "language" and "customs", as markers of difference between Europeans and Africans. And measured by all of these criteria he adjudged the Xhosa and colonist to be at opposite ends of the human spectrum.

Although there were dissenting voices, most humanitarian liberals endorsed the iron-fisted militarism of the *South African Commercial Advertiser* in the late 1840s and its reversed assessment of the Xhosa character. Fairbairn and his newspaper were closely allied with the rising commercial bourgeoisie in the Western Cape and leading local merchants echoed his hardened attitude towards frontier relations in private correspondence as well as print. H. E. Rutherford, an established Cape Town merchant and Fairbairn's long-standing ideological ally, wrote in an off-hand way to a friend in England of the sudden necessity of "powder and ball" solutions to the frontier conflict: "You will have heard of our Caffre war: it is very shocking for we must kill them by hundreds before we shall make them understand our power. They are tricky, dangerous fellows: the young men are all for war and began to think they could bully us."[26]

Liberal colonial officials like William Porter likewise expressed growing disillusion with Africans as a result of frontier wars in the late 1840s and the early 1850s. Porter arrived at the Cape in 1839 and played a major role in Cape politics as attorney-general and parliamentarian over the middle decades of the century. In his early years at the Cape, his colonial policies and attitudes towards Africans had shared the optimism of humanitarian liberals like Fairbairn. He too railed against "the wretched aristocracy of the skin" and vocally supported the Treaty System. In 1845 Porter was still convinced of the importance of a diplomatic policy and the independence of Africans beyond the frontier: "By avoiding annexation an experiment will be tested which has never yet been tried, viz. whether the extinction of the coloured races before whites, usually ascribed to the civilisation of the latter, may not, with greater truth, be ascribed to their defective form of civilisation, and whether the contact of white with coloured, when the former are more highly civilised, may not merely consist with the safety, but advance the political independence of the latter . . . But once advance your boundary in name to any great extent and you must soon advance it in reality to the full extent and the result will be the old oil and water process and the natives will sink into servitude and the whites will by force, or otherwise, usurp the entire soil."[27]

In a speech before the Cape Legislative Council in October of that year Porter declared his continued opposition to frontier war at a time when British frontier settlers were clamouring for conquest. He acknowledged the depredations of the Xhosa, but emphasized that only one hundred colonists and soldiers had been killed in the last war as opposed to four thousand Xhosa, and recommended to the war party, "never draw your sword until you have tried every other means".[28]

But the renewed military conflict in 1846–47 convinced him that "every other means" had been exhausted. Like John Fairbairn and his merchant allies, William Porter reversed his judgement of the Treaty System in the mid-1840s, turning to military rather than diplomatic solutions. He now insisted that the colonists were blameless and that the Xhosa should be severely punished for their treachery. The grand experiment of African independence was no longer deemed feasible. Subjugation and firm British rule over Xhosaland was seen as the only possible way of avoiding the outright extinction of indigenous peoples.[29]

Humanitarian disillusion in the wake of the 1846–47 war deepened in a climate of political instability and more extended military conflict in the early 1850s. The Khoikhoi of the Kat River Settlement were advertised as model reconstituted Africans by abolitionist propagandists like Philip and Buxton in the 1830s. During the War of Mlanjeni, which raged from 1851 to 1853, these once idealized subjects colluded with the Xhosa enemy, prompting nagging doubts about whether Africans could be civilized. In the mid-1830s humanitarian liberals expressed outrage at Governor D'Urban's statement that Africans were "treacherous and irreclaimable". By the early 1850s their views on the possibilities of African "improvement" now inclined towards those of D'Urban.

It was the Kat River Rebellion of 1851 that entrenched the more pessimistic liberal assessment of the Khoikhoi. The uprising of the Kat River rebels was typically interpreted not as a last desperate stand by a community whose lands were being encroached upon by white settlers and used as a dumping-ground for dispossessed people from other parts of the colony,[30] but as the product of Khoikhoi and missionary delusion. For William Porter, whose ideas were published in the settler newspaper in the Eastern Cape, the *Graham's Town Journal*, the treachery was inspired by a "foolish notion of nationality" based on the Khoikhoi belief that they were the ancient owners of the land of which the white man had dispossessed them, and their envy at the prosperity and industry of the whites which contrasted with their own poverty, "sloth and inactivity".[31] In his anger at their rebellion, Porter relapsed into the crass racism more characteristic of the racial discourse of his ideological enemies. He insisted that in their pre-colonial state "the Khoikhoi had had no more idea of nationality than the baboons, and as little notion of rights and privileges".[32]

Just as British settler imperialists in the Eastern Cape had blamed the humanitarian liberals for fomenting war in the mid-1830s, Porter blamed the Khoikhoi Rebellion of 1851 on "the indiscreet zeal of certain missionaries" like James Read. "There was, Porter said, no nobler gospel in the entire Bible than 'God hath made of one blood all the nations that dwell upon the face of the earth', but it was a gospel which required to be preached with soberness and some degree of caution, 'lest the ignorant and unstable among them should wrest it, as they do all other scripture, to their own destruction'."[33]

But Porter had little reason to fear the spread of radical evangelicalism, among white missionaries at least, by the middle of the nineteenth century. In accordance with Porter's wishes and the changing attitudes of other liberals, the Cape missionary movement, that seedbed of humanitarian reform in the 1820s, was preaching a more sober and cautious message by the 1840s. As Elizabeth Elbourne indicates, the egalitarian ethos of the London Missionary Society under Van der Kemp had been eclipsed by a more respectable, mainstream, middle-class evangelicalism in the early nineteenth century, which grew increasingly conservative by mid-century.[34]

John Philip had owed his political influence in the 1820s and 1830s to personal contacts with leading Whig reformers in the British parliament, notably Thomas Fowell Buxton. But in the early 1840s, Buxton no longer enjoyed the same access to the corridors of power. The select committee on aborigines of the late 1830s which Buxton chaired was

> the product of the last parliamentary session in which the middle- and upper-class "Saints" remained committed to an Africanist parliamentary platform with broadly-based popular pressure groups "out of doors". These "pro-Negro" pressure groups dissipated after the abolition of slavery removed their primary focus, while parliamentary evangelicals in the 1840s became more conservative, less united and more concerned with domestic religious issues . . . Buxton's arguments that Britain had a duty to spread Christianity and commerce proved more enduring than his opposition to the further acquisition of white territory in Africa.[35]

As Kale's article in this volume highlights, the British anti-slavery movement was riddled with contradiction and schism by 1840.[36]

The decline of humanitarian evangelicalism at the Cape was highlighted by the open conflicts that ruptured the London Missionary Society in the 1840s.

In the first of these conflicts the majority of white missionaries in Xhosaland led by a relatively new recruit, Henry Calderwood, turned on James Read, the long-standing political ally of John Philip, and attacked his vision of the evangelical task in southern Africa. Beneath the Calderwood faction's vague general charges of "dishonorable and unworthy conduct", "clandestine and most unchristian proceedings" and "incalculable injuries done to the cause of Christ"[37] lay a more fundamental challenge to James Read's egalitarian vision of the evangelical mission among Africans.

The clash between Calderwood and Read was at heart a dispute about racial politics and attitudes towards indigenous peoples. Calderwood and his supporters not only resented the influence that James Read and his son still exercised over John Philip, but warned of the seditious consequences of the unlicensed distribution of information among Africans on the frontier. In a letter of complaint to their London directors, they charged that: "Considering the circumstances and natural disposition of the Natives generally all who know this country will admit that a more serious offence against the souls of the people & comfort & influence of his brethren could scarcely be committed than that which Mr. Read had many a time committed on speaking and writing to the Natives" in an unguarded way. In more general terms, they criticized the humanitarian image that the Reads projected: "It has long been known that the Reads are in the habit of representing themselves to the people as more than others the Friends of the Natives, and that too in the most unscrupulous manner in order to get people to regard them 'as Martyrs to the liberties of the Hottentots' [which] amounts to 'a covert attack even upon the Society – represented as ready to oppress the Hottentots'."[38]

The attacks by his fellow missionaries and the rising current of conservatism within the London Missionary Society left unrepentant humanitarian liberals like James Read ostracized and despairing. In letters written to his friend at Bethelsdorp, James Kitchingman, in the mid-1840s, the ageing Read confided: "I am at present an outcast among my Brethren," "James [his son] and I are cut off, and our Brethren in these quarters seem determined on our ruin." Read wrote poignantly of his personal anguish: "I have suffered very much in my mind for fear of considerable blame being attached to me . . . I hope, my dear Brother, you will pray for me."[39]

Kitchingman himself, another of Philip's followers, was also increasingly prone to depression and gloom at this time. In the late 1820s John Philip had advertised his mission station, Bethelsdorp, as a model of industry and laboratory for the reconstruction of South African indigenes. In the late 1830s, as newly emancipated slaves flocked to mission stations in the Western Cape, Kitchingman still furnished Philip with relatively enthusiastic accounts of new converts and evangelical revival. By the time Jane Philip visited the mission station in the mid-1840s, however, the decline of Bethelsdorp and its long-resident missionary were painfully evident: "Mr. Kitchingman is an excellent man and has been very useful at Bethelsdorp, but [is] labouring under discouragement . . . Bethelsdorp and his own family seem to occupy all his thoughts, and thus a general feeling of depression rests on his mind."[40]

This pervading pessimism was shared by London Missionary Society evangelicals throughout the colony. By the late 1840s John Philip's Cape Town office was being flooded with missionary complaints about the immoral behaviour of the newly emancipated. In one particularly severe "year of trial for our Brethren", the missionary at Paarl referred to the "demoralising influence" of those "sinks of iniquity", the canteens; the Graham's Town report lamented the "scenes of dissipation daily presented in the streets"; that from Graaff Reinet complained of a "fearful" increase in drunkenness.[41] In 1848 William Elliot, one of the Society's more seasoned campaigners, wrote to the directors of his change of heart:

> He [the Hottentot] now needs no city of refuge. In proportion as the necessity of our missionary institutions has been superseded by the altered state of things, the evils incident to them have increased. The authority of the missionary has been diminished; the population of the missionary institutions has become injuriously dense, by a vast influx of late apprentices and other persons of colour, who prefer abundant leisure and unrestrained freedom to those habits of industry and those salutary restraints, which must be sustained and submitted to in ordinary social life.[42]

It is scarcely surprising that Philip himself became thoroughly despondent in the final decade of his life. Heightened conflicts with his conservative rival, Robert Maffat, provoked him to offer his resignation to the London directors in 1843. Though persuaded to retain his position as superintendent, he was troubled by the schisms between the frontier missionaries. The Xhosa War of 1846, which had prompted a reversal of attitudes among humanitarian liberal allies like Fairbairn, Rutherford and Porter, was interpreted as another sign of defeat. In his letters to the directors, Philip emphasized the extent to which the war had disrupted mission work within and beyond the colony's borders: "On them [our missions] the war has fallen with double weight; while our missions in Caffreland have been entirely broken up, and the labours of the missionaries suspended; the Hottentots at our different stations within the Colony, have been called into Caffreland and compelled to bear the greatest burden."[43] The fact that Philip viewed the war "in the light of a judgement" as well as "a heavy calamity" points to a more fundamental sense of failure.[44]

A year after the war Philip informed Kitchingman that "Many of our friends are dissatisfied with the smallness of our success . . . [and] begin to doubt whether our missions are not in a state of retrogression . . . Tahiti, Madagascar and South Africa are appealed to justify the surmise."[45] He wrote gloomily of the state of the missions in southern Africa in the late 1840s: "I feel at present the care of the churches as a heavy burden pressing me to the earth. Things are very dark with us at present. Our Society was among the first in the field of missions, and I am afraid that we shall be among the first out of it."[46] This was a time of personal trauma for Philip. His wife, eldest son and grandson all died within a year of each other. In July 1848 he informed his superiors, "I beg you to recollect that I am working in the service of the Society with one foot in the grave and the other in Heaven."

The humanitarian evangelical movement of the first half of the nineteenth century had, quite literally, run its natural term. Philip wrote in 1848 of the "heavy losses which the Society's Missions in South Africa have sustained by the extraordinary mortality that has prevailed".[47] In that year alone seven of the missionaries died, most of whom were aged and faithful agents. The Rev. J. Kitchingman, the Rev. J. H. Schmelen and his wife, the Rev. J. Helm and Mrs Anderson, had all spent nearly four decades in the field. The death of the leading humanitarian evangelicals Philip and James Read in 1851 and 1852 symbolized the closure of an evangelical epoch at the Cape.

The conservative consensus

The decline of the Cape humanitarian movement in the 1840s made way for the rise of a new racial conservatism in the 1850s. It was ironically the disillusioned humanitarians themselves, ideologues like John Fairbairn, William Porter and their merchant allies, who formed the core of this mid-century conservative consensus. They were supported by a faction of Cape Afrikaner urban professionals and rural farmers, as well as "liberal" Cape governors with increasingly imperialist ambitions.

It was in the debate over representative government and the Cape franchise between 1848 and 1853 that the new conservatives first came together. Despite the popular rhetoric of the rights of all "races" and the justice of assimilating coloured voters into a new political order, the classic liberal argument for a low, non-racial franchise was squarely based on considerations of white security and solidarity.[48] At the height of the abolitionist campaign, when rural slave-owners had come out in outright rebellion against British reforms, John Fairbairn had shelved his proposals for Cape self-government on the grounds that English and Afrikaner colonists were too politically divided. By 1848 a more conservative Fairbairn had become convinced that inter-ethnic, middle-class, white unity defined in opposition to Africans rendered the Cape ripe for representative government: "[T]here is no difference between these two classes [English and Afrikaner], in rank, place, or consideration in society. They are all engaged in the same pursuits, and meet each other everywhere on a footing of perfect equality. They do not stand apart, like the European and African, in the characters of rich and poor, capitalists and labourers, employers and employed. Their interests are identical, and cannot be separated, or opposed to each other . . . By local intermixture, by intermarriages, and by connections in business, these two classes have to a great extent, lost their original distinctions."[49]

It was Fairbairn's disillusioned humanitarian ally, the Cape attorney-general William Porter, who was given the task of drawing up a draft constitution for the Cape in 1848. Porter's political intervention proved decisive: after substantial delays occasioned by frontier war and Colonial Office intransigence, his proposal for a non-racial franchise based on the relatively low £25 property qualification was endorsed by the British government. But, as in the case of Fairbairn, Porter's arguments for the low franchise qualification were motivated more by expedience and the dictates of white unity than humanitarian sentiment. Porter was sympathetic to Afrikaner colonists from his arrival in the colony and English–Dutch union was central to his vision of the Cape's political future. In campaigning for the low franchise qualification, he predicted that

> When the Dutch majority, long depressed, shall have got over the temporary elation of acquiring power, and the English minority shall have got over, in like manner, their temporary mortification at being less influential than before, the fusion of race . . . which is undoubtedly in progress will be promoted and the peace and prosperity of the colony . . . ultimately advanced.[50]

Demands for white unity were particularly pressing in the light of the heightened African resistance around mid-century. For disillusioned humanitarians the selective incorporation of members of the coloured elite in Cape politics was a matter of political necessity rather than civil rights. William Porter provided the classic exposition of their "safety valve" argument. In the wake of the Kat River Rebellion he warned that "It is better to meet the Hottentot at the hustings than in the wilds with a gun slung over his shoulder."[51]

The overarching emphasis on Afrikaner inclusion and colonial security also dominated the discourse of the Cape liberal Afrikaner faction led by the newspaper editor and lawyer Christoffel Brand, and the Swellendam farmer F. W. Reitz. Brand, Rietz and Fairbairn (along with the controversial Afrikaner frontiersman Andries Stockenstrom) were elected as leaders of a "popular" party in 1850 and took their constitutional demands to Britain. Given the heated conflicts between Fairbairn and Brand over the slave question in earlier decades, they made strange companions as "popular" party allies. Brand's newspaper, the mouthpiece of Afrikaner farmers and urban professionals, echoed Porter's view that "the low qualification [is] the surest and only way of obviating serious opposition at home".[52] Afrikaner liberals of the 1860s continued to warn that "it would still be better for Parliament to listen now and again to a little native eloquence than it would be for us to quieten Hottentot mutiny or Malay commotions from time to time".[53]

Neither were humanitarian considerations of much importance in the British Colonial Office's attitudes towards the Cape franchise or, indeed, in their attitude towards colonial politics more generally by the early 1850s. As Trapido has indicated, the Cape would not have been granted representative government if James Stephen's anxieties regarding white domination in the early 1830s were still taken seriously.[54] Colonial Office support for low franchise qualifications was based rather on the necessity of securing a wider class of white collaborators for the effective administration of informal empire. In Kirk's overview of British imperial policy in southern Africa, the simultaneous granting of representative government to the Cape Colony and independence to Afrikaner republics in the early 1850s is epitomized as "an attempt to regain, not to devolve, power in southern Africa. The imperial government was shifting its grip, not relaxing it. The tactics involved a temporary retreat to the Cape Colony in order to build up an alliance with the mass of inhabitants and wait for their own expansive tendencies to carry them – and the imperial power – into the interior."[55]

In the pursuit of their imperialist ambitions, metropolitan officials found enthusiastic allies among the humanitarians of yesteryear. The attitudes of Fairbairn and his allies towards the frontier in the late 1840s and 1850s were a far cry from the protectionist policies and treaty systems advocated by Cape humanitarians in the 1830s. The clamour of the disillusioned humanitarians for Xhosa retribution and dispossession in the wake of the 1846–47 Frontier War was supported by their Afrikaner allies, Christoffel Brand and F. W. Reitz.

Following the Seventh Frontier War, Brand echoed Fairbairn's scepticism concerning policies based on treaties and negotiations and saw "complete subjugation" as the only viable solution. This view was taken further by Reitz in 1855 who spoke before the Cape parliament of the "one strong feeling" of English and Afrikaner for an end to "all little Kaffir Wars" and declared that:

They [the colonists] expected that our Governors would no longer be led by a false philanthropy to pursue a vacillating policy which but renders our savage neighbours more insolent, more independent, and which ultimately brings ruin upon themselves, and on the colony greater evils. They expected that if ever unfortunately a Kaffir war should break out again, such a number of colonists would be enabled to crush the power of our barbarous neighbours from one ocean to the other, and thus prevent them, for many years, at least, from disturbing the safety of the colony, and then will be the time for a Christian people to tame and civilise them . . . [W]here a civilised and a barbarous nation come together, the savage must learn to fear the punishment which will follow upon an act of aggression committed by him.[56]

By the middle of the nineteenth century there was every indication that the colonial governors and the Colonial Office endorsed the aggressive expansionism of this inter-ethnic alliance. When Harry Smith returned to the colony as Cape governor in the late 1840s, he was acclaimed by the disillusioned humanitarians, who offered to build a statue in his honour. The same ideologues who had denounced Smith's military expansionism when he served as commander under the "rogue" imperialist Benjamin D'Urban in the mid-1830s welcomed him as a political ally a decade later.

Smith's frontier policies did not disappoint the new conservatives. The Cape governor was bent on the moral and material upliftment of the Xhosa by coercive means and sought the ruthless suppression of traditional culture. After the 1846–47 war, he brashly implemented these policies. Vast tracts of Xhosaland were annexed to the Colony and administered as British territory under military officers and magistrates. He tore up treaties before the eyes of the Xhosa chiefs, bluntly informing them: "this land is mine".[57]

Smith's imperial ambitions were shaken in the early 1850s by African resistance on an unprecedented scale and colonists grew resentful when he applied his high-handed methods to the politics of representative government. It was left to Sir George Grey, governor at the Cape from 1856 to 1862, to hammer the nail in the Xhosa coffin. Grey came to the Cape from New Zealand, where his decade as governor had embroiled him in protracted wars with the Maori. Through Grey's agency the Maori had lost six million acres of the disputed North Island and all the South Island's thirty million acres. At the Cape, as in New Zealand, the dispossession of indigenous peoples and the destruction of traditional culture formed the cornerstone of Grey's programme of assimilation.[58]

In much of the liberal historiography of the twentieth century, George Grey has been invoked as a symbol of humanitarian liberalism. His policies for

African upliftment included the building of hospitals and schools in Xhosaland and the education of the children of Xhosa chiefs in Cape Town.[59] But as Peires so vividly demonstrates in his analysis of the Xhosa cattle-killing movement, Sir George Grey's liberalism was dominated by a darker utilitarian aspect and a bloodless political economy. In the aftermath of the Xhosa cattle-killing, Grey's policies towards the Xhosa were unsympathetic to the point of brutality.[60]

Grey seized on the cattle-killing as a golden opportunity for securing labour and suppressing Xhosa culture. Magistrates were instructed not to give food to those Xhosa unwilling to register as labourers. "The willing volunteers in question were literally starving to death. The only way they could get food was to give themselves bodily into the hands of the Chief Commissioner, who could send them wherever he liked to do any sort of work at any wage under any conditions for any length of time not exceeding five years."[61] The newly established Cape parliament passed laws, the Kaffir Pass Act and the Kaffir Employment Act, to ensure that the Xhosa became labourers, and the potential threat posed to this enlistment programme by the Kaffir Relief Committee led Grey to stifle colonial charity towards the starving Xhosa systematically. The Government took over the relief operations with great success. Of the 25,363 distressed Xhosa to be relieved by February 1858 no fewer than 22,150 were placed in colonial service.[62]

Far from criticizing this brutality, the disillusioned humanitarian liberals actively promoted the governor's "trampling on the human wreckage".[63] William Porter was outspoken in his support for the suppression of the Kaffir Relief Committee. In addressing the Cape Town branch of the Committee, Porter declared that

> he had once mistakenly thought that Kaffir Relief was a fit object for private charity, like famine in his native Ireland. But he had come to realise that the Xhosa were "a very difficult people to deal with" and that "it is impossible in British Kaffraria to separate private charity from public policy". The problem was that the Xhosa wanted to "be supported in idleness, for he has no desire for work, and we know that idleness is their besetting sin".[64]

On such grounds, he insisted that the Relief Committee should be dissolved and the Chief Commissioner of British Kaffraria, John Maclean, be made responsible for administering the fund.[65]

The liberal press enthusiastically backed the governor's actions. Fairbairn praised Grey's ambitions to cripple the power of the Xhosa chiefs: "Sir George Grey quickly discovered that the root and spring of innumerable evils in Caffraria and what rendered them dangerous and formidable to the Colony lay in the relation which subsisted between the Chiefs and the people, and . . . the power and influence of the Chief."[66] He insisted on the necessity of strict influx control in the ensuing debate over the Kaffir Employment Bill in the Cape parliament. It was reported that "He objected to the introduction of large numbers of people into the colony. They would form a savage element in the population, and he thought that the armed savage was even less to be dreaded than the domestic savage". In editorials at the time, Fairbairn declared that Xhosa "manners are brutish, their passions violent and irrepressible" and warned that "It is contrary to all principle, to all precedent, to all experience to attempt to civilise a savage continent by directing the flood of barbarism down upon the single spot where a feeble civilisation has but recently taken root."[67]

Conclusion

The disillusion of the humanitarians and rising settler racism in the Cape Colony in the 1840s needs to be integrated into Bolt's standard chronology of the transition from the era of humanitarianism to the era of imperialism. Although this article has focused on the ideological reversal among colonial humanitarians, I would suggest that the Xhosa wars on the Cape Colony's eastern frontier had more of an impact on metropolitan thinking than has generally been acknowledged. The writings of Victorian ideologues of the 1840s and 1850s still need to be reassessed in this light, but there is preliminary evidence that the Cape colonial experience exercised an important influence on the British imperial imagination. For example, Robert Knox, the leading figure of the new mid-century scientific racism in Britain, based his widely publicized theories of race conflict and racial war on anatomical lessons learnt during years of experience as a military surgeon to British forces locked in conflict with the Xhosa.[68]

But the premature demise of the Cape humanitarian movement also challenges cherished beliefs that liberalism in South Africa only went into decline at the end of the nineteenth century. Disillusioned humanitarians formed the core of a new conservatism in the 1850s and articulated a racial discourse that was stridently imperialist and often strikingly anti-humanitarian. The civilizing mission of merchants, missionaries and colonial officials became increasingly compatible with the views of their ideological enemies of earlier decades, the Cape Afrikaner slave-owners and British frontier settler imperialists.

Colonists were now united in support of conquest over the Xhosa and a policy of incorporating the "coloured classes" that was, at most, highly selective. The calls for a policy of conquest of Xhosaland by Eastern Cape settlers after the 1835 Xhosa War were endorsed by disillusioned humanitarians and Cape Afrikaner leaders after the 1846–47 War. The tensions between the Cape abolitionists and Afrikaner slave-owners of the early 1830s had dissipated, giving way to shared visions of English–Dutch unity in the 1840s and a common struggle for representative government on the basis of white unity and security in the 1850s. Indeed, the only group that lay outside the new mid-Victorian conservative consensus were Cape Dutch ultra-conservatives,[69] whose thought was expressly antagonistic to ideas of assimilation and later informed the Afrikaner nationalism of the 1870s.

Notes

1 P. Curtin, *The image of Africa: British ideas and action* (London, 1965), p. vi.
2 P. Brantlinger, "Victorians and Africans: the genealogy of the myth of the dark continent", *Critical Enquiry* **12**, 1985, p. 166.
3 C. Bolt, *Victorian attitudes to race* (London, 1971).
4 *Ibid.*, Chapter 1.
5 Dr Cumming cited in Bolt, *Victorian attitudes to race*, p. 183. On British attitudes towards Indians after the Mutiny, see T. R. Metcalf, *The aftermath of revolt: India, 1857–1870* (Princeton, N. J., 1965), pp. 289–327.
6 Bolt, *Victorian attitudes to race*, Chapter 3.
7 D. A. Lorimer, *Colour, class and the Victorians: English attitudes to the negro in the mid-nineteenth century* (Leicester, 1978), p. 12.
8 J. Bellich, *The New Zealand wars and the Victorian interpretation of racial conflict* (Auckland, 1988), p. 328.
9 See especially C. Crais, *White supremacy and Black resistance in pre-industrial South Africa: the making of the colonial order in the Eastern Cape, 1770–1865* (Cambridge, 1992), pp. 125–46; A. Bank, *Liberals and the enemies: racial ideology at the Cape of Good Hope, 1820 to 1850* (PhD thesis, Cambridge University, 1995), pp. 189–236.
10 For recent liberal accounts, see R. Davenport, "The Cape liberal tradition to 1910", in *Democratic liberalism in South Africa: its history and prospects*, J. Butler et al. (eds) (Cape Town, 1987), pp. 26–32; A. Du Toit, "The Cape Afrikaners' failed liberal moment, 1850–1870", in J. Butler et al. (eds), *Democratic liberalism*, pp. 37–40. For the most influential revisionist account, see S. Trapido, " 'Friends of the Natives': merchants, peasants and the political and ideological structure of liberalism in the Cape, 1854–1910", in *Economy and society in pre-industrial South Africa*, S. Marks and A. Atmore (eds) (London, 1980), pp. 247–74.
11 Trapido, " 'Friends of the Natives' ", pp. 270–74.
12 See Bank, *Liberals and the enemies*, pp. 82–140.
13 John Philip, *Researches in South Africa* (London, 1828), vol. 2, p. 316.
14 *South African Commercial Advertiser*, 27 June 1829.
15 See Bank, *Liberals and the enemies*, pp. 91–100.
16 See, for example, *South African Commercial Advertiser*, 22 June 1842.

17 See N. Worden, "Adjusting to emancipation: freed slaves and farmers in the mid-nineteenth century South-Western Cape", in *The Angry Divide: Social and Economic History of the Western Cape*, M. Simons and W. James (eds) (Cape Town, 1989), pp. 37–8.

18 See J. Frye, *The South African Commercial Advertiser and the eastern frontier, 1834–1847* (MA thesis, Rhodes University, Grahamstown, 1968), pp. 56–76 for a detailed discussion of Fairbairn's coverage of the war and the Eastern Cape settler reaction.

19 *South African Commercial Advertiser*, 3 July 1839.

20 See J. B. Peires, *The house of Phalo: a history of the Xhosa people in the days of their independence* (Johannesburg, 1981), pp. 109–34; B. Le Cordeur and C. Saunders, *The War of the Axe* (Johannesburg, 1981) for recent historiographical assessments of the causes of war which contrast with Fairbairn's settler interpretation.

21 *South African Commercial Advertiser*, 14 October 1846.

22 *South African Commercial Advertiser*, 19 December 1846.

23 Frye, *The South African Commercial Advertiser and the eastern frontier*, p. 119.

24 *South African Commercial Advertiser*, 24 April 1847.

25 *South African Commercial Advertiser*, 18 June 1831.

26 Cited in Frye, *The South African Commercial Advertiser and the eastern frontier*, p. 101.

27 Cited in J. L. McCracken, *New light at the Cape of Good Hope: William Porter: father of Cape liberalism* (Belfast, 1993), p. 108.

28 Cited in *The letters and speeches of John Mitford Bowker* (Grahamstown, 1864), p. 176.

29 McCracken, *New light at the Cape of Good Hope*, p. 108.

30 See T. Kirk, "Progress and decline in the Kat River Settlement, 1829–1854", *Journal of African History* **3**, 1973, pp. 411–28; "The Cape economy and the expropriation of the Kat River Settlement", in Marks and Atmore (eds), *Economy and society*, pp. 226–46.

31 McCracken, *New Light at the Cape of Good Hope*, p. 109.

32 *Ibid.*, p. 109.

33 *Ibid.*, p. 109.

34 E. Elbourne, "*To Colonize the Mind*": *evangelical missionaries in Britain and the Eastern Cape, 1790–1837* (DPhil. thesis, Oxford University, 1992).

35 *Ibid.*, p. 332.

36 The Anti-Slavery Society's Convention held in London's Exeter Hall in June 1840 was marked by deep-rooted tensions over the meanings of slavery and indenture. William Knibb's utopian visions of the reconstituted black subject were met with caution as the leading abolitionists now echoed the West Indian planter's insistence on the dangers of unbridled liberty and the absolute necessity of maintaining levels of production.

37 Cited in C. Hummel (ed.), *Rev. F. G. Kayser: journals and letters* (Grahamstown, 1990), pp. 165, 170.

38 *Ibid.*, pp. 172–3.

39 B. Le Cordeur and C. Saunders, *The Kitchingman papers: missionary letters and journal, 1817 to 1848* (Johannesburg, 1976), pp. 248–9.

40 Jane Philip cited in *ibid.*, p. 21.

41 London Missionary Society, Cape Town Auxiliary, 1847 Report, p. 10.

42 Cited in R. A. Lovett, *The history of the London Missionary Society, 1795–1899* (London, 1899), vol. 1, p. 573.

43 South African Library, Cape Town Auxiliary to the London Missionary Society, 1846 Report, p. 5.

44 *Ibid.*, p. 5.

45 *Ibid.*, p. 27.

46   Cited in Le Cordeur and Saunders, *The Kitchingman Papers*, p. 27.

47   London Missionary Society, Cape Town Auxiliary, 1848 Report, p. 5.

48   See S. Trapido, "The origins of the Cape franchise qualifications of 1853", *Journal of African History* **5**(1), 1964, pp. 37–54.

49   *South African Commercial Advertiser*, 20 September 1848, cited in J. L. Meltzer, *The growth of Cape Town commerce and the role of John Fairbairn's* Advertiser, *1835–59* (MA thesis, University of Cape Town, 1989), p. 133.

50   Cited in J. L. McCracken, *New light at the Cape of Good Hope*.

51   Trapido, "Origins", p. 48.

52   *De Zuid-Afrikaan*, 8 May 1851, cited in Meltzer, *Cape Town commerce*, p. 150.

53   B. J. van der Sandt, cited in A. Du Toit, "The Afrikaners' failed liberal moment, 1850–1870", in *Democratic Liberalism in South Africa: its History and Prospects*, J. Butler, R. Elphick, D. Welsh (eds) (New Haven (CT), 1987), p. 47.

54   Trapido, "Origins", p. 39.

55   T. Kirk, *Self-government and self-defence in South Africa: the inter-relations between British and Cape politics, 1846–1854* (DPhil thesis, Oxford University, 1972), p. 502. This challenge to Galbraith's image of "reluctant empire" in the 1850s and 1860s is developed in Tim Keegan's recent work. See J. S. Galbraith, *Reluctant empire: British policy on the South African Frontier, 1834–1854* (Berkeley, 1963); T. Keegan, *Colonial South Africa and the origins of the racial order* (Cape Town, 1996), pp. 248–80.

56   Cited in A. Du Toit and H. Giliomee, *Afrikaner political thought* (Cape Town, 1983), p. 186. As Du Toit and Giliomee and especially Keegan emphasize, many Afrikaners did not share these expansionist ambitions in the mid-century decades.

57   Keegan, *Colonial South Africa*, pp. 220–21.

58   See J. B. Peires, *The dead will arise* (Johannesburg, 1989) for a brilliant analysis of the ambiguities of Grey's racial ideology. This has been taken up more recently in J. Gump, "The imperialism of cultural assimilation: Sir George Grey's encounter with the Maori and the Xhosa, 1845–1868", paper presented at the Conference on the British Encounter with Indigenous Peoples, London, February 1997.

59   See J. Rutherford, *Sir George Grey* (London, 1964); J. Hodgson, "Zonnebloem College and Cape Town, 1858–1870", paper presented at Cape Town History Conference 1978.

60   J. B. Peires, *The dead will arise*.

61   J. B. Peires, "Sir George Grey versus the Kaffir Relief Committee", *Journal of Southern African Studies* **10**(2), 1984, p. 152.

62   *Ibid.*, p. 163.

63   The phrase is from Peires, *The dead will arise*.

64   Peires, "Sir George Grey versus the Kaffir Relief Committee", p. 158.

65   *Ibid.*, p. 158.

66   *South African Commercial Advertiser*, 14 April 1857, cited in Meltzer, "Cape Town commerce", p. 180.

67   *South African Commercial Advertiser*, 16, 23 June 1857, cited in Meltzer, "Cape Town commerce", p. 182.

68   See Bank, Liberals and the enemies, pp. 320–22; S. Dubow, *Scientific racism in modern South Africa* (Cambridge, 1995).

69   See A. Du Toit, "The Afrikaners' failed liberal moment", pp. 35–63, for an incisive analysis of the split between the liberal and conservative wings of Afrikaner thought over these decades.

Index